AIDS TO THE STUDY & COMPOSITION OF ENGLISH

IN FIVE PARTS

AIDS TO THE STUDY & COMPOSITION OF ENGLISH

IN FIVE PARTS

BY

J. C. NESFIELD

GYAN

Published by

Gyan Publishing House
5, Ansari Road
Daryaganj, New Delhi-110002
Phone: 011-47034999, 9811692060
E-mail: books@gyanbooks.com

Distribution Network
gyanbooks.com
India, USA, Canada, UK, Australia

ISBN: 978-93-6280-202-6 (HB)
First Published, 1912

2nd Impression 2024

Printed at: Gyan Press, Delhi.

AIDS TO THE STUDY AND COMPOSITION OF ENGLISH
AUTHOR: J. C. NESFIELD

AIDS TO THE

STUDY & COMPOSITION OF ENGLISH

AIDS TO THE STUDY & COMPOSITION OF ENGLISH

IN FIVE PARTS

BY

J. C. NESFIELD, M.A.

AUTHOR OF 'ENGLISH GRAMMAR PAST AND PRESENT,' 'HISTORICAL ENGLISH AND DERIVATION,' ETC.

MACMILLAN AND CO., LIMITED
ST. MARTIN'S STREET, LONDON
1912

PUBLISHERS' NOTICE.

Part I., "**The Foundations of English Speech**," contains a series of chapters (I.-XIII. inclusive) on Accidence, Parsing, and Analysis of Sentences, all of which are a reprint, without any change, of the corresponding chapters in the *Manual of English Grammar and Composition*, by the same author. To these chapters two more have been added,—Chapter XIV. on Sounds, Symbols, and Spellings (a subject not much attended to hitherto, but likely to become more and more important),—and Chapter XV. on Word-building. These fifteen chapters have been placed under the general heading, "Foundations of English Speech," because a knowledge of their contents is indispensable as a grounding for what is to follow, and reference will frequently be made to them in subsequent Parts of this book.

Part II. consists of "**Studies and Exercises Subsidiary to Composition.**" These are dealt with in a series of chapters from XVI. to XXII. (inclusive), most of which nearly coincide with what has been told already in different parts of the *Manual* above referred to. There is, however, a new and important chapter on Direct and Indirect Speech.

Part III., "**Composition in Five Stages,**" is almost entirely new. The five stages referred to are the Structure and Synthesis of Sentences, the Structure and Analysis of Paragraphs, Paraphrasing, Précis-writing, and Essay-writing, to each of which a separate chapter has been given. The Essays in Part III. are all on general subjects.

Part IV., "**Composition Continued**," contains two chapters on Idiom and Construction, which are for the most part a reprint of what has been told already by the same author in his *English Grammar Past and Present*. In addition to these two chapters there is a third chapter that is entirely new, the subject of which is Essay-writing on the basis of English History and of General Geography.

Part V., "**Aids to the Study of English Literature.**" As its name implies, this part is not intended to help the student either in Grammar or in Composition, but in the Study of English Literature, both Prose and Verse. The last chapter, "Style in Prose and Verse," is entirely new; the other chapters (on the Figures of Rhetoric, Prosody, and Poetic Diction) are partially so.

CONTENTS.

PART I.—THE FOUNDATIONS OF ENGLISH SPEECH.

PART I.—THE FOUNDATIONS OF ENGLISH SPEECH.

CHAPTER I.

ANALYSIS IN OUTLINE.

This chapter assumes that the student has a rough knowledge of the Parts of Speech to start with. Analysis is worked out more fully below, in Chapter XIII.

1. Sentence.—When one person says something to another, or puts what he says into writing, he uses a combination of words which is called a sentence :—

Fire burns.

Here "fire" is the thing talked about. The word "fire," though it names the thing, does not make a sentence. It is a *name*, and nothing more. It is only by adding such a word as "burns" to the word "fire," that is, by *saying* what the thing (fire) does, that we can make a sentence.

Definition.—A sentence is a combination of words, in which something is *said* about something else.

Note.—That which is "*said*" may be an assertion, or a command, or a question, or a wish, or an exclamation,—whatever, in fact, can be expressed by a Finite verb (on the meaning of Finite verb see § 5). Thus there are five different kinds of sentences :—

(*a*) **Assertive**, affirming or denying. (*Indicative Mood.*)

A man's success *depends* chiefly on himself. (*Affirmative.*)
He *did* not *get* much help from others. (*Negative.*)

(*b*) **Imperative**, commanding or prohibiting. (*Imperative Mood.*)

Rely chiefly on your own efforts. (*Command, Advice.*)
Do not *rely* much on the help of others. (*Prohibition.*)

(*c*) **Interrogative**, asking a question. (*Indicative Mood.*)

Have you *finished* that task ?

(*d*) **Optative**, expressing a wish. (*Subjunctive Mood.*)

Thy kingdom *come*, thy will *be done*.

(*e*) **Exclamatory**, expressing some emotion. (*Indicative Mood.*)

What a foolish fellow you have been !

2. Subject and Predicate.—Every sentence, when it is expressed in full, consists of two parts, a Subject and a Predicate.

In a very short sentence like "fire burns," the word "fire" (which is called a Noun) expresses the whole of the Subject, and the word "burns" (which is called a Finite Verb) expresses the whole of the Predicate.

However long a sentence may be, it can always be divided into the same two parts as the shortest sentence:—

Subject.	*Predicate.*
(1) Fire	burns.
(2) A fierce fire	burnt down my house.
(3) A fierce fire, breaking out yesterday,	completely burnt down my house.
(4) A fierce fire, suddenly breaking out yesterday afternoon,	completely burnt down my house and many others in the same street.
(5) A fierce fire, suddenly breaking out yesterday afternoon at four o'clock,	completely burnt down my house and all the other houses in the same street except five.

Definitions.—The Subject of a sentence is a word or words denoting what we speak about.

The Predicate is a word or words by which we say something about the thing denoted by the Subject.

Note 1.—In *grammar* the Subject is not "what we speak about," but "the *word or words denoting* what we speak about." Grammar deals exclusively with words, and this fact has to be recognised in all the definitions.

Note 2.—Such a sentence as "Go!" is elliptical. Here the Subject "thou" or "you" is understood. Still more elliptical is a sentence in which the Subject and the Finite verb are both understood:—

Companion, hence!—SHAKSPEARE.

To express this sentence in full, we have to say—

Companion, *go thou* hence!

3. Nominative or its equivalent.—The predicate-verb has for its Subject some noun or noun-equivalent of the same number (Singular or Plural) and the same person (First, Second, or Third) as the verb itself. The noun that stands as Subject to a verb is invariably in the Nominative case, and so it is best to call it a Nominative at once.

Fire | burns.

Here "fire" is the Nominative to the predicate-verb "burns."

A pronoun is a very common form of noun-equivalent:—

He | is standing outside.

We cannot say "*Him* is standing outside." So the pronoun like the noun must be in the Nominative case.

Another form of Nominative is a Gerund or Verbal noun ending in *-ing* :—

Walking | is good for health.

Sometimes an Infinitive is used as an equivalent to the Nominative :—

To walk | is good for health.

Sometimes a **clause** (that is, a sentence which is part of a larger sentence) is used as an equivalent to the Nominative. This is called a Noun-clause, because it does the work of a noun :—

Whom the gods love | die young.—*Proverb.*

4. **Enlargement of Nominative.**—The Nominative is sometimes enlarged by a word or words that add something to its meaning.

The commonest form of enlargement is an adjective or a participle; and both forms of enlargement may occur together :—

A *fierce* fire
A *fierce* fire, *breaking out* yesterday, } burnt down my house.

Another very common form of enlargement is a noun or pronoun in the Possessive case :—

My prospects | are not bad.
A *fox's* tail | is of a tawny colour.

Another form of enlargement is a noun in apposition (*i.e.* referring to the same thing as the other noun) :—

John, *the baker*, has taken a new shop.

Another form of enlargement is a preposition followed by a noun :—

My prospects *in life* | are not bad.
A bird *in the hand* | is worth two in the bush.

Sometimes a clause can be used to enlarge the Nominative. This is called an Adjective-clause, because it enlarges the noun as an adjective would do.

The house *in which we live* | has been sold.

5. **Finite Verb.**—Any part of a verb that can be used for saying something about something else (in any of the five senses shown in § 1) is called Finite.

The word "finite" means "limited." A Finite verb is so called, because it is limited to the same person (*First, Second*, or *Third*) and to the same number (*Singular* or *Plural*) as its Nominative :—

(*a*) I *see* him. (*b*) They *see* him.

In both sentences the *form* of the verb "see" is the same.

But in (*a*) the verb is in the *First* person, because its Nom. "I" is in the *First* person, and in the *Singular* number, because its Nom. "I" is *Singular*. Similarly in (*b*) the verb is in the *Third* person, because its Nom. "they" is in the *Third* person, and *Plural*, because its Nom. "they" is Plural.

Note.—Those parts of a verb which are not finite, that is, are not limited to number and person, are of three kinds :—(1) the **Infinitive** mood, as "I wish *to retire*"; (2) a **Participle**, as "a *retired* officer"; (3) a **Gerund** or Verbal noun, as "I think of *retiring*." These, though they are parts of a verb, have lost what is most essential in the verb-character; that is, they do not enable us to *say* anything about anything else, and therefore they can never be the verb of a Predicate.

6. Completion of Finite Verb.—Some verbs make a complete sense by themselves. If so, they are called Intransitive verbs of Complete Predication :—

Fish *swim*. Rivers *flow*. All animals *die*.

Other verbs do not make a complete sense by themselves, but require some word or words to be added for this purpose. Such additional word or words are called the **Completion**.

The Completion may be either (*a*) an Object, or (*b*) a Complement; and there is one class of verb (Factitive, see below) that requires both :—

(*a*) **Object** :—

A verb that requires an object is called Transitive. "Transitive" means "passing over" or "passing on." A verb is Transitive, when the action denoted by it does not stop with the doer, but passes on to something else :—

Ships traverse *the ocean*. He shot *a tiger*.

There is no sense, or at least a very imperfect sense, in saying "Ships traverse," "He shot."

A Transitive verb may even have *two* objects :—

He asked *me a difficult question*.

To say "he asked" gives a very incomplete sense. "He asked me" brings the sense a step nearer to completion. But the sense is not really completed till we say, "He asked me a difficult question."

(*b*) **Complement** :—

This word is used to denote any kind of completion except the object or objects to a Transitive verb. Transitive verbs which need a complement as well as an object are called **Factitive**; Intransitive verbs which need a complement are called **Copulative**.

That grief drove him (Object) *mad* (Complement) (*Factitive.*)
He seems *to be mad* (Complement) . . . . (*Copulative.*)

If we omit the complement, and say "That grief drove him," or "He seems," the sentences are almost meaningless. It is the complement which furnishes what was wanted to complete the sense in either sentence.

7. Extension of Finite Verb.—The Finite verb is said to be "extended," when its meaning is increased by an adverb or by some word or words that have the force of an adverb :—

That grief *nearly* drove him mad.
That grief drove him mad *all of a sudden.*

Here the meaning of "drove" is extended in the first sentence by the adverb *nearly*, and in the second by the adverbial phrase *all of a sudden.*

Sometimes the Finite verb is extended by a clause. A clause so used is called an Adverb-clause, because it has the force of an adverb :—

The news drove him mad, *as soon as he heard it.*

The sentence italicised extends the meaning of "drove" by mentioning the time of the action.

8. Scheme of Analysis.—Sentences are analysed according to the following scheme, the details of which have been already explained in §§ 3-7 :—

The new master soon put the class into good order.
A bird in the hand is worth two in the bush.
Evil communications corrupt good manners.
Without any necessity, he asked me a rude question.

I. SUBJECT.		II. PREDICATE.			
			Completion of Finite Verb.		
Nominative or Equivalent.	Enlargement of Nominative.	Finite Verb.	Object.	Complement.	Extension of Finite Verb.
master	(1) The (2) new	put	the class	into good order	soon.
bird	(1) A (2) in the hand	is	...	worth two in the bush.	
communications	Evil	corrupt	good manners.		
He	...	asked	(1) me (2) a rude question	...	without any necessity.

Analyse the following sentences according to the model:—

1. A certain fowler, having fixed his net, withdrew to a little distance, that the birds might not be afraid to come.
2. A flight of pigeons, led by their king, was by chance passing through the sky at this time.
3. They caught sight of the rice-grains scattered by the fowler near the net.
4. The pigeon who was king of the rest then asked his rice-loving followers this question—
5. Why are rice-grains lying here in this lonely place?
6. We will see into this thing.
7. We must be cautious in our movements.
8. One conceited pigeon among the rest gave them bad advice.
9. He told them to fly down to the rice-grains and satisfy their hunger.
10. Having listened to this bad advice and flown down, they began to pick up and swallow the grains.
11. On beginning to peck they were all caught in the net.
12. Then they blamed their rash and imprudent friend for having given them such bad advice.
13. They ought rather to have blamed themselves for having listened to him.
14. The king now told them what to do.
15. At one moment and with one united movement springing suddenly up fly off with the net.
16. Small things become strong by being united among themselves.
17. Even mad elephants can be held fast by a rope made of thin blades of grass.
18. The pigeons acted on this advice.
19. Making a sudden spring together, they flew up into the air, carrying the net with them.
20. At first the fowler hoped to see them come down again to the earth.
21. Flying along as fast as they could, they passed out of sight with the net about them.
22. In this way the fowler lost both his net and the pigeons.
23. The pigeons then said to their king:—"O king, what is the next thing to be done?"
24. The king directed them to a certain place.
25. There his friend, the king of the mice, received them kindly.
26. The king of the mice set them all free by nibbling through the net.
27. Thus the whole troop of pigeons escaped by means of union.
28. All men should profit by this lesson.
29. A chariot will not go on a single wheel.
30. A creeper, having nothing to support it, must fall to the earth.—*Digest of Eastern Fable.*

SUMMARY OF CHAPTER I.

Sentence: a combination of words in which something is said about something else (§ 1).

Subject: the word or words denoting what we speak about (§ 2).

Predicate: the word or words by which we say something about the thing denoted by the subject (§ 2).

Clause: a sentence that is part of a larger sentence (§ 3).

Nominative or its equivalent: the noun or noun-equivalent that fixes the number and person of the Finite verb (§ 3).

Noun-clause: a clause that does the work of a noun (§ 3).

Enlargement of Nominative: an adjective or adjective-equivalent that enlarges the meaning of the Nominative (§ 4).

Adjective-clause: a clause that does the work of an adjective (§ 4).

Finite verb: any part of a verb that is limited to number and person (§ 5).

Non-finite parts of a verb: those parts of a verb that are not limited to number or person, viz. the Infinitive, the Participle, and the Gerund (§ 5).

Transitive verb: one that requires an object (§ 6).

Intransitive verb: one that does not require an object (§ 6).

Factitive verb: a Transitive verb that requires both a complement and an object (§ 6).

Copulative verb: an Intransitive verb that requires a complement (§ 6).

Extension of Finite verb: an adverb or adverb-equivalent that extends the meaning of a Finite verb (§ 7).

Adverb-clause: a clause that does the work of an adverb (§ 7).

CHAPTER II.—THE PARTS OF SPEECH IN OUTLINE: PHRASES.

Section 1.—The Parts of Speech.

The definitions given in this chapter will not be repeated in subsequent chapters.

9. **The Parts of Speech.**—The different kinds of words used for different purposes in a sentence are called Parts of Speech.

Until we see a word *in a sentence*, we are often unable to say to what part of speech it belongs:—

(*a*) *Water* the roses. (*b*) Take some *water*. (*c*) A *water* bird.

In (*a*) *water* is a verb. In (*b*) it is a noun. In (*c*) it is an adjective, or a noun used as an adjective.

10. **Noun.**—Take such a sentence as the following:—

The *howling* of the *wolf* filled the *flock* with *terror*.

Here *howling* is the name of an action; *wolf*, of an animal; *flock*, of a multitude; *terror*, of a feeling. So *howling*, *wolf*, *flock*, *terror* are all nouns.

Definition.—A noun is a word used for naming anything.

Note 1.—The word "thing" in this definition stands for person, place, quality, action, feeling, collection, etc., anything, in fact, that we can speak about. It is so used in all the definitions that follow.

Note 2.—*Noun* and *name* both mean the some thing at bottom. *Noun* is from Latin *nomen*, a name. *Name* is from Anglo-Saxon *nama*, a name.

11. Pronoun.—Take such a sentence as the following:—

I told James that the snake *which you* saw in the garden would do *him* no harm, if *he* let *it* go *its own* way.

Here *I* is used for the speaker; *you* for the person spoken to; *him* and *he* for "James"; *which*, *it*, and *its own* for "snake." So all these words are pronouns.

Definition.—A pronoun (Latin *pro*, for, instead of) is a word used instead of a noun. (It is, in fact, a substitute word or proxy. It denotes a thing without being a name for it.)

Note 1.—Pronouns in the First and Second persons save the *mentioning* of a noun, and in the Third the *repetition* of one. The speaker, however, can give his own name, if he chooses:—

We, *John Cade*, so termed of our supposed father, etc.
2 *Henry VI.* iv. 2, 33.

Usually, however, the speaker simply says "I" without giving his own name, and in addressing any one he simply says "you" without mentioning the name of the person spoken to.

Note 2.—Pronouns are also used as substitutes for a noun-equivalent:—

Climbing up rocks is an amusement to me; but *that* (=climbing up rocks) is a labour to you.

12. Adjective.—A noun standing by itself is sometimes of too general a meaning to indicate the thing to which the writer or speaker is referring.

Supposing the noun to be "house," the speaker might wish to point out some particular house. He would then have to say "*this* house," or "*that* house," or "*the other* house."

Or he might wish to allude to the quantity, as "the *whole* house"; or to the number, as "*one* house," "*four* houses"; or to the serial order, as "the *first* house," "the *fourth* house."

Or he might wish to describe the kind of house, as "a *little* house," "a *comfortable* house," "an *untidy* house," etc.

Or he might wish to speak about several houses in a distributive sense, as "*each* house," "*every* house."

Any word thus added to a noun is called an Adjective (Lat. *adjectivus*, "used for adding on"). The noun and adjective thus combined make a kind of compound noun. Sometimes this compound noun can be written as a single word, as "greatcoat," "blackguard," "nobleman," "halfpenny," "quicksands," "sweetheart," etc., every one of which can easily be broken up into a simple noun and an adjective that precedes it.

Definition.—An adjective is a word that enlarges the meaning and narrows the application of a noun.

Enlargement of meaning is necessarily accompanied by a narrowing of application. This is a vital point. Thus the noun "house," so long as its meaning remains unenlarged, that is, so long as no adjective is added to it, can be applied to an almost countless number of things called by the general name of "house." But if I add to the noun the adjective "fourth," the noun so enlarged can be applied to only one house, viz. to that house which stands fourth in a certain row or terrace.

Observe that when we enlarge the meaning of "house" by adding "fourth," we do not alter the meaning of "house." "Fourth house" means all that "house" means, and more besides.

Shorter definition.—An adjective is a word used to qualify a noun.[1]

This shorter definition is intended to signify exactly the same thing as the longer one. On account of its shortness it is more convenient for parsing. Thus in parsing "fourth house" we can say that "fourth" is an adjective qualifying the noun "house."

Note.—Amongst adjectives we must not omit to include the Definite article *the* (a short form of *this*) and the Indefinite article *a* (a short form of *one*).

13. Verb.—This has been described already in §§ 2, 5.

Definition.—A verb is a word used for *saying* something about something else.

"Verb" is from Latin *verbum*, a word. A verb has been called pre-eminently "the word," because it is the chief word in a sentence. In fact, it is the most important kind of word in human speech. "James laughs": we might designate James by pointing to him with our finger; but we cannot express any fact about him, as "laughs," without using our voice and saying the word *laughs*.

14. Preposition.—Take such sentences as the following:—

(*a*) I put my hand *on* the table.
(*b*) A bird *in* the hand is worth two (birds) *in* the bush.
(*c*) He is opposed *to* severe measures.

In (*a*) the preposition *on* shows the relation between the thing denoted by *table* and the action denoted by "put." The hand might be held *above* the table, or *under* it, or *on* it. It is the preposition which defines the relation.

---

[1] Observe that *qualify* simply means *modify*. In grammar it means precisely the same thing that it does in ordinary language, and is not by any means limited to adjectives that express some quality or attribute.

In (*b*) the preposition *in* shows the relation between the thing denoted by the noun *bird* and the thing denoted by the noun *hand*; also between the things denoted by the noun *birds* and the thing denoted by the noun *bush*.

In (*c*) the preposition *to* shows the relation between the things denoted by *severe measures* and the quality (opposition) denoted by the word *opposed*.

Definition.—A preposition is a word used for showing in what relation one thing stands to another thing, or (more briefly) for showing what one thing has to do with another thing.

The noun or noun-equivalent that comes after a preposition is called its **Object**.

Note 1.—Avoid such definitions as the following:—

"A preposition is a word used before a noun or pronoun to show its relation to some other word in the sentence."

According to this, "a Jack in the box" does not mean that a Jack is in the box, but that the noun "Jack" is in the noun "box."

Nor is it enough to say that "a preposition connects a noun with a verb, an adjective, or other noun." In the phrase "time *and* tide," we have one noun connected with another noun; and in the sentence "men *are* mortal," we have a noun connected with an adjective by the copulative "are." Yet neither *and* nor *are* is a preposition.

Note 2.—When a single preposition does not express all that is needed, two prepositions may be used for the purpose:—

The mouse crept out *from under* the floor.
The rabbit escaped by running *into* its hole.

15. Conjunction.—Take such examples as the following:—

(*a*) He is a humble-minded *and* contented man.
(*b*) We admire the character of a poor, *but* honest, man.
(*c*) That man is disliked, *because* he is ill-tempered.

In (*a*) the notion of humility expressed by *humble-minded* is connected (in the sense of addition) with the notion of contentment expressed by *contented*. The one notion is simply added to the other. The conjunction used for this purpose is *and*.

In (*b*) the notion of poverty expressed by *poor* is connected (in the sense of contrast) with the notion of honesty expressed by *honest*. The one notion is contrasted with the other. The conjunction used for this purpose is *but*.

In (*c*) the thought expressed by the sentence "he is ill-tempered" is connected (in the sense of cause or reason) with the thought expressed by the sentence "that man is disliked."[1] The one thought is given as the reason for the other.

[1] When the mind apprehends a single object, as "father," "son," "honesty," "poverty," the result is called a *notion*; and this is expressed

Definition.—A conjunction is a word used for showing in what relation one notion stands (in the mind of the speaker or writer) to another notion, or one thought to another thought.

Note 1.—A detail of the different relations expressed by conjunctions will be given hereafter. Meanwhile it may be pointed out that three different relations have been exemplified already—addition in example (*a*), contrast in (*b*), and causality in (*c*).

Note 2.—In parsing, it is convenient for the sake of brevity to say that "a conjunction joins words to words, and sentences to sentences." But this is not enough for the purposes of definition. Prepositions also join words, as "a bird *in* the hand." Some verbs, too, join words, as "time *is* money" (in fact, the verb *is* is called "copulative" for no other reason than that it couples or joins words). Some adverbs, too, like *where*, *when*, etc., join sentences, as "We found out *where* he was." Relative pronouns also join sentences, as "We have found the house *that* you were looking for"; and for this reason they are called conjunctive.

Note 3.—Prepositions and conjunctions have been bracketed sometimes as "connective words," and sometimes as "relational words." If there is any truth in what we have laid down, there is much more point in bracketing them as "relational" words than as "connective" ones. Both kinds of words express relations—prepositions a relation between one *thing* and another *thing*; conjunctions a relation between one *notion* and another *notion*, or between one *thought* and another *thought*.

16. Adverb.—What an adjective does for a noun or pronoun, an adverb does for any part of speech except a noun or pronoun: it enlarges or extends the meaning of a word and narrows its application. Take such sentences as the following:—

(*a*) *With verb.*—I *much* admire his industry.
(*b*) *With adjective.*—He is *deservedly* successful.
(*c*) *With preposition.*—The body floated *partly* above and *partly* below the water.
(*d*) *With conjunction.*—He was despised, *merely* because he was poor.
(*e*) *With other adverb.*—He writes *remarkably* well.

In (*a*) the verb "admire" is qualified by the adverb "much."

In (*b*) the adjective "successful" is qualified by the adverb "deservedly."

In (*c*) the preposition "above" is qualified by the adverb "partly"; and the preposition "below" by the same adverb.

In (*d*) the conjunction "because" is qualified by the adverb "merely."

---

by a single word or phrase. When the mind compares two notions and connects them by a Finite verb, the result is called a *thought*; and this is expressed by a sentence (Latin, *sententia*, a thought).

In (*e*) the adverb "well" is qualified by the adverb "remarkably."

Definition.—An adverb is a word that extends the meaning and narrows the application of any part of speech except a noun or pronoun.[1]

Note.—Example (*c*). Observe that in extending the meaning of "above" by the addition of "partly," we do not alter the meaning of "above." The phrase "partly above" expresses all that is implied in the preposition "above," and something more. It shows that the relation of above-ness denoted by "above" is not entire, but partial. The same remarks apply to the preposition "below."

Example (*d*). Here the meaning of the conjunction "because" is extended, not altered, by the adverb "merely." The phrase "merely because" expresses all that is implied in "because," and something more. It shows that the relation of cause denoted by the conjunction "because" is to be understood in a sense that excludes every other cause. If we change the order of the words and say, "He was merely despised, because he was poor," the meaning of the sentence is not the same: this would mean, "He was merely despised (not hated or attacked), because he was poor." Or, if we leave out the adverb "merely," the sense would again be different. The sentence would then imply that there may have been other reasons besides poverty for which he was despised.

17. Interjection.—All Parts of Speech except interjections have some grammatical connection with some other word in the sentence in which they occur. An interjection is the only part of speech that stands alone—isolated. It scarcely deserves to be called a part of speech; for it lies on the borderland of language, halfway between articulate speech and the inarticulate cries of animals. We must give it a name, however, because it is a *word*; for grammar takes account of every kind of word that can occur in human speech.

My son, *alas!* died yesterday.

Definition.—An interjection is a word thrown into a sentence to express some feeling of the mind, but forms no part of the construction of the sentence.

"Interjection" is from Latin *interjectus*, thrown between.

Note.—The meaning of an interjection might be expressed by a parenthetical sentence:—

My son (I am sorry to say) died yesterday.

Observe that a sentence substituted for an interjection is always

---

[1] In § 17 it is shown that an interjection is, properly speaking, not a Part of Speech. Hence no mention is made of interjections in this definition. An interjection, being absolute or isolated, cannot be qualified by any other word.

parenthetical. The sentence "I am sorry to say" is as completely isolated from the sentence "My son died yesterday" by the parenthesis as the interjection "alas!" is isolated from it by its own nature.

18. **Double Parts of Speech.**—Besides the eight Parts of Speech already described, there are four kinds of words which are double parts of speech, that is, two combined in one:—

(1) A **Participle.**—This is a verb and adjective combined.

A *retired* officer lives next door.

"Retired" is a verb, being part of the verb "retire." It is also an adjective, because it qualifies the noun "officer." Hence a participle may be called a verbal adjective.

(2) A **Gerund** or **Verbal Noun.**—This is a verb and noun combined.

I think of *retiring* soon from service.

"Retiring" is a verb, being part of the verb "retire." It is also a noun, because it is object to the preposition "of."

(3) An **Infinitive.**—This too is a verb and noun combined.

I wish *to return* that book.

Here "to return" is a verb, in the Infinitive mood. It is also a kind of noun, because it is the object to the Transitive verb "wish."

(4) **Relative Adverb.**—This is partly an adverb and partly a conjunction. It has hence been called a "Conjunctive adverb."

We shall be glad *when* the risk is over.

Here "when" is an adverb, because it qualifies the verb "is." It has also the character of a conjunction, because it connects the thought expressed by "we shall be glad" with the thought expressed by "the risk is over."

Exercise.

In the following sentences point out the Part of Speech in which each italicised word is used, and give your reason for saying that it belongs to one Part of Speech rather than to another:—

1. A square thing does not fit into a *round* hole. Draw a circle *round* a given centre. The flies are flying *round* and *round*. Men must go their daily *round* of duty. Vasco da Gama was the first to *round* the Cape of Good Hope.

2. The earth is very dry, and *needs* rain. He must *needs* know the reason of this. Our *needs* or wants are few.

3. I will wait for you at the *next* house. He stood *next* me in the class. Who came *next*?

4. We must *all* die some day. We lost our *all* on that day. The road was *all* covered with sand.

5. He returned *after* a week's absence. He returned *after* he had been absent for a week. The man died of fever, and his son died a few days *after*.

6. A beggar is standing *before* the gate. I never saw such a thing *before*. He took the book, *before* he had paid for it.

7. My book is a *better* one than yours. You are working *better* to-day. Do not despise your *betters*.

8. There is *but* one man present. Who *but* you would have made such a mistake. He is a man of common sense, *but* not learned in books.

9. He had *enough* to do. We have wages *enough* for three men.

10. *Half* measures do not succeed. One *half* of his task is now done. He was *half* dead with fear.

11. He has eaten *more* bread to-day than yesterday. *More* has been done than was expected. I like him *more* than I like you.

12. *Near* our house there is a fine tree. He is a *near* relative of mine. Stand *near*, while I whisper something into your ear.

13. He has wasted *much* time. I am *much* pleased with your conduct. You will not get *much* from me.

14. We should pity the sorrows of *others*. *Other* men besides you deserve pity.

15. You will *save* him if you try. All the men *save* one perished.

16. I have not seen him *since* Monday last. I took this house four weeks *since*. We shall trust you, *since* you were always honest.

17. I am not a student in *that* school. A student *that* works hard will get promotion. I heard *that* you were coming.

18. We must stop here a little *while*. *While* the cat is away, the mice play.

SECTION 2.—CLASSIFICATION OF PHRASES.

19. Phrase defined.—A phrase is a combination of words in which no Finite verb is either expressed or understood.

A phrase is therefore intermediate between a single word and a sentence.

20. Kinds of Phrases.—Phrases may be classified according to the parts of speech for which they are used as substitutes. There is no phrase which can be substituted for a pronoun, since a pronoun is a substitute word already (§ 11).

(*a*) *Noun-phrase:* one which does the work of a noun :—

How to do this is a difficult question.

(*b*) *Adjectival phrase:* one which does the work of an adjective :—

A bird *in the hand* is worth two (birds) *in the bush*.

(*c*) *Adverbial phrase:* one which does the work of an adverb :—

I shall wait *a few minutes*.
He shouted *at the top of his voice*.
The sun having set, they all retired.

(*d*) *Prepositional phrase:* one which does the work of a preposition :—

He went *on board* ship.

(e) *Conjunctional phrase:* one which does the work of a conjunction :—

In case we fail, we must try again.

(f) *Interjectional phrase:* one which does the work of an interjection :—

What a pity! For shame! Good gracious!

The result, then, is that any combination of words which can be substituted for some part of speech may be called a phrase; and we have seen that nouns, adjectives, adverbs, prepositions, conjunctions, and interjections may all be expressed by phrases.

The one exception is a Finite verb. Nothing but a Finite verb can do the work of a Finite verb,—which corroborates what is said in § 13, that a verb is the most important kind of word in human speech.

Exercise.

Show for what Parts of Speech the italicised phrases are used in the following sentences:—

1. I am sorry that he behaved *with so much rudeness.*
2. A sharp ride *on a spirited horse* is the best kind of exercise.
3. The beauties of nature are *beyond description.*
4. *Dinner being over*, let us now go into the next room.
5. He will be dismissed *in the event of* his doing such a thing again.
6. The young have to learn *how to profit by experience.*
7. He was not often *behind time.*
8. An English sailor had been shut up *for several years*, but he was set free *at the peace.*
9. Bind him *hand and foot* and take him away.
10. A man *in bad health* can seldom be happy.
11. He was not a man *to tell a lie.*
12. *The two chief points having been gained*, success is now certain.
13. He took medicine *in order that* he might recover.
14. He still feels tired, *notwithstanding that* he had ten hours' sleep.

SUMMARY OF CHAPTER II.

Parts of Speech: the different kinds of words that serve different purposes in a sentence (§ 9).

Noun: a word used for naming anything (§ 10).

Pronoun: a word used instead of a noun (§ 11).

Adjective: a word that enlarges the meaning and narrows the application of a noun (§ 12).

Verb: a word used for *saying* something about something else (§ 13).

Preposition: a word used for showing in what relation one thing stands to another thing, or for showing what one thing has to do with another thing (§ 14).

Conjunction: a word used for showing in what relation one notion stands to another notion, or one thought to another thought (§ 15).

Adverb: a word that extends the meaning and narrows the application of any part of speech except a noun or pronoun (§ 16).

Interjection: a word thrown into a sentence to express some feeling of the mind, but forming no part of the construction of the sentence (§ 17).

Double Part of Speech: a word in which the characters of two parts of speech are combined (§ 18).

Phrase: a combination of words in which no Finite verb is either expressed or understood (§ 19).

Noun-phrase: one which does the work of a noun (§ 20).

Adjectival phrase: one which does the work of an adjective (§ 20).

Adverbial phrase: one which does the work of an adverb (§ 20).

Prepositional phrase: one which does the work of a preposition (§ 20).

Conjunctional phrase: one which does the work of a conjunction (§ 20).

Interjectional phrase: one which does the work of an interjection (§ 20).

CHAPTER III.—NOUNS.

SECTION 1.—THE KINDS OF NOUNS.

21. Nouns classified.—Nouns are of five different kinds:—

I. Concrete	Proper (one thing at a time)	1
	Common (any number of things)	2
	Collective (a group of things)	3
	Material (what a thing is made of)	4
II. Abstract (quality, state, or action)		5

22. A Proper Noun is a name for *one particular* thing as distinct from every other; as *James* (a person), *Kenilworth* (a book), *Paris* (a city), *France* (a country).

Note.—"Proper" (Lat. *proprius*) means "own." Thus a Proper name is "*own* name." It cannot be given to more than one thing at a time.

23. A Common Noun denotes no one thing in particular, but is *common to any number of things of the same kind*; as "man," "book," "country."

Note 1.—Many nouns now Proper were originally Common. A common name, as Brown, Smith, Baker, Clark (clerc), Shepherd, Butcher, Parson, Mason, etc., being frequently applied to some individual by way of distinction, was eventually restricted to that individual and his family, and so the Common name became a Proper name.

Note 2.—"Common" (Lat. *communis*) means "shared by several."

Things of the same kind, *i.e.* possessing some property in common, have an equal right to be called by the same name.

Note 3.—A Proper noun becomes a Common noun, when it is used in a descriptive or general sense :—

The *Czar* of Russia. The *Pharaohs* of Egypt.
He is the *Newton* (greatest astronomer) of the century.

24. A **Collective Noun** is a name for a *group of similar individuals*, the group being one complete whole.

For instance, there may be *many sheep* in a field, but only *one flock*. Here "sheep" is a Common noun, because it may stand for any and every sheep; but "flock" is a Collective noun, because it stands for all the sheep at once, and not for any one sheep taken separately.

Note 1.—A Collective Noun may be either Common or Proper :—
Thus the term "flock" may stand for many different flocks. But *Parliament, the House of Commons*, can stand for only one body.

Note 2.—A Noun of Multitude, since it denotes a specific group, must be classed as Collective; but with a difference.

(*a*) A Collective noun denotes *one undivided whole*; and hence the verb following is singular :—

The jury *consists* of twelve persons.

(*b*) A noun of Multitude denotes the *individuals* of the group; and hence the verb is plural, although the noun is singular :—

The jury (the men on the jury) *were* divided in their opinions.

25. A noun of **Material** is a name for some particular **kind** of *matter* or *substance*.

Thus "sheep" is a Common noun; but "mutton" (or the flesh of sheep) is a Material noun.

Note.—The same word can be a Material noun or a Common noun according to the sense :—

Fish live in water (*Com.*). *Fish* is good for food (*Mat.*).

26. An **Abstract Noun** denotes some *quality, state*, or *action*, apart from anything possessing the quality, etc.

Quality—Cleverness, height, humility, roguery, colour.
State—Poverty, manhood, bondage, pleasure, youth.
Action—Laughter, movement, flight, choice, revenge.

The four kinds of nouns first named are all **Concrete**; *i.e.* they denote *objects of sense*, viz. what can be seen, heard, touched, smelt, or tasted, or what can be perceived by the muscular sense, as weight, extension, etc. But an abstract noun relates to *qualities, states*, etc., which cannot be seen or touched, etc., and which are thought of *apart from* any object of sense.

For example: We know that a stone is *hard*. We also know that iron is *hard*. We also know that a brick is *hard*. We can therefore speak of *hardness* apart from stone, or iron, or brick, or any other object having the same quality. "Abstract" (Lat. *abstractus*) means "drawn off" (abstracted in thought) from the object. Hence *hardness* is an abstract noun; while *stone* or *brick* or *iron* is a concrete noun.

27. The same word may be an Abstract noun or a Common (*i.e.* Concrete) noun, according to the purpose for which it is used:—

(a) *Examples of Persons.*

Justice	1. Justice is a virtue	*Abstract*
	2. He is a justice of the peace	*Concrete*
Beauty	1. She is admired for her beauty	*Abstract*
	2. She is the beauty of the town	*Concrete*
Authority	1. He has no authority	*Abstract*
	2. The best authorities differ	*Concrete*
Nobility	1. I admire nobility of character	*Abstract*
	2. He is one of the nobility	*Concrete*

(b) *Examples of Things.*

Judgment	1. He is a man of sound judgment	*Abstract*
	2. The magistrate passed a severe judgment	*Concrete*
Sight	1. Sight is a valuable faculty	*Abstract*
	2. That was a fine sight	*Concrete*
Wonder	1. The news fills me with wonder	*Abstract*
	2. We have seen a wonder to-day	*Concrete*
Kindness	1. Kindness is part of his character	*Abstract*
	2. He did me a great kindness	*Concrete*

Note 1.—Sometimes there is one form of adjective for an Abstract noun used as such, and another for the same noun used as Concrete.

(1) An *industrious* man (=man of *industry, Abstract*).

(2) This town has no *industrial* works (=has no local *industry, Concrete*).

Note 2.—Sometimes an Abstract noun has a collective sense:—

The *rank* and *fashion* (=persons of rank or fashion) all went out to hear him speak.

Note 3.—Abstract nouns are often personified:—

But *Melancholy* marked him for her own.—GRAY.

How Abstract Nouns are formed.

28. Abstract Nouns can be formed from Adjectives, or from Common nouns, or from Verbs:—

(a) *Abstract Nouns formed from Adjectives.*

Adj.	*Abstract Noun.*	*Adj.*	*Abstract Noun.*	*Adj.*	*Abstract Noun.*
Wise	wisdom	Prudent	prudence	Bitter	bitterness
Poor	poverty	Sweet	sweetness	Wide	width
High	height	Young	youth	Sole	solitude
Short	shortness	Proud	pride	Broad	breadth
Honest	honesty	Just	justice	Deep	depth
Dark	darkness	Great	greatness	True	truth
Long	length	Hot	heat	Cold	coldness
Brave	bravery	Sleepy	sleepiness	Humble	humility

(b) *Abstract Nouns formed from Common Nouns.*

Common Noun.	*Abstract Noun.*	*Common Noun.*	*Abstract Noun.*	*Common Noun.*	*Abstract Noun.*
Man	manhood	Agent	agency	Mother	motherhood
Child	childhood	Regent	regency	Rascal	rascality
Friend	friendship	King	kingship	Rogue	roguery
Boy	boyhood	Bond	bondage	Slave	slavery
Captain	captaincy	Hero	heroism	Infant	infancy
Priest	priesthood	Thief	theft	Owner	ownership

(c) *Abstract Nouns formed from Verbs.*

Verb.	*Abstract Noun.*	*Verb.*	*Abstract Noun.*	*Verb.*	*Abstract Noun.*
Serve	service	Relieve	relief	Seize	seizure
Live	life	Believe	belief	Laugh	laughter
Hate	hatred	Please	pleasure	Free	freedom
Obey	obedience	Advise	advice	Expect	expectation
Choose	choice	Defend	defence	Protect	protection
Move	motion	Judge	judgment	Think	thought
See	sight	Conceal	concealment		

Note.—All Verbal Nouns (§ 3 and § 18) ending in *-ing* are Abstract nouns :—

The *reading* of books is good for the mind.

(d) *Abstract Nouns of the same form as Verbs.*

Verb.	*Abstract Noun.*	*Verb.*	*Abstract Noun.*	*Verb.*	*Abstract Noun.*
Fear	fear	Fall	fall	Sob	sob
Hope	hope	Stay	stay	Laugh	laugh
Desire	desire	Stop	stop	Taste	taste
Regret	regret	Walk	walk	Ride	ride
Order	order	Run	run	Touch	touch
Move	move	Step	step	Love	love
Rise	rise	Cry	cry		

29. There are two ways in which a Proper, Material, or Abstract noun can be used as a Common noun—(*a*) by putting an article ("a" or "the") before it; (*b*) by putting it in the plural number.

Proper Noun.	*Common Nouns.*
Daniel was a learned Jew.	*A Daniel* come to judgment. There are more *Daniels* than one.
Material Noun.	
Apple is my favourite fruit.	Give me *the apple* in your hand. Give me one of your *apples*.
Abstract Noun.	
Justice is a noble quality.	He is *a justice* of the peace. There are four *justices* present.

SECTION 2.—GENDER.

30. Gender.—Nouns are now classified according to sex or absence of sex, and not, as once, by *form* or *declension*:—

(1) **Masculine**—*male* animals: *bull, horse, hog.*
(2) **Feminine**—*female* animals: *cow, mare, sow.*
(3) **Common**—of *either* sex: *parent, child.*
(4) **Neuter**—of *neither* sex: *box, flock, pain.*

Note 1.—It is only in the pronouns *he, she, it,* that gender according to *form* has survived.

Note 2.—When no account is taken of sex, we often speak of animals as neuter:—

The *child* is asleep: let *it* sleep on.
You have a *horse*: will you let me ride *it*?

31. Modes of denoting Gender or Sex.—There are three different ways in which the gender (or sex) of living beings is indicated:—

1. *By a Change of Ending.*

Masculine.	*Feminine.*	*Masculine.*	*Feminine.*
Abbot	abbess	Marquis	marchioness
Actor	actress	Master	mistress
Author	authoress	Murderer	murderess
Duke	duchess	Negro	negress
Emperor	empress	Patron	patroness
Executor	executrix	Poet	poetess
Giant	giantess	Priest	priestess
God	goddess	Prince	princess
Heir	heiress	Prophet	prophetess
Hero	heroine	Shepherd	shepherdess
Host	hostess	Songster	songstress
Hunter	huntress	Testator	testatrix
Lad	lass	Tiger	tigress
Lion	lioness	Widower	widow

Note.—There are some Feminines that have no Masculines:—*blonde, brunette, dowager, dowdy, drab, prude, shrew, siren, termagant, vixen.* (But *vixen* was originally the Fem. of *fox.*)

2. *By a Change of Word.*

Masculine.	*Feminine.*	*Masculine.*	*Feminine.*
Bachelor	maid, spinster	Drake	duck
Boar	sow	Earl	countess
Boy	girl	Father	mother
Brother	sister	Friar (or monk)	nun
Buck	doe	Gander	goose
Bull	cow	Gentleman	lady
Bullock (or steer)	heifer	Hart	roe
Cock	hen	Horse	mare
Colt	filly	Husband	wife
Dog	bitch (or slut)	King	queen

Masculine.	*Feminine.*	*Masculine.*	*Feminine.*
Lord	lady	Sloven	slattern, slut
Man	woman	Son	daughter
Milter	spawner	Stag	hind
Nephew	niece	Uncle	aunt
Ram	ewe	Wizard	witch
Sir	madam		

3. *By placing a Word Before or After.*

Masculine.	*Feminine.*	*Masculine.*	*Feminine.*
Bride-groom	bride	He-goat	she-goat
Cock-sparrow	hen-sparrow	Land-lord	land-lady
Grand-father	grand-mother	Man-servant	maid-servant
Great-uncle	great-aunt	Pea-cock	pea-hen

4. *Nouns in the Common Gender ;* i.e. *denoting either Sex.*

Baby—male or female.
Bird—cock or hen.
Calf—bullock or heifer.
Child—boy or girl.
Cousin—male or female.
Deer—stag or hind.
Fallow-deer—buck or doe.
Foal—colt or filly.
Fowl—cock or hen.
Friend—Enemy—male or female.
Monarch—king or queen.
Orphan—boy or girl without parents.
Parent—father or mother.
Person—man or woman.
Pig—boar or sow.
Pupil—boy or girl.
Relation—male or female.
Servant—man or maid.
Sheep—ram or ewe.
Student—boy or girl.
Teacher—master or mistress.

Note.—Some Masculines, as *colt*, *dog*, *horse*, and some Feminines, as *duck*, *goose*, are used to denote either sex, provided that no question arises as to whether the animal is male or female :—

A *goose* is a much bigger bird than a *duck*.

SECTION 3.—NUMBER.

32. When a Noun denotes *one* object, it is **Singular.** When it denotes *more than one*, it is **Plural.**

33. Proper, Material, and Abstract nouns have no Plural, unless they can be used as Common nouns :—

(*a*) **Proper** { *Egypt* is a country in Africa. (*Proper.*)
Many *Egypts* (=countries as large as Egypt) could be contained in India. (*Common.*)

(*b*) **Material** { *Tea* is a pleasant drink. (*Material.*)
The best *teas* (=kinds of tea). (*Common.*)

(*c*) **Abstract** { *Kindness* is part of his character. (*Abstract.*)
He did many *kindnesses* (=kind acts). (*Common.*)

34. The general rule for forming the Plural number of a noun is by adding *s* to the Singular :—

Singular.	*Plural.*	*Singular.*	*Plural.*
Hand	hand-*s*	House	house-*s*
Map	map-*s*	Stone	stone-*s*

But if the Noun ends in *s*, *x*, *sh*, or *ch*, the Plural is formed by adding *es* to the Singular :—

Singular.	*Plural.*	*Singular.*	*Plural.*
Glass	glass-*es*	Gash	gash-*es*
Gas	gas-*es*	Brush	brush-*es*
Tax	tax-*es*	Bench	bench-*es*
Box	box-*es*	Coach	coach-*es*

35. If the Noun ends in *y* and the *y* is preceded by a *consonant*, the Plural is formed by changing the *y* into *ies* :—

Singular.	*Plural.*	*Singular.*	*Plural.*
Duty	dut-*ies*	Army	arm-*ies*
Fly	fl-*ies*	Lady	lad-*ies*

But if the final *y* is preceded by a *vowel*, as in *ay*, *ey*, or *oy*, the Plural is formed by simply adding *s* to the Singular :—

Singular.	*Plural.*	*Singular.*	*Plural.*
Day	day-*s*	Monkey	monkey-*s*
Play	play-*s*	Toy	toy-*s*
Key	key-*s*	Boy	boy-*s*

Note.—In *colloquy* the *qu* = *kw* : so *y* becomes *ies*.

36. If the Noun ends in *o* and the *o* is preceded by a *consonant*, the Plural is generally (not always) formed by adding *es* to the Singular :—

Singular.	*Plural.*	*Singular.*	*Plural.*
Cargo	cargo-*es*	Volcano	volcano-*es*
Hero	hero-*es*	Potato	potato-*es*
Buffalo	buffalo-*es*	Echo	echo-*es*
Motto	motto-*es*	Negro	negro-*es*

Note.—The chief exceptions are :—*grotto, halo, memento, proviso, tiro, piano, canto, solo.*

But if the *o* is preceded by a *vowel*, the Plural is formed by simply adding *s* to the Singular :—

Singular.	*Plural.*	*Singular.*	*Plural.*
Folio	folio-*s*	Hindoo	Hindoo-*s*
Cameo	cameo-*s*	Bamboo	bamboo-*s*

37. If the Noun ends in *f* or *fe*, the Plural is generally formed by changing *f* or *fe* into *ves* :—

Singular.	*Plural.*	*Singular.*	*Plural.*
Loaf	loa-*ves*	Thief	thie-*ves*
Wife	wi-*ves*	Half	hal-*ves*
Wolf	wol-*ves*	Myself	oursel-*ves*
Knife	kni-*ves*	Shelf	shel-*ves*
Life	liv-*es*	Leaf	lea-*ves*
Calf	cal-*ves*	Sheaf	shea-*ves*

(*a*) Some Nouns ending in *f* form the Plural by adding *s* :—

Singular.	*Plural.*	*Singular.*	*Plural.*
Reef	reef-*s*	Dwarf	dwarf-*s*
Chief	chief-*s*	Turf	turf-*s*
Roof	roof-*s*	Cliff	cliff-*s*
Hoof	hoof-*s*	Gulf	gulf-*s*
Proof	proof-*s*	Grief	grief-*s*

(*b*) Three Nouns in *fe* form the Plural by adding *s* :—

Safe—safe-*s* ; strife—strife-*s* ; fife—fife-*s*.

38. Peculiar Plurals.—(*a*) Eight Nouns in common use form the Plural by a change of inside vowel :—

Singular.	*Plural.*	*Singular.*	*Plural.*
Man	men	Tooth	teeth
Woman	women	Louse	*lice*
Foot	feet	Mouse	m*ice*
Goose	geese	Dormouse	dorm*ice*

(*b*) There are three Nouns which form the Plural in *en* :

Ox—ox-*en* ; child—childr-*en* ; brother—brethr-*en*.

The word "cow" has two plurals—"cows" or "kine."

(*c*) Some Nouns have the same form in both numbers :—

Animals.—Deer, sheep, fish (rarely fishes), swine, grouse, salmon, trout, cod, heathen.

Collective numerals.—Yoke, brace, dozen, score, gross.

Measures of weight.—Stone, hundredweight.

(*d*) Some Nouns have no Singular :—

Annals	Gallows	Pincers	Victuals
Shears	Statistics	Scissors	Tidings
Bellows	Suds	Shambles	News
Tongs	Nuptials	Thanks	Means

Note.—In spite of the Plural form we say, "By *this* means," "*This* news is not true."

(*e*) Some Nouns, that take a Plural at ordinary times, use a Singular to express some specific quantity or number :—

A twelve-*month.* A three-*foot* rule. An eight-*day* clock. A six-*year* old horse. A fort-*night* (=fourteen nights). Forty *head* of cattle. Twelve *pound* weight. Ten *sail* of the line. A six-*penny* piece.

Note.—Such a phrase as "A hundred thousand men" does not come under this heading. Here "a hundred thousand" is a Collective noun in the Singular number, and the preposition "of" is understood after it.

(*f*) A Noun of Multitude, being plural already in sense (§ 24, *b*), has no need of a plural form :—

The *poultry* are doing well. These *cattle* are mine. These *vermin* do much harm. These *people* have come. No *gentry* live here.

(*g*) Foreign Plurals :—

Latin : Sing. in *-um* ; *agend-a*, *addend-a*, *dat-a*, *effluvi-a*, *errat-a*. Sing. in *-us* ; *alumn-i*, *foc-i*, *radi-i*. Sing. in *-a* ; *formul-æ*. From other Singulars ; *genera* (genus), *series* (series), *appendices* (appendix). **Greek** : Sing. in *-is* ; *bas-es*, *hypothes-es*, *parenthes-es*. Sing. in *-on* ; *phenomen-a*, *criteri-a*. **French** : *beaux*, *bureaux*, *messieurs*, *mesdames*. **Italian** : *banditti*, *dilettanti*. **Hebrew** : *cherubim*, *seraphim*.

(*h*) Compound Plurals. The principal word is pluralised :—

Step-sons, *sons-in-law*, *hangers-on*, *maid-servants*, *courts-martial*.

(*i*) Double Plurals :—*Men-servants*, *lords-justices*.

Section 4.—Case.

39. Case defined.—The *relation* in which a noun stands to some other word, or the *change of form* (if any) by which this relation is indicated, is called its **Case.**[1]

40. Three Cases in modern English.—These are the *Nominative*, the *Possessive*, and the *Objective*.

But the Possessive is the only case that is *now* indicated by a case-ending or *change of form*. The other cases have lost their case-endings, and are indicated only by grammatical relation.

Note.—A change of form is called an **inflexion.** All our noun-inflexions except (1) the plural, and (2) the possessive, are lost. The ending *-ess* (§ 31) is not an inflexion, but a suffix. See Appendix II.

41. When a noun is used as the *subject* to a verb (§ 3), or for the sake of *address*, it is said to be in the **Nominative** case :—

Rain falls. (*Nominative of Subject.*)
Are you coming, my *friend?* (*Nominative of Address.*)

42. When a noun is the *object* to a verb (§ 6, *a*), or to a preposition (§ 14), it is said to be in the **Objective** case :—

The man killed a *rat*. (*Object to Verb.*)
The earth is moistened by *rain*. (*Obj. to Prep.*)

43. The **Possessive** case is so called, because it usually denotes the *possessor* or owner. It is formed by adding *'s* (called *apostrophe s*) to Singular nouns, and sometimes to Plural ones :—

Singular—man's. | *Plural*—men's.

Note 1.—The old inflexion for the Possessive case was *es*. When the *e* was omitted, as it now always is, the absence of the *e* was indicated by the comma or apostrophe ; as *moon*, *moones*, *moon's*.

---

[1] *Case* lit. means "falling" (Lat. *cas-us*). The Nom. was considered the upright or perpendicular, and the other cases were said to fall off to one side of it, and were hence called *oblique* or slanting. Since English nouns have lost every case-ending but one (the Possessive), the term "case" is etymologically inappropriate. We retain it, however, to denote grammatical relation as well as change of form.

Note 2. There are three different senses in which this case can be used :—

(*a*) **Subjective** :—

England's power is very great. (*Possession.*)
A good son will repay his *father's* benefits. (*Origin.*)
Shakspeare's plays are excellent. (*Authorship, Agency.*)
His friendship (the friendship felt by him) is sincere. (*Subject.*)

(*b*) **Objective** (rather uncommon) :—

His friendship (friendship for him) must be given up.
Cæsar's murderers were conquered at Philippi.

(*c*) **Descriptive** (rather uncommon) :—

I'll break your *knave's* (=knavish) pate.—SHAKSPEARE.
The *mother's* (motherly) nature of Althæa.—LOWELL.
Her *woman's* heart, to which love was all, could at first scarcely comprehend the mystery.—Mrs. CRAIK, *Ogilvies*, ch. 1.

44. Omission of "s."—There are three kinds of instances in which the *s*, but not the apostrophe, is omitted :—

(*a*) After all plural nouns ending in *s* ; as—

Horses' tails ; the *birds*' nests ; the *dogs*' kennels.

(*b*) Whenever the last syllable of a Singular noun begins and ends with *s* ; as—

Moses' law. (But we must say *Venus's* beauty ; *James's* hat, etc.)

(*c*) Whenever the last syllable of a Singular noun ends with *s* or *ce*, and the noun is followed by "sake" ; as—

Conscience' sake ; for *goodness*' sake. (But we must say—a *mouse's* skin ; *James's* smile.)

45. Rare use of Possessive.—The Possessive case was once used with any kind of noun ; but it is now restricted to such examples as those shown below :—

(1) Nouns denoting *persons* or other kind of *living thing* ; as—

Henry's book ; a *man's* foot. (But we cannot say "a library's book," "the stocking's foot," since "library" and "stocking" are inanimate objects.)

A *cat's* tail ; a *horse's* head ; a *bird's* feathers.

(2) Nouns denoting *personified* things ; as—

Fortune's favourite ; *Sorrow's* tears ; *England's* heroes.

(3) Nouns denoting time, space, or weight ; as—

Time.—A *day's* journey ; a *month's* holiday ; three *weeks'* leave ; a *year's* absence ; at six *months'* sight ; three *days'* grace.
Space.—A *boat's* length ; a *hand's* breadth ; a *hair's* breadth ; a *razor's* edge ; a *stone'* a throw ; a *needle's* point.
Weight.—A *pound's* weight ; a *ton's* weight.

(4) Nouns signifying certain dignified objects ; as—

The *court's* decree; the *sun's* rays; the *moon's* crescent; *nature's* works; the *earth's* axis; the *soul's* delight; *heaven's* will; the *law's* delays; *truth's* triumph; the *mind's* eye; the *ocean's* roar; *duty's* call; the *country's* good.

Let all the ends thou aim'st at be thy *country's*,
Thy *God's*, and *truth's*.—*Hen. VIII.* iii. 2.

Note.—The Possessive is also used in a few familiar phrases, in which it has been retained for the sake of shortness:—

Out of *harm's* way; at his *wit's* end; for *mercy's* sake; he did it to his *heart's* content; the *ship's* passengers; at his *fingers'* ends; he got to his *journey's* end; the *boat's* crew.

CHAPTER IV.—ADJECTIVES.

SECTION 1.—THE KINDS OF ADJECTIVES.

46. There are altogether seven different kinds of Adjectives:—

(1) **Proper**: describing a thing by some *Proper noun.*
(2) **Descriptive**: showing *of what quality* or *in what state* a thing is.
(3) **Quantitative**: showing *how much of* a thing is meant.
(4) **Numeral**: showing *how many* things or *in what order.*
(5) **Demonstrative**: showing *which* or *what* thing is meant.
(6) **Interrogative**: asking *which* or *what* thing is meant.
(7) **Distributive**: showing that things are taken *separately* or *in separate lots.*

Proper Adjectives.

47. These restrict the application of a noun to such persons or things as come within the scope of some Proper name:—

A *Portuguese* sailor = a sailor from Portugal.
The *Turkish* empire = the empire of the Turks.
The *English* language = the language of England.

Note.—Proper adjectives, like Proper nouns, may be used in a general sense; as, *French* leave (leave like that taken by the French); *British* pluck (pluck like that of a Briton).

Descriptive Adjectives:—Quality or State.

48. These restrict the application of a noun to such persons or things as possess the *quality* or *state* denoted by the adjective:—

A *brave* boy; a *sick* lion; a *tame* cat; a *large* field; a *black* horse.

Quantitative Adjectives:—Quantity or Degree.

49. These restrict the application of a noun to such things as are of the *quantity* or *degree* denoted by the adjective.

The only adjectives of this class are—*Much, little; no; some, any; enough* or *sufficient; all* or *whole, half.*

He ate *much* (a large quantity of) bread.
He ate *little* (a small quantity of) bread.
A *half* loaf is better than *no* bread.
He ate *some* (a certain quantity of) bread.
He did not eat *any* (any quantity of) bread.
He ate *enough* or *sufficient* bread.
He ate *all* the (the *whole* quantity of) bread.

Note.—"No" is always followed by a noun, and is therefore an adjective. "None" is never followed by a noun, and is therefore a pronoun. It is a negative pronoun: see § 73.

Numeral Adjectives.

50. These restrict the application of a noun to such persons or things as are of the *number* or *serial order* denoted by the adjective.

Numeral Adjectives are subdivided into two main classes:—

I. Definite. II. Indefinite.

51. **Definite** numerals denote some *exact* number.

Those which show *how many* things there are (as one, two, three, four, etc.) are called **Cardinals.**

Those which show the *serial order* are called **Ordinals.**

Those which show *how often* a thing is *repeated* are called **Multiplicative.**

Cardinals.	*Ordinals.*	*Multiplicatives.*
One	first	one only, single
Two	second	twofold, double
Three	third	threefold, treble, triple
Four	fourth	fourfold, quadruple (four times one)
Six	sixth	sixfold (six times one)
Seven	seventh	sevenfold (seven times one)

52. **Indefinite** numerals denote number of some kind without saying precisely what the number is:—

All, some, enough, no or *none; many, few; several, sundry.*

All men are mortal. *Some* men die young.
No men were present. Ten men will be *enough.*
Many men are poor. *Few* men are rich.
Several men came. *Sundry* men went away.

A Definite numeral can be made Indefinite by placing the word *some* or *about* before it:—

Some twenty men (=*about* twenty men, twenty men *more or less*) were present.

53. The words "some," "enough," "all," "no," are adjectives of *Number* or of *Quantity*, according to the noun following.

If the noun is Material or Abstract, the adjective is Quantitative. If the noun is Common, the adjective is Numeral :—

Quantitatives.	*Numerals.*
Much ; he had much bread.	*Many* ; he had many loaves.
Little ; he had little bread.	*Few* ; he had few loaves.
Enough ; he had enough bread.	*Enough* ; he had loaves enough.
Some ; he had some bread.	*Some* ; he had some loaves.
No ; he had no bread.	*No* ; he had no loaves.
All ; he had all the bread.	*All* ; he had all the loaves.
Any ; have you had any bread ?	*Any* ; did you bring any loaves?

Demonstrative Adjectives.

54. These restrict the application of a noun to those persons or things that are intended to be *pointed out* by the adjective.

They are subdivided, like Numerals, into two classes :—

I. Definite. II. Indefinite.

When a person or thing is pointed out *exactly*, as "this man," the adjective is called a **Definite** Demonstrative.

When it is pointed out in a certain sense, but *not exactly*, it is called an **Indefinite** Demonstrative.

Definite.		*Indefinite.*	
Singular.	*Plural.*	*Singular.*	*Plural.*
The	the	A, an	*nil.*
This	these	One, any	any
That, yon, yonder	those, yon, yonder	A certain	certain
Such	such	Such and such	such and such
The same, or self-same	the same, or self-same	Some	some
The other	the other	Another, any other	other, any other

All purely Demonstrative adjectives are given in the above list.

Note.—In some books, however, the Ordinals (§ 51) are classed as Demonstratives, because they point a thing out by showing its place in a list or series. But it is better to call them Numerals, because they cannot show the place of a thing without showing its numerical order.

55. **Articles.**—"The" (short for *this, that*) is a Definite Demonstrative. "A" or "an" (short for *one*) is an Indefinite.

An is used before an open vowel, a silent *h*, or unaccented *h* ; as—

An apple ; *an heir* ; *an honest* man ; *an historical* fact.

A is used before a consonant, before *u* or *ew* or *eu* sounded as *yoo*, and before *one* sounded as *wun* :—

A kite; *a* cart; *a* bottle; *a* useful thing; *a* one-eyed man; *a* European; *a* ewer; *an* unusual, but *a* unique case.

Interrogative Adjectives.

56. These restrict the application of a noun by asking a question:—

What book is that? *Which* book do you like best?

Note.—"What" has a general sense, "which" a selective one. "What" can also be used in an exclamatory sense, as "*What* folly!" It can also be used when no question is asked, as, "I do not know at *what* time he came."

Distributive Adjectives.

57. Distributive Adjectives show that the persons or things denoted by the noun are taken *singly*, or *in separate lots*. There are only four Adjectives of this class:—

(*a*) **Each.**—One of *two* or of any number *exceeding two*:—

The *two* men had *each* (man) a gun.
The *twenty* men had *each* (man) a gun.

(*b*) **Every.**—Never used of *two*. Denotes *each without exception*:—

Every man (out of the *twenty present*) had a gun.

"**Every six hours**" and similar expressions.—This means every *space of six hours*, six hours being taken collectively as *one* period:—

He came *every five hours* (= at the close of every space of five hours).

"**Every other.**"—This means *every second* or *each alternate*; as—

He was attacked with fever *every other day* (= on every second day).

(*c*) **Either.**—(1) *One of two*, or (2) *each of two*,—that is, *both*.

(1) You can take *either* side; that is, one side or the other.
(2) The river overflowed on *either* side; that is, on both sides.

(*d*) **Neither.**—This is the negative of "either":—

"You should take *neither* side"; neither this nor that.

Section 2.—The Two Uses of Adjectives.

58. There are two different ways in which an Adjective can be used—(*a*) the Attributive, and (*b*) the Predicative.[1]

(*a*) *Attributive use.*—An adjective is used attributively, when it qualifies its noun *directly*, so as to make a kind of compound noun. All true adjectives can be used attributively:—

A *lame* horse. A *noble* character. A *true* tale.

---

[1] We would not go so far, however, as to say (as Mr. Mason does in *English Grammar*, p. 37, § 87) "that all true adjectives can be used in both ways." A Distributive adjective cannot be used predicatively. For instance, we can say "every man," but we cannot say, "man is every." Again, Quantitatives cannot in all cases be used predicatively. We can say "some bread," but we cannot say "bread is some."

Note.—When no noun is expressed, the adjective is used as a noun:—

A noble (=nobleman). The brave (=brave men). The true (=truth).

When an adjective assumes a noun-inflexion, it has become a real noun, and is not merely used as one:—

Nobles (=noblemen). Secrets (=secret things).

(*b*) *Predicative use.*—An adjective is used predicatively, when it qualifies its noun *indirectly*—through some verb going before:—

That horse went *lame*. His character is *noble*.

Section 3.—Comparison of Adjectives.

59. The degrees of comparison are three in number,—the Positive, the Comparative, and the Superlative.

The **Positive** denotes the simple quality; as, "a *beautiful* horse."

The **Comparative** denotes a higher degree of the quality; as, "a *more beautiful* horse." This is used when *two* things are compared.

The **Superlative** denotes the highest degree of the quality; as, "the *most beautiful* horse." This is used when *one* thing is compared with *all other* things of the same kind.

60. In all adjectives of *more than two syllables*, and in most adjectives of two syllables, the Comparative is formed by adding "*more*" and the Superlative by adding "*most*," as in § 59.

61. But adjectives of one syllable and some adjectives of two can also form the Comparative by adding *er* or *r*, and the Superlative by adding *est* or *st*. This is the **inflexional** method.

(*a*) If the Positive ends in a consonant, *er* and *est* are added:—

Small	smaller	smallest
Great	greater	greatest
Thin	thinner	thinnest
Fat	fatter	fattest

(*b*) If the Positive ends in *e*, only *r* and *st* are added, and not *er* and *est*:—

Brave	braver	bravest
True	truer	truest

(*c*) If the Positive ends in *y*, and the *y* is preceded by a *consonant*, the *y* is changed into *i*, when *er* and *est* are added:—

Happy	happier	happiest
Dry	drier	driest

(*d*) If the *y* is preceded by a *vowel*, the *y* is not changed:—

Gay	gayer	gayest
Grey	greyer	greyest

62. **Irregular Comparisons.**—In the examples marked *

the Positive has had a Comp. and a Superl. allotted to it from some other root. These are defective rather than irregular.

Bad, ill, evil *	worse	worst
Fore	former, further	foremost, first, furthest
Good *	better	best
Hind	hinder	hindmost
Late	later, latter	latest, last
Little *	less	least
Much (quantity) *	more	most
Many (number) *	more	most
Nigh	nigher	nighest, next
Old	older, elder	oldest, eldest

63. There are five words which are adverbs in the Positive degree, but adjectives in the Comparative and Superlative :—

Far	farther	farthest
In	inner	innermost, inmost
Out	outer, utter	uttermost, utmost
Be-neath	nether	nethermost
Up	upper	uppermost

64. Latin Comparatives.—All of these end in *or*, and not in *er*; and all are followed by *to* instead of *than* :—

Superior to, inferior to, anterior to, prior to, posterior to, senior to.

CHAPTER V.—PRONOUNS.

65. There are four different kinds of Pronouns :[1]—

(1) **Personal**; as, *I, thou, he, she,* etc.

(2) **Demonstrative**; as, *this, that, such, one,* etc.

(3) **Relative** or **Conjunctive**; as, *which, who, that, as,* etc.

(4) **Interrogative**; as, *who? which? what?*

---

[1] A different classification of Pronouns is given in Mason's *English Grammar*, p. 48, ed. 1891. After giving eight classes of Pronouns, he subdivides each class, wherever this is possible, into two columns, one for Substantive pronouns and the other for Adjective pronouns. Under adjective pronouns he includes Distributive and Demonstrative adjectives, which in this book have already been disposed of in the chapter on Adjectives. It is difficult to see how such adjectives as "every," "each," "some," "other," "any," etc., or, in fact, any adjective, can be correctly called a Pronoun. A Pronoun is a *substitute* word,—a word used *for* another word. But "every," "each," "some," "other," "any" are simply *qualifying* words. They are not *substitute* words. There are no other words for which they are used as substitutes, and therefore they are not pronouns. The same author has a class of pronouns which he calls **Indefinite**, and subdivides into Substantives (*one, aught, naught*) and Adjectives (*any, other, some, no*). We have already shown that the last four are not pronouns at all. *Aught* and *naught* are not pronouns either, because they are not *substitutes* for any other words. *One* is a pronoun in certain contexts, as shown below in § 73.

This classification excludes all words that are *adjectives*, and all words that are not *substitutes* for other words. It is shown in § 72 that *this, that, such* are not here adjectives, but substitutes for nouns.

Section 1.—Personal Pronouns.

66. The **Personal Pronouns** are so called, because they stand for the three persons, and have a different form for each.

(*a*) The First, which stands for the person *speaking*:—

I (*the person now speaking*) hope to win a prize this term.

(*b*) The Second, which stands for the person *spoken to*:—

You (*the person now spoken to*) should leave off this habit of idleness.

(*c*) The Third, which denotes the person or thing *spoken of*:—

He (*the person already mentioned*) did good work with his tutor.

67. **Forms of Personal Pronouns.**—Personal Pronouns have the same differences of gender, number, and case that nouns have.

I. *The First Person, Masculine or Feminine.*

Case.	Singular.	Plural.
Nominative . .	I	We
Possessive . .	My, mine	Our, ours
Objective . . .	Me	Us

II. *The Second Person, Masculine or Feminine.*

Case.	Singular.	Plural.
Nominative . .	Thou	Ye or you
Possessive . .	Thy, thine	Your, yours
Objective . . .	Thee	You

III. *The Third Person, of all Genders.*

Case.	Singular.			Plural.
	Masculine.	Feminine.	Neuter.	All Genders.
Nominative .	He	She	It	They
Possessive .	His	Her or hers	Its	Their or theirs
Objective .	Him	Her	It	Them

68. Two Forms of Possessive.—Most of the Personal Pronouns have two forms for the Possessive :—

	Singular.			Plural.		
First Form .	My	Thy	Her	Our	Your	Their
Second ,, .	Mine	Thine	Hers	Ours	Yours	Theirs

The first is used, when the Possessive is placed *before* its noun. It qualifies the noun like an adjective :—

This is *my* book. That is *their* house.

The second is used—(*a*) when it is separated from the qualified noun by a verb coming between; (*b*) when the noun is not expressed; (*c*) when the Possessive is preceded by "of":—

(*a*) This book is *mine*. That house is *theirs*.
(*b*) My horse and *yours* (your horse) are both tired.
(*c*) That horse *of yours* is tired.

69. Reflexive or Emphatic Forms.—These are made by adding "self" in the Nom. or Obj. and "own" in the Possessive.

I. *The First Person.*

Case.	Singular.	Plural.
Nom. or Obj. . .	Myself	Ourselves
Possessive . .	My or mine own	Our own

II. *The Second Person.*

Case.	Singular.	Plural.
Nom. or Obj. . .	Thyself	Yourselves
Possessive . .	Thy or thine own	Your own

III. *The Third Person.*

Case.	Singular.			Plural.
	Masculine.	Feminine.	Neuter.	All Genders.
Nom. or Obj.	Himself	Herself	Itself	Themselves
Possessive .	His own	Her own	Its own	Their own

I hid *myself* (Reflexive). I *myself* saw it (Emphatic).

SECTION 2.—DEMONSTRATIVE PRONOUNS.

70. **A Demonstrative Pronoun** is one that *points to* some noun going before, and is used instead of it. This noun is called the Antecedent.

71. The chief pronouns of this class are :—*this, that, these, those ; one, ones, none ; such.*

The student will have observed that these words have appeared already in the list of Demonstrative *Adjectives.* Where, then, is the difference? This depends entirely on their use.

When they **qualify** *some noun expressed or understood, they are* **Adjectives.**

When they are **substitutes** *for some noun expressed or understood, they are* **Pronouns.**

(*a*) He came to my house *one* day.

Here *one* is an adjective (Indefinite Demonstrative) qualifying its noun "day."

(*b*) Your coat is black ; mine is a white *one.*

Here *one* is a pronoun, because it is a substitute for the previously mentioned noun "coat," and is qualified by the adjective "white."

72. **This, that, these, those.**—The uses of these words as *pronouns,* and not as *adjectives,* are as follows :—

(*a*) When two nouns have been mentioned in a previous sentence or clause, "**this**" is a substitute for the *latter,* and "**that**" for the *former* :—

(1) Work and play are both necessary to health; *this* (=play) gives us rest, and *that* (=work) gives us energy.

(2) Dogs are more faithful animals than cats ; *these* (=cats) attach themselves to places, and *those* (=dogs) to persons.

Observe that in the first of these sentences "*this*" does not specify *which* or *what* play is meant, and therefore it is not a Demonstrative Adjective. It is simply put as a *substitute* for the noun "play," and therefore it is a Demonstrative Pronoun.

A similar explanation holds good for the other example.

(*b*) The word "**that,**" together with its plural form "**those,**" is used as substitute for a single noun previously mentioned :—

(1) The air of hills is cooler than *that* (=the air) of plains.

(2) The houses of the rich are larger than *those* (=the houses) of the poor.

Observe the word "that" in the first example does not qualify the noun "air" by saying *which* air or *what* air, and therefore it is not an Adjective. It stands for "air" in general, and is a *substitute* for the noun "air" ; and therefore it is a Pronoun.

(c) The words "**this**" or "**that**" can be used as substitutes for a *clause* or *sentence* previously mentioned :—

(1) I studied Greek and Latin when I was young, and *that* (= I studied Greek and Latin) at Oxford.

Here by using the pronoun "*that*" as a substitute for the sentence "I studied Greek and Latin," we not only avoid repeating this sentence a second time, but we give some emphasis to the words "at Oxford."

(2) Make the best use of your time at school ; *that*'s a wise boy.

Here "*that*" = "one who makes the best use of his time at school." All this repetition is avoided by using the pronoun "*that*" as a substitute for the implied sentence.

(3) You paid your debts ; and *this* (= the payment of your debts) is quite sufficient to prove your honesty.

73. **One, ones, none.**—When the antecedent noun is in the Singular number, we use "*one*"; but when the antecedent noun is Plural, we use "*ones*" :—

(1) He gained a prize last year ; but he did not gain *one* (= a prize) this term. (*Singular.*)

(2) There were six lazy boys and four industrious *ones* (= boys) in our class. (*Plural.*)

None (= *no one*) was originally used only as a Singular :—

None but the brave *deserves* the fair.—DRYDEN.

But "none" has also acquired a Plural meaning :—

None have gone away yet.

74. **Such.**—"Such" can be substituted for a noun in either number :—

(1) He is the judge appointed to hear this case, and as *such* (= as the appointed judge) you must not speak to him before the trial. (*Singular.*)

(2) Kings are constituted *such* (= kings) by law, and should be obeyed. (*Plural.*)

Examples for Practice.

Show whether the words printed in italics are Demonstrative **Adjectives** *or Demonstrative* **Pronouns** :—

This horse is stronger than *that*.

Health is of more value than money ; *this* cannot give such true happiness as *that*.

I prefer a white horse to a black *one*.

You will repent of this *one* day, when it is too late.

You have kept your promise ; *this* was all that I asked for.

The faithfulness of a dog is greater than *that* of a cat.

One Mr. B. helped his friend in need ; *that* was a true friend.

Return to your work, and *that* immediately.

Bring me *that* book, and leave *this* where it is.

The step you have taken is *one* of much risk.
Such a book as yours deserves to be well read.
Prosperous men are much exposed to flattery; for *such* alone can be made to pay for it.
Prosperous men are not always more happy than unlucky *ones*.
A pale light, like *that* of the rising moon, begins to fringe the horizon.
Will you ride *this* horse or *that*?
A stranger could not be received twice as *such* in the same house.
The plan you have chosen does not seem to me to be a wise *one*.
One man says *this*, another *that*; whom should I believe?

75. Indefinite Demonstrative Pronouns.—Sometimes Demonstrative Pronouns are used as substitutes, not for some noun previously mentioned, but for some noun understood or implied. These are Indefinite, because they have no antecedent.

All Indefinite pronouns are in the Third person. *I* and *you* cannot be indefinite, because we know who is speaking or who is spoken to.

(*a*) **They.**—This pronoun is sometimes used for *men in general*, or some person whose name is purposely concealed:—

They say that truth and honesty is the best policy.

(*b*) **One.**—Used in the sense of *any person* or *every person*:—

One should take care of *one's* health.
=*A man* (any and every man) should take care of *his* health.

Note 1.—Whenever "one" is the subject to a verb, it must be followed by "one" and not by "he." Thus we cannot say, "*one* must take care of *his* health."

Note 2.—When *they* and *one* are used as above, they are not true pronouns, because strictly speaking they are not substitute words. They are pronouns used as Common nouns.

(*c*) **It.**—In such sentences as the following, "*it*" is the subject to the verb, and the noun or other pronoun is the complement:—

Who is *it*? *It* is I. Is *it* you? No; *it* is he.

"*It*" gives **emphasis** to the noun or pronoun following:—

It was I who told you that. *It* is the men who work hardest, not the women. *It* was the queen who died yesterday. *It* is little things that chiefly disturb the mind.

Section 3.—Relative or Conjunctive Pronouns.

76. A Relative Pronoun not only refers to some noun going before (as a Demonstrative pronoun does), but it also *joins two sentences together* (which a Demonstrative pronoun does not do).

This is a good house; I live in *it*. (*Demonstrative Pronoun.*)
The house in *which* I live is a good one. (*Relative Pronoun.*)

77. Who, which.—These are declined as follows for Singular and Plural alike:—

Nom.	Who, . . .	which.
Poss.	Whose, . . .	(of which).
Obj.	Whom, . . .	which.

The forms *who*, *whose*, *whom* are used for persons only. The form *which* is used for things without life and for animals of any kind except men and women.

In poetry, and occasionally in prose, *whose* can be used as the Possessive form of *which*:—

The tree, under *whose* shade we are sitting.

78. Forms of Antecedent.—The antecedent may have the form of a noun, or any kind of noun-equivalent (§ 3 and § 204).

You have paid your debts, which (=the fact that you have paid your debts) is a clear proof of your honesty. (*Clause.*)

79. Antecedent understood.—When no antecedent is expressed, the neuter Relative takes the form of "**what**," while the Masculine and Feminine retain the form of "who."

(*a*) *Who*=*he who*, or *she who*, or *they who*.

Who (=he who) steals my purse, steals trash.—SHAKSPEARE.
Whom (=those persons whom) the gods love, die young.—*Proverb.*

(*b*) *What*=*the thing which*, or *the things which*.

I cannot tell you now *what* (=the thing which) has happened.
The laws are *what* (=the things which) you say they are.

(*c*) *So*, *ever*, or *soever* added to a Relative pronoun or to a Relative adverb gives the meaning of totality:—

Whosoever (=any and every person who) breaks this law will be punished, *wherever* (in any and every place where) he may live.

Note 1.—"**What**" has been called a "Compound Relative," because the antecedent is said to be contained in it. But this is not correct; for the antecedent is sometimes expressed, either (*a*) in a subsequent clause, or (*b*) immediately after the Relative itself:—

(*a*) *What* I tell you in darkness, *that* speak ye in the light.
(*b*) Take *what* (or *whatever*) *help* you can get.

Note 2.—Whenever the so-called antecedent is placed after *what*, as in example (*b*), the *what* is not a *substitute* word, but an adjective (see § 56, *Note*). Note also the following:—

Take *whichever book* (=that book of all books which) you prefer.

80. That.—The word "*that*" is often use for "who," "whom," or "which," but never for "whose":—

This is the house *that* (=which) Jack built.
The man *that* (=whom) we were looking for has come.

Note.—Whenever "that" is the object to a preposition, the preposition is invariably placed after the verb of its sentence, and never before its own object:—

The house *that* we live *in*.

81. As.—The word "as" can be used for a Relative pronoun, provided it is preceded by "such," or "as," or "the same." It may be in the Nominative or the Objective case, but not in the Possessive.

This is not *such* a good book *as* I expected.
As many men *as* came were caught.
Yours is not *the same* book *as* mine (is).

82. But.—The conjunction "but," *when some Demonstrative pronoun is understood after it*, is used in the sense of "who not" or "which not."

There was no one present, *but* saw (= but *he* saw = *who* did *not* see) the deed.
There is no vice so simple, *but* may (= but *it* may = *which* may *not*) become serious in time.

Note.—The student must avoid the common mistake of saying that *but* is a "negative relative." It is not a pronoun, but a conjunction with some Demonstrative pronoun understood after it. This pronoun is sometimes expressed, as in the common saying—

It never rains, *but it* pours.

The uses of Who and Which

83. Restrictive, Continuative.—These words denote two distinct uses of "who" or "which":—

(*a*) *Restrict.*—The man *who lived there* died yesterday.
(*b*) *Contin.*—I have seen my friend, *who recognised* me at once.

In (*a*) the Relative clause does the work of an *adjective* to the noun "man," because it *restricts* the application of this noun to that particular man who is said to have "lived there" (see § 4).

In (*b*) the Relative cause "who recognised me at once" has no restrictive force on the noun "friend." It simply *continues* what was said in the previous clause:—"I found my friend, *and he* (= who) recognised me at once."

Note.—"*Who*," "*which*" in a restrictive sense are less commonly used than "*that*," which is invariably restrictive.

SECTION 4.—INTERROGATIVE PRONOUNS.

84. An **Interrogative Pronoun** is one that asks a question. It has been well called a pronoun in search of an antecedent.

Who spoke? (Nominative to the verb.)
Of *whom* did he speak? (Objective after preposition.)
What did he say? (Objective after verb "say.")
Whose book is that? (Possessive Case.)
Which of these boys will win the prize? (Selective.)

CHAPTER VI.—VERBS.

SECTION 1.—THE KINDS OF VERBS.

85. Verbs are subdivided into three main classes:—

Notional or Principal	Transitive	Class I.
	Intransitive	Class II.
Auxiliary		Class III.

An explanation of "Notional" is given in § 88, *Note*.

86. *A verb is* **Transitive,** *if the action does not stop with the doer, but passes from the doer to something else* (see § 6):—

(1) The man killed *a snake*.
(2) I do not know *whether he has come*.

The word or words denoting that person or thing, to which the action of the verb is directed, are called the **Object**.

87. *A verb is* **Intransitive,** *when the action stops with the doer, and does not pass from the doer to anything else* (§ 6):—

Men sleep to preserve life.

Sleep what? This is nonsense. No word or words can be placed as object to such a verb as "sleep."

88. An **Auxiliary** verb is one which (*a*) *helps* to form a tense, or a mood, of some Principal verb, and (*b*) *forgoes its own signification as a Principal verb* for that purpose:—

A merchant buys that he *may* sell.

Here *may* is not used either in its early sense of "power" or in its present sense of "permission." It helps to form a subjunctive.

I *have* come from home to-day.

Here *have* forgoes its proper signification—"possession," and helps the verb "come" to form a Present Perfect tense.

Note.—Principal verbs are called "Notional," because (unlike Auxiliaries) they express a notion or full meaning of their own.

SECTION 2.—TRANSITIVE VERBS.

89. Forms of Object.—There are seven forms at least.

(*a*) **Noun**:—The man killed a *snake* with his stick.
(*b*) **Pronoun**:—The man lifted *me* up out of the water.
(*c*) **Adj. used as Noun**:—He helped the *needy*.
(*d*) **Infinitive**:—He desires *to leave* us to-morrow.
(*e*) **Gerund**:—He disliked *sleeping* in the daytime.
(*f*) **Phrase**:—No one knew *how to make a beginning*.
(*g*) **Clause**:—We do not know *who has come*.

Note.—The Relative pronoun as object is often left out:—

The books (that) I bought have been lost.

90. The Double Object.—Some Transitive verbs take two objects, one denoting a *thing*, and the other a *person*.

The *thing* named is called the **Direct** object; the *person or other animal* named is called the **Indirect** (§ 6):—

I forgave him (*Indirect*) his faults (*Direct*).

The Indirect always stands first. If it is placed after the Direct, it is preceded by the preposition "*for*" or "*to*":—

He taught Euclid (*Direct*) to his sons (*Indirect*).

91. Factitive Verbs.[1]—Those Transitive verbs which take *one* object only, but still require some other word or words to make the predication *complete*, are called **Factitive** (§ 6).

The word or words so added are called the **Complement** (§ 6).

92. Forms of Complement.—There are at least eight.

	Subject.	*Verb.*	*Object.*	*Complement.*
Noun . .	They	made	him	king.
Possessive .	She	made	A.'s quarrel	her own.
Adjective .	The judge	set	the prisoner	free.
Participle.	They	found	her	still weeping.
Prep. with Object	This plot	filled	us all	with terror.
Infinitive .	I	like	a rascal	to be punished.
Adverb .	They	found	the man	asleep.
Clause .	We	have made	him	what he is.

Note.—The necessity of adding a Complement to certain verbs, to make the predication complete, can be seen at once from the example, "I like a rascal to be punished." If you merely say, "I like a rascal," you are saying the opposite to what you intended: for you do not like a rascal, but a rascal *to be punished*, or the *punishment* of a rascal.

93. Transitive Verbs used Intransitively.—There are two ways in which Transitives can become Intransitive:—

(*a*) When the verb is used in such a general sense that no object or objects are thought of in connection with it:—

Men *eat* to preserve life (Intr.). He never *eats* meat (Trans.).
A new-born child *sees*, but a kitten is born blind.
He *writes* well (Intr.). He *writes* a good letter (Trans.).

(*b*) When the Reflexive pronoun is omitted:—

He *drew* (himself) near me. He *made* (himself) merry.

---

[1] In books on Latin grammar the term "Factitive" is usually limited to those Transitive verbs that are followed by an adjective agreeing with the object, or by a noun in apposition with the object. In English grammar it is more convenient to extend the name to *all* Transitive verbs that require a complement in any form whatever.

The following are common examples of Transitive verbs which have acquired an Intransitive force by omitting the Reflexive pronoun :—

Transitive Verb.	*Intransitive Counterpart.*
Get you (yourself) gone.	*Get* out of my way.
Give him a penny.	The shoe *gives* (stretches).
He *obtained* a place.	This doctrine *obtained* (maintained itself) for a long time.
The fire *burnt* up the house.	He *burnt* with rage.
Do not *stop* me.	Let us *stop* here a little.
They *open* the doors at nine.	School *opens* at ten o'clock.
A man *breaks* stones with a hammer.	The day *breaks* at six.
The ox *drew* this cart.	He *drew* near to me.
Move away this stone.	*Move* on a little faster.
He *broke up* the meeting.	School *broke up* at three.
The mouse *steals* food.	The mouse *steals* into its hole.
They *bathed* the child.	Let us *bathe* here.
He *rolls* a ball down the hill.	The ball *rolls* down the hill.
He *burst* the door open.	The monsoon has *burst*.
Bad men *hide* their faults.	Bats *hide* during the day.
He *turned* me out of the room.	He *turned* to me and spoke.
They *drop* the boat into the water.	Rain *drops* from the sky.
They *keep* the boat on the left bank.	The boat *keeps* on the left bank.
He *sets* the school in order.	The sun *sets* at six P.M.
He *feeds* the horse on grain.	Many men *feed* on rice.
He *rested* his horse.	The horse *rested* in the stable.
He *lengthened* his journey.	The days begin to *lengthen*.
He *spread* his garment.	The mist *spreads* over the earth.
The shepherd *gathered* the sheep.	The sheep *gathered* round their shepherd.
The wind *dispersed* the clouds.	The clouds *have dispersed* from the sky.
He *closed* the business.	The day *closed* at six P.M.
The sun *melts* the snow.	The snow *melts* in the sun.
He *dashed* down the cup.	He *dashed* out of the room.
We must *widen* the road.	The road *widens* at this point.
Lift the box.	The fog *has lifted*.

SECTION 3.—INTRANSITIVE VERBS.

94. Of Complete Predication.—This is the name given to any Intransitive verb, which makes a complete sense by itself, and does not require a Complement :—

Rivers *flow*. Winds *blow*. Horses *run*, or *walk*, or *graze*, or *lie down*. Birds *fly*. All animals *sleep*. All animals *die*.

95. Of Incomplete Predication.—This is the name given to those Intransitive verbs, which do not make a complete sense by themselves, but require a Complement to supply what the verb left unsaid (§ 6). Such verbs are more briefly called **Copulative,** because they couple one idea with another.

The Complement of Copulative verbs can be in the same eight forms as that of Factitive ones.

	Subject.	*Verb.*	*Complement.*
Noun . .	That beggar	turned out	a thief.
Possessive	This book	is	mine (§ 68, *a*), not James's.
Adjective .	The man	has fallen	sick.
Participle	The stag	continued	running and jumping.
Prep. with Object	That book	proved	of no use.
Infinitive	The flower	seems	to be fading.
Adverb .	The man	has fallen	asleep.
Clause .	The results	are	what we expected.

Note 1.—When the Complement comes after a Copulative verb, it is called a **Subjective Complement,** because it relates to the Subject. But when it comes after a Factitive verb in the *Active* voice, it is called an **Objective Complement,** because it relates to the Object.

Note 2.—The same verb, whether Trans. or Intrans., may in different connections be of either complete or incomplete predication :—

The world *is* (exists)	(*Comp.*)
The world *is round*	(*Incomp.*)
They *made* a snow-man	(*Comp.*)
They *made* him *king*	(*Incomp.*)
The tree *is growing*	(*Comp.*)
He *is growing strong*	(*Incomp.*)
The water *filled* the pipe . .	(*Comp.*)
They *filled* the pipe *with water* .	(*Incomp.*).

96. The Cognate Object.—An Intransitive verb, though it is never followed by a noun denoting an *outside* or foreign object, may sometimes be followed by a noun *already implied more or less in the verb itself.* ("Cognate" means "kindred.")

There are five different forms of Cognate object :—

(*a*) *Cognate noun formed directly from the verb.*

He laughed a hearty *laugh.*	He slept a sound *sleep.*
He died a sad *death.*	He prayed an earnest *prayer.*
He lived a long *life.*	He sighed a deep *sigh.*

(*b*) *Cognate noun of similar meaning.*

He went a long *way.*	He ran his own *course.*
He fought a hard *battle.*	It blows a brisk *gale.*
He struck a deadly *blow.*	The bells ring a merry *peal.*

(*c*) *A noun descriptive of the Cognate noun understood.*

They shouted *applause* = they shouted a *shout* of applause.
He served his *apprenticeship* = he served his *service* as an apprentice.
He ran a great *risk* = he ran a *course* of great risk.

He played *the fool* = he played the *part* of a fool.
He looked *daggers* at me = he looked me a *look* of daggers.

(*d*) *An adjective qualifying the Cognate noun understood.*

He shouted his loudest (shout). He ran his fastest (run or pace). He fought his best (fight). She sang her sweetest (song). He breathed his last (breath). He tried his hardest (trial or attempt).

(*e*) *Cognate noun expressed by "it."*

We must fight *it* (= the fight) out to the end.
Lord Angelo dukes *it* (= acts the part of a duke) well.—SHAKSPEARE.

97. **Reflexive Object.**—In older English, Intrans. verbs were often followed by a Personal pronoun, either reflexive or used reflexively, in the objective case. Examples still occur:—

Hie *thee* home. Fare *thee* well. Haste *thee* away. They sat *them* down. He over-ate *himself*. To over-sleep *oneself*. Vaulting ambition which o'erleaps *itself*.—SHAKSPEARE.

98. **Intransitive Verbs in Causal sense.**—An Intrans. verb, used in a causal sense, becomes Transitive.

Intransitive.	*Causal.*
The horse trotted out.	They trotted out the horse (= caused it to trot out).
Water boils.	He boils the water.
The prisoners walk out.	He walks out the prisoners.
A thorn ran into his hand.	He ran a thorn into his hand.
That horse will starve.	Do not starve the horse.
The bell rang twice.	Ring the bell.
The kite flew into the air.	He flew the kite.
The soldiers march out.	He marches out the soldiers.
Wheat grows in the field.	He grows wheat in the field.
The boat floated.	He floated the boat.
He talks hoarsely.	He talks himself hoarse (= he makes himself hoarse by talking).

99. There are a few Intransitive verbs, in which the causal sense is indicted by *some change of vowel.*

Intransitive.	*Transitive or Causal.*
The tree *falls.*	He *fells* the tree with an axe.
The sun will *rise* at six.	I cannot *raise* this box.
The cow *lies* on the grass	The man *lays* down his coat.
We must not *sit* here.	He *set* the books in order.
He will *fare* well.	He will *ferry* me over.
The enemy *quails.*	He *quells* the enemy.

100. **Prepositional Verbs.**—An Intransitive verb can be made Transitive by adding a preposition to it. Such verbs are real Transitives, if they can be used in the Passive voice.

{We *act on* this rule. (*Active.*)
{This rule is *acted on* by us. (*Passive.*)
{No one *relies on* his word. (*Active.*)
{His word cannot be *relied on*. (*Passive.*)

Observe that when the verb is in the Passive voice, the *on* cannot be parsed as a preposition, since there is no object to it. It must therefore be parsed as part of the verb itself.

Note 1.—In prepositional verbs, the preposition is almost always placed after the verb; but "*with*" and "*over*" are often placed before it:—

He *withstood* (stood against, endured) the attack.
He was *overcome* (defeated) by the enemy.
The banks were *overflowed* (inundated) with water.
The field is *overgrown* (covered) with weeds.
The boundary has been *overstepped* (transgressed).

All these verbs, when they are used apart from the preposition, are Intransitive. It is the *preposition which makes them Transitive.*

Note 2.—It sometimes happens that the preposition after the Intransitive verb is not expressed, but the verb is none the less followed by an object:—

They *laughed* (at) *him* to scorn. He *looked* (at) *me* in the face.
Leonidas *fought* (against) *the Persians* at Thermopylæ.
I cannot *sit* (on) that horse.
I cannot *stand* (with-stand) your impertinence.

101. Summary.—There are thus two ways in which an Intransitive verb can become Transitive—(1) when it is used in a Causal sense (§ 98); (2) when it is connected with a preposition so closely that the verb, compounded with the preposition, can be made Passive (§ 100).

Similarly, there are two kinds of objects that can come after an Intransitive verb, although the verb itself continues to be Intransitive—(1) the Cognate object (§ 96); (2) the Reflexive or Personal object (§ 97).

SECTION 4.—AUXILIARY VERBS.

102. List of Auxiliary Verbs.—The Auxiliary verbs make up a very small class:—*have, be, shall, will, may, do*—only six, all told.

But their fewness is compensated by their usefulness; for no Transitive or Intransitive verb can be conjugated without them, except in two tenses, the Present and Past Indefinite.

Note 1.—*Have, be* are always followed by Participles. The other Auxiliaries are always followed by Infinitives.[1]

[1] The Infinitive that follows all the Auxiliaries except *be* and *have* might be parsed (if we wish to parse it separately) as the object to the Auxiliary verb going before: thus in "I shall go," *go* is object to the

Note 2.—Auxiliary verbs help not only Principal verbs, but one another. "I *shall have been going*"; here three Auxiliaries combine to form a single tense. *Shall* is followed by an Infinitive *have*; *have* is followed by a Participle *been*. The last Auxiliary "been" is then followed, as per rule in *Note* 1, by a Participle, "going."

Note 3.—*Can*, *ought*, and *must*, though Defective, are Principal verbs. *Let* is also a Principal verb. They are not Auxiliary—(*a*) because they do not help to form any tense, mood, or voice; and (*b*) because they do not discard their meanings as Notional verbs for auxiliary purposes. The Infinitive that follows is their object, as in the case of *shall*, *will*, *may*, *do*.

103. Auxiliary and Principal.—The same verb may be an Auxiliary at one time and a Principal at another:—

Have	I *had* a fine horse	(*Principal.*)
	I *had* gone away	(*Auxiliary.*)
Be	The earth *is* (exists). A horse *is* a quadruped	(*Principal.*)
	He *was* going. He *is* loved	(*Auxiliary.*)
Shall	You *shall* leave the house (Command, Authority)	(*Principal.*)
	I *shall* leave the house (Simple Futurity)	(*Auxiliary.*)
Will	I *will* go to-day (Determination)	(*Principal.*)
	You *will* go to-day (Simple Futurity)	(*Auxiliary.*)
May	I *may* go (=am permitted to go)	(*Principal.*)
	He works that he *may* live (Purpose)	(*Auxiliary.*)
Do	You *did* that work well	(*Principal.*)
	You *did* indeed work hard	(*Auxiliary.*)

Note.—**Be** as a Principal verb has two uses, as below:—

(*a*) There *are* some who deny this . . (*Complete predication.*)
(*b*) This coat *is* of many colours . . (*Incomplete predication.*)

As an Auxiliary, it helps to form all tenses in Passive verbs, and all continuous tenses in Active ones.

Have as a Principal verb denotes possession:—"I *have* a watch." As an Auxiliary it helps to form all the Perfect tenses, in all the Moods, Active and Passive, of all verbs, Transitive and Intransitive.

Shall as a Principal verb denotes command; **should** denotes duty.

Thou *shalt* not steal. He *should* do it at once.

As an Auxiliary, "**shall**" helps to form the *first* person, Future, Indicative (§ 115), and "**should**" to form *any* person in the Subjunctive mood (§ 122):—"He worked hard lest he *should* fail."

Will as a Principal verb denotes intention, and **would** denotes habit.

I *will* never do such a thing again . . . . . (*Intention.*)
The dog *would* come every day to the door . . (*Habit.*)

---

verb *shall*. This, at all events, is the way in which the Future tense came into existence. Nevertheless, we cannot consider the verb *shall* to be an ordinary Transitive. We must still call it an Auxiliary for two reasons—(1) because it helps to form a tense; (2) because it foregoes its own meaning for an auxiliary purpose. *Has*, when it is not an Auxiliary, is a full Transitive verb signifying "possesses." We cannot, however, parse it as a Transitive in "He *has* gone," Pres. Perf. tense.

As an Auxiliary, "**will**" helps to form the *second* and *third* persons Future (§ 115), Indicative, and "**would**" to form the same persons of the Subjunctive (§ 122).

May, might, as a Principal verb denotes permission or possibility.

You *may* now go. (*Permission.*) It *may* be true. (*Possibility.*)

As an Auxiliary, "**may**" expresses a wish, and "**may**" and "**might**" express a purpose;—both in the Subjunctive mood (§ 122).

Do, did.—On the Auxiliary uses, see below (§ 114 and § 119).

"**Do**" is also used as a **Pro-verb**, *i.e.* a *substitute* verb, and in this capacity it saves the repetition of some Principal verb going before; as, "I awoke at six A.M., and so *did* (=awoke) you"; "He worked more industriously than his brother *does* (=works)."

SECTION 5.—ACTIVE AND PASSIVE VOICES.

104. A *Transitive* verb has two voices, the **Active** and the **Passive.**

In the Active voice the person or thing denoted by the Subject is said to *do something to* something else:—

Tom *kills* a snake. (Here Tom *does something to* a snake.)

In the Passive voice the person or thing is said to *suffer something from* something else:—

A snake *is killed* by Tom. (Here a snake *suffers something from* Tom.)

Note.—*Active* (from Latin "activus") means "doing." *Passive* (from Latin "passivus") means "suffering."

105. An *Intransitive* verb is not used in the Passive voice, unless it takes a Cognate object in the Active:—

The Athenians fought a hard battle at Marathon. (*Active.*)
A hard battle was fought by the Athenians at Marathon. (*Passive.*)

Here the subject "battle" does not really *suffer* anything. Nevertheless, the verb "fight," although it is Intransitive, can be conjugated all through the Passive voice in the *third* Person. It has no Passive forms, however, in the *first* and *second* Persons. In the third person it is conjugated throughout.

106. Retained Object.—Verbs that take *two* objects in the Active can still retain *one* in the Passive.

(*a*) The Indirect object of the Active verb; as—

Active Verb.	*Passive Verb.*
I forgave *him* his fault.	The fault was forgiven *him* by me.
We allowed *him* two pounds.	Two pounds were allowed *him* by us.

Or (*b*) the Direct object of the Active verb; as—

Active Verb.	*Passive Verb.*
I forgave him *his fault.*	He was forgiven *his fault* by me.
We allowed him *two pounds.*	He was allowed *two pounds* by us.

Note 1.—It has now been shown that there are five different kinds of objects which can be used with verbs:—

(1) **Direct** (with Trans. verbs).—He taught *Euclid* (§ 90).
(2) **Indirect** (with Trans. verbs).—He taught *his sons* Euclid (§ 90).
(3) **Retained** (with Pass. verbs).—His sons were taught *Euclid* (§ 106).
(4) **Cognate** (with Intrans. verbs).—The fever must run its *course* (§ 96).
(5) **Reflexive** (with Intrans. verbs).—He sat *himself* down (§ 97).

In (1), (3), and (4) the verbs are followed by a *Direct* object; in (2) and (5) by an *Indirect*. It should be also noted that in (3) the verb is Transitive without being Active, while in (4) it is Active without being Transitive.

Note 2.—Whenever a Factitive verb is changed from the Active voice to the Passive, the Objective Complement becomes Subjective.

Active: Comp. to Object.	*Passive: Comp. to Subject.*
They proclaimed him *king*.	He was proclaimed *king* by them.
They did not crown him *king*.	He was not crowned *king* by them.

107. Verbs Active in form, but Passive in sense.—Transitive verbs, Active, are sometimes used in a Passive sense.

(*a*) Verbs with a Complement:—

The stone *feels* rough (is rough when it is felt).
Honey *tastes* sweet (is sweet when it is tasted).
The milk *smells* sour (is sour when it is smelt).
Your blame *counts* for nothing (is worth nothing when it is counted).
Your composition *reads* well (sounds well when it is read).
The house *does* not *let* (is not taken when it is meant to be let).
The horse *does* not *sell* (is not taken when it is meant to be sold).
That cloth will *wear* thin (will become thin when it is worn).

(*b*) Verbs without a Complement:—

The house *is building* (=is in a state of being built).
The trumpets *are sounding* (=are being sounded).
The cannons *are firing* (=are being fired).
The drums *are beating* (=are being beaten).
The house *is finishing* (=is being finished).
The book *is printing* (=is being printed).
The cows *are milking* (=are being milked).

Note.—The generally received and best supported opinion regarding this construction is that what looks like a present participle is in reality a gerund, with the preposition *on* or *in* omitted.

This house was three years in *building* (Ger. or Verbal noun).

Others, however, think that it is a real Active participle used in a Passive sense, like the verbs in examples (*a*).[1]

---

[1] The word ending in *-ing* must certainly be a participle in such colloquialisms as "I want a button *sewing on*." In such a sentence as "The wall is rapidly building," *building* must certainly be parsed as a participle, as otherwise the adverb *rapidly* could not be parsed.

Section 6.—Moods and Tenses, Active and Passive.

108. **Moods.**—Mood means the mode or manner in which an action is spoken of. There are three Finite moods (*i.e.* limited by number and person), and one Infinitive (not so limited).

(*a*) Three Finite moods:—

1. Indicative, the mood of **Assertion** or **Inquiry**.—*He comes.*
2. Imperative, the mood of **Command** or **Advice**.—*Come.*
3. Subjunctive, the mood of **Supposition**.—*If he come.*

(*b*) Infinitive mood . . . . *To come.*

109. **Number and Person.**—The number and person of a Finite verb depend upon the nature of its Subject.

Number
- If the subject is Singular, the verb must be Singular; as, Rain *is* falling.
- If the subject is Plural, the verb must be Plural; as, Raindrops *are* falling.

Person
- If the subject is in the First person, the verb must be in the First person: as, I love. We come.
- If the subject is in the Second person, the verb must be in the Second person; as, Thou lovest. You come.
- If the subject is in the Third person, the verb must be in the Third person; as, He loves. The teacher *has* come.

Hence arises the following rule (which is called a Concord or Agreement):—*A Finite verb must be in the same number and person as its Subject.*

110. **Tense defined.**—Tense is the form assumed by a verb (by means of inflexion or with the help of Auxiliaries) for indicating either (*a*) the *time* in which an event occurs, or (*b*) the *degree of completeness* ascribed to an event at the time of its occurrence.

As regards the question of time, the verb may tell you:—

(1) That an action *is done* in **Present** time; as, "he *comes.*"
(2) That it *was done* in **Past** time; as "he *came.*"
(3) That it *will be done* in **Future** time; as, "he *will come.*"

111. To express the different degrees of completeness there are four different forms to each tense:—

I. **Indefinite**; which denotes Present, Past, or Future time in its simplest form; as, "I see," "I saw," "I shall see."

II. **Continuous**; which denotes that the event (in Present, Past, or Future time) is still *continuing*, and is not yet completed; as, "I am seeing," "I was seeing," "I shall be seeing."

Note.—This tense is sometimes called the **Imperfect**, because it denotes an event which is imperfect or not completed.

III. **Perfect**; which denotes that the event (in Present, Past, or Future time) is in a completed or *perfect* state; as, "I have seen," "I had seen," "I shall have seen."

IV. **Perfect Continuous**; which combines the meanings of the two preceding forms; as, "I have been seeing," "I had been seeing," "I shall have been seeing."

Complete Conjugation of a Verb in the Finite Moods.

In this scheme 1 stands for First person (*I, we*); 2 for Second person (*thou, you*); 3 for Third person (*he, she, it, they*). The non-Finite parts of a verb are shown in sections 10, 11, 12.

From the following scheme it will be seen that the only tenses formed by inflexion are two in number, viz. the Present Indefinite and the Past Indefinite, Active voice, in the Indicative and Subjunctive moods.

All the other tenses in the Active voice, and all the tenses in the Passive voice without any exception, are formed by means of Auxiliary verbs (§ 102).

A. Active Voice of Do.

I.—*Indicative Mood.*

Tense.		Singular. 1	2	3	Plural. 1 2 3
Present	*Indefinite*	do	doest or dost[1]	does	do
	Continuous	am doing	art doing	is doing	are doing
	Perfect	have done	hast done	has done	have done
	Perf. Cont.	have been doing	hast been doing	has been doing	have been doing
Past	*Indefinite*	did	didst	did	did
	Continuous	was doing	wast doing	was doing	were doing
	Perfect	had done	hadst done	had done	had done
	Perf. Cont.	had been doing	hadst been doing	had been doing	had been doing
Future	*Indefinite*	shall do	wilt do	will do	1. shall 2, 3. will } do
	Continuous	shall be doing	wilt be doing	will be doing	1. shall 2, 3. will } be doing
	Perfect	shall have done	wilt have done	will have done	1. shall 2, 3. will } have done
	Perf. Cont.	shall have been doing	wilt have been doing	will have been doing	1. shall 2, 3. will } have been doing

[1] When "*do*" is used as an Auxiliary (§ 103), the form is *dost*; when it is used as a Notional or Principal verb (§ 85), or as a Pro-verb (§ 103), the form is *doest*. In all other respects the Auxiliary and the Principal forms are identical.

II.—*Subjunctive Mood.*

	Tense.	Singular. 1	2	3	Plural. 1 2 3
Present	*Indefinite* .	do	do	do	do
	Continuous.	be doing	be doing	be doing	be doing
	Perfect . .	have done	have done	have done	have done
	Perf. Cont. .	have been doing	have been doing	have been doing	have been doing
Simple Past	*Indefinite* .		(*Same as Indicative*)		
	Continuous.	were doing	wert doing	were doing	were doing
	Perfect . .		(*Same as Indicative*)		
	Perf. Cont. .		(*Same as Indicative*)		
Compound Past	*Indefinite* [1].	should do	wouldst do	would do	1. should, 2, 3. would } do
	Continuous.	should be doing	wouldst be doing	would be doing	1. should, 2, 3. would } be doing
	Perfect [2]. .	should have done	wouldst have done	would have done	1. should, 2, 3. would } have done
	Perf. Cont. .	should have been doing	wouldst have been doing	would have been doing	1. should, 2, 3. would } have been doing

III.—*Imperative Mood.*

Present Singular 2. do (thou). *Plural* 2. do (ye or you).

B. Passive Voice of **See.**

This, if we omit the Past Participle "seen," gives a complete conjugation of the Finite moods of the verb "*to be.*"

I.—*Indicative Mood.*

	Tense.	Singular. 1	2	3	Plural. 1 2 3
Present	*Indefinite* .	am seen	art seen	is seen	are seen
	Continuous.	am being seen	art being seen	is being seen	are being seen
	Perfect . .	have been seen	hast been seen	has been seen	have been seen
	Perf. Cont. .		(*None*)		
Past	*Indefinite* .	was seen	wast seen	was seen	were seen
	Continuous.	was being seen	wast being seen	was being seen	were being seen
	Perfect . .	had been seen	hadst been seen	had been seen	had been seen
	Perf. Cont. .		(*None*)		
Future	*Indefinite* .	shall be seen	wilt be seen	will be seen	1. shall, 2, 3. will } be seen
	Continuous.		(*None*)		
	Perfect . .	shall have been seen	wilt have been seen	will have been seen	1. shall, 2, 3. will } have been seen
	Perf. Cont. .		(*None*)		

[1] This tense, though it has the Past forms *should, would*, can be used to denote a conditional or contingent futurity, and hence it is sometimes called the Subjunctive future, answering to the Indicative future *shall, will*, "should" being substituted for "shall, and "would" for "will"—

I *shall* do this, if you *will* let me—*Indic. Future.*
I *should* do this, if you *would* let me—*Subjunct. Future.*

[2] On the other hand, the Perfect forms denote a conditional past, as is shown below in § 122 (3). The Perfect forms cannot be used in a future sense, but only in a past sense.

II.—*Subjunctive Mood.*

Tense.		Singular. 1	2	3	Plural. 1 2 3
Present	*Indefinite* .	be seen	be seen	be seen	be seen
	Continuous .		(*None*)		
	Perfect . .	have been seen	have been seen	have been seen	have been seen
	Perf. Cont. .		(*None*)		
Simple Past	*Indefinite* .	were seen	wert seen	were seen	were seen
	Continuous .	were being seen	wert being seen	were being seen	were being seen
	Perfect . .		(*Same as Indicative*)		
	Perf. Cont. .		(*None*)		
Compound Past	*Indefinite* .	should be seen	wouldst be seen	would be seen	1. should be seen; 2, 3. would be seen
	Continuous .		(*None*)		
	Perfect . .	should have been seen	wouldst have been seen	would have been seen	1. should have been seen; 2, 3. would have been seen
	Perf. Cont. .		(*None*)		

III.—*Imperative Mood.*

Present Singular 2. be (thou) seen. *Plural* 2. be (ye or you) seen.

SECTION 7.—INDICATIVE MOOD.

112. The Present Indefinite can be used to denote :—

(*a*) What is always and necessarily true :—

The sun *shines* by day and the moon by night.

(*b*) What is habitual in life or character :—

He *keeps* his promises. He *has* good health.

(*c*) What is present, if this is helped by the context :—

I *understand* what you *say*. The door *is* open.

(*d*) What is future, if this is helped by the context :—

When *do* you (=will you) start for Edinburgh ?

(*e*) What is past, provided that the event is known to be past. (This is called the Historic or Graphic Present.)

Baber now *leads* (=then led) his men through the Khyber Pass, and *enters* (=entered) the plains of India.

113. The Perfect tenses are used as follows :—

(1) The *Present* Perfect connects a past event in some sense or other *with present time* :—

The British Empire in India *has succeeded* to the Mogul.

The series of events by which the British Empire superseded the Mogul took place more than a century ago. The events are therefore long past. But the state of things arising out of these past events is *still present*. The British Empire *still exists*. Hence it is right to say "has succeeded."

Some Intransitive verbs (Transitive ones never), and especially those Intransitive verbs that signify going, coming, becoming, changing, etc., may use the Auxiliary **is** instead of *has*, and **was** instead of *had* :—

(*a*) The flower *is* faded. (*b*) The flower *has* faded.

In (*a*), however, the *state* of the flower (faded) is more prominently indicated; in (*b*) the *time* of the fading. So the two sentences are not quite equivalent.

(2) The *Past* Perfect (called also the Pluperfect) is never used, except when we wish to say that some action was either (*a*) completed, or (*b*) supposed to be completed, before another was commenced :—

(*a*) He *had been* ill two days, when the doctor was sent for. (*Fact.*)
(*b*) If I *had seen* him, I should have known him. (*Supposition.*)

(3) The *Future* Perfect denotes the completion of some event (*a*) in future time, (*b*) in past time :—

(*a*) He *will have reached* home before the rain sets in.
(*b*) He *will have heard* this news already; so I need not repeat it.

It seems like a contradiction to make a *Future* tense have reference to *Past* time. But the future here implies an inference regarding something which is believed to have passed rather than past time itself. "You will have heard" means "I infer or believe that you have heard."

114. Do and Did.—The Present and Past Indefinite in the Active voice can also be formed by the Auxiliary "*do*" (§ 103).

Present Tense.

	Singular.	*Plural.*
1st Person	I do love	We do love
2nd ,,	Thou dost love	Ye or you do love
3rd ,,	He does love	They do love

Past Tense.

	Singular.	*Plural.*
1st Person	I did love	We did love
2nd ,,	Thou didst love	Ye or you did love
3rd ,,	He did love	They did love

This form is used for three different purposes :—

(*a*) For the sake of emphasis; as, "I *do* love," "I *did* love."

(*b*) For the sake of bringing in the word "not"; as, "I *do not* love" (which is better than saying "I love not"), "I *did not* love" (which is better than saying "I loved not").

(*c*) For the sake of asking a question; as, "*Does* he love?" "Why *did* he love?" "*Did* he not love?"

115. Shall and Will.—Beginners are sometimes puzzled to know when to use "*shall*" and when to use "*will*."

It should be understood that there are *three* senses in which the future tense can be used :—

(*a*) To express *merely future time*, and nothing more.
(*b*) To combine future time with an implied *command*.
(*c*) To combine future time with an implied *intention*.

(*a*) *Merely future time.*

When nothing but future time is intended—*mere futurity*, without any idea of command or intention being mixed up with it—*shall* must be used for the *First* person, and *will* for the *Second* and *Third* persons, as below :—

	Singular.	*Plural.*
1*st Person*	I *shall* go	We *shall* go
2*nd* ,,	Thou *wilt* go	You *will* go
3*rd* ,,	He *will* go	They *will* go

In these persons *shall* and *will* are strictly *tense-forming*, that is, Auxiliary verbs (see §§ 102, 103).

(*b*) *An Implied Command, Promise, or Threat.*

Whenever we desire to express, not merely future time, but some *command*, or *promise*, or *threat* in addition, *shall* is put for *will* in the Second and Third persons ;[1] as—

You *shall* be hanged (by some one's command).
You *shall* receive your prize to-morrow (promise).
If you do this you *shall* be hanged (threat).

In these examples, the *shall* is not a tense-forming or Auxiliary verb, but a Principal or Notional one (see §§ 102, 103).

(*c*) *An Implied Intention.*

When the speaker wishes to express some intention of his own, then *will* is put for *shall* in the First person :[2]—

I *will* call on you to-day, and I *shall* then say good-bye.

Here *will* denotes the *intention* of calling, while *shall* denotes *merely future time*. Therefore *will* is a Principal verb, and *shall* is an Auxiliary.

Note.—In a command, promise, threat, or intention there is necessarily some sense of futurity. Nevertheless, the verb *shall* in all such contexts as (*b*) and *will* in such a context as (*c*) are in the

---

[1] In Old Eng. *sceal* (shall) means "I must," "I owe," "I am liable for" ; and it still means this in the Second and Third persons.

[2] *Will* in Old Eng. means to intend or desire ; and it still means this in the First person. In some contexts *will* or *would*, if it is accentuated, still means intention even in the Second and Third persons :—

> The government *will* not and dare not look our difficulties in the face.—*Daily Tel.* p. 10, Oct. 19, 1907.

Present tense, not in the Future. They are simply Notional verbs (Transitive) in the Present tense, and the Inf. following is their object.

I shan't as an angry reply to *You shall* is a colloquialism.

SECTION 8.—IMPERATIVE MOOD.

116. The **Imperative** mood is used only in the Present tense, Second person: the Subject is seldom expressed.

Singular.	*Plural.*
Speak.	Speak.

117. To express our will in connection with the *First* or *Third* person we either (*a*) use the Transitive verb *let*, which is itself the Second person of the Imperative mood of the verb "to let," or (*b*) we employ the Subjunctive mood:—

		Singular.	*Plural.*
(*a*)	1*st Person*	Let me speak	Let us speak
	3*rd* ,,	Let him speak	Let them speak

(*b*) Every soldier *kill* his prisoner.—SHAKESPEARE.
Thither our path lies; *wind we* up the height.—BROWNING.

The Third person of the Subjunctive occurs in the common phrases *suffice it* = "let it suffice"; *so be it* = "so let it be."

Suffice it to say that all the prisoners were acquitted.

Note.—In such a construction as *Let me speak*, "speak" (Infin.) is the direct object to "let," and "me" the indirect (§ 90).

118. The chief uses of the Imperative mood are to express (*a*) *command*, (*b*) *precept*, or (*c*) *entreaty*:—

(*a*) *Command*:—

Awake, *arise*, or *be* for ever fallen.—MILTON.

(*b*) *Precept* or *Invitation*:—

Go to the ant, thou sluggard; *consider* her ways and *be* wise.
—*Old Testament.*

(*c*) *Entreaty* or *Prayer*:—

Give us this day our daily bread.—*Lord's Prayer.*

119. When the verb is negative, that is, prohibitive, the Imperative is now formed by the Auxiliary "*do*." See § 114 (*b*).

Older Form.	*Present Form.*
Fear not.	*Do* not fear.
Taste not that food.	*Do* not taste that food.

Note.—Sometimes, even when the verb is affirmative, the Imperative is formed by "do," in order to give more emphasis to an entreaty. See § 114 (*a*). This, however, occurs only in colloquial English:—

Do help me to lift this box.

120. The Imperative mood is sometimes used to express a **Supposition.**

Take care of the pence, and the pounds will take care of themselves (= If you take care of the pence, the pounds will, etc.).

121. Sometimes an Imperative is used **absolutely**; *i.e.* in isolation from the rest of the sentence :—

A large number of men, *say* a hundred, are working on the railroad.

Section 9.—Subjunctive Mood.

122. The Subjunctive mood expresses *a purpose*, *a wish*, *a condition*, or *a doubt*, anything rather than a fact.

(1) *A Purpose.*

In this case the verb in the Subjunctive mood is preceded by the conjunction *that* or *lest* (lest = that not). The Auxiliary verbs "*may*" and "*might*" are used after "*that*," and "*should*" after "*lest*."

	Indicative.	*Subjunctive : Purpose.*
Present or *Future*	I give you a prize, .	that you *may work* well again.
	I shall keep your book,	lest you *should lose* it.
		that you *may* not *lose* it.
Past	I gave you a prize, .	that you *might work* well again.
	I kept your book, .	lest you *should lose* it.
		that you *might* not *lose* it.

Note.—In the Tudor Period, and somewhat beyond it, the Subjunctive of purpose was commonly expressed in the Present Indefinite tense, without the help of the Auxiliary "may" or *should* :—

Love not sleep, lest thou *come* to poverty.—*Old Test.*

Speak to my brother, that he *divide* the inheritance with me. —*New Test.*

(2) *A Wish or Order.*

To express a wish or order, there are two forms of the Subjunctive that may be used : either (*a*) the simple form, without an Auxiliary ; or (*b*) the compound form, with the Auxiliary "*may*" :—

Thy kingdom *come*, thy will *be* done.
May he live long and see not the grave !
Would that (= I wish that) he were here.
Far *be* it from me to say anything false.
My sentence is that the prisoner *be hanged.*

(3) *Condition and its Consequence.*

When the verb expresses a *condition*, it is generally preceded by the conjunction "*if*." The verb denoting the *consequence* is expressed by the Auxiliary "*would*" in the Second and Third persons, and by "*should*" in the First :—

	First Sentence : Condition.	*Second Sentence : Consequence.*
Present or *Future*	If he *should meet* me,	he *would know* me at once.
	If I *were* in his place,	I *should pay* the money.
Past	If he *had met* me,	he *would have known* me.
	If I *had been* in his place.	I *should have paid* the money.

Sometimes the *if* is left out. In this case the *should*, or the *had*, or the *were* must be placed before its subject :—

Present or Future	*Should* he *meet* me,	he *would know* me at once.
	Were I in his place,	I *should pay* the money.
Past	*Had* he *met* me,	he *would have known* me.
	Had I *been* in his place,	I *should have paid* the money.

Sometimes the Conditional sentence is left out or understood, and only the Consequent sentence is expressed :—

He *would* never agree to that ("if you asked him," understood).
He *would* be very thankful to you for this kindness ("if you were to do him the kindness," understood).

(4) *A Doubt or Supposition.*

A verb in the Subjunctive mood, preceded by some conjunction or conjunctive pronoun, implies some *doubt* or *supposition* :—

I will not let thee go, *except* thou *bless* me.—*Old Test.*
Murder, *though* it *have* no tongue, will speak.
Whoever he *be*, he shall not go unpunished.

The conjunction is not always expressed :—

"*Come* weal, *come* woe, by Bruce's side,"
Replied the chief, "will Donald bide."—SCOTT.

Note.—The Subjunctive mood in some form or other is always used to express (1), (2), and (3). But to express (4) the Indicative is now often used instead of it. The Subjunctive, however, ought still to be used, whenever we express something that we know or believe to be either doubtful or contrary to the fact :—

If he *were* guilty (which I know he is not), I should never get over it.

SECTION 10.—INFINITIVE MOOD.

123. The Infinitive may denote either Present or Past time :—

	Form.	*Active.*	*Passive.*
Present	*Indefinite* .	To send	To be sent
	Continuous .	To be sending	(*Wanting*)
Past	*Perfect* . .	To have sent	To have been sent
	Perf. Contin.	To have been sending	(*Wanting*)

Future time can be expressed only by some phrase ; as, "to be about to send" ; "to be going to send."

124. The Perfect form of Infinitive.—After verbs expressing wish, intention, duty, etc., the Perfect form of the Infin. is used, to show that the wish, etc., was not carried out :—

He intended *to have gone* (but something stopped him).
He would *have gone* (but he was not able).
He ought *to have gone* (but he neglected to do so).

It is a mistake, however, to use the Perfect Infinitive in any other connection. Thus we cannot say—

It was unkind of him *to have gone* without saying good-bye.

Here *to have gone* should be changed to "*to go*."

His going (= to go) without saying good-bye was unkind.

Note.—After the verbs "said," "known," "believed," "supposed," and such-like the Perfect Infinitive is used to denote past time:—

He is said *to have gone* = It is said that he *went*.

125. Infinitive without "to."—The word "*to*" is usually, but not always, the sign of the Infinitive mood.

(*a*) Most of the verbs not followed by "*to*" occur in the following examples:—

I *hear* thee speak (to speak) of a better land.
I *saw* him take (to take) aim with his bow.
You *need* not send (to send) those books to me.
I *feel* the cold air strike (to strike) against my face.
He *dared* not say (to say) this in open day.
He *made* me come (to come) and sit (to sit) beside him.
I *let* him go (to go) back to his own house.
They *bade* me tell (to tell) them the right road.
We *watched* him go (to go) and come (to come).
We *beheld* the fish rise (to rise).
I have *known* him laugh (to laugh) for nothing.

(*b*) The "*to*" is also left out after Auxiliary and Defective verbs, as may be seen below:—

I shall *go*; I will *go*; I can *go*; I may *go*; I do *go*; I must *go*.
(But "I ought *to* go" is an exception.)

(*c*) The "*to*" is left out after *than* and *but*:—

He did nothing *but* laugh.
He did nothing else *than* laugh.

(*d*) The "*to*" is left out after certain phrases:—

You had better not *remain* here.
I had rather *take* this than that.

The Uses of the Infinitive Mood.

126. There are two main uses of the Infinitive mood:—

I. The Noun-Infinitive (also called Simple).
II. The Qualifying Infinitive (also called Gerundial).[1]

---

[1] The name Gerundial, though unfortunately it is now well established, is misleading. It implies that the Qualifying Infinitive has some connection with what we now call the Gerund or Verbal noun. In point of fact, it has no connection with it whatever, either historically or syntactically. They are as distinct in origin as they are in use. The one does

127. I. The Noun-Infinitive may be used in any way in which Nouns are used; *i.e.* (*a*) as the Subject to a verb, (*b*) as the Object to a Transitive verb or to a Preposition, (*c*) as the Complement to a verb, or (*d*) as a form of exclamation :—

(*a*) Subject to a verb :—

To err is human; *to forgive*, divine.

(*b*) Object to a Transitive verb or to a Preposition :—

A good man does not fear *to die*.
He was about (=near) *to die* (=death).

(*c*) Complement to a verb (see § 92 and § 95) :—

He appears *to be* a wise man. (*Intrans.*)
We considered him *to be* the best in the class. (*Factit.*)

(*d*) As a form of **exclamation** :—

To think that he told so many lies!

II. The Qualifying Infinitive may be used in any way in which an adjective or adverb is used; and sometimes it is used absolutely :—

(*a*) After a verb (here its use is adverbial) :—

He came *to see* (=for the purpose of seeing) the sport.
He wept *to see* (=at seeing) that shocking sight.

(*b*) After a noun (here its use is adjectival) :—

He hopes to be rewarded in the world *to come*.
Give him a chair *to sit* on.

Note.—The Qualifying Infin., when used with a noun, can be either attributive or predicative (§ 58) :—

A house *to let* (Attrib.). This house is *to let* (Predic.).

(*c*) After an adjective (here its use is adverbial) :—

He is quick *to hear* and slow *to speak*.

(*d*) Absolutely, for bringing in a **Parenthesis** :—

I am,—*to tell* you the truth,—quite tired of this work.
They were thunderstruck,—so *to speak*,—on hearing this news.

SECTION 11.—PARTICIPLES.

128. The forms of the different Participles are as follows :—

Transitive Verbs.

	Active Voice.	*Passive Voice.*
Present or Continuous	Loving	Being loved
Past Indefinite . .	(*Wanting*)	Loved
Past Perfect . .	Having loved	Having been loved

---

the work of an adjective or adverb, the other of a noun; and so they have nothing at all in common. The Gerund so-called in *-ing* was never an Infinitive, and it is a great mistake to call it so.

Intransitive Verbs.

Present or Continuous . .	Fading
Past Indefinite . . .	Faded
Past Perfect . . .	Having faded

Note 1.—The form *loving* or *fading* stands for both Present and Continuous participles. These are not the same in meaning :—

(*a*) *Hearing* this he was much surprised. (*Pres.*)
(*b*) He went away *sorrowing*. (*Cont.*)

In (*a*) the action is completed. In (*b*) it is continuous.

Note 2.—There is no Future Participle in English. Futurity can be expressed by the Qualifying Infinitive, as "the world *to come*," or by a periphrasis, as "about (*prep.*) to fall" (*Noun Infin.*), "going to see" (*Qual. Infin.*), "going to be beaten" (*Qual. Infin.*).

129. Double Character of Participles.—A Participle has two distinct functions, and can be defined as that part of a verb which may be used either (*a*) for helping to form a tense, or (*b*) as an adjective for qualifying some noun or noun-equivalent.

I. *As part of a tense.*

130. Many of the tenses of English verbs are formed with the help of the Past or the Present Participle.

Thus all the tenses of the Passive voice are formed out of the verb "to be," followed by the Past Participle ; as, "I am loved," "I was loved," "I shall be loved."

Again, all the Continuous tenses in the Active voice are formed out of the verb "to be," followed by the Present Participle ; as, "I am loving," "I was loving," "I shall be loving."

Again, the Perfect tenses in the Active voice are formed out of the verb "to have," followed by the Past Participle ; as, "I have loved," "I had loved," "I shall have loved."

II. *As an Adjective.*[1]

131. A Participle, when it is not part of a tense, belongs to the class of Descriptive adjective (§ 48). Like other adjectives, it can (*a*) qualify a noun, (*b*) be qualified by an adverb, (*c*) admit of degrees of comparison, (*d*) be used as a noun :—

---

[1] To show how completely a Participle can assume the function of an adjective, there are instances in which it forgoes its verb-character altogether :—

Astonishing to any one. *Disturbing* to any one. *Surprising* to any one.

When the words italicised are used as verbs, they are Transitive, and do not allow the prep. *to* to come between them and their object. We could not say, "This astonishes *to* me, or disturbs *to* me, or surprises *to* me."

(a) *Being tired* of work, *the men* went home.
(b) The man was picked up in an *almost dying* state.
(c) This flower is *more faded* than that.
(d) Let *bygones* be *bygones*. (This kind of use is rare.)

132. Since a Participle is a verb as well as an adjective, it can take an Object, which may be of five different kinds (§ 106):—

Having shot *the tiger*, he returned home. (*Direct Obj.*)
He is busy, teaching *his sons* Greek. (*Indirect Obj.*)
Having been taught *Greek*, he was a good scholar. (*Retained Obj.*)
We saw him fighting *a hard battle*. (*Cognate Obj.*)
Having sat *himself* down, he began to eat. (*Reflexive Obj.*)

133. Past Indefinite.—The use of such participles depends upon whether the verb is Transitive or Intransitive:—

(a) If the verb is *Transitive*, the Past Indefinite Participle is never used in the Active voice, but only in the Passive:—

This much-*praised* man proved to be a rogue.
Gold is a metal *dug* out of the earth.

(b) If the verb is *Intransitive*, the Past Indefinite is not used at all in most verbs. But whenever it is used (which depends entirely on custom), it must *precede* its noun, and not follow it:—

The *faded* rose. A *retired* officer. The *returned* soldier. The *fallen* city. The *risen* sun. A *withered* flower. A *departed* guest.

If the speaker or writer desires to place the Past Participle of an Intransitive verb *after* its noun, he must insert the Relative pronoun and change the participle into a Finite verb; as—

The horse of Mr. A., *gone* to America, is for sale. (This is wrong. The sentence should be—"The horse of Mr. A., *who has gone* to America, is for sale.")

But the Past Participle of an Intransitive verb is sometimes put *after* its noun *in poetry*:—

A Daniel *come* to judgment.—SHAKESPEARE, *Mer. Venice.*
Toll for the brave—the brave that are no more,
All *sunk* beneath the wave, fast by their native shore.—COWPER.

Even in prose the Past Participle of an Intransitive verb is sometimes, *but very rarely*, placed after its noun:—

In times *past*=in times which have passed.
He is a man *descended* from a high family.

134. The Past Participle of verbs is sometimes used to express some *permanent habit*, *state*, or *character*:—

A well-*read* man=a man who has read much and read well.
A well-*behaved* man=a man whose habitual behaviour is good.
An out-*spoken* man=a man who habitually speaks out his mind.
A *retired* man=a man who dislikes appearing in public.
A *mistaken* man=one who errs by habit or in some specific case,

From this use of the Past Participle has arisen a large class of Adjectives, which are formed from nouns by adding "*ed*" to the end of the noun :—

An evil-*heart*-ed man. A *talent*-ed man. A *land*-ed proprietor. A long-*tail*-ed ape. A smooth-*skin*-ned cat. His *saint*-ed mother. A red-*colour*-ed rose. A rough-*face*-d youth. A *hood*-ed snake. A long-*leg*-ged spider. A purple-*crest*-ed helmet. A many-*page*-d book. A long-*arm*-ed monkey. A thickly-*wood*-ed hill. A noble-*mind*-ed man. A warm-*blood*-ed animal.

Section 12.—Gerunds and Verbal Nouns.

135. A Gerund has four forms—two for the Active voice and two for the Passive.

	Active.	*Passive.*
Present or Continuous	Loving	Being loved
Perfect . . .	Having loved	Having been loved

136. The *forms* of a Gerund, then, are the same as those of a Participle, and both are parts of a verb. What, then, is the difference? A Gerund is a kind of *Noun*; but a Participle is a kind of *Adjective*. So, in spite of the resemblance in *form*, they are quite distinct in *nature*.[1]

The reason of the resemblance in form is a matter of history. In Old Eng. the *forms* of the Verbal Adjective and the Verbal Noun were quite distinct. The suffix *-ing* originally belonged to the latter only.

Participle . . *Writ-ende*, or *-inde*, or *-and*.
Verbal noun . . *Writ-ung*, or *writ-ing* (both forms occur in Anglo-Saxon).

In later English the suffix *-inde* took the form of *-ing*, while *-ende* and *-and* died out; and *-ung* became obsolete. Hence we have now only one form instead of two for the two parts of speech :—

Participle . . . . *Writing*.
Verbal noun . . . . *Writing*.

137. Gerund defined.—A Gerund is that part of a verb which, if the verb is Intransitive, has the function of a noun only, but if the verb is Transitive, retains the function of a verb also, and can be followed by an object in the same way as if it were a Finite verb :—

Fond of *sleeping* . . . (*Noun-function only.*)
Fond of *hunting* foxes . . (*Noun- and verb-function combined.*)

In point of *function* there is no difference between a Gerund and an Infinitive. Either may be correctly defined as "that part of a verb

[1] In some books the Gerund is called a Participial noun. This name should be avoided, since a Noun is one part of speech and a Participle is another.

which names the action, without naming the doer." Both are Abstract nouns. The difference between them is not in function, but in *form*; observe the suffix *-ing*. They differ also in syntactical usage; for a Gerund has case, and can be preceded or followed by any kind of preposition, and it can be preceded by the Def. art. *the*; the same cannot be said of Infinitives.

Subsequently the other forms of Gerund (sometimes called Compound), *being loved, having loved, having been loved,* were formed in modern English, on the analogy of corresponding participles.

138. Gerund as Noun.—Since a Gerund is a *kind of noun*, it may be the subject to some verb, or object to some verb, or complement to some verb, or object to some preposition; as—

Subject to a verb.—*Sleeping* is necessary to life.
Object to a verb.—He enjoyed *sleeping* in the open air.
Complement to a verb.—His almost constant habit was *sleeping*.
Object to a preposition.—He was fond of *sleeping*.

In the following sentences say whether the words noted below are Gerunds or Participles:—

The rice will grow well in the *coming* rains. We heard of his *coming* back to-day. Did you hear of his *having won* a prize? The boy *having won* a prize was much praised. She was fond of *being admired*. *Being admired* by all she was much pleased. The cow *having been killed* by a tiger yesterday could not be found. The boy was ashamed of *having been beaten* in class by his sister. I am tired of *doing* this work. *Doing* this work every day you will soon improve. *Spelling* is more difficult than *writing*. He was in the habit of *boasting* of his cleverness. A *boasting* man is much despised.

Note.—In such phrases as "a hunting whip," "a drinking fountain," the words *hunting* and *drinking* are Gerunds, not participles: "a whip for hunting," "a fountain for drinking." The Gerund or Verbal noun is here used as a substitute for an adjective; see § 180.

139. Gerund as a Verb.—Since the Gerund of a Transitive verb retains its verb-character (§ 137), the object by which it is followed may be of any of the five kinds shown in § 106, *Note.*

Direct (with Trans.).—He is clever at teaching *Euclid*.
Indirect (with Trans.).—He is clever at teaching *his sons* Euclid.
Retained (with Passive).—He is pleased at being taught *Euclid*.
Cognate (with Intrans.).—He is proud of having fought a good *fight*.
Reflexive (with Intrans.).—He is in the habit of oversleeping *himself*.

140. Gerund with Possessive.—A noun, when it is placed before a Gerund, should be in the Possessive case, provided it can be used in that case:—

He was displeased at the *barber's* not coming.

Avoid such constructions as the following:—

He was displeased at the *barber* not coming.
Would you mind *me* asking you a question?

Note.—Sometimes the letter "*a*" (an abbreviation of "*on*") is placed before a Gerund in a prepositional sense :—

This set him *a* (=on) *thinking.*

141. Gerundive use of Participles.—Such participles are not Gerunds, but participles used in a Gerundive sense :—

I depend on the wall *being built* immediately.

How are we to parse "being built" in such a connection? We must parse it as a participle; but it is not used as such in the ordinary way; for it does more than qualify the noun "wall." The sentence does not mean "I depend on the wall that was being built," or "the wall when it was being built"; but "I depend on the *wall-being-built* immediately," that is, "on the immediate *building of* the wall." There is therefore a Gerund or Verbal noun implied in the participle "being built," and hence it may be said that such participles are used Gerundively. (Dr. Abbott calls this the "Noun-use of the Participle." But he also uses the phrase "Gerundive use of Participles."—*How to Parse*, § 405, p. 235.)

142. A **Verbal noun** is the same thing at bottom as a Gerund, but a distinction has been drawn between them.[1]

A Verbal noun is preceded by the Definite article and followed by the preposition "*of*"; whereas a Gerund has no article preceding it and no preposition following it. The former construction is the original one. The latter is modern, and arose simply out of the omission of the preposition "of."[2]

(*a*) I am engaged in *the* careful reading *of* a book (*Verbal noun.*)
(*b*) I am engaged in carefully reading a book . (*Gerund.*)

In (*a*) "*reading*" is a *single* part of speech,—a noun and nothing more. In (*b*) "*reading*" is a double part of speech,—a noun and verb combined. Observe, too, that a Verbal noun is qualified by an **Adjective**, a gerund by an **Adverb.**

Note 1.—Sometimes the "*of*" is left out, even when there is a Definite article going before :—

---

[1] It has been said that "a word ending in *-ing* may be a participle, or an adjective, or a noun, or *a verb in the Infinitive Mood.*" For the last see Professor Earle's *Simple Grammar of English*, p. 241, where he calls it a "Flexional Infinitive," derived from the old Infinitive ending in *-en*; as "build-*en*," "build-*ing*." I cannot find any evidence for this theory, which he has borrowed, as he says, from Carlyle! The inflexion *-en* was dead by about 1500 A.D., and it died without leaving anything behind it. The noun-suffix *-ing* is as old as Anglo-Saxon. What we now call the Gerund has not sprung out of any Infinitive, but is simply the Verbal noun itself with the "*of*" omitted. See my *English Grammar Past and Present*, § 523, or *Historical English and Derivation*, § 148. That a word ending in *-ing* may be a participle or an adjective has been shown already; see § 131 and footnote. *It never is and it never was an Infinitive* of any kind whatever.

[2] Compare the omission of "*of*" in such phrases as "on board (of) ship," "inside or outside (of) the door." "a thousand (of) men."

The *giving* to the courts the power to review hard and unconscionable bargains will control the rest.—*Review of Reviews*, August 1898, p. 165.

Here there is no "*of*" after the word "giving." In such a construction we cannot distinguish between a Verbal noun and a Gerund.

Note 2.—The Abstract noun, which we call a Verbal noun or Gerund, can be used in a Concrete sense :—

I am pleased with my *surroundings*.
He went away with all his *belongings*.

SECTION 13.—THE STRONG AND WEAK CONJUGATIONS.

143. Strong and Weak.—Verbs are distinguished according to *function* into Transitive, Intransitive, and Auxiliary (§ 85). According to *form* or Conjugation, they are distinguished into **Strong** and **Weak**. (All our borrowed verbs are Weak.)

Note.—The names "Irregular" and "Regular" for Strong and Weak are misleading; for in point of fact the Strong conjugation is, in its own way, not less regular than the Weak, besides being the older of the two. The name Irregular is reserved in this book for certain verbs mentioned below in § 147.

Tests of a Weak verb :—

(*a*) All verbs, whose Past tense ends in a *-d* or *-t*, which is not in the Present tense, are Weak :—

Live, live-*d*. Fan, fann-*ed*. Think, though-*t*. Sell, sol-*d*.

(*b*) All verbs, whose Past tense is formed by shortening (not changing) the vowel of the Present tense, are Weak :—

Bleed, bled. Shoot, shot. Lead, led. Light, lit or light-*ed*.

(*c*) All verbs, whose Past tense is the same as the Present, are Weak :—

Cut, cut. Hurt, hurt. Put, put. Rid, rid. Spread, spread.

Tests of a Strong verb :—

(*a*) All verbs, which form the Past tense by *changing* (not merely shortening) the inside vowel, and do *not* add on a final *-d* or *-t*, are Strong :—

Fight, fought (but "buy, bough-*t*" is Weak, because, after changing the inside vowel, it adds a final *-t*). Hold, held. Stand, stood.

(*b*) All verbs, which form the Past participle in *-en* or *-n*, are either wholly or partly Strong :—

Wholly.—Draw, drew, draw-*n*.
Shake, shook, shake-*n*.
Partly—Saw, saw-*ed*, saw-*n*.
Cleave, clef-*t*, clov-*en*.

144. Lists of Strong Verbs.—The list of Mixed verbs given under Group III. exemplifies the tendency of Strong verbs to become Weak.

Group I. (50 *verbs*).—Final *-n* or *-en* retained in Past Participle.

Present Tense.	*Past Tense.*	*Past Part.*
Arise	arose	arisen
Bear (produce)	bore	born
Bear (carry)	bore	borne
Beget	begot begat	begotten begot
Bid	bade, bid	bidden, bid
Bind	bound	*bounden, bound
Bite	bit	bitten, bit
Blow	blew	blown
Break	broke	broken
Chide	chid	chidden, chid
Choose	chose	chosen
Draw	drew	drawn
Drink	drank	*drunken, drunk
Drive	drove, drave	driven
Eat	ate	eaten
Fall	fell	fallen
Fly	flew	flown
Forbear	forbore	forborne
Forget	forgot	forgotten
Forsake	forsook	forsaken
Freeze	froze	frozen
Get	got	*gotten, got
Give	gave	given
Go, wend	went	gone
Grow	grew	grown

Present Tense.	*Past Tense.*	*Past Part.*
Hide	hid	*hidden, hid
Know	knew	known
Lie	lay	lain
Ride	rode	ridden
Rise	rose	risen
See	saw	seen
Shake	shook	shaken
Shrink	shrank	*shrunken, shrunk
Sink	sank	*sunken, sunk
Slay	slew	slain
Slide	slid	slidden, slid
Smite	smote	smitten, smit
Speak	spoke	spoken
Steal	stole	stolen
Stride	strode	stridden
Strike	struck	*stricken, struck
Strive	strove	striven
Swear	swore	sworn
Take	took	taken
Tear	tore	torn
Throw	threw	thrown
Tread	trod	trodden, trod
Wear	wore	worn
Weave	wove	woven
Write	wrote	written writ (rare)

Note.—The seven participles marked * are now chiefly used as Verbal adjectives only, and not as parts of some tense:—

Verbal Adjective.	*Part of some Tense.*
Our *bounden* duty.	He was *bound* by his promise.
A *drunken* man.	He had *drunk* much wine.
A *sunken* ship.	The ship had *sunk* under the water.
A *stricken* deer.	The deer was *struck* with an arrow.
The *shrunken* stream.	The stream has *shrunk* in its bed
Ill-*gotten* wealth.	He *got* his wealth by ill means.
A *hidden* meaning.	The meaning is *hid* or hidden.

Group II. (32 *verbs*).—Final -*n* or -*en* lost in Past Participle.

Present Tense.	*Past Tense.*	*Past Part.*	*Present Tense.*	*Past Tense.*	*Past Part.*
Abide	abode	abode	Sing	sang	sung
Awake	awoke	awoke	Sit	sat	sat
Become	became	become	Sling	slung	slung
Begin	began	begun	Slink	slunk	slunk
Behold	beheld	beheld, beholden[1]	Spin	spun	spun
			Spring	sprang	sprung
Cling	clung	clung	Stand	stood	stood
Come	came	come	Stick	stuck	stuck
Dig	dug	dug	Sting	stung	stung
Fight	fought	fought	Stink	stank	stunk
Find	found	found	String	strung	strung
Fling	flung	flung	Swim	swam	swum
Grind	ground	ground	Swing	swung	swung
Hold	held	held	Win	won	won
Ring	rang	rung	Wind	wound	wound
Run	ran	run	Wring	wrung	wrung
Shine	shone	shone			

Group III.—Mixed or Strong-Weak Verbs (28 *in number*).

Present Tense.	*Past Tense.*	*Past Participle.*
Beat	beat	beaten
Cleave (split)	clave, cleft	*cloven, cleft
Climb	clomb, climbed	climbed
Crow	crew, crowed	crowed, crown (rare)
Do	did	done
Grave	graved	*graven, graved
Hang[2]	hung, hanged	hung, hanged
Hew	hewed	*hewn, hewed
Lade	laded	laden
Melt	melted	*molten, melted
Mow	mowed	mown
Prove	proved	†proven, proved
Rive	rived	riven
Rot	rotted	*rotten, rotted
Saw	sawed	sawn
Seethe	seethed	*sodden, seethed
Sew	sewed	*sewn, sewed
Shape	shaped	†shapen, shaped
Shave	shaved	shaven
Shear	sheared	*shorn, sheared
Show	showed	shown
Sow	sowed	sown

[1] "Beholden" means "indebted."

[2] The Intransitive verb is conjugated in the Strong form only. The Transitive verb is conjugated in both forms. *Hanged* means "killed by hanging"; as, "The man was *hanged.*" *Hung* is used in a general sense; as, "He *hung* up his coat."

Present Tense.	*Past Tense.*	*Past Participle.*
Stave	stove, staved	stove, staved
Strew	strewed	strewn or strown
Swell	swelled	swollen
Thrive	throve, thrived	thriven, thrived
Wake	woke, waked	woke, waked
Wash	washed	* washen, washed
Writhe	writhed	† writhen, writhed

Note 1.—The participles marked * are now chiefly used as Verbal adjectives, and not as parts of some tense:—

Verbal Adjective.	*Part of some Tense.*
A *graven* image.	The image was *engraved* with letters.
A *molten* image.	The image was *melted* with heat.
A *rotten* plank.	The plank was *rotted* by water.
The *sodden* flesh.	The flesh was *seethed* in hot water.
A well-*sewn* cloth.	I have *sewed* or *sewn* it.
Un-*washen* hands.	I have *washed* my hands.
A *shorn* lamb.	The lamb was *sheared* to-day.
A *hewn* log.	The log is *hewed* or *hewn*.

Note 2.—The participles marked † are now seldom seen except in poetry.

145. Lists of Weak Verbs.—The mode of adding the suffix of the Past tense is not uniform; and the two rules given below should be observed:—

(1) If the verb ends in *e*, then *d* only is added; as—

Live, lived (not *liveed*).
Clothe, clothed (not *clotheed*).

To this rule there is no exception.

(2) The final consonant is doubled before *ed*, provided (*a*) that the final consonant is *single*, (*b*) that it is *accented* or *monosyllabic*, (*c*) that it is preceded by a *single vowel*; as—

Fan, fanned (not *faned*); *drop, dropped* (not *droped*).
Compel, compelled; control, controlled.

But in a verb like *lengthen*, where the accent is not on the last syllable, the Past tense is *lengthened*; in a verb like *boil*, where the vowel is not single, the Past sense is *boiled*; and in a verb like *fold*, where the last consonant is not single, the Past tense is *folded*.

To this rule there are very few exceptions. One exception occurs in the final *l*. The final *l* is doubled, even when it is not accented; as, travel, tra*velled* (not tra*veled*). But the final *l* is not doubled, if it has two vowels going before it; as *travail, travailed* (not *travailled*.

Group I.—Shortening (if possible) of Inside Vowel: Past tense in t.

Present Tense.	*Past Tense.*	*Past Part.*	*Present Tense.*	*Past Tense.*	*Past Part.*
Creep	crept	crept	Sweep	swept	swept
Sleep	slept	slept	Keep	kept	kept

Present Tense.	*Past Tense.*	*Past Part.*	*Present Tense.*	*Past Tense.*	*Past Part.*
Weep	wept	wept	Smell	smelt	smelt
Burn	burnt	burnt	Spell	spelt	spelt
Deal (dēl)	dĕalt	dĕalt	Lean (lēn)	lĕant or leaned	lĕant or leaned
Dream (drēm)	drĕamt or dreamed	drĕamt or dreamed	Mean (mēn)	mĕant	mĕant
Dwell	dwelt	dwelt	Spill	spilt	spilt
Feel	felt	felt	Spoil	spoilt or spoiled	spoilt or spoiled
Kneel	knelt	knelt			

Exceptional Verbs.—Make, made, made. Have, had, had. Hear, heard, heard. Leave, left, left. Cleave, cleft, cleft. Lose, lost, lost. Shoe, shod, shod. Flee, fled, fled. Say, said, said. Lay, laid, laid. Pay, paid, paid.

Group II.—Changing of Inside Vowel: Past tense in **d** *or* **t**.

Present Tense.	*Past Tense.*	*Past Part.*	*Present Tense.*	*Past Tense.*	*Past Part.*
Beseech	besought	besought	Work	wrought, worked	wrought, worked
Bring	brought	brought			
Buy	bought	bought	Owe	ought, owed	owed
Catch	caught	caught	Dare	durst or dared	dared
Seek	sought	sought	Can	could	(*Wanting*)
Sell	sold	sold	Shall	should	(*Wanting*)
Teach	taught	taught	Will	would	(*Wanting*)
Tell	told	told	May	might	(*Wanting*)
Think	thought	thought	Clothe	clad, clothed	clad, clothed

Group III.—Verbs whose Present tense ends in **d** *or* **t**.

Verbs ending in *d* or *t* in the Present tense have discarded the suffix of the Past tense, to avoid the repetition of *d* or *t*.

(*a*) Some verbs in this group have the three forms (Present tense, Past tense, and Past Participle) all exactly alike:—

Present Tense.	*Past Tense.*	*Past Part.*	*Present Tense.*	*Past Tense.*	*Past Part.*
Burst	burst	burst	Slit	slit	slit
Cast	cast	cast	Spit	spit or spat	spit
Cost	cost	cost			
Cut	cut	cut	Split	split	split
Hit	hit	hit	Spread	spread	spread
Hurt	hurt	hurt	Sweat	sweat	sweat
Let	let	let	Thrust	thrust	thrust
Put	put	put	Bet	bet	bet
Rid	rid	rid	Quit	quit or quitted	quit or quitted
Set	set	set			
Shed	shed	shed	Knit	knit or knitted	knit or knitted
Shred	shred	shred			
Shut	shut	shut			

Note.—"Spit" is a Weak verb, although it has a form *spat* for the Past tense. In Anglo-Saxon the Present had two forms also.

(*b*) Other verbs in this group end in *d* in the Present tense, but form the Past tense and Past Participle by changing *d* into *t*. (There are at least nine such verbs in English.)

Present Tense.	*Past Tense.*	*Past Part.*	*Present Tense.*	*Past Tense.*	*Past Part.*
Bend	bent	bent	Rend	rent	rent
Build	built	built	Send	sent	sent
Gild	gilt, gilded	gilt	Spend	spent	spent
Gird	girt, girded	girt	Wend	went	(*Wanting*)
Lend	lent	lent			

Exceptions :—end-ed, mend-ed, blend-ed or blent, defend-ed.

(*c*) Other verbs of this group have the three forms all alike, except that they shorten the vowel in the Past forms :—

Present Tense.	*Past Tense.*	*Past Part.*	*Present Tense.*	*Past Tense.*	*Past Part.*
Bleed	bled	bled	Lead	led	led
Breed	bred	bred	Read	r*e*ad	r*e*ad
Feed	fed	fed	Light	lit, lighted	lit, lighted
Speed	sped	sped	Shoot	shot	shot
Meet	met	met			

SECTION 14.—DEFECTIVE, IRREGULAR, AND IMPERSONAL VERBS.

146. Defective Verbs.—It has been shown that verbs can be classified (1) according to function into Notional (Trans. or Intrans.) and Auxiliary, see § 85 ; and (2) according to Conjugation or form into Strong and Weak, see § 143.

"Defective" does not constitute a separate class. This word merely means that a verb, whether Weak or Strong, is not conjugated in all its parts.

The verbs *shall*, *will*, *may*, *can* are Defective, because they have no other forms besides that of the Past tense, viz. *should*, *would*, *might*, *could*.

The verbs *quoth*, *must*, *ought* are Defective, because these are the only forms of tense in which they are now seen ; and *quoth* is further Defective, because it is never used in the Second person.

The verb *wit* is Defective, because it is seen chiefly in the Infinitive mood, "*to wit*" (used only in legal documents.) (The Present *wot* and Past *wist* are almost obsolete.) The verb *worth* is Defective, because it is seen only in the Subjunctive mood, as in the phrase "Woe *worth* (= be to) the day." The verbs *wont* and *yclept* are now seen only as participles. *Hight* = *is* or *was called* is almost obsolete even in poetry.

Anomalous is the name given to those verbs that are pieced together from parts of two or more Defective verbs ; as, *am, was, been*; *go, went, gone*. The verb "to be" is a patchwork of three distinct Anglo-Saxon roots, *es* (cf. Latin *es*, *est*), *beó* (cf. Latin *fi-o*), and *wes*.

147. Irregular Verbs.—The verbs *shall, will, may, can, wot, quoth* are called Irregular, because in the Third person Singular they do not take a final *s*.

For the same reason *dare* and *need* are Irregular, whenever they are followed by an Infinitive without "to"; as, "He *dare* not go," "He *need* not go."

The Past tense *could* is Irregular, because it has taken an intrusive *l*, in imitation of *should*, *would*. *Did* is an Irregular Past tense of *do*, *made* of *make*, and *had* of *have*. *Made* has lost the medial *k*, and *had* the medial *v*.

148. Impersonal Verbs.—These take "it" for their Subject, and are followed by some Personal pronoun in the Objective case, which in Personal verbs would be the Subject in the Nom. case:—

It shames *me* to hear this = I am ashamed to hear this.
It repents *me* of my folly = I repent of my folly.
It behoves *me* to do this = I ought to do this.

There are three instances in which the *it* is omitted, and the pronoun is placed *before* the verb instead of after it:—

Methinks = it seems to me.
Meseems = it seems to me.
Melists = it seems to me, or it pleases me.

Note.—In Modern English there is no difference of spelling between *thinks* Impersonal and *think* Transitive. But in Old Eng. the former was *thync-an* (to seem) and the latter *thenc-an* (to think).

CHAPTER VII.—ADVERBS.

Section 1.—The Functions of Adverbs.

149. It has been shown already (§ 16) that an Adverb can qualify Prepositions and Conjunctions, as well as Verbs, Adjectives, and other Adverbs.

(*a*) **Prepositions**:—

The bird flew *exactly over* the sleeper's head.
He paid the money *quite up to* date.
His abilities are *decidedly above* the average.
He was sitting *almost outside* the door.
He arrived *long before* the time.
He held his hand *partly on* and *partly off* the table.

(*b*) **Conjunctions**:—

A man is truly happy *only when* he is in sound health.
I dislike this weather *simply because* the air is too hot.

I wish to know *precisely how* it happened.
They locked the door *shortly before* the thieves came.
The watch was found *long after* the thieves had been caught.
He has been ill *ever since* he left us.

Note.—If for an adverb proper we substitute an adverbial phrase, we find that such a phrase can qualify a preposition or a conjunction in the same way as an adverb proper does :—

Preposition.—He arrived *a few hours after* midnight.
Conjunction.—He recovered *ten days after* he had been taken ill.

150. An Adverb can also qualify an entire sentence. *In this case it must stand first :—*

Unfortunately the thief was not caught.
Evidently you were much distressed at the news.

We could rewrite these sentences in the following form :—

It is unfortunate that the thief was not caught.
It was evident that you were much distressed.

151. *Adverbs do not qualify Nouns or Pronouns.* This is the work of adjectives.

The apparent exceptions to the above rule can all be explained :—

(*a*) I am *sincerely yours.* That book is *certainly mine.*

Here the words "yours" and "mine" are the Possessive forms of "you" and "I," and are therefore equivalent to *adjectives.*

(*b*) A by-path ; a fore-taste ; an out-house.

Here the adverbs do not qualify the several nouns, but are *compounded* with them, so that each compound makes a *single* word.

(*c*) In the following examples the adverb that precedes the noun does not qualify the noun, but some participle or adjective understood :—

The then king = the king then *reigning.*
The late king = the king lately *reigning.*
The above account = the account *given* above.
A far country = a country far *distant.*
An up mail = an up-*going* mail.

(*d*) In the following example the adverb "almost" or "quite" does not qualify the noun "drunkard," but the verb "is" :—

He is *almost* or *quite* a drunkard.

To say, "He is an almost or a quite drunkard," would be incorrect.

Note.—A slovenly practice is springing up, however, by which the adverb "quite" is made to qualify nouns :—

Quite a panic (= a serious panic) was caused.
They had *quite a run* (= a long run) of ill luck.

Section 2.—The Kinds of Adverbs.

152. Adverbs are subdivided into three distinct classes :—

I. Simple. II. Interrogative. III. Conjunctive.

153. Simple Adverbs.—These can be distinguished from one another according to their meaning:—

(1) **Time.**—He did this *before*, and you have done it *since*.

The chief adverbs of this class are:—*Now, then, before, since, ago, already, soon, presently, immediately, instantly, early, late*, etc.

(2) **Place.**—We must rest *here*, and not *there*.

The chief adverbs of this class are:—*Here, there; hence, thence; hither, thither; in, out; within, without; above, below; far, near.*

Note.—Sometimes *there* is merely introductory, and has no meaning of place:—

There is some one knocking at the door.

(3) **Number.**—He did this *once*, but he will not do it *again*.

The chief adverbs of this class are:—*Once, twice, thrice, again, seldom, never, sometimes, always, often, firstly, secondly, thirdly*, etc.

(4) **Description** (§ 46, 2).—He did his work *slowly*, but *surely*.

This class is very numerous. Most of them are formed by adding *-ly* to some adjective. But some do not end in *-ly*; cf. *thus, so, well, ill, amiss, asleep.*

(5) **Quantity, Extent,** or **Degree.**—He is *almost*, but not *quite*, the cleverest boy in the class. He was *too* tired to go on.

To this class of adverb belong:—*Very, much, the, too, quite, almost, little, a little, rather, somewhat, half, partly, wholly, so*, etc.

Note.—The adverb "the" is quite distinct from the Definite article. It is an Adverb of Degree, derived from the Anglo-Saxon Instrumental case (*thī*) of the Demonstrative, and is never used except before an adjective or adverb in the *Comparative* degree: "*the* more, *the* merrier."

(6) **Affirming** or **Denying.**—He did *not* come after all.

Yes, no, not, perhaps, probably, certainly, not at all, etc.

Note.—*Yes* and *no* are pro-sentence or substitute adverbs:—

(1) Did he come? Yes (=He did come). *Affirm.*
(2) Did he come? No (=He did not come). *Negat.*

In (1) *yes* is substituted for an affirmative sentence, and in (2) *no* is substituted for a negative sentence. As pro-nouns save the repetition of a noun, so these adverbs save the repetition of a sentence.

Note 1.—In some books a 7th class is added, viz. adverbs of Cause or Consequence:—*Therefore, then, consequently, because, for.* It appears, however, that these words do not exactly modify any word or words in a sentence, but are rather conjunctions combining the sense of one sentence with that of another by way of inference. They have therefore been included amongst Conjunctions in this book.

Note 2.—**Phrase-adverbs.**—Adverbs can be expressed by phrases (§ 19) as well as by single words:—*now and then, to and fro, at present, by all means, up and down, how long? how far? now-a-days*, etc.

154. Interrogative Adverbs.—Used for asking questions:—

(*a*) **Time.**—*When* did he *come?* *How long* will he remain here?
(*b*) **Place.**—*Where* did he stop? *Whence* has he come? *Whither* is he going?
(*c*) **Number.**—*How often* did the dog bark?
(*d*) **Description** (manner, quality, or state).—*How* did he do this? *How* (in what state of health) is he to-day?
(*e*) **Quantity** or **Degree.**—*How far* (to what extent) was that report true?
(*f*) **Cause** or **Reason.**—*Why* did he do this? *Wherefore* did he go?

155. The adverbs "*how*" and "*what*" are sometimes used in an exclamatory sense:—

How kind of you to do that!
What a foolish fellow you are!

156. Conjunctive Adverbs.—These are the same in *form* as Interrogative adverbs; but instead of asking questions, they join sentences, being partly adverbs and partly conjunctions (§ 18).

(*a*) *The antecedent understood.*

This is *where* (=the place in which) we dwell.
Let me know *when* (=the time by which) you will come.

(*b*) *The antecedent expressed.*

This is the place *where* we dwell.
Let me know the time *when* you will come.

Section 3.—Comparison of Adverbs.

157. Adverbs of Quality have degrees of comparison, which are formed in the same way as those of adjectives:—

(*a*) If the Adverb is a word of *one* syllable, the Comparative is formed by adding *er* and the Superlative by adding *est*:—

Fast	faster	fastest	Loud	louder	loudest
Hard	harder	hardest	Late	later	latest or last
Near	nearer	nearest	Far	farther	farthest
Long	longer	longest	Rathe	rather	...

Till *rathe* (=early) she rose, half cheated in the thought.—Tennyson.

(*b*) Some Adverbs have had a Comparative and Superlative allotted to them from another root:—

Well	better	best	Much	more	most
Ill or badly	worse	worst	Little	less	least

(*c*) Adverbs ending in *ly* form the Comparative by adding *more* and the Superlative by adding *most*:—

Wisely	more wisely	most wisely
Beautifully	more beautifully	most beautifully

Note.—The Adverb "*early*," however, has "*earlier*" for its Comparative.

SECTION 4.—VERBS COMPOUNDED WITH ADVERBS.

158. A Verb is said to be compounded with an Adverb, when the two words are so habitually used together, that one is considered to be a part of the other.

Such Adverbs are almost always (except in poetry) placed *after* the verb; as "speak out," "rise up." Here the *out* should be parsed as part of the verb "speak"; and *up* as part of the verb "rise."

But in forming the corresponding noun, the adverb is put first:—

Verb.	*Noun.*
The crops will *come out* well.	The *outcome* was a good crop.
No profits will *come in*.	His *income* is small.
Cholera did not *break out*.	There was no *outbreak* of cholera.
He *set out* on his journey.	He had no trouble at the *outset*.

Similar instances are:—*Set off* (verb), *offset* (noun); *put out* (verb), *output* (noun); *fit out* (verb), *outfit* (noun); *shoot off* (verb), *offshoot* (noun); *spring off* (verb), *offspring* (noun); *shoot up* (verb), *upshot* (noun); *turn out* (verb), *outturn* (noun); *cast out* (verb), *outcast* (noun); *set on* (verb), *onset* (noun); *lay out* (verb), *outlay* (noun); *look out* (verb), *outlook* (noun); *draw in* (verb), *indraught* (noun); *let out* (verb), *outlet* (noun); *let in* (verb), *inlet* (noun).

Note.—"Set-off," "turn-out," and a few more are also used as nouns.

SECTION 5.—THE TWO USES OF ADVERBS.

159. Adverbs, like Adjectives (see § 58), have two different uses, viz. (*a*) the Attributive, (*b*) the Predicative.

(*a*) *Attributive use.*—An Adverb is used attributively, when it qualifies in the ordinary way the word associated with it:—

He is *entirely wrong*. He *shouted loudly*. He *did* his work *very badly*. *Half through* the door. I dislike him *only because* he is lazy.

(*b*) *Predicative use.*—An Adverb is used predicatively, when it is made part of the Predicate of a sentence, or in other words, when it is used as the Complement of the verb going before it:[1]—

Subject.	*Verb.*	*Complement*, etc.
My son	is	*well* (in good health) to-day.
He	will be	*better* (in better health) soon.
He	was turned	*adrift* (to go where he could).
The two boys	are	much *alike* (like to each other).
The bear	was caught	*alive* (in a living state).
Those men	are	*aware* (conscious) of their faults.

[1] We cannot endorse what is said in Mason's *English Grammar*, p. 157, ed. 1891: "*An Adverb or adverbial phrase never forms the complement of a predicate.*" The examples given in the text show how very common the predicative or complementary use of Adverbs is.

Subject.	*Verb.*	*Complement*, etc.
The game	is	*over* (finished).
Some money	was	still *over* (remaining).
The results	are	*out* (published).
The stars	are	*out* (visible).
He	was heard	*out* (to the very end).
The bargain	is	*off* (cancelled).
The train	is	*off* (started).
He	is	*well off* (in good circumstances).
Our side	is	*in* (having their innings).
The late minister	is	*in* (holding office) again.

CHAPTER VIII.—PREPOSITIONS.

160. Kinds of Objects.—Besides nouns and pronouns, we sometimes have adverbs, infinitives, phrases, and clauses as objects to a preposition :—

(*a*) *Adverbs* :—

We must be ready by *then* (= that time). By *far* the best.
He has worked hard from *then* to *now*.
He walks about from *here* to *there*.
I have heard of worse things being done before *now*.
Until *now* it has not ceased raining.
Many strange things may happen between *now* and *then*.
You must go at *once*. This will last for *ever*.

(*b*) *Infinitives* ; see § 127 (*b*) : this construction is rare except in such examples as the following :—

He was about *to die*. He desired nothing but *to succeed*.

(*c*) *Phrases* :—

The day-spring from *on-high* hath visited us.
He did not return till *about-ten-days-afterwards*.
These books are sold at *over-one-shilling* each.
I bought this for *under-half-its-value*.
The question of *how-to-do-this* is difficult.

(*d*) *Clauses* :—

This depends upon | whether-he-will-consent-or-not.
He told every one of | what-he-had-heard.
Go whenever you like except | that-you-must-not-go-in-the-rain.
In | that-he-died | he died unto sin once.—*New Testament*.

161. (*a*) **Omission of Object.**—There are two cases of this :—
Relative Pronoun.—The man (*whom* or *that*) we were looking for.
Demons. Pronoun.—A chair to sit on (*it*).

(*b*) **Omission of Preposition.**—This occurs chiefly with the prepositions *to*, *of*, and *at* :—

(1) **To** :—
He went (to) home. Give (to) me that book.
On the Indirect object, see § 90 and § 360 (*e*).

(2) **Of**:—

On board (of) ship. A hundred (of) pounds. A many (=a multitude, of) tears (§ 38 (*e*), *Note*).

What we now call the Gerund in *-ing*, as "telling lies," has come into existence solely through the omission of "*of*" after the Verbal noun in *-ing*; as "telling of lies." (See § 142.)

(3) **At**: see § 100, *Note* 2:—

They laughed (at) him to scorn. He stared (at) me in the face. He looked (at) me in the face.

162. Disguised Prepositions.—"*On*" is changed into "*a*" in such phrases as "to go *a fishing*."

Similarly "*of*" can be changed into "*o*," as in "four o'clock," "Jack o' lantern," etc.

In such phrases as the following *a* was originally *on*:—

Flour sells at tenpence *a pound*.
He called to see me once *a week*.
He gave the men four shillings *a piece*.

The "a" *looks* so much like the Indefinite Article, that by a false analogy "the" is sometimes used in its place; as—

Flour sells at tenpence *the pound*.

163. Than.—This word has been used as a Preposition by the best English writers:—

No mightier than thyself or *me*	SHAKESPEARE.
A stone is heavy, and the sand weighty; but a fool's wrath is heavier than *them* both .	*Old Testament.*
She suffers hourly more than *me* . . .	SWIFT.
You are a much greater loser than *me* . .	*Ibid.*
Lined with giants deadlier than *them* all . .	POPE.
For thou art a girl as much brighter than *her*	
As he was a poet sublimer than *me* . . .	PRIOR.
Thou hast been wiser all the while than *me* .	SOUTHEY.
You know that I am, not less than *him*, a despiser of the multitude	GOLDSMITH.

She should look worse than *him*.—*Time*, July 1883, p. 83.

It struck me then that God knew better than *me*.—*Review of Reviews*, Aug. 1898, p. 126.

Even so far back as Caxton, the first English printer, we find *than* used as a preposition, followed by an objective case:—

For ther is nothyng more suspecte to evyl people than *them*, whom they know to be wyse and trewe.—*The Curial*, 4, 18.

These are not errors or solecisms of the illiterate. But in current books on Grammar the prepositional character of *than* is denied.[1]

[1] For example, in Mason's *English Grammar*, p. 177, ed. 1891, we are told that "no *syntactical* explanation can be given of the relative *whom* after *than*." The syntax, however, is very simple, if we parse *than* as a

Originally "than" was not a conjunction, but an adverb (another form of *then*). In modern English it has been further developed into a preposition, and has been used as such by good authors, and is still used. The best course to take is to parse it as a Conjunction, whenever it is possible to supply a Finite verb understood :—

No animal is larger than a whale.
No animal is larger than a whale (is large).

But in such constructions as the following "than" must still be parsed as a Preposition, because there is no Finite verb understood which could make it a Conjunction :—

	Kind of Object.
I will not take less than *ten shillings* . .	*Noun.*
No one other than a *graduate* need apply [1] .	*Noun.*
Here is my son, than *whom* a better does not exist	*Rel. Pron.*
He did nothing else than *laugh*	*Noun-Infin.*
I will suffer myself rather than (that) *he should suffer*	*Noun-clause.*
He got more *than* (what) he asked for . .	*Noun-clause.*
He has said so more than *once*	*Adverb* (§ 160, *a*).

164. But.—In such examples as the following "but" must be parsed as a Preposition. Otherwise it is a Conjunction :—

All *but* (except) one fulfilled their promises.
He was all *but* (=everything except) ruined. (Here "ruined" is an elliptical form of the Gerund "being ruined"; and this Gerund is the object of the preposition "but.")

---

preposition. There is ample analogy for the use of "than" as a preposition, besides ample authority. "Superior *to* mine" = "better *than* mine." If *to* is a preposition, why not *than*? The Scotch say, "He is taller *be* (=*by*) onie o' thaim." If *by* is a preposition, why not *than*? "He was not only equal to, but taller than, me in height." Here we have *to* and *than* used as prepositions for the same object.

[1] "No other than *he* need apply" is an exceptional phrase that proves nothing; cf. "but *he*" in "Whence all but *he* had fled" (Mrs. Hemans). In the sentence given, "No other than a graduate need apply," the phrase "other than"=different from, except, but. We cannot expand "than a graduate" into a clause containing a Finite verb, and hence *than* is a preposition. In some editions of Shakespeare we have the phrase "no other than *him*" :—

That you elect *no other* king than *him*.—1 *Hen. VI.* iv. 1, 4.

The editor who makes Shakespeare say "than *him*," evidently regards "than" as a preposition.

Sometimes the preposition *from* is used instead of *than* after "other" :—

This is a far *other* tone *from* that
In which the Duke spoke eight, nine years ago.
COLERIDGE, *Piccolomini*, i. 12.

Mrs. Craik, in *The Ogilvies*, chap. x., uses *but* after *other*, where *but*, though undoubtedly a preposition, is followed by *he* :—

How could I hear such words from any other man *but he*?

But for your help (=except on account of your help=if you had not helped me) I should have been ruined. (Here the phrase "for your help" is object to the preposition *but.*)

I cannot *but* fear (=I cannot do anything except fear) that you are ill. (Here the Noun-Infinitive "fear" is the object of *but.*)

CHAPTER IX.—CONJUNCTIONS.

165. According to the definition given in § 15, a "conjunction is a word used for showing in what relation one notion stands to another notion, or one thought to another thought."

As notions are expressed by single words or phrases, and thoughts by sentences or clauses, we can substitute a shorter, though less accurate, definition, which is more convenient for parsing and analysis,—"a conjunction joins one word to another word, or one sentence to another sentence." Conjunctions are subdivided into two main classes:—

I. **Co-ordinative**, which join sentences of co-ordinate (that is, of *equal*) rank, or words that stand in the same relation to some other word in the sentence.[1]

II. **Subordinative**, which join a *subordinate* or dependent sentence to a *principal* sentence (that is, to a sentence of *higher* rank).

SECTION 1.—CO-ORDINATIVE CONJUNCTIONS.

166. *Sentences are of* **Co-ordinate** *or* **equal** *rank, when one is not dependent on the other, nor enters at all into its construction.*

167. Sentences of equal rank can be related to one another in four different senses, and this gives rise to four different kinds of Co-ordinative Conjunctions:—

---

[1] Conjunctions for the most part join sentences, not words. We cannot, however, accept Mr. Mason's statement that "*and* is the single exception," the only instance of a conjunction which may join words; for in point of fact, *all* the Co-ordinative conjunctions can join *adjectives.*

(1) A captious *and* conceited man is not fit to review a book (*Cumulative.*)
(2) We admire the character of a poor, *but* honest man . (*Adversative.*)
(3) A drunk *or* mad Malay ran amuck yesterday . . (*Alternative.*)
(4) An iron (and) *therefore* durable box was procured . (*Illative.*)

In (1) the notion of self-conceit is added to that of captiousness. In (2) the notion of honesty is contrasted with that of poverty. In (3) the notion of madness is given as an alternative to that of drunkenness. In (4) the notion of durability is inferred from that of iron.

The Conjunction "*and*" will join *nouns* as well as adjectives. In this respect, and this only, it is unique:—

Youth *and* experience cannot exist together.

(*a*) **Cumulative.**—By these one thought is simply *added* to another :—*and, both . . . and, not only, but also, as well as* :—

He was *both* degraded *and* expelled.
He *as well as* you is guilty.

(*b*) **Alternative.**—By these a *choice* is offered between one thought and another :—*either . . . or, else, or, otherwise* :—

Leave the room, *or* take the consequences.
He was *neither* an idler *nor* a gambler.

(*c*) **Adversative.**—By these conjunctions one thought is *contrasted* with or set against another :—*but, still, yet, nevertheless, however* :—

He is very rich, *still* or *yet* or *but* he is not contented.

(*d*) **Illative.**—By these conjunctions one thought is *inferred* or proved from another :—*for, therefore, then, so then* :—

He was found guilty, and *therefore* he was hanged.
It is time to go ; let us start *then*.

SECTION 2.—SUBORDINATIVE CONJUNCTIONS.

168. One sentence is said to be *subordinate* to another, when it depends upon the other, that is, forms part of its construction, doing the work of a noun, adjective, or adverb.

That sentence on which the subordinate sentence depends is called the **Principal** sentence

Principal.	*Conj.*	*Dependent.*	
I will read that book,	if	you advise me.	(*Adverb-clause.*)
We still hope	that	you may get well.	(*Noun-clause.*)

169. The chief modes of dependence are nine in number :—

(*a*) Apposition, (*b*) Causation, (*c*) Effect, (*d*) Purpose, (*e*) Condition, (*f*) Concession or Contrast, (*g*), Comparison, (*h*) Extent or Manner, (*i*) Time.

Apposition.—He made a promise, *that* he would soon return.
Causation.—I will do this, *because* or *as* or *since* you desire it.
Effect.—He talked so much *that* he made himself hoarse.
Purpose.—Men work *that* they may earn a living.
Condition.—I will do this, *if* I am allowed (=*unless* I am prevented).
Concession.—He was a contented man, *although* he was poor.
Comparison.—He is quite *as* clever *as* I am. (Equal degrees.)
,, He is more clever *than* I am. (Unequal degrees.)
Extent, Manner.—Men will reap *as* they sow.
Time.—He returned home *after* he had finished work.

170. As well as.—This conjunctional phrase is Co-ordinative in one sense and Subordinative in another—

(*a*) *Co-ordinative.*—In adding one co-ordinate sentence to another, it gives emphasis to the *first* :—

He as well as you is guilty =
Not only you, but he also is guilty.

(*b*) *Subordinative* :—

Principal.	*Dependent.*
He does not write	as well as you do

= His writing is not as good as yours.

171. Though, but.—Both of these conjunctions (the first Subordinative, the second Co-ordinative) denote concession or contrast :—

(*a*) He is honest, *though* poor.
(*b*) He is poor, *but* honest.

These two sentences mean precisely the same thing, because in (*a*) "He is honest" is the *Principal* clause, and in (*b*) the Co-ordinate clause, "but he is honest," is more *emphatic* than the clause preceding it. Thus the Principal clause and the Emphatic clause are the same.

If, however, we rewrite the two sentences thus :—

(*a*) He is honest, though poor ;
(*b*) He is honest, but poor,

the two sentences are not equivalent. The first emphasises the fact that he is honest in spite of his poverty. The second emphasises the fact that he is poor in spite of his honesty.

Conjunctive and Interrogative Adverbs.

172. It was explained in § 18 that a Conjunctive adverb is a *double* part of speech,—a conjunction and adverb combined in one :—*when, why, where, whence, how, whether.*

The same is true of Interrogative adverbs, when they are used as conjunctions :—

Let me ask you *how* you did this.

There is no difference in *form* between a Conjunctive and an Interrogative adverb. The former qualifies some noun expressed or understood in the Principal sentence. The latter is preceded by some verb that signifies *asking* or *inquiring.*

CHAPTER X.—INTERJECTIONS.

173. An Interjection is unlike every other Part of Speech, since it does not enter into the construction of a sentence.

It is merely an *exclamatory sound,* thrown into a sentence to denote some strong feeling or emotion (see § 17) :—

Joy.—Hurrah! huzza!
Grief.—Oh! ah! alas! alack!
Amusement.—Ha! ha!
Approval.—Bravo!
Weariness.—Heigh-ho!
Attention.—Lo! hark! hush! hist!
Reproof.—Fie! fie!
Contempt or ridicule.—Stuff! bosh! tut-tut! pooh! pish! pshaw! tush!
To call some one.—Ho! holloa!

174. There are certain moods of verbs and parts of speech which can be used for an exclamatory or Interjectional purpose:—

(*a*) *Noun-Infinitive.*—*To think* that he should have died! (§ 127, *d*).
(*b*) *Subjunctive.*—*Would* that I had gained that prize! (*Wish.*)
(*c*) *Imperative.*—*Hear! hear!* (*Applause.*)
(*d*) *Noun.*—Dreadful *sight!* Foolish *fellow!* *Fool!* *Dunce!*
(*e*) *Adjective* (with some noun understood).—*Strange!* *Shocking!*
(*f*) *Adverb.*—*How* very kind of you! *How* wonderful!
(*g*) *Pronoun.*—*What* a sad thing it is!
(*h*) *Conjunction.*—*If* I could only see him once more!

175. Sometimes in a rapid or exclamatory sentence an Auxiliary verb with its subject is left out, and only the main verb is expressed:—

Why dream and wait for him longer?—LONGFELLOW.
(=Why *dost thou* or why *do we* wait for him longer?)

CHAPTER XI.

THE SAME WORD USED AS DIFFERENT PARTS OF SPEECH.

A. *Indef. Article.* The sportsman shot *a* tiger.
Prep. He has gone *a* hunting. Three times *a* day (§ 162).

All. *Adj. of Quantity.* He ate *all* the bread.
Indef. Num. Adj. We must *all* die some day.
Adj. used as Noun. We lost our *all* on that day.
Adv. *All* bloodless lay the untrodden snow.

Any. *Adj. of Quantity.* Have you *any* bread?
Adv. of Qu. We must stop and rest before going *any* farther.
Indef. Num. Adjective. Did you bring *any* loaves?
Indef. Dem. Adjective. Take *any* book that you like best.

As. (*a*) *Conjunctive pronoun*:—
He is not such a fool *as* he looks.
As many men *as* came were caught.
Yours is not the same book *as* mine.

(*b*) *Conjunctive adverb* (or subordinative conjunction):—
Time. He trembled *as* (at what time) he spoke.
Manner. Do not act *as* (in what manner) he did.
State. He took it just *as* (in what state) it was.
Extent. He is not as (to that extent) clever *as* (to what extent) you are.
Hot *as* (to whatever extent) the sun is (=however hot the sun is), we must go out in it.
Reason. The air is now cool, *as* (for what reason or for the reason that) the rain has fallen.

(c) *In Elliptical Phrases*:—all of these imply "extent."

I condemn you *as* a judge (to what extent or so far as I am a judge), but *as* a man (to what extent I am a man) I pity you.

I will inquire again *as* to (to what extent the question relates to) that matter.

As regards this journey (to what extent the question regards this journey), we can now decide nothing.

Better. *Comp. Adj.* My book is a *better* one than yours.
Comp. Adv. You are working *better* to-day.
Adj. used as Noun. Do not despise your *betters*.

Both. *Def. Num. Adj.* *Both* the men have arrived.
Conj. Co-ord. He is *both* a fool and a knave.

But. *Adv.* There is *but* (only) one man present.
Prep. Who could have done this *but* (except) him?
I cannot *but* believe that you are lost. (I cannot believe anything *except* that, etc.)
Conj. Co-ord. He is a man of common sense, *but* not learned in books.
Conj. Subord. There was no one present, *but* (he) pitied (= who did not pity) the lame horse.
Perdition catch my soul, *but* I love thee.—SHAKESPEARE. (May perdition catch my soul, *if* I do *not* love thee.)

Either. *Distrib. Adj.* He is ruined in *either* case.
Conj. Co-ord. He is *either* a fool or a knave.

Else. *Adv. used as Adj.* We could not find any one *else* (=any *other* person).
Conj. Co-ord. He has some real object; *else* he would go.

Enough. *Adj. of Quantity.* He has eaten *enough* bread.
Adj. of Number. We have *enough* loaves.
Adj. used as Noun. He had *enough* to do.

Half. *Adj. of Quantity.* *Half* measures do not succeed.
Adj. used as Noun. One *half* of his task is now done.
Adv. of Quantity. He was *half* dead with fear.

Little. *Adj. of Quality.* A *little* blow may give much pain.
Adj. of Quantity. He has eaten a *little* bread.
Adv. of Quantity. Let us wait here a *little*.
Adj. used as Noun. Man wants but *little* here below.

More. *Adj. of Quantity.* He eats *more* bread than you.
Adj. used as Noun. *More* is done than was expected.
Adv. of Quantity. I like him *more* than (I like) you.
Adj. of Number. *More* men came to-day than yesterday.
Adv. of Number. I saw him once *more*.

Much. *Adj. of Quantity.* He has wasted *much* time.
Adv. of Quantity. I am *much* pleased with your son.
Adj. used as Noun. You will not get *much* from me.

Neither. *Adj. Distrib.* I agree with *neither* side.
Conj. Co-ord. *Neither* you nor I can do that.

Near. *Adv.* Stand *near*, while I speak to you.
Prep. There is a fine tree *near* our house.
Adj. He is a *near* relative of mine.

Needs. *Verb.* The earth is very dry and *needs* rain.
Adv. He must *needs* know the reason of this.
Noun. Our *needs* or wants are few.

One. *Def. Num. Adj.* There is but *one* shilling left.
Indef. Dem. Adj. He came here *one* day.
Indef. Dem. Pron. *One* is apt to waste *one's* time.
Def. Dem. Pron. Your horse is white; mine is a black *one.*

Only. *Adj.* The *only* dog I had was stolen.
Adv. I heard of this *only* yesterday.
Conj. Co-ord. Do what you like; *only* (=but whatever else you may do) keep silence.

Round. *Adj.* A square thing does not fit into a *round* hole.
Prep. Draw a circle *round* a given centre.
Adv. The flies are flying *round* and *round.*
Verb. Gama was the first to *round* the Cape of Good Hope.
Noun. Men must go their daily *round* of duty.

Since. *Prep.* I have not seen him *since* Monday last.
Adv. I took this house four weeks *since.*
Conj. Subord. We must trust you, *since* you are in earnest.

Single. *Verb.* *Single* out the best.
Adj. He is a *single* (unmarried) man.

Such. *Def. Dem. Adj.* He is not *such* a man *as* I expected.
Indef. Dem. Adj. He came to me on *such* a day.
Def. Dem. Pron. You are a coward; I am not *such.*

That. *Def. Dem. Adj.* I am no admirer of *that* book.
Def. Dem. Pron. The light of the sun is brighter than *that* of the moon.
Relat. Pron. The book *that* you gave me is lost.
Conj. { *Effect.* He aimed *so* well *that* he hit the mark.
Apposit. He heard (the news) *that* you had come.
Purpose. We must eat *that* we may live. }

Than. *Conj. Subord.* I like this more *than* (I like) that.
Prep. { These workmen, *than* whom I have never seen men more industrious, have left me.
He was fond of any drink other *than* wine. }

Then. *Adv. of Time.* He was better *then* than he is now.
Conj. Co-ord. I see, *then,* we ought to start at once.

The. *Def. Article.* *The* ass is a dull animal.
Adv. of Quantity. *The* more, *the* merrier (§ 153 (5), *Note*).

Too. *Adv. of Quantity.* He is *too* fond of play.
Conj. Co-ord. We *too* must expect to die some day.

Well. *Adv. of Quality.* He has done the work very *well.*
Adv. used as Noun. Leave *well* alone.
Conj. Co-ord. He has finished his work in time; *well,* I did not expect it of such a lazy man.

What. *Inter. Pron.* *What* did you say?
Rel. Pron. I do not know *what* you mean (§ 79).
Indef. Demons. I tell you *what* (=something).
Adverb. *What* (=partly) with illness and *what* (=partly) with losses, the poor man is almost ruined.

Yet. *Conj. Co-ord.* I have called; *yet* no one answers.
Adv. of Time. You may *yet* (=even now, still) find him.

CHAPTER XII.—SYNTAX AND PARSING.

PARSING CHART.

I. *Nouns.*

Kind of Noun.	Gender.	Number.	Case.
Concrete { Proper Common Collective Material } Abstract	Masculine Feminine Common Neuter	Singular Plural	Nominative Possessive Objective

II. *Pronouns.*

Kind of Pronoun.	Gender.	Number.	Person.	Case.
Personal { Simple Reflexive } Demons. { Definite Indefinite }	Masculine Feminine Common Neuter	Singular Plural	1st 2nd 3rd	Nominative Possessive Objective
Conjunctive Interrogative	Agreeing (if Demonstrative or Conjunctive) in Gender, Number, and Person with its antecedent.			

III. *The Cases of Nouns or Pronouns.*

Nom. to Verb ,, as Compl. to Verb ,, in Apposition ,, of Address ,, Absolute *Possessive*	*Obj.* to Verb Direct ,, ,, Indirect ,, ,, Retained ,, ,, Cognate ,, ,, Reflexive ,, as Compl. to Verb	*Obj.* in Apposition ,, to Preposition ,, Adverbial ,, after certain Adjectives ,, Interjectional

IV. *Adjectives.*

The Kind of Adjective.	Degree.	Use.
Proper Descriptive Quantitative Interrogative Distributive Numer. { Def. Indef. } Demons. { Def. Indef. }	Positive Comparative Superlative	Attributive Predicative

V. *Adverbs.*

Kind.	Degree.	Use.	Attributive Uses.
Simple Conjunctive Interrogative	Positive Comparative Superlative	Attributive Predicative	To qualify Verb ,, ,, Adjective ,, ,, Adverb ,, ,, Preposition ,, ,, Conjunction ,, ,, Sentence

VI. *Finite Verbs.*

Kind of Verb.	Conjug.	Voice.	Mood.	Tense.	Form of each Tense.
Trans. Intrans. Auxil.	Strong Weak Mixed	Active Passive	Indic. Imper. Subjunc.	Present Past Future	Indefinite Continuous Perfect Perf. Contin.

Number.	Person.	
Singular Plural	1st 2nd 3rd	Agreeing in Number and Person with its subject or subjects, expressed or understood.

VII. *Infinitive.*

Form.	(*a*) Use as Noun-Inf.	(*b*) Use as Qualifying Inf.
Indefinite Continuous Perfect Perf. Contin.	Subject to Verb Object to Verb Complement to Verb Object to Preposition Exclamatory	To qualify— ,, a Verb ,, a Noun { Attributively / Predicatively ,, an Adjective To introduce a Parenthesis

VIII. *Gerund.*

Form.	Voice.	Kind of Verb.
Present Perfect	Active Passive	Transitive Intransitive

IX. *Participle or Verbal Adjective.*

Form.	Voice.	Kind of Verb.	Use.
Present Past Perfect	Active Passive	Transitive Intransitive	Attributive Predicative {Complement, Absolute} Gerundive

X. *Conjunctions.*

Co-ordinative.	Subordinative.

Some of the following rules have been incidentally given already in different places. They are here collected and summarised; and others not given before have been added, so as to make the account more complete.

176. Nominative case.—See No. III. of Parsing Chart.

(1) As Subject to a verb (see § 3 and § 41):—

I did this. *Rain* is falling. *You* are tired.

(2) As *Subjective* Complement to a verb (see § 95):—

I am *the man*. Cæsar was declared *emperor*.

Note.—An Infinitive can come between the verb and the noun:—

He appeared *to be* a wise man.

(3) In Apposition with a noun or pronoun (§ 4):—

John, *the carpenter*, has succeeded well in business.

(4) For purposes of Address (see § 41):—

How art thou fallen, *O Cæsar!*

(5) In the Absolute construction:—

(*a*) *With Participle*, in **past** or **present** sense:—

Off we started, he *having given* the signal.
Off we start, he *remaining behind*.

Note.—Without altering the sense, we could substitute the clause "while he remains behind" for the phrase "he remaining behind." In the absolute construction the noun or pronoun is in the Nominative case, because (as we see from this) it is *the Subject to the Finite verb that is implied in the Participle.*

(*b*) *With the Qualifying Infinitive*, in **future** sense:—

The caul was put up in a raffle, *the winner to pay* five shillings.—DICKENS, *David Copperfield.*

The estate has been divided between us, *you to have* two-thirds of it, and *I* one-third.

177. Possessive case.—See No. III. of Parsing Chart.

(*a*) A noun or pronoun in the Possessive case qualifies Nouns and Gerunds as an adjective would do :—

My son. The *barber's* shop. The *tiger's* claw.—*Noun.*
I was displeased at *his* going away without leave. } *Gerund*
This was a plan of *your* contriving. } (§ 140).

(*b*) When two Possessive nouns are in apposition with each other, the apostrophe *s* is added either to the first or last, but not usually to both :—

Herod married his *brother* Philip's wife.
For the *queen's* sake, his sister.—BYRON.

(*c*) When two nouns are connected by "*and*," the apostrophe *s* is added to both to denote *separate* possession, and to the last only to denote *joint* possession :—

A.'s and B.'s horses were sold yesterday.
A. and B.'s horses were sold yesterday.

(*d*) A noun or pronoun in the Possessive case can be the Complement to a verb (see §§ 92, 95) :—

That book is *mine*, not *James's*.

178. Objective case.—See No. III. of Parsing Chart.

(1) As Object to a verb, or in connection with some verb (§ 106, *Note* 1) :—

(*a*) The master teaches *Euclid*. (*Direct.*)
(*b*) He teaches *his sons* Euclid. (*Indirect.*)
(*c*) His sons were taught *Euclid*. (*Retained.*)
(*d*) The fever will run its *course*. (*Cognate.*)[1]
(*e*) He sat *himself* down. (*Reflexive.*)

(2) As Objective Complement to a verb (§ 95) :—

The citizens made him their *king*.

Note.—An Infinitive can come between the verb and the noun :—

The people considered him *to be* a wise man.

(3) In Apposition with a noun or pronoun :—

The people of England beheaded Charles I., their *king*.

(4) As Object to a preposition (§ 42) :—

He fought against *me*. A house built on *sand*.

(5) Adverbial Objective :—called "Adverbial," because such phrases qualify words as an adverb would do :—

---

[1] It is maintained in Mason's *English Grammar*, p. 150, ed. 1891, that "the cognate objective should more properly be classed among the Adverbial Adjuncts," that is, as an Adverbial objective, see § 178 (5). This we cannot admit, because when the verb of the sentence is changed from Active to Passive, as "He fought a good fight," "A good fight was fought by him," the cognate object becomes the Subject; whereas, if the cognate object were adverbial, it would remain adverbial.

He lived ten *years* (Time). He walked ten *miles* (Space). This cost ten *shillings* (Price). That box weighs ten *pounds* (Weight). The air is a *trifle* hotter to-day (Degree). Bind him *hand* and *foot* (Attendant circumstance).

(6) Objective after the adjectives "like" or "unlike," "near," "next." (This has arisen from the omission of the preposition "*to*," which is still sometimes used after these adjectives):—

No man could bend the bow *like him*.
The house *nearest the grove* is the one that I prefer.

(7) Objective after Interjections or in exclamatory phrases:—

Oh unhappy *man*! Oh dear *me*!
Foolish *fellow*! to have wasted his time as he has done!

179. Two uses of Adjectives.—See No. IV. of Parsing Chart.

(*a*) Attributive use (§ 58):—

An *industrious* student will generally succeed.

(*b*) Predicative use (§ 58):—

He was *industrious*, and therefore he succeeded.

180. Noun or Gerund used as an Adjective.—It can be used attributively for an adjective, but not predicatively:—

A *village* watchman. *Drinking* water. A *bathing* place.

181. Adjective substituted for Adverb.—An Adverb qualifying a *verb* can be changed into an adjective qualifying the *subject* to the verb. (More common in poetry than in prose.)

And *furious* every charger neighed.—CAMPBELL.
They neither toil nor spin, but *careless* grow.—THOMSON.
First they praised him *soft and low*.—TENNYSON.

Note 1.—When the adverb qualifies *any part of speech except a verb*, we cannot substitute an adjective for it. Thus we cannot say, "He is *immense* clever" for "He is *immensely* clever."

Note 2.—In poetry an adjective and adverb are sometimes coupled together by *and*.

Very *carefully* and *slow*.—TENNYSON.
Good gentlemen, look *fresh* and *merrily*.—SHAKESPEARE.

Here one *-ly* does duty for both adjectives; or the construction is mixed, the adj. qualifying the subject, and the adv. the verb.

182. Pronoun and Antecedent.—See Nos. II. and III. of Parsing Chart.

(*a*) A Pronoun is of the same person, number, and gender as the noun it stands for; but in case it depends upon the requirements of its own sentence. (This is called a Concord or Agreement.)

After Cæsar was declared *emperor* (Nom.), they slew *him* (Obj.).
You must return the *book* (Objective), *which* (Nominative) was lent.

(*b*) A Conjunctive Pronoun, if it has two Antecedents not of the same person, agrees in person with the Antecedent *nearest to it* :—

You are the man who *is* (not *are*) chosen.

183. Two uses of Adverbs.—See No. V. of Parsing Chart.

(*a*) Attributive use (§ 159).

(1) *Adjective.*—He is *remarkably clever.*
(2) *Verb.*—*Act decisively,* if you act at all.
(3) *Other Adverb.*—He explained his views *remarkably well.*
(4) *Preposition.*—The sun stood *exactly over* our heads.
(5) *Conjunction.*—You may go *only if* you promise to return.
(6) *Sentence.*—*Fortunately,* all the thieves were caught (§ 150).

(*b*) Predicative use (§ 159).

(1) *Intrans. verb.*—The results will soon be *out* (=published).
(2) *Trans. verb.*—We have found him *out* (=in his true character).

184. Verb and Subject.—See No. VI. of Parsing Chart.

A Finite Verb must be in the same number and person as its Subject (§ 109). (This is another Concord or Agreement.)

Note.—Avoid such a mistake as "The man with his dog *have* just come." Such a mistake arises from confounding "*with*" with "*and*."

185. Subjects not of the same Person.—(*a*) When two or more Subjects, not of the same Person, are joined by "*and*," the verb is in the First person rather than the Second, and in the Second rather than the Third; and *the First person should be mentioned last* :—

James and I *are* (=we are) great friends.

(*b*) When two Subjects are joined by "*or*" or "*nor*," the verb agrees in person with the Subject nearest to it :—

Either James or I *am* at the top of the class.
Either you or James *has* done it.
Neither James nor you *were* present.

It would be better, however, to repeat the verb for each Subject. The sentences would then be rewritten as follows :—

Either James *is* at the top of the class, or I *am*.
Either you *have* done it, or James *has*.
Neither James *was* present, nor *were* you.

(*c*) When two Subjects are joined by "as well as," the verb agrees in number and person with the *first* one :—

My comrades as well as I myself *were* caught.

The reason of this rule is that "My comrades were caught" is the Principal clause, to which the other clause introduced by "as well as" is Co-ordinate (see § 170, *a*).

186. Two Singular Subjects with Plural Verb.—Two or

more Singular nouns, when they are joined by "*and*," require a verb in the Plural.

> A man and his wife *have* come here asking for work.
> Your horse and mine (=my horse) *are* both at the door.

To this rule there are a few exceptions:—

(*a*) If the two nouns joined by "*and*" refer to the same person or thing, the verb is Singular, and not Plural; as:—

> The great scholar and poet *is* dead.

Here "scholar" and "poet" refer to the same man, and the sentence might have been written:—

> The man, who was a great scholar and a great poet, is dead.

Note.—When the article is mentioned *only once*, as in the sentence "*the* great scholar and poet," it stands for *both the nouns*. This shows that *only one* person (and not two) is intended, and that hence the verb must be singular.

But if the article is mentioned twice, as in the sentence "*the* scholar and *the* poet," then two distinct persons are intended, and the verb following must be in the plural number; as—

> The scholar and the poet *are* dead.

(*b*) If the two nouns joined by "*and*" are regarded as denoting *a single object or notion*, the verb is Singular; as—

> Truth and honesty (=the practice of truth and honesty) *is* the best policy. Slow and steady *wins* the race.

(*c*) If the two nouns joined by "*and*" are qualified by a Distributive adjective (§ 57), the verb is Singular; as—

> Every man and every woman *is* gone. (This is really a condensed form of two sentences:—"Every man (is gone) and every woman is gone.")

(*d*) If the two Singular nouns are connected by *as well as*, the verb is Singular:—

> James as well as John *has been* promoted. (This is really a condensed form of two sentences: "James has been promoted, as well as John has been promoted." See above, § 185, *c*.)

187. One Singular Subject with Plural Verb.—A noun of *Multitude* (see § 24, *Note* 2), since it implies plurality, is followed by a Plural verb:—

> The jury (*i.e.* the individual jurors) *were* divided in *their* opinions.
> The jury (as one body) selected *its* speaker.

188. Noun-Infinitive.—See No. VII. of Chart.

The Noun-Infinitive may be (*a*) the Subject to a verb, (*b*) the Object to a verb, (*c*) the Complement to a verb, (*d*) the Object to a preposition (although this is very uncommon), (*e*) a form of exclamation (see § 127, I.):—

(a) *Subj. to Verb.*—*To sleep* is necessary to health.
(b) *Obj. to Verb.*—We desire *to improve*.
(c) *Compl. to Verb.*—He appears *to be clever*.
(d) *Obj. to Prepos.*—Your cow is about (=near) *to die* (=death).
(e) *Form of Exclam.*—*To think* that he should have deceived me!

189. Qualifying Infinitive.—See No. VII. of Chart.

The Qualifying Infinitive may be used—(a) to qualify a verb, in which case it does the work of an adverb; (b) to qualify a noun, in which case it does the work of an adjective; (c) to qualify an adjective, in which case it does the work of an adverb; (d) to introduce a parenthesis, in which case it is absolute (see § 127, II.):—

(a) *Verb.*—They went out *to see* the sport.
(b) *Noun.* { A house *to let*. (*Attributive.*) / This house is *to let*. (*Predicative.*) }
(c) *Adjective.*—Be quick *to hear* and slow *to speak*.
(d) *Parenthesis.*—He is,—*to speak* plainly,—a thief.

Note.—In qualifying a *noun*, the Infinitive is sometimes used in the Passive voice. No rule, however, can be given as to when the Active voice is the more idiomatic and when the Passive:—

A man *to be admired*. (*Attributive.*)
That man is *to be admired*. (*Predicative.*)

190. Three uses of Participles.—See No. IX. of Chart.

(a) Attributive use (see § 58 for Adjectives):—

A *willing* horse. A *fallen* tree. A *withered* flower.

(b) Predicative use.—This may occur either (1) when the Participle is Complement to some verb (see § 58 again), or (2) when the Participle is used absolutely with some noun going before (see § 176, 5).

(1) { We found him *sleeping*. (*Object. Complem.*) / He became *alarmed*. (*Subject. Complem.*) }
(2) Our pace was slow, the horse *being tired*. (*Absolute.*)

Note 1.—That the Participle is predicative in the Absolute construction is clear from the fact that an absolute *phrase* can be easily rewritten in the form of a *clause*, in which a Finite verb is substituted for the Participle:—

{ Our pace was slow, the horse *being tired*.
{ Our pace was slow, *because* the horse *was tired*.

Note 2.—When no noun or pronoun is expressed, the Participle is called an **Impersonal Absolute.**

Supposing this to be true, you are certainly guilty.

(c) Gerundive use (§ 141).—Here the Participle denotes

something that could be as well or better expressed by a Gerund or Verbal noun :—

{ This prevented the letter *being sent* ;=
{ This prevented *the sending of* the letter.

Note.—If we insert the preposition "*from*," "This prevented the letter *from* being sent," the form *being sent* is not a participle at all, but a Gerund or Verbal noun in the Passive voice. On this form see § 135.

191. Sequence of Tenses.—There are two main rules :—

I. A Past tense in the Principal clause must be followed by a Past tense in the Dependent clause :—

Principal.	*Dependent.*
He *would* come, ...	if you *sent for* him.
He *succeeded*, ...	because he *worked* hard.
He *worked* hard	that he *might* succeed.

II. A Present or Future tense in the Principal clause can be followed by any tense whatever in the Dependent clause :—

Principal.	*Dependent.*
I *am* quite aware . .	that he *was* angry. (*Past.*)
I *shall* soon know . .	why he *is* angry. (*Present.*)
He *has* told me . .	that he *will* soon return. (*Future.*)

Exceptions to Rule I.—There are three exceptions :—

(1) If the Dependent clause expresses some *universal* or *habitual* fact, its verb remains in the Present tense, and is not changed from Present to Past :—

Principal.	*Dependent.*
They *were* taught . .	that the earth *is* shaped like an orange.
He *was* glad to hear .	that I *take* regular exercise twice a day.

(2) If the Dependent clause is introduced by "than" or by "as much as," its verb can be in the Present or Future tense,—in fact, in any tense that suits the sense :—

Principal.	*Dependent.*
He *liked* you more . . .	than he *likes* or *will like* me.
He *liked* you as much . . .	as he *likes* or *will like* me.

(3) If the Dependent clause is an Adjective-clause, its verb may be in any tense that suits the sense. In fact, the above rule has no connection whatever with Adjective clauses, but applies only to Noun-clauses and to Adverb-clauses :—

Principal.	*Dependent.*
He *did* not see the event .	that he *has* described so well in the pamphlet which I *was* reading yesterday, and which I *shall* read again to-morrow.

CHAPTER XIII.—ANALYSIS IN DETAIL.

SECTION 1.—SENTENCES SIMPLE, COMPOUND, AND COMPLEX.

192. Simple Sentence.—A Simple sentence (Lat. *simplex*, single-fold) is one that has *only one Finite verb* expressed or understood.

Subject.	*Predicate.*
The merchant, having much property to sell,	*caused* all his goods to be conveyed on camels, there being no railway in that country.

In this sentence there are five different verbs, "having," "to sell," "caused," "to be conveyed," "being." Of these only one, viz. "caused," is *finite.* The sentence is therefore Simple.

193. Compound Sentence.—A compound sentence is one that is made up of two or more *Co-ordinate* clauses.

Co-ordinate clauses are joined together by the Co-ordinative conjunctions (§ 167).

(1) The sun rose with power, *and* the fog dispersed . (*Cumulative.*)
(2) He called at my house, *but* I was not at home . (*Adversative.*)
(3) *Either* he must go *or* I (must go) . . . . (*Alternative.*)
(4) He came back tired ; *for* he had been out all day . (*Illative.*)

In (1) one clause is simply added to another. In (2) one clause is contrasted with another. In (3) one clause is offered as an alternative to another. In (4) one clause is inferred from another.

Note.—When sentences are connected, not by any Co-ordinative conjunction, but merely by co-ordination of sense or by unity of construction, they are said to be **collateral** :—

The way was long ; the wind was cold ;
The minstrel was infirm and old ;
The harp, his sole remaining joy,
Was carried by an orphan boy.—SCOTT.

194. The Conjunctive pronoun *who* or *which*, or a Conjunctive adverb, such as *where*, *when*, etc., provided its sense is continuative, and not restrictive (§ 83), may be used to connect Co-ordinate clauses :—

He went to London, *where* (=and there) he stayed ten days.

195. Complex Sentence.—A Complex sentence consists of a Principal clause (*i.e.* the clause containing the main *Finite verb* of the sentence) with one or more Subordinate clauses.

Complex { A merchant, who *had* much property to sell, *caused* all his goods to be conveyed on camels, as there *was* no railway in that country.

Simple { A merchant, having much property to sell, *caused* all his goods to be conveyed on camels, there being no railway in that country.

The latter sentence is evidently Simple, since there is only one Finite verb, *caused*. The former cannot be Simple, since it has three Finite verbs, *have*, *caused*, *was* (all italicised). It cannot be Compound, because the clauses are not co-ordinate. It is therefore Complex, consisting of one Principal clause and two Subordinate ones.

195[A]. **Compound and Complex mixed.**—A Compound sentence can now be more fully defined than it was in § 193:—

"A Compound sentence is one that is made up of two or more Co-ordinate *parts*."

Here the wider word *parts* has been substituted for the narrower word *clauses* given in § 193.

He seized the hill | and | occupied the strongest position that he found there.

This sentence is Compound, the first part being connected co-ordinately by *and* with the second part. The first part is a Simple sentence; but the second part is Complex, consisting of a main clause, "he occupied the strongest position," and a Subordinate clause, "that he found there." (For a much longer example see below, § 210.)

196. There are three kinds of Subordinate clauses—the Noun-clause, the Adjective-clause, and the Adverb-clause:—

I. *A Noun-clause is one which does the work of a noun in relation to some* **word** *in some other clause.*

II. *An Adjective-clause is one which does the work of an adjective in relation to some* **word** *in some other clause.*

III. *An Adverb-clause is one which does the work of an adverb in relation to some* **word** *in some other clause.*[1]

Note.—The same clause may be a Noun-clause in one context, an Adjective-clause in another, an Adverb-clause in another.

Where Moses was buried is still unknown.
—Noun-clause, subject to the verb "is."

No one has seen the place *where Moses was buried.*
—Adj.-clause, qualifying the noun "place."

Without knowing it the Arabs encamped *where Moses was buried.*
—Adverb-clause qualifying the verb "encamped."

---

[1] In these three definitions **word** has been printed in black type, because, in stating the kind of clause, it is necessary to state the word to which it relates. Mason's three definitions (*Eng. Grammar*, p. 160) merely say "in relation to *the rest of the sentence*." This is rather too vague for purposes of guidance.

I. *The Noun-clause.*

197. A Noun-clause is subject to all the liabilities and duties of a noun proper. It may therefore be the subject to a verb, the object to a verb, the object to a preposition, the complement to a verb, or in apposition to a noun :—

That he will come back soon is certain . . .	*Subject.*
I shall be glad to know *when you will return* .	*Obj. to verb.*
This will sell for *what it is worth*	*Obj. to prep.*
This is exactly *what I expected*	*Comp. to verb.*
The rumour *that he is sick* is false	*App. to noun.*

Note 1.—From the above examples it will be seen that a Noun-clause can be introduced either by the conjunction "*that*" or by a Conjunctive pronoun or by a Conjunctive adverb. Sometimes, however, the conjunction *that* is left out :—

It seems (that) he is not clever.

Note 2.—A clause containing the very words used by a speaker is another form of Noun-clause :—

All that he said was, "*I have seen you before.*"

Here the italicised clause is the complement to the verb "was."

Examples of the Noun-clause.

I. *Pick out the Noun-clause in each of the following examples and say whether it is the Subject to some Verb, or the Object to some Verb, or the Object to some Preposition, or the Complement to some Verb, or in Apposition to some noun expressed. Supply the Conjunction* "that" *wherever it has been left out* :—

1. No one knows when he will come, or whether he will come at all, or whether he is even alive.
2. How this came to pass is not known to any one.
3. What is sauce for the goose is sauce for the gander.
4. It is quite evident rain will fall to-day.
5. The Equator shows where days and nights are of equal length.
6. What is one man's meat is another man's poison.
7. You must know that the air is never quite at rest
8. I think I shall never clearly understand this.
9. We heard the school would open in ten days' time.
10. The name "Volcano" indicates the belief of the ancient Greeks, that the burning hills of the Mediterranean were the workshops of the divine blacksmith, Vulcan.
11. Even a feather shows which way the wind is blowing.
12. Whatever faculty man has is improved by use.
13. The fool hath said in his heart, "There is no God."
14. "Know thyself," was the advice given us by a Greek sage.
15. He did not know that his father had been shot.
16. The fact that you have not signed your name to a letter shows that you lack moral courage.
17. It will be easily understood how useful even the simplest weapons were to the first dwellers on the earth.

18. The question first occurring to the mind of a savage is how is fire to be made.

19. Common-sense soon taught him that fire could be produced by rubbing two sticks together.

20. In chipping their flint weapons men must have seen that fire occasionally flashed out.

21. We learn from travellers that savages can produce fire in a few seconds.

22. He shouted out to the thief, "Leave this house."

23. We cannot rely on what he says.

24. It is quite evident you have made a mistake.

25. It was very unfortunate that you were taken ill.

26. He was a man of fine character except that he was rather timid.

II. *Expand each Simple Sentence into a Complex one containing a* **Noun-clause** *or* **clauses** :—

1. I was glad to hear of your having succeeded so well.
2. He is generally believed to have died of poison.
3. No one can tell the time of his coming.
4. One man's meat is another man's poison.
5. We have read of savages being able to produce fire by the friction of two pieces of wood.
6. He shouted to his neighbours to come to his help.
7. We can place no confidence in any of his words.
8. The fact of his having gone away without leaving us his address is a clear proof of the dishonesty of his intentions.
9. The usefulness of even the simplest weapons to men in the savage state will easily be understood.
10. His death at so young an age is much to be regretted.
11. We must hope for better times.
12. Tell me the time and place of your birth.
13. The verdict of the judge was in favour of the accused.
14. All his statements should be accepted.
15. They questioned the propriety of doing that.
16. The greatness of his labour could be seen from the result.
17. My departure will depend upon my getting leave.
18. He desired to know the nature of his offence.
19. The burial-place of Moses was never known to the Jews.
20. They explained to him the duty of confessing his fault.
21. He was reported to have lost most of his money.
22. We know the name of the writer of that letter.

II. *Adjective-clause.*

198. An Adjective-clause has but one function, viz. to qualify some noun or pronoun belonging to some other clause. In doing this it simply does the work of an adjective proper. Remember that the Conjunctive pronoun or Conjunctive adverb, by which an Adjective-clause is introduced, must have a Restrictive, not a Continuative, sense (§ 83); for if the sense is

Continuative, and not Restrictive, the sentence is Compound, not Complex (§ 194).

(1) We found it in the place *where* we had left it . *Complex.*
(2) We went to Brighton, *where* we spent a week . *Compound.*

In (1) the sentence is Complex, because the clause "where we had left it" qualifies the noun "place' as an adjective would do. *Where* is here Restrictive. In (2) the sentence is Compound, because the clause "where we spent a week" is merely Continuative,—co-ordinate with the preceding clause :—"We went to Brighton, *and* spent a week *there.*"

Note.—The Conjunctive pronoun (when used in a Restrictive sense) is sometimes left out. (It is never left out when the sense is Continuative) :—

The food (that or which) he needed was sent.

I. *Pick out the Adjective-clause or clauses in each of the following examples, and point out the noun or pronoun qualified by it in some other clause. If the Conjunctive pronoun has been omitted anywhere, supply it :—*

1. Man has the power of making instruments, which bring into view stars, whose light has taken a thousand years to reach the earth.
2. The first thing that man needed was some sharp-edged tool.
3. The exact time when the theft was committed was never found out.
4. The man by whom the theft was committed has been caught.
5. The house we lived in has fallen down.
6. This is the same story that I heard ten years ago.
7. It's an ill wind that blows no one any good.
8. This is not such a book as I should have chosen.
9. He made his living by the presents he received from the men he served.
10. All that glitters is not gold.
11. In ponds, from which but a week before the wind blew clouds of dust, men now catch the re-animated fish.
12. A river is joined at places by tributaries that swell its waters.
13. Of what use is a knowledge of books to him who fails to practise virtue?
14. Fortune selects for her lord a man, who reflects before acting.
15. Springs are fed by rain, which has percolated through the rocks or soil.
16. Nuncoomar prepared to die with that quiet fortitude with which the Bengalee, so backward as a rule in personal conflict, often encounters calamities for which there is no remedy.
17. I have seen the house where Shakspeare was born.
18. The plan you acted on has answered well.
19. They accepted every plan we proposed.
20. Surely the story you are telling me is not true.
21. Thrice is he armed that hath his quarrel just.
22. The night is long that never finds the day.

23. He travelled home by the way his father showed him.
24. There are times when every one feels a little sad.
25. Such men as are false to their friends should always be avoided.
26. I forgot to tell you the time when I shall return.

II. *Expand each Simple sentence into a Complex one containing an* **Adjective-clause** :—

1. Our present house suits us exactly.
2. This rule, the source of all our troubles, is disliked by every one.
3. That was a fault not to be forgiven.
4. The diamond field is not far from here.
5. He and his friend entered into a partnership binding themselves to incur equal risks.
6. Their explanation cannot be true.
7. The king took refuge in the fortress, being determined to make a last attempt in that place to save his kingdom.
8. The snow-line in India is about 20,000 feet high.
9. The troubles besetting him on all sides did not daunt him.
10. They soon forgot their past labours.
11. This spot, the first landing-place of the Pilgrim Fathers, is held to be sacred ground.
12. My leave-application has been dispatched.
13. Is this the way to learn your lessons?
14. A certain cholera-cure has not yet been found.
15. Egypt was one of the first countries to become civilised.
16. Death from snake-bite is of daily occurrence.
17. The benefits of his early training were thrown away.
18. That was the act of a coward.
19. Milton was the greatest poet in King Charles's reign.
20. These hills have never yet been trodden by the foot of man.

III. *The Adverb-clause.*

199. An Adverb-clause does the work of an adverb to some verb, adjective, or adverb belonging to some other clause.

An Adverb-clause can be introduced by any of the *Subordinative* conjunctions, or by the Conjunctive adverbs—*where*, *when*, *whether*, etc. —

Principal Clause.	*Adverb-Clause.*	*Subord. Conjunc.*
He will succeed,	*because* he works hard .	*Cause.*
He worked *so* hard,	*that* he was quite tired .	*Effect.*
He took medicine	*that* he might get well .	*Purpose.*
I will do this,	*if* I am allowed . . .	*Condition.*
He is honest,	*although* he is poor . .	*Contrast.*
He likes you *more*	*than* (he likes) me . .	*Comparison.*
Men will reap	*as* they sow . . .	*Extent or Manner.*
The tooth stopped aching	*when* the dentist came in .	*Time.*

200. After the conjunctions *though*, *when*, *unless*, *till*, *if*, *whether . . . or*, and *while*, the Predicate-verb "**to be**" and its Subject are often omitted. These must be supplied in the Analysis.

Though (*he was*) much alarmed, he did not lose all hope.
He sprained his foot, while (*he was*) walking in the dark.
His opinion, whether (*it is*) right or wrong, does not concern me.

201. When an Adverb-clause is introduced by "**than,**" its Finite Verb is not always expressed. It must then be borrowed *in the same tense* from the clause to which it is subordinate :—

He loves you better than (he loves) me.
He loves you better than I (love you).

202. The Conjunctive pronoun "**who**" or "**which**" makes an Adverb-clause, whenever it is substituted for a Subordinative conjunction signifying Cause or Purpose :—

Cause.—They should pardon my son, *who* (=*because he*) has never committed such a fault before.

Purpose.—A man was sent, *who* should deliver (=*that he* might deliver) the message.

Note.—The student can now therefore take note that four different kinds of clauses can be introduced by the pronoun "who" or "which" :—(1) A *Co-ordinate* clause, where the pronoun is used in a **Continuative** sense. This belongs to Compound sentences. (2) A *Noun*-clause, where no Antecedent to the pronoun is expressed. This belongs to Complex sentences. (3) An *Adjective*-clause, where the pronoun is used in a **Restrictive** sense. This belongs to Complex sentences. (4) An *Adverb*-clause, where the pronoun is used in the sense of **Cause** or **Purpose.** This also belongs to Complex sentences.

I. *Pick out the Adverb-clause or clauses in the following. Show what word or phrase is qualified by every such clause, and what Adverbial relation is denoted thereby* :—

1. He will succeed, because he has worked hard.
2. Men engage in some work, that they may earn a living.
3. He threatened to beat him, unless he confessed.
4. He was always honest, although he was poor.
5. This is not true, so far as I can tell.
6. He likes you as much as I do.
7. He tried for a long time before he succeeded.
8. Let us go to bed, as it is now late.
9. He walked with care, lest he should stumble.
10. I agree to this, provided you sign your name.
11. Though he punish me, yet will I trust in him.
12. He returned home, after he had finished the work.
13. Prove a friend, before you trust him.
14. When the cat's away, the mice will play.
15. He persevered so steadily, that he succeeded at last.
16. I will let off this man, who has been well punished already.
17. He sees very well, considering that he is sixty years of age.

18. I gave him a prize, that he might work harder next year.

19. They deserted their former associate, who had become poor and unfortunate.

20. As the tree falls, so will it lie.

21. Ever since we left the house, it has not ceased raining.

22. I should be glad to lend you that money, if I had as much in my own pocket.

23. Murder, though it have no tongue, will yet speak.

24. Unless you leave the house at once, I will send for a policeman.

25. A jackal, while prowling about the suburbs of a town, slipped into an indigo tank; and not being able to get out he laid himself down, so that he might be taken for dead.

26. Ambassadors were sent from Sparta, who should sue for peace.

II. *Expand each Simple sentence into a Complex one containing an* **Adverb-clause** *or* **clauses** :—

1. In the absence of any other helper, we must accept his aid.
2. The two chief points having been gained, success is now certain.
3. Owing to repeated failures, he made no further attempt.
4. The problem was too difficult to be solved.
5. He worked very well, to the astonishment of every one.
6. He fell under suspicion by becoming suddenly rich.
7. He worked hard for the purpose of gaining a prize.
8. Every precaution was taken against the failure of the plan.
9. He purposes to become rich by sticking steadily to his work.
10. Without leave from the master, we should not go out.
11. He would be very thankful to be relieved of all this trouble.
12. With or without his leave, I shall leave the room.
13. He would have been caught, but for his flight across the border.
14. Notwithstanding the heat of the sun we must go out.
15. In spite of all his riches, he is never contented.
16. For all his experience he is still incompetent.
17. The depth of the sea equals the height of the mountains.
18. With every man who came in, another went out.
19. Of all the boys in the class James is the most industrious.
20. Keep perfectly silent at peril of your lives.
21. Be it done unto thee according to thy belief.
22. The harvest will depend upon the sowing.
23. Nothing in my opinion will prosper under such a man.
24. He returned to duty immediately on the expiry of his leave.
25. With every cough he felt a good deal of pain.
26. In the performance of duty, no one should feel afraid.

Section 2.—Scheme of Analysis in Detail.

203. Scheme of Analysis.—The scheme of Analysis, given already in § 8, is here recapitulated to save reference :—

A man convinced against his will is of the same opinion still.

He made himself mean and of no reputation.

The second master of the school has been teaching my sons Euclid since Thursday last.

Whom the gods love die young.

I. Subject.		II. Predicate.			
			Completion of Finite verb.		
Nominative or Equivalent. 1	Enlargement of Nominative. 2	Finite verb. 3	Object. (1) Direct. (2) Indirect. 4	Complement. 5	Extension of Finite verb. 6
man	(1) A (2) convinced against his will	is	...	of the same opinion	still.
He	...	made	himself	mean and of no reputation.	
master	(1) The (2) second (3) of the school	has been teaching	(1) *Direct* Euclid (2) *Indirect* my sons	...	since Thursday last.
Whom the gods love	...	die	...	...	young.

204. Nominative or its equivalent : see heading to col. 1. This is the chief part of the Subject, and when there is no enlargement, it is the only part. It is this that fixes the number and person of the Finite verb. Its most typical form is that of a noun or pronoun in the Nominative case. The following is a list of the various forms in which a Nominative or its equivalent can be expressed :[1]—

(1) **Noun.**—A *ship* went out to sea yesterday.
(2) **Adj. used as Noun.**—The *brave* are always respected.
(3) **Pronoun.**—*He* (some one previously named) has gone.
(4) **Noun-Infinitive.**—*To walk* regularly is good for health.
(5) **Gerund or Verbal noun.**—*Reading* is good for the mind.
(6) **Noun-phrase.**—*How to do this* is a difficult question.
(7) **Noun-clause.**—*Whom the gods love* die young.

Note.—Sometimes a sentence begins with "it," and the Nominative or its equivalent is mentioned after the verb : "*It* is easy to do this." Here the "it" is redundant, and may be left out in the analysis :—"To do this is easy."

[1] There is no need to commit this list of forms to memory. They are enumerated merely to show what the student may expect to find. The same remark applies to the lists in §§ 205-209.

205. Enlargement: see heading to col. 2. The most typical form is an Adjective. We call this "*enlargement*," because an adjective, according to the definition given in § 12, "is a word that *enlarges* the meaning of a noun and narrows its application."

The following is a list of the various forms in which an "enlargement" can be expressed :—

(1) **Adjective.**—*Just* men deserve to prosper.
(2) **Participle.**—A *fertilising* shower fell to-day.
(3) **Qualifying Infin.**—Water *to drink* is scarce in this place.
(4) **Possessive noun or pronoun.**—*Your* teacher has come.
(5) **Noun used as Adj.**—The *village* school opens at eight A.M.
(6) **Gerund used as Adj.**—*Drinking* water is scarce here.
(7) **Prep. with object.**[1]—A man *of virtue* does not tell lies.
(8) **Adverb with Def. article.**—*The then* king died suddenly.
(9) **Noun in Apposition.**—Charles, my *son*, has come.
(10) **Noun-clause in Appos.**—The rumour *that he was dead* is false.
(11) **Adjective-clause.**—The house *in which we live* has been sold.

206. Finite verb : see heading to col. 3. This is the chief part of the predicate, and, when the verb is Intransitive and of Complete predication (§ 6), it can be the only part ; as, "Hogs *grunt.*"

If the tense or mood of the Finite verb is formed, not by inflexion, but by the help of one of the six Auxiliary verbs (§ 102), remember that the Auxiliary verb and the Principal verb together make up the Finite verb, and must be mentioned together in column 3.

Subject.	Finite verb.	Object.
I	have been examining	the pictures.

But if the previous verb is not Auxiliary, as "*will*," for instance, when it occurs in the *first* person of the Future tense (§ 115), in such a sentence *will* alone makes the Finite verb, and the Noun-Infinitive that follows is its Object :—

Subject.	Finite verb.	Object.
I	will	see him to-morrow.

[1] In such a phrase as "a brute of a man," the "*of*" denotes apposition, "a man a brute," *i.e.* a brutish man, a man who is a brute. In such a phrase, therefore, the sense is analogous to (9), and not to (7).

207. Object, direct or indirect: see col. 4. The different forms in which a *Direct* object can be expressed are the same as those in which the Nominative can be expressed (§ 204):—

(1) **Noun.**—The snake bit the *man.*
(2) **Adj. used as Noun.**—He satisfied the *public.*
(3) **Pronoun.**—My friend will not deceive *me.*
(4) **Noun-Infinitive.**—He deserves *to succeed.*
(5) **Gerund or Verbal noun.**—He likes *riding.*
(6) **Noun-phrase.**—We did not know *how to do it.*
(7) **Noun-clause.**—We do not know *who he is.*

There are only two forms in which an *Indirect* object can be expressed, viz. a noun denoting some person or other animal, or some personal pronoun:—

He gave *James* a book . . . . (*Trans. verb.*)
He overslept *himself* . . . . (*Intrans. verb.*)

208. Complement: see heading to col. 5. The following are the various forms in which a Complement can be expressed (§§ 92, 95):—

(1) **Noun**	The citizens made him their *king*	(*Fact.*)
	That beggar turned out a *thief*	(*Cop.*)
(2) **Possessive**	She made A.'s quarrel *her own*	(*Fact.*)
	This book is *mine*, not *James's*	(*Cop.*)
(3) **Adjective**	The judge set the prisoner *free*	(*Fact.*)
	The prisoner is now *free*	(*Cop.*)
(4) **Participle**	They found her *weeping*	(*Fact.*)
	He seemed much *pleased*	(*Cop.*)
(5) **Prep. with object**	I prefer a dog *to a cat*	(*Fact.*)
	He is *in a sad plight*	(*Cop.*)
(6) **Qualifying Infinitive**	I like a thief *to be punished*	(*Fact.*)
	This house is *to let*	(*Cop.*)
(7) **Adverb**	That noise sent him *asleep*	(*Fact.*)
	The man has fallen *asleep*	(*Cop.*)
(8) **Noun-clause**	We have made him *what he is*	(*Fact.*)
	The result is *what we expected*	(*Cop.*)

209. Extension: see heading to col. 6. The most typical form is an Adverb. We call this "*extension*," because an adverb, according to the definition given in § 16, "is a word that *extends* the meaning and narrows the application of any part of speech except a noun or pronoun."

Two points should be noticed: (1) In the analysis of sentences (not in parsing, which is a different kind of operation), extension applies *only to the Finite verb* of its own clause: if an adverb or adverb-equivalent belongs to any part of a sentence except the Finite verb, it must not be placed in column 6. (2) "Extension" means the same thing as "enlargement." But as one relates to the Finite verb, and the other to the Nominative or its equivalent, it is convenient in analysing sentences to give them separate names.

The following are the various forms in which "extension" can be expressed :—

(1) **Adverb.**—He slept *soundly.*
(2) **Prep. with object.**—He slept *for six hours.*
(3) **Adjective.**—He went away *sad.*
(4) **Participle.**—He went away *disappointed.*
(5) **Qualifying Infin.**—He came *to see* the horse.
(6) **Adverbial objective.**—Bind him *hand and foot.*
(7) **Absolute phrase.**—We all set off, *he remaining behind.*
(8) **Adverb-clause.**—We all set off, *while he remained behind.*

Note.—The student must not be surprised that in (3) an *adjective* is included among forms of extension, the typical form of which is an *adverb.* Analysis is not the same thing as parsing: there are three differences at least. (1) In analysis the unit to be dealt with is a sentence; in parsing a single word. (2) Analysis deals with grammar on its logical side; parsing on its syntactical. The word "sad," though it is an adjective in form and in syntax, is adverbial in function. In what manner or in what state of mind did he go away? In a sad state. The word "sad" therefore qualifies the verb "went away" in just the same way as if it were expressed in the form "sadly." The same remark applies to the participle "disappointed" in the fourth sentence. (3) There are some words which can be parsed, but do not come within the framework of analysis at all; such as an interjection, an exclamatory phrase, a nominative of address.

SECTION 3.—DEGREES OF SUBORDINATION.

210. Degrees of Subordination.—The following sentence may be taken as an example for analysis :—

One man in the audience, who was chief magistrate of the town and happened to be present, on seeing that the lion fawned on Androcles, when it was expected to tear him to pieces, called out with a loud voice, and ordered Androcles to explain how a savage beast could have so forgotten its innate disposition all of a sudden, that it became converted into a harmless animal, which chose to spare its intended victim rather than devour him.

Now, when we come to divide this sentence into its component clauses, we find, firstly, that it is a Compound sentence, consisting of two co-ordinate *parts* (§ 195[A]) connected by "*and*," and secondly, that each of these co-ordinate parts contains subordinate *clauses*, the former containing three, and the latter four.

The two co-ordinate parts, which are connected by "*and*" and make the sentence a Compound one, are marked A and B.

(A) One man in the audience, (*a*) who was chief magistrate of the town (*b*) and happened to be present, on seeing (*x*) that the lion fawned on Androcles, (*y*) when it was expected to tear him to pieces, called out with a loud voice, (B) and ordered Androcles to explain (*a*) how a savage beast could have so forgotten its innate disposition all of a sudden, (*b*) that it became converted into a harmless animal, (*c*) which chose to spare its intended victim rather (*d*) than to devour him.

In (A) we see that clause (*a*) is an adjective-clause in the first degree, qualifying the noun "man"; clause (*b*) is co-ordinate to clause (*a*), and therefore a second adjective-clause to the noun "man"; clause (*x*) is a noun-clause in the first degree, object to the verb "seeing"; clause (*y*) is an adverb-clause in the second degree, qualifying the verb "fawned."

In (B) we see that clause (*a*) is a noun-clause in the first degree, object to the verb "explain"; clause (*b*) is an adverb-clause in the second degree, qualifying the verb "forgotten"; clause (*c*) is an adjective-clause in the third degree, qualifying the noun "animal"; and clause (*d*) is an adverb-clause in the fourth degree, qualifying the verb "chose."

The degree of subordination (as first, second, third, fourth, etc.), is shown by the number of lines drawn under the clause concerned.

211. Tabular form of Analysis.—Before beginning to analyse a sentence of many clauses in tabular form, it will be best to write it out with the clauses marked off in the manner shown in § 210. This will serve as a key to the tabulation, of which a complete example is given on page 106.

Words that are understood must be supplied: they can be shown in brackets in their proper column.

Words which do not come within the framework of analysis must be left out; as, for instance, an interjection, an exclamatory phrase, a noun used for purposes of address; see *Note* to § 209.

> This heavy rain, *alas!* has spoilt the harvest this year.
> The farmers, *poor fellows!* have lost heavily.
> *Friends, Romans, countrymen,* lend me your ears.

A parenthetical sentence cannot be considered a *clause* of the sentence into which it has been wedged.

> Mr. R. (so at least his friends say) will soon retire.

Here there are two distinct sentences to be analysed:—

> (1) Mr. R. will soon retire.
> (2) So at least his friends say.

Clause.	Kind of Clause.	Connective.	I. Subject.		II. Predicate.			
			Nominative or Equivalent. 1	Enlargement of Nominative. 2	Finite Verb. 3	Completion of Finite Verb. Object. (1) *Direct.* (2) *Indirect.* 4	Completion of Finite Verb. Complement. 5	Extension of Finite Verb. 6
A. One man in the audience called out with a loud voice, on seeing that etc.	Principal.	..	man	(1) One (2) in the audience	called out	..	..	(1) with a loud voice, (2) on seeing that etc.
(*a*) who was chief magistrate of the town	Adj.-clause to "man" in A.	who	who	..	was	..	chief magistrate of the town	..
(*b*) and happened to be present,	Co-ord. to (*a*).	and	(who)	..	happened	..	to be present,	..
(*x*) that the lion fawned on Androcles	Noun clause, object to "seeing."	that	lion	the	fawned on	Androcles,	..	..
(*y*) when it was expected to tear him to pieces,	Adv. clause, qualifying "fawned."	when	it	..	was expected	..	to tear him to pieces,	..
B. and ordered Androcles to explain	Principal, co-ord. to A.	and	(man)	..	ordered	Androcles	to explain etc.	..
(*a*) how a savage beast could have so forgotten its innate disposition all of a sudden,	Noun-clause object to "explain."	how	beast	(1) a (2) savage	could	have so forgotten its innate disposition all of a sudden,	..	..
(*b*) that it became converted into a harmless animal,	Adv.-clause to "have forgotten."	that	it	..	became	..	converted into a harmless animal,	..
(*c*) which chose to spare its intended victim	Adj.-clause to "animal."	which	which	..	chose	to spare its intended victim	..	rather than etc.
(*d*) rather than to devour him.	Adj.-clause to "chose."	than	(it)	..	(chose)	to devour him.		

I.—*Examples in Parsing and Analysis.*

For parsing a word the student can follow the Parsing Chart given at the opening of Chap. XII. The method there shown is as follows :—

I. **Noun.**—What kind (Proper, Common, Collective, Material, or Abstract)? What gender (Masc., Fem., or Neut.)? What number (Sing. or Plur.)? What case (Nom., Poss., or Obj.)? Why in such a case (see all possible reasons in Parsing Chart No. III.)?

II. **Pronoun.**—What kind (Pers., Dem., Conj., or Interr.)? What gender (depends on antecedent)? What number (depends on anteced.)? What person (depends on anteced.)? What case (depends on the requirements of its own clause, see Parsing Chart No. III.).

IV. **Adjective.**—What kind (Proper, Descriptive, Quantit., Interr., Distrib., Numeral, or Demons.)? What degree of Comparison (Pos., Comp., or Superl.)? Which use (Attributive or Predicative)? What noun or pronoun does it qualify?

V. **Adverb.**—What kind (Simple, Conj., or Interr.)? What degree (Pos., Comp., or Superl.)? Which use (Attrib. or Predic.)? If Attrib., to qualify what word or words (Verb, Adj., Adv., Prep., Conj., or Sentence)? If Predic., complement to what verb?

VI. **Finite Verb.**—What kind (Transitive or Intransitive)? What Conjug. (Strong, Weak, or Mixed)? What voice? What mood? What tense? Agreeing with what subject? and therefore in what number (Singular or Plural)? and in what person (first, second, or third)?

VII. **Infinitive.**—What form (Indefinite, Continuous, Perfect, or Perf. Contin.)? Which Infin. (Noun-Infin. or Qualif. Infin.)? If Noun-Infin., in what connection? If Qual. Infin., in what connection?

VIII. **Gerund.**—What form (Pres. or Perf.)? What voice? What kind of verb? If Trans., governing what object?

IX. **Participle.**—What form (Pres., Past, or Perf.)? What voice? What kind of verb? If Trans., governing what object? What use (Attributive, Predicative, Absolute, or Gerundive)?

X. **Conjunction.**—What kind (Co-ordinative or Subordinative)? Joining what words or phrases, or what sentences?

Analyse the following sentences, and parse (with any explanation that may be necessary) the words printed in italics :—

1. By torch and trumpet *fast* arrayed,
   Each horseman *drew* his *battle* blade,
   And *furious* every charger neighed,
     To join the dreadful revelry.—CAMPBELL.
2. Let *me hear what* you have *to say*.
3. *Week in, week out,* from morn till night,
   You *may hear* his *bellows blow*.—LONGFELLOW.
4. On Linden, when the sun was *low*,
   All bloodless lay the untrodden snow,
   And dark as winter was the flow
     Of Iser rolling rapidly.—CAMPBELL.

5. Perdition *catch* my soul, *but* I love thee.—SHAKESPEARE.

6. I cannot *but believe* that you are lost.

7. These men, *than* whom I have never known men more unwilling, have suddenly left me, *merely* because I asked them *to work* a *little* overtime on account of the orders *that* I unexpectedly received this *morning* from headquarters.

8. Toll for the *brave*!
Bravè Kempenfelt is gone;
His *last* sea-fight *is fought*,
His work of glory *done*.—COWPER.

9. Cowards die many *times* before their death;
The *valiant only* taste of death *but* once.—SHAKESPEARE.

10. I now gave *over* any more thoughts of the ship, or of *getting* anything out of her, *except* what might *drive a*-shore from the wreck, *as* indeed divers pieces of her afterwards *did*; but those things were of small use to me.—*Robinson Crusoe*.

11. I like a rascal *to be punished*,[1] when I am quite sure that his guilt *has been proved* to the satisfaction of a *jury who* had no prejudice against him, before they began *hearing* his case.

12. The reason *why* the seven stars are *no more than* seven is a pretty reason.—SHAKESPEARE.

13. *Just* so we have heard a baby, mounted on the shoulders of its father, *cry out*, "How *much* taller I am *than* papa!"—MACAULAY.

14. *There* is no despair so absolute as *that* which comes with the *first* moments of our first great sorrow, when we havè not yet known *what* it is *to have suffered* and be healed, to have despaired and to have recovered hope.—G. ELIOT.

15. Music, when soft voices die,
Vibrates in the memory;
Odours, when sweet violets sicken,
Live within the sense they *quicken*.—SHELLEY.

16. Woe *worth* the chase, woe worth the day,
That cost thy *life*, my gallant *grey*!—SCOTT.

17. What must the king *do* now? Must he *submit*?
The king shall *do* it.—SHAKESPEARE.

18. At four o'clock P.M. we reached York, *which* is a fine old town dating back to the time of the Romans, though they called it by a different name, *that* I cannot now remember.

19. For *what* are men better than sheep and goats
That nourish a blind life within the brain,
If, knowing God, they lift not hands of prayer
Both for *themselves* and those who call them friend?—TENNYSON.

---

[1] The explanation given in § 92 is that *to be punished* is the Infin. form of Complement; and this agrees with that given by Abbott in § 97 and § 105 in *How to Parse*. Dr. Gow, however, in *Method of English*, p. 117, has expressed the view that *to be punished* (= punishment) is the Direct object to the verb "like," and "a rascal" (= for a rascal) the Indirect. Both views appear to be tenable; but on grounds of convenience I have adopted the former. It covers the ground of such a sentence as "I saw him come." This could scarcely be broken up into "I saw *come* (Direct object) for *him* (Indirect)."

20. Our deeds shall *travel* with us from afar,
And what we have been makes us *what-we-are.*—G. ELIOT.

21. Because half a dozen grasshoppers under a fern make the field *ring* with their importunate chink, while thousands of great cattle, reposing beneath the shadow of the British oak, chew the cud and are silent, *pray do* not imagine that those who make the noise are the only inhabitants of the field.—BURKE.

22. For when the noble Cæsar saw him *stab*,
Ingratitude, more strong than traitors' arms,
Quite vanquish'd him: then *burst* his mighty heart;
And, in his mantle muffling *up* his face,
Even at the base of Pompey's statua,
Which all the *while* ran *blood*, great Cæsar fell.—SHAKESPEARE.

23. *Let me* now *tell you* that *every* six hours of study will be injurious to your health, unless you break the period with half an hour's *walk* in the open air or with some light form of recreation that *can give* relief to the brain.

24. He was proud, when I praised; he was submissive, when I reproved him; but he did never *love* me, and what he now mistakes for justice and kindness for me, is *but* the pleasant sensation *that* all persons feel at *revisiting* the scenes of their boyish hopes and fears, and the *seeing* on equal terms the man they were accustomed to look up *to* with reverence.

II.—*General Questions.*

1. When a Singular noun ends in an *s* sound, how is the Possessive sign (or case-ending) affected? How is the Possessive expressed in plurals?

2. What are Weak verbs? Classify *bring*, *sing*, *take*, *seek*, *teach*, *set*, *bleed*, *eat* as Strong or Weak. Give reasons in each case.

3. Name all the Auxiliary verbs. Why are they so called? Distinguish them from every other class of verb.

4. Distinguish the uses of *but* in the following sentences:—

> There is *but* one man present.
> I cannot *but* believe that you are lost.
> He is a clever man, *but* not learned in books.
> There was no one present *but* pitied the lame horse.
> He was all *but* ruined by that investment.

5. Explain and exemplify the difference between Extension and Completion of a Finite verb, and between a Direct and an Indirect object.

6. Point out the grammatical difference between *the* in such a sentence as "He did his duty, and was *the* happier for it," and *the* in such a sentence as "He was *the* happier of the two."

7. Account for the resemblance in form between the Verbal noun and the Present Participle. Parse all the words ending in *-ing* in this sentence: "Darkling, we went singing on our way, with our walking-sticks in our hands, weary of toiling in town."

8. Show by what means Transitive verbs in English can be used Intransitively and *vice versa*. Can Intransitive verbs be conjugated in the Passive voice? If so, to what extent?

9. Classify verbs of Incomplete predication, and exemplify the different forms that the Complement may assume with each class of verb.

10. What principle would you adopt in classifying nouns in English? Exemplify each class.

11. Exemplify the uses of the Qualifying or Gerundial Infinitive. Is there any connection in origin between this and what we now call a Gerund or Verbal noun?

12. Explain and exemplify the meaning of each of the Auxiliary verbs, when the said verbs are not used as Auxiliaries.

13. Under what circumstances are we debarred from parsing *than* as a conjunction? To what part of speech must we then assign it? Give examples.

14. Explain the points of resemblance and the points of difference between (*a*) adjectives and adverbs, (*b*) prepositions and conjunctions.

15. Explain and exemplify the terms *Impersonal verbs, Defective verbs, Irregular verbs, Auxiliary verbs, Factitive verbs, Copulative verbs.*

16. What is meant by the *case* of a noun? How did the word come to be used in such a sense?

17. How do we express simple futurity (1) in Finite verbs, (2) in the absolute construction? Give examples.

18. What form of the Indefinite article do you use before the words—*history, historical, European, usual, humble, ewe*? Give reasons.

19. Specify, with examples, the various meanings and uses of *one* in our language.

20. Give instances of the conversion of Abstract nouns into Concrete, Proper into Common, Material into Common.

21. Define a sentence. How would you deal with the following? (1) *go;* (2) *hence!* (3) *does it rain? yes; let us return.*

22. Explain and exemplify "*pro*-noun," "*pro*-verb," "*pro*-sentence."

23. Explain *finite* in the phrase "Finite verb." Mention those parts of a verb which are not finite.

24. Examine the following definitions of a preposition:—

> "A word used before a noun or pronoun to show its relation to some other word."
>
> "A word that connects a noun with a verb, an adjective, or other noun."

25. Give examples of the three main senses in which the Possessive case can be used. To what class or classes of instances is the use of this case now restricted?

26. How would you distinguish between a Demonstrative adjective and a Demonstrative pronoun? Give examples.

27. Distinguish the uses of *as* in the following sentences:—

> Yours is not the same book *as* mine.
> He trembled *as* he spoke.
> Do not act *as* he did.
> Hot *as* the sun is, we must go out in it.
> I will inquire again *as* to that matter.
> *As* a judge I condemn you, *as* a man I pity you.

28. Describe and exemplify the different kinds of objects that can be used in connection with verbs.

29. Describe the main tests by which a Weak verb is distinguished from a Strong. Apply these tests to *hang, fight, read, beseech, see, saw, say, sow, sew, sue, sit, seethe, sell.*

30. Show how the distinction between Attributive and Predicative is applied to adjectives and Simple adverbs, and how that between Continuative and Restrictive is applied to Relative pronouns or Relative adverbs.

31. Exemplify the uses of (*a*) *though*, *but*, (*b*) *as well as*, as Co-ordinative or Subordinative conjunctions.

32. What exceptions are there to the rules (1) that two Singular subjects are followed by a Plural verb, (2) that one Singular subject is followed by a Singular verb?

33. Explain the cases of the words italicised below:[1]—

(*a*) Knock *me* this gate and rap *me* well.—SHAKESPEARE.
(*b*) Fare *thee* well. He overslept *himself*.
(*c*) *Methinks*. It likes *us* well (SHAKES.).
(*d*) Woe worth *the day*! Woe is *me*!
(*e*) I hope you will do *me* this favour.

III.—*Correct or justify the following.* (From London Matriculation Papers, Jan. 1879 to Jan. 1897.)

1. I am verily a man who am a Jew.
2. Too great a variety of studies distract the mind.
3. Who do you speak to?
4. The river has overflown its banks.
5. Man never is, but always to be blest.
6. Neither our virtues or our vices are all our own.
7. If I were old enough to be married, I am old enough to manage my husband's house.
8. I am to blame, not you.
9. Art thou proud yet? Ay, that I am not thee.
10. Whoever the king favours
The cardinal will find employment for.
11. Here you may see that visions are to dread.
12. Nothing but wailings was heard.
13. Neither of them are remarkable for precision.
14. I cannot tell if it be wise or no.
15. It must be confessed that a lampoon or a satire do not carry in them robbery or murder.—*Spectator*.
16. Whose own example strengthens all his laws,
And is himself the great sublime he draws.
17. They were both fond of one another.
18. Thersites's body is as good as Ajax, when neither are alive.
19. Thou art much older than thy looks.
20. There were no less than five persons concerned.
21. Recite the first six lines of *Paradise Lost*.
22. Neither he nor we are disengaged.

---

[1] These are all now parsed as Objective cases. For (*b*) see § 97; for (*c*) see § 148; for (*e*) see § 90. In all of them the preposition *to* or *for* is understood. In Old English all these cases were Datives. The construction in (*a*) is still called the **Dative of Interest**: "Knock this gate *for* me and rap well *for* me." In (*d*) the prep. *to* is understood: "Woe happen *to* the day!": woe is *to* me" (Latin, *hei mihi*).

23. One of the best books that has been written on the subject.
24. I like it better than any.
25. And since I never dare to write
As funny as I can.
26. Laying the suspicion on some one, I know not who.
27. Well is him that hath found prudence!
28. Neither he nor I have any doubt of his success.
29. One of the best treatises that has been written on the subject.
30. I am one of those who cannot describe what I do not see.
31. The country was divided into counties, and the counties placed under magistrates.
32. Nobody ever put so much of themselves into their work.
33. He hath given away above half his fortune to the Lord knows who.
34. Friendships which we once hoped and believed would never grow cold.
35. Nepos answered him, Celsus replied, and neither of them were sparing of censure on each other.
36. Such are a few of the many paradoxes one would cite from his writings, and which are now before me.
37. The largest circulation of any Liberal newspaper.
38. Injustice springs only from three causes. . . . Neither of these can be found in a being wise, powerful, and benevolent.
39. This dedication may serve almost for any book that has, is, or shall be published.
40. In the best countries a rise in rents and wages has been found to go together.
41. He belongs to one caste, and the hewers of wood and drawers of water to another.
42. The second assault was met by Buckingham by a counter attack on the Earl of Bristol, whom he knew would be the chief witness against him.
43. And many a holy text around she strews,
That teach the rustic moralist to die.
44. This view has been maintained by one of the greatest writers that has appeared in this country.
45. The administration of so many various interests, and of districts so remote, demand no common capacity and vigour.
46. He having none but them, they having none but he.
47. Breaking a constitution by the very same errors that so many have been broke before.
48. They are not only the most charitable of any other nation, but most judicious in distinguishing the properest objects of compassion.
49. The part of this reed used by the Indians is from 10 to 11 feet long, and no tapering can be perceived, one end being as thick as another.
50. If he had writ one word by the next post, this had been just and civil.
51. Thou lovest, but ne'er knew love's sad satiety.
52. *Macbeth.* There's blood upon thy face.
Murd. 'Tis Banquo's then.
Macb. 'Tis better thee without than he within.

53. This is he, my master said,
Despised the fair Athenian maid.

54. Luckily the monks have recently given away a couple of dogs which were returned to them, or the breed would have been lost.

55. It was the most amiable, although the least dignified, of all the party squabbles by which it had been preceded.

56. Having perceived the weakness of his poems, they now reappear to us under new titles.

57. Neither you nor I am right.

58. I am one of those who cannot describe what I feel.

59. Whom they were I really cannot specify.

60. Whom do you say that I am.

61. His is a poem, one of the completest works that exists in any language.

62. He was shot by a secretary under notice to quit, with whom he was finding fault,—very fortunately without effect.

63. It is characteristic of them to appear but to one person, and he the most likely to be deluded.

64. I think it may assist the reader by placing them before him in chronological order.

65. Few people learn anything that is worth learning easily.

66. My resolution is to spare no expense in education; it is a bad calculation, because it is the only advantage over which circumstances have no control.

67. Image after image, phrase after phrase, starts out vivid, harsh, and emphatic.

68. Books that we can at a glance carry off what is in them are worse than useless for discipline.

69. He preferred to know the worst than to dream the best.

70. Humanity seldom or ever shows itself in inferior minds.

71. You have already been informed of the sale of Ford's theatre, where Mr. Lincoln was assassinated, for religious purposes.

72. The Moor, seizing a bolster, full of rage and jealousy, smothers her.

73. Nor do I know any one with whom I can converse more pleasantly or I would prefer as my companion.

74. They drowned the black and white kittens.

75. The then Ministry were in favour of the bill.

76. The people is one; they have all one language.

77. George and myself went up the mountain together.

78. The Duke of Wellington is one of those who never interfere with matters over which he has no control.

79. Her voice was ever soft, gentle, and low; an excellent thing in woman.

80. Peter the Hermit's diet was abstemious, his prayers long and fervent.

81. I shall have great pleasure in accepting your invitation.

82. Each of the girls went to their separate rooms to rest and calm themselves.

83. Being early killed, I sent a party in search of his mangled body.

CHAPTER XIV.—SOUNDS, SYMBOLS, AND SPELLINGS.

SECTION 1.—LETTERS, ACCENT, QUANTITY, SYLLABLES.

212. **A Letter** (Latin *litera*, Fr. *lettre*) is a mark or symbol that stands for a certain sound. Without letters men can talk as fast as they like, but they cannot either read or write. A word, until it is written, is merely a sound, perceptible to the ear, but not to the eye.

Letters are subdivided into two great classes, vowels and consonants.

213. **Vowel** is from Lat. *vocalis*, Fr. *voyelle*,—L. *vox*, *vocis*, the voice. A vowel, as its etymology implies, stands for a *voice*-sound, *i.e.* a sound or tone produced by the unimpeded passage of the breath, without the help of a consonant. Thus it is quite as easy to say *e* as *be*.

214. **Consonant** (L. *con*, together with, *sonant*-em, sounding). This, as its name implies, stands for a sound that cannot be easily, if at all, produced except in company with a vowel. Thus it is not easy to pronounce the letter *b*, until we connect it with some vowel, as *be*. In fact, we find it so difficult to sound *b* by itself, that we have called the consonant *be*, not *b*.

215. **The English Alphabet.**—Our alphabet consists of 26 letters, of which 5 are vowels, 19 are consonants, and 2 are semivowels, *i.e.* dubious letters.

Vowels.—A, a; E, e; I, i; O, o; U, u.

Consonants.—B, b; C, c; D, d; F, f; G, g; H, h; J, j; K, k; L, l; M, m; N, n; P, p; Q, q; R, r; S, s; T, t; V, v; X, x; Z, z.

Semivowels.—Y, y; W, w.

The letter *y* is superfluous as a vowel; for it expresses precisely the same sound as *i*. Thus there is no difference of sound between the first syllables of *sin*-ner and *syn*-tax. As a consonant, however, the y is indispensable; for we could not express such words as *yoke*, *yet* without it.

The letter *w* as a vowel is even less useful (if this were possible) than *y*; for it cannot stand alone as *y* can, but is seen only in such combinations as *aw*, *ew*, *ow*, all of which can be quite as easily spelt *au*, *eu*, *ou*. As a consonant, however, the letter *w* is indispensable; for it enables us to express such words as *will*, *wax*, *wet*.

Note.—The vowels *i* and *u* (care being taken that *u* here stands for the *u* in *full*, and *not* for the *u* in *tune*) acquire the consonantal sounds of *y* and *w* respectively, when they are followed by other vowels. Thus *opinion* is sounded as if it were spelt *o-pin-yon* (three syllables). Similarly if we attempt to sound *uilliam* we get *William*. The letter *w* is merely a double *v*, though it is called a "double *u*." The symbol *v* is merely another form of *u*, and in Latin during the classical period *u* was the only symbol used.

216. Digraph, Diphthong.—It is necessary to understand clearly what is meant by these two words.

A *digraph* is a compound **letter**; a *diphthong* is a compound **sound.** "Digraph" is from Greek *di*, two or twice, and *graph*, to write: it therefore means "a double letter." "Diphthong" is from Greek *di*, two or twice, and *phthong*-os, a sound: it therefore means "a double sound."

Owing to the fewness of our vowel-*symbols* and the multiplicity of our vowel-*sounds* we are sometimes forced to use a digraph for expressing a vowel-sound that is simple or uncompounded, as *au*. On the other hand, it sometimes happens (such is the perversity of our spelling) that we use a single letter to express a vowel-sound that is compound; as *u* in *tu-bu-lar*, sounded as *tyōō-byōō-lar*.

Similarly we sometimes use a digraph to express a single consonantal sound, as *ph* in *Philip*; and a single consonant to express a double sound, as *x* in *tax*, sounded as *taks*.

217. Voiceless and Voiced Consonants.[1]—Consonants are subdivided into two great classes, the Voiceless and the Voiced. Voiced is the name given to those consonants which can be sounded to a slight extent *without the help of a vowel*; the Voiceless are those to which no sound whatever can be given without this help. The Voiced therefore have something of a vocalic character, and are a connecting link between Voiceless consonants and Vowels.

Consonants as thus distinguished go for the most part in pairs. All consonants not included amongst these pairs are Voiced, with the exception of *h*, which is Voiceless.

Voiceless.	*Voiced.*	*Voiceless.*	*Voiced.*	*Voiceless.*	*Voiced.*
k	g	s	z	p	b
ch	j	t	d	f	v
sh	zh	th(in)	th(is)	wh	w

[1] *Voiceless* and *Voiced* are the names adopted by Professor Skeat. **Surd** (silent) and **Sonant** (sounding) are equally suitable. The names Hard and Soft, Sharp and Flat, are also used; but they are not suitable. An apple may be hard or soft, but not a consonant.

The distinction between Voiceless and Voiced can be easily verified by any one who will make the experiment on his own organs. We can sound *ka*, for instance, so long as the *k* is followed by a vowel. But if we cut off the *a* and try to sound the *k* alone, we cannot produce any sound whatever, though we are conscious of a feeling of muscular tension in the tongue. There is no *voice* in it; and hence the consonant *k* is classed as Voiceless.

On the other hand, if we take the combinations *ga*, and cut off the *a*, we find that without the assistance of this or any other vowel it is possible to make an audible guggle. This consonant is therefore classed among the Voiced.

The following facts are of very wide application :—

I.—When two consonants come together, voiceless consonants are assimilated in sound to voiced ones, or voiced to voiceless.

(*a*) In monosyllables the first letter usually holds its ground, and the second has to give way to it. Compare the *s* in *cats* with that in *lads*. In the first the *s* remains voiceless, because it is preceded by the voiceless *t*. In the second the *s* becomes a voiced letter, *i.e.* receives the sound of *z*, because it is preceded by a voiced *d*. Similarly compare the *d* in *looked* with that in *loved*, the *s* in *caps* with that in *cabs*.

(*b*) In dissyllables and compound words the first letter usually gives way to the second one; as in *five*-teen, sounded and spelt as *fif*-teen; *cup-board*, sounded, though not spelt, as *cub-board*; *black-guard*, sounded, though not spelt, as *blag-guard*.

This process is very commonly at work in prefixes. Thus we have a*c*cent for a*d*cent, a*ff*lict for a*d*flict, a*p*pear for a*d*pear, a*s*sent for a*d*sent, a*t*tain for a*d*tain, a*g*grieve for a*d*grieve, a*l*lot for a*d*lot, a*n*nul for a*d*nul, a*r*rive for a*d*rive, inte*l*lect for inte*r*lect, o*c*cur for o*b*cur, o*f*fer for o*b*fer, o*p*pose for o*b*pose, pe*l*lucid for pe*r*lucid, po*l*lute for po*r*lute, su*c*ceed for su*b*ceed, su*p*port for su*b*port, etc.

II.—A voiceless consonant often receives the sound of a voiced one, when it is placed between two vowels. Thus in *breath* the *th* is voiceless; but in *breathe*, where it stands between two vowels, it is voiced. Again *rise* is sounded as *rize*, not as *rice*. *Lathe* is sounded, not as *lath*, but with the sound *th* as in *th*(is).

III.—When one consonant is substituted for another, as sometimes happens, a voiceless consonant is displaced by a voiceless one, and a voiced by a voiced. This is especially seen in doublets,—that is, pairs of words derived from the same original elements, but differently spelt :—

Crook, cross (*k* substituted for *s*, both voiceless). Aptitude, attitude (*p* and *t*, both voiceless). Apricock (older spelling) and apricot (*k* and *t*, both voiceless). Bark, beard (*b* and *d*, both voiced). Wrap, lap (*r* and *l*, both voiced). Prune, plum (*r* and *l*, *n* and *m*, both pairs voiced). *W*ard, *g*uard (*w* and *g*, both voiced).

In *sh*oe (A.S. *scó*) we find *sh* substituted for *sk* (both voiceless). So too in *sh*e (Midland *scæ*). In "see*th*e," "so*dd*en," voiced *th* is interchanged with voiced *d*; so too in mur*th*er (older spelling), mur*d*er. In the 3rd Sing. "cast-*s*" (older form, cast-*es*, cast-*eth*) we find the voiceless *s* substituted for the voiceless *th*.

In A.S. final or medial *h* was sounded almost like *k*, as in "Lo*ch* Lomond." A survival of this occurs in the word *next* (= *nekst*), which in A.S. was spelt *nehst*. In modern English this *h* has been usually respelt as *gh*. In the words "lou*gh*" and "hou*gh*" (sounded as *lok*, *hok*), the original sound of the *k* has been retained. But in certain other words, as *enough*, *laugh*, *rough*, *trough*, *tough*, *cough*, the sound of *f* has been substituted for the sound of *k*, both letters being voiceless.

218. Accent, Emphasis, Quantity.—Roughly speaking, both accent and emphasis are the effect of *loudness* (which helps to produce distinctness), while quantity depends on the *time* that it takes to pronounce a syllable.

When we lay stress upon a *single syllable*, *i.e.* pronounce it more loudly and distinctly than any other syllable or syllables of the same word, this is called **Accent** (Latin *ad*, to, *cantus*, a song).

Sup-ply′, sim′-ply. Re-bel′ (verb), reb′-el (noun).

When we lay stress upon *an entire word*, *i.e.* pronounce it more loudly and distinctly than any other word of the same sentence or phrase, this is called **Emphasis** (Greek *en*, in or on, *phasis*, speech).

I appeal from Philip *drunk* to Philip *sober*.

Quantity means "the amount of *time* occupied in uttering a vowel or syllable." If the time so occupied is short, the vowel or syllable is said to be short; otherwise, it is said to be long.

A vowel can be long either by nature or by position. (1) Vowels long by nature are exemplified in *fate*, *fraud*, *smote*, *bite*, etc.; vowels short by nature are seen in *fat*, *pod*, *hit*, *wet*, etc. (2) Vowels long by position, but short by nature, are seen in *west*, *land*, *flint*, *stump*, *bond*. The vowels themselves in such words or syllables are not long, but they are said to be made long by position, because they are followed by a strong combination of consonants, which prevents the syllable from being sounded rapidly.

219. Importance of Accent in English.—In English as now spoken quantity counts for very little: accent is all-important. Thus the word *guard* is certainly a long syllable when it stands alone; but in the combination "blackguard" (sounded as *blag'-guard*) the accent thrown upon the first syllable compels us to make the second syllable as short as we can pronounce it. Again, the diphthong *u* (i.e. *u* sounded as *yoo*) is long by nature, as in *tube*. But in the adjective *tu'-bu-lar* the second *u*, though long by nature like the first one, is, owing to the want of accent, made as short as we can pronounce it.

Such is the effect of accent in our language that an unaccented syllable sometimes disappears altogether. Thus *ap-pren'-tice* has been reduced to *pren'-tice*; *dam'-o-sel* (older spelling) to *dam'-sel*; *co-rone'* (Lat. "corona") to *crown*; *la-ven'-der-ess* to *laun'-dress*; *with-draw'-ing-room* to *draw'-ing-room*; *pun'-ish* to *punch*; *sa'-cris-tan* to *sex'-ton*; *pa-ral'-y-sis* (Gr. "paralysis") to *pal'-e-sy*, *pal'-sy*; *en-sam'-ple* to *sam'-ple*; *dis-port'* to *sport*; *hy-drop'-sy* to *drop'-sy*; *af-fray'* to *fray*; *es-quire'* to *squire*; *a-mend'* to *mend*; *ap-peal'* to *peal*; *de-spite'* to *spite*.

The part of speech to which a word belongs often depends upon the accent. If the choice lies between a verb and a noun, both spelt alike, the verb has the accent on the last syllable, the noun on the first. Of this we have at least sixty examples.

Com-pound' (verb), com'-pound (noun). Con-duct' (verb), con'-duct (noun). Con-fine' (verb), con'-fine (noun). Con-vert' (verb), con'-vert (noun). Con-vict' (verb), con'-vict (noun), etc.

If the choice lies between a verb and an adjective, the erb has the accent on the last syllable, as before:—

Ab-sent' (verb), ab'-sent (adj.). Fre-quent' (verb), fre'-quent (adj.).

If the choice lies between a noun and an adjective, the noun has the accent on the first syllable, as before, and the adjective on the second:—

Com'-pact (noun), com-pact' (adj.) Min'-ute (noun), mi-nute' (adj.). In'-va-lid (noun), in-val'-id (adj.).

Note.—Sometimes, however, there is no difference of accent; as *con-tent'* (adj. and verb), *con-tents'* (noun); *con-sent'*, *re-spect'*, *her'-ald*, *sup-port'* (all nouns and verbs); *con'-crete*, *pa'-tient* (both nouns and adjectives). Such examples are not common.

220. Syllabic division is ruled by accentuation, and not, as has been sometimes maintained, by etymology. "Word-division has nothing to do with etymology. From a practical point of view *im'-pu-dence* is right, being based on true phonetic principles, *i.e.* on the spoken language. It is only when we take the word to pieces that we discover that it is formed from *im-* (for *in*), the base *pud*, and the suffix *-ence*. The spoken language has *pe-ruse'* at one moment, and *pe-ru'-sal* at another. It rightly regards ease of utterance, and nothing else" (Skeat).

It may be added that syllabic division by etymology is impracticable for two reasons: (1) the component parts of a word are sometimes so mixed together as to be indistinguishable; cf. *monkey* (2 syll.), from Old Ital. *monicchio* (4 syll.); (2) the etymologies of words can be known only to those few persons who have studied the subject, whereas all men should know how a word ought to be sounded; cf. *banqu-et* (lit. little bench), which is divided phonetically as *ban'-quet.*

La-ment', lam'-en-ta'-ble. At'-om, a-tom'-ic. At'-tri-bute (noun), at-trib'-ute (verb). Or'-tho-dox, or-thog'-ra-phy. Pro-vide', prov'-i-dence. Tel'-e-gram, te-leg'-ra-phy. Ex-pect', ex'-pec-ta'-tion. Me-chan'-ic, mech'-a-nism. Do-min'-ion, dom'-i-nant. Fi-nite, fin'-ish. Ta'-ble, tab'let. Nu'-me-ral, nu-mer'-i-cal. O'-cean, o'-ce-an'-ic.

The terminations *-cial, -cious, -cean, -sion, -gion, -tion, -tial, -tious,* since they are sounded as one syllable, should not be divided into two:—

So'-cial, o'-cean, le'-sion, le'-gion, con'-scious, mo'-tion, par'-tial, cap'-tious, fi-nan'-cial.

Section 2.—Vowel-Sounds and How They are Spelt.

Twenty Vowel-sounds.[1]—If our alphabet were more perfect than it is, we should have one separate symbol to express each separate sound. Unfortunately it is very imperfect; for we have only five vowel-signs (*y* having been excluded as super-

[1] The list of twenty sounds here given, though not the same as that given in some school-books, will, I trust, be accepted as correct; for it is the one on which all the best authorities are agreed,—Professor Skeat, Mr. Sweet, Miss Laura Soames, and Dr. Murray (in the introduction to the Oxford Dictionary). Dr. Murray's system is much more elaborate, but the basis is the same. As to the phonetic symbol most suitable for each sound, authorities are not equally unanimous. I have myself adopted those symbols which seemed likely to cause the least difficulty to a beginner, and which come nearest to those used in the current Dictionaries.

fluous) to express four times as many sounds. Of these twenty vowel-sounds, sixteen are simple, and four are diphthongs. (The phrase "phonetic symbol" used below means the symbol used to express or denote the *one particular sound* assigned to it. The reason why some are bracketed as pairs is explained in § 222.)

A. Four sounds[1] frequently denoted by the symbol *a*; one short, and three long; all simple, none diphthongal.

{ 1. Short: the sound of *a* in *marry*. Phonetic symbol **ă**.
{ 2. Long: the sound of *a* in *Mary*. Phonetic symbol **â**.
3. Long: the sound of *a* in *mason*. Phonetic symbol **ā**.

Note.—Observe that (3) is quite a distinct sound from (2). In sounding (2) you have to open the mouth a great deal wider than in sounding (3). In (2) the *a* is always followed by an *r*; in (3) it never is. No. (2) is merely No. (1) drawled or lengthened.

4. Long: the sound of *a* in *path*. Phonetic symbol **ȧ**.

E. Two sounds commonly denoted by the symbol *e*; one short, and one long; both simple, neither diphthongal.

5. Short: the sound of *e* in *fed*. Phonetic symbol **ĕ**.
6. Long: the sound of *ee* in *feed*. Phonetic symbol **ē**.

I. Two sounds commonly denoted by the symbol *i*; one short, and one long; the short is simple, the long diphthongal.

7. Short: the sound of *i* in *bit*. Phonetic symbol **ĭ**.
8. Long: the sound of *i* in *bite*. Phonetic symbol **ī**.

O. Three sounds commonly denoted, and a fourth occasionally denoted, by the symbol *o*; two short and two long; all simple, none diphthongal.

{ 9. Short: the sound of *o* in *lot*. Phonetic symbol **ŏ**.
{ 10. Long: the sound of *o* in *lost*. Phonetic symbol **au**.

Note.—Since the usual spelling is *au*, as in "fraud," this has been made the phonetic symbol in preference to *o*. But the use of the digraph *au* does not make the sound less simple than it is. In fact (10) is nothing more than (9) drawled or lengthened. If *dog* is drawled, it has the sound of *daug*. If the first syllable of *laurel* is

[1] To the four *a* sounds given above, some writers add two more, viz. the *a* in *fall* and the *a* in *want*. The latter is evidently a mistake. It creates a redundancy and leads to confusion; for the *a* in *want* is identical in sound with the *o* in *not*, and it never has the sound of *o* except when it is preceded by *w*. In fact, it is an *o* sound, and its connection with *a* is both accidental and exceptional. The former is not an *a* sound either, and is not expressed by *a* except when the *a* is followed by *l*. Professor Skeat associates only four sounds with the symbol *a* (see his Note printed in page 459 of my *English Grammar Past and Present*).

shortened (as in practice it always is), it has the sound of *lŏrel*, rhyming with "moral." *Not* is merely the short of *naught*.

{ 11. Short: the sound of *o* in *o*-mit. Phonetic symbol **o'**.
{ 12. Long: the sound of *o* in *tone*. Phonetic symbol **ō**.

Note.—There is a great difference between (11) and (9). In sounding (9) you have to open your mouth rather wide, whereas in sounding (11) you almost close it. No. (12) is merely No. (11) drawled or lengthened.

OO. Two sounds commonly denoted by the digraph *oo*; one short, the other long; both simple, neither diphthongal.

{ 13. Short: the sound of *oo* in *stood*. Phonetic symbol **ŏŏ**.
{ 14. Long: the sound of *oo* in *stool*. Phonetic symbol **ōō**.

U. Two sounds commonly denoted by the symbol *u*; one short, the other long; the short simple, the long diphthongal.

15. Short: the sound of *u* in *duck*. Phonetic symbol **ŭ**.
16. Long: the sound of *u* in *duke*. Phonetic symbol **ū**.

Oi. One sound commonly denoted by the digraph *oi*; diphthongal.

17. Long: the sound of *oi* in *toil*. Phonetic symbol **oi**.

Ou. One sound commonly denoted by the digraph *ou*; diphthongal.

18. Long: the sound of *ou* in *mouse*. Phonetic symbol **ou**.

Lastly, we come to two sounds, one short, the other long, and both simple or non-diphthongal. These have been called the Obscure, Neutral, or Indefinite sounds. For the expression of these sounds we have no vowel in our alphabet. So the expedient which the best authorities have agreed upon is to use *ə* (inverted *e*) for the phonetic symbol.

{ 19. Short: the sound of *er*[1] in gath'-*er*. Phonetic symbol **ə**.
{ 20. Long: the sound of *er*[1] in con-*fer'*. Phonetic symbol **əə**..

222. General results.—We have thus twenty vowel-sounds, of which sixteen are pure or simple, and four are mixed or diphthongal. The sixteen simple sounds are subdivided into

[1] In Scotland, however, and in some of the northern counties of England, the *r* is trilled, that is, distinctly sounded as *r*. Owing to this peculiarity of the Northern dialect, I have been reluctantly compelled to adopt from Mr. Skeat, Mr. Sweet, Miss Soames, and Dr. Murray the awkward-looking symbol **ə**. This sound is so natural to human speech that hesitating speakers use it to fill up the pauses in their sentences. In books such pauses are printed thus:—"I—*er*—am aware—*er*—that," etc.

(*a*) eight short, viz. ă, ĕ, ĭ, ŏ, o', ŏŏ, ŭ, and ə; and (*b*) eight long, viz. â, ā, å, ē, au, ō, ōō, and əə. The four diphthongs are ī, ū, oi, and ou.

Sounds which in the above description are bracketed together as short and long are real pairs. Thus the *a* of *Mary* is the drawled or lengthened sound of the *a* in *marry*; the *o* of *lost* is the lengthened sound of the *o* in *lot*; the *o* of *tone* is the lengthened sound of the *o* in *o*-mit; the *oo* of *stool* is the lengthened sound of the *oo* in *stood*; the *er* in con-*fer'* is the lengthened and accented sound of the *er* in gath'-*er*.

On the other hand, the sounds which are not bracketed together as short and long are not pairs. Thus the *ee* in *feed* is not the long sound of *e* in *fed*; the *i* of *bite* is not the long sound of *i* in *bit*; the *u* in duke is not the long sound of *u* in *duck*. Though the same vowel is used in each case, the sounds are entirely distinct. For instance, the sound of *ee* in *feed* pairs not with *ĕ*, but with *ĭ*. The sound of *ĭ* is actually expressed by *ee* in the word "breeches" (sounded short as if it were spelt *brĭches*). Again, the sound of *ā* pairs not with *ă*, but with *ĕ*; thus *waist'*-coat is sounded short as if it were spelt *wĕst'*-coat.

223. How the four Diphthongs are produced.—Let us take each diphthong in turn.[1]

ī. The first vowel-sound that helps to make this diphthong is obsolete in modern English, though still heard in the north-country dialects, where the *a* of *man* has retained a sound intermediate between ă and å (Nos. 1 and 4). This intermediate sound rapidly followed by the *i* of *bit* produces a third sound that is distinct from both. The spelling, *ai*, is seen in the word *aisle* (sounded as *īl*).

Note.—The sound of *ä*, when added to *i*, would produce a diphthong, like the sound of *ai* in *Isaiah*, *naive*, *Kaiser*.

ū. Made up of *ĭ* + *ōō*. These, when sounded rapidly in succession, give *yōō*, like the *u* in *duke* (sounded as "dyōōk").

oi. Made up of *au* (see No. 10 in § 221) + *ĭ*. The utterance

[1] It has been pointed out by phoneticians (Skeat, Sweet, Soames, Dr. Murray) that the long vowels which I have written as ā and ō are usually sounded with the glides *i* and *u* respectively, as *a*[i], *o*[u], and that hence these vowels are in a certain sense diphthongal. They are not diphthongal, however, to the same extent that ī, ū, oi, and ou are. For the sake of simplicity I have followed Miss Laura Soames in treating them as simple vowels, not as diphthongs.

of these two simple sounds in rapid succession produces a mixed sound distinct from both.

ou. Made up of *ä* (see No. 4 in § 221) + *ŏŏ*. The utterance of these two simple sounds in rapid succession produces a mixed sound distinct from both.

Note.—We now see very clearly what was stated above in § 216, that the use of a digraph or two letters to express a sound is no proof that the sound is diphthongal or mixed. Thus **ī** and **ū**, though expressed by single vowels, are both diphthongs; while **au**, **ŏŏ**, **ōō**, **ee**, though expressed by digraphs, are all simple sounds.

224. Spellings of the twenty Vowel-sounds.—We shall follow the order of vowels, simple and diphthongal, given in § 221.

1. **ă**: mad, plaid, have, salmon, thresh.
2. **â**: Mary, airy, bearer, heiress, mayoralty, therein.
3. **ā**: fatal, fate, tail, play, campaign, straight, vein, they, reign, weigh, steak, gaol, gauge, eh, dahlia, halfpenny. French words: fête, congé, ballet, champagne, demesne.
4. **ä**: path, art, heart, clerk, aunt, bazaar, palm, hurrah, plaister. Fr. words: vase, éclat.
5. **ĕ**: bed, head, any, said, says, leopard, leisure, reynard, ate, friend, bury.
6. **ē**: me, theme, seen, each, field, seize,[1] key, Cæsar, police, invalid, quay, people, receipt, Beauchamp.
7. **ĭ**: bit, nymph, pretty, give, surfeit, married, happy, guinea, donkey, women, busy, breeches, sieve.
8. **ī**: idol, try, mine, lyre, sign, high, height, die, rye, island, aisle, choir, indict, eye.
9. **ŏ**: from, want, shone, laurel, knowledge, yacht, hough.
10. **au**: haul, law, lost, tall, talk, pour, ought, broad, sore, lord, war, water, aught, Vaughan, gone.
11. **o'**: hero, follow, heroes, followed, furlough. Fr. dépôt.
12. **ō**: no, note, both, toad, toe, dough, mow, brooch, oh, yeoman, sew, Cockburn. Fr. mauve, beau.
13. **ŏŏ**: stood, full, could, wolf.
14. **ōō**: fool, tomb, shoe, move, soup, through, truth, blue, juice, sleuth-hound, slew, rude, manœuvre.
15. **ŭ**: shut, blood, son, come, touch.
16. **ū** (=yōō): du-ty, tune, due, suit, few, feud, lieu, view, impugn.
17. **oi**: coil, boy.
18. **ou**: loud, down.
19. **e**: Chi'-na, Sa'-rah, suf'-fer, squir'-rel, but'-ton, Eu'-rope, thor'-ough, tor'-toise, fa'-mous, meer'-schaum, waist-coat, cup'-board,

---

[1] The following is a list of all the words in which *ei* has the sound of *ē*:—conceive, deceive, perceive, receive (and their derivatives), ceiling, seize, either, neither, plebeian, weir, weird, seignory, inveigle, counterfeit.

pleas′-*ure*, col′-*lar*, mar′-*tyr*, bun′-*kum*, an′-*chor*, ran′-*cour*, mur′-*mur*. (All in unaccented syllables. This sound is never accented.)

20. **əə**: h*er*d, *err*ed, h*ear*d, b*ir*d, st*irr*ed, t*ur*n, bl*urr*ed, w*or*d, *colo*-nel (sounded as k*er*′-nel). (All in accented syllables.)

One hundred and ninety spellings (not counting the French words) for twenty vowel-sounds.

225. Same spelling with different sounds.—We may now invert the process, and show how the same symbol (*i.e.* the same spelling) may be used to denote different sounds :—

a: r*a*t, t*a*ll, p*a*th, m*a*ny, m*a*de, c*a*re, w*a*nt, stew*a*rd.
a—e: r*a*v*e*, h*a*v*e*, *a*r*e*, *a*t*e*.
ai: m*ai*d, s*ai*d, pl*ai*d, *ai*sle.
au: *au*nt, h*au*nt, g*au*ge, m*au*ve, meer-sch*au*m.
e: h*e*, h*e*r, cl*e*rk, b*e*d, pr*e*tty.
e—e: th*e*r*e*, h*e*r*e*.
ea: h*ea*t, st*ea*k, h*ea*rt, h*ea*d.
ei: v*ei*n, l*ei*sure, s*ei*ze, sur-f*ei*t, h*ei*ght.
ey: th*ey*, k*ey*, *ey*e.
ew: n*ew*, s*ew*.
i—e: b*i*t*e*, n*i*ch*e*, pol*i*c*e*.
ie: f*ie*ld, d*ie*, s*ie*ve.
o: h*o*t, c*o*ld, w*o*lf, w*o*men, wh*o*m, s*o*n, butt*o*n, l*o*st, her*o*.
o—e: c*o*v*e*, pr*o*v*e*, l*o*v*e*, sh*o*r*e*.
oa: l*oa*d, br*oa*d, cup-b*oa*rd.
oe: sh*oe*, t*oe*.
oo: h*oo*k, f*oo*l, br*oo*ch, fl*oo*d, d*oo*r.
ou: p*ou*r, y*ou*ng, th*ou*, s*ou*p, s*ou*l.
ough: r*ough*, hicc*ough*, c*ough*, h*ough*, tr*ough*, b*ough*, th*ough*, thr*ough*.
al: f*al*l, p*al*m, sh*al*l, hospit*al*.
ol: c*ol*d, w*ol*f, g*ol*f, sym′-b*ol*.
ar: *ar*′-row, *ar*t, col-l*ar*.

Note.—The reasons why our vowels came to express so many different sounds are—(1) because the Norman scribes, when they addressed themselves to the study of English, discarded the marks or accents denoting vowel-length in Anglo-Saxon words, and their example has been followed ever since; (2) because our vocalic symbols, though sufficient for the simple and pure language for which they were originally intended, are not sufficient for the very composite language that English has since become; (3) because one of the vocalic symbols (æ) used in A.S. has disappeared in modern English, though the sounds that it expressed have remained; (4) because in the sixteenth and seventeenth centuries a general shifting of the vowel-sounds took place, which was very seldom accompanied by a change of spelling; (5) because the sounds of certain vowels are affected by the proximity of certain consonants, by the presence or absence of an accent, and by syllabic division; in short, the sound of a vowel varies with its surroundings.

For example, the vowel *a*, as shown above, is now used to express at least eight different sounds, viz. those exemplified in *rat*, *tall*, *path*, *many*, *made*, *care*, *was*, *steward*. (1) The sound of *a* in *rat* was represented in A.S. by the symbol *æ*; as this has become obsolete, *a* is made to do duty for it. (2) The sound of *a* in *tall* is produced by the liquid *l*, which has had the effect of prolonging the vowel and deepening its tone. (3) The sound of *a* in *path* was represented in A.S. by *á*; but as the accent has gone out of use, there is nothing but the simple *a* left to express this sound. (4) The sound of *a* in *many* (A.S. *manig*) may be ascribed to the frequent interchange of *a* and *e* in English; cf. A.S. *thenc-an*, *thank*: the sound of the *a* in *manig* has changed, but the spelling has remained. (5) The sound of *a* in *made* was represented in A.S. by *é* (very nearly); but as the sound of A.S. *é* has since shifted to that of *ee* in *seem*, the vowel *a* has been made to do duty for it. (6) The sound of *a* in *care* was represented in A.S. by *ǽ* (very nearly); but as this symbol has become obsolete, the vowel *a* followed by *re* has had to take its place. (7) The sound of *a* in *was* (= *wos*) is produced by the rounding of the lips in sounding the *w* that goes before; and in sounding the vowel *o*, the lips are somewhat rounded also. (8) The indefinite or neutral sound of *a* in *steward* arises from the want of accent on the syllable in which it stands.

Section 3.—Consonantal Sounds and How They are Spelt.

226. Twenty-five consonantal sounds.—In English as now spoken there are altogether *twenty-five* consonantal sounds. The symbols used to denote these sounds, if we place them as nearly as we can in the order of the alphabet, run as follows:—

1. b	4. g	7. k	10. n	13. s	16. w	19. ch	22. th(in)
2. d	5. h	8. l	11. p	14. t	17. y	20. ng	23. sh
3. f	6. j	9. m	12. r	15. v	18. z	21. th(is)	24. zh
							25. wh

227. Simple and Compound.—Out of the twenty-five sounds enumerated above, all are simple or uncompounded except two, viz. *j* and *ch*. These are called by Dr. Murray (in the Oxford Dictionary) "consonantal diphthongs," because he, with other phoneticians, has analysed *ch* into *t* + *sh*, and *j* into *d* + *zh*. Thus the sound of *ritshes* cannot be distinguished from that of *riches*; nor the sound of *ridzhid* from that of *rigid* = *rijid*.

Though we have to accept this analysis on the word of the best authorities and on the evidence of our own experience, it would be very inconvenient to write *tsh* for *ch*, and *dzh* for *j*. Moreover, the two sounds in question are of such frequent occurrence in our language, that *j* and *ch*, even if the sounds are diphthongal, deserve a place in the list of our consonantal symbols.

228. Redundant Consonants.—It has been said that "our alphabet contains four redundant consonants—*c*, *j*, *q*, *x*." The statement may be admitted for the following reasons:—

C is superfluous, because (1) when it precedes *a*, *o*, or *u*, it expresses the sound of *k*; (2) when it precedes *e* or *i*, it expresses the sound of *s*; (3) when it is combined with *h*, as in *church*, the digraph *ch* has been analysed into *tsh*.

J is superfluous, because it has been analysed into *dzh*. But we are glad to have it, because it is conveniently short.

Q is superfluous, because it is never used except in combination with *u*, and the combination can be expressed equally well by *kw*, as in *awkward*. In A.S. the letters used were *cw*, as in *cwén*, a woman.

X is superfluous, because in such words as *extra* it is equivalent to *ks*, and in *example* to *gz*.

229. Main divisions of Consonants.—The consonantal sounds can be classified according to the organ chiefly used in uttering them. Any part of our bodily structure that helps us to utter articulate sounds may be called an organ of speech. The chief organs are the tongue, the throat, the palate, the teeth, and the lips. By means of these organs the breath is modified as it passes through the larynx.

The most important of all these organs is the tongue; for the loss of this organ involves the loss of articulate speech. Since the tongue is the necessary helpmate to the other four organs, there is no separate class of Lingual (Lat. *lingua*, tongue).

The main divisions of consonants are as follows:—

I. **Gutturals** (Lat. *guttur*, throat): *k*, *g*, *ng*.
II. **Palatals** (Lat. *palatum*, palate): *ch*, *j* | *sh*, *zh* | *y*, *r*.
III. **Dentals** (Lat. *dent-em*, tooth): *t*, *d* | *s*, *z* | *n*, *l* | *th*(in), *th*(is).
IV. **Labials** (Lat. *labium*, lip): *p*, *b*, *m* | *f*, *v* | *wh*, *w*.

I. **Gutturals**: these three sounds are produced by raising the *back* of the tongue towards the *soft* palate, viz. that part of the palate that lies farther back in the throat (Lat. *guttur*):—*k*, as in *k*een; *g*, as in *g*ood; *ng*, as in thi*ng* or fi*n*-ger. The last, though expressed by a digraph, is as simple a sound as the other two. It occurs only when it is followed by another guttural, *k* or *g*, as in bla*n*-ket, fi*n*-ger, or when it comes at the end of a word, as in thi*ng*, ridi*ng*. There is a great difference of sound between the *n* of fi*n*-(ger) and the *n* of fi*n*. The former is a guttural, which you cannot utter without opening your jaws; the latter a dental, which you can utter only with closed teeth.

II. **Palatals**: all these sounds are produced by raising the *front* of the tongue towards the *hard* palate, or palate proper (viz. that part of the palate that lies farther forward than the soft palate):—*ch*, as in *ch*air; *j*, as in *j*oke; *sh*, as in *sh*ip; *zh*, as in sei*z*ure; *y*, as in *y*ield; *r*, as in *r*ob. All of these are simple sounds with the exception of the first two (§ 227).

III. **Dentals**: all these are produced by bringing the point of the tongue towards the upper teeth or upper gums:—*t*, as in *t*ail; *d*, as in *d*og; | *s*, as in *s*eal; *z*, as in *z*eal; | *n*, as in *n*ame; *l*, as in *l*ine; | *th*(in), as in brea*th*; *th*(is), as in brea*th*e. In sounding the first pair, *t* and *d*, the point of the tongue touches the upper teeth. In sounding the second pair, *s* and *z*, it comes very near the roots of the upper teeth, but does not quite touch them. In sounding the third pair, *n* and *l*, it touches the upper gums. In sounding the fourth pair, *th*(in) and *th*(is), it is placed between the upper and the lower teeth.

IV. **Labials**: all these sounds are produced by closing the lips: *p*, as in *p*oor; *b*, as in *b*oon; *m*, as in *m*oon; | *f*, as in *f*ox; *v*, as in *v*ixen; | *wh*, as in *wh*ine; | *w*, as in *w*ine. In sounding *p*, *b*, and *m* the lips are closed against each other, while the tongue is left to rest on the lower jaw. In sounding *f* and *v* the edges of the upper teeth are pressed against the lower lip, while the tongue rests on the lower jaw. In sounding *wh* and *w* the lips are rounded with the corners drawn together, while the tongue is almost in the same position as in sounding *g*. Hence *w* and *g* are liable to be interchanged, as in *w*ard (A.S. *w*eard), *g*uard (Fr. spelling of the same word).

230. The Glottal "h" (Greek, *glottis*, mouth of the wind-pipe). "Glottal" is the name given to the open throat-sound expressed by the letter *h*. In sounding *h* we make no use of the palate, tongue, teeth, or lips. It is a mere breath-sound or aspirate, and stands alone in our alphabet.

The uncertainty about sounding or not sounding this unfortunate letter appears to have arisen in some way from the collision between English and French, which resulted from the Norman Conquest. In

Anglo-Saxon the *h* was very distinctly sounded; in French very indistinctly. Hence the confusion.

231. Minor subdivisions of Consonants.—There are a few subdivisions of consonants, which cross with the four main divisions described above, and sometimes with one another.

Sibilants (Lat. *sibilantes*, hissing). On account of the hissing sound which they express, the name "sibilant" has been given to the letters *s*, *z*, *sh*, and *zh*.

Liquids (Lat. *liquidus*, flowing). This is the name given to the letters *l*, *m*, *n*, *r*, *ng*.

Nasals (Lat. *nasus*, nose); the name given to the three letters *n*, *m*, *ng*. These are called nasals, because in forming the sounds which they express the breath passes up the nose-passage and escapes through the nostril. If the nose-passage is blocked by a cold, *ng* (a guttural) is sounded almost as *g* (another guttural), *n* (a dental) almost as *d* (another dental), and *m* (a labial) almost as *b* (another labial).

Note.—When an *intrusive* consonant, *i.e.* one not belonging to the root, is inserted into a word, the intruder is usually of the same class as the consonant going before:—

Num-*b*-er (Lat. *nu-mer-us*); hum-*b*-le (Lat. *hum-il-is*); ten-*d*-er (Lat. *ten-er*); gen-*d*-er (Lat. *gen-er-is*). Observe the *m* and *b* are both labials, while the *n* and *d* are both dentals.

232. Spellings of the consonantal sounds.—We shall take each of the twenty-five sounds in the order in which their respective symbols are given in § 226:—

1. **b**: *b*ond (initial), e*bb* (final), *b*uoy, cu*p*-board.
2. **d**: bon*d*, la*dd*er, call*ed*, hor*d*e, wou*ld*.
3. **f**: *f*elt, whi*ff*, *ph*legm, lau*gh*, ha*lf*, o*ft*en, sa*pph*ire, li*eu*-tenant (where *ieu*=*ef*).
4. **g**: *g*ame, e*gg*, *gh*ost, *gu*ard.
5. **h**: *h*ot, *wh*o.
6. **j**: *j*ob, *g*ist, *G*eor*g*e, ju*dg*e, ju*dg*ment, sol*di*er, Greenwi*ch*, *g*aol.
7. **k**: *k*ill, *c*all, a*cc*ount, ba*ck*, bis*cu*it, *q*uell, li*qu*or, grotes*que*, a*ch*e, lou*gh*.
8. **l**: *l*ake, ki*ll*, is*l*and, ais*le*, gaze*lle*, scra*gl*io, Woo*lw*ich.
9. **m**: *m*end, ha*mm*er, hy*mn*, la*mb*, progra*mme*, phle*gm*, Ha*mp*den, dra*chm*.
10. **n**: pi*n*, i*nn*, dei*gn*, *kn*ee, *gn*aw, Jo*hn*, Linco*ln*, We*dn*esday, rib*and*, bor*ne*, A*nne*, coi*gne*.
11. **p**: *p*lace, ha*pp*y, ste*ppe*, Cla*ph*am, hiccou*gh*.
12. **r**: *r*ain, bo*rr*ow, *rh*ythm, *wr*ite, No*rw*ich.
13. **s**: *s*elf, ki*ss*, den*se*, *c*ell, dan*ce*, *sc*ene, coale*sce*, *sc*hism, quar*tz*, *sw*ord, ha*st*en, is*th*mus, *ps*alm, creva*sse*.
14. **t**: we*t*, ke*tt*le, gaze*tte*, *Th*ames, look*ed*, *tw*o, de*bt*, indi*ct*, recei*pt*, ya*cht*, cas*te*.

15. **v**: *v*est, ha*v*e, na*vv*y, o*f*, ne*ph*ew, hal*v*e.
16. **w**: *w*ine, *wh*en, s*u*ave, ch*o*ir.
17. **y**: *y*ield, un*i*on, hallelu*j*ah. French vi*gn*ette (*gn*=ny) cotil*l*on.
18. **z**: *z*eal, fi*zz*, hi*s*, clean*se*, sci*ss*ors, *X*erxes, fur*ze*, We*d*n*es*day, Chis*w*ick, Win*ds*or, ven*i*son, *cz*ar, bus*i*ness.
19. **ch**: *ch*ur*ch*, ni*che*, la*tch*, na*tu*re, ques*ti*on, righ*te*ous, violon*c*ello.
20. **ng**: thi*ng*, fi*n*ger, to*ngue*, ha*nd*kerchief, Birmi*ngh*am.
21. **th**(is): *th*en, soo*the*.
22. **th**(in): brea*th*, Ma*tth*ew.
23. **sh**: *sh*all, A*s*ia, ti*ss*ue, pen*si*on, mousta*che*, fu*chs*ia, mi*ssi*on, fa*shi*on, offi*ci*ate, so*ci*al, o*ce*an, cons*ci*ence, *sch*edule, vi*ti*ate, por*ti*on, lun*che*on, *ch*aise.
24. **zh**: sei*z*ure, lei*s*ure, occa*si*on, transi*ti*on. Fr. rou*ge*, ré*g*ime, *j*ujube (sometimes sounded as *j*u*j*ube).
25. **wh**: *wh*ile (often sounded merely as *w*, except in North Britain).

One hundred and sixty-six spellings (not counting the French words) for twenty-five different sounds.

233. Same spelling with different sounds :—

c: violon*c*ello, *c*at, *c*ity.
ch: a*ch*e, *ch*aise, su*ch*, dra*ch*m (silent).
j: *J*ew, *j*u*j*ube, hallelu*j*ah.
ge: rou*ge*, villa*ge*, *ge*t.
gi: *gi*ve, *gi*nger.
ti: no*ti*on, ques*ti*on, transi*ti*on.
s: ha*s*, ga*s*.
sc: *sc*ene, *sc*arce.
sch: *sch*eme, *sch*edule.
si: occa*si*on, disper*si*on.
th: *th*in, *th*is, *Th*ames.
x: e*x*tra, e*x*ample, *X*erxes. Fr. beau*x*.
ph: nym*ph*, ne*ph*ew.
gh: *gh*ost, lau*gh*, hou*gh*.
qu: li*qu*or, *qu*een.

234. Silent Consonants.

(1) **b** (after *m*): lam*b*, lim*b*, dum*b*, num*b*, plum*b*, clim*b*, clom*b*, tom*b*, wom*b*, crum*b*, thum*b*, com*b*, bom*b*: (the *b* is excrescent in *crumb*, *limb*, *numb*, and *thumb*; in the rest it is part of the root).

b (before *t*): dou*b*t, de*b*t, de*b*tor.

(2) **ch**: ya*ch*t, dra*ch*m, s*ch*ism.

(3) **g** (before *n* and *m*): *g*nat, *g*naw, *g*nash, *g*narled, *g*neiss, dei*g*n, fei*g*n, rei*g*n, champai*g*n, campai*g*n, coi*g*ne, impu*g*n, phle*g*m.

(4) **gh** (final): hi*gh*, nei*gh*, wei*gh*, dou*gh*, slou*gh* (mire), plou*gh*, thou*gh*, throu*gh*, bou*gh*, thorou*gh*.

gh (before *t*): cau*gh*t, hau*gh*ty, frau*gh*t, fou*gh*t, nau*gh*t, thou*gh*t, sou*gh*t, bou*gh*t, tau*gh*t, mi*gh*t, ri*gh*t, etc.

(5) **h**: *h*eir, *h*our, *h*onour, *h*umour (where u=yoo), *h*onest, Jo*h*n.

Note.—*h* is sometimes silent in the middle of a word, as "ex*h*ibitor."

(6) **k** (before *n*): *k*now, *k*nack, *k*nave, *k*nead, *k*nee, *k*nell, *k*night, *k*nit, *k*nob, *k*nock, *k*not, *k*nuckle, *k*nout, *k*noll, *k*nacker, *k*napsack, *k*nife.

(7) **l**: cou*l*d, shou*l*d, wou*l*d; yo*l*k, fo*l*k; wa*l*k, ta*l*k; psa*l*m, pa*l*m; ha*l*f, ca*l*f; Linco*l*n.

(8) **n** (after *m*): autum*n*, hym*n*, condem*n*, dam*n*, colum*n*, lim*n*.

(9) **s**: viscount, puisne (= puny), isle, island, aisle.

(10) **t** (after *s* or *f* and before *le* or *en*): has*t*en, lis*t*en, glis*t*en, mois*t*en, this*t*le, whis*t*le, wres*t*le, jos*t*le, of*t*en, sof*t*en.

(11) **w** (before *r*): *w*rap, *w*retch, *w*raith, *w*rath, *w*roth, *w*reath, *w*reck, *w*rite, *w*right, *w*rench, *w*rest, *w*rinkle, *w*riggle, *w*rist, *w*rithe, *w*rong, *w*rought, a*w*ry.

w: s*w*ord, ans*w*er, t*w*o, *w*ho, Kes*w*ick, Chis*w*ick.

235. The letter "r."—In the Midland and Southern dialects the letter *r* in such words as *hair*, *deer*, *moor*, *pour*, is not sounded as a consonant (unless the next word or the next syllable begins with a vowel), but has the sound of the Indefinite vowel ə (described in § 221, (19)), so that here it helps to make a diphthong; as *hāə* (hair), *dēə* (deer), *mōōə* (moor), *pauə* (pour). It is not sounded as a *consonant* except before a word or syllable beginning with a vowel. Compare "*hair*" with "the *hai***r** of a man"; "*boor*" with "a *boo***r**-ish man."

In the same dialects the letter *r* helps to form a triphthong or treble vowel-sound, in such words as *fire*, *pure*, *destroyer*, *power*, unless the next word or the next syllable begins with a vowel, in which case the *r*, as before, is sounded as a consonant.

In the Northern dialect, however, *i.e.* the dialect commonly spoken in Scotland and in the most northerly of the northern counties of England, the *r* is trilled. Here, then, the letter *r* retains in full its consonantal character, and no such diphthongs or triphthongs are formed.

Exercise

(*a*) 1. Distinguish between *emphasis*, *accent*, *quantity*. 2. Give two instances in which words, identical in spelling, are distinguished one from another by accent. 3. "A perfect alphabet would contain a separate letter to represent every simple or elementary sound." Show that the letter *a* in English represents several simple or elementary sounds. 4. What single letters in our alphabet represent compound sounds? 5. "Our alphabet contains four redundant letters—*c*, *j*, *q*, *x*." Discuss this statement. 6. Write two words of one syllable, in the first of which the letter *i* represents a pure vowel sound, and in the second a diphthongal sound. 7. How do you account for the fact that the spelling of English words is often at variance with their pronunciation? 8. Give one example under each of the following to show that in some words—

(i.) The letter *i* represents a diphthongal sound.
(ii.) The letter *s* is written where *z* is sounded.
(iii.) A letter is not sounded at all.

9. State and illustrate the different sounds of the letter *s*. (*Oxford and Cambridge Locals.*)

(*b*) 1. What consonants are redundant in the English alphabet, and in what respects is our alphabet defective in consonants? 2. The sound of *a* in *hate* is expressed in several different ways in written English (as in *bait, may, whey, weight, gaol, gauge,* etc.). Show that there are also several ways in which the sound of *e* in *me* is represented in writing. 3. Give four true Diphthongs, four Liquids, four Sibilants, and four Labials. 4. Explain the terms *letter, diphthong, labial, palatal.* How many sounds has the combination *ough*? 5. Quote examples of English words containing *ei* or *ie* (four of each), and of verbs ending in *ceed* or *cede* (two of each). 6. What is a *diphthong*? Give six examples, all different, of so-called diphthongs which are not really diphthongs. By what name should such compounds be called? 7. How many *true* diphthongs have we in the English language? Quote three words as examples of each of them. (*College of Preceptors.*)

CHAPTER XV.—WORD-BUILDING.

SECTION 1.—COMPOUNDS AND DOUBLETS.

236. Simple Words.—A word that is not combined with any other word or syllable is called a Simple or Primary word; such as *buy, walk, come* (verbs); *bench, fire, name* (nouns); *hot, cold, stiff* (adjectives); *well, ill, much* (adverbs); *in, by, with* (prepositions); *he, she, it* (pronouns); *and, but, for* (conjunctions).

237. Compounds, Derivatives.—Most of our words, however, are not Simple, but either Compounds or Derivatives.

When one *word* is added to another, the combination is called a **Compound**; as *man-kind.*

When a *particle* (*i.e.* a syllable which does not make a complete word, or is not *now* used as one) is added to a word, the combination is called a **Derivative**; as *man-ly.*

If one Simple word is formed from another Simple word by means of some internal change, as *graze* from *grass, bleed* from *blood, raise* from *rise,* this is called a **Primary** Derivative; but a Derivative formed by adding a particle to the beginning or end of a word, as "man-*ly*," "*un*-man-*ly*," is called **Secondary.**

238. Compounds.—Such words fall into six main classes :—

(1) *Noun Compounds.*

(1) *Adjective + Noun:* blue-bell, mid-day, sweet-heart, noble-man.
(2) *Noun + Noun:* noon-tide, plough-man, sports-man, rail-road.

Note.—In *sportsman* the noun *sports* is Possessive = *sport's.* Cf. salesman, oarsman, etc.

(3) *Gerund + Noun:* cooking-stove, looking-glass, drinking-water.
(4) *Pronoun + Noun:* he-goat, she-goat, she-ass.
(5) *Verb + Noun:* tell-tale, dare-devil, pick-pocket, break-fast.
(6) *Verb + Adverb:* keep-sake, break-down, stand-still, draw-back.
(7) *Adverb + Verb:* out-come, off-spring, out-lay, in-come.
(8) *Adverb + Noun:* by-path, after-life, up-land, in-land, over-coat.

(2) *Adjective Compounds.*

(1) *Noun + Adject.:* sky-blue, blood-red, foot-sore, air-tight.
(2) *Adject. + Adject.:* red-hot, high-born, blue-green, ready-made.
(3) *Prep. + Noun:* over-land, under-hand, over-hand.

(3) *Verb Compounds.*

(1) *Noun + Verb:* back-bite, way-lay, hen-peck, brow-beat.
(2) *Adject. + Verb:* white-wash, rough-hew, safe-guard, rough-shoe (chiefly seen in the participial form "rough-shod").
(3) *Adverb + Verb:* back-slide, over-awe, up-set, with-hold.
(4) *Verb + Adverb:* doff (do off), don (do on), turn out, put on.

(4) *Adverb Compounds.*

(1) *Adject. + Noun:* mean-time, other-wise, mid-way, yester-day.
(2) *Adverb + Prep.:* here-in, forth-with, there-for(e), here-upon.
(3) *Noun + Noun:* length-ways, side-ways.

(5) *Double Compounds.*

(1) The notion that realism is somehow immoral faintly suggests a French-novel-reading Bishop.—*Times Weekly*, p. 329, 28 Sept. 1906. (A bishop who is a reader of French novels).

(2) A seventeen-year-old girl is alleged to have attacked a woman with a chopper, etc.—*Daily Express*, p. 6, 4th Oct. 1906. (A girl seventeen years old. On the use of *year* for *years*, see § 88, *c.*)

(6) *Phrase Compounds.*

Forget-me-not (noun); hand-and-glove (adj. said of friends that fit each other as closely as hand and glove); man-of-war; would-be (adj. used for one who intended to be or do something, but was stopped); barrister-at-law; note-of-hand; ticket-of-leave; Jack-o'-lantern: hole-and-corner (adj. clandestine); son-in-law; four-in-hand; spic-and-span new (lit. spike and spoon new; new as a nail or spike just made, or a spoon (chip, Norse, *spánn*) just cut).

Note.—Such phrase-compounds as the above are all well established; but the student is not at liberty to coin fresh ones whenever he likes.

239. Spelling of Compounds.—In words of two or more syllables the accent is usually thrown back on the first syllable, and in many cases this has the effect of altering the spelling:—

Bon-fire from *bone-fire*. *Hus-band* from *house-band* (lit. house-dweller). *Hus-sif* or *hus-sy* from *house-wife*. *Nos-tril* from *nose-thril*. *Star-board* from *steer-board*. *Tad-pole* from *toad-poll*. *Fort-night* from *four-teen-night*. *Suf-folk* from *South-folk*. *Fur-long* from *furrow-long*. *Sus-sex* from *South-Sex* (i.e. *Sax-on*).

In some words, however, the change of sound produced in this first syllable by the accent is not accompanied by any change in the spelling:—

Black-guard. Cup-board. Break-fast. Two-pence, three-pence, four-pence, five-pence. Row-lock (sounded as *rullock*).

240. Doublet defined.—Words derived from the same original elements, but differing in form and generally differing in meaning, are called **Doublets**. They are a special and important class of Primary Derivatives (§ 237).

241. Origin of Doublets.—Doublets have come into existence from various causes :—

(*a*) The Saxon semi-vowel *w* was seldom sounded in French ; so by the time that Norman-French began to make itself felt, it was usually changed to a *g* or *gu*, and in this way a kind of doublet was formed :—

Wile, guile ; ward, guard ; wise (manner), guise.

(*b*) Words of Romanic or Greek origin frequently appear in two different forms,—one "Popular," and the other "Learned." In the following pairs the "Learned" form is the one mentioned second, and is called "Learned" because it is most like the original Latin. The word mentioned first is called "Popular" because it shows how the word became corrupted in popular speech :—

Abridge, abbreviate ; aggrieve, aggravate ; allow, allocate ; amiable, amicable ; antic, antique ; appraise, appreciate ; benison, benediction ; chance, cadence ; challenge, calumny, etc.

(*c*) Substitution of one letter for another :—

Fabric, forge ; boss, botch ; locust, lobster ; deck, thatch ; aptitude, attitude ; cask, casque ; prune, plum ; servant, serjeant ; ant, emmet ; sect, sept ; wrap, lap ; porridge, pottage, etc.

(*d*) *Metathesis*, or change of place among consonants :—

Granary, garner ; wight, whit ; scarp, scrap ; task, tax ; ask, ax (vulgar) ; thrill, thirl ; gabble, jabber (here *r* is substituted for *l*).

(*e*) Palatalisation, or the substitution of a palatal consonant for a guttural (§ 229) :—

Bank, bench ; dike, ditch ; kirk, church ; trickery, treachery ; gaud, joy ; gabble, jabber ; gig, jig ; lurk, lurch ; disc, dish, desk, dais ; etc.

(*f*) A change of inner vowel :—

Brown, bruin ; shock, shake ; these, those ; dune, down ; grove, groove ; hale, whole ; load, lade ; lust, list ; truth, troth ; cavalry, chivalry ; clause, close ; custom, costume ; one, an ; assay, essay.

(*g*) Excision of an initial letter or syllable :—

Adamant, diamond ; engine, gin ; defence, fence ; appeal, peal ; history, story ; affray, fray ; etiquette, ticket ; ensample, sample ; estrange, strange, etc.

(*h*) Interchange of words derived from cognate roots :—

Name, noun ; barb, beard ; beaker, pitcher ; knot, node ; foam, spume ; corn, horn ; eatable, edible ; brother, friar, etc.

SECTION 2.—PREFIXES AND SUFFIXES.

242. Root, Stem, Prefixes, Suffixes.—A word reduced to its simplest etymological form is called a **Root**.

A **Stem** is the change of form (if any) assumed by the root, before a suffix is added to it. Thus in the word "fals-i-ty" the root is *fals* (Lat. *fals*-us), the stem is *falsi*, and the suffix is *ty*. The stem and the root, however, often coincide; as in *man* (root or stem) + *ly* (suffix).

Particles added to the *end* of a stem are called **Suffixes**. Those added to the *beginning* are called **Prefixes**. The name "Affix" stands for either, though more commonly used for Suffix.

As a general rule Prefixes alter the meanings of words, while Suffixes show to what Part of Speech they belong. Thus there is a very radical difference of meaning between "*pre*-scribe," to order, and "*pro*-scribe," to prohibit. Again, "dark-*ness*" is a noun, "dark-*ly*" is an adverb, "dark-*en*" is a verb.

243. Sources of Prefixes and Suffixes.—The three sources from which our Prefixes and Suffixes have come are:—

I. Teutonic (Anglo-Saxon, with a few Norse and Dutch). These are sometimes, but wrongly, called "English."

II. Romanic (Latin or French, with a few Spanish and Italian).

III. Greek (either directly from Greek or through French).

Note.—There are two reasons why it is wrong to call affixes of Class I. "English": (1) because, as is stated in the text, some of them are of Norse, and some others of Dutch, origin; (2) because those of Classes II. and III., whatever their origin may have been, have become English, *i.e.* have been naturalised, and are now an integral part of our language.

244. Hybrids.—The name "hybrid" (which means "of mixed origin") is applied to any Compound or Derivative word, whose parts have come from different sources, *i.e.* are neither purely Teutonic, nor purely Romanic, nor purely Greek. Hybrids are very common in our language.

Thus in *en-dear* the prefix is Romanic, the stem is Teutonic. In *starv-ation* the stem is Teutonic, the suffix is Romanic. In *be-siege* the stem is Romanic, the prefix is Teutonic. In *false-hood* the stem is Romanic, the suffix is Teutonic. In *bi-cycle* the stem is Greek, the prefix is Romanic. In *art-ist* the stem is Romanic, the suffix is Greek.

SUFFIXES: TEUTONIC, ROMANIC, GREEK.

245. I. Noun-forming.—We may classify the principal suffixes under the following headings:—

(*a*) Denoting agent, doer, or one appointed to act:—

Teutonic:—

-er, -ar, -or (modern forms of A.S. *-ere*): bak-*er*, do-*er*, li-*ar*, tail-*or*, London-*er*, law-y-*er*, saw-y-*er*.

-nd (*old ending of Pres. Part.*): fie-*nd*, frie-*nd*, husba-*nd*.

-wright (*workman*): wheel-*wright*, play-*wright*, cart-*wright*.

-ther, -der (A.S. *-ther*, *-der*): fa-*ther*, bro-*ther*, daugh-*ter*, spi(n)-*der*.

-monger (trader): fish-*monger*, iron-*monger*, coster-*monger*.

Romanic:—

-or, -eur (Latin *-or*, *-ator*, French *-eur*): aggress-*or*, doct-*or*, amat-*eur*, emper-*or*, cens-*or*, specul-*ator*.

ary, -aire, -ar, -eer, -ier (Latin *-arius*, *-aris*): secret-*ary*, million-*aire*, schol-*ar*, volunt-*eer*, cash-*ier*, brigad-*ier*.

-an, -ain, -en, -ian, -on (Latin *-anus*): public-*an*, capt-*ain*, citiz-*en*, guard-*ian*, sext-*on*.

-ant, -ent (Latin, *-antem*, *-entem*): merch-*ant*, tru-*ant*, ten-*ant*, combat-*ant*; stud-*ent*, rod-*ent*, cli-*ent*.

-ate (Latin *-atus*, *-atem*): candid-*ate*, magistr-*ate*, prim-*ate*.

-ee, -ey, -y (French *-é*, from Latin *-atus*): deput-*y*, jur-*y*, attorn-*ey*, grand-*ee*, employ-*é*.

-ive, -iff (Latin *-ivus*, Fr. *-if*): fugit-*ive*, mot-*ive*; plaint-*iff*, bail-*iff*.

Greek:—

-ist, -ast (Greek *-ist-es*, *-ast-es*): soph-*ist*, art-*ist*, psalm-*ist*, botan-*ist*, nihil-*ist*; enthusi-*ast*.

-ot (Greek *-ot-es*): patri-*ot*, zeal-*ot*, idi-*ot*, Iscari-*ot*.

-ite, -it (Greek *-it-es*): Israel-*ite*, erem-*ite*, herm-*it*, Jesu-*it*.

(*b*) Marking the Feminine gender:—

Teutonic:—

-ster (A.S. *-es-tre*), **-en** (A.S. *-en*): spin-*ster*, vix-*en* (Fem. of "fox").

Romanic:—

-ess (Latin *-ix*, Late Lat. *issa*, French *-esse*): testatr-*ix*, shepherd-*ess*.

Note.—In the words "sultan-*a*," "donn-*a*," the *a* is Italian.

Greek:—

-ine (Greek, *in-e*, French *-ine*): hero-*ine*, czar-*ina*.

(*c*) Denoting patronymics:—

Teutonic:—

-ing: Vik-*ing*, k-*ing* (A.S. cyn-*ing*), Brown-*ing*, Mann-*ing*.

-kin: Peter-*kin* (hence Per-*kin*), Sim-*kin* (Simon-*kin*), Wil-*kin*-s.

-son: Ander-*son*, Collin-*son*, David-*son*.

(*d*) Suffixes having usually, not always, a depreciatory force:—

Teutonic:—

-craft: priest-*craft*, state-*craft*, witch-*craft*.
-erel, -rel: mong-*rel*, dogg-*erel*, dott-*erel*, wast-*rel*.
-ling: hire-*ling*, ground-*ling*, under-*ling*, world-*ling*, weak-*ling*.
-monger: ballad-*monger*, crotchet-*monger*, grievance-*monger*.
-ster: trick-*ster*, young-*ster*, rhyme-*ster*.

Romanic:—

-ard: cow-*ard*, drunk-*ard*, slugg-*ard*, dot-*ard*. See also below (*f*).
-aster: poet-*aster*, critic-*aster*.

(*e*) Diminutives (denoting smallness, endearment, contempt):—

Teutonic:—

-en (A.S. *-en*): maid-*en*, chick-*en* (from *cock*), kitt-*en* (from *cat*).
-ing, **-ling** (A.S. *-ing*, *-el+ing*); farth-*ing*, tith-*ing*; hire-*ling*, duck-*ling*, gos-*ling*, dar-*ling*.
-kin (Dutch *-ken*): fir-*kin*, nap-*kin*, Peter-*kin*, or Per-*kin*.
-ock, -k (A.S. *-uc*, *c*): bull-*ock*, hill-*ock*, stir-*k* (little steer).
-y, -ey, -ie (A.S. *-ig*): bab-*y*, Tomm-*y*, Charl-*ey*, bird-*ie*, lass-*ie*.
-el, -le, -l (A.S. *-el*): sack, satch-*el*; corn, kern-*el*; scythe, sick-*le*; nave, nav-*el*; spark, spark-*le*; speck, speck-*le*; fow-*l*, hai-*l*, gir-*l*.
-erel, -rel (A.S. *-er+el*): cock-*erel*, mong-*rel*, dogg-*erel* (?)
-ster (A.S. *-es-tre*): trick-*ster*, pun-*ster*, young-*ster*, rhyme-*ster*.

Romanic:—

-aster (Lat. *-aster*, cf. A.S. *-estre*): ole-*aster*, pil-*aster*.
-ule, -le (Lat. *-ulus*): pill-*ule*, sched-*ule*; circ-*le* (hence circ-*ul*-ar).
-cule, -cle (Lat. *-cu-lus*, Fr. *-cle*): animal-*cule*, pinna-*cle*.
-el, -le, -l, elle (Lat. *-ellus*): dams-*el*, cast-*le*, vea-*l*, bagat-*elle*, vermi-c-*elli*, umbr-*ella*, violon-c-*ello* (Ital.).
-et, -ot, -ette (Fr. *-et*, Fem. *-ette*; Ital. *-etto*): lock-*et*, lanc-*et*; ball-*ot*; brun-*ette*, cigar-*ette*; stil-*etto*.
-let (Double suffix, *-el+et*): brook-*let*, rivu-*let*, ham-*let*, cut-*let*.
-ito (Span. *-ito*): negr-*ito*, mosqu-*ito*.

Greek:—

-isk (Gr. *-iskos*): aster-*isk*, obel-*isk*.

(*f*) Augmentatives (denoting greatness, or excess to a fault):—

Romanic:—

-ard, -art (Low Lat. *-ardus*): drunk-*ard*, wiz-*ard*, bragg-*art*.
-oon, -on, -one (Fr. *-on*, Ital. *-one*): ball-*oon*, flag-*on*, tromb-*one*.

(*g*) Abstract suffixes (denoting act, state, quality, etc.):—

Teutonic:—

-dom (A.S. *dóm*): free-*dom*, martyr-*dom*, earl-*dom*, wis-*dom*.
-hood, -head (A.S. *hád*): man-*hood*, priest-*hood*, maiden-*head*.
-ing: learn-*ing*, writ-*ing*, walk-*ing*, sleep-*ing*.
-lock, -ledge (A.S. *lác*): wed-*lock*, know-*ledge*.
-red (A.S. *réd*): hat-*red*, kind-*red*.
-ric (A.S. *rice*): bishop-*ric*.
-ness (A.S. *-nis*, *-nes*): dark-*ness*, aloof-*ness*, holi-*ness*.

-ship (A.S. *scipe*): friend-*ship*, wor-*ship*, owner-*ship*.
-t, -th (A.S. *-ith*): leng-*th*, tru-*th*, heigh-*t*, ligh-*t*, sigh-*t*.
-ter, -der (A.S. *-ther*, *-der*): slaugh-*ter*, laugh-*ter*, mur-*der*.

Romanic:—

-age (Fr. *-age*): cour-*age*, hom-*age*, umbr-*age*, bond-*age*.
-al (Fr. *-aille*): refus-*al*, tri-*al*, surviv-*al*, bestow-*al*.
-ance, -ence, -ancy, -ency (Lat. *-antia*, *-entia*): dist-*ance*, prud-*ence*, guid-*ance*, const-*ancy*, urg-*ency*.
-cy, -acy (Lat. *-tia*): cur-*acy*, prel-*acy*, secre(t)-*cy*, idiot-*cy*.
-ice, -ise, -ess (Lat. *-itia*, Fr. *-esse*): serv-*ice*, exerc-*ise*, prow-*ess*.
-ion (Lat. *-ionem*): relig-*ion*, fash-*ion*, suspic-*ion*, relat-*ion*.
-ment (Lat. *-mentum*): enjoy-*ment*, fer-*ment*, attach-*ment*.
-mony (Lat. *-monia*, or *-monium*): parsi-*mony*, matri-*mony*.
-or, -our, -eur (Lat *-or*, Fr. *-eur*): err-*or*, fav-*our*, grand-*eur*.
-ry, -ery (Fr. *-rie*, *-erie*): slave-*ry*, trick-*ery*, brave-*ry*.
-tude (Lat. *-tudo*): forti-*tude*, longi-*tude*, magni-*tude*.
-ty (Lat. *-tas*, Fr. *-té*): cruel-*ty*, certain-*ty*, frail-*ty*.
-ure (Lat. *-ura*): seiz-*ure*, cult-*ure*, capt-*ure*, us-*ury*.
-y (Lat. *-ia*, *-ium*): infam-*y*, stud-*y*, perjur-*y*.

Greek:—

-ism, -asm (Gr. *-ismos*, *-asmos*): optim-*ism*, enthusi-*asm*.
-y (Gr. *-ia*): monarch-*y*, energ-*y*, sympath-*y*.

(*h*) Collective (denoting a collection, or the place of one):—

Romanic:—

-ade (Fr. *-ade*): arc-*ade*, colonn-*ade*, balustr-*ade*.
-age (Fr. *-age*): foli-*age* plum-*age*, vill-*age*, cott-*age*.
-ry, -ery (Fr. *-rie*, *-erie*): tenant-*ry*, rook-*ery*, gent-*ry*.
-ory (Lat. *-orium*): dormit-*ory*, fact-*ory*, invent-*ory*.
-ary (Lat. *-arium*): gran-*ary*, libr-*ary*, gloss-*ary*.

(*i*) Miscellaneous suffixes, not included in the above:—

Teutonic:—

-el, -le: shov-*el* (a thing to shove with), gird-*le* (a thing to gird with), spind-*le* (from *spin*), shutt-*le* (from *shoot*), hand-*le*, thimb-*le* (from *thumb*), sadd-*le* (from *sit*), sett-*le* (from *sit* or *set*), bund-*le* (from *bind*).

-m, -om (A.S. *-m*, *-ma*): bloo-*m* (from *blow*), doo-*m* (from *do*), bes-*om* (A.S. *besma*). Random (Old Fr. *randon*) is excluded.

-en, -on (*that which acts*): hav-*en* (have): mai-*n* (may), wag-*on*, wai-*n* (weigh).

-fare (*going*): war-*fare*; thorough-*fare*, wel-*fare*, chaf-*fer* (cheap fare).

-lock, -lic (*plant*): hem-*lock*, gar-*lic*.
-stead (*place*): home-*stead*, bed-*stead*, in-*stead* of, Hamp-*stead*.
-tree (*sawn timber*): axle-*tree*, rood-*tree*.
-ow, -w (A.S. *-u*, *-we*): mead-*ow*, shad-*ow*, stra-*w*, de-*w*.

Romanic:—

-ace (Lat. *-atio*, *-atium*; Fr. *-ace*): popul-*ace*, terr-*ace*, pal-*ace*.
-ine, -in (Lat. *-inus*): libert-*ine*, cous-*in* (Lat. consobr-*inus*).

-me, -m (Lat. *-men*): cri-*me*, char-*m*, real-*m* (Lat. regali-*men*).
-o (Lat. *-us*, *-um*; Span. *-o*): studi-*o*, grott-*o*, incognit-*o*.
-cre, -chre (Lat. *-crum*): sepulch-*chre*, lu-*cre*.

Greek:—

-on (Gr. *-on*): criteri-*on*, skelet-*on*, col-*on*, phenomen-*on*.
-ic, -ics (Gr. *-ikos*, *-ika*): log-*ic*, mus-*ic*, phys-*ics*, eth-*ics*.

246. II. Adjective-forming:—

(*a*) Possessing a quality of any kind:—

Teutonic:—

-ed (A.S. *-d*): wretch-*ed*, gift-*ed*, fabl-*ed*, money-*ed*, ragg-*ed*.
-en (A.S. *-en*): wheat-*en*, gold-*en*, heath-*en*, op-*en*, wood-*en*.
-ly (A.S. *-lic*): god-*ly*, woman-*ly*, man-*ly*, love-*ly*, god-*like*.
-some (A.S. *-sum*): toil-*some*, hand-*some*, whole-*some*, bux-*om*.
-y, -ey (A.S. *-ig*): might-*y*, wood-*y*, clay-*ey*, drear-*y*, an-*y*.

Romanic:—

-al (Lat. *-alis*): vit-*al*, parti-*al*, mort-*al*, comic-*al*.
-an, -ane, -ain (Lat. *-anus*): pag-*an*, hum-*an*, hum-*ane*, cert-*ain*.
-ant, -ent (Lat. *-antem*, *-entem*): dist-*ant*, abs-*ent*, pres-*ent*.
-ar, -ary, -arious (Lat. *-aris*, *-arius*): lun-*ar*, contr-*ary*, vic-*arious*.
-esque (Lat. *-iscus*, Fr. *-esque*): pictur-*esque*, grot-*esque*.
-ile, -il, -eel, -le, -el (Lat. *-ilis*): frag-*ile*, fra-*il*, gent-*eel*, gent-*le*, hum(b)-*le*, cru-*el*.
-ic, -ique (Lat. *-icus*, *-iquus*): rust-*ic*, com-*ic*, un-*ique*, obl-*ique*.
-ine (Lat. *-inus*): div-*ine*, clandest-*ine*, infant-*ine*.
-lent (Lat. *-lentem*): pesti-*lent*, corpu-*lent*, vio-*lent*.

(*b*) Possessing a quality in a high degree:—

Teutonic:—

-ful (A.S. *-ful*, Eng. *-full*): plenti-*ful*, beauti-*ful*, master-*ful*.

Romanic:—

-ous, -ose (Lat. *-osus*): numer-*ous*, fam-*ous*, verb-*ose*.

Note.—The equivalent of these suffixes is seen from the fact that the same stem sometimes takes both forms—plenti-*ful*, plente-*ous*; beauti-*ful*, beaute-*ous*; joy-*ful*, joy-*ous*; grace-*ful*, graci-*ous*.

(*c*) Possessing a quality in a slight degree; hence sometimes used in a depreciative sense:—

Teutonic:—

-ish (A.S. *-isc*): pal-*ish*, redd-*ish*, woman-*ish* (fit for a woman, but not fit for a man), snapp-*ish*, upp-*ish*, slav-*ish*, baby-*ish*.

Romanic:—

-ile: puer-*ile* (child-*ish*), infant-*ile* (baby-*ish*), serv-*ile* (slav-*ish*).

Note.—The prefix *sub-* (Latin) sometimes means "slightly"; as, *sub*-acid, *sub*-tropical (not quite tropical).

(*d*) Conveying an Active sense :—

Romanic :—
-ive (Lat. *-ivus*) : recept-*ive*, act-*ive* : (capt-*ive* is exceptional).
-ory, -orious (Lat. *-orius*) : illus-*ory*, cens-*orious*.
-fic (Lat. *-ficus*) : terri-*fic*, honori-*fic*, beati-*fic*.

(*e*) Conveying a Passive sense :—

Romanic :—
-able, -ible (Lat. *-bilis*) : laugh-*able*, eat-*able*, ed-*ible*, cred-*ible*.

(*f*) Describing nation, sect, creed, etc. :—

Teutonic :—
-ish, -ch (A.S. *-isc*) : Engl-*ish*, Ir-*ish*, Span-*ish*, Fren-*ch*.

Romanic :—
-an (Lat. *-anus*) : Rom-*an*, Austri-*an*, Belgi-*an*, Christi-*an*.
-ese (Lat. *-ensis*) : Chin-*ese*, Siam-*ese*, Portugu-*ese*.

Greek :—
-ite (Gr. *-it-es*) : Israel-*ite*, Irving-*ite*, Carmel-*ite*.

(*g*) Miscellaneous suffixes, not included in the above :—

Teutonic :—
-th (*order*) : six-*th*, seven-*th*, etc.
-teen, -ty (A.S. *-tén*, *tig*, ten) : thir-*teen* (3 + 10), (thirt-*ty* 3 × 10).
-ern (A.S. *irn*-an, to turn) : north-*ern*, north-*er*(n)-ly.
-ward (*direction*) : fro-*ward*, for-*ward*, way-*ward*, down-*ward*.
-ther (A.S. *ther*, comp. degree) : o-*ther*, fur-*ther*, whe-*ther*, ne-*ther*.
-less (*without*) : faith-*less*, shame-*less*, home-*less*.
-most (*superlative*) : fore-*most*, in-*most*, ut-*most*.
-fold (*repeated*) : two-*fold*, mani-*fold*, hundred-*fold*.
-ow, -w : call-*ow*, fall-*ow*, mell-*ow*, fe-*w*, ra-*w*, slo-*w*.
-fast (*firm*) : stead-*fast*, shame-*faced* (misspelt for *fast*).

Romanic :—
-ior (Lat. comp. degree) : exter-*ior*, pr-*ior*, super-*ior*.
-monious (Lat. *-monius*) : cere-*monious*, sancti-*monious*.
-ple, -ble (Lat. *-plex*, Fr. *-ple*, fold) : tri-*ple*, tre-*ble*.

Greek :—
-astic, -istic (Gr. *-astikos*, *-istikos*) : dr-*astic*, art-*istic*.

247. III. **Verb-forming** :—

(*a*) Causative ; hence forming Transitive verbs :—

Teutonic :—
-en (A.S. *-en* or *-n*) : dark-*en*, sweet-*en*, length-*en*, height-*en*.

Romanic :—
-fy (Lat. *facio*) : magni-*fy*, terri-*fy*, stupe-*fy*.

Greek :—
-ise (through French *-iser*) : galvan-*ise*, brutal-*ise*, fertil-*ise*.

Note.—Some Prefixes are also used for the same purpose :—

Teutonic **be-**, as *be*-friend, *be*-calm, *be*-numb; *Romanic* **im-**, **en-**, as *im*-peril, *en*-dear.

(*b*) Frequentative, denoting frequency or continuance:—

Teutonic:—

-el, -le, -l: cack-*le*, jost-*le*, sniv-*el* (sniff), draw-*l* (draw).
-er, -r: batt-*er* (beat), sputt-*er* (spout), glimm-*er* (gleam).
-k: har-*k* (hear), hear-*k*-en, lur-*k*, tal-*k* (tell).

(*c*) Other verb-forming suffixes:—

Romanic:—

-ate (Lat. *-atum*): captiv-*ate*, gradu-*ate*, filtr-*ate*.
-ish (Lat. *-isc*, Fr. *-iss*): pun-*ish* (pun-*ch*), per-*ish*, flour-*ish*.
-esce (Lat. *-esco*, inceptive): coal-*esce*, acqui-*esce*.

248. IV. **Adverb-forming**:—

Teutonic:—

-ly (A.S. *lic-e*, in a like way): on-*ly*, bad-*ly*, dark-*ly*, open-*ly*.
-ling, -long (A.S. *linga*): head-*long*, dark-*ling*, side-*long*.
-meal (A.S. *mæl*, a time): piece-*meal*, inch-*meal* (Shakespeare).
-wards (A.S. *weard*, direction): back-*wards*.
-wise (A.S. *wis-e*, manner): like-*wise*, other-*wise*.
-way, -ways (A.S. *weg*, way): straight-*way*, al-*ways*.
-s, -ce (sign of Possessive): need-*s*, twi-*ce*, back-ward-*s*, some-time-*s*.
-n: whe-*n*, the-*n*, the-*n*-*ce*. (The *n* in *often* is an intruder.)
-re: whe-*re*, the-*re*, he-*re*.
-om (old Dative ending; cf. who-*m*, the-*m*, hi-*m*): whil-*om*, seld-*om*.
-ther (direction): whit-*ther*, hi-*ther*, hi-*ther*-to.

Note.—We have no Romanic or Greek suffixes for forming Adverbs.

Prefixes: Teutonic, Romanic, Greek.

249. **Teutonic Prefixes.**—These have been distinguished into (*a*) Separable, and (*b*) Inseparable:—

(*a*) *Separable*; *i.e.* capable of being used as separate words; such as *after*-life, *a*-do (for *at* do), *al*-one (for *all* one), *by*-path, *fore*-cast, *forth*-coming, *fro*-ward (for *from*-ward), *in*-sight, *off*-shoot, *on*-set, *out*-let, *through*-ticket, *to*-gether, *up*-start, *wel*-fare. Such words might be called Compounds (§ 237). These do not require further explanation. The four mentioned below are somewhat peculiar.

Out-.—This sometimes gives certain verbs the sense of surpassing; as *out*-live (to live beyond), *out*-vote (to defeat by votes), *out*-run.

Over-.—This sometimes denotes excess; as *over*-eat (eat too much), *over*-sleep (sleep too long), *over*-worked (worked too much).

Under-.—This sometimes denotes deficiency, too little; as *under*-fed, *under*-paid, *under*-valued, *under*-cooked.

With-.—This denotes "back," "against"; as *with*-stand, *with*-hold, *with*-draw. ("Drawing-room" means "with-drawing-room.")

(*b*) *Inseparable; i.e.* not used as separate words:—

A- (*on, in*): *a*-bed, *a*-shore, *a*-jar, *a*-stir, *a*-sleep, etc.
A- (*of, from*): *a*-down (off a down or hill), *a*-fresh, *a*-kin, *a*-new.
A- (Intensive): *a*-rise, *a*-waken, *a*(f)-fright, *a*(c)-cursed.
Al- (*all*): *al*-one, *l*-one, *al*-most, *al*-ready, *al*-together.
Be- (*by*): (1) Transitive force; as *be*-calm. (2) Intensive force; as *be*-smear. (3) Forming adverbs or prepositions; as *be*-sides, *be*-fore. (4) Privative force in *be*-head.
For- (not the prep. "for"): (1) Intensive; as *for*-bear, *for*-lorn. (2) Privative; as *for*-bid, *for*-get, *for*-swear, *fore*-go (a bad spelling for *for*-go). The prefix *fore* is quite distinct from *for*.
Gain (A.S. *gegn*, against): *gain*-say, *gain*-strive (out of use).
N- (Indef. article "a," the *n* being wrongly detached): *n*-ewt (for *an ewt*), *n*-ugget (for *an ingot*), *n*-ickname (for *an eke-name*).
N- (Negative prefix): *n*-or, *n*-either, *n*-ay.
Mis- (*miss*): *mis*-take, *mis*-hap, *mis*-deed, *mis*-trust.
Twi- (A.S. *twi*, double): *twi*-light, *twi*-n, *twi*-ce, *twi*-st.
Un- (A.S. *un-*): (1) Negative: *un*-wise. (2) Reversal: *un*-twist. (In "*un*-loose" the *un-* is merely Intensive.) (3) Up to: *un*-to.

250. Romanic Prefixes.—The following are of frequent occurrence:—

A-, ab-, abs- (*from*): *a*-vert, *ab*-use, *ab*-normal, *abs*-tain.
Ad- (*to*): *ad*-vice, *ab*-breviate, *ac*-cent, *af*-fable, *ag*-gressor, *al*-lude, *an*-nex, *ap*-pear, *ar*-rears, *as*-sert, *at*-tain.
Ambi- (*on both sides, around*): *amb*-iguous, *amb*-ition.
Ante-, anti-, ant- (*before*): *ante*-cedent, *anti*-cipate, *ant*-ique.
Bene- (*well*): *bene*-fit, *bene*-volent, *ben*-ison.
Bis-, bi-, bin- (*twice*): *bis*-cuit, *bi*-ped, *bi*-cycle, *bin*-ocular.
Circum-, circu- (*around*): *circum*-stance, *circu*-it, *circum*-ference.
Cis- (*on this side*): *cis*-Alpine, on this side of the Alps.
Con- (*with*), **coun-** (Fr.): *con*-tend, *col*-lege, *com*-pete, *cor*-rect, *coun*-sel, *con*-temporary.
Contra- (*against*), **counter** (Fr.): *contra*-dict, *contra*-st, *counter*-act.
De- (*down, from, astray*): *de*-grade, *de*-part, *de*-viate.
,, (Reversal): merit, *de*-merit; *en*-camp, *de*-camp.
,, (Intensive): *de*-liver, *de*-clare, *de*-file, *de*-fraud.
Dis-, di- (*asunder*): *dis*-tract, *dis*-miss, *dis*-member, *di*-vulge.
,, (Intensive): *dis*-sever, *dis*-annul, *di*-minish.
,, (Reversal): en-chant, *dis*-enchant; illusion, *dis*-illusion.
,, (Negative): ease, *dis*-ease; honour, *dis*-honour; *dif*-ficult.
Ex-, e-, extra- (*out*): *ex*-ample, *e*-lapse, *extra*-vagant.
,, (*loss of office*): *ex*-king, *ex*-empress.
In-, en-, em- (*in*): *in*-ject, *im*-pute, *ir*-ritate, *en*-close, *em*-ploy.
In- (*not*): *in*-firm, *il*-literate, *im*-pious, *ir*-regular, *i*-gnorance.
Inter-, enter- (*among*): *inter*-est, *intel*-lect, *enter*-prise.
Intro-, intra- (*within*): *intro*-duce, *intra*-tropical, *intr*-insic.
Male-, mal- (*badly*): *male*-volent, *male*-factor, *mal*-ady.
Mis- (Lat. *minus*, badly): *mis*-chance, *mis*-chief, *mis*-nomer.
Non-, ne-, neg- (*not*): *non*-sense, *ne*-uter, *neg*-lect.

Ob- (*against*): *ob*-ject, *oc*-cur, *of*-fer, *op*-press, *os*-tensible, *o*-mit.
Pen- (Latin, *pæne, almost*): *pen*-insula, *pen*-ultimate.
Per- (*through*): *per*-form, *per*-haps, *pel*-lucid.
„ (*wrong direction*): *per*-vert, *per*-jury, *per*-fidy, *per*-ish.
Post- (*after*): *post*-script, *post*-pone, *post*-ern.
Pre- (Latin *præ, in front, before*): *pre*-occupy, *pre*-tend, *pre*-dict.
Preter- (Latin, *præter, beyond*): *preter*-natural, *preter*-ite.
Pro-, por-, pur- (Latin, *pro, for, before*): *pro*-fess, *pour*-tray, *por*-trait, *pur*-pose.
Re-, red- (*back*): *re*-fer, *re*-new, *red*-eem, *red*-undant.
Retro- (*backwards*): *retro*-cession, *retro*-grade.
Se-, sed- (*apart*): *se*-cret, *se*-cure, *se*-parate, *sed*-ition.
Semi-, demi- (*half*): *semi*-circle, *demi*-god.
Sub- (*under*): *sub*-ject, *suc*-cour, *suf*-fice, *sug*-gest, *sum*-mon, *sup*-pose, *sur*-render, *sus*-pend, *sub*-marine, ("under the sea").
„ (*slightly*): *sub*-acid, *sub*-tropical.
„ (*of lower rank*): *sub*-judge, *sub*-committee, *sub*-division.
Subter- (*under, secretly*): *subter*-fuge.
Super-, sur- (*above*): *super*-fluous, *sur*-face, *sur*-vive.
Trans-, tra- (*across*): *trans*-mit, *trans*-gress, *tra*-duce, *tra*-ffic.
Tri-, tre- (*three, thrice*): *tri*-angle, *tri*-nity, *tri*-vial, *tre*-ble.
Ultra- (*beyond, excess*): *ultra*-marine, *ultra*-radical.
Vice-, vis- (*instead of*): *vice*-roy, *vis*-count.

251. Greek Prefixes ;—

Amphi- (*on both sides*): *amphi*-bious, *amphi*-theatre.
An-, a- (*not*): *an*-archy, *an*-ecdote, *a*-pathy, *a*-theism.
Ana- (*again, back*): *ana*-logy, *ana*-lyse, *ana*-tomy.
Anti-, ant- (*against*): *anti*-podes, *anti*-pathy, *ant*-agonist.
Apo-, aph- (*from*): *apo*-logy, *apo*-state, *apo*-stle, *aph*-orism.
Archi-, arch- (*chief*): *archi*-tect, *arch*-bishop.
Auto- (*self*): *auto*-car, *auto*-graph, *auth*-entic.
Cata-, cath- (*down*): *cata*-ract, *cath*-edral, *cat*-echism.
Dia- (*through*): *dia*-logue, *dia*-meter, *dia*-gnosis.
Dis-, di- (*in two*): *dis*-syllable, *di*-phthong, *di*-lemma.
Dys- (*ill, badly*): *dys*-entery, *dys*-pepsia.
Ek-, ex- (*out*): *ec*-stasy, *ex*-odus.
En- (*in*): *en*-thusiasm, *em*-phasis, *el*-lipsis.
Eu-, ev- (*well*): *eu*-phony, *eu*-logy, *ev*-angelist.
Epi-, ep-, eph- (*on*): *epi*-taph, *ep*-och, *eph*-emeral, *ep*-isode.
Hemi- (*half*): *hemi*-sphere, *hemi*-stich.
Hyper- (*above, beyond*): *hyper*-critical, *hyper*-bole.
Hypo-, hyph- (*under*): *hypo*-crite, *hypo*-thesis, *hyph*-en.
Meta-, meth-, met- (*after*): *meta*-phor, *meth*-od, *met*-eor.
Mono-, mon- (*single*): *mono*-poly, *mon*-arch, *mon*-k.
Pan-, panto- (*all*): *pan*-orama, *panto*-mime.
Para-, par- (*beside*): *para*-ble, *para*-graph, *par*-allel.
Peri- (*around*): *peri*-od, *peri*-phrasis, *peri*-phery.
Pro- (*before*): *pro*-gramme, *pro*-phet, *pro*-blem.
Syn- (*with*): *syn*-od, *syl*-lable, *sym*-bol, *sym*-pathy, *sy*-stem.
Tri- (*thrice*): *tri*-pod, *tri*-syllable.

252. *Lat. and Gr. equivalent Prefixes*, spelt nearly alike :—

Latin.	*Greek.*	*Meaning.*
Ambi-, amb-iguous	**Amphi-**, amphi-bious	On both sides
Ab-, ab-solute	**Apo-**, apo-logy	From
Ex-amine	**Ec-**, ec-stasy	Out of
In-, in-spection	**En-**, **Em-**, em-phasis	Into, in
Semi-, **demi-**, demi-god	**Hemi-**, hemi-sphere	Half
Super-, super-vise	**Hyper-**, hyper-bole	Above
Sub-, sub-stantive	**Hypo-**, hypo-thesis	Under
Pro-, pro-portion	**Pro**, pro-phet	Before or for
Tri-, tri-angle	**Tri-**, tri-pod	Thrice

253. General results, regarding the uses of Prefixes :—

(*a*) Prefixes denoting the **undoing** of something done :—

Teutonic :—
un- : *un*-bolt, *un*-tie, *un*-lock, *un*-fold.

Romanic :—
dis- : *dis*-mount, *dis*-arm, *dis*-appear, *dis*-close, *dis*-abuse.
de- : *de*-odorise, *de*-plete, *de*-camp, *de*-throne.

(*b*) Prefixes denoting a **Negative,** with one Suffix :—

Teutonic :—
for- : *for*-bid.
un- : *un*-happy, *un*-safe, *un*-ready, *un*-certain.
-less : hap-*less*, law-*less*, hope-*less*, spot-*less*.
n- : *n*-one, *n*-ever, *n*-or, *n*-either.

Romanic :—
ne-, **neg-**, **non-** : *ne*-uter, *neg*-lect, *non*-sense.
dis-, **di-** : *dis*-contented, *dif*-ficult, *dif*-fident, *dis*-honour.
in- : *in*-human, *ir*-rational, *im*-moral, *ig*-noble, *il*-legible.
ab- : *ab*-normal.

Greek :—
a-, **an-** : *a*-pathy, *an*-archy.

(*c*) Prefixes indicating something **good** :—

Teutonic :—
well- : *wel*-fare, *wel*-come, *well*-bred.

Romanic :—
bene- : *bene*-volent, *bene*-fit, *ben*-ignant, *ben*-ison.

Greek :—
eu-, **ev-** : *eu*-phony, *ev*-angelist.

(*d*) Prefixes indicating something **bad** :—

Teutonic :—
mis- (from *miss*) : *mis*-deed, *mis*-take, *mis*-hap.

Romanic :—
mis- (from *minus*) : *mis*-carry, *mis*-use, *mis*-fortune.
male-, **mal-** : *male*-factor, *mal*-ignant, *mal*-treat.

Greek :—
dys- : *dys*-entery, *dys*-pepsia.

I. *Exercise on Word-Building.*

(*a*) 1. Supply the feminine forms of *sultan, hero, testator, shepherd, spinner, fox.* 2. Break up *mistrustfully, unwholesomeness* into syllables, and show how each syllable contributes to the meaning of the words. 3. What are the suffixes in the following words:—*farthing, foremost, kingdom, fatten, English, thirsty.* 4. Reverse the meaning of each of the following words by adding a prefix:—*happy, possible, rational, contented, valid, noble, sense.* 5. Give four examples of diminutive forms in English nouns. 6. Form adjectives from *disaster, two, wheat,* and adverbs from *gay, holy, other, south, week.* 7. How are verbs formed (*a*) from nouns; (*b*) from adjectives; (*c*) from other verbs. Give two examples of each, and show the exact force of the change of the word. 8. By the use of a suffix, change each of the following nouns into an adjective, and give the force of each suffix:—*sister, fame, quarrel, slave, silver.* 9. What is meant by saying that the word *bicycle* is a hybrid? Write words (one in each case) containing the following prefixes and suffixes:—*ante-, anti-, auto-, vice-, -ess, -ness, -ry, -kin.* (*Oxford and Cambridge, Junior and Senior.*)

(*b*) 1. How are Compound verbs formed? Write down ten Compound verbs with different prefixes, giving the meaning of these. 2. Give the diminutive forms of *stream, hill, duck, lass*; and the meaning of the prefix in each of the following words:—*mischance, importunate, retrospect, subterfuge, constant.* 3. Why is *co*-temporary an incorrect form? What different forms do *cum, in, ad, inter, per* assume in composition? 4. Write down suffixes employed to denote (1) the agent, (2) diminution, (3) gender. 5. Give with examples three affixes (suffixes) of Latin origin, by which Abstract nouns in English are formed. 6. Give the exact force of the following prefixes and affixes (suffixes):—man*hood*, spin*ster*, tire*some*, spark*le*; *mis*give, *for*get, *be*troth, *in*nocent. 7. What is the force of the prefixes in the words *impossible, except.* From what languages are they respectively taken? Write down three other examples of the use of each of these prefixes. 8. Explain the meaning of the following prefixes, and write words formed by means of them:—*un-, ante-, bi-, circum-, inter-.* 9. Give (i.) three prefixes of Latin origin, and (ii.) three noun suffixes; and by examples show what effect they have upon words in which they are introduced. (*Preceptors', Second and Third Classes.*)

(*c*) 1. Give the different ways of forming adverbs in English. 2. Explain the force of the syllables in *italics* in the following words:—spin*ster*, head*long*, twent*y*, *im*proper, hill*ock*, eld*est*, king*dom*, *be*sprinkle. 3. In the following words what is the force of the parts printed in *italics*?—*a*round, numer*ous*, *a*loud, gover*nesses*, *re*cite, Eng*lish*, Itali*an*. 4. Mention *two* ways in which *abstract* nouns can be formed from *common* nouns, and give *two* examples of each. 5. What is meant by *diminutives* and *augmentatives.* Illustrate by examples the suffixes used in the formation of such words. 6. What are *compound* adjectives? Give *three* examples. 7. Give the meanings of the following Latin Prefixes, and illustrate each by *two* English words:—*ab-, bis-, con-, non-, pro-, se-.* 8. Give the meanings of the following *prefixes*, and *two* instances of the use of each:—*in-, per-, dis-, re-.* (*Preceptors', Second and Third Classes.*)

(*d*) 1. Say what you know about the Feminine endings in *vixen, spinster, duchess, baxter, margravine, infanta,* and *testatrix.* 2. Mention six English Inseparable prefixes; and give two examples of words formed with each of them. 3. What is the force of the prefix *un*dismayed, *mis*lay, *be*hind, *for*give, *with*stand, *pre*fix, *extra*vagant, *post*pone, *super*scription, *an*archy, *epi*taph, *peri*meter? 4. Give the meaning of the following prefixes (with *two* examples in each case), and state which are English (Teutonic) and which Latin:—*be-*, *con-*, *for-*, *gain-*, *in-*, *pro-*, *re-*, *with-*. 5. Give the derivation and meaning of each of the following suffixes, with two examples of each:—*-ard* or *-art*, *-fy*, *-kin*, *-ock*, *-ous*, *-some* *-ster*, *-tude*. 6. Give the meaning and function of the following suffixes; and state whether they are added to nouns, or verbs, or adjectives:—*-ing*, *-lock*, *-m*, *-red*, *-ther*, *-s*, *-ward*. 7. Give examples of the following suffixes, and state their derivation and their meaning:—*-ster*, *-kin*, *-ly*, *-tude*, *-let*, *-ous*, *-fy*, *-ise*. 8. Explain with examples the force of the following prefixes and suffixes:—*be-*, *for-*, *with-*, *cata-*, *intro-*, *-der*, *-nd*, *-ship*, *-eer*, *-le*, *-ment*. 9. Give the origin and meaning of the prefix in each of the following words:—*ad*vent, *contra*dict, *for*lorn, *hyper*critical, *inter*pose, *mis*take, *re*open, *trans*marine, *un*kind, *with*stand. 10. Give the meaning and derivation of the suffixes (distinctly specifying these) of the following words:—*wisdom*, *bounty*, *slavish*, *clayey*, *worship*, *blackness*, *longitude*, *sepulchre*, *strengthen*, *gamble*. 11. Explain the force of the termination in any five of the following:—*oxen*, *vixen*, *maiden*, *holden*, *wooden*, *open*, *often*. 12. With what different suffixes, and derived from what sources, do we form Abstract nouns? Give one or two examples of each. 13. Point out the force of the prefix in each of the following, explaining the words themselves:—*hypercritical*, *antechamber*, *cisalpine*, *synchronous*, *percolate*, *cataract*. (*Preceptors'*, *First Class*.)

II. *Write short sentences illustrating the differences of meaning in each of the following pairs of Abstract nouns formed with different suffixes:—*

(*a*) *Teutonic suffixes:—*

Dearth, dearness.
Drought, dryness.
Hardness, hardihood.
Sleight, slyness.
Sloth, slowness.
Truth, trueness (truism, *Gr.*).
Witness, wisdom.

(*b*) *Romanic suffixes:—*

Acquitt-ance, acquitt-al.
Appar-it-ion, appear-ance.
Benefact-ion, benefic-ence.
Committ-al, commiss-ion.
Compos-ure, compos-it-ion.
Content-ment, content-ion.
Continu-ance, continu-at-ion.
Creat-ure, creat-ion.
Degener-at-ion, degener-ac-y.
Depart-ment, depart-ure.
Destin-y, destin-at-ion.
Dispos-al, dispos-it-ion.
Eject-ment, eject-ion.
Expos-ure, expos-it-ion.
Fixt-ure, fix-ity.
Fract-ure, fract-ion, frag-ment.
Impost-ure, impos-it-ion.
Impress-ment, impress-ion.
Intim-at-ion, intim-ac-y.
Luxur-y, luxur-i-ance.
Observ-ance, observ-at-ion.
Post-ure, posit-ion.
Propos-al, propos-it-ion.
Protest-er, protest-ant.
Serv-i-tude, serv-ice.
Signific-ance, signific-at-ion.
Stat-ure, stat-ion.
Tempera-ment, tempera-ture.
Vac-ancy, vac-at-ion.

(c) *Romanic and Teutonic suffixes* :—

Appropriate-ness, appropriat-ion.
Apt-ness, apt-i-tude.
Close-ness, clos-ure.
Complete-ness, complet-ion.
Direct-ion, direct-ness.
Distinct-ness, distinct-ion.
Exact-ness, exact-ion.
False-hood, fals-ity, false-ness.
Human-ity, humane-ness.
Ingenu-ity, ingenu-ous-ness.
Just-ness, just-ice.
Lax-ity, lax-ness.
Pall-or, pale-ness.
Proced-ure, proceed-ing.
Quiet-ude, quiet-ness.
Remiss-ness, remiss-ion.
Secure-ness, secur-ity.
Till-age, til-th.

(d) *Greek and Romanic suffixes* :—

Barbar-ism, barbar-ity.
Commun-ism, commun-ity.
Fatal-ism, fatal-ity.
Formal-ism, formal-ity.
Vulgar-ism, vulgar-ity.

(e) *Write a sentence showing the difference of meaning, if any, in each word of each of the following pairs of adjectives* :—

Beneficial, beneficent.
Ceremonious, ceremonial.
Childlike, childish.
Comic, comical.
Comprehensive, comprehensible.
Congenial, congenital.
Contemptible, contemptuous.
Continual, continuous.
Corporate, corporal.
Credible, creditable.
Definite, definitive.
Dramatic, dramatical.
Elemental, elementary.
Exceptional, exceptionable.
Expedient, expeditious.
Godlike, godly.
Illusive, illusory.
Imaginary, imaginative.
Imperial, imperious.
Industrial, industrious.
Ingenious, ingenuous.
Innocent, innocuous.
Judicial, judicious.
Luxurious, luxuriant.
Masterly, masterful.
Momentary, momentous.
Notable, notorious.
Official, officious.
Ordinal, ordinary.
Permissive, permissible.
Politic, political.
Popular, populous.
Respective, respectful.
Reverend, reverent.
Sanatory, sanitary.
Sensitive, sensible.
Sensual, sensuous.
Silvery, silvern.
Spirituous, spiritual.
Temporal, temporary.
Tragic, tragical,
Transitory, transitional.
Verbal, verbose.
Virtual, virtuous.

III. *Substitute a single word for the words italicised* :—

1. This writing is *such as cannot be read.*
2. The plan you mention *cannot be put into practice.*
3. He is *one who cannot according to the rules be elected.*
4. That herb is *fit to be eaten.*
5. The colour is *beyond my perception.*
6. You are *liable to be called to account* for your actions.
7. The plan you propose is *open to objections.*
8. That word is *no longer in use.*
9. This is a bird *of passage.*
10. Your office is *one for which no salary is paid.*

11. His motive was merely *to get some money.*
12. His position was *beyond all hope of improvement.*
13. His manners are *more like those of a woman than of a man.*
14. He is *one who takes no trouble* about his work.
15. His style is *too full of words.*
16. He is *inclined to find fault.*
17. A wolf is an animal *that cannot be tamed.*
18. That problem is *one which is never likely to be solved.*
19. His character *has an evil reputation.*
20. The use of opium is *likely to do much injury.*
21. That impression is *too vivid ever to be effaced.*
22. He is *unable to pay his debts.*
23. This was *the original pattern or model of the work.*
24. You will never find *a remedy for all diseases.*
25. Some animals are *without any backbone.*
26. *A remedy to counteract the effects of poison* is needed.
27. Both fell *at the same moment.*

IV. *To each word given below add some Abstract suffix :—*

Serve, coward, right, grand, err, miser, apt, victor, acrid, just, merchant, trick, pass, seize, try, judge, compel, admit, patron, repent, regent, bankrupt, accurate, poor, rely, captive, fragile, facile, felon, sole, assist, scarce, secret, defy, father, real.

V. *To each word given below add some Diminutive suffix :—*

Animal, code, pouch, brook, poet, cigar, vase, lance, globe, mode, pill, bill, car, cellar, statue, part, song, sign, table, home, wagon, hump, park, maid, cut, lamb, hill, change, bird, lad, scythe, corn.

VI. *Distinguish the senses of* "**age**" *in the following :—*

Herbage, hermitage, courage, postage, breakage, personage.

VII. *Describe the uses of* "**en**" *in the following :—*

Maiden, flaxen, vixen, fatten, drunken, kitten, alien, rotten, golden, oxen, haven.

VIII. *Explain the senses of* "**sub-**" *and* "**re**" *in the following :—*

(*a*) Sub-terranean, sub-montane ; (*b*) sub-acid, sub-tropical ; (*c*) sub-judge, sub-deputy ; (*d*) remark, re-mark.

IX. *Show the differences of meaning implied in the following words by the prefix* "**non-**" *and the prefix* "**in**" *or* "**un-**" :—

(*a*) Non-active, inactive ; (*b*) non-effective, ineffective ; (*c*) non-Christian, unchristian ; (*d*) non-professional, unprofessional.

X. *Separate the stem from the affixes (prefixes or suffixes) of the following words, and the affixes from each other :—*

Undenominationalism, valetudinarian, unsophisticated, renegade, instrumentality, disproportionate, talkativeness, protestantism, absenteeism, accidentally, miscreant, indentures, intoxicate, interest, intellectual, demonetise, telephone, introspection, captivate, insignificant, homogeneous, inaccessible, procedure, likelihood.

PART II.—STUDIES AND EXERCISES SUBSIDIARY TO COMPOSITION.

CHAPTER XVI.—STOPS AND OTHER MARKS USED IN COMPOSITION.

254. Punctuation divides one sentence or one part of a sentence from another, to help the reader's eye. Much confusion is caused by using wrong stops, or by putting them in wrong places, or by leaving them out where they are wanted, or by putting them in where they are not wanted. Punctuation is therefore an important element in written composition.

To take a very simple example, there is a vast difference in meaning between the two following sentences:—

May I be promoted?
May I be promoted!

And this difference turns, not upon the grammatical construction, nor upon the order of the words, nor (if the sentences are read aloud) upon the modulation of the voice, but solely on the punctuation.

255. The names and forms of the different points, stops, or marks are the following:—

Comma, indicated by	,	Note of exclamation, indicated by	!
Semicolon, indicated by	;	Brackets, indicated by	( ) or [ ]
Colon, indicated by	:	Dash, indicated by	—
Full stop or period, indicated by	.	Hyphen, indicated by	-
Note of interrogation, indicated by	?	Inverted commas, indicated by	" "
Apostrophe, indicated by	'		

The Comma.

256. The shortest pause in the sense or voice is represented by a comma. Its chief uses in a **simple** sentence are the following:—

(*a*) Between nouns or pronouns in apposition; as—

Alexander, the *son* of Philip, *king* of Macedon.

(*b*) Between words of the same Part of Speech:—

A dull, heavy sound was heard. (*Adjectives.*)
Greece, Italy, and Spain are peninsulas of Europe. (*Nouns.*)
We should live soberly, prudently, and industriously. (*Adverbs.*)
Steam propels, elevates, saws, prints, threshes, etc. (*Verbs.*)

(*c*) After the Nominative of address:—

Friends, Romans, countrymen, lend me your ears.

(*d*) Before and after an absolute construction, or before and after words interpolated in the middle of a quotation:—

The sun having set, we all went home.
"Leave the room," said he, "and do not come back."

(*e*) When words of the same class or rank go together in pairs, each pair is separated by a comma:—

By night or by day, at home or abroad, asleep or awake, he is a constant source of anxiety to his parents.

(*f*) After an adverbial phrase at the commencement of a sentence. (Here, however, the use of the comma is optional.)

In fact, his poetry is no better than prose.

(*g*) Before and after a participial phrase, provided that the said phrase might be expanded into a sentence, and that the participle is not used in a merely qualifying sense:—

Cæsar, having defeated the Gauls, led his army into Britain. (Here "having defeated" means "after he had defeated.")
Convinced of the accuracy of his facts, he stuck to his opinion. (Here "convinced" means "because he was convinced.")

But when the participle merely qualifies the noun as an adjective would do, no comma need be used:—

A dog lying asleep on a public road is likely to be run over.
A man convinced against his will is of the same opinion still.

(*h*) Explanatory phrases are separated by commas:—

The field was oblong, 60 yards in length, 40 in breadth.

(*i*) Before and after a Qualifying Infinitive (§ 126), when this is used in an explanatory or parenthetical sense:—

I am, to tell you the truth, thoroughly sick of work.
To sum up, the man was accused of three offences.

(*j*) To introduce the words actually or apparently used by a speaker. The sentence so quoted must begin with a capital :—

What I say unto you, I say unto all, Watch.—*New Testament.*
The question is, What shall we do with it?

(*k*) To mark the omission and save the repetition of a verb :—

My regiment is bound for India ; yours, for Gibraltar.

257. (*a*) In a **compound** sentence the co-ordinate clauses, when expressed at full length, are separated by a comma :—

His vanity is greater than his ignorance, and what he lacks in knowledge is supplied by impudence.

But when the two sentences are not expressed at full length and have the same Subject, the comma is not used :—

I made haste and caught him.
I took up a stone and threw it at the mad dog.

(*b*) If no conjunction is used between Co-ordinate clauses, these must be separated either (1) by a comma, when they are short, or (2) by a semicolon, when they are long :—

(1) Steam propels, elevates, lowers, pumps, drains, pulls, etc.
(2) Between fame and true honour there is much difference : the former is a blind applause ; the latter is an internal and more silent homage.

258. In **complex** sentences the following are the main rules regarding the use of commas :—

(*a*) A Noun-clause is not separated by a comma from the word to which it stands in grammatical relation :—

It is generally allowed that the art of teaching is difficult.
No one knows when he will come.
His pardon depends upon whether he will confess his fault or not.

But two or more Noun-clauses must be separated by commas, when they stand in the same relation to the same word :—

No one knows when he will come, or whether he will come at all, or whether he is even alive.
Who he was, or why he came, or what he intends to do, will all be found out in time.

(*b*) An Adjective-clause is not separated from its noun or pronoun, unless it is rather lengthy :—

The man *we saw* yesterday has come again to-day.
The man, *who reflects carefully before acting*, is more likely to be successful than one, *who thoughtlessly takes a leap in the dark.*

(*c*) An Adverb-clause is separated from the Principal clause :—

He will succeed, because he works hard.
I will gladly do this, if I am allowed.

The comma is never omitted, unless the Adverb-clause is either very short or is expressed elliptically :—

He likes you better than me.
Send me word before you start.

Insert commas, where necessary, in the following sentences :—

The triple alliance consists of Germany Austria and Italy. My son so far from being blamed for his conduct was commended and even rewarded. The roof of the house having caught fire the inmates fled and remained outside the house until the fire was put out. Towns villages and hamlets were all alike attacked with the epidemic of cholera. I shall be happy to make the attempt that you speak of if I am permitted. From morning till noon from noon to evening from evening to midnight this same grief never leaves him. Early this morning when we had just left the house we met the man that we had been looking for. He found as I expected he would that the house he had lately purchased was a bad one. What was the cause of so much grief to him was never known to any of us. I hope my friend that you will come and spend at least a week with us. He has now grown so old that he spends most of his time in sleeping taking his food or sitting in an easy chair. I remain my dear sir yours faithfully William Matthews. I shall not leave home for business unless you set the example. Example as the proverb says is the sincerest form of precept. To tell you the plain truth I should be glad to retire from business altogether considering that I am now past sixty years of age and have a son to succeed me. The boatman shouted to a man on shore throw out the rope. A snake sleeping in the grass will bite if any one treads upon it. The prisoner having been convicted of the crime of which he was accused must make up his mind to suffer the penalty. The building is a noble structure of red brick and comprises a reading-room a library a room for writing letters and a room for refreshments. It is quite true that this fine building was erected by private subscriptions. In fact of all that was subscribed L. gave the largest amount in cash but M. was not less liberal because he gave the land on which the building was erected. A dog barking at nothing is a nuisance.

The Semicolon.

259. A **Semicolon** indicates a longer pause than one indicated by a comma. Its chief uses are as follows :—

(*a*) To separate *longer* Co-ordinate clauses (see § 257, *b*). A longer pause gives greater emphasis to each clause in the series, as it gives the mind more time to dwell on each of them separately :—

Honesty of purpose in worldly affairs has many advantages over deceit. It is a safer way of dealing with men ; it is an easier mode of despatching business ; it inspires men with greater confidence ; it acquires more and more confidence in itself, while deceit becomes more and more diffident.

(*b*) To divide clauses, which are connected by some Alternative or some Illative conjunction. (Here a greater pause is needed, because the mind requires a little more time to perceive the alternative or the inference.)

I met him as he was leaving his house; *otherwise* I should not have known where he lived.

I refused to do what he asked me to do; *for* I was convinced that he had been misinformed of the facts.

The Colon.

260. **Colon**: The main uses of the colon are the following:—

(*a*) To introduce a sentence in continuation or in explanation or in confirmation of a previous one:—

Strive above all things, in whatever station of life you may be, to preserve health: there is no happiness in life without it.

(*b*) To introduce a quotation: usually followed by a dash:—

Then Peter stood forth and said:—"Of a truth I perceive that God is no respecter of persons," etc.

(*c*) To introduce or to sum up a series of Co-ordinate clauses. Here, too, the colon is followed by a dash:—

You must now hear what I have to say about the uses of iron:—we sleep on iron; we travel on iron; we float on iron; we plough the fields with iron; we shoot with iron; we chop down trees with iron:—in fact, there is scarcely anything that we can do without the help of this wonderful metal.

(*d*) To introduce an enumeration of particulars:—

Send me the following articles:—a pen, a brush, a pencil, a portfolio, and some fine-pointed nibs.

Insert commas, colons, or semicolons, where necessary, in the following sentences:—

1. According to an old belief if a sick man sneezes it is a sure sign of recovery but when a man is going on a journey or about to commence some business should any one about him sneeze the sneeze indicates that the object in which he is interested will not be accomplished.

2. In Rome the army was the nation no citizen could take office unless he had served in ten campaigns.

3. The drill was unremitting at all times so long as a man continued to be a soldier when the troops were in winter quarters sheds were erected in which the soldiers fenced with swords buttoned at the points or hurled javelins also buttoned at the points at one another.

4. The Carthaginian army was composed entirely of mercenary troops Africa Spain and Gaul were their recruiting grounds and these countries were an inexhaustible treasury of warriors as long as the money which the recruits received as pay did not run short.

The Full Stop or Period.

261. The **Full Stop** or **Period** indicates the close of a complete sentence. The sentence following must invariably be commenced with a capital letter. See § 271 (1).

The full stop is also used after abbreviations; as, A.D. (for Anno Domini); B.L. (for Bachelor of Law); Bart. (for Baronet); the Hon. (for the Honourable).

But if the last letter is given, the stop is sometimes not used; as, Dr Jones, Mr Clark, Mrs Jones, Messrs Scott and Sons.

Inverted Commas.

262. **Inverted Commas** are used for indicating the beginning and end of a quotation, or of the actual words used by a speaker:—

The councillors stood up, and with one voice exclaimed:—"Death before dishonour."
"Wine is a mocker," said the wise king.

To introduce a quotation within a quotation, a single comma is used at either end:—

"What did they say to you?" inquired the man.
"They gave me," he answered, "strict orders, 'That gate is not to be opened under any circumstances whatever.'"

Insert any stops or marks needed in the following:—

1. While I was still wondering at my sudden deliverance a man came suddenly forward and said my good sir there is nothing to be surprised at I was sent here to find you and rescue you from these robbers well I have succeeded in finding you and so I have accomplished what I was sent for.

2. Whenever you hesitate about beginning to do something which must be done eventually remember the maxim a thing begun is half done.

Note of Exclamation.

263. A **Note of Exclamation** is used after words or sentences which express emotion:—

How are the mighty fallen in the midst of the battle! I am distressed for thee, my brother Jonathan!
"Land ahead!" shouted the delighted crew.

The Apostrophe.

264. The **Apostrophe** (') is inserted to show that some letter or letters have been omitted:—

The Hon'ble (for *Honourable*); e'en (for *even*); 'tis (for *it is*); ta'en (for *taken*); don't (for *do not*); shan't (for *shall not*); won't (for *will not*); tho' (for *though*); an ox's head (for *oxes head*); and all other instances of the Possessive case.

Note of Interrogation.

265. A **Note of Interrogation** is used after sentences which ask questions. The sentence following must be commenced with a capital :—

Where was he born? When did he die?

Insert the proper stops and capitals, where necessary, in the following sentences :—

Whats the matter Thomas ist that old pain of yours again no its not that at all said he but something a good deal better would you believe it my poor old uncle is dead and he has left me five thousand pounds that was very good of him she replied but its come too late why he inquired because she answered you are now old and broken in health what a pity it is that he did not die twenty years ago or give you the money while he was still alive.

Dashes.

266. The **Dash** has five main uses :—

(*a*) To mark a break or abrupt turn in a sentence :—

Here lies the great—false marble where?
Nothing but sordid dust lies here.

(*b*) To mark words in apposition or in explanation :—

They plucked the seated hills with all their loads—
Rocks, waters, woods—and by the shaggy tops
Uplifting bore them in their hands.—*Paradise Lost.*

(*c*) To insert a parenthesis. Here *two* dashes are required.

At the age of ten—such is the power of genius—he could read Greek with facility.

(*d*) To resume a scattered subject :—

Health, friends, position,—all are gone.

(*e*) To indicate a hesitating or faltering speech :—

I—er—I—that is,—I don't care.

Brackets.

267. **Brackets** are used like a couple of dashes in (*c*), as just explained, for inserting a parenthesis, which may be either a sentence, or a phrase, or a word. There is no difference in use between [ ] and ( ), § 255.

At the age of ten (such is the power of genius) he could read Greek.
I gave all I had (twopence) to that noble cause.

The Hyphen.

268. A **Hyphen** is used for joining the parts of a compound word; as "bathing-place." It is a shorter line than the Dash.

A hyphen is also used to indicate syllabic division (see § 247); as "for-mer-ly."

Insert a dash, a hyphen, or brackets, wherever necessary, in the following sentences, and add any other appropriate stops :—

England and Russia the two greatest empires on the face of the earth have no real cause for enmity. I could tell you all about my but perhaps you have heard enough by this time. My dog such is the power of jealousy attacked its rival whenever they met. This is very uphill work. If you read without spectacles and I believe you can be so good as to read out to me the contents of this letter. When I took my degree and this was twelve years ago I had good prospects before me. I will never but I need not finish my sentence for you know already what I was going to say.

Diæresis.

269. Diæresis (separation) consists of two dots placed over the second of two vowels, to show that the two vowels are to be sounded separately :—

Coöperation = co-operation.

Asterisks.

270. Asterisks denote that some words or clauses have been omitted :—

The Jews * * * * * had to pay heavy taxes to the Norman kings.

When to use Capital Letters.

271. Capitals are used as follows :—

(1) With the first letter of a sentence following a full stop :—

She adopted the boy and gave him an Egyptian name. He was educated as a priest and became a member of the University of Heliopolis.—READE, *Martyrdom of Man*, p. 185.

(2) With the first letter of a sentence following a note of interrogation :—

Who could disprove the evidence of a tradition? He made no secret of his design ; it was to drive the Phœnician strangers out of Africa.—READE.

(3) With the first letter of proper names, and with that of all adjectives derived from proper names :—

England, English. Japan, Japanese. Milton, Miltonic.

Note.—When an adjective formed from a proper name has come into such general use that no one thinks of its origin, it is written without a capital :—as a *hansom* cab.

(4) With the first letter of a common or abstract noun, when the thing denoted by the noun is personified :—

Fair Science frowned not on his humble birth,
But Melancholy marked him for her own.—GRAY.

(5) With the first letter of the names of months, the days of a week, and the names of holidays, seasons, or festivals :—

He arrived on August 16th and left on the following Saturday. Good Friday. Christmas. Lent. A Bank Holiday.

(6) With the first letter of titles of honour or office, and in addressing any one as Mr. or Mrs. :—

The First Lord of the Treasury. The Commander-in-chief. The Prime Minister. The Colonial Secretary.

Similarly, when letters are used instead of whole words to represent titles, the letters are written with capitals :—

M.A. (for Master of Arts). M.D. (for Doctor of Medicine).

(7) With the first letter of a descriptive noun or adjective used as a kind of surname or additional name :—

Aristides the Just. Herod the Great. Charles the Fat. William the Conqueror. Edward the Confessor. Henry the Fifth. Edward the Seventh.

(8) With the first letter of the name of the Deity or any person of the Trinity, or of a pronoun that stands for any such name :—

Trust in Providence. In all thy ways acknowledge Him, and He will direct thy paths.

(9) With the pronoun "I" and with the interjections "O" or "Oh" and "Ah!"

(10) With the first letter of every line of poetry :—

Only the pure and virtuous soul
Like seasoned timber never gives ;
And though the whole world turn to coal,
Then chiefly lives.—HERBERT.

(11) With the first letter of a speech or sentence quoted in the Direct form :—

Another of the disciples said unto him, "Lord, let me first go and bury my father." But Jesus said unto him, "Follow me, and leave the dead to bury their dead."

(12) With the first letter of a technical term :—

Note.—When a technical term is first introduced and defined in a treatise, it is usual to print the first letter of every such term in a capital. As the work proceeds, the use of the capital may be continued or not at the option of the writer.

(13) With the first letters of titles of books, poems, chapters, and magazines, and of words expressing some great historical event :—

The Daily Telegraph. The Daily Express. The Ancient Mariner. The Norman Conquest. The Revival of Learning.

(14) In the "salutation" of a letter the words *sir* or *madam*, *lord* or *lady*, are capitalised, as in—

My dear Sir. Dear Madam. My Lord. My Lady.

When to Underline a Word.

272. Uses of Underlining or Italics.—When we draw a single line under a word or words in writing, this is intended to have the same effect on the eye and mind of the reader as that which a printer indicates by italics.

There are three uses of underlining or italics:—

(1) To give particular emphasis to some word or words:—

If we were reading such words aloud, we should lay stress on them with the voice, *i.e.* we should utter them more loudly, more distinctly, and more slowly. In reading a book out to an audience, or in conversation, it adds much to the effect to throw more stress of voice upon the more important words. But in written composition we should avoid the practice of frequent underlining, and rely more on the position of the words and the clearness of the language.

(2) To indicate the name of a book, of a part of a book, or of a newspaper:—

Have you seen the *Telegraph* office?
I am well acquainted with *The Ancient Mariner.*

If the words italicised above were not underlined in writing, the sense of both sentences would be entirely different from what it is.

(3) To indicate that the word or words used are foreign:—

I have studied this subject *ad nauseam.* (Latin.)
We shall meet him *en route.* (French.)

We must point out, however, that though it is a very common practice to use foreign words (especially French and Latin ones) in English, it is very much better to shun the use of such words altogether. It would be quite as easy to say: "I have studied this subject, till I am sick of it"; "We shall meet him on the way."

Exercises on §§ 256-272.

Remove redundancies and supply deficiencies of stops, wherever they may occur in the following sentences; correct errors, wherever you find any; and supply the necessary capitals:—

(*a*) *Preceptors' Third Class Examination.*

1. useful indeed said the man come you had pinched and ground me down for some years before that but i had served you faithfully up to

that time in spite of all your dogs usage had i ralph made no reply had i said the man again you had had your wages rejoined ralph and had done your work—June 1889.

2. at last calling serjeant thompson aside i asked him am i too old to be accepted in johns place why i dont know said he you are rather old to be sure but yet money may do much i put the money into thompsons hand and said jack you are free i will go in your stead—Xmas 1889.

3. it is not unlikely that your highness will one day command your governor to show you some of our productions to which he will answer for I am informed of his designs by asking your highness where are they and what is become of them and pretend it is a proof that there never were any because they are not then to be found not to be found who has mislaid them your highness will exclaim—Xmas 1895.

4. The pass of thermopylæ was favourable to the greeks for the persians could not avail themselves of their superior numbers xerxes sent messengers to leonidas king of sparta bidding him give up his arms he replied come and take them lands were then offered to the defenders of the pass on condition that they should become allies of the great king but the lacedæmonians answered it was their custom to win lands by valour not by treachery—June 1897.

5. You are mad said the curate starting up astonished is thy master such a wonderful hero as to fight a giant at two thousand leagues distance then they heard don quixote bawling out stay villain since i have thee here thy scimiter shall but little avail thee—Xmas 1897.

6. i opened the boxes and to andersons surprise i counted out gold coin to the amount of four hundred pounds not a bad legacy said mr wilson then you knew of this of course i answered i have known it some time ever since the attempt to rob her but what are these papers said the lawyer—June 1898.

7. the traveller made three quick steps towards the jail then turning short tell me said he has that unnatural captain sent you nothing to relieve your distress call him not unnatural replied the other gods blessing be upon him he sent me a great deal of money but i made a bad use of it—Xmas 1898.

8. miss matty could hardly drink for looking at her brother peter and as for eating that was out of the question i suppose hot climates age people quickly she said almost to herself when you left cranford you had not a grey hair in your head but how many years ago was that said mr peter smiling ah true yes i suppose you and i are getting old—Xmas 1894.

9. the man was a rough bearded old sea dog who had just burst in from the tavern through the low thatch upsetting a drawer with all the glasses and now came panting and blowing straight up to the high admiral my lord my lord theyre coming i saw em off the lizard last night who my good sir you seem to have left your good manners behind you the armada your honour.

10. we all withdrew mr rochester stayed a moment behind us to give some further orders poole the solicitor addressed me as he descended the stair you madam said he are clear from all blame your uncle will be glad to hear it if indeed he should still be living when mr mason returns from Madeira my uncle what of him do you know him—June 1893.

(b) *Calcutta Matriculation Papers.*

1. a valiant knight sir giles de argentine much renowned in the wars of palestine attended the king till he got him out of the press of the combat he would retreat no further it is not my custom he said to fly with that he took leave of the king set spurs to his horse and calling out his war cry of argentine argentine he rushed into the thickest of the scottish ranks and was killed—1891.

2. he invited heilburg to avail himself of the opportunity which would then be afforded to effect his escape what exclaimed the noble dutchman and leave my unfortunate countrymen to perish no I will never desert the brave fellows who have fought so well for their country the english officer affected by the generosity of heilburgs noble reply answered bravo my good fellow god bless you here is my hand i give you my word i will stay with you—1893.

3. indeed his whole character is most forcibly expressed in his own words which every young man might well stamp upon his soul the longer i live said he the more certain i am that the great difference between men between the feeble and the powerful the great and the insignificant is energy invincible determination a purpose once fixed and then death or victory that quality will do anything that can be done in this world and no talents no circumstances no opportunities will make a two-legged creature a man without it—1894.

4. in the wise words of Shakespeare all places that the eye of heaven visit are to the wise man ports and happy havens happiness indeed depends i repeat it much more on what is within than without us o how careful we should therefore be that we be well furnished within written on friday the sixth of june in london england by john grant solicitor—1895.

5. after school in the evening as he was standing silently beside hardy who was ruling a sheet of paper for him tarlton in his brutal manner came up and seizing him by the arm said come along with me lovatt ive something to say to you i cant come now said lovatt drawing away his arm ah do come now said tarlton in a voice of persuasion well ill come presently nay but do pray theres a good fellow come now because ive something to say to you what is it youve got to say to me i wish youd let me alone said lovatt—1896.

6. having arrived at cardiff he called on blind walter ross the baker for lodgings what caused you to come here asked the blind man and what may be your business in cardiff robert jones the peat cutter advised me to come here he said you were honest and respectable my business is to build for mr john morris in high street theres a clear ring in your voice young man yes yes I shall be glad to have you come in sir—1897.

(c) *Examples from the Press.*

1. A somewhat ungenerous attempt had been made by certain of the trade union leaders to make trade union capital out of this fact, and to press for a rule that the fireman on an express train shall always be a fully-qualified man. The answer is that T. was fully qualified in practice if not in trade union theory. He had been selected for conspicuous merit.—*Daily Telegraph*, 26th Sept. 1906, p. 11.

2. In a portion of the address which, owing to its length, I had to withhold I alluded to the recreational utility of pursuits which can be

carried on in museums such as Mr. H. advocates, and particularly insisted on the benefit to be derived from natural history studies—*Times Weekly*, 28th Sept. 1906, p. 622.

3. On the solace brought to town-pent workers by bird fancying and window-gardening I need not enlarge.—*Ibid.*

4. In the large towns of Lancashire there are many men who in a humble way may claim kindred with Hugh Miller and Edwards, weavers who struggle with Newton's "Principia" at meal-times, and broad-speaking factory hands who dip into mathematics.—*Ibid.*

5. A fatal motor accident occurred on Saturday afternoon about a quarter of a mile from Newton Abbot, the victim being C. H., aged eight years, the son of a labourer working at the locomotive works.—*Ibid.*

6. His temperament was that of the man who inclines to the essay in writing; a bachelor, a gardener, a lover of books, and quiet, and easy living.—*Ibid.* p. 29, 25th Jan. 1907.

7. The thick foliage of the branching oaks and elms in my grounds afforded grateful shade and repose to the entire body, while the tranquil loveliness of the woodland and meadow scenery, comforted and soothed the equally tired mind.—CORELLI.

8. A final word may be said about the spirit in which this language is being evolved, for by some complicated mental process the American people assert their independence of all hampering forms of the ancient tongue while still hotly proclaiming adherence to classic accuracy.—*Monthly Review*, Oct. 1906, p. 32.

9. Politics affords a tremendous scope for the diner-out; political life depends a good deal on dining, only, in this case, young Tucker must make up his mind about the party to which he means to belong, for political dinner-givers are peculiarly vindictive, and to be seen at a house of the wrong complexion is fatal.—Quoted in *Daily Telegraph*, 5th Oct. 1906, p. 5.

10. It is to analyse and to bring into full daylight the true nature of this mystic being that the present article has been written, for, absurd spectre of the Brocken though he be, his is the power and the glory to-day.—*Monthly Review*, Oct. 1906, p. 32.

11. While he claims more ruthlessly, and devours more greedily than any fetish of Central Africa, he has nothing to give to his starving votaries, no material from which the wise or the simple can derive any guidance, or thought-centralising support.—*Monthly Review*, Oct. 1906, p. 32.

12. Until his Majesty's reply reaches me, although there is no doubt as to what it will be, official etiquette prevents my saying more, for, nominally, I am still in office.—Quoted from *Daily Telegraph*, 16th Oct. 1906, p. 9.

13. It was ideal motor-country, and Dick recalled with sneers the sixty horse-power man in Biarritz, who had feared the experiment.—WILLIAMSON, *The Car of Destiny*, ch. xxv., 1907.

14. His poems are eloquent, and their music is not the ordered sound of art but the music of motion and activity, of a rushing river, or of the train which crossed the Hex mountains.—*Times Weekly*, p. 429, 8th Dec. 1905.

15. The apples of discord must lie untouched which are being showered down between the two governments.—*Daily Tel.* p. 10, 10th April 1906.

CHAPTER XVII.—DIRECT AND INDIRECT SPEECH.

273. Two Ways of Reporting a Speech.—A speech is said to be in *Direct* Narration, when the very words used by the speaker are reported without any change; in *Indirect*, when the words are given with some change of construction, the third person being used throughout instead of the first or second.

In Indirect Narration the verbs are bound by the same rules as those given in § 191 for the Sequence of Tenses.

Thus by Rule I., when the reporting or principal verb is in the Past tense, the Present tense in the reported speech must be changed into its corresponding Past form. Thus we change—

Shall	into	*should*	*See*	into	*saw*
Will	,,	*would*	*Is seeing*	,,	*was seeing*
May	,,	*might*	*Has seen*	,,	*had seen*
Can	,,	*could*	*Has been seeing*	,,	*had been seeing*

Observe also that when the Present tense is changed into the Past by Rule I., an adjective or adverb expressing *nearness* is similarly changed into one expressing *distance*. Thus we change—

Now	into	*then*	*To-day*	into	*that day*
This or *these*	,,	*that* or *those*	*To-morrow*	,,	*next day*
Hither	,,	*thither*	*Yesterday*	,,	*the previous day*
Here	,,	*there*	*Last night*	,,	*the previous night*
Hence	,,	*thence*	*Ago*	,,	*before*
Thus	,,	*so*			

1. **Direct.**—"What *is this* strange outcry?" said Socrates; "I *sent* the women away mainly in order that they might not offend in *this* way; for I *have heard* that a man should die in peace. *Be* quiet then and *have* patience."

Indirect.—Socrates *inquired* of them what *that* strange outcry *was*. He *reminded* them that he *had sent* the women away mainly in order that they might not offend in *that* way; for he *had heard* that a man should die in peace. He *begged* them therefore *to be* quiet and *have* patience.

2. **Direct.**—The teacher became angry with the student and *said*, "Why *have* you again *disturbed* the class in *this* way? I *have told* you before, that when I *am speaking*, you should be silent. *Leave* the room, and *do not return* again *to-day*."

Indirect.—The teacher became angry with the student and *inquired* of him why he *had* again *disturbed* the class in *that* way. He *reminded* him that he *had told* him before that he (the student) should be silent when he (the master) *was speaking*. He *ordered* him therefore *to leave* the room, and *forbade* him *to return* again *that* day.

(1) *Convert the following sentences from Direct to Indirect, making all necessary changes in punctuation :—*

1. And Reuben said unto them, "Shed no blood; cast Joseph into this pit that is in the wilderness, but lay no hand upon him."—*Old Testament.*

2. And Judah said unto his brethren, "What profit is it, if we slay our brother and conceal his blood? Come, let us sell him to the Ishmaelites, and let not our hand be upon him; for he is our brother and our flesh."—*Old Testament.*

3. Joseph said to James, "I can tell you what strikes me as the most useful machine in the world." James replied, "Can you, Joseph? I should like to hear about it. What is it used for?"

4. "What do you mean?" asked the man; "how can a rope be used for binding flour?" "A rope may be used for anything," replied the man, "when I do not wish to lend it."

5. A rich man once said to his poorer brother, "Why do you not enter the service of the king, so that you may be relieved of the baseness of labour?"

6. Finding no remedy, he said to himself, "It is better to die than to live in such misery as I am compelled to suffer from a master who treats me and always has treated me so unkindly."

7. And they said one to another, "We are verily guilty concerning our brother, in that we saw the distress of his soul, when he besought us, and we would not hear: therefore is this distress come upon us."—*Old Testament.*

8. The violent man said, "What violence have I done? What anger have I been guilty of?" Then the others laughed and said to him, "Why should we speak? You have given us ocular proof of your violent temper."

9. The robber said to Alexander, "I am thy captive: I must hear what thou art pleased to say, and endure what thou art pleased to inflict. But my soul is unconquered; and if I reply at all to thy reproaches, I will reply to thee like a free man."

10. "You are old, Father William," the young man cried,
"The locks that are left you are grey;
You are hale, Father William, a hale old man;
Now tell me the reason, I pray."

11. "I am sorry indeed," replied the king, "that my vessel is already chosen, and that I am therefore unable to sail with the son of the man who served my father."—DICKENS.

12. He cried to them in agony, "Row back at any risk! I cannot bear to leave her behind to be drowned."—DICKENS.

13. He made a promise to the king's surgeon, saying:—"Bleed the king to death with this lancet, and I will give you a thousand pieces of gold; and when I ascend the throne, you shall be my chief minister."

14. "That's the road we want," said Ladislas, pointing upwards; "once on it, we can't well miss the hill-track over to Clant. Then we shall have done with these many streams and this cross-country work, which is very like bad English hunting. You were not hurt just now?"

"No," said Ralph, "and I don't think the mare is. I was afraid she'd overreached at first, but she's getting better now."—*Ralph Elliott*, ch. xi.

15. (*a*) In this speech Mr. B. said:—"Our great self-governing colonies have one and all expressed a desire for closer relations with the mother-country. They have shown no desire for anything in the nature of organic political union, such as would be provided, let us say, if possible, by a Council of the Empire. But what they have said, and what they have shown that they are in earnest in saying, is that they desire a closer relation, and that they believe is to be attained by this commercial transaction."

(*b*) "That is what they have said. Now, I ask anybody, be his opinions what they may, is it not a serious reflection that the result of the last election has been, apparently at all events, to show that the people of this country will have nothing to do with any commercial arrangements? Is it not a serious thing that our colonial ministers are coming here in a few weeks, and that the party in power has said, so far as I know, not one single word in public indicating that they sympathise with the movement for mutuality of trade-preference between the colonies and the mother-country? We may think the problem very difficult, I admit that it is not easy. But ought we to draw the conclusion that we are not to consider the problem at all? I trow not. For my part, I am glad that there is one party in the State who welcome the idea of such closer union, and who would do much, and sacrifice much, to see it carried into effect."—Quoted from *Times Weekly*, Feb. 8, 1907.

16. (i.) *Specify the clauses of the following paragraph, and the functions of each*:—

By this time, my Lord, I doubt not but that you wonder why I have run off from my bias so long together and made so tedious a digression from satire to heroic poetry. But if you will not excuse it by the tattling quality of the age, which, as Sir William Davenant says, is always narrative, yet I hope the usefulness of what I have to say on this subject will qualify the remoteness of it; and this is the last time I will commit the crime of prefaces, or trouble the world with my notions of anything that relates to verse.

(ii.) *Turn the above paragraph into Reported (Indirect) Speech.*—*Lond. Matric. Exam.*, Sept. 1905.

17. *Convert the following from Direct to Indirect, making the necessary changes in punctuation*:—

I know of no way of judging the future but by the past. And judging by the past, I wish to know what there has been in the conduct of the British ministry for the last ten years to justify those hopes, with which gentlemen have been pleased to solace themselves in this House? Is it that insidious smile with which our petition has lately been received? Trust it not, Sir; it will prove a snare. Suffer not yourselves to be betrayed with a kiss. Are fleets and armies necessary to a work of love and reconciliation? Let us not deceive ourselves, Sir. These are the implements of war and subjugation, the last arguments to which kings resort.—*London Matric.*, June 1905.

18. (*a*) *Analyse into clauses, merely stating the grammatical function and connection of each clause* :—

Let thy voice
Rise like a fountain for me night and day.
For what are men better than sheep or goats
That nourish a blind life within the brain,
If, knowing God, they lift not hands of prayer
Both for themselves and those who call them friend?

(*b*) *Turn the following passage into a Reported (Indirect) Speech* :—

As to the wealth which the colonies have drawn from the sea by their fisheries, you had all that matter fully opened up at your bar. You surely thought those acquisitions of value; for they seemed even to excite your envy: and yet the spirit, by which that enterprising employment has been exercised, ought rather in my opinion to have raised your esteem and admiration. And, pray Sir, what in the world is equal to it? Pass by the other parts, and look at the manner in which the people of New England have of late carried on the whale fishery. Whilst we follow them among the tumbling mountains of ice, and behold them penetrating into the deepest frozen recesses of Hudson's Bay and Davis's Strait; whilst we are looking for them beneath the Arctic Circle, we hear that they have pierced into the opposite region of polar cold, that they are at the antipodes.—BURKE.

London Matric., Sept. 1904.

(2) *Convert the following sentences from Indirect to Direct, making all necessary changes in punctuation* :—

1. Damon, before his execution, requested but one favour from Dionysius, which was that he might be permitted to visit his wife and children, who were at that time a considerable distance from him, and he promised faithfully to return on the day appointed.

2. This Dionysius refused to grant, unless some person could be found who would consent to suffer death in his stead, if he did not perform his promise and return by the appointed time.

3. In a short speech Pythias told the surrounding multitude that his dear friend, Damon, would soon arrive; but he hoped not before his own death had saved a life so dear as Damon's was to his family, his friends, and his country.

4. He sent his compliments to Francis, Clavering, and Monson, and charged them to protect Raja Guru Das, who was about to become the head of the Brahmans of Bengal.

5. The governor of the town then called out with a loud voice, and ordered Androcles to explain to them how a savage and hungry lion could thus in a moment have forgotten its innate disposition, and be converted all of a sudden into a harmless animal.

6. Androcles then explained to them that that very lion, which was standing before them, had been his friend and partner in the woods, and had for that reason spared his life, as they now saw.

7. Socrates then suggested to Glaucon that the entire abolition of the guards, which he (Glaucon) recommended, could not remedy the evils which he desired to remove, and he inquired of Glaucon whether he knew

by personal examination that the guards did their work as badly as he imagined.

8. When he reached home, his father asked him where his ship was and what had become of his merchandise. The son in reply told him what had happened,—how he had given up his vessel with its cargo, and had taken in exchange the slaves and set them free, and how he had consented to take this girl back with him and make her his wife.

9. When they asked Thales what thing in the world had the best claim to be called universal, he replied that Hope had the best claim to be so called, because Hope remained with those who had nothing else left.

10. When Solon and Periander were sitting together over their cups, Periander, finding that Solon was more silent than usual, asked him whether he was silent for want of words or because he was a fool. Solon told him in reply that no fool could be silent over his cups.

11. Fears had been occasionally expressed that the opening of this railway might do harm to Egypt, and it had, therefore, been urged that the resources of Egypt should not be employed in its construction. He was glad to observe that these complaints were gradually dying out. It could not be too clearly understood that the construction of this railway would not divert any existing trade to any considerable extent. It would create a trade, which, unless the railway were made, could never exist.—Speech by Lord Cromer, *Daily Telegraph*, Feb. 2, 1906.

12. Mr. Ritchie congratulated the Chancellor of the Exchequer upon the great ability with which he had discharged what he rightly described as a heavy duty. The right hon. gentleman had succeeded in making his proposals perfectly plain and simple to the Committee,—a task which he knew from experience to be by no means easy. He very much regretted that his right hon. friend was placed in the difficult position of having to face a falling revenue, and he regretted it still more, because it had been contended in many quarters that it was his (Mr. Ritchie's) proposals of last year which had landed the right hon. gentleman in his present difficulties. He had had many congratulations from his friends, that it was not his duty this year to introduce the Budget; but although these congratulations were well grounded, he would have been glad if he could have done anything to relieve his right hon. friend of his difficulties. In preparing his Budget last year he made full inquiry into all the circumstances that were likely to affect the revenue, and he did not feel justified in making any material reductions in the estimates of income which his advisers laid before him.—*London Matric.*, Jan. 1905.

13. (*a*) Sir Clements Markham said the time had come for taking stock of their Arctic knowledge, and for deciding what work of importance remained to be done. Until lately they had before them many unconnected stories of discoveries in one direction or another, but now, thanks to the researches of scientific thinkers and explorers, each discovery was falling naturally into its place.

(*b*) The discovery by Dr. Nansen of a polar ocean with a depth of 2000 fathoms drew the veil from the Arctic mystery and made all things clear. That this ocean extended to and beyond the pole was shown by convincing evidence, and it probably covered the greater part of the unknown area. This polar basin was almost surrounded by continental lands, whence shelves at no great depths extended to the edge of the deep ocean, where there was a more or less rapid descent.

(c) All undiscovered Arctic land probably rose from the continental shelves, just as all discovered Arctic land did. There could scarcely be any land rising out of an ocean with a depth of 2000 fathoms. Of the continental shelves they had least knowledge of the shelf to the north of Greenland, Ellesmere Island, and the Parry Archipelago. From the Parry Islands towards the New Siberia Islands there was an area probably occupied by a continental shelf; and this area was now the least known part of the Arctic regions, and the one which contained the most interesting geographical problems. Great part of it was occupied by a sea bounded on the south by the American continent and on the east by the west coast of Banks and Prince Patrick Islands. It had received the name of the Beaufort Sea.

(d) Ever since he was serving in the Arctic regions, more than fifty years ago, he had taken a special interest in the Parry Archipelago and the region between it and Siberia. All along the southern shores of the Parry Islands, facing Barrow Strait, there were the remains of Eskimo encampments. He had examined many himself, and collected relics. Two facts appeared to be clear—that the people who had thus left so many vestiges of their presence were moving eastward, and that the emigration took place at some very distant period.

CHAPTER XVIII.—COMMON ERRORS IN THE USE OF COMMON WORDS.

274. Common Errors.—Under the above heading has been placed a miscellaneous collection of words and their uses about which mistakes are sometimes made. Some hints are added to show how such errors may be corrected or avoided.

Nouns.

(1) **Concrete, Abstract.**—If a noun can be used in both senses (see § 27), take care to use it in one sense only within the *same sentence*:—

He is a man of clear judgment; but as regards this case I still think it was too severe for the offence. (For *it* say *his sentence*, or *his verdict*. *It* is here improper, because it stands for "judgment" in a concrete sense, whereas in the former clause "judgment" is used in an abstract sense.)

(2) **Collective** nouns must not be associated with adjectives that imply individual attributes, nor with verbs that imply individual action:—

The average population of England is tall. (For *average population of England* say *the average Englishman* or *most Englishmen.*)

Mankind seeks for happiness in both worlds. (For *mankind* say *most men* or *men in general.* Change *seeks* to *seek.*)

(3) **Abstract** nouns must not be pluralised, unless authority exists for using them as common nouns (§ 33) :—

Leave off such stupidities. (For *stupidities* say *acts of stupidity*.)

(4) **Possessive Case.**—Be careful how you use this case with nouns denoting anything inanimate or not personified (see § 45) :—

Beware of life's shortness. (Say *the shortness of life*.)
Look at this letter's signature. (Say *the signature to this letter*.)

(5) **Apostrophe "s."**—If the apostrophe "*s*" is given to the ear, it should also be given to the eye. In other words, it must be written, if it is pronounced :—

Epps' cocoa. (Write *Epps's* for *Epps'*.)

(6) **Subject, Object.**—If a noun or a pronoun is used once as subject and once as object in the same sentence, it must be expressed twice :—

This is a weakness, *which* some admire and seldom fails to command respect. (Say *and which seldom*, etc.)

Note.—For Plurals in a special sense see appendix to this chapter.

Pronouns.

(7) **We, I.**—If *we* is substituted for *I*, avoid coupling it with a singular noun :—

We did things in a much better way, when we were manager. (Either change *we* to *I*, or change *were manager* to *held the office of manager*.)

(8) **I.**—Take care to place the first personal pronoun last, if it appears in company with nouns or other pronouns :—

I and Herbert return to school to-morrow. (For *I and Herbert* write *Herbert and I*.)

(9) **Them.**—Avoid using this Demonstrative pronoun as if it were a Demonstrative adjective :—

Leave them books alone. (For *them* say *these* or *those*.)

(10) **Myself**, etc.—A Reflexive or Emphatic pronoun (§ 69) cannot stand alone as the subject of a verb :—

In October last George and myself spent ten days at Hampton Court. (For *myself* say *I* or *I myself*.)

(11) **They.**—This is less suitable than "those" as an antecedent to "who" or "that" :—

They who have large private means need not for that reason lead an idle life. (For *they* write *those*.)

(12) **One,** as an Indefinite Demonstrative pronoun (§ 75, *b*).

This must not be followed by "he," "his," or "him," since a Definite Demonstrative cannot have an Indefinite for its antecedent :—

> One must not be too confident of his own success. (For *his* write *one's.*)

(13) **My, our, your, his, her, their.**—The use of these Possessive pronouns as antecedents to a Relative, though defensible and used occasionally by good writers, is not common and had better be avoided :—

> The more accurately we search into the human mind, the stronger traces we everywhere find of His wisdom who made it.—BURKE. (For *His wisdom* write *the wisdom of Him.*)

(14) **Who, which** (as Subjects of a verb).—These cannot be omitted, as "whom," "which" (objects) can be :—

> I had several men in my ship died of calentures.—SWIFT. (Insert *who* before *died.*)

(15) **Which, whom, that** (as Objects of a verb).—When one of these words is the connective between two rather long clauses, it is better not to leave it out :—

> The action for libel recently brought in the City Magistrate's Court by Miss ——, a nurse, against Mr. ——, in respect of a letter the latter had written to a relative who was being nursed by the plaintiff, terminated in favour of the defendant. —*Daily Telegraph.* (Insert *which* or *that* after *a letter.* Or change *the latter had written* to *written by the latter.*)

(16) **Which.**—If this word stands for two different cases in the same sentence, it must be mentioned twice, once for each case. (This is a re-assertion of (6) in other words) :—

> This is a point, which is very important and all men acknowledge to be so. (Insert *which* after *and.* Or reconstruct the second clause by saying "and is acknowledged to be so by all men.")

(17) **Which, that.** — In a restrictive or limiting sense, "who" or "which" is less suitable than "that" (see § 83, *Note*) :—

> This is the house which Jack built. (Say *that.*)

(18) **Same.**—After "same" use *as* or *that* for the following Relative, not *who* or *which* (see § 81) :—

> This is the same man who came yesterday. (Say *that.*)

(19) **As.**—Avoid the vulgarism of using *as* for "who" or "which" or "that," unless it is preceded by "such" or "same" :—

> This is not the book as I bought. (For *as* say *that.*)

(20) **And which.**—These words must not be used to introduce a Relative clause, unless another Relative clause similarly introduced by *which* has been expressed already :—

(*a*) It is a doctrine not very easily adapted to his habitual creed, and which drops out of his mind whenever, etc. (Insert *which is* after *doctrine*, and leave out *which* after *and*.)

Note.—In the sentence as now amended the second *which* is unnecessary, because it stands for the same case as the first one. A second *which* is necessary only when it is in a different case ; see (16).

(*b*) Have we not hereditary possessions in our just laws, our free constitution, our rich literature, incomparably above material wealth, and which we are beyond all things bound to maintain, improve, and hand down in safety?—JEVONS, *The Coal Question*, p. 371.

Here say *which are incomparably above material wealth*. The words *and which* must both be retained, because this *which* is in the Objective case, while the previous one is in the Nominative ; see (16).

Adjectives.

(21) **A, an.**—Observe the invariable rule, that the *n* of *an* must be written if it is pronounced, but not otherwise (see § 55) :—

A clock is an useful thing.
He is an one-eyed man. } For *an* write *a*.
That is not a ho-tel'.
A his-tor'-i-cal record. } For *a* write *an*.

Note.—In the last two examples the *h* is silent, or so nearly silent as to be inaudible, because the syllable following is accented.

(22) **A, the.**—Take care to repeat the article after *and*, when a separate person or thing is introduced by *and* (see § 186, *a*, *Note*) :—

The styles of a poet and historian are not the same. (Insert *an* after *and*.)

An equal amount of care must be taken *not* to repeat the article when one and only one person or thing is intended :—

The great eater and *the* great drinker, seen from the outside, is a pleasant fellow, a good sort : we like him, we admire him, we emulate him.—*Macmillan's Magazine*, p. 126, Dec. 1906. (Cancel *the*.)

(23) **Other.**—Take care to use this word with a Comparative, and to abstain from using it with a Superlative :—

He is more learned than any person now living. (Insert *other* before *person*.)

Of all other scholars he is the most accurate. (Omit *other*.)

(24) **Each other, one another.**—The first is generally used for two things, and the second for more than two :—

His knees smote one against another.—*Dan.* v. 6. (For *one against another* say *against each other*, or *the one against the other*. Observe that a dual sense can be given to "one another" by the insertion of *the*.)

(25) **Other . . . but.**—Avoid using the preposition *but* after *other* :—

He had no other object but to get his money. (For *but* say *than*, which is appropriate, since "other" is etymologically a Comparative adjective; or retain *but* and omit *other*. The two constructions must not be confused.)

(26) **Few, little.**—Remember that these are implied negatives (= not many, not much), unless they are preceded by *a* :—

Few men escaped, and these were rewarded. (Insert *a* before *few*.)
Little hope remained, but that was soon disappointed. (Insert *a* or *one* before *little*.)

Also remember that "*few*" denotes number, and "*little*" quantity or degree :—

To-day there is less than eight hours of full daylight. (For *is less* say *are fewer*.)

(27) **Any, either.**—Observe that *either* is used for two things, and *any* for more than two :—

He was first groom, then coachman, then stable-boy; and he did not do well in either capacity. (For *either* say *any*. Or say "in any of these capacities.")

(28) **Comparatives.**—Use the Comparative in preference to the Superlative, when two things are referred to :—

This picture is the best of the two. (For *best* say *better*.)

Note.—There are, however, certain well-established phrases or sayings in which the Superlative is used :—

Of two evils choose the *least*.

(29) **Comparatives in -or.**—Avoid using "than" after Latin comparatives in *-or* :—

His work is superior and deserves to be better paid than yours. (Say *superior to yours and deserves to be better paid.*)

(30) **Like.**—Avoid the vulgarism of using this adjective as if it were a conjunction :—

A timid, nervous child like Martin was. (Say *as* or *such as* for *like*. Or put *what* after *like*. Or leave out *was*.)

Verbs.

(31) **Shall, will.**—Remember that these are Principal verbs in some persons and auxiliaries in others (see § 103 and § 115) :—

I will be drowned; nobody shall save me. (Let *shall* and *will* change places.)

Will I accompany you? (For *will* say *shall*.)

(32) **Present, Past.**—Avoid putting an Historic Present (§ 112, *e*) in the same sentence with the Past Indefinite:—

While the governor is thus quietly kept in bonds, the prisoners were triumphantly paraded through the streets. (For *is* say *was*. Or change *were* to *are*.)

(33) **Perfect Infinitive.**—Use the Perfect form, when you wish to show that some expectation, supposition, or desire *was not realised* (§ 124). Use it also after the verb "said" in the Passive voice, when you wish to express *past time* (§ 124, *Note*). In all other connections use the Present form:—

They, supposing him *to have been* in the company, went a day's journey.—*Luke* ii. 44. (Correct.)

But for his illness he would *have come*. (Correct.)
I should *have liked* to see him. (Correct.)
I intended *to have seen* him, and I succeeded. (Wrong.)
(In the last line change "*to have seen*" to "*to see*."
He is said *to have been* once an honest man. (Correct.)

(34) **Noun-Infinitive, Gerund.**—The Noun-infinitive (§ 127, I.) and the Verbal noun or Gerund are equivalent in sense, both being equivalent to Abstract nouns. But if the verb or other word going before requires a preposition, the Infinitive (with few exceptions) must not be used:—

He persisted to say this. (Change to *in saying*.)
I insisted to have my fee paid. (Say *on having*.)
I am confident to win. (Say *of winning*.)
I assisted to do this. (Say *in doing*.)
Disqualified to compete. (Say *from* or *for competing*.)

In some few contexts, however, the Infinitive is more idiomatic than the Gerund, even though the word going before usually requires a preposition:—

I have a great desire of seeing you. (Say *to see*.)

(35) **The Qualifying Infinitive** (§ 127, II.).—When this is used to qualify an *adjective*, the Active voice is more common than the Passive; but the rule is not absolute:—

The road, on account of robbers, was difficult to be passed. (For *to be passed* write *to pass*.)

(36) **Two Subjects or Objects to the same verb.**—If the same verb suits one of the two subjects or objects mentioned, but does not suit the other, add a second verb which suits the other:—

That phrase is often heard in talk and in literature. (After *and* insert *seen*.)

Very few of the Sultans of Turkey have enjoyed a life of peace or a natural death. (After *or* insert *died*.)

(37) **One Auxiliary with two Principal verbs.**—Repeat the Auxiliary, if the voice or number of the two principal verbs is not the same :—

The growth of tobacco has been established in India for the last 300 years and overspread the country. (Insert *has* before *overspread*.)

Three were killed, and one taken prisoner. (Insert *was*.)

(38) **Two Auxiliaries with one Principal verb.**—When two Auxiliaries are used with the same Principal verb, use the Principal verb in two forms, if one form is not sufficient :—

I never have, and I never will, accuse a man falsely. (After *have* insert *accused*, and cancel the comma after *will*. A comma should be placed after *accuse*.)

(39) **Mixed use of verbs.**—If the use of the verb is not the same in two successive clauses, give the full form of the tense in each clause :—

Happily we have not and could not have seen a repetition of the scandalous scenes which took place at the Assize Court.—*Times Weekly*, 8th April 1898, p. 213.

The sentence should begin, "Happily we have not *seen*," etc. The "*seen*" must be inserted. In the first clause "have seen" is the Present Perfect tense, *Indicative* mood; in the second clause "have seen" is the Perfect *Infinitive*, object to the verb *could*.

Adverbs.

(40) **Quite.**—(*a*) Avoid the impropriety of using this adverb as if it were an adjective and competent to qualify nouns. "Quite" means "perfectly," "entirely," and should not be used in any other sense or for any use other than adverbial :—

Quite an item. (*A considerable item.*)
Quite a place. (*An important place.*)
Quite a sensation. (*A startling sensation.*)

(*b*) Avoid the impropriety of using this adverb in the sense of "very" :—

Quite a unique and interesting document has been published here. —*Daily Telegraph*, 13th Jan. 1898.

(*Quite unique* is unmeaning; for there cannot be degrees of uniqueness. Erase *quite* and insert *very* between *and* and *interesting*.)

(41) **Since, ago.**—These adverbs mean "from the present time reckoning backwards." They must always be preceded by a verb in the Past Indefinite tense :—

My house has fallen two weeks since (*or* ago). (Say *fell.*)

(42) **That.**—Avoid the vulgarism of using *that* as if it were an adverb signifying "so":—

I am that tired that I can scarcely walk. (Say *so tired.*)

(43) **Scarcely, hardly.**—Avoid using a negative with these adverbs, which are implied negatives already. Two negatives make an affirmative, not a negative:—

I don't hardly know how to answer you. (Omit *don't.*)
We won't go no further. (Change *no* to *any.*)

Prepositions.

(44) **Sequence of Prepositions.**—Take care that nouns, adjectives, verbs, and adverbs are followed by the right preposition, that is, the preposition prescribed by idiom and required by the sense:—

Lord Salisbury has now in his disposal the whole future of South Africa. (Say *at* for *in.*)
China's resistance of Japan was vain. (Say *to.*)
A sad picture was presented before our sight. (Say *to.* Or change *presented* to *placed.*)
All the examples can be reduced under three heads. (Say *to.* Or change *reduced* to *summed up.*)
Marred, as you see, with traitors.—SHAKESPEARE. (Say *by.*)
I have no sympathy for his opinions. (Say *with.*)
A testimonial of my industry. (Say *to.*)
McArthur's history treats only with his own time. (Say *of.* Or change *treats* to *deals.*)
I do not concur with that. (Say *with you in that.*)
Dutch is of the same origin with Anglo-Saxon. (Say *as.*)
I prevailed with him to let me go. (Say *on.*)
I never interfere with other men's affairs. (Say *in.*)
I never interfere in other people. (Say *with.*)
This is not the question which we were contending. (Add *about.*)
His style is characterised with verbiage. (Say *by.*)

(45) **One preposition for two.**—If one preposition is not fit to do the work of two, fill up the gap with one that is fit:—

This fact did not add but detract from his merits. (Put *to* after *add*; we cannot say *add from.* The sentence would stand better thus:—"This fact did not add to his merits, but it detracted from them.")

(46) **Than.**—This must not be used after "different," nor after "prefer," nor after "scarcely":—

His ideas are different than those of the majority. (Say *from.*)
He had scarcely gone than a letter was brought in. (For *scarcely* say *no sooner*, or change *than* to *when.*)
I prefer to do this than that. (Say *doing this to doing that.*)

(47) **Except, without, against.**—These prepositions are not now used as conjunctions. Their former use as conjunctions was through the omission of *that*, which introduced a Noun-clause :—

> Except ye repent. (Say *unless.*)
> Without you apologise. (Say *unless.*)
> Have it ready against I come. (Say *my coming.*)

Conjunctions.

(48) **Since.**—This word, when used as a conjunction, must be preceded by a Present Perfect tense and followed by a Past Indefinite :—

Two years passed since my father has died. (Say *have passed* for *passed*, and *died* for *has died.*)

(49) **Not only . . . but also.**—Take care that the first of these is followed by *the same part of speech* as the second (§ 294) :—

He not only built a house, but also a stable. (Put *not only* before *a house.*)

(50) **Both . . . and.**—If a preposition occurs after *both*, repeat it after *and* :—

Excess of any kind is bad both for mind and body. (Insert *for* before *body*, or else say *for both mind and body.*)

(51) **Than . . . as.**—*As* will not do duty for *than* as well as for itself :—

My prospects are no better, and not even as good, as they were before. (Say *my prospects are no better than they were before, and not even as good.*)

(52) **That.**—This must not be used as a general hack, to save the repetition of *when, though, if, whether, unless*, etc. It is, however, a common trick with careless writers to misuse it in this way :—

If I do not speak of them, it is because they do not come within my subject, and not that they are lightly esteemed by me. (For *that* say *because.*)

(53) **As.**—Avoid the vulgarism of using *as* for *that* to introduce a noun-clause :—

I do not know as I need say anything more. (Say *that.*)

(54) **And that.**—If this is used for introducing a noun-clause, take care that it is preceded by another noun-clause which also begins with *that*. When the first *that* has been mentioned, a second one need not be repeated unless the subject of the verb is changed :—

(*a*) I fancied I should get on well by degrees and that I had a good chance of ultimate success. (Insert *that* after *fancied*. *That I* need not be repeated in the subsequent clause.)

(*b*) There seemed to be some hope of his recovery and that he would live to make a fresh effort. (For *of his recovery* say *that he would recover*. *That he would* need not be repeated in the subsequent clause.)

(*c*) Physicians declare lung-disease to be difficult to cure in England, and that the patient must go to a more equable climate. (Say *that lung disease is difficult*, etc. Here *that* must be repeated in the second clause, because the subject is changed.)

(55) **Though, but.**—Remember that *though* is a subordinative conjunction, while *but* is a co-ordinative one, and therefore more emphatic (see § 171):—

He is an honest man, but poor; and honesty is always rewarded. (The context shows that in the first clause the emphasis is on the word *honest*. Hence *but* must be changed to *though*.)

(56) **Whether . . . whether.**—When contradictory alternatives are offered by a couple of verbs, repeat the word *whether*; but if they are not contradictory, simply say *or*:—

(1) I beg to ask whether our minister at Pekin has protested against, or in any way recognised, the claims made by the German minister and consul.—*House of Commons*, 10th August 1898. (Insert *whether he has* after *or*.)

(2) I beg to ask whether our minister has protested against or in any way opposed the claims, etc. (This is correct, because protesting against and opposing, though not synonymous, are not contradictory.)

(57) **Or.**—When the noun following *or* is contrasted with the noun preceding it, put an article or a preposition, if possible, before the second noun:—

Has he gained a prize or scholarship? (Insert *a* before *scholarship*.)

Tell me whether he influenced you with promises or threats. (Insert *with* before *threats*.)

Exercise.

Correct any errors that you may find in the following sentences. (These might all be answered orally and at sight in class.)

1. The creed of Zoroaster assumes the coexistence of a malevolent and benevolent principle, which divide the sovereignty of the world between them.

2. The failure of the spring and autumn harvest in 1897 led to a serious famine in India that year.

3. Is that house in the distance a hospital or a hotel?

4. He mistook James' hat for his own.

5. Sir Roger was saying last night that he was of opinion none but men of fine parts deserve to be hung.—*Spectator*, No. 6.

6. A coxcomb, flushed with many of these infamous victories (over young women), shall say he is sorry for the poor fools, protest and vow he never thought of matrimony.—*Spectator*, No. 288.

7. The jury summoned to attend the court was a clever body of men.

8. Mazzini did more for the emancipation of his country than any living man of his own time.

9. The squadron consisted of about 200 men, and divided the booty among themselves after the victory.

10. A masterly genius does not care what men say of him.

11. I heard the multitude's shout.

12. The stamina of a plant consists of the anther and filament.

13. The violences of a mob must be suppressed.

14. Bring them books down from the shelf.

15. No one as yet had exhibited the structure of the human kidneys, Vesalius having only examined them in dogs.—HALLAM.

16. The claim to inspiration, which is made for these persons and they would not perhaps claim for themselves, cannot be proved.

17. There were very few passengers who escaped without serious injury. (Why is this sentence ambiguous? remove the ambiguity.)

18. In Palestine at the time of Christ the three chief sects were the Pharisees, the Sadducees, and Essenes; and they thoroughly disliked each other.

19. My readers too have the satisfaction to find that there is no rank or degree among them who have not their representation in this club.—*Spectator*, No. 34.

20. You shall seldom find a dull fellow of good education, but if he happens to have any leisure upon his hands, will turn his head to one of those two amusements for all fools of eminence—politics or poetry.—*Spectator*, No. 43.

21. Your Englishman is just as serious in his amusements as in any act of his life.

22. I prefer a profitable occupation and which I can look back upon afterwards without regret.

23. There is no popular *Life of Oliver Cromwell* in print; those by Guizot and Carlyle being too bulky for general use.

24. I have read of a man who was very rich, but he considered himself poor all the same.

25. On a subject in which the feelings of others are entitled to respect, one must keep his thoughts to himself.

26. How do you distinguish between a poet and orator, and what is there in common between them?

27. I have few things more to talk about, but I have no time now; you shall hear them to-morrow.

28. "A little knowledge is a dangerous thing," says Pope; but with all due deference to Pope, even little knowledge is better than none.

29. My friend sent me a pair of turkeys to choose from; but I returned them with thanks, and told him I did not want any of them.

30. Several neighbouring gentlemen contributed works, for which they had either given commissions direct to our most distinguished artists, or had purchased them during this exhibition at the Royal Academy.

31. You will perceive that this is the same horse which yourself possessed four years ago.

32. I do not think that the Squire and myself ever had better sport together than we had that day.

33. On comparing his gun with mine, they pronounced his to be the best.

34. In selecting this house in preference to any others, I had no other object in view but to get the one that was nearest the railway station.

35. In commerce it often happens that they who have abilities want capital, and they who have capital want abilities.

36. Were he still disposed to go there, my purse shall be open to him.

37. I shall have great pleasure in accepting your invitation.

38. If he has been the cause of all this trouble, it would weigh heavily on his conscience.

39. I have lived ten years of my life in Canada, but left it for good and all two years ago.

40. I never have and never will attack a man for speculative opinions. —BUCKLE.

41. Quite an innovation in the mode of dressing the hair has come into fashion this year.

42. My almost drunkenness of heart.—BYRON.

43. My success or otherwise will be communicated to me by post this evening.

44. From my point of view Grote is a greater historian than Gibbon, though his style is much less grand.

45. I really believe that except to doctors and clergymen, and the very few intimate friends who have seen me frequently, even my state of extremity has been doubted.—Miss MITFORD.

46. In his translation of the *Iliad*, Pope has sometimes given us a picture of a very different kind than what Homer intended.

47. It was in such a situation of affairs that Hastings was made Governor-General of India.

48. Breaking a constitution by the very same errors, that so many have been broken before.—SWIFT.

49. The trees have cast their leaves a month ago.

50. I will not let thee go, except thou bless me.—*Gen.* xxxii. 26.

51. He not only gave them his advice, but a good deal of pecuniary help besides.

52. It is contrary both to justice and common sense to do such a thing as that.

53. This building is both superior in size and more suitable in design than any other town-hall that I have seen.

54. No one ever worked more regularly or so carefully as he.

55. We decidedly prefer reading the *Swiss Family Robinson* at this moment than the rather characterless *Masterman Ready*.—Miss YONGE.

56. The modern Germans are fond of metaphysics like the ancient Athenians were.

57. But scarce were they hidden away, I declare,
Than the giant came in with a curious air.—TOM HOOD.

58. I am not that fond of my books that I like to stay in the house reading them all the afternoon.

59. I consider him to be very clever, and that he will do great credit to his teachers.

60. If any such rash project were attempted and that any serious trouble came of it, the fault would be yours, not mine.

61. I pass over this subject in silence, because it does not come within my present purpose, and not that I feel at all incompetent to deal with it.

62. He is an industrious boy, but naturally rather dull, and industry is almost always rewarded in the long run.

63. Whether this conflagration was the work of an incendiary, or that some one employed by the firm was guilty of carelessness, will never be ascertained.

64. This statement was repeated and impressed upon the audience.

65. The man as came here yesterday went away to-day.

66. That operation was first performed on rabbits; it is now performed with success on the human family.

67. It is interesting to observe the various substitutes for paper before its invention.

68. The virtuous and the vile, the learned and ignorant, the temperate and debauched, all give and return the jest.—BROWN's *Characteristics.*

69. This bold statement of fact will be sufficient to show that the permanency of the Yukon goldfields is established beyond peradventure. —*Liverpool Daily Post,* 29th Jan. 1898.

70. How should I look to have any part of my desire herein satisfied, unless myself be careful to satisfy the like desire which is in other men? —HOOKER.

71. Air, when carefully tested, is found to contain something else than nitrogen and oxygen.—GEIKIE.

72. The misreading of a person's character is an error rather difficult to be avoided.

73. He is as likely to make a good living for himself as his brothers have done.

74. Driving down the street, his horse ran off, and he was thrown out.

75. There have been three famous talkers in Great Britain, either of whom would illustrate what I say about dogmatists well enough for my purpose.—HOLMES.

76. We already possess four times as great a trade with China as every other nation put together.—*Report of G. Balfour's Speech,* 4th Feb. 1898.

77. The Zulu chief, Dinizulu, after some years of exile in St. Helena, has now been reinstated, to rank as a hereditary chief.—*Daily Telegraph,* 8th Feb. 1898.

78. France has obtained a firm footing at Tonkin; England is settled at Hong-Kong for some time past; Russia is at the Amoor; and even Spain, and Portugal, and Holland have their resting-places in East Asia. —*Daily Telegraph,* 8th Feb. 1898.

79. No one would accuse the representative of an English newspaper as an Irishman desirous of exaggerating the distress and grievances of his country.—*Dillon's Speech,* 10th Feb. 1898.

80. Quite a record gallop fell to the Whaddon Chase from Wing, where Lord Orkney kept open house.—*Daily Telegraph,* 10th Feb. 1898.

81. We were no sooner sat down, but after having looked upon me a little while, she said, etc.—*Spectator,* No. 7.

82. It is difficult to imagine a rougher experience than that involved by his attempt to carry out the adventurous project of reaching Paris from New York by land.—*Times Weekly*, 11th Feb. 1898, p. 92.

83. It (the work of Abbé Dubois) records the impressions of an acute and a patient observer of the actual life of the Hindus.—*Times Weekly*, 11th Feb. 1898, p. 92.

84. The predicate of a sentence always is or contains a verb."

85. Few of his friends except myself knew of his being in the kingdom.

86. The public and private good are so far from being inconsistent that they promote one another.

87. He regretted that the pupil-teacher did not prevent the boys from writing so fast, as he noticed that is done in the absence of such immediate supervision as the master, otherwise engaged, would have prevented.

88. Men and women who have no object or aim than amusement.—*Daily Telegraph*, 16th Feb. 1898, p. 8.

89. Though these nine warships were built in different dockyards, the design of the whole nine is the same, with slight differences in points of detail.—*Daily Telegraph*, 16th Feb. 1898, p. 9.

90. Bounteous harvests in the Punjaub and in the wheat lands of the River Plate are expected to furnish supplies from the Southern Hemisphere to the extent of about 5,000,000 quarters, etc.—*Daily Telegraph*, 29th April 1898.

91. Mr. Gladstone was able to sit for a short while in an easy-chair on the small lawn by the side of the house, which is charmingly sheltered by quite a small pine forest.—*Daily Telegraph*, 22nd March 1898.

92. I shall leave this house at once without you put it in proper repair.

93. You will have to get that lesson by heart like I did.

94. He preferred to take a sweep-crossing than beg his bread from door to door.

95. The army liked their quarters so well, that neither officers nor soldiers was in any degree willing to quit them till they should be thoroughly refreshed.—CLARENDON.

96. The recent fighting has led many people to reconsider the whole question of the relations between the Cape, the Imperial Government, and the natives.—*Review of Reviews*, Feb. 1898, p. 147.

97. I am anxious for the time when he will talk as much nonsense to me as I have to him.—W. S. LANDOR.

98. From this coalition, and not from the spirit of its own laws and institutions, he attributed the harsh and ungenerous treatment of our fallen enemy, Napoleon Buonaparte.—MRS. FLETCHER.

99. The position of the Cabinet is exceedingly difficult between the danger of foreign and civil war, either of which may be precipitated by a simple error.—*Telegram from Madrid*, 14th April 1898.

100. The image and name of Goethe occurs to us at once when we try to evoke the man of most perfect brain who ever existed.—*Fortnightly Review*, May 1898, p. 766.

101. The condition of Mr. Gladstone, who is without pain, is not quite so favourable.—*Daily Telegraph*, 21st April 1898.

102. The nurses for the Spanish Royal family are always chosen from the peasantry of Asturias; a large number are sent for, and from them the most handsome of the province is finally selected.—*Cassell's Family Magazine*, Jan. 1898, p. 152.

103. By that time he will have come in contact with some of the most gifted genius of the earth.—*Cassell's Family Magazine*, Jan. 1898, p. 158.

104. Here is a specimen from *Hamlet* which illustrates the unmethodical character conversation will assume when a principal interlocutor is pursuing a private train of thought with intense eagerness.—ABBOTT AND SEELEY, *English Lessons for English Readers*, p. 231.

105. The whole question is accordingly remitted to a committee, the composition of which has already been announced in our columns, who will consider and report upon with all convenient speed the proposals of the Government of India.—*Times*, 3rd May 1898.

106. Chung Chih Tung, Viceroy of Nankin, a thorough Chinaman, a Progressive, though disliking foreigners, but who has the unique distinction of being absolutely honest and incorruptible, has engaged German instructors for his army.—*Daily Telegraph*, 19th April 1898.

107. He gathered that the Government were not altogether satisfied with each other.—MORLEY, quoted in *Daily Telegraph*, 23rd June 1898.

108. Throughout the whole of the north-east of the Soudan trade and industry are reviving surely, but no doubt slowly.—Sir M. HICKS-BEACH, quoted in *Daily Telegraph*, 28th June 1898.

109. How could I hear such words, how could I meet such looks, from any other man but he?—Mrs. CRAIK, *The Ogilvies*, chap. x.

110. No one is more fully alive than himself to the heavy burden of his responsibilities.—*Standard*, 11th August 1898, p. 4.

111. These agents should be authorised to (and capable of) discussing industrial questions, and of availing themselves of the best markets.—*Daily Telegraph*, 15th August 1898, p. 2.

112. At any other time, and in any other person, such an exhibition might have been conducive of pity.—*Windsor Magazine*, August 1898, p. 258.

113. The adulteration of food generally occurs in some wholesome form. Margarine is an excellent food substance, though it is not butter; the potato is very nourishing, but it should not be found in bread.—*Daily Telegraph*, 27th August 1898.

114. Would not a man of far inferior abilities than Bismarck have become cognisant from that moment of France's exact power of resistance?—*Fortnightly Review*, September 1898, p. 407.

115. There was that early *Letter of Advice to Queen Elizabeth*, written in 1584-5, thought for a time to be Lord Burghley's work, but now known to be written by Bacon.—*Is it Shakespeare?* p. 320.

116. On the 20th, as Mr. E. G. was returning in his motor-car from a fishing expedition, he ran his car on to a bank, with the result that he and a companion were thrown out and the car overturned and smashed.—*Times Weekly*, 28th September 1906, p. 622.

117. On the other hand, the authors and nearly the whole of public opinion took the opposite view, and cordially supported the dissentient booksellers and free trade in books.—*Ibid.*, 28th September 1906, p. 629.

118. A Japanese and English instructor from London have been engaged to give instruction in ju-jitsu at the Gunnery School on Whale Island and the Naval Barracks at Portsmouth.—*Ibid.*, 28th September 1906, p. 620.

119. Grave doubts are entertained that these statements are far too optimistic, and that the sudden stress of work, which will succeed his

return to the capital, will bring on a relapse.—*Daily Telegraph*, 16th October 1906, p. 10.

120. The recent action of the *Times* Book-Club, which, we are informed, is owned, originated, and directed by the *Times* newspaper, must be my excuse for troubling you with a letter.—RUDYARD KIPLING, letter to the *Times*, 30th October 1906.

121. It is true that as a "compound householder," who, by the way, constitute nearly half the electors of London, he pays indirectly, and he does not understand that this very system adds something quite appreciable to his rent.—*Daily Telegraph*, 30th October 1906, p. 11.

122. Which do you like best, the English or Russian armies?—*Century Magazine*, September 1906, p. 654.

123. If any one were asked to name the reason that the French have a national drama and the English have none, he would say, "The French drama is a part of French literature and is honoured as a fine art: not so the English."—*Daily Telegraph*, 1st December 1906, p. 11.

124. I found her accompanied with one person only, a commonplace talker, who upon my entrance arose, and after a very slight civility sat down again.—STEELE, *Spectator*.

125. In France the dispute between Church and State has reached an acute crisis. The Pope, having ordered the Catholic clergy to disobey the law of the French Government, is now taking drastic measures, among which prominently figures the expulsion of the Pope's semi-official representative.—*Daily Telegraph*, 12th December 1906, p. 10.

126. Though the glutton or the drunkard may be considered bores, the great eater and the great drinker, seen from the outside, is a pleasant fellow: we like him, we admire him, we emulate him.—*Macmillan's Magazine*, December 1906, p. 126.

127. A weakness, which some would miscall gratitude and is oftentimes the corruption of a heart not ignoble.—RICHARDSON.

Appendix to Chapter XVIII. Plurals in Special Senses.

(*a*) Nouns which have two forms in the Plural,—each form with a separate meaning of its own:—

Brother	Brothers,	*sons of the same mother.*
	Brethren,	*members of the same society, profession, etc.*
Cherub	Cherubim,	*angels of a certain rank.*
	Cherubs,	*images or models of a cherub.*
Cloth	Cloths,	*kinds or pieces of cloth* (Distributive).
	Clothes,	*articles of dress* (Collective).
Cow	Cows,	*individual cows* (Distributive).
	Kine,	*cattle* (Collective).
Die	Dies,	*stamps for coining* (Distributive).
	Dice,	*small cubes used in games* (Collective).
Genius	Geniuses,	*men of genius or talent.*
	Genii,	*fabulous spirits of the air.*
Index	Indexes,	*tables of contents.*
	Indices,	*signs used in algebra.*
Pea	Peas,	(Distributive), as "a pod with 9 *peas*."
	Pease,	(Collective), as "pease-pudding."

Penny	Pennies,	=*penny-pieces* (Distributive).
	Pence,	(sometimes Collective).[1]
Staff	Staves,	*sticks or poles.*
	Staffs,	*departments in the army.*
Stamen	Stamens,	*male organs of flowers* (Distributive).
	Stamina,	*endurance, vigour,* lit. *threads* (Collective).
Shot	Shot,	*little balls discharged from a gun.*
	Shots,	*discharges; as, "he had two shots."*

(*b*) Nouns which have one meaning in the Singular and another in the Plural :—

Singular.	*Plural.*
Advice, counsel.	*Advices*, information.
Air, atmosphere.	*Airs*, assumed demeanour.
Ban, a curse (under a *ban*).	*Banns*, announcement (*banns* of marriage).
Beef, flesh of ox.	*Beeves*, cattle, bulls and cows.
Compass, range or extent.	*Compasses*, an instrument for measuring.
Copper, a kind of metal.	*Coppers*, pennies.
Domino, a kind of mask.	*Dominoes*, the game so-called.
Force, strength or energy.	*Forces*, army.
Good, benefit.	*Goods*, movable property.
Iron, a kind of metal.	*Irons*, fetters and other things made of iron.
Physic, medicine.	*Physics*, natural science.
Return, coming back.	*Returns*, statistics.
Salt, seasoning substance.	*Salts*, smelling salts.
Sand, a fine particle of rock or shell.	*Sands*, a tract of sandy land.
Vapour, invisible steam.	*Vapours*, dejection.
Vesper, evening.	*Vespers*, evening prayers.
Water, the liquid element.	*Waters*, springs or rivers.

(*c*) Nouns which have two meanings in the Plural against one in the Singular :—

	Singular.		*Plural.*
Colour,	hue, tint.	*Colours*	1. Kinds of colour. 2. *Flag of regiment.*
Custom,	habit.	*Customs*	1. Habits. 2. *Toll* or *tax*.
Element,	simple substance.	*Elements*	1. Simple substances. 2. *Conditions of the air.*
Effect,	result.	*Effects*	1. Results. 2. *Goods and chattels.*
Letter,	1. Of alphabet. 2. Epistle.	*Letters*	1. Of alphabet. 2. Epistles. 3. *Learning.*

[1] Hence *six-pence* has a Collective sense, denoting a single coin, which makes the noun appear to be Singular, so that we say *a sixpence* (Singular), *sixpences* (Plural).

Singular.		Plural.	
Manner,	mode or way.	*Manners*	1. Modes, ways. 2. *Behaviour.*
Number,	as in counting.	*Numbers*	1. As in counting. 2. *Poetry.*
Pain,	suffering.	*Pains*	1. Sufferings. 2. *Trouble, care.*
Part,	portion.	*Parts*	1. Portions. 2. *Abilities.*
Premise,	a proposition.	*Premises*	1. Propositions. 2. *Buildings.*
Quarter,	a fourth part.	*Quarters*	1. Fourth parts. 2. *Lodgings.*
Spectacle,	anything seen.	*Spectacles*	1. Things seen. 2. *Eye-glasses.*

(*d*) Nouns which have two meanings in the Singular against one in the Plural :—

Singular.		Plural.	
Abuse	1. Wrong use. 2. Reproaches.	*Abuses*,	wrong uses.
Foot	1. Part of body. 2. Infantry.	*Feet*,	parts of body.
Horse	1. A quadruped. 2. Cavalry.	*Horses*,	quadrupeds.
Issue	1. Result. 2. Offspring.	*Issues*,	results.
Light	1. A lamp. 2. Radiance.	*Lights*,	lamps.
People	1. A nation. 2. Persons.	*Peoples*,	nations.
Powder	1. A medicinal mixture. 2. Gunpowder.	*Powders*,	medicinal mixtures.
Practice	1. Habitual act. 2. Professional connection.	*Practices*,	habitual acts.
Stone	1. A piece of rock. 2. Fourteen pounds.	*Stones*,	pieces of rock.
Wood	1. A forest. 2. Timber.	*Woods*,	forests.

CHAPTER XIX.—THE NORMAL ORDER OF WORDS.

275. The Rule of Proximity.—If words, phrases, and clauses are not put in their right places, the sense of a sentence is either rendered doubtful or destroyed altogether. Observe how the sense of the following sentences is marred by the misplacement of some of the words :—

(1) *Paradise Lost* is the name of Milton's great epic poem on the loss of Paradise divided into twelve separate parts.
(2) You have already been informed of the sale of Ford's theatre where Mr. Lincoln was assassinated for religious purposes.
(3) Few people learn anything that is worth learning at all easily.
(4) He was shot by a secretary under notice to quit with whom he had found fault very fortunately without effect.
(5) He repeated these lines after he had read them only once with perfect accuracy.
(6) Our correspondent saw several soldiers dead or wounded riding over the battlefield.

The cardinal rule is that *things which are to be thought of together must be mentioned as closely as possible together.* This is called **The Rule of Proximity.** In no language is this more important than in modern English, which has lost almost all the inflexions, that in Old English, as in other freely inflected languages, served as a guide to the grammatical relations of words. In every one of the above examples this rule has been violated. By attending to this rule, we can correct these sentences one by one in the order in which they stand:—

(1) *Paradise Lost,* divided into twelve separate parts, is the name of Milton's great epic poem on the loss of Paradise.
(2) You have already been informed of the sale, for religious purposes, of Ford's theatre, where Mr. Lincoln was assassinated.
(3) Few people learn anything easily that is worth learning at all.
(4) He was shot, fortunately without effect, by a secretary under notice to quit, with whom he had found fault.
(5) After he had read these lines only once, he repeated them with perfect accuracy.
(6) Our correspondent, riding over the battlefield, saw several soldiers dead or wounded.

A correspondent addressed the following letter to the editor of a newspaper:—

Dear Sir—Please inform a constant reader how to cure bunions in to-day's issue.

He ought to have placed the phrase *in to-day's issue* at the beginning of the sentence instead of at the end. But the editor published the following answer:—

There are no bunions in to-day's issue, nor in yesterday's, nor in to-morrow's, nor in any that is to come, and were you a careful as well as a constant reader you would have grasped this fact without being told.

Note.—The correspondent might have retaliated on the editor by telling him that his own English was at fault. The first sentence should have been,—"There are no bunions in to-day's issue, nor in yesterday's, nor *will there be any* in to-morrow's," etc.

Sometimes it is necessary to recast a sentence, a mere change of order being insufficient:—

> Very tenderly does Arethusa appeal to her son not to deprive her of his protection, companionship, and help, who had devoted her life to him, by retiring into a monastery.—*Academy*, 15th May 1872, p. 196.

The sentence can be recast as follows:—

> Very tenderly does Arethusa appeal to her son not to retire into a monastery and thereby deprive her, who had devoted her life to him, of his protection, companionship, and help.

In an inflected language, like Latin for example, the order of words is of less importance, because the sense is shown by the endings. The following words cannot have more than one meaning. The inflexions leave no choice.

Brut*us* et Cassi*us* Cæsar*em* interfec*erunt*.

The same five words, when translated into English without reference to their Latin inflexions, can, by being arranged in six different orders, give six different senses:—(1) "Brutus slew Cassius and Cæsar," (2) "Cæsar slew Brutus and Cassius," (3) "Cassius slew Cæsar and Brutus," (4) "Brutus and Cassius slew Cæsar," (5) "Cæsar and Brutus slew Cassius," (6) "Cæsar and Cassius slew Brutus."

All that we have to say in this chapter about "the normal order of words" in English consists of the various applications of the Rule of Proximity.

Nouns.

276. Nouns must be placed as near as possible to the nouns or pronouns with which they are connected in sense:—

> (1) The death is announced of Dr. Scott, the joint-author with Dr. Liddell of the well-known Greek dictionary.

Here "joint-author" is rightly placed close to "Dr. Scott," with which it is in apposition. So far, so good. But the noun "Scott" should, if possible, be nearer to the noun "death," and the noun "dictionary" to the noun "author." The sentence might be rewritten thus:—

> We regret to announce the death of Dr. Scott, who with Dr. Liddell was the joint-author of the well-known Greek dictionary.
>
> (2) As the leading and consistent champion of the oppressed, I trust you will permit me in your columns to advocate the cause of humanity towards helpless animals.—*To the Editor of the "Daily Telegraph,"* 6th Jan. 1898.

This sentence can be put right by changing "*I trust you will*" to "*you will, I trust.*" As it stands, the noun "champion" is wrongly placed in apposition with the pronoun "I."

Adjectives and Participles.

277. Attributive use.—When an adjective is used attributively (§ 58), it should as a rule be placed *before* the noun that it is intended to qualify:—

A *just* man. *Bright* prospects. *This* rose. *Other* roses.

There is a vast difference of meaning between an "English village" and "village English"; and it is the qualifying or adjectival word standing first that decides the meaning. In such examples as the following, however, the position of the adjective is exceptional:—

(*a*) If the adjective is enlarged by some qualifying phrase, it must be placed *after* its noun, to avoid a breach of the "rule of proximity":—

A matter too *urgent* to be put off any longer.

We could not separate *matter* from *urgent* by saying:—

A too urgent to be put off any longer matter.

(*b*) If several adjectives qualify a single noun, it often sounds better to place them *after* the noun than before it:—

God is the maker of all things *visible and invisible, animate and inanimate.*

(*c*) There are certain stock phrases, in which it has become idiomatic (chiefly through the influence of French) to place the adjective after its noun:—

The body *politic.* Malice *prepense.* Heir *apparent.* Lords *Temporal and Spiritual.* Notary *public.* Knight *errant.* Governor *General.* Bishop *elect.* The sum *total.* Point *blank* (the white or blank spot in the centre of a target). Letters *patent.* Price *current.* Lord *paramount.* Durance *vile.* Court *martial,* etc.

Note 1.—The adjective *alone*, as "he alone," is always placed after the noun or pronoun that it qualifies.

Note 2.—An adverbial phrase, when it is in the form of a preposition followed by its object, may have the force and do the work of a qualifying adjective. In this case it is always placed *after* the noun or pronoun which it qualifies:—

Maid *of Athens* = Athenian maid.
A change in theory = a theoretical change.

Observe the difference in meaning between:—

He worked hard to become a doctor *in London.*
He worked hard *in London* to become a doctor.

In the former sentence the italicised phrase (by the Rule of Proximity) qualifies the noun "doctor," and has the force of an adjective. In the latter it qualifies the verb "worked," and has the force of an adverb.

278. Predicative use.—When an adjective is used predicatively (§ 58), it is placed after its noun :—

All men are *mortal*. He lay *dead* on the ground. He became *very rich*. He was left *rich* by his father. The clouds hang *heavy* over the earth. (*Subjective Complement*, § 95.)

My father left me *poor*, but *well educated*. The judge declared him *guilty*. (*Objective Complement*, § 95.)

The difference in meaning between the two following sentences hinges on the position of the word "public" :—

He made *public* confessions. (*Attrib. use.*)
He made his confessions *public*. (*Predic. use.*)

279. Sometimes an adjective (§ 209, 3) is used instead of an adverb to qualify the predicate-verb of the sentence. In this case it must be placed as near as possible *after* the verb that it qualifies, as in example (*a*) given below :—

(*a*) I can do it *alone*.
(*b*) I *alone* can do it.

Observe that the sense of each sentence depends entirely on the position of the adjective "alone."

(*c*) He bought the material *cheap*.
(*d*) He bought *cheap* material.

In (*c*) "cheap" must be *parsed* as an adjective qualifying the noun "material" ; but in point of meaning it qualifies the verb "bought" and signifies "at a low price." The first sentence means that he bought good material at less than the market-price ; the second, that he bought inferior material at the market-price.

Adverbs.

280. If the word to be qualified is an Adjective, or an Adverb, or a Preposition, or a Conjunction, the qualifying Adverb is placed immediately *before it* :—

Adjective.—We are *half* pleased and *half* sorry.
Adverb.—He stood *far* apart from me.
Preposition.—He arrived *long* before the time.
Conjunctions.—This is *precisely* how it happened.
He has been ill *ever* since Monday.

Note.—But "enough" is placed *after* the adjective that it qualifies, because it is very often followed by a phrase :—

Your pay is good *enough* for your work.

281. If the Verb to be qualified is *Intransitive*, the Adverb, unless it is one of Time, is placed immediately *after* it :—

He *always* laughed *heartily* at a good joke.
He *never* spoke *boastfully* about his own merits.
He *often* wept *bitterly* on passing that tomb.
He *sometimes* slept *soundly* in my house.
He *seldom* slept *well* in any house but his own.

These sentences would all sound very awkward, if the adverbs in each changed places :—

He heartily laughed always at a good joke.

282. If the Verb to be qualified is *Transitive*, the qualifying Adverb must not be allowed to separate the verb and its object.

The Adverb must therefore be placed either *before the Verb* or (which is rather more common) *after the Object* :—

He bore his losses *cheerfully*.
He *briefly* explained his meaning.

But if the Object is qualified by a clause, or consists of a good many words, the adverb may come between the verb and its object :—

He rewarded *liberally* all those who had served him well.

But this is scarcely so idiomatic as, "He liberally rewarded," etc.

283. An Adverb is often placed *between* the Auxiliary verb and the Principal verb (whether Transitive or Intransitive) :—

The wind has *suddenly* risen. I have *quite* understood you.

An adverbial phrase follows the same rule of place as the adverbs :—

We shall *within the next few days* hear what he intends to do.

The sense would be quite different, if we said :—

We shall hear what he intends to do within the next few days.

The Negative adverb "*not*" is always placed between the Auxiliary verb and the Principal verb :—

We have *not* seen him since Monday last.

284. An Adverb is placed first in a sentence—(*a*) when it qualifies *the whole sentence*, (*b*) when it is emphatic.

Rewrite the following pairs of sentences, so as to show how the sense depends on the position of the Adverb :—

{ *Happily* he did not die. { *At length* he wrote to her.
{ He did not die *happily*. { He wrote to her *at length*.

285. **Divided Infinitives.**—An adverb should not be placed between the "to" and the Infinitive. The custom is springing up, but it is not sanctioned by the usage of good writers :—

I feel it my duty to plainly inform you, etc.
I feel it my duty to inform you plainly, etc.

286. Only.—This word should be placed immediately before the word that it is intended to qualify; otherwise there is a risk of ambiguity.

(*a*) *Only* he promised to read the first chapter of that book.

Here "only" is an Adjective qualifying the pronoun "he." *He alone* would be more suitable than *only he*.

He alone, and no one else, promised to read the first chapter, etc.

(*b*) He *only* promised to read the first chapter of that book.

Here "only" is so placed as if it were meant to qualify the verb "promised"; hence the meaning might be that he merely promised, but did not perform the promise.

(*c*) He promised *only* to read the first chapter of that book.

Here "only" is so placed as if it were meant to qualify the verb "to read"; and hence the meaning might be that he did not promise to study, analyse, or remember, but *only to read*.

(*d*) He promised to read *only* the first chapter of that book.

That is, he promised to read nothing more than the *first* chapter. Here "only" is rightly made to qualify the adjective "the first."

(*e*) He promised to read the first chapter of that book *only*.

That is, he promised to read the first chapter of no other book but that. Here "only" qualifies the phrase "of that book." To prevent ambiguity it is here placed last.

Subject and Object.

287. The Subject usually precedes its verb; but the following exceptions should be noted:—

(*a*) When the verb is Intransitive, and is preceded by the introductory adverb "there"; see § 153 (2), *Note*:—

On the whole *there* is nothing to prove his guilt.

(*b*) When the verb is used for asking a question:—

At what hour in the morning does *he* get up?

(*c*) When the verb is in the Imperative mood:—

Go *ye* into all the world, and preach the gospel to every creature.

(*d*) To express a wish or a condition:—

Wish { Long live *the king*.
May *he* never again come inside this house.

Condition { Should *he* meet me, he would know me at once.
Had *he* met me, he would have known me.

288. If the Object to a verb is expressed by a Conjunctive pronoun, or is qualified by an Interrogative, it is placed before the verb instead of after it:—

The house *that* we occupy suits us well. (*Conjunctive.*)
What kind of book do you like best? (*Interrogative.*)

289. If the Object is qualified by an Adjective-clause, it may be separated from its verb by an adverbial phrase :—

The captain took *with a thankful heart* the good things which the firm provided.

Nobler and loftier emotions lit up *with a generous enthusiasm* the hearts of men who had heavy sacrifices still to make.

If the italicised phrases were placed at the end of the sentence, the sense would be either obscured or radically altered.

Pronoun and Antecedent.

290. A Conjunctive pronoun or Conjunctive adverb must always be placed as close as possible to its antecedent :—

(1) I have read Plato's writings, who succeeded Socrates.

Here it would have been better to say "the writings *of Plato, who* succeeded," etc.

(2) It is the system, not the individual, which I condemn.

The clause *which I condemn* should be written after *system.*

(3) I now come to one of the objections to free trade, which has never yet been answered.

The sentence can be rewritten thus, "Among the objections to free trade, I now come to one which has never yet been answered."

291. Demonstrative and Conjunctive pronouns should not, as a rule, be mentioned until the Antecedent has been mentioned.

Avoid such an order of words as the following :—

Before we pay *them,* let us see what work *the men* have done.

The proper arrangement would be :—

Before we pay *the men,* let us see what work *they* have done.

Preposition and Object.

292. In prose (not always in poetry) the preposition is placed immediately before its Object. But the following exceptions occur in prose also :—

(*a*) When the Object is "whom," "which," or "what," the preposition *may be* placed last in the sentence and its Object first :—

That is the man *whom* we were looking *for.* (*Conjunctive.*)
Which of these chairs did you sit *on?* (*Interrogative.*)

(*b*) When the Object is the Conjunctive pronoun "that," the preposition *must be* put last. This rule is invariable.

This is the man *that* we were looking *for.*

Prepositions.

293. A Preposition must be placed immediately after the word with which it is intended to be construed :—

Books authorised by teachers as fit for use.
Books authorised as fit for use by teachers.

The meaning of each sentence turns entirely upon the position of the phrase *by teachers*.

Correlative Conjunctions.

294. When Conjunctions are used correlatively, that is, in pairs, each member of the pair must invariably be connected with words *of the same part of speech* or *of the same function*.

(1) *Not . . . but* :—

A wise physician endeavours *not* to cure diseases, *but* to prevent them. (*Infinitive mood.*)
Objections were raised *not* to his having spent the money, *but* to his having done so without leave. (*Preposition.*)

(2) *Not only . . . but also* or *but* :—

All his work was done *not only* with zeal, *but also* with judgment. (*Preposition.*)
He was *not only* sad, *but* disgusted. (*Adjective and Participle.*)
This *not only* amused, *but* enlightened them. (*Verb.*)

(3) *Not more . . . than* :—

I am *not more* amused, *than* surprised. (*Participle.*)

(4) *Both . . . and* :—

He is thoroughly tired out *both* in mind *and* in body. (*Preposition.*)

(5) *Either . . . or*, *neither . . . nor* :—

They have worked *either* stupidly *or* lazily. (*Adverb.*)
This wall was built *either* crookedly *or* of bad material. (*Adverb and Adverb-phrase.*)
Neither James *nor* I saw it. (*Noun and Pronoun.*)

Exercise.

Rewrite or rearrange the following sentences in such a way as to remove any impropriety that may exist in the order of the words. (These might be answered orally and at sight in class.)

1. The chair cost ten shillings on which he sat.
2. He shot the mad dog after driving it out of the house with a gun.
3. A gang of robbers entered the house at night armed from head to foot.
4. He is an undoubted man of honesty, and yet persons accused him of cheating who ought to have known him better.
5. This tablet was erected to the memory of a faithful dog that was accidentally shot as a mark of respect.
6. He left the house where he had slept next morning mounted on a horse.
7. All experience shows that they cannot deal with the difficulties of housing alone.
8. The judge saw more clearly that the man was innocent than the jury did.

9. The girl was conveyed from the house where she had just been married in a carriage and pair.

10. They found the house on the top of a hill where they wished to spend the night.

11. It is believed that they are most desirous of keeping up this practice who profit most by it.

12. There was a small house on the side of the mountain, out of which came a black slave.

13. The magistrate passed too severe a sentence, being young and inexperienced.

14. English is not only difficult to read, but also to speak.

15. Such were the Centaurs of Ixion's race,
Who a bright cloud for Juno did embrace.

16. The general ordered indignantly the deserters to be shot.

17. I only like a pear when it is ripe.

18. He wisely did this because he was ordered, not because he liked it.

19. Northern India is bounded by the Himalaya mountains, with at their base a very thick jungle.

20. The natives of the other islands only knew how to divide time by the sun and moon, whereas these had acquired some knowledge of the stars also.

21. They are as ready, nay more ready, to apply these things to their right uses than we are.

22. I soon arrived at the mansion of my friend, which was guarded by a huge mastiff that flew at me.

23. He cannot be said to have died prematurely whose work was finished, nor does he deserve to be lamented who died so full of honours. —SOUTHEY.

24. Sir Morton Peto spoke of the notion that the national debt might be repudiated with absolute contempt.

25. An unquestioned man of genius.

26. I am neither an ascetic in theory or practice.

27. Her success is neither the result of system nor strategy.

28. I never remember to have felt an event more deeply than Horner's death.

29. His last journey was to Cannes, whence he was never destined to return.

30. No one has been able to deny that there is a connection between virtue and vice on the one hand and happiness and misery on the other.—*Saturday Review*, 2nd Sept. 1865.

31. All goes on well at Winchester, the attention and attendance gradually deepening and increasing.

32. Since several thoughts may be natural which are low and grovelling, an epic poet should not only avoid such sentiments as are unnatural or affected, but also such as are mean and vulgar.—*Spectator*, No. 279.

33. This shipping is to a great extent now the product of German yards, which have developed rapidly to suit the requirements every day increasing of local shipbuilding.—*Daily Telegraph*, 27th Jan. 1898.

34. There are not meanwhile critics wanting here who assign this victory as regards moral and political supremacy in China to Russia.—*Berlin Telegram, Daily Telegraph*, 5th Feb. 1898.

35. The sitting closed definitely at five o'clock without the matter which had brought so many together having been practically entered upon.—*Daily Telegraph*, 8th Feb. 1898.

36. The death occurred last week in Madrid of Mr. W. Macpherson, formerly British Vice-Consul at Seville.—*Times Weekly*, 11th Feb. 1898.

37. The traveller received the good things which the company had provided with much thankfulness.

38. His daily custom is to tell anecdotes which amuse or excite the company after dinner.

39. Othello seizing a bolster, full of rage and jealousy, smothers Desdemona.

40. Some paintings by lady artists, well worthy of inspection, will be exhibited to-morrow.

41. The daughter of a civil officer retired from India, brought up in England, seeks employment.

42. Lost, a walking-stick belonging to a gentleman, with a curiously shaped head.

43. Here the train made a halt to take in water, which lasted only for a few minutes.

44. He wept in passing that tomb often.

45. Do you take the medicine that I send you regularly?

46. In all scientific books it is necessary to clearly define the technical terms employed.

47. I never remember to have spent a more agreeable visit.

48. Zedekiah was sent captive to Babylon, from which he was never destined to return.

49. His body was found floating lifeless on the water at a short distance from where the boat was upset by a fisherman.

50. No one is entitled to form or express an opinion on the relations between Nelson and Lady Hamilton, or on the parentage of Horatio, who has not carefully studied the letters to be found in this invaluable collection.—*Times Weekly*, 4th March 1898.

51. It will be a war on sea, instead of land, largely, and we do not know much about sea warfare of late years.—Quoted in *Daily Telegraph*, 15th April 1898.

52. Right from the birth of a Spanish monarch he is subject to an etiquette the most pronounced.—*Cassell's Family Magazine*, Jan. 1897, p. 149.

53. For this person to accuse us of want of knowledge can only create amusement in the minds of those who have studied the views and know the facts as I have and do.—*Middlesex County Times*, 30th April 1898.

54. We may well ask what is the use of it, if parallel action in shipbuilding is not accompanied by energetic action in diplomacy?—*Homeward Mail*, 25th July 1898.

55. With regard to the Ottoman bank, the government, in case of its leaving Cyprus, would undertake some measures to replace it.—*Report of Mr. Chamberlain's Speech*, 9th August 1898.

56. Mr. H., replying as to the action which had been taken on the report of the War Stores Commission by the Army Council, insisted that what had been done in the way of punishment was just, and that in every case the benefit of the doubt had been given to those concerned.—*Daily Telegraph*, 26th Oct. 1906, p. 8.

57. It was clearly inevitable that a man who regarded human love as the very centre and starting-point of all the good influences of life should look upon teaching thus understood with absolute detestation.—LESLIE STEPHEN, *Hours in a Library*, 3rd Ser. p. 378.

58. She is in that time of life which is neither affected with the follies of youth, nor the infirmities of age; and her conversation is so mixed with gaiety and prudence, that she is agreeable both to the young and the old. —STEELE, *Spectator*.

CHAPTER XX.—INVERSION OF THE NORMAL ORDER: EMPHASIS.

295. Inversion of Normal Order.—In the last chapter we showed what is the normal order of words in a sentence. We have now to show how emphasis may be given to a word by placing it out of the normal order. A word so placed excites surprise, and thereby attracts more attention. But no inversion must be made, if it obscures the meaning or offends the ear.

(1) The Object placed before its verb instead of after it:—

Direct object:—

Silver and gold have I none; but *such as I have* give I unto thee: in the name of Jesus of Nazareth, arise and walk.—*Acts* iii. 6.

If *heaven* I cannot summon to my prayer,
Hell will I move, and try mine interest there.
DRYDEN'S *Virgil: Æneid*, Book vii.

The sorrow for the dead is the only sorrow from which we refuse to be divorced. *Every other wound* we seek to heal, *every other affliction* to forget; but *this wound* we consider it a duty to keep open, *this affliction* we cherish and brood over in solitude. —WASHINGTON IRVING.

Indirect object:—

They held their peace, and glorified God, saying, Then *to the Gentiles also* hath God granted repentance unto life.—*Acts* xi. 18.

(2) The Complement placed before its verb instead of after it:—

On Linden, when the sun was low,
All bloodless lay the untrodden snow,
And *dark* as winter was the flow
Of Iser rolling rapidly.—CAMPBELL.

Great is Diana of the Ephesians.—*Acts* xix. 28.

Immense is the attention that the government in France is devoting to the Zola trial.—*Daily Telegraph*, 16th Feb. 1898.

Fallen, fallen is Babylon, the great city.[1]—*Rev.* xviii. 2.

(3) Adverb or Adverbial phrase placed first :—

Not at once was language adequate to receive or take up into itself the ideas that were asking for expression.—JOWETT.

On these two commandments hang all the law and the prophets.—*Matt.* xxii. 40.

In thy presence is fulness of joy ; *at thy right hand* there are pleasures for evermore.—*Psalms* xvi. 11.

(4) The verb placed first (rare except in poetry) :—

Stole a maiden from her place,
Lightly to the warrior stept,
Took the face-cloth from the face ;
Yet she neither moved nor wept.—TENNYSON.

Flashed all their sabres bare,
Flashed as they turned in air.—*Ibid.*

(5) Adverb with verb placed first :—

Thus came into prominence what are called sacred and profane knowledge : *thus came into the presence of each other* two opposing parties, one relying on reason, the other on revelation. —DRAPER.

Then burst his mighty heart.—SHAKESPEARE.

Up goes my grave Impudence to the maid.—*Tatler.*

(6) Adjective or Adjectival phrase placed after its noun :—

I appeal from Philip *drunk* to Philip *sober.*

Alfred *the Great.* Pliny *the Elder.* Pliny *the Younger.*

I will talk of things *heavenly* or things *earthly* ; things *moral* or things *evangelical* ; things *sacred* or things *profane* ; things *past* or things *to come* ; things *foreign* or things *at home* ; things *essential* or things *circumstantial* ; provided that all be done to our profit.—BUNYAN.

Absence of occupation is not rest ;
A mind *unoccupied* 's a mind *distressed.*—POPE.

I love thee, Cassio,
But nevermore be officer *of mine.*—SHAKESPEARE.

---

[1] This is the rendering given in the Revised Translation, 1885. In the Authorised Version of 1611 the wording is far less pointed :—

Babylon is fallen, is fallen, that great city.

Compare what Horace puts into the mouth of Hannibal :—

Occidit, occidit,
Spes omnis et fortuna nostri
Nominis, Asdrubale interempto.—Ode iv. 4, 70.

"Fallen, fallen is all the hope and fortune of our name ; for Hasdrubal is slain."

The retort *courteous* . . . The quip *modest* . . . The reply *churlish* . . . The reproof *valiant* . . . The countercheck *quarrelsome* . . . The lie *circumstantial* . . . The lie *direct*.—SHAKESPEARE, *As You Like It*, v. 4.

296. **Emphatic Positions.**—The middle of a sentence is less emphatic than the beginning, and the beginning in most cases is less emphatic than the end.

(*a*) *The beginning.*—If we take a word out of its normal order in order to place it first, the emphasis that it acquires arises partly from the surprise excited by its unusual position, and partly from the prominence that naturally belongs to the initial word.

The subject of a sentence is usually placed first, because that is its normal order. In this position it possesses a certain degree of prominence, because it names the person or thing that does or suffers what the verb asserts :—

Romulus, according to the ancient legend, founded Rome.

If that degree of prominence, however, happens not to be sufficient, additional emphasis can be given to the subject "Romulus" by placing it last :—

Rome, according to the ancient legend, was founded by Romulus.
The founder of Rome, according to the ancient legend, was Romulus.

(*b*) *The end.*—The end of a sentence is more emphatic than the beginning, because one's mind is held in suspense till we know the closing circumstance, and our interest is aroused to know what that circumstance is. This is called the PRINCIPLE OF SUSPENSE.

(1) Add to your faith *virtue*; and to virtue *knowledge*; and to knowledge *temperance*; and to temperance *patience*; and to patience *godliness*; and to godliness *brotherly kindness*; and to brotherly kindness *charity*.—2 *Peter* i. 5-7.

(2) Knowing that you are very inquisitive after everything that is curious in nature, I will wait on you *in the dusk of the evening with my show upon my back*.—*Spectator*, No. 271.

Here the emphatic phrases, the first of which shows the time of coming, and the second the purpose of coming, are rightly placed last.

Corollary.—If we do not wish a word to be emphatic, we must avoid placing it in an emphatic position :—

That all members of the same household should live together in peace is necessary.
He, deserted by his friends and pursued by his enemies, fled from the country.

The undue emphasis given in one sentence to the word "necessary," and in the other to "he," can be avoided by altering their positions:—

> It is necessary that all members of the same household should live together in peace.
>
> Deserted by his friends, and pursued by his enemies, he fled from the country.

297. Correlative Conjunctions and Phrases.—Conjunctions and phrases which go in pairs add to the energy of a sentence, because the first one keeps the mind in suspense (§ 296, *b*) till the second one has been mentioned:—

Either—or	Partly—partly	On the one hand—on the other hand
Neither—nor	In the first place—in the second place	Though—yet
Not only—but also	On this side—on that side	As—so
Both—and	Here—there	Indeed—but
If—then	Not—but	

(1) The use of language is to conceal the thoughts.

To emphasise *conceal* we could say:—"The use of language is not to express, but to conceal the thoughts."

(2) I regard the prospects of peace with confidence.

To emphasise *confidence* we could say:—"I regard the prospects of peace not only with hope, but with confidence."

(3) He is both a fool and a knave.

To emphasise *fool* we should say:—"He is not only a knave, but also a fool"; or, "He is a fool as well as a knave." To emphasise *knave*, we should say:—"He is not only a fool, but also a knave"; or "He is a knave as well as a fool."

298. Emphasis by Repetition.—Emphasis is sometimes added to a word by repeating it, or by adding some other word almost synonymous. Repetition, when it adds force, is "not like a bird flapping its wings uselessly in the air, but like a blacksmith repeating his blows on an anvil" (Nichol).

> If I were an American, as I am an Englishman, I would never lay down my arms, *never—never—never*.—BURKE.
>
> Christ being raised from the dead dieth no more; *death hath no more dominion over him*.—*New Test.*
>
> Let our watchword be Union,—*union* of the party, *union* of the kingdom, *union* of the empire.—JOS. CHAMBERLAIN.
>
> *They are dead.* They will never again be heard upon the heaths singing at morning their happy songs; they will never more drink with their peers in the deep ingle-nooks of home. *They are perished. They have disappeared.* Alas! the valiant fellows.—BELLOC, *Hills and the Sea.*

Our language abounds in phrases, in which words of the same or almost the same meaning go in pairs :—

They were driven out *bag and baggage*. He works only by *fits and starts*. His progress is by *leaps and bounds*. He was *fair and square* in all his dealings. Words full of *fire and fury*. He is a stickler for *forms and ceremonies*. He is *free and easy* in his manners. His presence is *gall and wormwood* to me. Where are my *goods and chattels*? He took to it *heart and soul*. He is very *high and mighty*. Turned out of *house and home*. To all *intents and purposes*. Eager for the *loaves and fishes* of office. He would not yield one *jot or tittle*. His will is *null and void*. Over *head and ears* in debt. The *pains and penalties* of the law. He arrived *safe and sound*. All *stuff and nonsense*. *Time and tide* wait for no man. If you do this, *well and good*. This is my *will and pleasure*. He worked with *might and main*. Drenched *through and through*. *First and foremost* be truthful.

299. "It is," "it was."—These introductory phrases are much used for giving prominence to the word that the writer wishes to emphasise (see § 75, *c*).

(1) Romulus, according to the ancient legend, founded Rome.

If "Romulus" is not sufficiently emphatic as it stands, we could say:—"*It was* Romulus who, according to the ancient legend, founded Rome."

(2) Cicero admired Pompey.

These words stand in their normal order, and one is not more emphatic than the other. Each in turn might be emphasised as follows :—"It was Cicero who admired Pompey"; "It was admiration, not blame, that Cicero expressed for Pompey"; "It was Pompey whom Cicero admired."

300. Conjunctions and Prepositions repeated.—If we wish to give equal emphasis to each word in a series of particulars, we can do so by repeating the conjunction or preposition before each of them instead of mentioning it once only before the first or last :—

Now, brethren, if I come unto you speaking with tongues, what shall I profit you, except I shall speak to you *either by* revelation, *or by* knowledge, *or by* prophesying, *or by* doctrine?—1 *Cor.* xiv. 6.

The latter part of this sentence would sound very feeble in comparison if it stood thus :—"Except I shall speak to you by revelation, knowledge, prophesying, or doctrine."

301. Recapitulation of Clauses.—A series of subjects or clauses can be recapitulated by the use of pronouns like "these" or "such"; and this adds to the energy of the sentence :—

Intellect, imagination, power of expression, humour, taste, truth to life, and truth to human nature,—*these* are not the qualities which to-day make a writer popular.—*Fort. Rev.*, Feb. 1898, p. 280.

The storm had passed, the sun was shining on the green leaves of the trees; the stream was dancing around the rocks; the birds hopped about him as they chirped with their cheerful notes; *such* were the pleasant scenes and sounds that welcomed the wanderer back to his home.

302. Antithesis.—Antithesis means "setting one word against another," like balancing opposite things against each other in a pair of scales. The balance of form and sound not only pleases the ear, but is an aid to memory, as we may gather from its frequent use in proverbs, and in the best-remembered sayings of great authors:—"It never rains, but it pours"; "A bird in the hand is worth two in the bush"; "Evil communications corrupt good manners"; "The Sabbath was made for man, not man for the Sabbath."

God, who at sundry times and in divers manners, spake in time past unto the fathers by the prophets, hath in these last days spoken unto us by his Son, whom he hath appointed heir of all things, by whom also he made the worlds.—*Hebrews* i. 1, 2.

The antithesis of this finely balanced sentence is marred in the Revised Version of 1885, where it is made to run as follows:—

God, having of old time spoken unto the fathers in the prophets by divers portions and in divers manners, hath at the end of these days spoken unto us in his Son, whom he appointed heir of all things, through whom also he made the worlds.

Exercises.

I. *Rearrange, or if necessary supplement or rewrite, the following sentences so as to throw the emphasis on certain words as directed:—*

1. I am not sure he said that. (Emphasise (1) *sure*, (2) *he*, (3) *said*, (4) *that*, (5) *I*.)

2. They brought home her dead warrior. (Emphasise *home*.)

3. No man hath greater love than this. (Emphasise *greater love*.)

4. Consummate men of business are almost as rare as great poets, and perhaps rarer than veritable saints and martyrs.—HELPS. (Emphasise *rare* and *rarer*.)

5. The battle of Hastings was fought in 1066. (Emphasise (1) *the battle of Hastings*, (2) *in 1066*.)

6. A greater mistake was never made. (Emphasise *never*.)

7. Thou didst not anoint mine head with oil.—*New Testament*. (Emphasise *mine head with oil*.)

8. The wind blows keen, and night is coming on. (Emphasise *keen*.)

9. If I have told you earthly things, and ye believe not, how shall ye believe if I tell you of heavenly things. (Emphasise *earthly* and *heavenly*.)

10. When all were seated, a noise was suddenly heard outside. (Emphasise *suddenly*.)

11. Moses led the children of Israel out of Egypt. (Emphasise (1) *Moses*, (2) *the children of Israel*, (3) *Egypt*.)

12. The reign of Constantine marks the epoch of the transformation of Christianity from a religion into a political system. (Emphasise *the reign of Constantine*.)

13. All classes of the population did not with equal rapidity adopt monotheistic views. (Emphasise (1) *not with equal rapidity*, (2) *all classes of the population*.)

14. All parties in the Roman commonwealth concurred in appointing Quintus Fabius to the command of the Roman forces against Hannibal. (Emphasise (1) *all parties*, (2) *Quintus Fabius*, (3) *concurred*.)

15. Nature conciliates and forms the mind of man to his condition.—GOLDSMITH. (Emphasise *mind*.)

II. *Give some additional point to the following sentences by a change of order, or by a change of words, or by any other means:—*

1. Which of you by taking thought can add one cubit to his stature? (cf. *Matt.* vi. 27 with *Luke* xii. 25).

2. The government prosecuted Watson for high treason and were defeated; had they indicted him for aggravated assault, they would have obtained a conviction.

3. The authors of a revolution are not like those whom the revolution produces.

4. Tully was the first who observed that friendship improves happiness and abates misery by the doubling of our joy and dividing of our grief; a thought in which he has been followed by all the essayers upon friendship, that have written since his time.—*Spectator*, No. 68.

5. A clever magistrate would see whether a witness was deliberately lying a great deal better than a stupid jury.

6. The air last night condensed the vapour into white particles, but was not cold enough to turn them into actual hoar-frost.

7. Nothing in this war threatened our interests more than the interests of other countries.

8. A coxcomb, flushed with victories over the fair young creatures whom he has deceived, will protest and vow he never thought of matrimony, and wonder talking civilly could be so strangely misinterpreted.—*Spectator*, No. 288.

9. Nor is the reason that has led to the establishment of this moral law difficult to be discerned.

10. In our search after God and contemplation of Him our wisdom doth consist; in our worship and obedience to Him our religion doth consist; in both of them our happiness doth consist.

11. It is not without a degree of patient attention, greater than the generality are willing to bestow, though not greater than the object deserves, that the habit can be acquired of examining and judging of our own conduct with the same accuracy and impartiality as that of another.

12. Every man calleth that which pleaseth and is delightful to himself good, and that evil which displeaseth him.

13. Our Berlin correspondent telegraphs that in diplomatic circles there confidence is placed in no reports about the Chinese loan.—*Daily Telegraph*, 8th Feb. 1898.

14. In the last few hours that preceded his death he was only able to make a few audible sounds, and no one understood them.

15. In this evil world guilt has a better chance than misfortune of being treated with indulgence.

16. He that tells a lie is not sensible how great a task he undertakes; for he must invent twenty more to maintain one.

CHAPTER XXI.—EUPHONY OR SMOOTHNESS OF DICTION.

303. What is meant by Euphony.—By euphony (a word of Greek origin, *eu*, well; *phon-e*, sound) is meant that kind of diction which sounds well to the ear. It might also be defined as "a smooth and easy flow of words." The writer himself must have a good ear, if he wishes to know what will please the ear of his readers. A few hints, however, are herewith offered.

(1) Avoid (if possible) the use of two different constructions in the same sentence:—

They suspected that he *had been bribed* and *given* an unjust sentence.

Here there is an abrupt change from the Passive voice "had been bribed" to the Active voice "given." It would sound much better to say—

They suspected that he had received a bribe and given an unjust sentence.

(2) Avoid using the same word twice in the same sense, but in a different connection:—

To enable us to make the *necessary* arrangements it is *necessary* for us to hear not later than noon on Friday, 21st current.—*Daily Telegraph*, 20th Jan. 1898.

Write "the *requisite* arrangements" for "the *necessary* arrangements."

Alarming statements having been published to the effect that the desertion of sailors had assumed *alarming* dimensions, the Naval General Staff announces that all such assertions are devoid of foundation.—*Weekly Times*, 12th Oct. 1906, p. 649.

Change the second "alarming" to "very serious."

(3) Avoid using words of the same or nearly the same sound within a very short distance of each other:—

(1) If all local authorities *affected acted* in the same manner, rate-payers might receive some benefit from unity.—*Daily Telegraph*, 8th Feb. 1898.

Write *concerned* for *affected*.

(2) The darling of his old age killed *before* him *before* her time.

Write "killed *in front of him*" for "killed *before him*."

Under this heading we may place the following :—

(*a*) The same Preposition repeated in the same sentence :—

In spite *of* the gloomy forebodings *of* prophets *of* evil, and in spite *of* the attacks *of* the partisans *of* the proposed change *of* policy, the empire will stand.

(*b*) The Conjunction *that* repeated in the same sentence :—

I heard *that* the rumour *that* he had been warned *that* the bridge was unsafe was not founded on fact.

(*c*) Words of similar endings :—

In Court to-day the defendants *apparently reluctantly* produced a small faded piece of newspaper.—*Daily Express*, 17th Oct. 1906, p. 1.

Change the italicised words to "with apparent reluctance."

(4) Avoid mixing Present participles with Verbal nouns :—

The Epistle to the Hebrews, *bearing* in its title a special form of address, is yet universal in its drift, as *designing* to convince all mankind of the necessity of *seeking* for happiness in a future life, and *avoiding* all things *leading* men to sin.

It will add to the clearness as well as to the smoothness of the sentence, if the sentence is rewritten as follows :—

The Epistle to the Hebrews, though it bears in its title a special form of address, is yet universal in its drift, as its design is to convince all mankind of the necessity of seeking for happiness in a future life and avoiding everything that may lead to sin.

(5) Avoid awkward constructions to which the ear is not accustomed :—

Flying visits to settlements of Finns, Poles, Bohemians, and Russians, located along the Northern Pacific, *disclosed them to have attained* a degree of Americanisation, etc. — *Harper's Magazine*, Feb. 1898.

Write "disclosed *the fact that these foreign settlers had attained*," etc.

(6) Avoid using, within the same sentence, words that are spelt and sounded alike, but differ from one another both in sense and in origin :—

He *means* (intends) to take advice as to the best *means* (method) of testing the fact.

(7) Avoid using verbs in different tenses within the same sentence without necessity :—

The lion *roared* to a false note, and then *rates* the jackals for yelping in unison.—*Daily Telegraph*, 5th Feb. 1898.

Write *rated* for *rates* ; or change *roared* into *roars*.

But in such a sentence as the following, no exception could be taken to the verbs being in different tenses, since the sense obviously demands it :—

The Emperor of Austria *has* now quite *recovered* his health, and *drove* from Schönbrunn to Vienna yesterday.—*Daily Telegraph*, 3rd Oct. 1906, p. 8.

Here the Present Perfect tense agrees well with "now," and the Past Indefinite with "yesterday."

(8) Avoid ending a sentence with a short and pointless word.

The walls of the fortress, battered with guns from the ships and artillery from the shore for a space of eight hours, *fell*.

Write, "were demolished and fell to the ground."

(9) Avoid using the same form of participle more than once in the same clause or phrase :—

Yesterday the vestry of St. George, Hanover Square, decided to seal the memorial to be presented to the Duke of Devonshire, *praying* for the introduction of a bill in the next session of Parliament, *providing* for the creation of metropolitan municipalities.—*Daily Telegraph*, 21st Jan. 1898.

For *providing*, write "which should provide."

(10) Avoid using a string of Relatives in the same sentence :—

The doctrine in question only appears a paradox, because it has usually been so expressed as apparently to contradict these well-known facts ; *which*, however, were equally well known to the authors of the doctrine, *who* therefore could only have adopted from inadvertence any form of expression *which* could to a candid person appear inconsistent with it.—J. S. MILL.

Write "the said facts" for the first "which."

Few, indeed, are those *who* still linger among us *who* took an active part in the great movement in 1848.—*Review of Reviews*, April 1898, p. 343.

The sentence must be reconstructed :—"Among those who still linger among us there are indeed but few left, who took," etc.

(11) Avoid using adverbs close together for qualifying either the same or different words, if the said adverbs can be separated without loss of idiom :—

In fact, those who study such matters *closely*, *already*, I think, perceive the tentative beginnings, etc.—*Fortnightly Review*, Feb. 1898, p. 261.

Write, "perceive already, I think."

(12) Adverbs or adverbial phrases that qualify the same word should be separated by some intervening word, if the construction admits of it:—

He, *at four o'clock p.m.*, *in spite of his contract*, *obstinately and with some acrimony declared* that he would not work another hour. (Write: "At four o'clock P.M. he, in spite of his contract, declared obstinately and with some acrimony that he would not work another hour.")

(13) Avoid mixing up one form of comparison with another in the same sentence; or, if this mixture is unavoidable, put the shorter one first:—

He is one of the *most beautiful* and *sweetest* characters of the Middle Ages.—GOLDWIN SMITH, *United Kingdom*, vol. i. p. 48. (It would sound better to say, "sweetest and most beautiful.")

304. Play upon Words.—Euphony as well as point is sometimes produced by repeating the same (or nearly the same) word in a different meaning or in a different relation:—

Evil (=evil consequences) be to him that evil thinks (=imputes misconduct).

Bad (=unlucky) accidents happen to bad (=unskilful) players.

The right (*noun*) divine of kings to govern wrong (*adj.*).—POPE.

These are all practical (=useful) and practicable (=workable) measures.—*Fortnightly Review*, Feb. 1898, p. 317.

When our vices leave us (give us no more relish), we flatter ourselves that we have left (given up as an act of virtuous self-denial) our vices.—*French Proverb.*

He who never changes his mind (opinion) has no mind to change (no capacity for forming an opinion).—*Proverb.*

Playing upon words, if this adds nothing either to force or clearness, produces not euphony, but a jingle. The following lines in *Paradise Lost* have been condemned by a distinguished critic. (See Addison's *Spectator*, No. 297.)

And brought into the world a world of woe.
This tempted our attempt and wrought our fall.
At one slight bound high overleapt all bound.

Exercise on Euphony or Smoothness of Diction.

Improve the euphony of the following sentences, wherever you see occasion to do so:—

1. This brings me to the question—the most important of all—of the final aims of British policy in the Far East.—*Fortnightly Review*, Feb. 1898, p. 329.

2. So it is that I must be forced to get home partly by stealth and partly by force.—SWIFT.

3. I look upon it as my duty, so far as good health enabled me and as long as I keep within the bounds of truth, of duty, and of decency, to do, etc.—SWIFT.

4. Buildings should not be put up unless in conformity with the bye-laws, unless we wish to encourage the jerry-builder.—*Middlesex County Times*, 23rd July 1898.

5. Two great sins, one of omission and the other of commission, were committed by him.

6. Far and wide the plain of the Vardu softened by a delicate blue haze, and in the extreme distance a thread of silver light—the Gulf of Salonica—stretches.

7. That Pre-Raphaelitism was not, any more than any other, the school in which the doctrine of art for art's sake was being forced upon its students, may be conceded.—*Fortnightly Review*, Feb. 1898, p. 196.

8. Of the western provinces which obeyed the Cæsars, Britain was the last that was conquered, while they (the Cæsars) gave it away before any other province.

9. Wit should be used as a shield for defence, rather than as a sword to wound others.

10. Knowledge in one of its senses is synonymous with sensation.

11. If the profession of anything is good for anything, practice is better.

12. It is a remarkable fact that some of the most remarkable men in ancient times combined warlike pursuits with political ambition.

13. The blessings of fortune are the lowest; the next are the bodily advantages of strength and health; but the superlative blessings, in fine, are those of the mind.

14. A. came here daily; every other man came every other day.

15. Innumerable failures occur every day in the numerous careers of life.

16. As one peruses the accounts, as they are issued, the outlook seems to be very serious.

17. We should cease persisting in trying to put a quart into a pint pot.—*Review of Reviews*.

18. Your not having hitherto paid the tithe, should such be the case, and the fact that the sum you are now called upon to pay does not rateably correspond with any previous payment made by you, cannot be raised as an objection.—*Tithe-collector's Notice*.

19. The friendless state that he was in, and that he wished to die, made every one pity him.

20. Accident having opened a new and most congenial career to him, and having become a great favourite of, and of much use to, Mr. Nash, he ultimately accompanied his patron to London.—C. J. MATHEWS.

21. Perhaps we might venture to add, that it is hardly explicable, except as a portrait drawn by a skilful hand guided by love, and by love intensified by the consciousness of some impassable barrier.—LESLIE STEPHEN.

22. We believe the freedom and happiness of a people are not the result of their political institutions, but that their political institutions are, in a great degree, the result of their own temper and aspiration.—PARNELL.

23. I have a book printed at Antwerp, and which was once possessed by Adam Smith.

24. Mr. B. is a handy man with his fists, and maintains, after long experience, that he would prefer to rely on the clenched hand to defend himself in a mêlée to any weapon yet invented.—*Review of Reviews*, Feb. 1898, p. 129.

25. Mr. J. H. C. said that there had been innumerable instances of bribery in the Guardians' Boards, leading to their supersession by the Government by paid guardians.—*Daily Telegraph*, 28th April 1898.

26. It is the men who have bridged the ocean with the steamship, who have tunnelled the mountains and severed the isthmus, who have made the empire.—*Ibid.* p. 130.

27. Notwithstanding his illness, and that he had lost nearly all his money, he still kept the business going, hoping for better times.

28. Prince Ferdinand of Bulgaria, who since the murder of M. Stambuloff, from which time the relations between Austria and Bulgaria changed considerably for the worse, has not appeared at the Vienna Court, was received in a long audience to-day at noon by the Emperor.—*Daily Telegraph*, 8th March 1898.

29. The first suggestion I would make is that usurers all over the country, who trade under false names and pretend to be banks, and issue circulars and prospectuses which are false and fraudulent, and who use these names for the purpose of securing contracts with borrowers in order to defraud them by a system of usury, should be dealt with.—*Evidence of Sir G. L.*, 11th March 1898.

30. The first thing the usurers do is to see who are the relatives of the young borrower. In the S. C. case we had a man whose bills were discounted, because a nobleman took them to them.—*Ibid.*

31. Our ministers cannot understand that England is sick of the parish pump and sickest of all of the Manchester school.—*Review of Reviews*, April 1898, p. 354.

32. The Americans are perhaps sincere in saying that the United States are not contemplating seizing Cuba in order to annex it.—*Times Weekly*, 6th May 1898, p. 276.

33. In 1874, though not then prepared to advocate the disestablishment of the Scotch Church, though he admitted an established church in a minority is an anomaly, he yet strenuously opposed when the Church Patronage Scotland Bill was before Parliament to invest this Church with powers never before entrusted to an ecclesiastical body.—*Middlesex County Times*, 4th June 1898.

34. The step was only decided upon at the very last moment; indeed, for reasons upon which it is unnecessary to dwell, it had appeared but a few hours previously utterly and absolutely impossible that it could be taken before to-day at the earliest.—*Daily Telegraph*, 16th June 1898, p. 7.

35. With a ministry without any authority any sudden course of action may be looked for.—*Daily Telegraph*, 23rd June 1898, p. 9.

36. When a person has attracted to himself by an elevated moral bond several other persons, when he dies, it always happens that the survivors, often divided up to that time by rivalries, beget a strong friendship the one for the other.—*Translation from* RENAN's "*Apostles.*"

37. This army is incapable because of sickness of marching anywhere

except to the transports.—*Telegram quoted in "Daily Telegraph,"* 8th August 1898.

38. The rest of the evening was devoted to voting away the nation's money, etc.—*Standard*, 9th August 1898.

39. The Carlists possessed an army of their own, now disbanded, but many of whose officers would expect to be reinstated in their former positions.—*Fortnightly Review*, 1st August 1898.

40. He discourses more or less discursively upon the various changes, etc.—*Review of Reviews*, August 1898, p. 165.

41. If there is one thing that strikes one more than another, it is His Majesty's ardent desire for peace.—*Times*, 31st August 1898.

42. Sir George says that he does not think property is divided properly, but he deals very vaguely with this part of his subject.—*Times Weekly*, 14th Sept. 1906, p. 584.

43. The document enumerates the laws ensuring to native workmen humanitarian and civilising assistance, they being Portuguese citizens, with the same rights as other citizens, and enjoying everywhere, always the broadest protection.—*Daily Telegraph*, 8th October 1906, p. 9.

44. They believe it (republicanism) to be for the healing of all nations, and that civilisation must advance or retrograde according as its supremacy is extended or curtailed.—*Fortnightly Review*, Dec. 1901, p. 1018.

45. For the first time since the establishment of the hall in 1884, the Warden, Canon Barnett and Mrs. Barnett were absent from the opening of the session. It was due to the new duties of the Warden as Canon of Westminster.—*Times Weekly*, 5th October 1906, p. 633.

46. In other words, we stand to-day, in our trade with Germany, in the position of an industrially undeveloped country trading with another country on a far higher level of industrial efficiency.—*Ibid.* 5th October 1906, p. 633.

47. Hence even the maximum quantity of boric acid present was quite small. By far the majority of the samples were good and clean, and certainly fit for food.—*Daily Telegraph*, 10th October 1906, p. 13.

48. All the experts expect that some 400,000,000 tons of the finest smokeless coal will be produced, and this is clearly the expectation of the German purchasers.—*Ibid.* 10th October 1906, p. 11.

49. This authority was not without hopes of the firms remaining outside the Combine being able eventually to make its operations in the direction of raising prices and the like ineffectual.—*Ibid.* 25th October 1906, p. 11.

50. It is exclusively those who are familiar with the tilling of the land who are being aided at the present time; for it is this class which, in the opinion of the authorities, constitute the greatest need of the Colony.—*Ibid.* 26th October 1900, p. 11.

51. This (the boycotting of English goods) has never been formally sanctioned by the Congress, but it has never denounced it.—*National Review*, November 1906, p. 557.

52. One system of education is the Secularist, which is logical and intelligible, but which is as strongly opposed by Nonconformists as a whole, as by Churchmen, Roman Catholics, and Jews.—*Daily Telegraph*, 12th December 1906, p. 11.

CHAPTER XXII.—PERSPICUITY OR CLEARNESS OF DICTION.

305. Perspicuity.—Of all qualities of composition the one that is of most general use is Perspicuity; for if the writer does not make himself understood, he writes to no purpose. "By perspicuity," says Quintilian, "care is taken, not that the reader *may* understand, if he will, but that he *must* understand, whether he will or not."

The original and once the only sense of the word "perspicuity" was "transparency,"—transparency of the medium through which objects can be seen. Afterwards, by a vigorous metaphor, it came to be applied, and was eventually restricted, to *transparency of language*,—language being the medium through which the thought or image intended by the writer can be seen by the reader, as light is the medium through which objects can be seen by the eye.

SECTION 1.—GRAMMATICAL PRECAUTIONS.

306. Grammatical Precautions.—Among the grammatical devices conducive to perspicuity the following deserve attention:—

(*a*) Repeat the Subject, if there is any fear of a wrong subject being construed with the next verb:—

He is endeavouring to help some friends, who are very grateful for his assistance, and (*he*) will not allow any one else to help them.

If the *he* had not been repeated, the word "who" would naturally have been considered the subject to the verb "will allow"; and this would have completely altered the sense. All ambiguity is removed by repeating "*he*."

(*b*) Repeat a Preposition, if the nouns to which it belongs are at some distance apart:—

(1) As soon as he had the power, he took vengeance on all those persons, who had injured his friends and relatives, and especially (*on*) his cousin John.

If the *on* had not been repeated, the reader would certainly have considered that "cousin John" was intended to be an object to the verb "injured."

(2) The concessions by China of Kiao-chau to Germany, and (of) Port Arthur and Ta-lien-wan to Russia, for terms of years, belong to a new development, etc.—*Times Weekly*, 8th April 1898.

The repetition of "*of*" (not given in the original) before "Port Arthur" improves the perspicuity. Cancel the comma after *Germany*.

(*c*) Repeat a Conjunction, if the verbs depending on it are at some distance apart :—

Some persons have maintained that Julius Cæsar did not destroy the republican constitution of Rome for the sake of making himself emperor; (*that*) the republic had, in fact, been destroyed already by the ambitious citizens who preceded him: and (*that*) he merely stepped into a position which had been left open for him by force of circumstances.

If the conjunction "*that*" is not repeated, the two last sentences might be taken to express the writer's own opinion, and not that of "some persons" referred to in the first sentence.

(*d*) Repeat an Auxiliary verb, when the Principal verbs are far enough apart to give rise to ambiguity :—

My powers, such as they were, had been cultivated at Oxford from the age of nineteen, when I was still young enough to be moulded into the shape that my advisers considered best for me, and (*had been*) trained to the study of science in preference to that of ancient philosophy.

Unless the auxiliary "*had been*" is repeated, the word "trained" would naturally be regarded as the sequel to the word "moulded."

(*e*) Repeat the Verb or use the pro-verb *do* after the conjunctions "than" and "as," if the omission of the verb would cause any ambiguity :—

The Presbyterians of Scotland disliked the Independents led by Cromwell as heartily as (*did*) the Royalists.

The Presbyterians of Scotland disliked the Independents led by Cromwell more heartily than the Royalists (*did*).

The ambiguity of both sentences is removed by using the pro-verb "*did*."

If the *did* is not inserted, the sentences might easily be taken to mean :—

The Presbyterians of Scotland disliked the Independents led by Cromwell as heartily as *they disliked* the Royalists.

The Presbyterians of Scotland disliked the Independents led by Cromwell more heartily than *they disliked* the Royalists.

(*f*) Antecedent clauses must not be mixed up with consequent ones :—

The prosperity of England will decline, if she loses her command of the sea, and other countries step into her place.

Does the last clause go with the consequent or with the antecedent? Begin with the antecedent or conditional clause first in any case, and then the sentence may be rewritten in two different ways, whichever meaning the writer may have intended :—

(1) If England loses her command of the sea, her prosperity will decline and other countries step into her place.

(2) If England loses her command of the sea and other countries step into her place, her prosperity will decline.

(*g*) Infinitives dependent on one word must not be mixed up with Infinitives dependent on another :—

He decided *to* take his daughter with him to the British Museum *to* see the Assyrian monuments and *to* compare these with the researches of Layard and Rawlinson.

This sentence might be rewritten so as to make at least three different senses. The third one might be considered rather far-fetched, but the first and second are perfectly natural, and there is no saying which to choose :—

(1) He decided to take his daughter with him to the British Museum that she might see the Assyrian monuments and compare these with, etc.

(2) He decided to take his daughter with him to the British Museum that they might see the Assyrian monuments and compare these with, etc.

(3) He decided to take his daughter with him to the British Museum that she might see the Assyrian monuments, and that he might compare these, etc.

SECTION 2.—THE OBSCURE.

307. Defective Expression.—Elliptical phrases or idioms, provided they are in current use and are generally understood, are unobjectionable. For instance, there is no lack of perspicuity in the sentence, "Do all you can," because the omission of the Relative pronoun as object to a verb, though unknown in other modern languages, is common in English. The same cannot be said, however, of ellipses that result from over-brevity or from rapidity of thought followed by carelessness of diction :—

(1) He is inspired with a true sense of that function, when chosen from a regard to the interests of piety and virtue.—*Guardian*, No. 13.

A function cannot be a sense or sentiment. The wording should have been "a true sense of the dignity or importance of that function, when the said function is chosen," etc.

(2) You ought to contemn all the wit in the world against you.—*Guardian*, No. 53.

The writer means "all the wit that can be employed against you."

(3) He talks all the way upstairs to a visit.—*Spectator*, No. 2.

The writer perhaps means, "He talks all the way as he goes upstairs to pay a visit."

(4) Arbitrary power I look upon as a greater evil than anarchy itself, as much as a savage is a happier state of life than a slave at the oar.—*Sentiments of a Church of England Man.*

Neither a savage nor a slave can be called a state of life. The writer means, "the life of a savage is happier than that of a slave."

(5) This courage among the adversaries of the court was inspired into them by various incidents, for every one of which the

ministers, or, if that was the case, the minister alone is to answer.—*Free Thoughts on the Present State of Affairs.*

If that was the case! He means, "if there was but one minister."

(6) Never let the glory of our nation, who made France tremble, and yet has the gentleness to be unable to bear opposition from the meanest of his own countrymen, be calumniated in so insolent a manner, etc.—*Guardian*, No. 53.

By "the glory of our nation," he means, "the man who was the glory of our nation,"—a fact that is by no means obvious on first reading.

(7) His chapters on these themes, or the commercial prospects of Siberia, are the pleasantest in his book.—*Daily Telegraph*, 25th Jan. 1898.

The writer means apparently "or *those on* the commercial prospects," etc.

(8) The ship was insured for a voyage from Cassis to Constantinople with cement.—*Syren and Shipping*, 9th Feb. 1898.

It looks at first as if the ship was insured with cement. The sentence should be worded: "The ship, with a cargo of cement, was insured," etc.

308. Bad Arrangement of Words.—The rules for the order of words, phrases, and clauses, with examples of their violation, have been given already in Chapters XIX. and XX. A few more examples may be given here, in illustration of the subject of obscurity:—

(1) It contained a warrant for conducting me and my retinue to Traldragdubb or Trildrogdrib, for it is pronounced both ways, as near as I can remember, by a party of ten horse.—SWIFT.

The sentence might be rewritten as follows:—"It contained, as near as I can remember, a warrant for having me and my retinue conducted to Traldragdubb or Trildrogdrib, (for the word is pronounced both ways), by a party of ten horse."

(2) I perceived it had been scoured with half an eye.—*Guardian*, No. 10.

The phrase *with half an eye* must be construed with the verb "perceived." The sentence should therefore be arranged as follows: "With half an eye I perceived it had been scoured"; or "I perceived with half an eye *that*," etc.

(3) The young man did not want natural talents; but the father of him was a coxcomb, who affected being a fine gentleman so unmercifully, that he could not endure in his sight, or the frequent mention of one who was his son, growing into manhood and thrusting him out of the gay world.—*Spectator*, No. 496, T.

The confused construction, together with the vile application of the word "unmercifully," is such that this sentence might with equal justice be ranked under solecism, impropriety, or obscurity (Campbell).

309. Using the same Word in different Senses.—The same word should not be repeated in the same sentence, unless it is used in the same sense and in the same part of speech :—

(1) Any reasons of doubt, which he may have in this case, would have been reasons of doubt in the case of other men, who may give *more*, but cannot give *more* evident, signs of thought than their fellow-creatures.—BOLINGBROKE, Essay 1, Sect. 9.

Here the first "more" is the Comparative degree of "many." It should be changed to "more numerous," to match and balance the phrase "more evident"; or the first "more" might be retained and "more evident" might be changed to "clearer."

(2) One may have an air *which* proceeds from a just sufficiency and knowledge of the matter before him, *which* may naturally produce some motions of his head and body, *which* might become the bench better than the bar.—*Guardian*, No. 13.

Here *which* is repeated three times, each time with a different antecedent. This is tantamount to using the same word in three different senses in the same sentence. The sentence is so awkward in other respects as to be almost obscure. Here "air" means "demeanour." "Just sufficiency" seems to mean "just appreciation." The second *which* might be changed to "and this knowledge." The word "one" ought not to be followed by "him," so it can be changed to "a man." With all these changes the sentence would run as follows :—

"*A man* may have a *demeanour* which proceeds from a *just appreciation* and knowledge of the matter before him, *and this knowledge* may produce some motions of his head and body which might become," etc.

(3) *They* were persons of such moderate intellects, even before *they* were impaired by *their* passions.—*Guardian*.

The first *they* refers to "persons," and the second to "intellects." *Their* refers back again to "persons." Change the second *they* to *their intellects*.

310. Uncertain Reference of Pronouns.—Pronouns must not be used in such a way as to cause any doubt about what noun they stand for :—

(1) Such were the centaurs of Ixion's race,
Who a bright cloud for Juno did embrace.—DENHAM.

What is the antecedent to *who*?

(2) There are other examples of the same kind, which cannot be brought without the utmost horror, because it is supposed impiously, against principles as self-evident as any of those necessary truths, which are *such* of all knowledge, that the Supreme Being commands by one law what He forbids by another.—BOLINGBROKE.

What word does *such* here stand for?

(3) When a man considers the state of his own mind, he will find that the best defence against vice is preserving the worthiest

part of his own spirit pure from any great offence against *it.* —*Guardian*, No. 19.

What does *it* (the last word in the sentence) refer to?

Note 1.—There is no uncertainty of reference, if the pronoun relates to a principal word, such as the subject of a verb or the object of one:—

But I shall leave this matter to your management, and question not but you will throw *it* into such a light as shall at once, etc. —*Spectator*, No. 628.

Here *it* relates to "matter," and not to the nearer word "management," for two reasons—(1) because "matter" is a chief word, while "management" is a subsidiary one; (2) because the rhythm of the sentence requires that the verb "throw" shall have the same object as the verb "leave."

Note 2.—If there is no other way of avoiding ambiguity, it is better to repeat the noun, as in the following example:—

The lad cannot leave his father: for if he should leave his father, *his father* would die.—*Gen.* xliv. 22.

311. Words changed without Change of Meaning.—When words are changed, not to alter the sense, but merely to save a repetition of the same sound, they must not be set against each other antithetically, as if they were intended to be understood in different senses:—

Scarlet rhododendrons 60 feet in *height* are surrounded by trees 200 feet in *elevation.*

Here *height* and *elevation*, though apparently balanced against each other by way of antithesis or contrast, are intended to mean exactly the same thing. Instead of 200 *feet in elevation* we could say *that reach to a height of* 200 *feet.*

SECTION 3.—THE DOUBLE MEANING.

312. Equivocal Words and Phrases.—Our language abounds, as most other languages do, in equivocal words; and there is no harm in using them, so long as the sense is clear from the context. Thus, if some one says that "he rents his house at fifty pounds a year," no one would suppose that he means pounds in troy-weight or pounds in avoirdupois. Sometimes, however, the context fails to give the requisite clue, or gives it so imperfectly, that the reader is forced to read the sentence twice and reflect a little upon its contents, before he can be quite sure that he has understood it. Whenever an author's style exacts such reflection from his reader, he has committed an offence against perspicuity.

There is no part of speech which, if used incautiously, is not susceptible of a double meaning:—

(a) *Prepositions* :—

(1) I am persuaded, that neither death, nor life . . . shall be able to separate us from the love *of* God.—*Romans*, viii. 38.

Does this mean God's love to us, or our love to God?

(2) A little after the reformation *of* Luther.—SWIFT.

To any one unacquainted with the history of the past dating back about 400 years, "the reformation of Luther" would indicate a change wrought *on* him, not *by* him.

(3) If I cannot be commended *for* the beauty of my style, I hope I may be pardoned *for* its brevity.

Here the preposition "for" is used in two different senses: the first "for" means "on account of," while the second "for" means "in consideration of." What the author intended to express (but the meaning is not as obvious as it should have been) is, that the brevity of his style may be taken as a set-off to its want of beauty.

(b) *Conjunctions* :—

(1) They were both much more ancient among the Persians than Zoroaster *or* Zerdusht.

Or is here equivocal. The mention of *both* suggests that the writer names two distinct persons by Zoroaster or Zerdusht, by way of balance. It is not every reader who would know that *or* is here used to denote an alternative spelling of the same name. All ambiguity can be removed by inserting the parenthesis (*as he is also called*) after *or*. On other means of avoiding the ambiguity of *or*, see § 274 (57).

(2) I did not sing yesterday *as* I wished.

Owing to the ambiguity of *as*, this sentence may give opposite senses: either "I did sing yesterday, but not in the manner that I wished," or "I did not sing yesterday, though I wished to have done so."

(3) And *seeing* dreams are caused by the distemper of the inward parts of the body, etc.

It requires something of an effort to find out that *seeing* here is equivalent to *seeing that* or *since*,—a conjunction, not a participle.

(c) *Pronouns* :—

She united the great body of the people in *her* and their common interest.

Is *her* here Objective or Possessive? The sense would have been clear at a glance, if the author had said "in *their and her* common interest."

(d) *Nouns* :—

(1) Your Majesty has lost all hopes of any future excises by their *consumption*.—*Guardian*, No. 52.

"Consumption" might be either Active or Passive. The sense appears to be "all hopes of levying any future excises on what they shall consume." But this is anything but obvious.

(2) A man who has lost his eyesight has *in one sense* less consciousness.

The words italicised might mean either "in one organ of sense" (eye-sight) or "in one respect." Which is it? Probably the latter.

(*e*) *Verbs*:—

I have long since learned to like nothing but what you *do*.—*Spectator*, No. 627.

Is *do* here a pro-verb (§ 103) to save the repetition of *like*, or is it a notional verb (§ 88, *Note*) signifying "perform"?

(*f*) *Adjectives*:—

He has a *certain* claim to a share in that property.

Does *certain* here mean "undoubted," or is it merely an Indefinite Demonstrative adjective? (see § 54).

(*g*) *Phrases*:—

Your character of universal guardian, joined to the concern you ought to have for the cause of virtue and religion, assure[1] me that you will not think that clergymen, when injured, have *the least* right to your protection.—*Guardian*, No. 80.
I will *have mercy*, and not sacrifice.—*Matt.* ix. 13.
He writes *as well* as you. (The sense is ambiguous, because *as well as* may be either Co-ordinative or Sub-ordinative; § 170.)
Much conversation was going on *about me*.
The counsel for the defence spoke *before the judge*.
Fish can scarcely be got now *at any rate*.
There seems to be no limit *to the scolding of the housekeeper*.

313. Ambiguous Construction.—Such ambiguities arise, not from the equivocal character of a word or a phrase, but from carelessness in the arrangement of the words, or from the omission of words that would have made the sense clear at a glance.

(1) Solomon, the son of David, who built the temple of Jerusalem, was the richest monarch that ever reigned over the Israelites.

Is "Solomon" the antecedent to *who*, or is "David"? According to the rule given in § 290, the antecedent should be "David," but the writer means "Solomon." Cancel the comma after *David*, and change *who built* into *and builder of*.

(2) I know that *all words which* are signs of complex ideas furnish matter of mistake and cavil.—BOLINGBROKE.

Is *which* here used in a Restrictive or in merely a Continuative sense? If the former, "all words" should be changed to "all *those* words," or *that* should be substituted for *which* (see § 83).

(3) God heapeth favours on His servants ever liberal and faithful.

Do the adjectives *liberal and faithful* refer to God or to His servants? If to the former, say, "God, ever liberal and faithful, heapeth," etc.

(4) The ecclesiastical and secular powers concurred in that measure.
The high and mighty states of Holland are against us.

[1] Observe that here the grammar is wrong.

The second sentence is quite correct, because the same "states" are both "high and mighty." But are we to understand that the epithets "ecclesiastical and secular" relate to the same powers or to different powers? The careless omission of *the* before "secular" would compel us, if we did not happen to know better, to understand the phrase in the former sense.

(5) At least my own private letters leave room for a politician, well versed in matters of this nature, to suspect as much, as a penetrating friend of mine tells me.—*Spectator*, No. 43.

Here, except for the comma after *much*, the ambiguity of the sentence as it stands would be insoluble. All doubt would have been removed, if the author had observed the Rule of Proximity given in § 275. The sentence would then run as follows: "At least my own private letters, as a penetrating friend of mine tells me, leave room for a politician well versed in such matters to suspect as much."

(6) I beseech you, sir, to inform these fellows, that they have not the spleen, because they cannot talk without the help of a glass, or convey their meaning to each other without the interposition of clouds.—*Spectator*, No. 53.

Is *because* intended to qualify the verb "beseech," or the verb "inform," or the verb "have," or the negative verb "have not"?

(7) He has by some strange magic arrived at the value of half a plumb, as the citizens call a hundred thousand pounds.—*Tatler*, No. 40.

Does this mean that a hundred thousand pounds was denoted by a plumb, or by half a plumb?

Exercise.

Rewrite the following sentences, so as to make each of them more perspicuous than it is in its present form; or if more than one meaning is possible, express each meaning more distinctly. If no ambiguity exists, give your reason for thinking so:—

1. Providence, my son, has given you strength of body and cleverness of mind; but instead of this you waste your time in frivolity and idleness.

2. The workmen decided to come to terms with their employers, but to ask for the same wages as before, and accept as much less as they possibly could.

3. Allahabad, one of the principal cities in Northern India, is situated between the junction of the Jumna and the Ganges.

4. I prefer doing this to that.

5. Looking at his own warm overcoat, he could not help wishing that he could cover the poor, whom he saw shivering around him, with the same.

6. The farmstead was always the wooden white-painted house, of which the small country towns are composed.

7. A river adds much beauty to natural scenery; but a mountain is the thing that carries grandeur in its idea.

8. I doubt the application of the German military system to England.

9. Lisias promised his father never to abandon his friends.

10. A box-tree was planted between each plane-tree.

11. The insincerity of Charles I. was suspected by his people, and with good reason.

12. Both sides confidently predicted victory for their candidate, and up to the time that the last vote was recorded, it was difficult to decide whether victory lay with Conservatives or Liberals.—*Daily Telegraph*, 13th Jan. 1898.

13. This prevents their attending enough to what is in the Bible, and makes them battle for what is not in the Bible, but they have put it there.—M. ARNOLD.

14. Nothing gave more or more just offence in this country than the characteristic passage in which Count Bülow hinted, etc.—*Fort. Rev.* p. 209, Feb. 1902.

15. Young Itylus, his parent's darling joy,
Whom chance misled the mother to destroy.
POPE'S *Odyssey*, Book xix.

16. I will spend a hundred or two pounds rather than be enslaved.—SWIFT.

17. My Christian and surname begin and end with the same letters.—*Spectator*, No. 505.

18. It has not a word but what the author religiously thinks in it.—*Guardian*, No. 4.

19. Mr. Dryden makes a very handsome observation on Ovid's writing a letter from Dido to Æneas, in the following words.—*Spectator*, No. 62.

20. As it is necessary to have the head clear as well as the complexion, to be perfect in this part of learning, I rarely mingle with the men, but frequent the tea-tables of the ladies.—*Guardian*, No. 10.

21. All orders not issued by the managing director must not be attended to.

22. The history of Natal during the past year has been, except for agricultural depression caused by rinderpest and locusts, the happy history of a colony which has none.—*Times Weekly*, 7th Jan. 1898.

23. To a barbarous and inhuman wit there cannot be a greater gratification than to stir up sorrow in the heart of a private person by secret charges, at the same time that he remains unseen and undiscovered.—*Spectator*, No. 23.

24. I must confess that we live in an age, wherein a few empty blusterers carry away the praise of speaking, while a crowd of fellows overstocked with knowledge are run down by them; I say overstocked, because they certainly are so as to their service to mankind, if from their very store they raise to themselves ideas of respect and greatness of the occasion, and I know not what, to disable themselves from explaining their thoughts.—*Spectator*, No. 484.

25. The German Mercantile Marine has, since 1871, more than trebled its capabilities; and since 1880 has more than doubled them.—*Daily Telegraph*, 27th Jan. 1898, p. 9.

26. The more faulty we consider the protective system to which Germany, together with all the other Great Powers of Europe, except Great Britain and the United States of America, adheres, the more surprising is the progress recorded.—*Daily Telegraph*, 27th Jan. 1898, p. 8.

27. Mr. B—— has issued invitations for a full-dress parliamentary dinner, and Lord ——, his colleague, has issued invitations for a full-dress banquet.

28. No one has now any idea of how the Powers will deal with the question of the evacuation of Thessaly, as it is certain that the Porte will not quietly abandon the only fertile province of Greece, if the selection of Prince George of Greece (for the governorship of Crete) is forced upon him.—*Daily Telegraph*, 28th Jan. 1898.

29. It is out of the question that Germany and Austria will join in measures of force against Turkey.—*Daily Telegraph*, 2nd Feb. 1898.

30. His (Hudson's) fall was like the crash of a cliff. He who had been slapping noble lords on the back and the king of his Company, was left a wreck on the shore, and deserted by all who had battened on him. —*Fortnightly Review*, Feb. 1898, p. 247.

31. In view of recent changes, and especially since the war between China and Japan, it seemed desirable that Germany should have a seaport there for safeguarding her interests.—*Speech from Berlin*, 7th Feb. 1898.

32. The hopes of parents are blighted, if their children are indolent, and the money spent on them is wasted.

33. He is a great admirer of the artist who painted that picture and lives in Brompton.

34. We have just heard that the two boys leave school at the end of next week, and hope that they will not return to the same school again.

35. Geddes is now one of the bright points of the world which lies in darkness, to which my spirit will often turn for light.—N. MACLEOD.

36. There is probably no one of this generation who bestows any thought upon the problems of history and politics who will not acknowledge his indebtedness to Mr. Carlyle.—*Times*, 18th Nov. 1870.

37. They forget to consult, and, as far as they are not vicious, conform to the tastes, feelings, and habits of those whose happiness they would promote, and think only of their own.—W. J. FOX.

38. Lord Chelmsford is put on his trial for an alleged mistake in the disposition of troops in war, and why not a police officer who has placed a young man's life in peril, and who but for public energy would have been executed?—W. E. STUTTER.

39. Sir Morton Peto spoke of the notion that the national debt might be repudiated with absolute contempt.—*Spectator*, 18th Nov. 1855.

40. Seldom has there been any great revolt of unskilled labour which attracted so much attention throughout the world, and which was fought out under circumstances of such constant peril of violence, which was brought to a close with so clean a sheet.—*Review of Reviews*, Feb. 1898, p. 127.

41. Antony was not less desirous of destroying the conspirators than his officers.

42. The amount which we annually devote to increasing our navy is, roughly speaking, identical with that expended by France, Russia, and Germany.—*Daily Telegraph*, 22nd April 1898.

43. The political demands of the party in power in Madrid have made it necessary for the political life of that party to resist in every form every attempt upon the part of the Cubans to secure their liberties, and to resist all attempts on the part of other countries to assert them.—*Fortnightly Review*, June 1898, p. 858.

44. Fresh attempts should be made to give shelter to a harbour by laying out not a few large, but a large number of small, floating breakwaters.—*Geograph. Journal*, May 1898.

45. By a narrow majority the Australian Federal Convention has reversed its decision making it compulsory for the Federation to take over the debts of the individual states.—*Daily Telegraph*, 3rd Mar. 1898.

46. It was part of the work of Alfred the Great to create little by little the love of country in place of the old love of tribe. He might, like the King of Mercia, have fled to Rome and religious life; in fact, he fought them for nine long years, growing every year weaker.—*Times Weekly*, 25th Feb. 1898.

47. The trial resulted in the binding over of the two boys who were charged with the stealing and the acquittal of the man who was charged with receiving.—*Daily Telegraph*, 8th August 1898.

PART III.—COMPOSITION IN FIVE STAGES:— SENTENCE, PARAGRAPH, PARAPHRASE, PRÉCIS, ESSAY.

CHAPTER XXIII.

STRUCTURE AND SYNTHESIS OF SENTENCES.

314. Rule of Proximity.—Subordinate clauses are subject to the Rule of Proximity (§ 275) to the same extent as the various parts of speech. A construction which violates this principle is called by the French *construction louche*, "a squinting construction"; or to adopt the more homely English phrase, "One eye is fixed on the kettle, while the other is looking up the chimney."

(*a*) *Noun-clause.*—A Noun-clause must be placed as close as possible to the verb or noun to which it belongs by grammatical relation:—

> Mr. J. S. Chapple points out in reference to our remark last week, that, with the exception of Sir G. Scott, no other architect of our time has erected a cathedral, that Mr. W. Burgess erected St. Fin Barré's Cathedral at Cork in the year 1862.—*Church Times*, 23rd Dec. 1897.

The chief fault of this slovenly sentence lies in the fact that it separates the object from its verb by a block of twenty-five words, and this without any necessity whatever. The sentence could easily have been arranged as follows:—

> In reference to our remark last week that, with the exception of Sir G. Scott, no architect of our time has erected a cathedral, Mr. J. S. Chapple points out that Mr. W. Burgess, etc.

(*b*) *Adverb-clause.*—An Adverb-clause must be placed as close as possible to the word that it qualifies:—

> He imprudently put all his money in that concern, as the event showed.

The adverbial clause "as the event showed" is intended to qualify and explain the adverb *imprudently*, and should therefore be placed immediately after it.

Imprudently, as the event showed, he put all his money in that concern.

To take another example :—

All this is meant to open the eyes of the Chinese, and to cause them to accept each and every claim that we make upon them as soon as possible.—*Daily Telegraph*, 3rd Jan. 1898.

The phrase *as soon as possible* should stand immediately after the verb *accept*, since it is not intended to qualify the verb *make*.

(*c*) *Adjective-clause.*—The position of such clauses is determined by the rule laid down in § 290 that a Conjunctive pronoun or Conjunctive adverb must be placed as close as possible to its Antecedent.

315. Rule of Priority.—The Rule of Proximity is supplemented by another—the Rule of Priority. According to this rule, qualifying clauses should, as far as possible, precede the clause or words to which they are subordinate.

The principle underlying this rule is that the mind of the reader is by this means *kept in suspense.* His interest is aroused to know what is coming, and when it does come, it comes with the greater force. The final or principal clause thus receives the emphasis that it ought to have. See § 296 (*b*).

(1) *Ghost.* If ever thou didst thy dear father love,
Hamlet. O heaven !
Ghost. Avenge his foul and most unnatural murder.

Observe how the effect of this dialogue would have been marred, if the order of the clauses had been reversed. Observe, too, how the interest of Hamlet has been awakened by the suspensive influence of the conditional clause. This is shown by the exclamation, "O heaven !"

(2) Though I speak with the tongues of men and of angels, and have not charity, I am become as sounding brass, or a tinkling cymbal.—1 *Cor.* xiii. 1.

Compare with this well-arranged sentence the following extract from Bacon, in which the limiting clause is awkwardly put last :—

A crowd is not company, and faces are but a gallery of pictures, and talk but a tinkling cymbal, where there is no love.

The sentence should have been arranged thus :—

Where there is no love, a crowd is not company, faces are but a gallery of pictures, and talk is but a tinkling cymbal.

316. Position of Qualifying Phrases.—What is true of subordinate clauses is no less true of qualifying phrases also. These, for the sake of their *suspensory influence*, should, whenever the idiom of our language allows it, be placed before, and not after, the word that they qualify. See § 315 and § 296 (*b*).

> A man who has mortgaged his estate up to almost its full value has, *to all intents and purposes*, ceased to be the owner of it.

This is very much better than saying, "Has ceased to be the owner of it to all intents and purposes."

In the following sentence the Rule of Priority and that of Proximity are both neglected :—

> With this small force the general determined to attack the foe, flushed with recent victory and rendered negligent by success.

The proper order would be as follows :—

> Flushed with recent victory and rendered negligent by success, the general determined with this small force to attack the foe.

317. Unity of Sentence.—A sentence should express one main fact at a time, and not more than one. This is called the **Unity** of a sentence. The sentence as a whole may, it is true, consist of several clauses or smaller sentences ; but if it does, the clauses must be so closely connected in sense, as to leave the impression that *one main fact* has been stated, and not more than one. Such a sentence as the following is devoid of unity, because here two perfectly distinct statements are muddled together as if they were one :—

> He invaded France, but Philip wisely declined a pitched battle, and having exhausted his money and loaded himself with debt, Edward returned the next year to England.—RANSOME, *Short Hist. Eng.* p. 48, ed. 1897.

This sentence should be broken up into two, a separate sentence being given for each separate statement :—

> Edward invaded France, but Philip wisely declined a pitched battle. Having exhausted his money and loaded himself with debt, Edward returned the next year to England.

Note.—Since a sentence is commenced with a capital letter to show that it stands apart from any preceding sentence, it ought not as a rule to be commenced with the conjunction *And*. The practice of commencing a sentence with *And* is, however, met with occasionally in the best writers. Among beginners it is so common, that the best way of getting rid of the nuisance is to prohibit the practice altogether.

318. Sentences Periodic and Loose.—A complex sentence can be either Periodic or Loose. It is *periodic*, if the sense is completed by the time that the sentence comes to an end ; *loose*, if after the chief statement has been made, a qualifying clause or clauses are tacked on to it.

The following sentence is Periodic, because the qualifying clauses are stated first (§ 315) :—

> Though I speak with the tongues of men and of angels, and have not charity, I am become as sounding brass, or a tinkling cymbal.—1 *Cor.* xiii. 1.

The following sentence is Loose, because the qualifying clause is placed last instead of first :—

> A crowd is not company, and faces are but a gallery of pictures, where there is no love.—BACON.

As a general rule, a Periodic sentence is to be preferred to a Loose one, on account of its superior force and lucidity. But sometimes it improves a sentence to place the principal clause between two qualifying clauses, as in the following example :—

> As the sun at this time of the year sets as early as four o'clock, we had better start at once, if we are to get to our journey's end in daylight.

The sentence would have an awkward sound, had the order of the clauses been as follows :—

> As the sun at this time of the year sets as early as four o'clock, if we are to get to our journey's end in daylight, we had better start at once.

319. Use of a Parenthesis.—If the writer wishes to say something, which is useful by way of comment or explanation, but has no direct bearing on the main point, he may do so by inserting a parenthesis into the body of the sentence : *provided the parenthesis is short*, this is not felt to be a breach of unity :—

> This gentleman (for I found he was treated as such by his audience) was entertaining a whole table of listeners with the project of an opera.—ADDISON, *Spectator*, No. 31, para. 4.

The unity of the sentence is not marred by the brief remark here made in brackets. In the following sentence, however, the length of the parenthesis creates an awkward break in the sense, and we feel that the unity of the sentence has been violated :—

> Failing as he does to recognise the obligation to speak the truth imposed by any of our solemn affirmations (you cannot make him put his hand on his son's head, and declare that the youth may die, if the witness speaks not the truth,—which is about the only way to save him from lying), and conscious that whatever course he may adopt, he will not lose the respect of his fellows, the mind of the (Hindoo) witness is almost in an equilibrium, till the weight of his interest thrown into the scale decides the matter.—CURRIE, *Behind the Surface*, pp. 165, 166.

This sentence might be broken up into two, in the following way. The structure of the first sentence can be improved by the insertion of *that* and of *is* :—

> Failing as he does to recognise *that* the obligation to speak the truth *is* imposed by any of our solemn affirmations, and conscious that whatever course he may adopt, he will not lose the respect of his fellows, the mind of the witness is almost in an equilibrium, till the weight of his interest thrown into the scale decides the matter. The only way to save him from lying would be to make him put his hand on his son's head, and declare that the youth may die, if the witness speaks not the truth ; but this you are not allowed to do.

320. Sentences can be too long.—No absolute rule can be laid down as to the length of a sentence. We may, however, safely advise the beginner to abstain from making very long sentences. When sentences are spun out to a great length, there is always a risk of the construction becoming confused or the sense obscured. Nothing in the way of clearness or force is gained, but much is lost, in such a prolonged sentence as the following :—

> There are girls, however, on whom the education and independence of to-day are having a deeper effect, and whose intellectual qualities and sympathies, being largely developed, welcome the freedom they enjoy, not from the standpoint of amusement or pleasure, but from the prospect it opens up to them of a wider and deeper life in which their mental powers may find an outlet, and who may probably be more impatient of old-fashioned opinions and restraints than were girls of a former generation. —*Fort. Review*, p. 635, Oct. 1900.

It cannot be said that this sentence is deficient in unity, since the parts are all well connected one with another in sense. The fault of the sentence is that it is long and straggling, that the construction is rather involved, and that the attention of the reader is somewhat wearied before it is finished. Most readers, we think, would prefer to see it broken up into three sentences as follows :—

> There are girls, however, on whom the education and (*the*) independence of to-day are having a deeper effect. The intellectual qualities and sympathies *of such girls*, being largely developed, welcome the freedom they enjoy, *and this* not from the standpoint of amusement or pleasure, but from the prospect it opens up to them of a wider and deeper life, in which their mental powers may find an outlet. *Girls so influenced* may probably be more impatient of old-fashioned opinions and restraints than were those of a former generation.

Observe that we have detached the second sentence from the previous one by substituting *of such girls* for *and whose*; and to give it more point we have inserted the words *and this.* In the last sentence we have written *girls so influenced* for *and who*; in the original sentence this Relative is separated from its antecedent "girls" by no fewer than fifty-nine words.

Observe also that in the first line we have repeated the Definite article *the* (see *the* in brackets) which is not in the original, as it should have been. See § 186 (*a*).

321. Sentences can be too short. — Though a long sentence is to be avoided, when the sense can be more lucidly expressed in two or three shorter ones, yet a succession of little periods, which are obviously connected in sense and could easily be put together in a single sentence without any violation of unity, is a fault in the opposite direction. One extreme should be avoided as much as the other :—

(1) Northumberland's triumph seemed to be complete. The heir to the throne was a Protestant, and his own son's wife.—*Short Hist. Eng.*

(2) Hyde's party opposed the Remonstrance. It was carried by a small majority of eleven. It was then printed and published. —*Ibid.*

The periods in (1) and (2) can be easily put together, so as in each case to make a single sentence of very moderate length :—

(1) Northumberland's triumph seemed to be complete, since the heir to the throne was a Protestant and his own son's wife.

(2) The Remonstrance, though it was opposed by Hyde's party, was carried by a small majority of eleven, and then printed and published.

On the other hand, the little periods quoted below cannot, without loss of effect, be combined into a complex or compound sentence, and no attempt should be made to do so :—

With the dead there is no rivalry. In the dead there is no change. Plato is never sullen. Cervantes is never petulant. Demosthenes never comes unseasonably. Dante never stays too long. No difference of political opinion can alienate Cicero. No heresy can excite the horror of Bossuet.—MACAULAY.

322. Synthesis of Sentences.—A student is sometimes asked to bind together a string of little sentences in the form of a Simple, or a Compound, or a Complex sentence. This kind of practice is called **Synthesis.** It is therefore the opposite to Analysis, which consists in breaking up a sentence into its component parts or clauses.

Two examples of Synthesis have been given incidentally in the preceding paragraph. I now give three more :—

(a) *Combine into a Simple sentence :—*

The horses were harnessed—they were driven to the court—His Imperial Majesty ascended his new English throne—he did so solemnly—there was a great flourish of trumpets—he had the First Lord of the Treasury on his right hand—he had the Chief Jester on his left.—*Lond. School-Leaving Certificate*, July 1904.

(b) *Combine into a Compound sentence :—*

This race is called the Iberian, Ivernian, or Silurian. It was probably sallow, dark-haired, and dark-eyed. It underlies the population of all Western Europe. It came from Asia. It travelled along the northern slopes of the Caucasus. It passed through South Russia. It left its monuments in the Crimea.—*Lond. Matric.* Jan. 1905.

(c) *Combine into a Complex sentence :—*

The followers of the Viceroy deserted him in the hour of need. They hated his cruelty and vices. They had often praised him to his face.—*History of India.*

These three groups of short disconnected sentences might be Synthesised as follows according to the above directions :—

(*a*) The horses having been harnessed and driven to the court, His Imperial Majesty, solemnly and with a great flourish of trumpets, ascended his new English throne, the First Lord of the Treasury being seated on his right hand and the Chief Jester on his left.

(*b*) This race, called the Iberian, Ivernian, or Silurian, probably sallow, dark-haired, and dark-eyed, and underlying the population of all Western Europe, came from Asia, and after travelling along the northern slopes of the Caucasus and passing through South Russia, left its monuments in the Crimea.

(*c*) The followers of the Viceroy hated him so much on account of his cruelty and vices, that though they had often praised him to his face, they deserted him in the hour of need. (Two Subordinate clauses.)

(or) The followers of the Viceroy hated him for his cruelty and vices, and though they had often praised him to his face, they deserted him in the hour of need. (One Co-ordinate and one Subordinate clause.)

323. Conversion of Sentences.—Sentences can be changed in form or character from Simple to Compound or Complex, from Compound to Simple or Complex, and from Complex to Simple or Compound. Examples of this kind of practice have been given already in pp. 96, 98, and 100. A few more very easy examples are given in this place :—

(a) *Convert into a Compound sentence :—*

To every man's surprise the project completely failed.

(b) *Convert into a Simple sentence :—*

He gained no honours and he lost no friend.

(c) *Convert into a Complex sentence:*—

Do this, or you will be punished.

Lond. School-Leaving Certificate, July 1905.

The corresponding conversions will be as follows:—

(1) The project completely failed, and every man was surprised.

or, The project completely failed, at which every man was surprised.

Observe *which* is here used in a Continuative, not in a Restrictive sense. It therefore makes a Co-ordinate, not a Subordinate, clause (see § 194); and so the sentence is Compound, not Complex.

(2) Having gained no honours, he lost no friend.

or, His having gained no honours did not entail the loss of any friend.

Observe, these two sentences are not equivalent in meaning. The original sentence will bear either sense; but without seeing the context we cannot tell which was the sense intended.

(3) If you do not do this, you will be punished.

or, Unless you do this, you will be punished.

These two sentences mean precisely the same thing.

I. *Convert the following Loose sentences into Periods:*—

1. The responsibility of managing such a large business was more than he could bear, as he had not been trained in book-keeping and office-accounts.

2. English may claim to be called the universal language, if any language deserves to be so called.

3. The order of nobility was exceedingly numerous in France before the outbreak of the Revolution, since all the children of a nobleman belonged to the class of their father, and the class was continually increased by the creation of new nobles.

4. Little good will be effected, notwithstanding the exertions that public-spirited individuals may make to dispel the ignorance and raise the moral tone of the lower orders, without the cordial co-operation of the government.

5. During his long imprisonment he was harassed with many bitter reflections, deprived of the consolations of friendship by the cruelty of the tyrant.

6. There was nothing out of place inside the house or outside.

7. William the Conqueror laid waste a tract of thirty square leagues in Hampshire, to make space for the New Forest, as it is still called.

8. On that occasion the men in the street behaved in a very unruly manner, and it was found necessary to read the Riot Act.

9. He has many irons in the fire and his affairs are getting into disorder.

10. I found all the shops closed next morning, as I went down the street.

11. We no longer understand the language of our stage, insomuch that I have often been afraid, when I have seen our Italian performers chattering in the vehemence of action, that they have been calling us names and abusing us among themselves.—*Spectator*, No. 18.

II. *Rewrite the following extracts in such a way as to remove the violation of unity (if it exists) or reduce the length of the sentence. Also say whether the sentence is Periodic or Loose, and reconstruct, if the sentence would be improved by the change:—*

1. Welbeck Abbey, the seat of the Duke of Portland, was seriously damaged on Thursday night by a fire which broke out in the Oxford wing, from which the Marquis of Titchfield, the heir, and his sister and brother were rescued.—*Daily Telegraph*, p. 8, 6th Oct. 1900.

2. Women are seeking for means to escape the mission that nature has cast on them, and they will probably continue so to struggle, while they will not realise how ineffably feeble they are in the fight, and until they are vanquished, we may possibly see even more wonderful developments than any we have yet witnessed.—*Fort. Review*, p. 636, Oct. 1900.

3. What is still worse, there is throughout the whole of this biography a dark uncharitable cast, by which the most unfavourable construction is put upon almost every circumstance in the character and conduct of my illustrious friend, who I trust will by a true and firm delineation be vindicated both from the injurious misrepresentations of this author, and from the aspersions of a lady who once lived in great intimacy with him. —BOSWELL'S *Life of Johnson*.

4. When his father's unsuccessful speculations reduced the family to straits, he obtained through the good offices of Lord Houghton a post in the British Museum, which he held for twenty years until his second marriage made him a rich man, when he bought an estate in Sussex, and settled down as a country gentleman, afterwards migrating to Hastings, and finally to Lymington.—*Spectator*, p. 845, 8th Dec. 1900.

5. A very widespread expression of sympathy has been obtained for the broad general principle, that the names of all our dead should be permanently preserved in an appropriate building in London, whether they were British born or whether they came from the colonies, whose assistance in this campaign has marked the birth of a coherent and united empire, in which every part is ready to share in the common responsibility and to bear the common burden.—*Daily Telegraph*, p. 5, 2nd Aug. 1900.

6. Without dwelling upon a most unlucky appointment, believed to be the result of a crooked intrigue, for which he must be held in part responsible—an avowed abetter of the "Plan of Campaign"—a swindling conspiracy of the basest sort—is not exactly a personage to place in high office—he has deeply offended thousands of the best men in Ireland.—*Ibid.* p. 264, Feb. 1901.

7. The Queen will with her own gracious hands lay the foundation-stone of the new buildings, which, under the name of the "Victoria and Albert Museum," and together with the "Science College," to be simultaneously constructed, are destined to complete the magnificent idea which the Prince Consort cherished in establishing at South Kensington the centre of the artistic life of the kingdom.—*Daily Telegraph*, p. 8, 17th May 1899.

8. Mr. Treves follows all the movements and activities of the hospital in his little book, which Messrs. Cassell and Co. have produced in

admirable taste as to paper, binding, and type.—*Daily Telegraph*, p. 11, 1st Nov. 1900.

9. General Buller was brought into telegraphic communication with Lord Roberts, who has returned to Pretoria, on Saturday afternoon, at which time he was advancing against the enemy's position at Spitz Kop. —*Ibid.* p. 8, 12th Sept. 1900.

III. *Combine each of the following groups of Simple sentences according to the form indicated below:—*

(*a*) *Combine into one Simple sentence:—*

1. The English nobles remembered the example set them by their fathers. This was set them in the reign of King John. The government by Henry III. was equally bad. He maintained foreign favourites. Their influence was predominant. The nobles were determined to put an end to this state of things.

2. Insurrections had come to an end. Henry VII. after this desired to marry his children. He desired to amass money. He devoted his attention to these two things.

3. The king spent the following year in Normandy. He desired to strengthen his position there. He desired to secure the succession of his son. The son was then eighteen years old.

4. There were 300 persons on board. Only one escaped. All the rest went down with the ship. One of the men drowned was Fitz-stephen. He was captain of the ship. The man who escaped was a butcher of Rouen.

5. Prince William had been drowned. Henry had only one object after this. His object was to secure the crown of England for his only daughter, Matilda. She had been married to the emperor of the west. The emperor's name was Henry V. He was now dead.

6. Henry was fond of his children. This was one strong point in his character. He was fond of learning. This was another strong point. In all other respects his character was devoid of any commendable qualities.

7. Richard I., the king of England, was seized with remorse. He had rebelled against his father. The father at that time was an old man. He was much attached to all his sons.

8. Two cats had stolen some cheese. They could not agree how to divide it equally between them. They decided on asking a monkey to settle the dispute for them. The monkey was seated by chance at the foot of a neighbouring tree.

9. The monkey agreed to hear and decide the case. He called the two cats before him for this purpose. He held out a pair of scales. He put one piece of cheese in one scale and one in another.

10. In private life he was amiable. In private life he was even fond of amusement. In public life he was severe. In public life he was a rigorous dispenser of justice.

(*b*) *Combine into one Compound sentence:—*

1. Henry was not in a position to follow up his victory. He gained this victory on the field of Agincourt. He proceeded to Calais. From

Calais he proceeded to Dover. At Dover he was received with the greatest enthusiasm. (*Three* Finite verbs.)

2. Perkin Warbeck was promised his life. He surrendered on that promise. He was carried in mock triumph to London A confession of the imposture was published in London. The object of this publication was to satisfy the people. (*Two* Finite verbs.)

3. A poor Arab came suddenly upon a spring of sweet water. He had never before tasted any but brackish wells. He thought such sweet water fit only for a king. He filled his leathern bottle from the spring. He set off to present it to the Khalif. (*Three* Finite verbs.)

4. The courtiers pressed forward. They desired to taste this precious water. The Khalif forbade them to taste even a drop. The water had turned sour on the way. The Khalif did not desire to give offence to the peasant. The peasant was simple-minded. The peasant was loyal. (*Four* Finite verbs.)

5. You have finished the job before the time. You have done it in good style. This is more than I expected from you. You have never before shown so much quickness and energy. I have seen a great deal of you for many years past. (*Five* Finite verbs.)

6. The Jews begged Pilate to release Barabbas. They begged him to condemn Jesus to death. Jesus was innocent. Barabbas was a robber. (*Three* Finite verbs.)

7. He is a fool. He is a knave. (Combine these sentences in three different ways, so as (1) to give equal stress to both statements; (2) to give most stress to the first; (3) to give most stress to the second.)

8. The monsoon (periodic rainfall) failed. The tanks became almost empty. The fields could not be irrigated. No grain could be sown. A famine was feared. The peasants looked anxiously for the next monsoon. It proved more abundant than usual. The danger was averted. (*Madras Matriculation*, 1888. *Six* Finite verbs.)

9. Henry III. had several times confirmed the Magna Charta. He regarded that document as an encroachment upon the rights of a king. He broke its provisions on several occasions. He looked upon the English barons with suspicion. They seemed to him to be desirous of lessening the kingly power. (*Three* Finite verbs.)

10. A boat was lowered. The prince at once put off from the sinking vessel. The nobles put off at the same time. He heard the cries of his half-sister. He returned to the vessel. He hoped thereby to save his half-sister. (*Two* Finite verbs.)

(c) Combine each set of Simple sentences into a Compound, or a Complex, or a Mixed sentence. The italicised word shows the Predicate verb of the Principal clause :—

1. Mr. Merriman *left* the cottage. He crossed the river. He returned almost immediately. He was accompanied by five Dyaks. He had met them in the Chinese quarters. They had arrived there with a boat-load of commodities. They had collected these from the jungle. (One co-ordinate clause and two subordinate clauses.)

2. Marsupials are a kind of animal. They have pouches for carrying their young. They *were* once scattered all over the world. Most of them have long since become extinct. The survivors are thus confined to two

quarters of the globe. One quarter is Australia. Here we find kangaroos, wombats, etc. The other quarter is a limited portion of America. Here we find only one small group. This group consists of the opossums. (Five clauses besides the principal.)

3. In the opossums the pouch *is* very small. It is thus useless as a receptacle for the little ones. The mother carries these on her back. The mother carries as many as a dozen. Their tails are lashed round hers. (One clause besides the principal.)

4. In former times there *was* a class of persons. They were called knights-errant. They were clad in coats of mail. They rode about singly. One object was to fight with each other at tournaments. The other object was to redress the wrongs of persons. These persons sought their assistance. (Three clauses besides the principal.)

5. (*a*) In those times two strong and warlike knights came from opposite directions. They *met* at a certain place. In that place a statue was erected. (One clause besides the principal.) (*b*) In the arm of the statue *was* a shield. One side of the shield was of iron. The other side was of brass. The two knights approached the statue from opposite quarters. Each saw only one side of the shield. (Four clauses besides the principal.) (*c*) They immediately *fell* into conversation in regard to the statue before them. One declared that the shield was made of iron. The other corrected him. It was made of brass according to his assertion. (Two clauses besides the principal.)

6. (*a*) Two persons sometimes attempt to decide a dispute by fighting. One man may be right on the disputed question. The other may be wrong. To settle such a question by fighting is very absurd. You *will* think so. (Three clauses besides the principal.) (*b*) But persons may be ignorant. They may be proud. They may be conceited. Among such people that mode of settlement *has been* a common practice in the history of mankind. A long and furious combat now ensued between the two knights. They fought earnestly over this petty question. They would not have fought more earnestly for their lives or their honour. (Three clauses besides the principal.) (*c*) They had fought for a long time. Both *were* at last exhausted. Both were unhorsed. Both lay bleeding on the ground. They then found out something new. It surprised and vexed them greatly. The sides of the shield were of different metals. They might have saved themselves the trouble of quarrelling and wounding each other for nothing. But they had not taken the trouble at first to look at both sides of the shield. (Five clauses besides the principal.)

CHAPTER XXIV.—STRUCTURE AND ANALYSIS OF PARAGRAPHS.

324. Unity of Paragraph: Theme.—A paragraph is a group of sentences.[1] An essay is a group of paragraphs. On what principle, then, is the division into paragraphs to be

---

[1] A paragraph is usually a *group* of sentences; but sometimes, for purposes of exposition, one very important or leading statement is placed in a paragraph by itself.

made? On the principle of Unity. A paragraph should be a separate whole; *i.e.* it must deal with one main division of the essay at a time, just as a sentence must make one main statement at a time. The subject or main purport of a paragraph, on which its unity depends, is called the **theme.** This is often expressed in a sentence of its own at the commencement of the paragraph, as in the following example:—

> Of Pau I shall say little or nothing. It would be real impertinence in one, who spent only three days in it, to describe a city which is known to all Europe; which is a permanent English colony, and boasts of one, sometimes two packs of English fox-hounds. But this I may be allowed to say. Of all delectable spots that I have yet seen, Pau is the most delectable. Of all the landscapes which I have yet beheld, that from the Place Royale is for variety, richness, and grandeur the most glorious,—at least as I saw it for the first time.—KINGSLEY, *Prose Idylls*, v. p. 182.

325. Violation of Unity.—In the following paragraph will be found a flagrant breach of the rule of Unity:—

The Royal Tour in Australia.

> The great event of the month in the Colonies has been the opening of the Australasian Parliament by the Duke and Duchess of Cornwall. The Royal progress in Australia has been one long triumphal procession. Colony has vied with colony as to which could make the most overwhelming manifestation of their loyalty and enthusiasm. So far everything has gone without a hitch, and when the Royal party returns, it will have to report that the stately ceremonial of the christening of the Commonwealth passed off in a fashion which bodes well for the future relations between the Commonwealth and the Empire. The King had a narrow escape from drowning last month. He was on board the *Shamrock II.* when Sir T. Lipton's yacht suddenly capsized in a squall. Fortunately no one was hurt. —*Rev. of Reviews*, p. 529, June 1901.

Here the theme of the paragraph, as distinctly given by the writer himself, is the "Royal Tour in Australia." Yet before concluding the paragraph he darts off, without giving a word of warning, into an entirely new subject,—an accident off the English coast. "Empire" should have been the last word of the paragraph. A new paragraph should begin with the words "The King."

326. Variable Positions of the Theme.—It has been pointed out already (§ 324) that "the theme is often expressed in a sentence of its own at the commencement of the paragraph." The opening sentence, standing as it does at the head of all the rest, is the first to arrest the reader's attention; and from the prominent place that it holds, it is expected to furnish a clue to the drift of what follows.

Sometimes, however, the theme is not given till towards the middle or even the close of the paragraph. In this case the previous sentences are merely preparatory, leading up to the theme by degrees. Several purposes may be served by this arrangement. It may be the intention of the writer to keep the reader's interest in suspense, or it may be his desire to lead the reader's mind by degrees to some conclusion, the full force of which could not have been perceived without some indication of the preparatory stages. An example of this latter process occurs in the following:—

> (1) The king cannot be blamed for determining that Monmouth should suffer death. (2) Every man who heads a rebellion against an established government stakes his life on the event. (3) He had declared against his uncle a war without quarter. (4) In the manifesto put forth at Lyme, James had been held up to execration as an incendiary, as an assassin who had strangled one innocent man and cut the throat of another, and lastly as the poisoner of his own brother. (5) To spare an enemy, who had not scrupled to resort to such extremities, would have been an act of rare, perhaps of blamable, generosity. (6) But to see him, and not to spare him, was an outrage on humanity and decency. (7) *This outrage the king resolved to commit.[1] (8) The arms of the prisoner were bound behind him with a silken cord; and thus secured he was ushered into the presence of the implacable kinsman whom he had wronged.—MACAULAY, *History of England*, ch. v.

The theme of the paragraph—"the outrage on humanity and decency" committed by James—is reserved for sentence (7), the last but one in the paragraph. Sentence (8) is in continuation of sentence (7), and adds a great deal to its force by mentioning one or two particulars as to the manner in which the outrage was perpetrated. All the sentences that precede sentence (7) are intended to lead the mind of the reader step by step to a just appreciation of "the outrage which the king resolved to commit." Sentence (1), which heads the paragraph, stands (as it should do in such a case) next in importance to sentence (7): it lays down the proposition that James cannot be blamed for determining that Monmouth should die,—an admission which appears to concede a great point in James's favour, and thus convinces the reader that the author's estimate of James is not dictated by prejudice. Sentences (2), (3), (4) enlarge upon this proposition, giving one after another the different reasons for which, in the opinion

---

[1] In this and the following examples the sentence containing the theme is indicated by an asterisk. To facilitate comment each sentence has been numbered.

of the writer, Monmouth deserved to die. Sentence (5) goes a step farther, and asserts that, far from blaming James for sentencing Monmouth to death, we should rather be inclined to blame him if he had spared his life. Then comes the climax expressed in sentence (6),—"but to see him, and not to spare him, was an outrage on humanity." By this time the reader's mind is fully prepared for the theme announced in sentence (7),—"This outrage the king resolved to commit."

327. Theme not always expressed.—If the theme is implied rather than expressed, it does not follow that the paragraph is deficient in unity. The following is an example:—

(1) The companion of the church dignitary was a man past forty—thin, tall, strong, and muscular; an athletic figure, to which long fatigue and constant exercise seemed to have left none of the softer parts of the human form. (2) His head was covered with a scarlet cap, faced with fur—of that kind which the French call *mortier* from its resemblance to the shape of an inverted mortar. (3) The expression of his face was calculated to impress a degree of awe, if not of fear, upon strangers. (4) High features, naturally strong and powerfully expressive, had been burnt almost into Negro blackness by constant exposure to the tropical sun, and might in their ordinary state be said to slumber after the storm of passion had passed away; but the projection of the veins of the forehead, the readiness with which the upper lip quivered upon the slightest emotion, plainly intimated that the tempest might be again and easily awakened. (5) His keen, piercing dark eyes told in every glance of difficulties subdued and dangers dared, and seemed to challenge opposition to his wishes.—SCOTT, *Ivanhoe*, ch. ii. para. 4.

Where then (it will be asked) is the theme of such a paragraph? The answer is, the theme is implied, not expressed. The theme is a description of "the companion of a certain church dignitary," and this is implied in the collection of sentences in which the different items of the description are conveyed. The first sentence is about the man's age, stature, and general appearance; the second about his head-dress; the third about the expression of his face; the fourth about his complexion; the fifth about his eyes, etc. Not only is there unity in every sentence, but unity in the paragraph as a whole.

328. Length of Paragraph.—The length of a paragraph depends upon the scope of the "theme" (§ 324), and the selection of the theme and the mode of stating it are at the option of the writer himself. The beginner, however, is advised to make his paragraphs short rather than long. A lengthy paragraph in a long book or a long essay may be quite appropriate, but in a short essay or in a letter a lengthy paragraph amounts almost to a fault; for in such compositions several different points have to be touched upon within a narrow space, and a separate paragraph should be given to each of them.

329. Parallel Construction.—Lastly, a brief allusion must be made to what has been called "the Rule of Parallel Construction." The rule has been stated thus:—

"When several consecutive sentences iterate or illustrate the same idea, they should, as far as possible, be formed alike" (BAIN).

> (1) *This old practice (the levying of ship-money) it was now determined, after a long interval, not only to revive, but to extend. (2) Former princes had raised ship-money only in time of war, it was now exacted in a time of profound peace. (3) Former princes, even in the most perilous wars, had raised ship-money only along the coasts; it was now exacted from the inland shires. (4) Former kings had raised ship-money only for the maritime defence of the country; it was now exacted by the admission of the Royalists themselves, not with the object of maintaining a navy, but of furnishing the king with supplies, which might be increased at his discretion to any amount and expended at his discretion for any purpose.—MACAULAY.

Sentence (1) contains the theme,—the king's determination to revive and extend the levying of ship-money. Then comes a series of parallel sentences, all bearing upon the theme. Each sentence expresses a telling contrast,—the first between the occasions on which the tax was levied (sentence 2), the second between the parts of the country to which it was applied (sentence 3), and the third between the objects for which it was levied (sentence 4). The three sentences are formed alike, the principal subject and the principal predicate having in each sentence a similar place allotted to it.

In the following example the rule of parallel construction is observed in all but sentence (4), where the contrast expressed by the writer puts the subject in the wrong place:—

> (1) *The most striking characteristic of the poetry of Milton is the extreme remoteness of the associations, by means of which it acts on the reader. (2) Its effect on the reader is produced not so much by the ideas which it directly conveys, as by other ideas which are connected with them. (3) He electrifies the mind through conductors. (4) The most unimaginative man must understand the Iliad; Homer gives him no choice, but takes the whole on himself, and sets his images in so clear a light that it is impossible to be blind to them. (5) Milton does not give a finished picture, a play for a mere passive listener. (6) He sketches and leaves others to fill up the outline; he strikes the key-note, and expects his hearers to make out the melody.—MACAULAY.

To make the parallelism perfect, we might rewrite sentence (4) as follows:—"The Iliad must be understood by the most unimaginative man: Homer gives him no choice," etc. In this way *Iliad* is made the subject of its sentence and placed in a parallel position with *Homer*—the reputed author of the poem named. Sentence (1) contains the theme, and sentence (2) reiterates it in other words. Or it might be said that the two sentences together contain and jointly express the theme, the second sentence supplementing the first. Sentence (3) illustrates the theme by a metaphor. Sentence (4) enforces the theme by a contrast. Sentences (5) and (6) illustrate the theme by metaphors drawn from painting and music.

Miscellaneous Questions on Sentences and Paragraphs.

1. Express with greater clearness the main ideas in the following extract by changing (i.) the sentence into a paragraph,[1] and (ii.) the phraseology as well as the order of the words so far as is necessary :—

To this succeeded the licentiousness which entered with the Restoration, and from infecting our religion and morals fell to corrupt our language: which last was not like to be much improved by those who at that time made up the court of Charles II. ; either such who had followed him in his banishment, or who had been altogether conversant in the dialect of those fanatic times : or young men who had been educated in the same company: so that the court which used to be the standard of propriety and correctness of speech was then, and I think hath ever since continued, the worst school in England for that accomplishment.—*Lond. Matric.* Sept. 1905.

2. (*a*) Subdivide the following very long sentence into a series of shorter sentences, making such changes of words and of punctuation as you may consider necessary. (*b*) Construct a heading which will approximately describe the theme of the paragraph thus formed :—

And after the king's blessed return to England, he had frequent conferences with many of those who had acted several parts towards the escape ; whereof some were of the Chancellor's newest alliance, and others his most intimate friends ; towards whom his Majesty always made many gracious expressions of his acknowledgment ; so that there is nothing in this short relation, the verity whereof can justly be suspected, though, as is said before, it is a great pity that there could be no diary made, indeed, no exact account of every hour's adventure from the coming out of Worcester, in that dismal confusion, to the hour of his embarkation at Bright-Hemsted, in which there was such a concurrence of good-nature, charity, and generosity in persons of the meanest and lowest extractions and conditions, who did not know the value of the precious jewel that was in their custody, yet all knew him to be escaped from such an action as would make the discovery and delivery of him to those who governed over and amongst them of great benefit and present advantage to them, and in those who did know him, of such courage, loyalty, and activity, that all may reasonably look upon the whole as the inspiration and conduct of God Almighty as a manifestation of His power and glory, and for

[1] Since a paragraph consists of a collection of sentences, the only way in which "a sentence can be changed into a paragraph" is to break up the given sentence into several smaller ones, care being taken that the rules relating to sentence-structure (§§ 314-319) are observed.

the conviction of the whole party which had sinned so grievously; and if it hath not wrought that effect in them, it hath rendered them the more inexcusable.—CLARENDON, *The Great Rebellion.*

3. State the main purport or theme of the following paragraph. Point out the sentences in which the rule of Parallel Construction is observed, and those in which it is not observed, if you find any such. Rewrite any sentence or sentences in which it is not observed:—

He enjoys great consequence and consideration along the road; has frequent conferences with the village housewives, who look upon him as a man of great trust and dependence; and he seems to have a good understanding with every bright-eyed country lass. The moment when he arrives where the horses are to be changed, he throws down the reins with something of an air, and abandons the cattle to the care of the ostler; his duty being merely to drive them from one stage to another. When off the box, his hands are thrust in the pockets of his great coat, and he rolls about the inn-yard with an air of the most absolute lordliness. Here he is generally surrounded by an admiring throng of ostlers, stable-boys, shoe-blacks, and those nameless hangers-on that infest inns and taverns, and run errands. These all look up to him as an oracle, treasure up his cant phrases, echo his opinion about horses and other topics of jockey-lore, and endeavour to imitate his air and carriage.—WASHINGTON IRVING.

4. Simplify and condense the following extracts, so far as this is possible, without altering the sense:—

(*a*) The power of speech in the direction of public affairs becomes more and more obvious, developed, and irresistible as we advance towards the culminating period of Grecian history—the century preceding the battle of Chæroneia. That its development was greatest among the most enlightened sections of the Grecian name, and smallest among the more obtuse and stationary, is matter of notorious fact; and it is not less true, that the prevalence of this habit was one of the chief causes of the intellectual eminence of the nation generally.—*Lond. Matric. Exam.* Sept. 1905.

(*b*) I have been told that if a man that was born blind could obtain and have his sight but for only one hour during his whole life, and should at the first opening of his eyes fix his eyes upon the sun when it was in its full glory, either at the rising or setting of it, he would be so transported and amazed, and so admire the glory of it, that he would not willingly turn his eyes from that first ravishing object, to behold all the other various beauties this world could present to him.—ISAAC WALTON.

(*c*) Avoid disputes as much as possible. In order to appear easy and well-bred in conversation, you may assure yourself that it requires more wit as well as more good humour to improve than to contradict the notions of another; but if you are at any time obliged to enter into an argument, give your reasons with the utmost coolness and modesty,—two things which scarce ever fail of making an impression on the hearers. Besides, if you are neither dogmatical, nor show either by your actions or words that you are full of yourself, all will then more heartily rejoice at your victory. Nay, should you be pinched in your argument, you may make your retreat with a very good grace. You were never positive and are now glad to be better informed.—*Spectator*, No. 197, Oct. 1711.

5. In the following extract there is a superabundance of full stops. Get rid of some of them by combining some of the sentences together into one sentence. Make the necessary changes in punctuation and the use of capitals. Show under one short heading what the theme or main purport of the paragraph is :—

Justinian was a great lawyer. His work in connection with Roman jurisprudence entitles him to high honour. But this is about all that can be said for him. Had he avoided aggressive warfare, his reign might have been a blessing. But he must eternally meddle with other peoples, so his reign became a curse. The weakness of the Roman Empire when he ascended the throne was already very great. Justinian bled it to death. Africa relapsed into barbarism. The fair provinces in which Phœnicians, Romans, and Vandals had thriven became deserts. Italy had recuperative power, and, though depopulated and impoverished, it recovered in the end. But Africa never did. Nor was the condition of the Eastern provinces much better. . . .—SOUTTAR, *Short History of Mediæval Peoples*, 1907.

6. (*a*) Divide the following into two paragraphs. Show where the second paragraph begins by quoting the three first words. (*b*) Construct a sentence or heading showing the theme of each paragraph. (*c*) Point out the instances in which the rule of Parallel Construction is observed, and those, if any, in which it is violated :—

No great general ever arose out of a nation of cowards; no great statesman or philosopher out of a nation of fools; no great artist out of a nation of materialists; no great dramatist except when the drama was the passion of the people. Acting was the especial amusement of the English from the palace to the village-green. It was the result and expression of their power over themselves and their power over circumstances. They were troubled with no subjective speculations, no social problems vexed them with which they were unable to deal; and in the exuberance of vigour and spirits they were able, in the strict and literal sense of the word, to play with the materials of life. The mystery-plays came first; next the popular legends; and then the great figures of English history came out upon the stage, or stories from Greek and Roman writers; or sometimes it was an extemporised allegory. Shakespeare himself has left us many pictures of the village drama. Doubtless he had seen many a Bottom in the old Warwickshire hamlets; many a Sir Nathaniel playing "Alissander," and finding himself "a little o'erparted." He had been with Snug the joiner, Quince the carpenter, and Flute the bellows-mender, and had acted with them and written their parts for them when a boy; and afterwards when he came to London and found his way into great society, he had not failed to see Polonius burlesquing Cæsar on the stage, as in his own person Polonius burlesqued Sir William Cecil. The strolling players in *Hamlet* might be seen at any country wake or festival; it was the direction in which the especial genius of the nation delighted to revel.—JAMES ANTHONY FROUDE (1818-1894), *Hist. of England*.

7. Rewrite the following in the form of Direct Speech; and in doing so subdivide into paragraphs, and write the theme at the top of each paragraph. Note also in one phrase, or in one very short sentence, what you consider to be the subject of the extract as a whole :—

Lord Roberts, who was enthusiastically received, said he imagined it did not often happen that an old soldier found himself in a position to address an assemblage of Oxford men, but, having been allowed to occupy so unique a position, he earnestly hoped that he might be able to induce some of his audience to feel with him on a subject he had greatly at heart and the intelligent understanding of which by the nation generally he believed of vital importance to the security of this great Empire. He had been much concerned to find how large a proportion of his fellow-countrymen took so small a practical interest in what he might call the possible objectives of the land forces of the Crown and how little they realised the enormous strain that would be placed upon them were they called upon to carry out a prolonged war against a formidable European Power. They were seemingly content with the fact that they had a powerful Navy, forgetting that a navy alone could not bring a war against an enemy possessing a land-frontier to a successful conclusion. It was with a view to pointing out that this was a matter worthy of grave consideration that he had selected as his subject the North-West Frontier of India, his reason being that, although the North-West Frontier of India was by no means the only part of the world where they might find themselves engaged in war, it was in India that this country to-day was in the position of a Continental nation, which they must be prepared to defend by Continental methods. During the last 42 years Russia had advanced more than 540 miles nearer to India, while England had practically remained stationary. The progress of Russia might possibly have been checked, had England 50 years ago responded to the wish of Persia that the friendly relations which formerly existed between her and Great Britain should be restored. But that opportunity was let slip, and nothing could now alter the fact that the termini of the two Russian railways were at the present time on the borders of Afghanistan. From what he had said it would be readily understood that England had now become a Continental Power, and she must henceforth be prepared to defend her eastern possessions. He had endeavoured to show them how step by step, he was going to say, involuntarily, but certainly with no great lust of conquest, they had been led on by the force of circumstances towards the north-west in the same manner that Russia had found her way to the south-east, until to-day we stood almost conterminous with that Power.

8. Write two paragraphs based upon the contents of the two extracts quoted below, and write them in such a way that the second shall appear to be a natural sequel to the first, and both to have been written by the same person. (The first must be changed from verse into equivalent and idiomatic prose; the second can be put in rather simpler language.) Write also (*a*) a brief heading which shall express the collective drift or main purport of the two paragraphs that you have made, (*b*) a brief heading which shall express the theme of each paragraph separately.

(1) We move, the wheel must always move,
Nor always on the plain,
And if we move to such a goal
As Wisdom hopes to gain,

Then you that drive, and know your craft,
  Will firmly hold the rein,
Nor lend an ear to random cries,
  Or you may drive in vain;

For some cry "Quick," and some cry "Slow,"
  But, while the hills remain,
Up hill "Too-slow" will need the whip,
  Down hill "Too-quick," the chain.—TENNYSON.

(2) Their recent speeches in the House of Commons would seem to suggest that the Government mean to take steps intended to lessen the legislative powers of the House of Lords. . . . The British people, however, will not consent to tamper with the Constitution under which they have enjoyed for so many centuries, in an unequalled degree, that stable and progressive liberty which is the chief end of civil government, without convincing proof that a change so incalculable in its consequences, and so irrevocable once it has been made, is imposed upon them by necessities that are imperative. They will resent any effort to deal with matters affecting so profoundly the very roots of the political life of the country in a spirit of levity or for mere reasons of party. They will hold that the burden of proving that any such change is required lies upon those who advocate it, and they will demand that the proof shall be clear and complete.—*Times*, 6th Feb. 1907.

9. Rewrite in the form of a continuous narrative, using the Third person only, the following dialogue between Alexander the Great and the Thracian robber. Subdivide the narrative into paragraphs, and write the theme at the top of each paragraph. Make all necessary changes in punctuation. If any brief explanation or comment seems to be needed, this may be added:—

Alex. What, art thou the Thracian robber of whom I have heard so much?

Rob. I am a Thracian and a soldier.

Alex. A soldier!—a thief, a plunderer, an assassin! the pest of the country! I could honour thy courage, but I must detest and punish thy crimes.

Rob. What have I done, of which you can complain?

Alex. Hast thou not set at defiance my authority, violated the public peace, and passed thy life in injuring the persons and properties of thy fellow-subjects?

Rob. Alexander, I am thy captive. I must hear what thou art pleased to say, and endure what thou art pleased to inflict. But my soul is unconquered; and if I reply at all to thy reproaches, I will reply to thee like a free man.

Alex. Speak freely. Far be it from me to take advantage of my power, to silence those with whom I deign to converse.

Rob. I must then answer your questions by another. How have *you* passed your life?

Alex. Like a hero. Ask Fame, and she will tell you. Among the brave I have been the bravest; among sovereigns the noblest; among conquerors the mightiest.

Rob. And does not Fame speak of me too? Was there ever a bolder captain of a more valiant band? Was there ever—but I scorn to boast. You yourself know that I have not been easily subdued.

Alex. Still, what are you but a robber, a base, dishonest robber?

Rob. And what is a conqueror? Have not you too gone about the earth like an evil genius, blasting the fair fruits of peace and industry; plundering, ravaging, killing, without law, without justice, merely to gratify an insatiable lust for dominion? All that I have done to a single district with a hundred followers, you have done to whole nations with a hundred thousand. If I have stripped individuals, you have ruined kings and princes. If I have burnt a few hamlets, you have desolated the most flourishing kingdoms and cities of the earth. What is then the difference, but that as you were born a king and I a private man, you have been able to become a mightier robber than I?

Alex. But if I have taken like a king, I have given like a king. If I have subverted empires, I have founded greater. I have cherished arts, commerce, and philosophy.

Rob. I too have given freely to the poor what I took from the rich. I know indeed little of the philosophy that you talk of; but I believe that neither you nor I will ever atone to the world for half the mischief that we have done to it.

Alex. Leave me. Take off his chains, and use him well. Are we then so much alike? Alexander like a robber! Let me reflect.

CHAPTER XXV.—PARAPHRASING.

330. Different Kinds of Paraphrasing.—The word "paraphrase" is of Greek origin (Gr. *para*, "along-side of," and *phras*-is, "wording"). It therefore signifies a parallel wording, *i.e.* a rendering from one form of diction to another. Such rendering may be seen in four different forms:—

I. The turning of prose into equivalent poetry.

II. The reproduction of prose in the form of a commentary.

III. The turning of poetry into equivalent prose.

IV. The turning of old idiom and old diction into modern.

Those kinds of paraphrase which are numbered I. and II. need not detain us long. But numbers III. and IV. will have to be treated more fully.

331. I. The Turning of Prose into Equivalent Poetry.—One short example will be amply sufficient. In the Authorised Version of the Bible dated A.D. 1611, verse 1 of Psalm xxiii., we read as follows:—

The Lord is my shepherd; I shall not want.

The following is Addison's rendering into verse. He calls it a "Paraphrase on Psalm xxiii."

The Lord my pasture shall prepare,
And feed me with a shepherd's care;
His presence shall my wants supply
And guard me with a watchful eye.

332. II. Reproduction of Prose in the Form of a Commentary.—Reverting again to the same psalm, we find that verse 2 runs as follows:—

> He maketh me to lie down in green pastures: he leadeth me beside the still waters.

The following is the paraphrase given by Bishop Patrick:—

> For as a good shepherd leads his sheep in the violent heat to shady places, where they may lie down and feed (not in parched, but) in green and fresh pastures, and in the evening leads them (not to muddy and troubled waters, but) to pure and quiet streams; so hath He (the Lord) already made a fair and plentiful provision for me, which I enjoy in peace without any disturbance.

This kind of expansion may be suitable for oral or unwritten exposition. But for practice in written composition it is more mischievous than useful. There was a time when books were published setting forth this kind of paraphrase or commentary; but the practice has completely died out.

333. III. The Turning of Poetry into Equivalent Prose.—This is the sense in which the word paraphrase is almost always used in the present day. To guide the student in this kind of exercise the following hints are offered:—

(1) Be certain that you have fully mastered the sense of the poetry before you begin to make any changes either in the words themselves or in their order.

(2) For all constructions that are uncommon in prose, but common in poetry, substitute the forms used in ordinary prose.

(3) Rearrange the parts of each sentence in the order commonly used in prose (see ch. xviii. on this point).

(4) Cancel epithets that contribute nothing to the purport of the sentence, but merely conduce to poetic ornament, or merely suit the necessities of the metre.

(5) For all words or phrases that are archaic or uncommon (provided that they help to express the main purport of the sentence, and are not used merely for ornament or for metre), substitute words or phrases such as are commonly met with in the present day.

(6) Substitute literal statement for figurative, if the figure used in the poetry appears to be unsuited to prose

(7) Supply all parts of speech, such as articles, prepositions, conjunctions, or relative pronouns, that have been omitted for the sake of the metre.

(8) Condense as much as you can, and avoid long and involved sentences. The shorter the prose version is, the better.

(9) Make no unnecessary changes of diction. It is not at all necessary for the student to find a prose-equivalent for any and every word used in the poetry, so long as the latter is suited to prose.

From the above instructions it will be seen that paraphrase of the kind here intended does not greatly differ from précis; in fact the only vital point of difference is, that of the two processes précis makes the greater demand for brevity or condensation.[1] The object of paraphrase, then, is not to spoil good poetry by turning it into prose, but to see whether the student has understood the poetry, and whether he can reproduce the main ideas idiomatically in prose-form, making no changes in the original except when change is demanded by prose-order, prose-diction, or prose-idiom.

After all, however, when all these precautions have been most carefully observed, paraphrasing, *i.e.* the turning of poetry into prose, is by no means applicable to all kinds of poetry. Poetry of the simple kind, when it is put into prose, often becomes doggerel, and poetry of the grander kind, when put into prose, becomes bombast. As a specimen of simple poetry, which we can admire if it is left as it stands, but which we cannot admire when it is stripped of its metrical form and turned into prose, I quote the following:—

Angels, ever bright and fair,
Take, O take me, to your care. (*Original.*)

Angels, always bright and beautiful, let me beg of you to take care of me. (*Paraphrase.*)

Still less can poetry of a high order be put into readable prose. It can, of course, be stripped of its metre and of its lofty diction, but it is murdered in the process. Such poetry, for example, as we meet with in *In Memoriam*, or in the *Ode on the Death of the Duke of Wellington* by the same poet, will not

[1] In the *London Matric. Exam.* of Jan. 1905, under the heading PARAPHRASE I find the following:—"State *in few words* the general sense of one of the following passages" given in verse. This kind of paraphrase appears to me to be undistinguishable from précis.

bear translation or paraphrase. The finer the poetry, the worse is the prose that can be got out of it. "Poetry," says Whately, "is not distinguished from prose by superior beauty of thought or of expression, but is *a distinct kind of composition*; and they produce, when each is excellent in its own way, distinct kinds of pleasure."

334. Examples of Paraphrase from Verse to Prose.—Let us now take one or two extracts from poetry, which are neither so simple nor so lofty as to be unfit for being paraphrased into prose.

(1) The lamb thy riot dooms to bleed to-day,
Had he thy reason, would he skip and play?
Pleased to the last, he crops the flowery food,
And licks the hand just raised to shed his blood.

POPE.

Here "riot," as the context shows, is used in the Tudor sense of banqueting, feasting, revelry. We see it so used in Luke xv. 13: "The younger son took his journey into a far country, and there wasted his substance with *riotous* living." The phrase "flowery food," besides being a little obscure, is not a suitable phrase for prose. The word "flowery" is perhaps meant to indicate the season of the year, when buttercups and daisies are seen in the midst of the rich and luxuriant grass. Since "lamb" is the subject of the verb "would," the pronoun "he" in the second half of the second line is superfluous,—admissible in verse, but considered a blemish in prose. In the prose-rendering, therefore, some change must be made in at least three points. The passage might be paraphrased thus:—

If the lamb, on whose flesh you are about to feast, had reason like yours, would he skip and play as you see him do? Fearless and happy to the last, he browses on the rich grass and licks the hand that is raised to shed his blood.

(2) "Paraphrase the following, and write an account of the historical events to which reference is made." When a question is given in this form, the student is advised to describe the historical events first; this will help to clear the ground, and give him confidence for turning the verse into prose.

Wrap them together in a purple cloak,
And lay them both upon the waste sea-shore
At Hastings, there to guard the land for which
He did foreswear himself—a warrior, ay,
And but that Holy Peter fought for us,
And that the false Northumbrian held aloof,
And save for that chance-arrow which the Saints
Sharpened and sent against him—who can tell?—
Three horses had I slain beneath me: twice

10. I thought that all was lost. Since I knew battle,
And that was from my boyhood, never yet—
No, by the splendour of God—have I fought men
Like Harold and his brethren, and his guard
Of English.—TENNYSON, *Harold*, V. ii.
(Quoted from *London Matric.* June 1905.)

A. *Historical Allusions:*—

Line 1. After winning the battle of Hastings, the Conqueror sees Edith of the Swan-neck, the ward of Edward the Confessor, lying dead on the battle-field, with her arms locked round the corpse of Harold, her husband or paramour. As the two bodies were rigidly fixed in death, and could not be separated without breaking some of their limbs, he gives an order that they are to be wrapped together in a purple cloak (purple being the badge of royalty, with which Harold had been invested before William disputed his claim) and buried on the waste sea-shore at Hastings.

Line 4. Harold had been made King of England by the votes of the Witenagemot ("Assembly of the Wise"), which, according to English notions in that day, made his title to the throne indisputable. But the Duke of Normandy gave out that Harold, while cruising in the Channel, had been thrown ashore by a storm, and had taken an oath at Rouen on the relics of certain Saints, by which he bound himself to renounce all claim to the crown of England as the price of his being allowed to return to England without the usual payment of a king's ransom; the Duke argued that Harold by accepting the crown from the National Assembly "did foreswear himself," *i.e.* was guilty of perfidy to the Duke and of perjury to the Saints.

Lines 5-9. In these lines William relates how very nearly he was defeated, and ascribes his deliverance to three different causes: (*a*) the aid of "Holy Peter," (*b*) the desertion of Harold by "the false Northumbrian," (*c*) the "chance-arrow" from an unknown hand, by which Harold, while victory was still hanging in the balance, was slain.

(*a*) *The Aid of Holy Peter.*—Edward the Confessor had spent most of his time, not in looking after the affairs of his kingdom, but in building a stately abbey at Westminster, which he dedicated—

To Holy Peter in our English isle.—Act II. Sc. 2.

This was built on the site where Westminster Abbey now stands. By the terms of the dedication England was placed under the special protection of St. Peter, as by the Roman Catholic Church it is still declared to be. Moreover, the Pope of Rome, in his capacity as successor of St. Peter, was on the side of William for reasons of his own. Stigand, the Archbishop of Canterbury, was the adherent of a rival pope; but Harold nevertheless recognised him as the primate of England:—

Old uncanonical Stigand—ask of me
Who had my pallium from an Antipope.—Act. I. i.

(*b*) "*The false Northumbrian.*"—This refers to Morcar, who had been made Earl of Northumbria in the place of Tostig, Harold's brother. Tostig had made himself so unpopular that he was banished from England, and the earldom was given to Morcar. Aided by Hardrada, the Norwegian king, Tostig had landed with a force in Yorkshire, but was defeated and slain in the battle at Stamford Bridge. Morcar, the Earl of Northumbria, was thus saved from destruction; but he was not grateful enough to accompany his benefactor and deliverer to the south, where his assistance would have been of great help to Harold in encountering William, who during Harold's absence in the north had sailed from Normandy and landed in the south coast of England with a large and formidable force.

(c) "*The chance-arrow.*"—This arrow struck Harold's right eye, which was of course a fatal spot. William in his speech says that "the Saints sharpened and sent this arrow against him." This is said in allusion to the relics of Saints, over which Harold is said to have sworn to William that he would never set up any claim to the throne of England.

> Stigand is not canonical enough
> To save them from the wrath of Norman Saints.
>
> Act III. Sc. i.

Line 11. William here refers to his early successes on other battle-fields. He was barely twenty years old, "a boy" as he calls himself, when he gained the duchy of Normandy by the brilliant dash that he made at Val-ès-dunes, where man and horse went down before his lance.—Green's *History of English People*, chap. ii. sec. iv.

Line 13. "Harold and his brethren." Besides the false Tostig, Harold had three other brothers, who were all slain that day.

B. *The Paraphrase*:—

Make no attempt to separate the two bodies; wrap them together in a purple-coloured shroud, and bury them on the barren sea-shore at Hastings, where their spirits may guard the land for which Harold perjured himself in vain. A warrior he was, —aye, of the first order. Who can say what the result of the battle might have been but for the assistance of Holy Peter, the absence of the false-hearted Morcar, and the chance-arrow (for such it seemed to be), which at a time when the result of the battle was still doubtful was sharpened and directed against him by the Saints whom he had offended? Three horses were slain under me in the course of the battle, and twice I thought that all was lost. From my boyhood upward have I been used to fighting. But never before,—no, never by the splendour of God,—have I fought men like Harold and his brothers and his guard of English warriors.

335. IV. The Turning of Old Idiom and Old Diction into Modern.—Of this kind of paraphrase several specimens written in *verse* have been given us by Dryden in his *Tales from Chaucer*,—which tales, as he states in his preface, he "has turned into modern English." The same kind of paraphrase can, of course, be applied to English prose; but for this purpose we need not go so far back as Chaucer. In our prose-literature of the last four hundred years we find that two different styles predominated in two different periods: (1) the *Older*, commencing from about A.D. 1500 and lasting for nearly two centuries; (2) the *Newer*, which has continued from about A.D. 1700 up to the present day. In the former we find among most writers long, elaborate, and cumbersome sentences written more in imitation of Latin idiom and Latin construction than in a strain of racy and genuine English. The first great writer of the "Older style" was Sir Thomas More, whose *Utopia* ("The Land of Nowhere") was written in Latin before it was put into English; the last, or one of the last, was Edward Hyde, afterwards known as the Earl of Clarendon, author of the *Great Rebellion*, who lived from 1608 to 1674. Almost contemporary with this historian there lived another,—Bishop Burnet (1643-1715), who wrote the *History of his own Times.* A comparison of these two writers, though they were separated from each other by only thirty-five years or so, shows the new turn that our prose-literature had taken in the interim. To read the long and involved sentences of Clarendon requires effort and close attention, and the most skilful reader or reciter could not put any rhythm or smoothness into them. On the other hand, Burnet's style is in most respects as easy and natural as could be found in any history or journal of the present day. Burnet was quite aware of the difference between himself and Clarendon; for he calls the new style (*i.e.* his own) "clear, plain, and short," while he describes the old as "long" and "heavy."

It was not the fault of our language, but of the men who handled it so unsuitably, that the "Clarendon style," as we might call it (for no other writer carried it to such an extreme as he did), came into vogue and held the ground so long. Even now on the side of Latin and Greek there are some fanatics, who insist that the ancient classics are the great, if not the only, model of a fine modern style. "It would be nearer the truth," says Morley, "if we said that our classical training is more aptly calculated to destroy the good qualities of good writing and fine speaking than any other system that could have been contrived."

The following extract from a sermon preached by Hugh Latimer, the Martyr (1485 ?-1555), shows very clearly that the English of the Tudor period could be as fresh and racy as the English of the present day, when it was used by a man who thought more of impressing his readers or hearers with the doctrines that he taught than of aping the idioms and constructions of Cicero or of Livy.

> And now I would ask a strange question: Who is the most diligent bishop and prelate in all England that passeth all the rest in doing his office? I can tell; for I know him who it is; I know him well. But now I think I see you listening and hearkening that I should name him. There is one that passeth all the other, and is the most diligent prelate and preacher in all England. And will ye know who it is? I will tell you; it is the devil. He is the most diligent preacher of all other; he is never out of his diocese, he is never from his cure; ye shall never find him unoccupied; he is ever in his parish; he keepeth residence at all times; ye shall never find him out of his way; call for him when you will, he is ever at home; etc.—*The Sermon of the Plough.*

There are three, but only three, peculiarities in the diction of the above extract. One peculiarity is the habit, at that time very common, of using words in pairs, where one word would have been sufficient,—"bishop and prelate," "listening and hearkening," "prelate and preacher." The second is the phrase "all the *other*," "of all *other*," which shows that Latimer was not acquainted, as every one now is, with the pluralised noun-form ("others") of the adjective "other." The third peculiarity is in the phrase "the most diligent preacher of all other"; we never now allow "other" to be used after a superlative. With these exceptions the language of Latimer could hardly be distinguished from what we hear or read in the present day.

336. Extract from Clarendon modernised.—I now give an extract from Clarendon, with a paraphrase or reconstruction in modern form:—

> The king's army was no sooner defeated at Worcester but the parliament renewed the old method of murthering in cold blood, and sent a commission to erect a High Court of Justice to persons of ordinary quality, many not being gentlemen and all notoriously his enemies, to try the Earl of Derby for his treason and rebellion; which they easily found him guilty of; and put him to death in a town of his own, against which he had expressed a severe displeasure for their obstinate rebellion against the king, with all the circumstances of rudeness and barbarity they could invent.—*Hist. of Great Rebellion.*

Paraphrase or reconstruction in modern form.

> No sooner was the king's army defeated at Worcester than the Parliament renewed their old method of putting their enemies to death in cold blood after a mock-trial. They commissioned a body of men to form a High Court of Justice and bring the Earl of Derby to trial on a charge of treason against the state. The men selected for this purpose were mostly persons of inferior rank, many of them not possessing an hereditary coat-armour, and all of them notoriously hostile to the earl. A court so constituted had no difficulty in finding him guilty.

Having declared their verdict they proceeded at once to carry it into effect in a way of their own. They put him to death with all the rudeness and barbarity that they could devise; and to add to the bitterness of his end they had him executed in a town of his own, whose inhabitants he had had occasion to censure severely for their persistent hostility to the king.

The original sentence has thus been broken up into six. "Quality" is used in the original in the older sense of "rank"; it has therefore been changed to "rank" in the paraphrase. For a similar reason "erect" has been changed to "set up"; and the word "gentlemen" has been given the sense that it bore in Clarendon's time.

I. Selections from Poetry.

Explain the historical allusions occurring in each of the following extracts, and turn each extract from poetry into prose:—

1. And you, my Lords, you make the people muse
 In doubt if you be of our Barons' breed—
Were those your sires who fought at Lewes?
 Is this the manly strain of Runnymede?
O fall'n nobility, that, overawed,
Would lisp with honeyed whispers of this monstrous fraud!

TENNYSON, *The Third of February* 1852.

2. The vernal sun new life bestows
Even on the meanest flower that blows;
But vainly, vainly, may he shine,
Where glory weeps o'er Nelson's shrine;
And vainly pierce the solemn gloom,
That shrouds, O Pitt, thy hallowed tomb.
Deep graved in every British heart,
O never let those names depart!
Say to your sons,—Lo, here his grave,
Who victor died on Gadite wave.
Nor mourn ye less his perished worth,
Who bade the conqueror go forth,
And launched that thunderbolt of war
On Egypt, Hafnia, Trafalgar.

SCOTT, Introd., *Marmion.*

3. If yet your thoughts are loose from state affairs,
Nor feel the burden of a kingdom's cares,
If yet your time and actions are your own,
Receive the present of a Muse unknown:
A Muse that in adventurous numbers sings
The rout of armies and the fall of kings,
Britain advanced and Europe's peace restored
By Somers' counsels and by Nassau's sword.

ADDISON, *To the Lord Keeper of the Great Seal.*

4. And turning to his men,
Quoth our brave Henry then,
"Though they to one be ten,
Be not amazèd.
Yet have we well begun,
Battles so bravely won
Have ever to the sun
By fame been raisèd.

Poitiers and Cressy tell
When most their pride did swell,
Under our swords they fell:
Nor less our skill is
Than when our grandsire great,
Claiming the regal seat,
By many a warlike feat,
Lopped the French lilies."

MICHAEL DRAYTON.

5. From town to town, from tower to tower
The Red Rose is a gladsome flower.
Her thirty years of winter past,
The Red Rose is revived at last;
She lifts her head for endless spring,
For everlasting blossoming.
Both Roses flourish, Red and White,
In love and sisterly delight;
The two that were at strife are blended,
And all old troubles now are ended.

WORDSWORTH, *The Good Lord Clifford.*

6. At Flores in the Azores Sir Richard Grenville lay,
And a pinnace, like a fluttered bird, came flying from far away:
"Spanish ships of war at sea! we have sighted fifty-three!"
Then sware Lord Thomas Howard: "'Fore God I am no coward;
But I cannot meet them here; for my ships are out of gear,
And the half my men are sick. I must fly, but follow quick.
We are six ships of the line; can we fight with fifty-three?"

Then spake Sir Richard Grenville: "I know you are no coward;
You fly them for a moment to fight with them again.
But I've ninety men and more that are lying sick ashore.
I should count myself the coward if I left them, my Lord Howard,
To these Inquisition dogs and the devildoms of Spain."

So Lord Howard passed away with five ships of war that day,
Till he melted like a cloud in the silent summer heaven;
But Sir Richard bore in hand all his sick men from the land
Very carefully and slow,
Men of Bideford in Devon,
And we laid them on the ballast down below;
For we brought them all aboard,
And they blessed him in their pain, that they were not left to Spain,
To the thumbscrew and the stake, for the glory of the Lord.

TENNYSON, *The Revenge.*

7. Proud Nimrod first the bloody chase began,
A mighty hunter, and his prey was man:
Our haughty Norman boasts that barbarous name,
And makes his trembling slaves the royal game.
The fields are ravished from the industrious swains,
From men their cities, and from gods their fanes.
Whom even the Saxon spared and bloody Dane,
The wanton victims of his sport remain.
But see, the man, who spacious regions gave
A waste for beasts, himself denied a grave.
Lo, Rufus, tugging at the deadly dart,
Bleeds in the forest like a wounded hart.
Succeeding monarchs heard the subjects' cries,
Nor saw displeased the peaceful cottage rise:
The forest wondered at the unusual grain,
And secret transports touched the conscious swain.

POPE, *Windsor Forest.*

8. Not a drum was heard, not a funeral note,
As his corse to the ramparts we hurried.
Not a soldier discharged his farewell shot
O'er the grave where our hero we buried.

We buried him darkly at dead of night,
The sod with our bayonets turning,
By the struggling moonbeam's misty light,
And the lantern dimly burning.

No useless coffin enclosed his breast,
Nor in sheet nor in shroud we wound him,
But he lay like a warrior taking his rest,
With his martial cloak around him.

C. WOLFE, *Burial of Sir John Moore.*

9. He was a scholar, and a ripe good one;
Exceeding wise, fair-spoken, and persuading;
Lofty and sour to them that loved him not;
But to those men that sought him sweet as summer.
And though he were unsatisfied in getting—
Which was a sin—yet in bestowing, madam,
He was most princely. Ever witness for him
Those twins of learning, that he raised in you,
Ipswich and Oxford! one of which fell with him,
Unwilling to outlive the good that did it;
The other, though unfinished, yet so famous,
So excellent in art, and still so rising,
That Christendom shall ever speak his virtue.

SHAKESPEARE, *Henry VIII.* IV. 2.

10. When Tumult lately burst his prison door,
And set plebeian thousands in a roar;
When he usurped authority's just place,
And dared to look his master in the face;
When the rude rabble's watchward was, Destroy!
And blazing London seemed a second Troy;

Liberty blushed and hung her drooping head,
Beheld their progress with the deepest dread,
Blushed that effects like these she should produce,
Worse than the deeds of galley-slaves broke loose.

COWPER, A.D. 1780.

11. Close by those meads, for ever crown'd with flowers,
Where Thames with pride surveys his rising towers,
There stands a structure of majestic frame,
Which from the neighb'ring Hampton takes its name.
Here British statesmen oft the fall foredoom
Of foreign tyrants and of nymphs at home:
Here thou, great Anna, whom three realms obey,
Dost sometimes counsel take, and sometimes tea.

POPE, *Rape of the Lock.*

12. And here perhaps by fate's unerring doom
Some mighty bard lies hid in years to come,
That shall in William's godlike acts engage,
And with his battles warm a future age.
Hibernian fields shall here thy conquests show,
And Boyne be sung when it has ceased to flow;
Here Gallic labours shall advance thy fame,
And here Seneffe shall wear another name.
Our late posterity, with secret dread,
Shall view thy battles, and with pleasure read
How in the bloody field too near advanced
The guiltless bullet on thy shoulder glanced.

ADDISON, *A Poem to His Majesty.*

13. Patron of else the most despised of men,
Accept the tribute of a stranger's pen;
Verse, like the laurel its immortal meed,
Should be the guerdon of a noble deed;
I may alarm thee, but I fear the shame
I must incur, forgetting Howard's name.
Blest with all wealth can give thee, to resign
Joys doubly sweet to feelings quick as thine,
To quit the bliss thy rural scenes bestow,
To seek a nobler amid scenes of woe,
To traverse seas, range kingdoms, and bring home,
Not the proud monuments of Greece or Rome,
But knowledge such as only dungeons teach,
And only sympathy like thine could reach,
Speaks a divine ambition and a zeal
The boldest patriot might be proud to feel.—COWPER.

II. SELECTIONS FROM PROSE (of the period between A.D. 1450 and 1700).

In dealing with each of the following extracts the student has three things to do:—

(*a*) To explain the historical allusions;

(*b*) To paraphrase the extract, *i.e.* reconstruct it according to modern idiom and modern diction: subdivide sentences, where necessary: give the correct punctuation, such as is required for the reconstructed extract: condense the original, wherever it may seem to be clogged with unnecessary verbiage: to divide a paragraph, if it seems to be too long;

(*c*) To write very short notes on the diction, the order of the words, or any other point requiring comment.

1. The king by this time was grown to such a height of reputation for cunning and policy, that every accident and event that went well was laid and imputed to his foresight, as if he had set it before; as in this particular of Perkin's design upon Kent. For the world would not believe afterwards but the king, having secret intelligence of Perkin's intention for Kent, the better to draw it on, went of purpose into the north afar off, laying an open side unto Perkin, to make him come to the close and so to trip up his heels, having made sure in Kent beforehand.—BACON.

2. Henry, Prince of Wales, eldest son of the king of Great Britain, happy in the hopes conceived of him, and now happy in his memory, died on the 6th November 1612, to the extreme concern and regret of the whole kingdom, being a youth who had neither offended nor satiated the minds of men. He had by the excellence of his disposition excited high expectations among great numbers of all ranks, nor had through the shortness of his life disappointed them. One capital circumstance added was the esteem, in which he was commonly held, of being fair to the cause of religion; and men of the best judgment were fully persuaded, that his life was a great support and security to his father from the danger of conspiracies; an evil against which our age has scarce found a remedy; so that the people's love of religion and the king overflowed to the prince: and this consideration deservedly heightened the sense of the loss of him. —BACON.

3. Sir Richard Grenville finding himself in this distress, and unable any longer to make any resistance, having endured in this fifteen hours' fight the assault of fifteen several armadoes, and by estimation eight hundred shot of great artillery besides many assaults and entries; and finding himself and the ship must needs be possessed by the enemy, who were now all cast in a ring round about him (the *Revenge* not able to move one way or the other, but as she was moved with the waves and billows of the sea), commanded the master gunner, whom he knew to be a most resolute man, to split and sink the ship that thereby nothing might remain of glory or victory to the Spaniards—seeing in so many hours' fight and with so great a navy they were not able to take her, having had fifteen hours' time, above ten thousand men, and fifty and three sail of men of war to perform it withal—and persuaded the company, or as many as he could induce, to yield themselves unto God and to the mercy of none else; but as they had, like valiant resolute men, repulsed so many enemies, they should not now shorten the honour of their nation by prolonging their own lives for a few hours or a few days.—SIR WALTER RALEIGH.

4. At their first sitting the committee began with the stating the manner of the king's (Charles I.) coming to the House, and all he did there; the several members mentioning all that they would take upon them to remember of His Majesty's doing or speaking, both as he came into the House and after he was there; some of them being walking in Westminster Hall when the king walked through, and so came to the House with him or near him; others reporting what they had heard some of the gentlemen who attended His Majesty say, as they passed by, every idle word having its commentary; and the persons, whoever were named, being appointed to attend, they having power given them to send for all persons and to examine them touching that affair. Nor had any man the courage to refuse to obey their summons; so that all those of the king's servants who were sent for appeared punctually at the hour that was assigned them, and were examined upon all questions which any one of the committee would propose to them, whereof many were very impertinent and of little respect to the king.—CLARENDON, *The Great Rebellion.*

5. Plato, a man of high authority indeed, but least of all for his Commonwealth, in the book of his laws, which no city ever yet received, fed his fancy with making many edicts to his airy burgomasters, which they who otherwise admire him wish had been rather buried and excused in the genial cups of an academic night-sitting; by which laws he seems to tolerate no kind of learning but by unalterable decree, consisting most of practical traditions, to the attainment whereof a library of smaller bulk than his own Dialogues would be abundant. And there also enacts that no poet should so much as read to any private man what he had written, until the judges and law-keepers had seen it and allowed it. But that Plato meant this law peculiarly to that Commonwealth which he had imagined, and to no other, is evident. Why was he not else a lawgiver to himself, but a transgressor, and to be expelled by his own magistrates, both for the wanton epigrams and dialogues which he made, and his perpetual reading of Sophron Mimus and Aristophanes, books of grossest infamy, and also for commending the latter of them, though he were the malicious libeller of his chief friends, to be read by the tyrant Dionysius, who had little need of such trash to spend his time on? But that he knew this licensing of poems had reference and dependence to many other provisos there set down in his fancied republic, which in this world could have no place; and so neither he himself nor any magistrate or city ever initiated that course, which taken apart from those other collateral injunctions, must needs be vain and fruitless. For if they fell upon one kind of strictness, unless their care were equal to regulate all other things of like aptness to corrupt the mind, that single endeavour they knew would be but a fond labour: to shut and fortify one gate against corruption, and be necessitated to leave others round about wide open.—MILTON, *Areopagitica.*

6. They had a captain called Wat Tyler, and with him in company was Jack Straw and John Ball; these three were chief sovereign captains, but the head of them all was Wat Tyler, and he was indeed a tiler of houses, an ungracious patron. These villains and poor people came to London, a hundred mile off, sixty mile, fifty mile, forty mile, and twenty mile off, and as they came, they demanded ever for the king. The same day that these unhappy people of Kent were coming to London, there

returned from Canterbury the king's mother, princess of Wales, coming from her pilgrimage. She was in great jeopardy to have been lost; for these people came to her chare (carriage) and dealt rudely with her, whereof the good lady was in great doubt lest they should have done some villainy to her or to her damosels. Howbeit God kept her, and she came in one day from Canterbury to London; for she never durst tarry by the way. The same time King Richard her son was at the Tower of London; there his mother found him, and with him there was the Earl of Salisbury, the Archbishop of Canterbury, Sir Robert of Namur, and divers other, who were in doubt of these people that thus gathered together, and wist not what they demanded.—LORD BERNERS (1467-1532), *Chronicles of Froissart.*

7. Then, when he had sitten still awhile, thus he began:—"What were they worthy to have, that compass and imagine the destruction of me, being so near of blood unto the king and Protector of his royal person and his realm?" At this question all the Lords sat sore astonished, musing much by whom this question should be meant, of which every man wist himself clear. Then the Lord Chamberlain, as he that for the love between them thought he might be boldest with him, answered and said, that they were worthy to be punished as heinous traitors whoever they were. And all the others affirmed the same. "That is," quoth he, "yonder sorceress, my brother's wife, and other with her," meaning the queen. At these words many of the other Lords were greatly abashed that favoured her. But the Lord Hastings was in his mind better content, that it was aimed at her, than at one whom he loved better. He was not ware that it had been already devised, that himself should the same day be beheaded in London. Then said the Protector: "Ye shall see in what wise that sorceress, and that other witch of her counsel, Shore's wife, with their affinity, have by their sorcery and witchcraft wasted my body." And therewith he plucked up his doublet-sleeve to his elbow upon his left arm, where he showed a werish (deformed) withered arm and small, as it was never other. No man was there present but well knew that his arm was ever such since his birth.—SIR THOMAS MORE (1478-1535).

8. With this answer the prince nothing appeased, but rather more inflamed, endeavoured himself to take away his servant. The judge considering the perilous example and inconvenience that might thereby ensue, with a valiant spirit and courage commanded the prince upon his allegiance to leave the prisoner and depart his way. With which commandment the prince, being set all in a fury, all chafed and in a terrible manner came up to the place of judgment,—men thinking that he would have slain the judge or have done to him some damage; but the judge sitting still, without moving, declaring the majesty of the king's place of judgment, and with an assured and bold countenance, had to the prince these words following:—"Sir, remember yourself: I keep here the place of the king, your sovereign lord and father, to whom ye owe double obedience; wherefore, eftsoons in his name, I charge you desist of your wilfulness and unlawful enterprise, and from henceforth give good example to those which hereafter shall be your proper subjects. And now for your contempt and disobedience, go you to the prison of the King's Bench, whereunto I commit you; and remain ye there prisoner, until the pleasure of the king, your father, be further known." With which words being abashed, and also wondering at the marvellous gravity

of that worshipful justice, the noble prince, laying his weapon apart, doing reverence, departed and went to the King's Bench, as he was commanded.—SIR THOMAS ELYOT (1490 ?-1456).

CHAPTER XXVI.—PRÉCIS-WRITING.

337. Précis described.—The word *précis*, though much used in English, is a French word signifying summary, compendium, abridgment, abstract, condensed statement, epitome (Greek, *epi-tom-e*). These words all mean the same thing at bottom. When a student is asked to write a précis of a paragraph or of a series of paragraphs, what he has to do is to pick out the salient points and omit what is merely subsidiary or what can be most easily spared. To do this successfully he must first, by dint of frequent reading and of careful thought, make himself thorough master of the contents of the passage that has been placed before him. For the sake of abridgment he may find it necessary to alter the diction here and there; but in doing so he must be careful to preserve the full force of the original, neither adding anything thereto nor detracting anything from it.

In making out a précis it should be the aim of the writer not merely to preserve the force of the original on all essential points, but to express the facts or the arguments in such a way that any one, who has seen the précis only, would suppose that the précis itself was an original piece of composition, and that no other original had existed. To arrive at this stage of proficiency will not be possible all at once, but it can be acquired by practice.

In this chapter I have given two kinds of examples to be worked out; these are distinguished from one another by the letters A, B. Under the heading A, a few of the examples set for practice are a good deal easier than what are usually set in examinations, so that the beginner may not be discouraged in making his first attempts at précis-writing.

338. A. First kind of Example.—As a specimen of one kind of example I quote in full the exercise in Précis set for London Matriculation in January 1905.

(i.) State under one heading or title the main purport—

(*a*) Of the following extract as a whole;

(*b*) Of each paragraph of the extract.

(ii.) Write a Précis of the extract, giving the substance of it without any superfluous details.

What, say some, can give us a more contemptible idea of a large State than to find it mostly governed by custom; to have few written laws and no boundaries to mark the jurisdiction between the Senate and the people? Among the number who speak in this manner is the great Montesquieu, who asserts that every nation is free in proportion to its written laws, and seems to hint at a despotic and arbitrary conduct in the present King of Prussia, who has abridged the laws of his country into a short compass.

As getting the ancients on our side is half a victory, it will not be amiss to fortify the argument with an observation of Chrysostom's: "The enslaved are the fittest to be governed by laws, and free men by custom." Custom partakes of the nature of parental injunction; it is kept by the people themselves, and observed with a willing obedience. The observance of it must therefore be a mark of freedom, and coming originally to a State from the reverenced founders of its liberty, will be an encouragement and assistance to it in the defence of that blessing. But a conquered people, a nation of slaves, must pretend to none of this freedom or these happy distinctions. . . . And the fixing a conquest must be done by giving laws, which may every moment serve to remind the people enslaved of their conquerors, nothing being more dangerous than to trust a lately subdued people with old customs that presently upbraid their degeneracy and provoke them to revolt.

The wisdom of the Roman republic in their veneration for custom, and backwardness to introduce a new law, was perhaps the cause of their long continuance and of the virtues of which they have set the world so many examples. But to show in what that wisdom consists, it may be proper to observe that the benefit of new written laws is merely confined to the consequences of their observance; but customary laws, keeping up a veneration for the founders, engage men in the imitation of their virtues as well as policy. To this may be ascribed the religious regard the Romans paid to their forefathers' memory, and their adhering for so many ages to the practice of the same virtues, which nothing contributed more to efface than the introduction of a voluminous body of new laws over the neck of venerable custom.[1]—*Lond. Matric.* Jan. 1905.

The above example can be worked out in the following way. in accordance with the instructions given.

[1] The above extract is a remarkable specimen both of bad English and of bad argument. Probably it was selected by the examiner for these very reasons. However faulty the extract may be in diction or in argument, the drift of its contents is plain enough; and the drift is the only thing that the précis-writer is allowed to think of. All that he has to do is to reproduce the argument (whether it be good or bad) in the clearest and fewest words.

(i.) (*a*) *Main purport of the extract as a whole:*

The superiority of customary to written law for the government of a State.

(*b*) *Theme of each paragraph:—*

First para.—In the opinion of Montesquieu and others, government by custom or unwritten law is incompatible with the dignity and freedom of a great State.

Second para.—This opinion, however, clashes both with the testimony of the ancients and with the nature of man.

Third para.—Nor is it in keeping with the teaching of history, especially of Roman history.

(ii.) *Précis of the arguments in the form of a single paragraph:—*

Written law, as some believe and as Montesquieu taught, is more conducive than custom or unwritten law can be to the collective dignity of a great State and to the personal freedom of its citizens. This theory, however, is not supported by the testimony of the ancients; nor is it in keeping either with the natural instincts of mankind or with the teachings of history. Written law is the mark of subjection; for it is only by written law that a conquered people can be held in check, and their enforced obedience to such law cannot fail to remind them of their subjection. Custom, on the other hand, is the mark of independence. Its observance is not forced, but voluntary; for custom is the legacy of revered ancestors and bears the stamp of an authority almost parental in its character. Only in the outward effects or consequences can a written code do any good. It cannot raise the national character from within, as custom does, by stimulating men to tread in the footsteps of their forefathers. To the backwardness of the Romans in introducing new laws may be ascribed the long continuance of their power and the possession of many virtues of which they set an example to the world.

339. B. Second kind of example.—As a specimen of another kind of example, I quote the exercise in Précis set for the School-leaving Certificate (London) in July 1905.

(*a*) State the general subject of the following extract.

(*b*) Indicate paragraphs into which it may be suitably divided, and state the particular subject of each.

(*c*) Write a Précis of the whole passage, that is, a summary of it in the form of a continuous narrative.

Nature does in no wise qualify us wholly, much less at once, for a mature state of life. Even maturity of understanding and bodily strength are not only arrived at gradually, but are also very much owing to the continued exercise of our powers of body and mind from infancy. But if we suppose a person brought into the world with both these in maturity, as far as this is conceivable, he would plainly at first be as unqualified for the human life of mature age as an idiot. He would be in a manner distracted with astonishment, and apprehension, and suspense; nor can one guess how long it would be, before he would be familiarised to himself and to the objects about him, enough even to set himself to anything. It seems that men would be strangely headstrong and self-willed, and disposed to exert themselves with an impetuosity which would render society insupportable and the living in it impracticable, were it not for some acquired moderation and self-government, some aptitude and readiness in restraining themselves and concealing their sense of things. But then as nature has endowed us with a power of supplying those deficiencies by acquired knowledge, experience, and habits, so likewise we are placed in a condition in infancy, childhood, and youth fitted for our acquiring those qualifications of all sorts, which we stand in need of in mature age. Hence children from their very birth are growing daily acquainted with the objects about them, with the scene in which they are placed and to have a future part, and learning somewhat or other necessary to the performance of it. The subordinations to which they are accustomed in domestic life prepare them for subjection and obedience to civil authority. Thus the beginning of our days is adapted to be and is a state of education in the theory and practice of mature life. We are much assisted in it by example, instruction, and the care of others, but a great deal is left to ourselves to do.—*School-leaving Certificate*, July 1905.

The example might be worked out in the following way :—

(a) *General subject, or main purport.*—The means by which we become qualified for the status of mature life.

(b) *Subdivision into paragraphs* :—

1. Nature does in no wise, etc.
2. But if we suppose a person, etc.
3. But then as nature has endowed us, etc.
4. Thus the beginning of our days, etc.

Particular subject or theme of each paragraph :—

1. Our preparation for the status of mature life is gradual.

2. Even if a man could come into the world fully equipped in mind and body, he would from lack of experience be as unqualified as ever.

3. Nature has given us the mental power of acquiring such experience, and the period of childhood and youth gives us the opportunity.

4. Whatever help we may get from without in acquiring this experience, we are mainly thrown upon ourselves.

(c) *Précis of the whole in the form of a continuous narrative* :—

A long and varied preparation is needed, before any one can be fit to enter the status of mature life. Such preparation is not furnished wholly by nature, much less is it furnished all at once. If we could suppose a man brought into the world with all his mental and bodily powers complete, how would he behave? Bewildered by his surroundings, a puzzle to himself, headstrong and impetuous, he would be no better than an idiot. Nature, however, has given us the power of acquiring the experience and self-restraint that enables us to submit to civil authority, and the period of childhood and youth, through which we all have to pass, gives us the time and the opportunity of cultivating this power. Thus the restraints of domestic life prepare us for those of civil life. However much we may learn from others in the way of precept and example, we are mainly thrown upon ourselves.

Note on Indexing and Précis-Writing.

In this book we are not concerned with the more elaborate process called "Indexing and Précis-writing," though the part called Précis-writing is virtually the same as that already described. For Indexing the student must suppose that he has a file of correspondence before him. For the Index four columns are provided in the form shown below:—

No. of Letter. 1	Date, Place, and Year of Despatch. 2	Names of Sender and Receiver. 3	Subject of the Letter. 4

The number of the letter (column 1) is that given to the letter by the office which receives it. The date, place, and year of despatch (column 2) are shown in the letter itself. The names of sender and receiver (column 3) are shown in the letter itself. The subject or main purport of the letter is stated in the first paragraph of the letter itself, which can be copied and entered in column 4; or the official who keeps the register may, if he prefers it, express the main purport of the letter in words of his own. So much for the Index. The Précis is a summing up of the contents of the correspondence as a whole, the summary being mainly based on the entries that have been made in column 4. This summary is written out in the form of a continuous *narrative* (not in the form of correspondence), and the wording of this narrative should be brief, simple, and to the point.

A. *Examples to be worked out on the plan indicated by A in* § 338 :—

I.—1. A large old house was so much infested with rats, that nothing could be made safe from their secret attacks. They scaled the walls and nibbled at flitches of bacon, though these were hung as high as the ceiling. Shelves hung against the wall gave no protection to the cheese and pastry. By mining through the wall they found their way into the storeroom, and plundered it of jams and sweetmeats. They gnawed through cupboards, undermined floors, and ran races behind the wainscots.

2. The cat could not get at them. The rats were too cunning and too well-fed to eat the poisoned food laid for them; and only now and then a few heedless stragglers were caught by traps. One of these, however, was once caught alive, and the master of the house determined to make this the occasion for trying a new plan. This was to fasten a collar with a small bell about the prisoner's neck and then to turn him loose again.

3. Overjoyed at recovering his liberty, the rat ran into the nearest hole, and went in search of his companions. They heard, at a distance, the bell tinkling through the dark passages; and, suspecting that some enemy had got among them, away they scoured, some one way and some another. The bell-bearer pursued; and soon, guessing the cause of their flight, he was greatly amused by it. Whenever he approached, it was all hurry-scurry, and not a tail of one of them was to be seen. He chased his old friends from hole to hole, from room to room, laughing all the while at their fears and increasing them by all the means in his power. Presently he had the whole house to himself. "That's right," quoth he, "the fewer companions, the better cheer." So he revelled alone among the good things, and stuffed till he could hardly walk.

4. For two or three days this course of life went on very pleasantly. He ate and ate, and played the bugbear to perfection. At length he grew tired of his lonely condition and longed to mix with his companions again upon the former footing. But the difficulty was how to get rid of his bell. He pulled and tugged with his fore-feet, and almost tore the skin off his neck in the attempt, but all in vain. The bell was now his plague and torment. He wandered from room to room earnestly desiring to make himself known to one of his companions; but they all kept out of his reach. At last, as he was moping about disconsolate, he fell in puss's way, and was devoured.

5. He who is raised so much above his fellow-creatures as to be the object of their terror, must suffer for it in losing all the comforts of society. He is a solitary being in the midst of crowds. He keeps them at a distance, and they keep him. Dread and affection cannot exist together.

II.—1. The majestic banyan-tree is lord of the forests of India, and is one of the marvels of the vegetable world. It rarely attains a great height, from 60 to 100 feet being the maximum. During the first hundred years of its life it behaves very much like other trees, developing a sturdy trunk and an immense dome-like head spreading far out on all sides. Its leaves are smooth and glossy and of a bright green. Its foliage is so dense as to afford a cooling shade and effectually prevent the growth of underbrush. It produces an abundance of mild, insipid, fig-like fruit, which is used both for food and for medicinal purposes.

2. At the end of the first century of its life the banyan begins to exhibit its singular propensities. From its arms, which have now grown out to a great length horizontally, it begins to send down fibres into the air; and these fibres do not stop growing, until their ends touch the earth. The rootlets at the ends strike into the ground, and when they have become well fixed in the earth, the sap, which previously was flowing downwards, changes its direction and flows upwards. The thin stems

grow by degrees into broad trunks, and afford an effectual support to the over-weighted branches from which they came down. The great horizontal branches are now supported at both extremities, like a bridge by a pier at both ends. The new trunks reach a gigantic size, and send out more lateral branches. These branches in their turn send down new stems or fibres, which take root like the previous ones and form new supports. The new trunks often surpass the parent stems, and this process of growth continues for many years, until the tree covers acres of ground, and presents the aspect of a colonnade of stems supporting numberless living rafters, all of which are covered with a dense canopy of perennial green.

3. On the banks of the Narbada, a river that rises from the hills of Central India, there is a tree, which measures a circuit of twenty-two hundred feet, whose larger trunks number three hundred and fifty-four, whose small ones exceed three thousand, and whose foliage makes a home for thousands of birds and monkeys. Under the shade of this wonderful tree the princes of the land used to encamp in magnificent style. Here the king entertained his guests on his tiger-hunting expeditions. The different parts of the ground under the tree were used as drawing-rooms, dining-rooms, smoking-rooms, kitchens, etc. Including all the animals and servants, there were seven thousand individuals in the retinue; yet the great banyan easily sheltered them all. Here, when the glow and glare of the fierce sun had given way to the cool dews of evening, the guests of the Oriental prince sipped their sherbet or champagne, and watched the movements of the dancing girls, while the monkeys chattered and the night-birds sang in the foliage above, and the pale moonshine glinted down through the openings in the vast leafy roof.

4. Such is the gigantic fig-tree of India, truly one of the wonders of the world, and not to be matched even in a country, where a hot sun combines with a rich soil to produce the most striking and luxuriant forms of life. It is supposed that some of the banyan-trees now standing were in existence, when Porus drove his squadron of elephants against the Macedonian phalanx of Alexander the Great, in the hope of saving his kingdom from falling under the dominion of the world's conqueror.

III.—1. The Abbotsford Library is rather more than forty feet long by eighteen feet broad. It is in appearance a well-proportioned room, but unless varied by some angles it would want relief, or, in the phrase of womankind, would be inexcusably devoid of a flirting corner. To remedy this defect an octagon is thrown out upon the northern side of the room, forming a recess which, corresponding to the uses of the whole apartment, contains two book presses with doors of latticed wire. These are meant to contain books of small size and some rarity which would otherwise run the risk of being lost or mislaid. . . . I have found it the best way to reserve some five or six cases which can be locked up at pleasure for the security of such books as are peculiarly valuable as well as those which for any reason seem unfit to be exposed to the general class of readers.

2. To return to the description of the library. Its roof—on a level with that of the Hall—is sixteen feet high and the presses rise to the height of eleven feet, having a space of five feet accordingly between the top of the shelves and the ceiling. This was a subject of great anxiety to me. A difference of six feet in height all round a room forty feet long would have added greatly to my accommodation. But on the other hand,

a bulky and somewhat ancient person climbing up to a height to pull a book down from a shelf thirteen feet high is somewhat too much in the position of a sea-boy on the dizzy shroud. Indeed, being one of those who hold that good people are valuable as well as scarce, I have remarked with anxiety that the lives of such worthies as myself are often embittered, if not ended, by the consequence of a fall from the steps of their own library staircase.

3. I remember wasting my invention in endeavouring to devise a mode of placing my volumes in an order easily attainable for the purpose of consultation. But I never could hit upon an idea more likely to answer than imagining a librarian who, like Talus in Spenser, should be in point of constitution "an yron man, and made of yron molde." He should be a creature without hopes, views, wishes, or studies of his own, yet completely devoted to assist mine; an unequalled clerk with fingers never weary, possessing that invariable local knowledge whereby my volumes, like the dishes at King Oberon's banquet, should draw near and retire with a wish. I have never been able to find for myself a mechanical aid of such a passive description, and the alternative to which I am reduced is the working room and study, in addition to my library, where I keep around me the dictionaries and books of reference which my immediate needs may require me to consult.—Sir WALTER SCOTT.

IV.—1. Numbers of men, who would never attain any extraordinary eminence in anything, are yet so constituted as to make a very respectable figure in the department that is suited for them and to fall below mediocrity in a different one. The world has been compared by some one to a board covered with holes of many different shapes, and pegs fitted for each, but which are scattered about at random, so that it is a mere chance whether a peg falls into a hole that fits it.

2. A. B. was the son of a schoolmaster, who had a great love of literature. The son had a perfect hatred of it, and was a mere dunce at his books. Various attempts were made, which proved perfect failures, to train him to some of what are called the learned professions; and he was to all appearance turning out what they call a "ne'er-do-weel." As a last resource he was sent out to a new colony. There he was in his element; for, when at school, though dull at learning and soon forgetting what he had read, he never saw a horse or a carriage once, that he did not always recognise; and he readily understood all that belonged to each. In the colony he became one of the most thriving settlers; skilful in making roads, erecting mills, draining, cattle-breeding, etc., and was advanced to a situation of trust in the colony.

3. C. D., again, was at a university, and was below the average in all academical pursuits; but he was the greatest mechanical genius in the university, not excepting the professors. He never examined any machine, however complex, that he could not with his own hands construct a model of it, and sometimes with improvements. He would have made a first-rate engineer; but family arrangements caused him to take Orders. He was a diligent and conscientious clergyman, but a dull and commonplace one, except that in repairing and altering and fitting up his parsonage and his church he was unrivalled.

4. E. F., when he entered the Navy, was thought by his friends to have made the mistake of not at all understanding what the hardships of

a sailor's life would be. So when at his earnest entreaty he was sent to sea, they secretly begged the captain to make his life as unpleasant as possible, being anxious to sicken him. He was accordingly snubbed and rated, and set to the most laborious duties, and never commended or encouraged. But he bore all and did all with unflinching patience and diligence. At last the captain revealed the whole to him, saying, "I can carry on this disguise no longer; you are the finest young man I ever had under me, and I have long admired your conduct, while I pretended to scold you."

5. G. H., who had as a youth a vehement longing to go to sea, was positively interdicted by his father. Hence, though possessing very good abilities, and not without aspirations after excellence, he never could be brought to settle down steadily to anything, but broke off from every promising pursuit that he was successively engaged in, in pursuit of some phantom.—WHATELY'S *Annotations on Bacon's Essays, Essay VII.*

V.—1. When Diogenes received a visit in his tub from Alexander the Great, and was asked, according to the ancient forms of royal courtesy, what petition he had to offer; "I have nothing," said he, "to ask, but that you would remove to the other side, that you may not by intercepting the sunshine take from me what you cannot give me."

2. Such was the demand of Diogenes from the greatest monarch of the earth; which those who have less power than Alexander may, with yet more propriety, apply to themselves. He that does much good may be allowed to do sometimes a little harm. But if the opportunities of beneficence be denied by fortune, innocence should at least be vigilantly preserved.

3. It is well known that time once past never returns, and that the moment which is lost is lost for ever. Time therefore ought, above all other kinds of property, to be free from invasion; and yet there is no man who does not claim the power of wasting that time which is the right of others.

4. This usurpation is so general, that a very small part of the year is spent by choice; scarcely anything is done when it is intended, or obtained when it is desired. Life is continually ravaged by invaders; one steals away an hour, and another a day; one conceals the robbery by hurrying us into business, another by lulling us with amusement; the depredation is continued through a thousand vicissitudes of tumult and tranquillity, till having lost all we can lose no more.

5. To put every man in possession of his own time and rescue the day from this succession of usurpers is beyond my power and beyond my hope. Yet perhaps some stop might be put to this unmerciful persecution, if all would seriously reflect that whosoever pays a visit which is not desired, or talks longer than the hearer is willing to attend to him, is guilty of an injury which he cannot repair, and takes away that which he cannot give. —SAMUEL JOHNSON (1709-1784), *Idler*.

VI.—1. In the case of the late Bribery Committee, it seemed to be the conclusion of the soundest practical minds that Bribery could not be put down; that Pure Election was a thing we had seen the last of, and must now go on without, as best we could. A conclusion not a little startling; to which it requires a practical mind of some seasoning to reconcile yourself at once! It seems then we are henceforth to get ourselves constituted Legislators not according to what merit we may have, or even what merit we may seem to have, but according to the length of our purse, and our frankness, impudence, and dexterity in laying out the contents of the same. Our theory, written down in all books and law-books, spouted forth from all barrel-heads, is perfect purity of Tenpound Franchise, absolute sincerity of question put and answer given:—and our practice is irremediable bribery, irremediable, unpunishable, which you will do more harm than good by attempting to punish!

2. A Parliament, one would say, which proclaims itself elected and eligible by bribery, tells the Nation that is governed by it a singular piece of news. Bribery—have we reflected what bribery is? Bribery means not only length of purse, which is neither qualification nor the contrary for legislating well; but it means dishonesty and even impudent dishonesty; brazen insensibility to lying and to making others lie; total oblivion and flinging overboard for the nonce of any real thing you can call veracity, morality; with dexterously putting-on the cast-clothes of that real thing and strutting about in them! What Legislation can you get out of a man in that fatal situation? None surely that will profit much, one would think. A Legislator who has left his veracity lying on the threshold, he, why verily *he*—ought to be sent out to seek it again.—*Lond. Matr.* Sept. 1905.

VII.—1. It was not from want of perceiving the beauty of external nature, but from a different way of perceiving it, that the early Greeks did not turn their genius to portray, either in colour or in poetry, the outlines, the hues, and contrasts of all the fair valleys, and bold cliffs, and golden noons, and rosy dawns, which their beautiful country affords in lavish abundance.

2. Primitive people never, so far as I know, enjoy what is called the picturesque in nature. Wild forests, beetling cliffs, reaches of Alpine snow, are with them great hindrances to human intercourse, and difficulties in the way of agriculture. They are furthermore the homes of the enemies of mankind, of the eagle, the wolf, or the tiger, and are most dangerous in times of earthquake or tempest. Hence the grand and striking features of nature are at first looked upon with fear and dislike.

3. I do not suppose the early Greeks differed in this respect from other people, except that the frequent occurrence of mountains and forests made agriculture peculiarly difficult and intercourse scanty, thus increasing their dislike for the apparently reckless waste in nature. We have even in Homer a similar feeling as regards the sea,—the sea that proved the source of all their wealth and the condition of most of their greatness. Before they had learned all this, they called it "the unvintageable sea," and looked upon its shore as merely so much waste land. We can therefore easily understand how, in the first beginning of Greek art, the representation of wild landscape would find no place, whereas fruitful fields did not suggest themselves as more than the ordinary background. Art in those days was struggling with material nature, to which it felt a certain antagonism.

4. There was nothing in the social circumstances of the Greeks to produce any revolution in this attitude during their greatest days. The Greek republics were small towns, where the pressure and fatigue of city

life was not felt. The Greeks themselves were essentially townsmen, who never desired to see more of the country than its olives and its grapes. . . . But as soon as the days of the Greek republics were over, and men began to congregate for imperial purposes into Antioch, or Alexandria, or lastly into Rome, then we see the effect of noise and dust and smoke and turmoil breaking out into the natural longing for rural rest and retirement, so that from Alexander's day . . . we find all kinds of authors —epic poets, lyrists, novelists, and preachers—agreeing in the praise of nature, its rich colours and its varied sounds.—[MAHAFFY's *Rambles in Greece*] *Lond. Matr.* June 1905.

VIII.—1. The best excuse that can be made for avarice is that it generally prevails in old men or in men of cold tempers, where all other affections are extinct. The mind, being incapable of remaining without some passion or pursuit, at last finds out this monstrously absurd one, which suits the coldness and inactivity of its temper.

2. At the same time it seems very extraordinary that so frosty, spiritless a passion should be able to carry us further than all the warmth of youth and pleasure. But if we look more narrowly into the matter, we shall find that this very circumstance renders the explication of the case more easy. When the temper is warm and full of vigour, it naturally shoots out more ways than one, and produces inferior passions to counterbalance in some degree its predominant inclinations. It is impossible for a person of that temper, however bent on any pursuit, to be deprived of all sense of shame or all regard to the sentiments of mankind. His friends must have some influence over him; and other considerations are apt to have their weight. All this serves to restrain him within some bounds. But it is no wonder that the avaricious, being from the coldness of his temper without regard to reputation, to friendship, or to pleasure, should be carried so far by his prevailing inclination, and should display his passion in such surprising instances.

3. Accordingly we find no vice so irreclaimable as avarice; and though there has scarcely been a moralist or a philosopher, from the beginning of the world to this day, who has not levelled a stroke at it, we hardly find a single instance of any person's being cured of it. For this reason I am more apt to approve of those who attack it with wit and humour than of those who treat it in a serious manner. There being so little hope of doing good to the people infected with this vice, I would have the rest of mankind at least diverted by our manner of exposing it; as indeed there is no kind of diversion, of which they are so willing to partake.—DAVID HUME (1711-1776), *Essays.*

IX.—1. There is a perennial nobleness, and even sacredness, in Work. Were he never so benighted, forgetful of his high calling, there is always hope in a man that actually and earnestly works: in Idleness alone is there perpetual despair. Work, never so Mammonish, mean, is in communication with Nature; the real desire to get Work done will itself lead one more and more to truth, to Nature's appointments and regulations, which are truth.

2. The latest Gospel in this world is, Know thy work and do it. "Know thyself": long enough has that poor "self" of thine tormented thee; thou wilt never get to "know" it, I believe! Think it not thy

business, this of knowing thyself; thou art an unknowable individual: know what thou canst work at; and work at it, like a Hercules. That will be thy better plan.

3. It has been written, "an endless significance lies in Work"; a man perfects himself by working. Foul jungles are cleared away, fair seed-fields rise instead, and stately cities; and withal the man himself first ceases to be a jungle and foul unwholesome desert thereby. Consider how, even in the meanest sorts of Labour, the whole soul of a man is composed into a kind of real harmony, the instant he sets himself to work! Doubt, Desire, Sorrow, Remorse, Indignation, Despair itself, all these like hell-dogs lie beleaguering the soul of the poor dayworker, as of every man: but he bends himself with free valour against his task, and all these are stilled, all these shrink murmuring far off into their caves. The man is now a man. The blessed glow of Labour in him, is it not as purifying fire, wherein all poison is burnt up? and of sour smoke itself there is made bright blessed flame!—CARLYLE, *Past and Present.*

X.—1. The impulse given to the study of Greek by exiles during the half century preceding the conquest of Constantinople, and by the enthusiasm of a series of scholars from Petrarch and Boccaccio down to 1453, was greatly stimulated by the increase of fugitives consequent on the capture of the city.

2. The arrival of numbers of scholars in Italy shortly before and shortly after 1453 is contemporaneous with the full spring-time of the great revival of learning. A series of remarkable efforts had been made to restore ancient Roman and Greek glory as seen in literature and architecture. Learning was regarded as a new and improved example. The learning of the ancients was compared with the ignorance of the Churchmen. The new movement marked a great reaction and went to unjustifiable extremes. Some of the advocates for classical influence went to the extent of discarding Christian in favour of Pagan morality. Paganism, because it was contemporaneous with the classical period, invaded the Church itself. All the architecture, art, and literature of Christianity was bad except in so far as it approximated to Pagan models. The careful study of the Latin classics, the marvellous development of painting, architecture, and sculpture, but, above all, the keen interest felt in the newly developed study of Greek, were all to produce wonderful fruit within a generation after 1453, and to culminate in Italy in an age of singular intellectual brilliancy.

3. The study of Greek, at first almost confined to Florence, gradually spread over the whole of the peninsula, and finally passed north of the Alps, into Germany, where it was taken up with great earnestness. In 1485 a Greek professor was appointed in Paris, and one in Rome. In the reign of Henry VII. Oxford consented to receive Grocyn and Linacre as teachers of Greek.

4. The movement known as the "Revival of Learning" was accomplished before the end of the fifteenth century, and all investigators are agreed that it had been very largely contributed to by Greek exiles during the half centuries preceding and following the Moslem conquest.

5. Its paganisation of Christianity proved temporary. But the critical examination of the text of the Greek New Testament had more durable results. It called attention to the contents of a book which had hitherto

been taken as outside controversy. When the study of Greek passed north of the Alps, the examination of the sacred writings was no longer in the hands of *dilettanti*, who looked upon the text with the contempt of scholars disposed to accept paganism as the complement of a higher form of civilisation, and who had so little patience with what they regarded as trivialities, but in those of religious and earnest German students, with results in Erasmus, Luther, Melanchthon, Calvin, and others, the end of which is not yet visible.

6. While it is beyond doubt that the dispersion of students from Constantinople aided the intellectual movement in Western Europe, there is no ground for the belief that, if the city had not been captured, Greek influence would not have made itself felt in the renaissance. The dispersion hastened the development of a movement which had already begun, awakened a spirit of inquiry, and conducted scholars into new fields of thought earlier than they would have arrived, if not thus aided. In this sense and to this extent it may be claimed as a beneficial result of the capture of Constantinople.—PEARS, *Destruction of the Greek Empire* (quoted from *Lond. Matric. Exam.* Sept. 1904).

Note 1.—A violation of the rule of Parallel Construction (§ 329) occurs in para. 3, which the student may be asked to remove.

Note 2.—Para. 4 contains an error of expression, which the student may be asked to correct.

B. *Examples to be worked out on the plan indicated by B in* § 339.

I. To appreciate thoroughly how very little the Tudors really did for schools, we have first to realise the extraordinary antiquity of grammar schools. It is a current superstition that Winchester, the oldest of the so-called "public schools," is one of the oldest of the existing schools. But this is an utter delusion. Winchester was only founded in 1385, and though of venerable and hoar antiquity compared with Harrow or Rugby, is a mere babe and suckling beside such institutions as St. Peter's School at York, the cathedral schools of Durham and Hereford, of Canterbury and Lincoln, or the grammar schools of Beverley and Southwell. In founding Winchester, the real step in advance taken by William of Wykeham was not that he liberated education from ecclesiastical control, or that he created an entirely novel institution for scholastic purposes and for those only. On the contrary, he merely followed a prevailing fashion, when he founded a collegiate church with a grammar school attached; for all collegiate churches were bound by canon law to maintain grammar schools. The advance consisted in assigning a definite portion of the collegiate buildings for a boarding school and making the school a part of the collegiate body, and in doing so in an independent foundation, and not in a cathedral or collegiate church already existing, or in a university. His example was followed by some of the first Wykehamists,—by Archbishop Chicheley at Higham Ferrers in 1422; by Henry VI., at Chicheley's instance, at Eton twenty years later; by William Wainfleet at Wainfleet in 1484, and by Archdeacon Rotherham, one of the first Etonians, at Rotherham in 1481,—all of whom founded collegiate churches, with grammar schools attached, and with rights of admission to colleges at the Universities. All these with many more were swept away by

Henry VIII. or Edward VI., except Winchester and Eton, and they were only saved by the skin of their teeth. But these foundations, magnificent as they were, are mere mushrooms compared with the school at York, which has enjoyed a continuous existence at least since 1080, when the earliest dignitary of the cathedral, afterwards and now called Chancellor, was called the schoolmaster, and had to teach (in the) school.—*School-leaving Certificate*, July 1904.

II. My hold of the Colonies is in the close affection which grows from common names, from kindred blood, from similar privileges, and (from) equal protection. These are ties which, light as air, are as strong as links of iron. Let the Colonists always keep the idea of their civil rights associated with your government; they will cling and grapple to you; and no force under heaven will be of power to tear them from their allegiance. But let it be once understood that your government may be one thing and their privileges another,—that these two things may exist without any mutual relation, the cement is gone, the cohesion is loosened, and everything hastens to decay and dissolution. As long as you have the wisdom to keep the sovereign authority of this country as the sanctuary of liberty, the sacred temple consecrated to our common faith, wherever the chosen race and sons of England worship freedom, they will turn their faces toward you. The more they multiply, the more friends you will have; the more ardently they love liberty, the more perfect will be their obedience. Slavery they can have anywhere. It is a weed that grows in every soil. They may have it from Spain; they may have it from Prussia. But until you become lost to all feeling of your true interest and your natural dignity, freedom they can have from none but you. This is the commodity of price, of which you have the monopoly. This is the true act of Navigation, which binds to you the commerce of the Colonies and through them secures to you the wealth of the world. Deny them this participation of freedom, and you break that sole bond, which originally made and must still preserve the unity of the Empire. Do not entertain so weak an imagination, as that your registers and your bonds, your affidavits and your sufferances, your cockets and your clearances, are what form the great securities of your commerce. Do not dream that your letters of office, and your instructions, and your suspending clauses, are the things which hold together the great contexture of the mysterious whole. These things do not make your government. Dead instruments, passive tools as they are, it is the spirit of the English communion that gives all their life and efficacy to them. It is the spirit of the English Constitution, which infused through the mighty mass pervades, feeds, unites, invigorates, vivifies every part of the Empire, even down to the minutest member.—EDMUND BURKE (1729-1797), *Speech on Conciliation with America.*

III. Since Romulus with a small band of shepherds and outlaws fortified himself on the hills near the Tiber, ten centuries had already elapsed. During the four first ages, the Romans in the laborious school of poverty had acquired the virtues of war and government. By the vigorous exertion of those virtues and by the assistance of fortune they had obtained, in the course of the three succeeding centuries, an absolute empire over many countries of Europe, Asia, and Africa. The last three hundred years had been consumed in apparent prosperity and internal decline. The nation of soldiers, magistrates, and legislators, who composed the thirty-five tribes of the Roman people, was dissolved into the common mass of mankind, and confounded with the millions of servile provincials, who had received the name, without adopting the spirit, of Romans. A mercenary army, levied among the subjects and barbarians of the frontier, was the only order of men who preserved and abused their independence. By their tumultuary election a Syrian, a Goth, or an Arab, was exalted to the throne of Rome, and invested with despotic power over the conquests and over the country of the Scipios. The limits of the Roman Empire still extended from the Western Ocean to the Tigris, and from Mount Atlas to the Rhine and the Danube. To the undiscerning eye of the vulgar, Philip appeared a monarch no less powerful than Hadrian or Augustus had formerly been. The form was still the same, but the animating health and vigour were fled. The industry of the people was discouraged and exhausted by a long series of oppression. The discipline of the legions, which alone after the extinction of every other virtue had propped the greatness of the State, was corrupted by the ambition or relaxed by the weakness of the emperors. The strength of the frontiers, which had always consisted in arms rather than in fortifications, was insensibly undermined; and the fairest provinces were left exposed to the rapaciousness or ambition of the barbarians, who soon discovered the decline of the Roman Empire.—GIBBON (1737-1794).

IV. The characteristics of a town or district in which married women are largely engaged in factory work repeat themselves with such monotonous regularity that they may be formulated without difficulty. In the first place we are confronted with severe poverty, a poverty from the pressure of which the married drudges, toil they ever so hard, appear to know no respite; next, we find a standard of domestic life so debased that every amenity of home is trodden under foot; third, the rate of infant mortality will be abnormally high; fourth, the standard of self-respect among the men will be proportionately low. Perhaps this fourth and last feature goes to the root of the whole matter. A nation, at least a great nation, must have certain ideals by which to live, if it hopes to prosper in the world. Such prosperity is not to be obtained through the violation of the primary and natural law that the man is to work for wife and child, and the woman is to be the guardian of the home. If these relations are inverted; if the responsibility of the man as bread-winner is broken down,—if he adopts the easy doctrine that less effort on his part is necessary, since his wife's wages may be counted upon to make up any deficiency in his own, what social conditions are likely to result from such a state of affairs? A plain answer to this question is to be found in the statistics of infant mortality which are forthcoming from the districts in which women's work is an economic feature. Such statistics, grievous though they are, speak only of those who die. They are silent as to the gamut of misery among those who live—the unfit children of toil—weary women—drugged, neglected, demoralised, and bereft of every influence which makes for health of mind and body. Left to the precarious care of friends and neighbours when the mother leaves the four weeks' old baby to drag herself back to the factory, such children who survive, reared on bread, gin, and sugar, struggle through a miserable infancy, in many cases to swell the ranks ultimately of the pauper and criminal classes. The general circumstances of the family are as lamentable as those of the children. If the greatness of any nation is proportionate to the strength of its family life—and this proposition seems indisputable—it is deplorable to realise the character of any home, from which the wife is absent all day and to which she returns in the evening, not for rest, but to commence her belated housework. Little wonder that from the discomforts of such an establishment the husband seeks refuge in the nearest public-house, and that the wife herself knows no better place of relaxation.—Miss V. MARKHAM (quoted from *Macmillan's Magazine*, November 1905).

V. It might appear at first sight,—and such is usually the expectation of a child of ordinary intelligence and of all those who are deficient in an intelligent study of history or in observation of what is passing in the world,—that whatever party might, in any meeting or in any community, obtain a majority, or in whatever other way a superiority, would be certain to carry out their own principles to the utmost, with a total disregard of all the rest; so that in a senate for instance consisting, suppose, of 100 members, a majority of 51 to 49 or of 70 to 30 or of 95 to 5 would proceed in all respects as if the others had no existence; and that no mutual concessions or compromises could take place except between parties exactly balanced. In like manner a person wholly ignorant of Mechanics might suppose that a body acted on by several unequal forces in different directions would obey altogether the strongest, and would move in the direction of that instead of moving, as we know it ordinarily does, in a direction not coinciding with any one of them. Experience shows that in human affairs as well as in Mechanics such expectations are not well founded. If no tolerably wise and good measures were ever carried except in an assembly where there was a complete predominance of men sufficiently enlightened and public-spirited to have a decided preference for those measures above all others, the world would, I conceive, be much worse governed than it really is. No doubt the larger the proportion of judicious and patriotic individuals, the better for the community: but it seems to be the appointment of Providence that the prejudices and passions and interests of different men should be so various as not only to keep one another somewhat in check, but often to bring about, or greatly help to bring about, mixed results, often far preferable to anything devised or aimed at by any of the parties. —ARCHBISHOP WHATELY, *The Kingdom of Christ*.

VI. Though most things which are wrong in their own nature are at once confessed and absolved in that single word Custom, yet there are some which, as they have a dangerous tendency, a thinking man will the less excuse on that very account. Among these I cannot but reckon the common practice of dedications, which is of so much the worse consequence, as it is generally used by the people of politeness, and whom a learned education for the most part ought to have inspired with nobler and juster sentiments. This misuse of praise is not only a deceit upon the gross of mankind, who take their notion of characters from the learned; but also the better sort must by this means lose some part of that desire of fame which is the incentive to generous actions, when they find it promiscuously bestowed on the meritorious and the undeserving: nay, the author himself, let him be supposed to have real respect for the patron, can find no terms to express it but what have been already used and rendered suspect by flatterers. Even truth itself in a dedication is like an honest man in a disguise or vizor-mask, and will appear a cheat by being dressed so like one. Though the merit of the person is beyond dispute, I see no reason that because one man is eminent, therefore another has a right to be impertinent and throw praises in his face. 'Tis just the reverse of the practice of the ancient Romans, when a person was advanced to triumph for his services. As they hired people to rail at him in that circumstance to make him as humble as they could, we have fellows to flatter him and make him as proud as they can. Supposing the writer not to be mercenary, yet the great man is not more in reason bound to thank him for his picture in a dedication, than to thank a painter for that on a sign-post; except it be a less injury to touch the most sacred part of him, his character, than to make free with his countenance only. I should think nothing justified me in this point but the patron's permission beforehand, that I should draw him as like as I could; whereas most authors proceed in this affair just as a dauber I have heard of, who not being able to draw portraits after the life was used to paint faces at random and look out afterwards for people whom he might persuade to be like them. To express my notion of the thing in a word: to say more to a man than one thinks, with a prospect of interest, is dishonest, and without it foolish. Whoever has had success in such an undertaking must of necessity at once think himself in his heart a knave for having done it and his patron a fool for having believed it.—ALEXANDER POPE (1688-1744).

VII. London, unique in the masses of its population, in the depths of its poverty, and the magnificence of its wealth, is also almost unique among the cities of Europe in omitting to provide a permanent home for either music or the drama, or for both, such as nearly every large town in England and in Europe generally has for generations past made an essential part of its municipal existence. A list has been prepared of some fifty continental towns, with populations ranging from the million one hundred thousand of Vienna to the thirty-two thousand of Coblentz, in every one of which land and buildings for music and the drama, or for both in combination, have been provided out of public funds to meet the requirements of a public, whose enjoyment and education in art have been cultivated and increased by an expenditure, which has added enormously to the intellectual assets of the community. A central concert-hall, if it is to be fit for a permanent home of music in London, should be planned to be as acoustically perfect as possible, whether for a full orchestra and chorus, or for the voice of a single speaker. Ventilation, lighting, warming, and the general equipment of the building should all be carefully arranged. It is generally found economical, as well as convenient, to have a larger and a smaller hall under the same roof. In the dignity of its architectural proportions, and by the harmonious beauty of colouring and of design in internal decoration, the building must be made worthy of the purposes for which it is intended. A central concert-hall provided out of public funds would act as a great encouragement to "private enterprise" in its true sense, for it would be an influence gaining a welcome and sympathetic entrance into thousands of homes where the germs of good music already exist, gradually making the caricature and degradation of music unpopular and ultimately impossible. And "private enterprise" in the money-making sense—to which, by some critics, the phrase is often unfairly restricted—would gain by a larger supply of more highly skilled performers, whom the wealth of London can always afford to pay well. To set up a high standard of music among the six millions of men inhabiting London would not only raise the musical ideal in concert-rooms and music halls, but it would lead to a large increase in musical experts for our cathedrals, churches, and chapels. It should not be forgotten that the sister arts of painting and literature are richly endowed out of public funds. There are our great national libraries, and year by year local public libraries are multiplying, not only in towns but in country villages, many of them being supplemented by private munificence in gifts of books as well as of money. In the same way large sums of public money are spent on picture galleries, at the head of them the National Gallery; and, of late years, in hundreds of elementary schools public money has been excellently well spent on pictures, many of them reproductions of the greatest works of art in existence. In Whitechapel, the very heart of one of the poorest parts of London, school-rooms during holiday time have been turned into picture galleries, filled by crowds of working people, who eagerly take advantage of seeing hung upon the walls, lent by their owners, some of the greatest works of art which enrich the world. A country's civilisation depends not at all on the richest people in it being able to purchase for their own enjoyment the sights and sounds created by the genius of painters and sculptors, of poets and musicians, but it does largely depend on the opportunity being given and taken for art in its highest forms, by entering into the life of the masses of the people, to ennoble and purify it. And if there is one place more than any other where this influence is wanted it is in the midst of London, where only a distant echo of the poetry, the music, and the drama of country life, and of the beauty of its sights and sounds, can ever find an entrance.—Compiled from *Macmillan's Magazine*, November 1905.

VIII. That history will provide for all boys useful information, and may give to some tastes and interests for their later life, will I think not be denied. But, after all, the chief object of education is to develop, to discipline, to draw forth the powers of the growing mind. Any subject which fails to do this must occupy only a subordinate place in any scheme of education: and it is often asserted that history cannot give the brain any intellectual exercise or discipline. Of course, if a boy is regarded as a sort of pitcher to be filled up with a certain number of useful facts, history will remain merely an exercise for the memory; but it seems to me that the study of history can be made, and should be made, a most valuable instrument for teaching a boy to express himself on paper in his own language. This can be done through written answers to questions and through historical essays. It is sometimes forgotten what a great variety of questions may be asked. Some, of course, may be set merely for the purpose of testing a boy's knowledge of bare facts and dates; each question may require only one word as an answer, or three or four lines. Questions which are set for this object ought only to require short answers, not so much because they may take up too much of the boy's time if they are longer, but because otherwise they take up too much of the master's in looking over. But history-questions should, as a rule, have as their object not merely to elicit a boy's information, but also to test and develop his abilities. The object of a history-question should be to teach a boy in a limited time how to disentangle from a mass of material the particular facts which he requires; how to arrange these facts so as to bring them to bear upon the particular question in the most effective order; how to argue from facts, or how to use them as illustrations, so that he may state his opinions convincingly and keep to the point; and finally, how to express his meaning concisely, forcibly, and attractively. The boy who can write an answer with these characteristics will at any rate have learnt an accomplishment which will be of value to him in after-life; but I do not for a moment pretend that all boys can be taught. The answers of some boys are always dull; other boys seem incapable of keeping to the point, or will, at the end of an answer, arrive at precisely the opposite conclusion to that which was intended when they began. Some are without any sense of style, others err from excess of it. Some boys, when they catch sight of any question which does not require a bald statement of facts, think that, if they cover a sufficiently large area of paper with rhetorical and empty sentences, they have done all that is required, and others will narrate facts instead of using them for argument or illustration. But I think that practice in these questions always leads to improvement, and that they do provide a valuable mental training.—C. H. K. MARTEN (History Master at Eton).

IX. When the division of labour first began to take place, the power of exchange or barter must have been very much clogged and embarrassed in its operations. One man, we shall suppose, has more of a certain commodity than he himself has occasion for, while another has less. The former consequently would be glad to dispose of, and the latter to purchase, a part of this superfluity. But if this latter should chance to have nothing that the former stands in need of, no exchange can be made between them. The first cannot be the merchant of the second, nor the second the customer of the first. In order to avoid the inconvenience of such situations, every prudent man in every period of society, after the first establishment of the division of labour, must naturally have endeavoured to manage his affairs in such a manner, as to have at all times by him, besides the peculiar produce of his own industry, a certain quantity of some one commodity or other, such as he imagined few people would be likely to refuse in exchange for the produce of their industry. Many different commodities, it is probable, were successively both thought of and employed for this purpose. In the rude ages of society cattle are said to have been the common instrument of commerce; and though they must have been a most inconvenient one, yet in old times we find things were frequently valued according to the number of cattle which had been given in exchange for them. The armour of Diomede, says Homer, cost only nine oxen; but that of Glaucus cost a hundred oxen. Salt is said to be the common instrument of commerce and exchanges in Abyssinia; a species of shells in some parts of the coast of India; dried cod in Newfoundland; tobacco in Virginia; sugar in some of our West India Colonies; hides or dressed leather in some other countries; and there is at this day a village in Scotland where it is not uncommon, I am told, for a workman to carry nails instead of money to the baker's shop or to the alehouse. In all countries, however, men seem at last to have been determined by irresistible reasons to give the preference, for this employment, to metals above every other commodity. Metals can not only be kept with as little loss as any other commodity, scarce anything being less perishable than they are; but they can likewise, without any loss, be divided into any number of parts, as by fusion these parts can easily be reunited again; a quality which no other equally durable commodities possess, and which more than any other quality renders them fit to be instruments of commerce and circulation. The man who wanted to buy salt, for example, and had nothing but cattle to give in exchange for it, must have been obliged to buy salt to the value of a whole ox or a whole sheep at a time. He could seldom buy less than this, whether he needed it or not, because what he was to give for it could seldom be divided without loss. If, on the contrary, instead of sheep or oxen, he had metals to give in exchange for it, he could easily proportion the quantity of the metal to the precise quantity of the commodity which he had immediate occasion for. Different metals have been made use of by different nations for this purpose. Iron was the common instrument of commerce among the ancient Spartans; copper among the ancient Romans; gold and silver among all rich and commercial nations.—ADAM SMITH (1723-1790), *Wealth of Nations.*

X. The chroniclers have given us many accounts of the masques and plays which were acted in the court, or in the castles of noblemen. Such pageants were but the most splendid expression of a taste which was national and universal. As in ancient Greece, generations before the rise of the great dramas of Athens, itinerant companies wandered from village to village, carrying their stage furniture in their little carts, and acted in their booths and tents the grand stories of the Greek mythology; so in England the mystery-players haunted the wakes and fairs, and in barns or taverns, in taprooms, or in the farm-house kitchen, played at saints and angels, and transacted on their petty stage the drama of the Christian faith. To us, who can measure the effect of such scenes only by the impression which they would now produce upon ourselves, these exhibitions can seem but unspeakably profane; they were not profane when tendered in simplicity and received as they were given. They were no more profane than those quaint monastic illuminations which formed the germ of Italian art; and as out of the illuminations arose those paintings which remain unapproached and unapproachable in their excellence, so out of the mystery-plays arose the English drama, represented in its final completeness by the creations of a poet who, it now begins to be supposed, stands alone among mankind. We allow ourselves to think of Shakespeare or of Raphael or of Phidias as having accomplished their work by the power of their own individual genius; but greatness like theirs is never more than the highest degree of an excellence which prevails widely round it and forms the environment in which it grows. No single mind in single contact with the facts of nature could have created out of itself a Pallas, a Madonna, or a Lear; such vast conceptions are the growth of ages, the creations of a nation's spirit; and artist and poet filled full with the power of that spirit have but given them form, and nothing more than form. Nor would the form itself have been attainable by any isolated talent. No genius can dispense with experience; the aberrations of power unguided or ill-guided are ever in proportion to its intensity, and life is not long enough to recover from inevitable mistakes. Noble conceptions already existing, and a noble school of execution which will launch mind and hand at once upon their true courses, are indispensable to transcendent excellence; and Shakespeare's plays were as much the offspring of the long generations that had pioneered his road for him, as the discoveries of Newton were the offspring of those of Copernicus.—FROUDE, *Hist. England.*

CHAPTER XXVII.—ESSAY-WRITING: GENERAL SUBJECTS.

SECTION 1.—PRELIMINARY REMARKS.

340. Unity of Essay.—A sentence is a complete thought expressed in words. A paragraph is a collection of sentences. An essay is a collection of paragraphs. These three products,—the sentence, the paragraph, and the essay,—however much they may differ in other respects, have, or ought to have, one factor in common,—UNITY.

The unity of a sentence (described in § 294) is realised, when the sentence is made to express one main fact or thought, and not more than one. The unity of a paragraph (§§ 301, 302) is realised, when the paragraph is made to deal with one main subject (which is called the theme), and not more than one. The unity of an essay is realised, when the essay is made to deal, as in the case of the paragraph, with one main subject, and not more than one. But the subject of an essay is of much wider scope than the theme of a paragraph; for it has to cover the ground of all the paragraphs contained in the essay. Thus, if any paragraph, that is irrelevant to the subject set, finds its way into an essay, that paragraph must be cancelled; or the essay will be condemned for lack of unity.

Denique sit quidvis, simplex dumtaxat et unum.
HORACE, *Ars Poetica*.

In short, whatever be the work begun,
Let it be something uniform and one.

341. How Unity is to be secured.—Unity in an essay implies three things at least,—Relevancy, Proportion, and Arrangement.

Relevancy.—This has been alluded to already. The student, before he begins to write, must note carefully the wording of the subject set, and convince himself that he has understood its scope, making it neither too narrow nor too broad, nor allowing his thoughts to wander away from the point. Thus, if the subject is "The Uses of Athletic Sports," he will take note of the word "Athletic," and abstain from dwelling on pastimes, which are sports, but not athletic ones. He will also take note of the word "Uses," and abstain from dwelling at length upon the abuses, which have no relevancy to the subject except indirectly by way of contrast to the uses. If the subject set were "The Uses *and Abuses* of Athletic Sports," the mode of treatment would of course be very different.

Proportion.—Reverting once more to the subject "The Uses of Athletic Sports," we might imagine the writer discussing the "Uses" under two separate headings, the physical and the mental. So far, so good. But if he gives three-quarters of his space to the physical and leaves only one-quarter to the mental (which are certainly of equal, if not of greater, importance), he violates the rule of proportion. What should we say of an artist who, in painting a fox-hunt, gives one-half of his space to the fox, one-third to the dogs, and only one-sixth to the riders?

Arrangement.—The paragraphs should be so arranged, that, when the reader has gone through one paragraph, his mind will be carried forward by an easy transition to the next one. If the subject is of the Narrative class, *i.e.* historical or biographical, the order of succession in *time* will probably be most natural. If the subject is of the Descriptive class, the order of succession in *place* will probably be the most natural. If the subject is of the Expository class, such as "The Uses of Athletic Sports," the writer will be careful not to mix up the physical uses with the mental uses. If he attaches more value to the mental than to the physical, he will dispose of the physical first and reserve his strength for the mental, which will thus occupy the latter part of the essay, and leave the final impression on the mind of the reader.

342. Style and Diction.—On diction or the use of words a great deal has been written already in Part II. of this book. There is no need to repeat. In this place, therefore, the subject will be dismissed with a few very obvious precepts, based upon what has been set forth already at greater length and in expository form.

1. Know what you have to say, and say it.

2. Say it in your own words, but in trying to be direct, simple, and vigorous, keep clear of colloquialisms and slang.

3. Make no attempt to ape the style of any great writer.

4. Follow your own bent, and then the style will be what it ought to be,—your own.

5. Do all that you can to make the reader understand what you write as readily and as clearly as you understand it yourself. (Chapter XXIV., on "Perspicuity.")

6. Abstain from bringing in hackneyed quotations from poetry, which add nothing to the force of the composition and are too stale to add anything to its beauty.

7. A short word and a short sentence are generally preferable to long ones; but on this point no absolute rule can be laid down, and on no account must clearness be sacrificed to brevity.

8. If owing to the nature of the subject you cannot always use short and simple words, this need not prevent you from using simple and well-known constructions in the forming of sentences.

343. The Method.—Lastly, as to the method. The plan that has been acted on in the present chapter is to make things as easy as possible to the student at starting, and then to carry him forward by degrees to what he will find more difficult. I begin therefore with giving him a few short essays written out in full, which, after mastering their contents, he might be expected to reproduce in his own words. I next give him a few subjects with notes appended. In writing an essay on such subjects he can make what use he likes of these notes, and add any fresh matter that he thinks fit. Lastly, I give him a list of subjects without notes or any other kind of help.

Section 2.—Essays for Reproduction.

344. How the System is meant to be Worked.—In the first three of the following essays the theme of each paragraph has been printed at the top in Italics. The student might be allowed, if the teacher thinks fit, to make a copy of the themes, before he closes the book and begins to reproduce the essay. It seems advisable that the writer of an essay, like the builder of a house, should at first have some plan placed before him on which he is to work, so that eventually, after sufficient practice has been obtained, the writer, like the builder, may become his own architect and originate any plan that commends itself to his judgment. The framework of an essay, *i.e.* its subdivision into paragraphs, each with a distinct heading of its own, has been well called "the architecture of composition."

In the essay that the student sends up he might be told to write the theme at the top of each paragraph and to underline it, as is done in three of the essays printed below. This will impress upon him, what cannot be impressed too often, the necessity of keeping the contents of each paragraph distinct from those of every other.

After the book has once been closed, it must not be reopened or referred to, until the reproduction has been completed.

Essay I. A River traced back to its Source.

This essay contains six paragraphs as shown below, and the last of these is made up of a single sentence. Provided the summing up is adequate, the brevity of a single sentence makes the summing up the more impressive.

1. The river traced back from the sea to its first streamlets.
2. The first streamlets traced back to rain or snow.
3. Rain or snow traced back to clouds.
4. Clouds traced back to vapour condensed by cold.
5. The alternation of cloud and vapour traced back to the sun.
6. The sun, then, is the ultimate source to which a river can be traced.

1. *The river traced back from the sea to its first streamlets.*

Let us try to find out what is the real beginning of a river. We see the current pass along unceasingly between its banks; where has it come from? If we start from where it empties itself into the sea and follow its course backwards, we find that at different points in its progress, and often at wide intervals apart, it has been joined by tributaries that swell its waters and widen its channel. The river becomes smaller and smaller as one tributary after another is passed. In this way it shrinks by degrees into a narrow stream; and this again, as we go further and further back, is divided into a number of still narrower streamlets, each of which ends at last in mere threads of water flowing down the sides of hills or down the declivity of some elevated plain. These threads and streamlets are in popular language said to be "the sources of the river."

2. *The first streamlets traced back to rain or snow.*

We have reached what are called "the sources of the river," but we are still very far from the real beginning; for we now have to ask ourselves, Whence do the first threads and streamlets, which are commonly called the sources, derive their water? If we visited the hills where these are first to be seen, we should perceive at once that they are fed by rain or by snow; and if we follow the lower courses of the stream, we find the same cause at work. After a long-continued drought the currents flow more and more feebly within their channels; and in extreme cases (as happens sometimes in Australia and South Africa) they dry up altogether in certain parts of their course, so that nothing but the channels remain. But if rain is abundant and continues for a certain period, these dry channels are again filled with water and become foaming torrents strong enough to carry everything before them. If, as is sometimes found among the first threads or streamlets, there happens to be one that has some spring for its source, we very soon become aware of the fact that such springs are also produced by rain, which has percolated through the rocks or through the soil, and comes back again to the light of day through some orifice that it has found or forced.

3. *Rain or snow traced back to clouds.*

But we cannot stop here, if we are to get to the real beginning of rivers. Whence comes the rain or the snow, out of which the river receives its waters? The question is easily answered. No one can help observing that neither rain nor snow comes from a clear sky, but from clouds.

4. *Clouds traced back to vapour condensed by cold.*

But what are clouds? Do we ever see anything in front of us that resembles a cloud? We certainly do. We cannot fail to notice the likeness between a cloud that is floating far above our heads and the condensed steam of a locomotive. At every puff of the engine a little cloud is projected into the air. On looking at this little cloud with some attention, we find that it begins to show itself, not in contact with the top of the funnel, but at a little distance above the top. Between the little cloud and the top of the funnel there is a perfectly clear space, in which there is nothing to be seen. Through that clear space, however, the thing of which the cloud is made must have passed. What, then, is this thing which at one moment is invisible as if it did not exist and at another is visible and becomes a cloud? It is the watery vapour, usually called steam, which comes out of the boiler. Within the boiler this steam, so long as it remains there, is invisible; but to keep it in this invisible state, after it has left the boiler, a heat outside the boiler would be required as great as that within the boiler. But the outside air does not possess such heat; it is a great deal colder. Herein lies the secret of the change. Every particle of steam, when it is chilled, becomes condensed and shrinks to a minute particle of water. The liquid particles thus produced out of condensed steam form a water-dust of exceeding fineness and so light that it floats in the air. This water-dust is the material of which clouds are made.

5. *The alternation of cloud and vapour traced back to the sun.*

Thus the formation of cloud from vapour or steam depends upon the alternation of heat and cold. If the water inside the boiler is sufficiently heated, it is converted into invisible vapour, *i.e.* into steam. If the steam thus formed is sufficiently cooled it is converted into cloud. If this cloud is sufficiently heated it is reconverted into steam; if not, it remains as cloud and adds to the amount of moisture already floating in the air. Eventually this moisture, when the air is saturated with it and can hold no more, falls upon the earth as rain or snow. Is there any fire in nature, similar to the fire of a boiler, which, acting upon the moisture that our atmosphere receives from the ocean, keeps up this perpetual alternation of steam and cloud? Yes; there is the fire of the sun.

6. *The sun the ultimate source to which a river can be traced.*

Thus by tracing a river backwards from its end to its beginning we come at last to the sun.

ESSAY II. WHY WE ARE TAXED.

The essay consists of the following paragraphs:—

1. Insecurity of person and property without settled government.
2. The office of settled government is to afford protection.
3. Settled government costs money, and taxes are levied to meet this cost.
4. The payment of taxes is as much an exchange as any other kind of payment.
5. The payment of taxes is compulsory, and justly so.

1. *Insecurity of person and property without settled government.*

There are some parts of the world (and a few centuries ago there were many more) where neither life nor property is safe, and where every one runs the risk of being robbed or killed, unless he is well armed and on his guard. In such countries there is no settled government; men are savages or nearly savages; or if a settled government nominally exists, it is managed so badly that it is useless or worse. In this state of things there can be very little agriculture; for if no one is certain of reaping or gathering in his own crop, no one will take the trouble to raise a crop. Commerce too is well-nigh impossible; for in such countries there are no roads, or if roads exist, they are not safe, and there is little or nothing to buy or sell.

2. *The office of settled government is to afford protection.*

The remedy for this state of things is, as we have said, settled government; and the office of settled government is to afford protection. It is for the purpose of protection that it provides ships of war and bodies of soldiers, whose duty it is to guard their country against foreign enemies, pirates, bands of robbers, or against rebels at home. It provides watchmen, constables, and other officers to apprehend criminals; judges and courts of justice for the trial of offenders; and prisons for placing in custody those who are found guilty.

3. *Taxes are levied to meet the cost of settled government.*

All these appliances cost money. Who is to find this money? Those who receive the benefit,—the people. Taxes, then, are the price that the community pays for the benefit of protection. They answer to the hire, which in private life we pay for services rendered.

4. *The payment of taxes is as much an exchange as any other kind of payment.*

Some persons are apt to look upon taxes as different from all other kinds of payment, quite forgetting that they receive something in exchange for the taxes that they pay. The payment of a tax is as much an exchange as any other kind of payment. You pay money to the baker for the bread that you eat, and to the miller for the flour of which bread is baked, or to the corn-factor for the grain of which the flour is made, or to the farmer for the labour by which the grain is produced in the field. Similarly you pay money to the government under which you live for the protection that it gives you from being plundered, cheated, or murdered. If you had the burden of protection thrown upon yourself, it would cost you a great deal more than the taxes that you pay to the government, and the protection would be far less effective.

5. *The payment of taxes is compulsory, and justly so.*

There is, however, one great difference between the payment of a tax and every other kind of payment. Every other payment is left to a man's own choice; that is to say, he is free to purchase or not to purchase the commodity for which payment is due. But the payment of taxes is compulsory. We have to pay them, whether we like it or not. If any one should say, "I prefer to protect myself, and therefore I decline to pay the taxes," the answer would be, "Then go away and live in some other country; go among the savages and live as they do; but while you live among us, you must pay your share of the public burden. You are profiting, whether you desire it or not, from the protection afforded by fleets and armies and all other appliances provided for the public safety. It is impossible for us to protect ourselves and leave you out. Therefore you must either pay or go."

Essay III. History of Football.

As this essay is rather long, half could be taken at a time. The paragraphs are as follows:—

1. Football the oldest and most popular of the athletic sports of England.
2. Not known to Greeks or Romans in ancient times.
3. Known only to England in the Middle Ages.
4. Football in the Tudor period.
5. Football under the Puritans, and after.
6. The Association game and the Rugby game.

1. *The oldest and most popular of the athletic sports of England.*

The game of football is the oldest of all the athletic sports of England. For the last six hundred years at least the people have loved the rush and struggle of this rough, but manly, game. Cricket may at times have excited greater interest among the leisured classes; boat-races may have drawn larger crowds of spectators from distant places; but football, which flourished centuries before cricket was known and before boating had become a pastime, may claim to be not only the oldest, but the most popular, of the athletic sports of our country.

2. *Not known to Greeks or Romans in ancient times.*

The ancient Greeks had a game, in which the players of one side had to carry a ball by any means in their power over a line defended by the players on the other side. The antagonists, we may presume, were not debarred by the rules of the game from using their feet; but the feet could not have been of much use to them; for the ball used, as its name in Greek implies, was a handball, of much smaller size than a football. The Romans, as we learn from some of their poets, had a pastime which consisted in striking a large inflated ball into the air and "keeping it up," so as to prevent it from falling on the ground,—a sport which may still be seen played with much skill in Paris. The French name for this ball was, according to the older spelling, *baloon*,—a word which, as need scarcely be added, has in our language been used in a very different, but still a kindred, sense. This pastime made a near approach to our own football: but still the difference was radical; for the ball was struck by the arms, not by the feet.

3. *Known only to England in the Middle Ages.*

Of the game, which in the Middle Ages was known as football, and is still so known, no trace has been found in any country, but our own. Fitzstephen, a monk of Canterbury, who died in 1191, alludes to it in his history of London. It was one of the sports of Shrove-Tuesday; "after dinner all the youths go into the fields to play at the ball."[1] Shrove-Tuesday continued to be the great football day in England for centuries. By the reign of Edward II. the game had become so popular in London, where, to the annoyance of merchants and quiet wayfarers, it was played in the streets, that street-playing was prohibited by statute. In 1349 football is mentioned by its present name, and condemned in a statute of Edward III., who objected to the game, not so much on its own account, as because it encroached upon the practice of archery, on which the military strength of England throughout the Middle Ages largely depended. Football held its ground against the House of Lancaster; all attempts to coerce the merry Englishman into giving it up were hopeless failures. Scotland liked the game not less than England. In 1491 James IV. decreed that "in na place of this realme ther be used futeball, golfe, or other sik unprofitable sportes." In Scotland as well as in England football was strong enough, especially among the labourers and the peasants, to defy the laws that were passed for prohibiting it.

4. *Football in the Tudor period.*

When we enter the Tudor period, we find football as popular as ever. In 1508, the year before Henry VIII. came to the throne, the poet Barclay in his fifth eclogue alludes to football in the following terms:—

> The sturdie ploughman, lustie, strong, and bold,
> Overcometh the winter with driving the foote-ball,
> Forgetting labour and many a grievous fall.

Not long afterwards Sir Thomas Elyot, in his "Boke called the Governour," inveighs against football, as being unfit for gentlemen owing to the violence with which it was played:—"In foote-balle verilie is nothing but beastlie furie and exstreme violence whereof proceedeth hurte, and consequently rancour and malice do remain with them that be wounded, wherefore it is to be put in perpetual silence." If in football there had been nothing but "beastly fury," the game would hardly have held its own so bravely as it has done to the present time. Sir Thomas

[1] Brand's *Popular Antiquities*, p. 36.

Elyot was not an unprejudiced witness; for in his day, and for several centuries before and after, any pedestrian sport that gave no scope for knightly skill was considered unworthy of a gentleman of equestrian rank; and this accounts for the adverse criticisms and statutes that were directed against it. About A.D. 1600 football was still in full vigour. Among the country sports mentioned by Randal Holmes, the Lancashire men challenge any one to—

> Try it out at football by the shinnes.

Shakespeare alludes to football in more than one of his dramas:—

> Am I so round with you as you with me,
> That like a football you do spurn me thus?
> You spurn me hence, and he will spurn me hither:
> If I last in this service, you must case me in leather.
>
> *Comedy of Errors*, ii. 1.

Here is a play on the word "round," being used partly in the sense of "plain-spoken," and partly in reference to the shape of a football. Another allusion is the following:—

> *Lear.* Do you bandy looks with me, you rascal?
> *Steward.* I'll not be struck, my lord.
> *Kent.* Nor tripped neither, you base foot-ball player.
> [*Tripping up his heels.*
> *Lear.* I thank thee, fellow; thou servest me, and I'll love thee.

"To bandy" means to strike to and fro. The allusions to shinning, to leather, and to tripping are significant. All this, common as it was three hundred years ago, when the above lines were written, is to be seen in the football field at the present day.

5. *Football under the Puritans, and after.*

While Puritans held the upper hand in England, football fell into neglect and was regarded with general disapproval. The hold that their ascetic creed, during its short career of triumph, took upon the feelings and manners of the nation, not only put a stop to football being played on Sunday, but made the game itself appear to be derogatory on other days of the week. With the fall of Puritanism the pastime rapidly recovered its lost ground. A most interesting allusion to it occurs in the *Spectator*, where Addison records what he saw (or says that he saw) in his visit to Sir Roger de Coverley:—

> "I was diverted from a further observation of these combatants (cudgel-players) by a football match, where Tom Short behaved himself so well, that most people seemed to agree, etc. . . . *Having played many a match myself*, I could have looked longer on the sport, had I not observed," etc.

Were it not for such unimpeachable testimony, one could hardly imagine the courtly Joseph Addison playing at such a rough game as football, unless he did so when he was a boy at Charterhouse. The interest attaching to the above extract lies in the fact that football had not only recovered from the slur that Puritans had cast upon it, but had made its way into a class of men above that of rustics, to which it had hitherto been confined, and was no longer considered to be unworthy of a gentleman.

6. *The Association game and the Rugby game.*

In recent times a well-marked distinction has been made between the "Association game," in which the players only kick the ball and may not strike it with their hands nor run with it nor throw it, and the Rugby game, in which all these things are allowed. The latter is very like what was played in olden days from the Middle Ages downwards. The former is the kind chiefly used in matches between one school, club, or county, and another. Thousands of persons will collect in a field to watch a game of this kind. The game is watched with as much zest as the gladiatorial combats were watched in pagan Rome, or as bull-fights are still watched in Spain and Mexico. Let us be thankful that the more humane sport of football gives excitement enough to satisfy the sportive instincts of our own countrymen.

ESSAY IV. CHARITY AND ALMSGIVING, ITS USES AND ABUSES.

In this and the following essays the themes of the paragraphs have not been given at the top, as they were in the three essays going before. It will be a profitable practice for the student to find out for himself what the theme of each paragraph is, and in the reproduction that he makes to write it at the top of the paragraph, as in the previous essays. I take the liberty of suggesting that, before the reproduction is commenced, the themes of all the paragraphs should be written out by the student and shown to the class teacher.

1. The motive to charity is not always pure benevolence; and even if it were, a benevolent motive is not always followed by a beneficial result. This fact suggests the duty of caution. If no caution is used, the donor may be doing more harm than good. He may be helping the unworthy, or if the receivers are worthy of the help, he may be helping them in the wrong way.

2. If the need of help is urgent and self-evident, no question of the duty of caution arises. In the Parable of the Good Samaritan the man who had fallen among thieves was picked up half-dead. It was no time to inquire either about his needs or about his deserts.

3. If the case is less urgent, indiscriminate charity, whatever the motive may be, is as much a vice as a virtue. It is a kind of pious selfishness, "a flattering unction" which the almsgiver "lays to his soul." It certainly encourages improvidence on the part of the receiver, and it may be so misplaced as to give him the means of indulging in some favourite vice.

4. Indiscriminate charity has been widely practised and widely commended, not because it will bear the test of being examined on its own merits, but because it seems to be enjoined in the New Testament, as in Matt. v. 42. The text, however, has been misunderstood and misapplied. See 2 Thess. iii. 10, "If any will not work, neither let him eat." Indiscriminate charity, by widening the area of charity which it seeks to contract, is a source of evil rather than of good.

5. The duty of charity, then, involves the duty of discrimination.

Discrimination is impossible without investigation; and investigation imposes personal trouble. Such charity is genuine unselfishness, real virtue.

6. Charity is made more effective as well as more safe by co-operation. Benevolent persons and benevolent institutions, since their aims are the same, should endeavour to pull together. The Charity Organisation Society is a good example of such union. A hospital supported by voluntary contributions is a vast charitable organisation: donations to such cannot be misplaced.

7. Besides relieving poverty we should try to ascertain its causes, and by removing its causes gradually get rid of poverty itself. We should strike at the roots of the upas-tree, and not keep for ever chopping at the branches, which only makes the tree throw out more branches. Of all the causes from which poverty may spring, there is none perhaps so common and so little deserving of pity as idleness. If a man is to be pushed up a ladder, he must do some of the climbing himself. Help should be given to those who are willing and striving to help themselves.

Essay V. The Force of Example.

The themes of the paragraphs should be written out by the student, as before.

1. Men are by nature imitators. All persons are more or less impressed by the speech, the manners, the gait, the gestures, and even the habits of thinking of those around them. "Example is the school of mankind," said Burke, "and they will learn from no other." In man, as in the lower animals, imitation is for the most part unconscious: impressions are made without our knowing it. But though they are unheeded, they sink none the less deeply and their effects are none the less permanent.

2. Though the force of example is for the most part spontaneous and is acquired unconsciously, the young need not necessarily be the passive followers or imitators of those about them. Not only can they select their companions and decide which are most worthy of imitation, but their own conduct tends to fix the purpose and form the principles of their lives.

3. Let a young man seek, if possible, the society of men better than himself, and especially of those who do not possess the kind of fault to which he finds himself peculiarly liable, or who possessed it once, but have conquered it. Their example is always inspiring. He corrects his own conduct by theirs, and becomes a partner in their wisdom. If they are stronger in will or character than he is, he becomes a participator in their strength. Dr. Arnold's own example was an inspiration, as is that of every great teacher. In his presence young men learnt to respect themselves; and out of the root of self-respect there grew up the manly virtues. The example of a good and great man is contagious and compels imitation.

4. Most young men of generous minds, especially if they are readers of books, find heroes to admire. On the contrary, small and ungenerous minds cannot admire any one heartily. To their own misfortune they cannot recognise, much less reverence, great men and great things. The

mean man admires what is mean, as the toad admires nothing but a toad. The small snob finds his ideal of manhood in the great snob. The slave-dealer values a man according to his muscles. Dennis, the hangman (in *Barnaby Rudge*), admired nothing but a man's neck. A glutton cannot look beyond his dinner. A man of the world can see nothing to admire but success. Men of inferior type, instead of trying to raise themselves to the level of their betters, are smitten with envy, and regard the success of others, even in a good cause, as a personal offence. On such men example is thrown away. A silk purse cannot be made out of a sow's ear.

5. One of the great uses of biography is to teach what a man can be and what he can do. The humblest, when they read of this, may admire and take hope. The examples set by the great and good do not die.

> He is not dead whose glorious mind
>   Lifts thine on high;
> To live in hearts we leave behind
>   Is not to die.

Essay VI. Howard the Philanthropist (1726-1790).

If this essay is considered too long to be taken in hand all at once, five paragraphs might be taken first, and the remaining five afterwards.

1. John Howard, surnamed the Philanthropist, was born in 1726, at Enfield, where his father, a retired London merchant, owned a country house. At the age of sixteen he inherited, by his father's death, a property which made him independent for life. For the next thirty-one years he beguiled his time at intervals with foreign travel, but mainly with looking after the country estate which he had acquired at Cardington in Bedfordshire. In one of his tours, on his way to Portugal (which had recently suffered from the earthquake at Lisbon), the ship he sailed in was captured by a French privateer, who conveyed both the crew and the passengers to Brest, where they were thrown into a dungeon, made to lie for several nights on a stone floor, and nearly starved. This was his first experience of the ill-treatment and sufferings, to which in those days men who met with misfortune of any kind might be exposed. At this time he was still a young man, and had formed no notion of the career that destiny had in store for him. But his experiences at Brest were remembered, and bore their fruit in due season.

2. As landlord of the estate that he owned at Cardington in Bedfordshire, he won a high reputation for beneficence by the neat and well-drained cottages that he had built for his farm-labourers, and by the schools that he had opened for their children. All this marked his disposition, but it gave no clue to the direction that his future career was destined to take. In 1773 (by which time he was forty-seven years of age) he was nominated High Sheriff of Bedfordshire, in spite of his being a Nonconformist, and therefore unfitted to undergo the tests imposed upon such officers by the bigotry of the age. He accepted the appointment, however, for the sake of the wider sphere of usefulness that he expected to find in it. After what he had experienced in the jail at Brest, he desired to see

how jails were managed in the county of which he had become High Sheriff. The resolution thus formed determined his future career. From this date the work that characterised his life may be said to have begun.

3. The age in which Howard lived was, in one respect, the most remarkable in our history. It witnessed an extraordinary revival of religion, and an outburst of public-spirited benevolence, such as had never been seen before and was indeed much needed to mitigate the harshness of the times. The religious movement was the work of a small band of Oxford students,—Whitfield, the great preacher,—Charles Wesley, the great hymn-writer,—and John Wesley, great organiser as well as great preacher, who survived the other two, and from whom the movement received the name that it still bears. The new philanthropy that accompanied the religious movement reformed our prisons, infused clemency and wisdom into our penal laws, abolished the slave-trade, and gave the first impulse to popular education. Mr. Raikes of Gloucester founded Sunday schools in his own town, and by his zealous advocacy of such schools in the journal of which he was himself the editor, he induced influential men of many other towns in England to follow his example. Hannah More, by her writings and by her example, drew the attention and sympathies of the public to the miseries with the attendant vices of the agricultural labourer. Clarkson and Wilberforce stirred up the conscience of England and of Parliament against the iniquities of the slave-trade. Cowper (1781-1800) set a new example in poetry (all of which had hitherto been based on classical models) by his advocacy of school reform, his praises of the simple life, his vindication of the negro in his celebrated Ode, and his detestation of cruelty and vice in every form. The list of capital crimes, among which was included the stealing of a turnip, was purged of some of its worst atrocities. The general outburst of sympathy with the afflicted and the oppressed raised hospitals, endowed charities, built churches, started Savings Banks for the benefit of the poor, and sent out missionaries to the heathen.

4. Among the many benefactors of mankind who lived in that day, John Howard holds a conspicuous, and (as most persons would admit) the highest, place. He at least is the only one of that or of any other day who has been distinguished by the name of Philanthropist. The sympathy that others felt for the wronged, the ignorant, and the afflicted he transferred to the wrong-doer himself,—the felon and the murderer. Moreover, his sympathy took the practical and realistic form of testing what prisoners suffered by going inside the jails and suffering the same things himself. What he saw of prison life inside the jails of Bedfordshire took possession of his soul; and the impression that it made clung to him for the rest of his life. Henceforth, at the age of forty-seven, when men not otherwise selfish begin to think most of personal comfort, especially men of delicate health, as Howard had always been and as he remained to the last, this quiet and retired country gentleman became the most energetic and zealous of reformers.

5. Before a year was over, he had visited almost every jail in England, and in nearly all of them he found frightful abuses, which had been noticed half a century before, but were left unredressed by Parliament. Jailers bought their situations as managers, were paid by prisoners' fees, and allowed to extort what they could. Even men who had been acquitted, and whose release had been notified, were dragged back to their

cells for want of funds to discharge what they owed or were said to owe to their keepers. Debtors and felons were huddled together in prisons, that were crowded and overcrowded by the cruel legislation of the day. In one jail he found a cell so narrow and noisome, that the poor wretch who was inhabiting it begged as a mercy to be taken out and hanged. Howard shut himself up in the cell and bore its darkness and its foul atmosphere, till nature could hold out no longer. It was by personal self-denying experience of this sort, and by the unvarnished pictures of prison life which it enabled him to draw, that he succeeded in bringing about the reforms, for which posterity has blessed his name.

6. The publication of Howard's report led at once to the passing of an Act of Parliament, which provided for the immediate and unconditional release of every prisoner against whom the jury failed to find a verdict of guilty, disallowed the exaction of fees from prisoners, and compensated the jailer by an equivalent sum from the county rate. This Act was soon followed by another, which required justices of the peace to see that the walls and ceilings of all prisons were scraped and whitewashed at least once a year, that the rooms were regularly cleansed and ventilated, that infirmaries and medical attendance were provided for the sick, and that underground dungeons should be used no longer. It was highly characteristic of the practical mind of Howard, and of the thoroughness with which he carried out his self-imposed task, that he had these new provisions printed in large type at his own cost, and sent a copy of them to every jailer and warder in the kingdom, so that no one could plead ignorance of the law, if detected in the violation of its requirements.

7. His labours by no means stopped with England, or even with the British Isles. After a tour of inspection through Scotland and Ireland he determined, before publishing his next report, to make a tour through the Continent, and see all that he could of jail management in foreign countries. In 1778 he set out on his Continental tour. He first went to Amsterdam; next he traversed Russia, Saxony, Bohemia, Austria, and Italy, everywhere inspecting prisons, hospitals, and workhouses, and carefully recording the merits and defects of each. From Italy he returned to England in 1779, by way of Lombardy, France, and Flanders. In 1780 he published his *State of Prisons*. Next year he started again, and had traversed Denmark, Sweden, and Prussia before he returned to his country. In 1783 he completed a tour through Spain and Portugal—all with the same object. In 1784 he found that he had travelled no less than 42,000 miles, or nearly as much as twice the circumference of the globe; and let it be remembered there were no railroads in those days to expedite the progress and promote the convenience of travellers. In the course of these tours he was received with marked consideration and respect at more than one royal court. Wherever he went, prisons and hospitals were thrown open to him, as to one who had acquired a right of censorship over the abodes of the unfortunate in every part of the world.

8. A new experience awaited him in 1785. He had heard much of the miseries which the plague, or "black death" as it was called, produced at many of the ports along the coasts of the Mediterranean; and he was determined to make a personal examination of the hospitals called "lazarettos," in which passengers landing from any ship that was supposed to be tainted were detained for forty days to make sure that they were quite free from the disease. He set out without a servant, having resolved that

no one's life should be risked except his own. He took his way by the South of France, through Italy to Malta, Zante, Smyrna, and Constantinople. Returning from Constantinople he visited Smyrna once more, where he knew that the plague was raging, and he chose this route for the purpose of going to Venice with a foul bill of health. In the course of the voyage the vessel was attacked by a Moorish privateer, and in the action which followed Howard took a prominent part and showed great bravery, proving for the hundredth time that valour is as closely allied to goodness of heart, as cowardice is to cruelty. At Venice, being then sixty years of age, and not in vigorous health, he went cheerfully into the lazaretto, knowing full well that he would have to remain there for the full period of forty days in the greatest discomfort, and at the risk of his life, day after day. The Emperor of Austria was so struck with the nobleness of his character, that when Howard, on his way homewards from Venice, passed through Vienna, he requested an interview with him, and would have erected a statue in his honour, if Howard—to whom personal ambition was abhorrent—had not begged him to desist. Wherever he went, he carried remedies with him, and though he had never received any medical training, he acquired a great reputation as a doctor. Having completed this tour, he reached England in February 1789, and published its results in a book called *An Account of the Principal Lazarettos in Europe*.

9. In July 1789 he embarked in what proved to be the last journey of his life. Travelling overland from Amsterdam by Hanover, Berlin, and Riga to St. Petersburg and Moscow, and so southward, he reached Cherson in November, having visited all the military hospitals that lay on the route. At Cherson he found more than enough to occupy his attention; for a malignant type of fever was raging there at the time. Towards the end of the year his medical advice was asked in the case of a young woman who was suffering from the fever. He went to her relief at once, but in doing so he caught the infection himself, and became one of its victims. He died on 20th January 1790. "Give me no monument," he had said, "but lay me quietly in the earth; place a sun-dial over my grave, and let me be forgotten." But a life like his had made such a burial impossible, even in a foreign land. Many thousands of foreigners, drawn by the magic of his name, followed his remains to the grave, where they now lie near the village of Dauphigny, on the road to St. Nicolas, and a simple monument marks the spot where they were buried. Pass it not by, traveller, for its simplicity. It conceals a noble dust.

10. Thus lived and thus died a man, who by sheer force of character and by unswerving singleness of purpose, receiving no help from any government on earth, and relying solely on his own resources, made himself as much honoured by the sovereigns of Europe as he was by the people of his own country, and by the unfortunate of all lands to whom he had given his life.

> The years are slow, the vision tarrieth long,
>   And far the end may be;
> But one by one the ancient fiends of wrong
>   Go out and leave earth free.

ESSAY VII.—DIALOGUE BETWEEN THE KING AND THE MILLER.

This dialogue is to be turned into narrative form, in which only the third person is to be used. It may be freely condensed, but no part of the drift is to be sacrificed. The paragraphs have been numbered. The theme or main purport of each paragraph is to be written at the top in the reproduction, as in the previous examples.

In turning the dialogue into the form of narrative, the writer will have to make use of the matter enclosed in brackets and printed in italics, no less than of the dialogue itself.

1. *King* (*to himself, on finding that he had lost his way in Sherwood Forest*). No, no; this cannot be a public road. I am lost, quite lost. Of what advantage now is it to be a king? Night shows me no respect. I cannot see better than any other man, nor walk so well as most do. What is a king? Is he not wiser than any other man? Not without his counsellors, I plainly find. Is he not more powerful? I have often been told so; but what now can my power command? Is he not greater and more magnificent? When he is seated on his throne and surrounded by nobles and flatterers, perhaps he may think so; but when lost in a wood, what is he, alas! but a common man? His wisdom knows not which is north and which is south; his power a beggar's dog could bark at; his greatness the beggar would not bow to, and yet how often are kings like myself, puffed up with such groundless attributes! Well, in losing the monarch I have found the man. (*The report of a gun is heard.*) Hark! some villain, sure, is near. What had I better do? Will my majesty protect me? No. Throw majesty aside then, and let manhood do it.

2. *Miller* (*enters*). Ho! here is the rogue that fired that gun.

King. No rogue, I assure you.

Miller. Very little better, I should think. Who fired that gun, then?

King. Not I, indeed.

Miller. You lie, I believe. Now, be careful what you say.

King (*aside*). Lie! lie! How strange it seems to me to be spoken to in such style! (*To the Miller.*) Upon my word I do not lie.

Miller. Come, come, sir, confess; you have shot one of the king's deer, have you not?

King. No, indeed; I owe the king more respect than to do such a thing. I heard a gun go off, indeed, and was afraid some robbers or poachers might be near. I thought I might be shot myself.

Miller. I am not bound to believe this, friend. Pray, who are you? What is your name?

King. Name?

Miller. Yes, name. You have a name, I suppose. Where have you come from? What are you doing in the king's forest at this time of night?

King. I have not been accustomed to be asked such questions, honest man.

Miller. Perhaps not, honest man. But they are questions that no honest man would be afraid to answer. So, if you can give no better account of yourself, I shall make bold to take you along with me, and place you in custody.

King. With *you*! what authority have you to take me away into custody?

Miller. The king's authority; if I must give you an account, sir, I am John Cockle, the Miller of Mansfield, one of his majesty's keepers in the forest of Sherwood; and I will let no suspected fellow pass this way, unless he can give a better account of himself than you have yet done.

3. *King* (*aside*). I must submit to my own authority. (*To the Miller.*) Very well, sir, I am glad to hear that the king has so good an officer; and since I find you have his authority, I will give you a better account of myself, if you will do me the favour to hear it.

Miller. It's more than you deserve, I think; but let us hear what you can say for yourself.

King. I have the honour to belong to the king as well as you, and perhaps should be as unwilling to see any wrong done him. I came down with him to hunt in this forest; and the chase leading us to-day a great way from home, I am benighted in this wood, and have lost my way.

Miller. This does not sound well. If you have been hunting, pray where is your horse?

King. I tired my horse so much that it lay down under me, and I was obliged to leave it.

Miller. Now, am I to believe this plausible tale?

King. I am not used to telling lies, honest man.

Miller. What! do you live at court, and not lie? What are courtiers but men who live by fine speeches, most of which are falsehoods?

King. Be that as it may, I am speaking truth *now*, I assure you. To convince you of it, if you will see me safe to Nottingham, or give me a night's lodging in your own house, here is something to pay you for your trouble [*giving him a purse*]. If that is not sufficient, I will satisfy you in the morning to your utmost desire.

4. *Miller.* Ay, now I am convinced that you are a false man, a courtier: here is a little bribe offered me to-day, and a large one promised me to-morrow, both in a breath. Here, take your purse back and be hanged; John Cockle is no courtier; he can do what he ought without a bribe.

King. Thou art a very extraordinary man, I must own, and I should be glad to be further acquainted with thee.

Miller. Thee! and thou! prithee, don't thee and thou me. I believe I am as good a man as yourself, at least.

King. Sir, I beg your pardon.

Miller. Nay, I am not angry, friend; only I don't like to be too familiar with anybody, before I know whether or not he deserves it.

5. *King.* You are in the right. But what do you wish to do with me?

Miller. If you are really a man of the court, I must not seize you as a poacher. Hear now my decision. You are at this moment twelve miles from Nottingham, and the way lies through a thick forest. If you are resolved upon going thither to-night, I will put you on the road, and direct you as well as I can; but if you will accept of such poor entertainment as a miller can give, you will be welcome to stay all night with me, and in the morning I shall go with you to Nottingham myself, and find out who you are.

King. And cannot you go with me to-night?

Miller. I would not go with you to-night, though you were the king: for if I did I should be deserting the post which the king has entrusted to me. It is my duty to remain here during the night and watch for poachers.

King. Then I must go with you to your house. I am ready. Let us start. I have had enough of this forest.

(*Enter a Courtier in haste.*)

6. *Courtier.* Ah! your majesty is safe? We have scoured the forest in search of you.

Miller. How! are you, sir, the king? (*Kneels.*) Your majesty will pardon the ill-usage that you have received. (*The king draws his sword.*) Your majesty will not kill a servant for doing his duty too faithfully?

King. No, my good fellow. So far from having anything to pardon, I am deeply in your debt. I cannot think but so good and honest a man will make a worthy and honourable knight. (*The king taps the shoulder of the kneeling miller with the flat of his sword—the ceremony used for conferring the order of knighthood.*)[1] Rise, Sir John Cockle, and receive this sword, which you saw me draw. I drew it on account of the honour that I was about to confer upon you. To support your dignity as a knight, and in some measure to requite you for the pleasure that you have given me, a thousand crowns a year shall be your revenue.

SECTION 3.—SUBJECTS FOR ESSAYS WITH NOTES APPENDED.

345. How the Notes can be Used.—The notes appended to the subjects given below are not intended to bind the student either as to the number or the order of the paragraphs into which the essay is to be divided. They are intended merely to suggest ideas and to save the student the labour of research, so that he may have more time to give to the composition. For this reason they have been made full enough to be self-explanatory.

[1] The same ceremony was performed by King Edward VII., on the formal opening of the South African Exhibition, 23rd Feb. 1907, in the Horticultural Hall, Westminster. The following is the account that appeared in the *Daily Telegraph*, p. 9, 25th Feb. 1907. This is known as the ceremony of "accolade."—"And now came a ceremony which had the charm of being unrehearsed, and which for other reasons is notable. The gathering awaited the next item in the order of ceremony when, of a sudden, his Majesty and Lord Elgin were seen whispering together, and King Edward turned to an officer in attendance. The officer unsheathed his sword, and at the same moment Lord Elgin motioned to Captain Bam. And before the crowd realised exactly what had happened, Captain Bam had knelt down before his Sovereign, the King had touched him lightly on the shoulder with the sword he had borrowed, and Captain Bam was a knight."

1. The Hand.

The hand is the most wonderful of all the organs of sense. The other organs—the eye, the ear, the tongue, and the nostrils—are merely passive; they can only see, hear, taste, and smell what comes or is placed in their way, and they do this whether they like it or not. But the hand is active: it selects what it shall touch, and it touches what it pleases.

The hand not only serves its own wants, but when other organs fail it takes their place. When the eye is blind, a man feels his way by means of his hand. When the tongue is dumb and the ears deaf, the fingers of the hand can be taught to speak. Those who can neither see nor speak nor hear, can be taught to read raised type by the finger-tips. The tongue and the palate depend almost entirely on what the hand gives them to taste.

The other organs, even when they are perfect, owe much to the hand. It is the hand that constructs the telescope and the microscope for the eye; makes musical instruments for the ear; plucks the flower or distils its fragrance for the nose; ploughs the field, sows seed, and gathers food for the tongue and palate. Thus the organ of touch is the helpmate of all.

The hand serves the mind no less than it serves the body. It gives expression to the genius and the wit, the courage and the affection, the will and the power of man. Put a sword into it, it fights for him; put a plough into it, it tills for him; put a harp into it, it plays for him; put a pen into it, it writes for him; put a brush into it, it paints for him; put a chisel into it, it carves and engraves for him; put a saw into it, it cuts for him; put a hammer into it, it shapes iron for him. A steam-engine is but a larger hand, made to extend its powers. An electric telegraph is but a longer pen for the hand to write with. Our huge cannon and other weapons of war are but the human hand made bigger, stronger, and fiercer. A ship, a railway, a lighthouse, a palace, a whole city, a whole continent of cities,—all are but works of that giant hand that is wielded by the human race.

It is the possession of the hand that has raised mankind above all the other animals inhabiting this earth. Other animals possess bodily faculties superior to ours, especially in hearing, seeing, and smelling; but none of them possesses a hand. The use of the hand stimulates the brain, and has done much to make the human intellect what it is. Other animals possess intelligence, as we do; but having reached a certain point they can go no further. Their intelligence is stunted, because without the possession of hands they can make nothing on which intelligence could be exercised.

2. The History of the Penny Post.

The postage stamp was first used in London on 10th January 1840; adopted by France in 1849, by Germany in 1850; now used everywhere. Long before 1840 there had been a postal service. What, then, gave rise to the postage stamp?

A traveller arrived at the door of an inn at the moment when a postman had stopped to deliver a letter. A young girl, recognising the handwriting of her brother, received the letter, but returned it with a sigh immediately afterwards on being told that she must pay a shilling. The traveller paid the shilling and handed the letter to the girl. When the postman was gone, the girl confessed to the traveller that there was nothing inside the envelope, and that she knew all that she cared to know from certain marks on the outside that had been agreed upon between herself and her brother.

This event gave the traveller food for reflection. Why should a letter cost so much as a shilling? Lower the price, have every letter prepaid and stamped, and make the difference of charge depend on weight, not on distance. The postman could then make no charge on delivery; the number of letters would be increased enormously; the public would reap much benefit; and the revenue derived from the postal service would not be diminished.

The name of the traveller was Rowland Hill. The scheme that he had formed in his brain was described by him in a pamphlet, which was published in 1837. It was opposed at first, as innovations, however valuable, always are; but it passed into law in 1840. It is amusing to hear how he described the postage stamp:—"A bit of paper just large enough to bear the stamp, and covered at the back with a glutinous wash, which by applying a little moisture might be attached to the back of the letter." From the year 1840 letters under a certain weight could be circulated over any part of the British Isles for one penny, and the revenue did not suffer. In 1846 Rowland Hill became Secretary to the Postmaster-General, and Chief Secretary in 1854. In this capacity he improved more and more the plans that he was the first to think of. In 1860 he received the honour of knighthood.

3. Tea—How it is Grown and how Manufactured.

Out of the many millions of persons who drink tea every day of their lives, how few there are who know how the tea-plant is grown and how tea is manufactured for the market!

The plant requires a hot sun with intervals of copious rain. These are needed to make the leaf grow luxuriantly; for the whole value of the plant lies in its leaf. But the plant suffers if it becomes water-logged; hence a plantation must be laid out, not on level, but on sloping ground.

The tea-plant is not allowed to grow to a height of more than six feet; otherwise the leaf could not easily be reached. The plant will grow to the height of a tall tree, if it is allowed; and it is said that in some parts of China monkeys are trained to climb up the trees and pick the leaves.

The leaf is from one to two inches in length. The edge is serrated. It is from the leaf that we get the drink called tea; and it is from the young and tender leaf that we get the best tea. The old leaf is dry and has a harsh flavour; and it cannot be rolled up, as the young leaf can.

In laying out a plantation the seeds of the tea plant are sown in rows, from four to six feet apart; and much care has to be spent in rearing the seedlings. In six or seven years the plant reaches a height of three or four feet, and then the plucking of leaf can be commenced. This must be done sparingly at first, as the plant has still to grow.

When the plant is grown up and in full bearing, there may be three or four pluckings of leaves in the same year; this all depends on sun and rain following each other at the needed intervals. A fresh outburst of leaf is called a flush. When the last of the summer rains is over, leaf-plucking must be stopped till the first flush in the following spring.

The preparation of the leaf for the market consists of the following processes :—(1) the withering of the leaves by exposure to the sun or dry air, which gives them a darker tint ; (2) the first or partial roasting ; (3) the rolling and the curling, now chiefly done by machinery, but formerly by the hand ; (4) the final roasting, which makes them dry, brittle, and fit for use.

Green tea is produced by rolling and roasting the leaf as soon as it has been plucked and while it is still green. Black tea is produced by the more gradual process already described.

The lands where the best tea is grown are the hill tracts of southern China, of northern India, especially Assam and Sikkim, of southern India, especially the Nilghiris, of Aracan and Burma, and of Ceylon. In all of these there is plenty of sloping land, a fertile soil, a hot sun, and a periodic rainfall called the monsoon. Good tea is also grown in parts of Japan.

4. The Story of the Railroad.

We find the first hint of the railroad in the "tramway," *i.e.* the way or road for trams—the trucks or wagons used one or two hundred years ago for conveying coal from the pits' mouth.

Log-roads were made to the pits' mouth by means of timbers (which we now call sleepers), half buried in the earth. Across these at right angles wooden rails were fastened at the ends of each side for the purpose of keeping the wheels of the car on the track. A little later the cars were drawn along on the rails themselves ; then to prevent the wooden rails from wearing out, they were coated with iron ; finally the rails were made wholly of iron. This answered very much to what we now call a railroad. Horses, however, were still used for traction.

No further improvement could be made, till Watt had invented the steam-engine. Then the idea of a locomotive, *i.e.* an engine that could move from place to place by means of steam, began to be thought of. The first trial of steam for purposes of locomotion was made on a tramway (which we must now call a railroad) in the west of England. The first locomotive was a lumbering thing. It moved slowly, consumed a great deal of coal, and was used for the conveyance of coal only. No one thought of its being used for the conveyance of passengers.

The man who brought the locomotive to perfection was George Stephenson, born in 1781 at a coal village near Newcastle. He began life as a cowherd ; but was afterwards employed about the engine at one of the mines. At the age of eighteen he had workmen placed under him, but he had never been taught to read or write. As soon as he had learned how to read at a night school, he studied all the books on engineering and mechanics that he could lay his hands on.

In 1815 Stephenson devised and built his first locomotive. In 1822 he induced the projectors of the Stockton and Darlington railroad to try his engine instead of using horses. This succeeded so well that the locomotive was used for conveying passengers as well as coals and other heavy traffic. The railway was now fairly started on its career.

The next railway on which the locomotive was used was that running between Liverpool and Manchester. The Company offered a prize of £500 for the best locomotive that could be built by a certain date. When the different locomotives were tested, Stephenson's was selected.

He was frequently consulted in regard to the construction of foreign railways, and in 1845 he visited Belgium and Spain for this purpose. In his old age he took up his residence in a country house, and devoted himself to rural pursuits.

5. Materials for Clothing.

Our remotest ancestors clothed themselves in the skins of beasts, as savages do still. The first step in advance was taken, when men changed the dress of leather and hair, *i.e.* of skin and fur, for one of hair only. This was the origin of felt. Felt is hair or wool damped and matted together into sheets or layers, which are then dried.

The next step taken was the spinning of wool into yarn and the weaving of yarn into cloth. The hairs or wool are first disentangled by being passed through a comb. One set of hairs is laid in one direction and another in the opposite direction, so that when the hairs are twisted together in pairs, they become firmly locked together in one thread by means of the scales with which they are covered. The threads thus made are doubled and twisted into fibres fit for weaving.

The animals that produce hairs or fleece fit for spinning into yarns are of various kinds. The sheep heads the list. The alpaca and llama of Peru yield a long and glossy wool. The goats of Angora in Turkey and of Cashmere in northern India are famous for the softness of their wool, and this wool is well suited for the manufacture of shawls. Silk is obtained from a caterpillar, which was first known in China.

Besides quadrupeds and caterpillars there are two vegetables that yield material for clothing. These are (*a*) the flax-plant, (*b*) the cotton-plant.

The flax-plant has a tall elegant stem of a green tint, and bears a bright blue flower about as large as a buttercup and rather like it in shape. This flower gives place to pods, from which linseed oil is extracted. The fibres, of which linen is made, are taken out from the stem. The stem is cut down, dried, beaten with a wooden instrument, drawn through a combing instrument, bleached, and finally handed over to the spinner. The manufacture of linen was known to the ancient Egyptians, as we learn from the Old Testament.

The cotton-plant bears a pale yellow flower, grows to a height of about two feet, and is perhaps the most beautiful of all field crops. The flower gives place to a triangular pod, which gradually dries and finally bursts, showing the soft white locks of cotton fibre peeping out from the brown shell. The husks are easily stripped off; but inside the fibre there are seeds (from which future crops are raised), and these, until machinery was invented, had all to be separated from the fibre by hand.

The cotton-plant has long been grown in India, in Central Asia, in Egypt, and in the southern states of America. Its cultivation is now being extended to many new lands, especially to the tropical regions situated within the British empire,—Jamaica, northern Queensland, and the Sudan. It needs a hotter sun than the flax-plant, and what it yields for the manufacture of cloth is more generally useful.

6. The Gentleman or Man of Feeling.

The word "gentleman" has become so vague, that for the sake of clearing the ground we had best go back to its original meaning.

The first part of the word ("gentle") is from Lat. *gens*, a clan of the patrician order. To be a *gentilis*, *i.e.* a member of such a clan, distinguished a patrician from a plebeian or man of low rank. From *gentilis* we get "gentle," "genteel," "gentle-man."

According to the Herald's College in London, "gentleman" still means one who possesses an hereditary coat-armour. This is still the legal or official meaning of the word. But in social life we have long given up this meaning. We now give the name to those who deserve to have it on grounds of character, conduct, and bearing. Even Chaucer, who wrote 500 years ago, speaks of "gentleman" in the modern sense. Our word "gentle-man" is a translation of the French "gentil-homme." The French, however, preserved the etymological meaning of the word very much longer than we did.

We have not space enough to enter upon all the qualities which go to make up the character of a gentleman, as the word is now understood. But there is one quality which is perhaps the most fundamental of all, viz. consideration for the feelings of others. If a man or woman is sore upon a certain subject, the subject should be avoided. A man should repress the display of his own feelings, if the occasion requires it. A gentleman will not ask inquisitive questions. He will not make rude or thoughtless remarks, which sometimes wound more deeply than injuries, and are less easily forgiven. He will not, without provocation, laugh at another's ignorance. Dekker, the dramatist, calls our Lord "the first true gentleman that ever breathed." A gentleman or man of feeling might be defined as "one who has too much self-respect to show disrespect to others."

Another unfailing test, closely allied to the preceding, is, How does a man behave towards his inferiors? How does the officer treat his men, the employer his servants or his workmen, the master his pupils? He who bullies those who are not able to resist may be a snob, but he cannot be a gentleman. Such a person may be a coward, but not a true man. Strength, with the consciousness of strength, in a right-hearted man, imparts a nobleness to his character which cannot be mistaken.

A gentleman will not boast of his wealth (if he has any), or of his abilities (if he has any), or of his superior position in life. He will not confer favours with a patronising air. Sir Walter Scott once said of Lord Lothian, "He is a man from whom one may receive a favour without being made to repent of it, and that's saying a good deal in these days."

Lastly, a man is not a gentleman because he has a good income, dresses well, lives in good style, and keeps up a good appearance in his house and surroundings. A poor man may have more of the gentleman in him than a rich man. "The appellation of gentleman," says Steele, *Tatler*, No. 207, "is never to be affixed to a man's circumstances, but to his behaviour in them."

7. How Vaccination was discovered and received.

Jenner, the discoverer of vaccination, was born at Berkeley in Gloucestershire in May 1749, and died in 1823. He was thus contemporary with Howard, who reformed prisons, hospitals, and lazarettoes all over Europe—with Clarkson and Wilberforce, who procured the abolition of the slave-trade, and with the Wesleys, who produced the revival of religion which bears their name. Our country has reason to be proud of having produced such men.

He was trained in London for the medical profession. One day he heard by accident a girl say in a chemist's shop, "I can't take the small-pox; for I have had the cow-pox." These words sank deep. He discussed the connection between the two maladies among some of his medical friends, and was laughed at. Innovators, projectors of new ideas, are almost always derided at first.

Having taken his medical degree he returned to his native county, where he obtained a private practice, but gave up all the leisure he could muster to studying the great problem which he was determined to solve. It took him more than two years. Having made himself quite certain that he had solved the problem, and that his method was sound (for he had vaccinated his own son and others with complete success), he published a treatise on the subject in A.D. 1798, by which time he was forty-nine years old.

His discovery was received at first with indifference, and then with active hostility. Not one medical man in London would give it a trial. Vaccination was denounced from the pulpit as "diabolical"; they said that it would make children "ox-faced," and that abscesses broke out to indicate "sprouting horns."

Meanwhile persons went on dying of small-pox, and at last two ladies of rank—Lady Ducie and the Countess of Berkeley—set an example by each of them having their children vaccinated. Others followed. The doctors came round, and there were some who tried to rob Jenner of the credit of the discovery. A man named Dr. Pearson called the discovery his own and published a pamphlet.

The discovery made extraordinary progress in the United States and in Europe. The Court of Spain in 1803 sent out an expedition which diffused the new remedy through all the Spanish possessions in the Old and New worlds, and returned after three years, having by this time circumnavigated the globe. Clergymen in Geneva and Holland urged vaccination upon their parishioners. In Sicily, South America, and Naples religious processions were formed by the priests for solemnising its reception: Jenner's birthday was long kept as a feast in Germany. The Czarina of Russia had the first child that was vaccinated baptised as "Vaccinoff." In these days we hardly realise what a blessing vaccination, when it was first discovered, was to mankind. Letters poured in upon Jenner, and he called himself "the vaccine clerk of the whole world."

In his own country Jenner's merits were less cordially recognised. But eventually (1806) the House of Commons took up the cause and made a suitable grant for the extension of vaccination. In 1808 the National Vaccine Establishment was founded.

Jenner ended his days in the quiet seclusion of country life. He outlived many of the fools in his own profession who had derided him.

8. The value of second-rate literature.

It might be supposed that second-rate books act as a bar to the appearance of books of genius, and are therefore mischievous; that from the reading of such books the public taste is corrupted; and that hence first-rate authorship will gradually disappear from want of encouragement.

This is absurd. A man of genius cares nothing about the public taste. He will not assimilate his work to that of the majority of contemporary writers. If he feels that he has something to say to the world, he will say it. Our great Puritan epic, *Paradise Lost*, was written in the dissolute reign of Charles II., when scarcely any one cared to read it. Bunyan did not consult the public taste (which was grossly corrupt) at the time, when he wrote his *Pilgrim's Progress*.

Second-rate literature must not be snubbed because it is second-rate. It may be very instructive—as much above the average intelligence as it is below literature of the first rank. Is all music, which is not of the very best quality, to be despised? Does not good music of the second or third quality give pleasure?

An author, who begins his literary career in the second or third rank, may rise to the first rank with the maturity of his powers. Tennyson, when his first poems appeared, was nothing to what he became eventually. It took time and experience to ripen his faculties. The same may be said of Byron, whose juvenile poems, *The Hours of Idleness*, were reviewed with derision, when they first appeared. Soon afterwards, however, the derision was turned against the reviewer himself.

There is a very large class of subjects, on which the public require to be informed, but on which first-rate literature is neither necessary nor even possible. The recent war in South Africa produced a flood of literature,—all necessary and useful in its way, but none of it first-rate. The daily newspaper is second-rate literature; but we cannot do without it: we read it every day.

The best novels written since 1860 are not, as some think, equal in merit to those published before. We have now no Scott, Dickens, or Thackeray. But we have had and still have a large number of very able and interesting writers. Are we to be perpetually going over the old ground, because the most recent writers happen not to be first-rate? If new ideas are started, are they to be stifled because there are no first-rate writers to give expression to them?

Since reading is practically universal among the rising generation, the greatest possible quantity and variety of sound literary work, even though it may not be first-rate, should be given to them to read. Many from reading what is second-rate may come to appreciate what is first-rate. Moreover, between first and second-rate literature no clear line of difference can be drawn: genius is not always detected in the age in which it first appears.

Section 4.—Subjects for Essays without Notes.

346. Sources of Selection of Subjects.—This section consists of subjects on which essays are to be written without the help of notes. They have been selected from subjects set in the various public examinations held in England, Scotland, and Wales, of which a list is given below:—

(*a*) Teachers' Certificate (England and Wales), 1891-1901.
(*b*) Teachers' Certificate (Scotland), 1892-1901.
(*c*) Queen's Scholarship (England and Wales), 1891-1900.
(*d*) Leaving Certificate (Scotland), 1892-1901.
(*e*) Central Welsh Board, 1897-1901.

(*f*) Oxford Local Examinations (Senior), 1892-1901.
(*g*) Cambridge Local Examinations (Senior), 1896-1901.
(*h*) College of Preceptors, 1900-1901.

(*a*) *Teachers' Certificate* (*England and Wales*), 1891-1901.

1. Thrift.
2. Patriotism.
3. Tragedy.
4. Reverence for antiquity.
5. International exhibitions.
6. The use of laws.
7. Training for citizenship.
8. Manners maketh man.
9. Time is money.
10. The child is father of the man.
11. The victories of peace.
12. Party-government.
13. The influence of the press.
14. Compulsory military service.
15. Use and abuse of newspapers.
16. Educational value of athletics.
17. Use and abuse of novel-reading
18. Constitutional monarchy.
19. A man's character as shown in his behaviour to other men.
20. "Revenge triumphs over death ; Love slights it ; Honour aspireth to it ; Grief flieth to it ; Fear preoccupieth it."
21. The increasing use of English as a spoken language in various parts of the world.
22. National character as affected by climate and other geographical conditions.
23. Minds that have nothing to impart find little to perceive.
24. "What should they know of England who only England know ?"
25. The advantages and disadvantages of cheap literature.
26 The best prophet of the future is the past.

(*b*) *Teachers' Certificate* (*Scotland*), 1892-1901.

1. Courtesy.
2. Trial by combat.
3. A general election.
4. Procrastination.
5. Habit is second nature.
6. The study of nature.
7. Technical education.
8. Knowledge is power.
9. The choice of a profession.
10. A railway bookstall.
11. Rational recreation.
12. Cycling as a recreation.
13. Local government.
14. Easter holidays.
15. The power of kindness.
16. The pleasures of hope.
17. Life insurance.
18. Market-day in a county town.
19. Physical training in schools.
20. From the Cape to Cairo.
21. The conquest of the Soudan.
22. Moral courage.
23. Masques : their origin and development.
24. A religious pilgrimage in England in the fourteenth century.
25. Great men : their characteristics and their uses.
26. "Cut your coat according to your cloth."
27. Fear makes men look aside, and so their footing miss.—DRYDEN.
28. The position of the Magazine in modern literature.
29. "The apparel oft proclaims the man."
30. The special characteristics of your favourite author, and the benefits that you have obtained from the study of his writings.
31. Use and abuse of reading as a recreation.
32. Lights and shadows of a teacher's life.
33. The connection between commerce and civilisation.
34. "If you wish peace, prepare for war."

35. "Sweet are the uses of adversity."
36. "Raw haste half-sister to delay."
37. Use and abuse of athletics.
38. Industrial and material progress in the nineteenth century.
39. "Prosperity doth discover vice; but adversity doth but discover virtue."
40. The value of colonial possessions.
41. All things that are
Are with more spirit chaséd than enjoy'd.
42. England's position and outlook at the beginning of the twentieth century.

(c) *Queen's Scholarship (England and Wales)*, 1891-1900.

1. Fruit trees.
2. School friendships.
3. Parliament.
4. Your favourite pursuit.
5. The Japanese.
6. Strikes.
7. Dress as an index of character.
8. The pleasures of gardening.
9. A winter landscape.
10. The evils of war.
11. Give in substance the contents of any interesting book that you have recently read.
12. Holidays and the way to use them.
13. On the value of the study of history.
14. Words are like leaves; and when they most abound,
Much fruit of sense beneath is rarely found.
15. Hope springs eternal in the human breast;
Man never is, but always to be blest.
16. How may the spirit of patriotism be promoted in elementary schools?
17. How far is it true that "history is the biography of great men"?
18. A short life of some great naval or military hero.
19. The darkest day,
Wait till to-morrow, will have passed away.
20. The life of the teacher: its difficulties and ideals.
21. "Great offices will have (*i.e.* need) great men."
22. What can be gained by the study of geography?

(d) *Leaving Certificate (Scotland)*, 1892-1901.

1. The place in which you live.
2. The uses of novel-reading.
3. Æsop's Fables.
4. Courage, its nature and kinds.
5. "The Pilgrim's Progress."
6. Spring wildflowers.
7. Your favourite holiday occupation.
8. Domestic animals.
9. Birds.
10. Your favourite periodical.
11. Our rights and duties in regard to animals.
12. The qualities required for successful public speaking.
13. The mental and moral uses of athletic sports.
14. What trade or profession would you like to enter, and why?
15. The character and career of Richard I., or of Oliver Cromwell, or of the young Pretender.
16. A letter to a friend, containing an invitation to spend a holiday with you.
17. A letter to a friend, giving a short account of a journey, real or imaginary, by land or by sea.

18. Changes which steam-power has wrought on the cond. in our country.

19. Which is the most useful foreign language to study, and why

20. Examinations as a test of knowledge and capacity.

21. Some points of interest connected with your neighbourhood.

22. The distinction between a liberal and a professional or technical education.

23. The influence of climate upon national character.

24. A comparison of the present methods of warfare with those of an earlier century.

25. A comparison of the benefits accruing to Britain from her colonies with those accruing to her colonies from Britain.

26. A comparison of the army and the navy as careers.

27. The conditions of modern civilisation, as favourable or as deleterious to health.

28. The relative value of classics and of modern languages in a school curriculum.

(e) *Central Welsh Board*, 1897-1901.

1. England, the mother of nations.
2. Cycles and cycling.
3. The story of an adventurer.
4. Your ideal friend.
5. Your favourite book.
6. The British navy.
7. Ships and boats.
8. "A stitch in time saves nine."
9. Egypt.
10. An ideal home.
11. An incident in world-history.
12. The uses of steam.
13. The scenery of Wales.
14. A voyage round the world.
15. Music.
16. The study of nature.
17. Feudalism.
18. The age of chivalry.
19. Hero-worship.
20. The triumphs of science.
21. What country do you most wish to visit, and for what reasons?
22. The progress of science during the late Queen's reign.
23. A walk in the country or by the sea-shore.
24. The identification of Prospero with Shakespeare.
25. The moral and social conditions of the Roman empire in the time of Augustus.
26. The character of Brutus in *Julius Cæsar*.
27. A description of some poem that you have read.
28. How best may we promote peace among the nations of Europe?
29. The pen is mightier than the sword.
30. The conditions of society described by any one of our great novelists.
31. A description of some scene of natural beauty with which you are familiar.

(f) *Oxford Local Examinations (Senior)*, 1892-1901.

1. Russia.
2. Colonies.
3. Tennyson.
4. Printing.
5. Enthusiasm.
6. Japan.
7. Fashion.
8. Democracy.
9. Brain.
10. Photography.
11. The United States of America.
12. Coal.
13. International disarmament.
14. Bismarck.

(g) *Cambridge Local Examinations (Senior)*, 1896-1901.

1. Clouds.
2. South Africa.
3. The fairy tales of science.
4. We live in deeds, not years.
5. The sun.
6. Greater Britain.
7. A ruined abbey.
8. Nelson.
9. Arctic exploration.
10. Alfred the Great.
11. The river Nile.
12. A storm at sea.
13. Westminster Abbey.
14. A flower-garden.
15. The English Lakes.
16. Moorland scenery.
17. Vesuvius.
18. Wit and humour.
19. April.
20. Simple pleasures.
21. Fashion.
22. Aerial navigation
23. One of Sir Walter Scott's novels.
24. Duty, "stern daughter of the voice of God."
25. The old order changeth, giving place to new.
26. "He is the freeman, whom the truth makes free
    And all are slaves beside."
27. "He prayeth well, who loveth well
    Both man and bird and beast."
28. "Take up the white man's burden."
29. "The stately homes of England,
    How beautiful they stand
    Amid their tall ancestral trees,
    Through all this pleasant land."
30. Our colonies and the mother country.

(h) *College of Preceptors (First Class)*, 1900-1901.

1. Your favourite picture.
2. The Australian confederation.
3. The House of Commons.
4. The Battle of Agincourt.
5. The game of hockey.
6. A cycling tour.
7. Any favourite flower and its cultivation.
8. The best subject for a photograph.
9. Moral courage—is it greater in men or in women?
10. The influence of climate on character.

PART IV.—COMPOSITION CONTINUED.

IDIOM AND CONSTRUCTION WITH FURTHER PRACTICE IN ESSAY-WRITING: SUBJECTS MAINLY HISTORICAL.

CHAPTER XXVIII.—IDIOM AND CONSTRUCTION.

347. Idiom Described.—The term "idiom" is applied to any special use of a word or words, that does not directly proceed from the general structure of a language, and therefore requires some specific description of its usage or some explanation of its origin.

As the contents of this chapter are very various, it has been considered better to deal with the several points in their alphabetical order, instead of attempting to classify them subject-wise under different headings.

Note.—For exercises in this chapter the student is referred to those given at the end of the chapter following.

348. Absolute Constructions.—There are altogether five different kinds of absolute construction in English:—

(1) A Nominative of noun or pronoun followed by a participle denoting **past** or **present** time; see § 176 (5), (*a*):—

Off we started, *he having given* the signal (*Past*).
Off we start, *he remaining* behind (*Present*).

(2) A Nominative of noun or pronoun followed by an Infinitive, to denote **future** time; see § 176 (5), (*b*):—

The estate has been divided between us, *he to have* two-thirds, and *I* one-third.

(3) Impersonal absolute; see § 190, *Note* 2:—

Supposing this to be true, you are guilty.

(4) Imperative absolute; see § 121:—

A large number of men, *say* a hundred, had come.

(5) Infinitive absolute; see § 127, II. (*d*):—

I am, *to speak* plainly, very much hurt.

Note.—We sometimes find an Absolute construction placed inside another Absolute construction, as in the following example, where the inner one is printed in italics. This is not to be commended.

The House of Commons reassembled after the Easter recess, the Speaker, *the new rules coming into operation for the first time*, taking the chair at a quarter to three.—*Daily Telegraph*, p. 8, 25th April 1906.

349. Adjective used as Noun.—This is a very common idiom in our language. The change from Adjective to Noun is complete when the word can be used in the Plural number or in the Possessive case; for adjectives proper have no inflexions to denote either number or case.

Nobles =noble men or noblemen.
A *noble's* house=a nobleman's house.
I have told you many *secrets*=secret things.

The different purposes for which Adjectives can be used as Nouns are shown under the following headings:—

(*a*) To denote some language; no article is used:—

He speaks *French*, but not *German*.
The grammar of *English* is simpler than that of *Greek*.

(*b*) To denote anything possessing number, quantity, or quality. Some are used as Nouns in the Singular only, some in the Plural only, and some in both.

(1) *Singular only*:—

Our all. Our best. Our worst. Much (as, Much has been done). More (as, More has been done). Little (as, Little has been done). Less (as, Less has been done). The future.

(2) *Plural only*:—

Morals. Movables. Eatables. Drinkables. Valuables. Greens (=green vegetables). Sweets and bitters (=the sweet and bitter contingencies of life). Our betters (=men better than ourselves). The ancients. The moderns. The Commons. The actuals. Futures (this word is used only in commercial transactions, to denote the future or anticipated values of merchandise or stocks).

Note.—"These presents" (that is, *present letters, literæ præsentes*, the present document) is a legal term borrowed from French. "News" was formed on the analogy of Fr. *nouvelles*. "Means" is plural of the adjective *mean* used as a noun.[1]

---

[1] "Mean" in the sense of "intermediate" is from Anglo-French *meien*, Late Lat. *medianus*. "Mean" in the sense of "common" is from Anglo-Saxon *ge-mæne*. The plural *means* is from the former.

(3) *Singular and Plural* :—

A secret; secrets. A liquid; liquids. A solid; solids. A total; totals. A capital; capitals. An elder; elders. A senior; seniors. A junior; juniors. A native; natives. A mortal; mortals. An inferior; inferiors. A superior; superiors. A criminal; criminals. An opposite; opposites. The contrary; contraries. This particular; these particulars. My equal; our equals. If *equals* be added to *equals*, the *wholes* are equal.

(*c*) Participles (which, in fact, are Verbal adjectives, see § 18) are sometimes used as Nouns in the Plural number, in the same way as ordinary adjectives are:—

He sent all his *belongings* (things belonging to him).
Let *bygones* be *bygones* (= let past offences be forgotten).

Unseens.—This word is used by examiners to denote "passages from authors" which have not been prescribed in the course, and presumably have not been seen by the examinee.

In Old English we meet with nouns whose origin was traceable to Present participles:—

Feó-nd (= fiend): akin to Pres. part. of *feón* (to hate).
Freó-nd (= friend): akin to Pres. part. of *freón* (to love).

(*d*) There are certain phrases in which adjectives go in pairs, some noun being understood after them:—

From bad to worse = from a bad state to a worse one.
The long and short = the sum and substance of the matter.
In black and white = written with black ink on white paper.
Through thick and thin = through difficult obstacles or easy ones.
From first to last = from the beginning to the end.
At sixes and sevens = in a state of disorder.
High and low = in high places and low ones, everywhere.
Right or wrong = whether the act is right or not.
For better, for worse = for any good or evil that may happen.
Fast and loose = with a tight hold or a loose one; at random.
Black and blue. "He beat them black and blue" (so as to leave black and blue marks on the skin).
Right and left. "He looked (on the) right (side) and (the) left."
Slow and steady. "Slow and steady (progress) wins the race."
For good, for good and all = for all future contingencies, good or evil; permanently, finally.

350. Adjective preceded by "the."—An adjective preceded by the Definite article can be used as a Noun in the three senses shown below:—

(*a*) As a Common noun (*Plural*) denoting *Persons*:—

None but *the brave* (= those men who are brave) deserves the fair.
To *the pure* = (those persons who are pure) all things are pure.

Note.—In earlier English this construction was common in a *Singular* sense also, and the article was sometimes omitted :—

For he nought helpeth *needful* in *his* neede.—CHAUCER.

(*b*) As an Abstract noun (*Singular*) :—

The good = that quality which is good, = goodness in general.
The beautiful = that quality which is beautiful, = beauty in general.

Note.—Sometimes we find the Superlative used instead of the Positive. This is done for the sake of heightening the effect.

He fell in *the thickest* (= the thickest part) of the battle.
He has got over *the worst* (= the worst phase) of his illness.

In poetry, adjectives are sometimes used as nouns, without having an article placed before them :—

Fair is foul, and *foul* is fair.—SHAKESPEARE.
O'er *rough* and *smooth* she trips along.—WORDSWORTH.
And fold me in the riches of thy *fair*.—GREEN.
Say what you can, my *false* o'erweighs your *true*.—SHAKESPEARE.
My *earthly* by his *heavenly* overpowered.—MILTON.
From *grave* to *gay*, from *lively* to *severe*.—POPE.

(*c*) As a name for some particular part of a thing :—

The white (= the white part) of the eye.
The vitals (= the most vital parts) of the body.
The thick (= the thickest part) of the forest.
The wilds (= the wild parts) of a country.
The middle (= the middle part) of a river.
The small (= the smallest part) of the back.

351. Adjective used as Adverb.—Since adjectives and adverbs are both qualifying words, an adjective qualifying the subject to a verb can be substituted for an adverb qualifying the verb itself, as has been explained in § 181. How far is this admissible in prose? and how far in poetry?

In prose and poetry alike :—

(*a*) When the adjective describes the state of the agent :—

He went away *sad* (that is, he was sad when he went away).

(*b*) When the adjective describes the effect of the action :—

The moon shines *bright* (the moon shines, and the effect of its shining is brightness).

Note.—This use of the adjective is *in prose* limited to monosyllables. Thus in prose we should not say, "The moon shines *brilliant*," but "The moon shines *brilliantly*."

In poetry only :—

(*c*) When the adjective is intended to describe neither the state of the agent, nor the effect of the action, but *the manner of doing the action* :—

> Then they praised him *soft and low*.—TENNYSON.
> (Their manner of praising him was soft and low).
> The green trees whispered *low and mild*.—LONGFELLOW.
> (The kind of whisper was low and mild).
> I'll have this crown of mine cut from my shoulders,
> Before I'll see the crown so *foul* misplaced.—SHAKESPEARE.

352. Adverbs qualifying Nouns.—In § 151 the principle is laid down that adverbs do not qualify nouns or pronouns, and explanations are given showing how the apparent exceptions can be met and accounted for.

As a general rule the above principle must be maintained. It might be urged, however, that there are a few examples in which the adverb has acquired the force of an adjective and for purposes of grammar may be regarded as one. This remark applies especially to the examples (*c*) in § 151; such as the "the *then* king," where the adverb is enclosed between the Definite article and the noun.

There is also a kind of construction in which an adverb is made to qualify a noun, when it is placed after it :—

> The world *above* = the upper world.
> My correspondence *abroad* = my foreign correspondence.

Here the adverb is used exactly in the same way as if it were an adverbial phrase consisting of a preposition with its object :—

> Maid *of Athens* = Athenian maid.
> A man *of letters* = a literary man.

In complex sentences an Adverb-clause is sometimes used to qualify a noun, as in the following example :—

> Of man's first disobedience and the fruit
> Of that forbidden tree, whose mortal taste
> Brought sin into the world and all our woe
> With *loss* of Eden, *till* one greater man
> Restore us and regain the blissful seat.
> *Paradise Lost*, i. 1-5.

Here the adverb-clauses introduced by *till* qualify the noun *loss*.

353. Articles how used.—The chief uses of Articles are shown below.

(*a*) To *particularise* the noun we use the *Definite* article :—

Let us go and bathe in *the* river (that is, the river near our house, or the river where we usually bathe).

This settles *the* matter (that is, the matter in which we are engaged).

(*b*) To *generalise* the noun we use the *Indefinite* article for the Singular, and no article for the Plural :—

A tiger is a fierce animal (that is, any tiger; or tigers generally).
Cats are not so faithful as dogs.

(*c*) An article is not used with a Proper, Material, or Abstract noun, except to make it a Common noun :—

He is *the Nestor* (=the oldest man) of the service.—*Proper.*
Sugar-cane is one of *the grasses* (=kinds of grass).—*Material.*
He is *a justice* of the peace.—*Abstract.*

Note 1.—"The" may, however, be placed before an Abstract noun, when this noun is followed by a qualifying phrase :—

The injustice of the world. *The shortness* of life. *The love* of money.

Note 2.—The Definite article is placed before (1) names of rivers, as *the Thames*; (2) mountain-ranges, as *the Alps*; (3) groups of islands, as *the Hebrides*. Before an isolated mountain and before other geographical names the article is not used.

(*d*) "*The*" is sometimes used to indicate a *class* or *kind* :—

The lion is a noble beast=
A lion is a noble beast=
Lions are noble beasts.

(*e*) When "*the*" is placed before a *Common* noun denoting a person, it can give it the meaning of an *Abstract* noun :—

He felt *the patriot* (the patriotic spirit) rise within his breast.
He acted *the lord* (the lordly character) wherever he went.

354. Articles not a Distinct Part of Speech.—It is opposed to history as well as to reason to consider the articles a distinct part of speech.

It is opposed to history, because out of a base *tha*, signifying "that," was formed the Anglo-Saxon *the*, which has come down to our own time. The other article *an* (of which *a* is merely an abridgment) is formed from A.S. *án*, signifying "one." Our article *a* is still used sometimes in the sense of "one" :—

A stitch (=one stitch) in time saves nine.
A bird in the hand is worth two in the bush.

It is opposed to reason, because whenever they are used they discharge, as their origin would imply, the function of Adjectives in limiting or defining the application of a noun. In fact *a* is a Numeral adjective, and *the* a Demonstrative one. The universality of their use gives them an exceptional character, which distinguishes them from ordinary Adjectives; but this does not make them distinct parts of speech.

355. Comparison of Adjectives.—Most adjectives of Quality, two adjectives of Quantity, viz. *much* and *little*, and two adjectives of Number, viz. *many* and *few*, can be used in different degrees of comparison. Adjectives which cannot be so used may be classified thus :—

(1) Quantitative, all except *much*, *little*.
(2) Numeral, all except *many*, *few*.
(3) Proper, as *English*, *African*, etc.
(4) Demonstrative, as *this*, *that*, *other*, etc.
(5) Distributive, as *either*, *every*, etc.
(6) Descriptive, when they denote qualities which from the nature of their meaning cannot be more or less.
   (*a*) Shape, as *round*, *square*, *oblong*, *triangular*, *four-footed*.
   (*b*) Material, as *golden*, *milky*, *vegetable*, etc.
   (*c*) Time, as *weekly*, *monthly*, *annual*, etc.
   (*d*) Place, as *Kentish*, *American*, *insular*, etc.
   (*e*) Natural objects, as *solar*, *lunar*, *sidereal*, etc.
   (*f*) Qualities in the highest degree, as *eternal*, *perpetual*, *perfect*, etc.
   (*g*) Qualities in a moderate degree, as *pal-ish*, *redd-ish*.

Such a phrase as "more perfect" is a short, but inaccurate, way of saying "more nearly approaching perfection."

356. Comparatives how used.—The uses of the different degrees of comparison are shown below :—

(*a*) **Positive.**—When two persons or things are said to be *equal* in respect of some quality, we use the *Positive* degree with *as* . . . *as* ; or we can use the Comparative adverb (*less* or *more*) with "not" :—

This boy is *as* clever *as* that=
This boy is *not less* clever *than* that=
That boy is *not more* clever *than* this.

(*b*) **Comparative.**—When *two* persons or things are said to be *unequal* in some quality, we use the *Comparative* degree :—

(*a*) This boy is more clever or cleverer *than* that.
(*b*) This boy is *the* cleverer *of the two*.

Note 1.—Forms (*a*) and (*b*) do not mean entirely the same thing. Form (*a*) merely denotes *superiority*. Form (*b*) denotes the *selection* of the one in preference to the other.

Note 2.—Observe that whenever the Comparative degree is used in the (*b*) or *selective* sense, it must be preceded by the Definite article, as might be expected ; for the proper function of this article is to particularise or select, see § 353 (*a*).

(*c*) **Superlative.**—When one person or thing is said to surpass all other persons or things of the same kind, we use the *Superlative* degree with *the* . . . *of*.

Chaucer was *the* greatest *of* all the poets of his age.

The same thing can be expressed by the Comparative degree followed by *all others*, or *all the others* :—

Chaucer was greater than *all the other* poets of his age.

Note 1.—Care must be taken not to omit the word *other* after a Comparative. To say, "Chaucer was greater than all the poets of his age" makes nonsense: for this can only mean that Chaucer was greater than himself.

Note 2.—Milton, by a poetical licence, and in imitation of a Greek idiom, confounds the Comp. with the Superl. in the following lines:—

> Adam, the goodliest man of men since born,
> His sons; the fairest of her daughters, Eve.

357. Comparatives which have lost their Force.

(*a*) Latin Comparatives:—*interior*, *exterior*, *ulterior*, *major*, *minor*. These are now never followed by *to*, but are used as if they were adjectives in the Positive degree:—

> A fact of *minor* (secondary) importance.
> He had an *ulterior* (further) purpose in doing this.
> The *interior* (inside) parts of a building.

Some, when preceded by an article, can be used as nouns:—

> He is a *minor* (a person under age).
> He is a *major* (in the military rank).
> The *interior* of the room was well furnished.

(*b*) English Comparatives:—*former*, *latter*, *elder*, *hinder*, *inner*, *outer*, *utter*, *upper*, *nether*. These are now never followed by *than*:—

> The *former* and the *latter* rain.—*Old Testament.*
> The *inner* meaning; the *outer* surface.
> The *upper* and the *nether* mill-stones.
> He talks *utter* nonsense.

The words *elder* and *elders* can also be used as nouns, as, "the village elders."

358. Comparatives and Superlatives in Special Senses.

—Observe the differences of meaning between (a) *eldest* and *oldest*; (b) *farther* and *further*; (c) *later* and *latter*; (d) *nearest* and *next*; (e) *outer* and *utter*; (f) *foremost* and *first*.

> (*a*) { My *eldest* son died at the age of twelve.
> He is the *oldest* of my surviving sons.

"Eldest" means first-born, and hence stands only for *persons*. "Oldest" is applied to things as well as to persons. Both denote the greatest age. "That is the *oldest* tree in the grove." In the Comparative degree the same distinction holds good; and besides this, *older* has retained its Comparative force, whilst *elder* has lost it.

> (*b*) { Liverpool is *farther* from London than Dover is.
> The *further* end of the room. A *further* reason exists.

The word "farther" (comparative of "far") denotes a greater distance between two points. The word "further" (comparative of *fore*, see § 62) has the sense of additional or more in advance.

(c) { This is the *latest* news.
This is the *last* boy in the class.

The words "later" and "latest" denote time; the words "latter" and "last" denote position.

(d) { This street is the *nearest* to my house.
This house is *next* to mine.

The word "nearest" denotes distance; ("this street is at a less distance from my house than any other street"). But "next" denotes position; ("no other house stands between this house and mine").

(e) The *outer* surface. An *utter* failure. An *utter* fool.

"Outer" means that which is outside; "utter" means extreme or complete, in a bad sense.

(f) { The *first* occasion. The *first* student in the class.
That struck the *foremost* man in all this world.—SHAKESPEARE.

"First" is a word of much wider application than "foremost." "Foremost" means most prominent, most distinguished, most conspicuous. The quotation from Shakespeare refers to Julius Cæsar, who at the time of his murder was the most conspicuous man in the world. Both are Superlatives of "fore" (§ 62).

359. Dative Absolute.—In medieval English the Absolute case was the Dative, not the Nominative:—

They have stolen away the body, *us* sleeping.—*Wyclif's Bible.*

In Milton we find "me overthrown," "us dispossessed," "him destroyed," which he introduced in imitation of the classical languages. Elsewhere he uses the Nominative:—

I should not lag behind or err the way, *Thou leading.*

360. Dative case.—In Old English there was a Dative case distinct from the Objective. What we now call the Indirect Object was then a Dative. Other examples of what in Old English was a Dative are given below:—

(a) **Dative of Interest.**—The Jew ate *me* (to my astonishment) a whole ham of bacon.—ADDISON.

"Archers," he cried, "send *me* (for my satisfaction) an arrow through yon monk's frock."—SCOTT, *Ivanhoe.*

Knock *me* this gate, and rap *me* well.—SHAKESPEARE.

Prophet, curse *me* the blabbing lip,
And curse *me* the British vermin, the rat.
TENNYSON'S *Maud.*

Note.—The Dative of Interest has been also called the *Ethical Dative*, to signify that the person or thing spoken of is regarded with interest by some one.

(b) **Reflexive Dative** (see § 97).—Fare *thee* well (=fare well *for thyself*).

He overslept *him*self (slept too long *for himself*).

But hear *thee*, Gratiano;
Thou art too wild, too rude, and bold of voice.
Merchant of Venice, ii. 2, 189.

(c) **With Impersonal Verbs.**—*Me*thinks; *me*seems; it likes *us* well.—*Hamlet*, ii. 2, 81.

(d) **With the Verbs "be," "worth."**—

Woe worth *the day*!
Woe is *me*!

(e) **As Indirect object to a Transitive verb** (see § 90).—He taught *my sons* Euclid.

I hope you will do *me* this favour.

361. Familiar "your" and "my."—These possessives are used indefinitely (*i.e.* without any distinct reference either to you or to me), and with some implication of contempt:—

Your worm is *your* only emperor for diet; *your* fat king and *your* lean beggar is but variable service.—*Hamlet*, iv. 3, 24.

When he entered the room, on seeing a servant coming towards him to order him out, up goes *my* grave Impudence (= the grave-faced, impudent fellow whom I was watching) to the maid, etc. —*Tatler.*

He saw more than *your* fool of a tourist usually sees.—Mrs. WARD.

For the loss of public and private virtue we are beholden to *your* men of fine parts forsooth.—STEELE, *Spectator*, No. 6.

362. Gerundive Use of Participles.—This construction has been explained already in §§ 140, 141. It is allowable only when the noun going before the Participle is one which does not take the Possessive inflection:—

(a) I have no hope of the *book* being found.
(b) I have no hope of the *man's* being found.

Since we do not use such a word as "book's," we have no choice but to use the construction exemplified in (a), where "being found" is not a gerund, as it is in (b), but a participle used in a gerundive sense. It was a very common construction in Latin. In our own language, however, it is not older than the sixteenth century,[1] and is not to be commended.

---

[1] Mr. Kellner, however (in *Historical Syntax*, p. 262), quotes two examples of a much earlier date than the sixteenth century:—

(1) Tó-janes þo sunne risinde.—*Old Eng. Misc.* p. 26.
(2) After the sunne goyng down.—WYCLIF, *Gen.* xxviii. 11.

But here he appears to be mistaken. Ex. (1) is from Old Kentish Sermons, that were copied by a Norman scribe, who betrays his imperfect knowledge of English by spelling the Verbal noun at first as *-inde*, then as *-inke*, and then at last correctly as *-inge*. The misspellings of such a scribe cannot be set up as an authority for Old English. The word *risinde* is not a pres. part., but a misspelling for *risinge*, a Verbal noun, and this noun is preceded by *sunne*, the *Genitive* case, which originally was spelt *sunnan*, then *sunnen*, then *sunne*. So example (1) means "at the time of the *sun's* rising," where "rising" (*risinde*) is a noun, and not

363. Infinitive after Relative Adverbs.—The Infinitive is placed after Relative adverbs in such phrases as the following:—

He did not know *how to write* (=the way to write).
He was not told *when to come* (=the time for coming).
I wish I knew *where to begin* (=the place for beginning).

Here the Relative adverb stands for the corresponding noun denoting manner, time, place, etc. Similarly, *somehow* stands for "some way or manner"; *somewhere* stands for "some place."

364. Infinitive after Relative Pronouns.—This occurs in such sentences as the following:—

(*a*) He had no money *with which to buy* food.

This is equivalent to "He had no money to buy food *with it*"; or "He had no money to buy food *with*" (§ 161).

(*b*) He is not such a fool *as to say* that.

Here the construction is elliptical. "He is not such a fool as *he would be* a fool to say (=for saying, or if he said) that."

365. "Of" followed by a Possessive.—This occurs in such phrases as "that book *of James's*," "that handsome face *of my father's*," "that book *of yours*."

Two explanations have been offered—both conceivable:—

(1) "Of my father's" is an ellipse for "of my father's faces." Here "faces" is the Object to "of" used in a Partitive sense. This is good grammar, but bad sense, since "my father" cannot have more than one face. But it is defensible on grounds of analogy with instances where it makes sense, as in "That book of my father's (books)."

(2) "Of my father's" is a Double Possessive. This explanation is the most natural, and seems to be the right one. The construction so explained has been called "the French Prepositional Idiom combined with the English Inflectional Idiom."—ABBOTT.

Note.—The ambiguity of the preposition "of" is removed by

---

a pres. part. Ex. (2) is equally clear. Here *sunne*, as before, is a Genitive case coupled with the Verbal noun *goyng-down*.

I am glad to find that the account which I have given of the above use of Participles is in substantial agreement with that given at an earlier date by Dr. Abbott in § 405 of *How to Parse*. Here he not only gives the same explanation that I do, but in a footnote he sanctions the phrase, "Gerundive use of participles." In the text he calls it "the Noun-use of the Participle," which is really the same thing; for a gerund is closely akin to a verbal noun (see §§ 138, 141, 142).

I am also glad to see that Mr. Sweet, in his *New English Grammar*, § 2330, calls the participle in such constructions a "half gerund." He thus endorses the explanation which I had given several years before his own grammar was published, although I do not suppose for a moment that he had seen or even heard of the grammar written by me more than ten years before the date of his own publication.

placing a Possessive noun after it. Thus, "a picture of the Queen" means a picture consisting of a likeness of the Queen. But "a picture of the *Queen's*" means a picture of which the Queen is owner.

The construction by which "of" is placed before a Possessive is not a modern idiom, but is frequently met with so far back as Chaucer, and has continued in constant use up to the present day :—

An old felawe (fellow, partner) *of youres.*—*Pardoner's Tale.*
A trusty frende *of Sir Tristram's.*—MALORY (15th cent.).

366. "Of" in the sense of Apposition.—This can be traced back as far as the fifteenth century :—

He was a ryght good knight *of a yonge man.*
MALORY (15th cent.).
There was in the castell a vii score prisoners *of Frenchmen.*
BERNERS (16th cent.).
This frail sepulchre *of our flesh.*—SHAKESPEARE, *Rich. II.* i. 3.

Compare the modern phrases "a fool *of a man*"; "the two *of us*" (=we two); "he made an ass *of himself*"; "he made a great success *of it*" (=made it a great success); "the sum *of* 40 *pounds.*"

The use of "*of*" in an appositional sense is common before Proper names :—

The island *of* Ceylon. The province *of* Ulster. The city *of* Paris. The continent *of* Asia. The county *of* Kent. The lake *of* Geneva. The title *of* colonel. The name *of* Brighton.

On the other hand, we cannot place "*of*" before the Proper names of rivers, mountains, or capes. Thus we cannot say "the river *of* Thames"; "the mountain *of* Blanc"; "Cape *of* St. Vincent."

367. "Of" in Adverbial Phrases.—This is seen in such phrases as *of course, of necessity, of a truth,* and in reference to time, *of a Sunday*: "He used to come here of a Sunday." This use of "*of*" has superseded the Possessive inflection -*s*, which used to be freely used for forming adverbs from nouns, and is not even now extinct. It was common in Tudor English :—

The other two would straightway-*s* balance it.—BACON.
Anyway-*s* afflicted or distressed.—*Prayer-book.*
He would have tickled you other gate-*s* (in another way or gate than he did).—*Twelfth Night,* v. 1, 198.
Come a little nearer this way-*s.*—*Merry Wives of Windsor,* ii. 1, 50.
'Tis but early day-*s.*—*Troilus and Cressida,* iv. 5, 12.

The Possessive inflection is sometimes attached to a phrase formed with a noun and the prep. *be* (=by) or *a* (=on).

Be-time-*s*, be-side-*s*, un-a-ware-*s*, now-a-day-*s*, a-night-*s* (colloquial), a-Sunday-*s* (colloquial).

Other examples of Possessive Adverbs are seen in such words as the following, all of which, whatever their spelling may now be, were originally Possessives :—

Need-*s*, el-*se* (A.S. ell-es), sin-*ce*, then-*ce*, hen-*ce*, when-*ce*, on-*ce* (A.S. *án-es*), twi-*ce*, thri-*ce*, sometime-*s*, alway-*s*, sideway-*s*, lengthway-*s*, the while-*s*(t), again-*s*(t), amid-*s*(t), eftsoon-*s* (archaic), longway-*s*, backward-*s*, wondrou-*s* (a corruption of wonder-*s*).

368. Participle expanded into a Clause.—Participles must of course be parsed as Verbal Adjectives qualifying their nouns. But sometimes there is a further *meaning* implied in them, which can be more fully expressed by expanding them into clauses.

(*a*) *Time.*

Walking along the street (= *while* I was walking), I met a friend.
Having met my friend (= *after* I had met my friend), I went back with him to his house.

(*b*) *Cause or Reason.*

Being tired (= *because* he was tired) with the toil, he sat down to rest.
The letter, *having been addressed* (= *because* it was addressed) to the wrong house, never reached me.

(*c*) *Condition.*

Turning to the left (= *if* you turn to the left), you will find the place you want.

(*d*) *Concession or Contrast* (rare).

Admitting (= though I admit) what you say, I still think that you made a mistake.
He *being* dead (= although he is dead) yet speaketh.—*New Testament.*

369. Participle with Implied Noun or Pronoun :—

(*a*) *Having stated* our first reason, the second must now be taken up and disposed of.
(*b*) *Defeated* on all sides, his courage began to fail.

In (*a*) the construction cannot be defended, although the mistake is often made. It would be correct if we added the words "by us" at the end of the sentence, because the participle "having stated" would then qualify the pronoun "us."

In (*b*) the construction, besides being very common in practice, is defensible, because "his" = *of him*, and "defeated" qualifies the implied pronoun "*him.*" See below, § 372.

370. Participial Prepositions.—There are some prepositions of participial or adjectival origin. These participles and adjectives were once used absolutely [in the manner described in § 176 (5)] with nouns, which have now become the objects of the prepositions.

He went *past* the house (the house having been passed).
All *except* two (two being excepted).
During two weeks (two weeks (en)during or continuing).
All *save* three (three being safe, saved, or reserved).
Notwithstanding his age (his age not-withstanding or not preventing).

Note.—"Notwithstanding" is still often placed as an Absolute participle after its noun:—

Fog notwithstanding (=not preventing) there was a large attendance yesterday afternoon.—*Daily Telegraph*, p. 9, 12th Dec. 1905.

There are other prepositions that have come from participles used as Impersonal Absolutes; see § 190 (*b*), *Note* 2.

Regarding this matter, what is your opinion?
Considering his age, he has done well.

Compare *touching*, *owing to*, *concerning*, *respecting*, etc.

371. Perfect Infinitive.—On the idiomatic use of the Perfect form of the Infinitive the student is referred to § 124.

372. Personal Possessives.—In Old English *mine*, *thine*, *our*, and *your* (=A.S. *mín*, *thín*, *úre*, *eówer*) had two distinct functions—(1) as independent pronouns in the Possessive case, where we now have to say *of me*, *of thee*, *of you*, *of us*; (2) as adjectives, declined in A.S. like other adjectives, so as to be in the same number, gender, and case as the noun following.

In Mod. Eng. function (1) is obsolete; yet some traces of it can be seen in such examples as the following:—

(1) Having heard of A.'s death, *my* mind was much disturbed.

Here *my*=*of me*, and the implied *me* is qualified by "having heard."

(2) Poor is *our* sacrifice, whose eyes
Are lighted from above.—NEWMAN.

Here *our*=*of us*, and *us* is the antecedent to "whose."

(3) Have I not *all their* letters to meet me in arms?—1 *Henry IV.* ii. 3, 28.

Here *all their letters* mean "letters from them all"; and *all* qualifies the pronoun *them*.

(4) At *your only* choice (=at the choice of you only).—*Coriol.* i. 9, 36.

(5) I took *her* leave (=leave of her) at Court.—*All's Well that Ends Well*, v. 3, 79.

(6) But I have sworn to frustrate *both their* hopes (=the hopes of both of them).—MARLOWE.

(7) Tell her 'tis *all our* ways (=the ways of all of us); it runs in the family.—SHERIDAN.

(8) Hungry and thirsty, *their* soul fainted in them.—*Psalms* cvii. 5.

(9) 'Tis liberty of heart derived from heaven,
Bought with *his* blood, who gave it to mankind.—COWPER.

(10) Nor mourn ye less *his* perished worth,
Who bade the conqueror go forth.—SCOTT.

The common phrase "in my despite" means "in spite of me"; cf. the obsolete phrase "maugre myn," which in the Middle period of English meant the same thing as "in my despite." (*Maugre* is from Old French *maugré*, Middle French *mal-gré*, ill will).

Note.—A construction similar to the above is used with nouns in the Possessive case as well as with Pronouns:—

(1) *Perched* on his wonted eyrie high
Sleep sealed the *tercelet's* wearied eye.—SCOTT.

Here the participle "perched," notwithstanding its distance, must be construed with the Possessive noun "tercelet's."

(2) Creation's *heir*, the world, the world is *mine*.—GOLDSMITH.

Here the noun "heir" is in apposition with the pronoun "me" implied in *mine* (=of me).

373. Phrases and words suggested by French:—

(*a*) "How do you *do*?" See chap. xxix. (48), where it is shown that *do* is a translation of the French *faire*.

(*b*) "It's *me*." A translation of Fr. "c'est *moi*"; see chap. xxix. (62).

(*c*) "The window *gives* upon the street." Here *gives* is a translation of the Fr. *donne*, which, though lit. "gives," means *looks, abuts*. Here we must parse *gives* as a Transitive verb used Intransitively on the principle shown in § 93 (*b*).

(*d*) "That goes *without saying*." A translation of Fr. *sans dire*; so evident that there is no need to mention it.

(*e*) "That subject came *upon the carpet*." A translation of Fr. *sur le tapis*; we often say "on the *tapis*," that is, on the tablecloth, before the meeting. "Carpet" once meant a covering of any kind, a tablecloth as much as a floorcloth.

(*f*) "*As to*," followed by a noun: "I am indifferent *as to* his success." A translation of Fr. *quant à*, as much as relates to. See explanation in chap. xxix. (15). The phrase *as to* is at least as old as Wyclif.

(*g*) "*Solidarity* of interests." A phrase lately borrowed from French Communists. Entire union of interests.

(*h*) "He *affects* the latest fashion." Translation of Fr. *affect-er*, follows, adopts.

(*i*) "To *exploit* a new invention." From Fr. *exploit-er*, to make the most of for the sake of trade, to utilise to the utmost.

374. Possessive Case.—On the three senses in which this case can be used, the student is referred to § 43, *Note* 2. In Shakespeare we have the Descriptive use of the Possessive (see again § 43, *Note* 2, *c*) exemplified in a Proper name:—

And wither'd Murder,
Alarum'd by his sentinel, the wolf,
With *Tarquin's* ravishing strides, towards his design
Moves like a ghost.—*Macbeth*, ii. 1.

375. Shall and will in Interrogative sentences:—

In Assertive sentences, *merely future time* is denoted by "shall" in the First person, and by "will" in the Second and Third; a *command* is denoted by "shall" in the Second and Third persons; an *intention* is denoted by "will" in the First person (see § 115).

In Interrogative sentences, however, the change of situation from asserting a fact to asking a question modifies to some extent the uses of "shall" and "will." The meanings of "shall" and "will," when they are used interrogatively, are shown in the following examples, which apply to the Plurals no less than to the Singulars:—

Shall I?	(*a*) *Shall I* be sixteen years old to-morrow? (Here the "shall" merely inquires after something future.) (*b*) *Shall I* post that letter for you? (Here the "shall" inquires about a command. Do you command or desire me to post that letter for you?)
Will I?	(This is not used at all, because "will" in the First person would imply intention, and it would be foolish to ask such a question about oneself.
Shall you?	*Shall you* return home to-day? (This is not at all uncommon. It merely inquires about something future. It cannot imply command, because it would be foolish to inquire of any one whether he commands himself to do so and so.)
Will you?	(*a*) *Will you* return home to-day=*shall you* (merely future time). (*b*) *Will you* do me this favour? (Here the "will" denotes willingness or intention. Are you *willing* or do you *intend* to do me this favour? Hence "will you" is the form used for asking a favour.)
Shall he?	*Shall he* call for the doctor? (Here the "shall" implies a command. Do you desire or command him to call for the doctor?)
Will he?	*Will he* be fourteen years old to-morrow? (Here the "will" merely inquires about something future.)

376. Transitive use of Intransitives.—It has been shown already in §§ 98-101 how Intransitive verbs can be made to assume a Transitive sense. A further method is exemplified in such sentences as the following:—

(1) She will *sing* the savageness out of a bear.—SHAKESPEARE.

That is, She will *drive* the savageness out of a bear *by her singing.*

(2) A foot that might have *danced*
The greensward into greener circles.—TENNYSON.

That is, A foot that might have *changed* the greensward into greener circles *by its dancing*.

(3) Dashed on every rocky square,
Their surging charges *foamed* themselves away.—TENNYSON.

That is, Their surging charges *dispersed themselves in foam*, as a wave disperses itself on rocks.

Note.—It can scarcely be doubted that in the composition of these two lines Tennyson was indebted to *Par. Lost*, vi. 18-20.

Or surging waves against a solid rock,
Though all to shivers dashed, the assault renew
(Vain battery !) and in froth and bubble end.

377. "Thou" and "thee" supplanted by "you."—In the fourteenth century, and throughout the Tudor period, *you* was the more formal, distant, and respectful mode of address, and *thou* the more familiar, such as a father could use to a son, but not a son to a father :—

(1) *Grat.* I have a suit to *you*.
Bass. *You* have obtained it.
Grat. *You* must not deny me. I must go with *you* to Belmont.
Bass. Why, then *you* must. But hear *thee*, Gratiano ;
Thou art too wild, too rude, and bold of voice.
Merchant of Venice, ii. 2. 187-190.

So long as the two friends are talking to each other in a formal way on a matter of business, they adopt the respectful and more distant *you*. But as soon as the one begins to address the other in a more confidential and intimate tone, he at once uses the more familiar *thee* and *thou*.

(2) All that Lord Cobham did was at *thy* instigation, *thou* viper ! for I *thou* thee, *thou* traitor.

This language was used at Sir Walter Raleigh's trial (A.D. 1603), when Coke, finding that argument and evidence were wanting, insulted the illustrious prisoner by applying to him the familiar "*thou*."

378. True Singulars used as Plurals.—By a "True Singular" it is meant that the final *s* is part of the original Singular noun, and not a sign of the Plural. Such nouns, though Singular by etymology, are liable to be considered Plural on account of the final *s* :—

Summons (Fr. *semonce*).—This noun is still correctly used as a Singular; as "I received *a* summons to attend"; "*This* summons reached me to-day." The plural form is *summonses*.

Alms (A.S. *ælmesse*).—"He asked *an alms*" (New Testament). But now the word is generally used as if it were Plural; as, "I gave alms to the beggar, and for *these* he thanked me."

Eaves (A.S. *efese*).—The edge or lower borders of the roof of a house. The word is now always used as a Plural; as, "The eaves *are* not yet finished."

Riches (Fr. *richesse*).—This too is really a Singular; as, "In one hour *is* so great riches come to naught" (New Testament); but now, on account of the final *s*, this noun is always used as a Plural; as, "Riches *do* not last for ever."

379. True Plurals used as Singulars.—In such nouns the final *s* is really a sign of the Plural:—

Amends.—This is sometimes used as a Singular and sometimes as a Plural; as, "*An* honourable amends" (Addison).

Means.—This is now almost always used as a Singular; as, "By *this* means."

News.—This is now almost always used as a Singular; as, "Ill news *runs* apace."

Innings.—This word is used as a Singular; as, "We have not yet had *an* innings."

Gallows.—The frame-work from which criminals are hanged. This noun is used as a Singular; as, "They fixed up *a* gallows."

Odds.—A word used in betting, to denote the difference of one wager against another. "We gave him *a* heavy odds against ourselves."

380. Verbal noun in -ing.—The suffix *-ing* is from A.S. *-ing* or (as it was more commonly spelt) *-ung*. A word formed by adding *-ing* to a verb-stem, as "binding," was a noun pure and simple. The *-ung* or *-ing* was purely a noun-forming suffix, like *-th* in steal-*th*, or *-r* in stai-*r*, or *-l* in aw-*l*, or *-m* in doo-*m*. Though we now call such a word a gerund, it is properly speaking a noun in Modern English also. In this respect there is no breach of continuity from the time of Alfred the Great up to the present day.

As we approach the modern period, the habit grew up of omitting the preposition *of* after such nouns; cf. a similar omission in "on board (of) ship," "a thousand (of) pounds," "a many (of) tears," "despite (of) those riches" (Scott). Thus men began to say "showing compassion" for "showing (of) compassion." The omission of the preposition "of" made the noun "showing" look like a verb with the noun "compassion" as its object. "Showing" as a Pres. part. was known to be a verb already, and so "showing," the abstract noun, looked like a verb also.

It was thus the identity in form between the Pres. part. "show-*ing*" and the abstract noun "show-*ing*" which gave rise to the notion that the latter must be a verb like the former; and it was the omission of the preposition "of" which completed the illusion.

When the abstract noun "showing" was thus made out to be a part of the verb "show," it was very easy to coin a Past form "having shown" corresponding to the form of the Past participle :—

He was praised for *having shown* compassion.

For words thus used, such as "showing" and "having shown," "grammarians in despair have invented the term *gerund*" (Skeat); and we must now accept these forms as "developments of modern English" (Sweet).

But it should be clearly understood that there is no connection whatever between this modern Gerund and the old Gerundial Infinitive. The latter invariably ended in *-anne*, or *-enne*, or simply *-en*, until (by about A.D. 1500) the inflexion died out altogether. The final *-enne* never took the form of *-inge* or *-ing*, and in fact it has no connection with it whatever.

381. "Ye" supplanted by "you."—In Old English, and in the English Bible, *ye* (= A.S. *gé*) is a Nominative, and *you* (= A.S. *eów*) is an Accusative or a Dative :—

Ye have not chosen me, but I have chosen *you*.—*John* xv. 16.

But prior to the date of the first Authorised Version some confusion had already been springing up in profane literature. Hence in the Elizabethan dramatists and later, when our language was still in some respects unsettled, we find *ye* and *you* apparently used indiscriminately, as if there was no difference between them :—

I do beseech *ye*, if *you* bear me hard.—*Julius Cæsar*, iii. 1. 157.
His wrath, which one day will destroy *ye* both.—*Par. Lost*, ii. 734.
Believe it, Lords and Commons, they who counsel *ye* to such a suppressing (of knowledge) do as good as bid *ye* suppress yourselves.—MILTON, *Areopagitica*.

Note.—*Ye* took the place of *you* in such examples as the above, because the unaccented *you* was pronounced as *y'*,—a sound very unlike that of the accented *you*. It was written as *ye*, because this spelling, though far from suitable, made a nearer approach to the sound of *y'* than the spelling of *you* did. We still say colloquially, "I tell *yer*," though this is chiefly heard in low life.

CHAPTER XXIX.—IDIOM AND CONSTRUCTION—*Continued.*

382. Alphabetical Order.—The present chapter is a continuation of the preceding. It deals with phrases and words rather than with constructions; but the distinction cannot always be preserved. In this chapter, as in that, it was found more convenient to the writer (as it certainly will be to the reader) to arrange the contents in alphabetical order.

(1) **All but.** This means "everything except," "everything short of." Here *all* is used as a noun, and *but* is a preposition signifying "except." See § 164.

He is *all but* perfect = He is everything short of being perfect, *i.e.* very nearly perfect.

By supplying the understood gerund "being," we give a grammatical object to the preposition "but." The phrase is now so well established that we may call it an adverbial phrase signifying "very nearly." It is by no means of recent date; for we meet with it in the Stuart period:—

Society is *all but* rude
In this delicious solitude.—MARVELL (1621-1678).

Carlyle in one passage gives it the force of an adjective; but this is a solecism, and is not recommended for imitation:—

The *all but* (=almost complete) omnipotence of early culture.—*Sartor Resartus*, II. ii. 111.

(2) **"All,"** as adverb. The word "all" is used as an adverb in such phrases as those given below. As an adverb it is made to qualify prepositions (§ 160), other adverbs, conjunctions, adjectives, and participles, but not Finite verbs. When it is used as an adverb it generally means "altogether," "completely." Sometimes it has a merely intensive force, especially when it stands before a preposition.

My friend is *all for* (=entirely in favour of) going.
I have *all along* (=from first to last) said so.
It is *all one* (=entirely the same thing) to me.
If you can do it, *all the better* (=better by the whole difference).
She is her mother *all over* (=in every part of her). (*Colloq.*)
It is difficult *all the same* (=nevertheless).
He was *all too* (=much too) sharp, as it proved.
He was *all* (=entirely) covered with dust.
He said that, *all because* (only because) he was angry.
Trust me not at all, or *all* in all (=entirely in everything).

In the sentence last quoted the italicised *all* is the only one that is used adverbially. The line quoted is by Tennyson.

Note.—In the *Book of Judges* ix. 53 we have the following:—

A certain woman cast a piece of a millstone upon Abimelech's head, and *all to brake* his skull.

The italicised words mean "entirely brake or fractured." They are sometimes printed as *all-to-brake*. But *all* is not compounded with the verb *to-brake*; it merely qualifies it, as any other adverb might do. "*To*," however, is an intensifying prefix, and the verb should be written as one word, *to-brake* or *tobrake*. Thus in Wyclif's Bible we have :—

> The veil of the temple was *to-rent*.
> He (Judas) was hanged and *to-burst* the middle.

(3) **"All"** as noun. Besides the phrase "all but" discussed in (1), other examples can be given, in which "all" is used as a noun :—

Death, as the Psalmist says, is certain to *all* (=all men).
All (=everything) that thou seest is mine.
He came out best *after all* (=in spite of everything to the contrary).
Above *all* (=everything else), keep out of debt.
I do not like it at *all* (=at any price, under any terms).
This coat is called an *over-all* (=one that covers everything).
Trust me not at *all*, or all in *all*.

In the line last quoted, the "all" which is not italicised is adverbial, as has been explained in (2).

(4) **All of them, both of them** :—

> All of them (=they all) consented.
> Both of them (=they both) consented.

In phrases like "some of them," "one of them," "two of them," the "*of*" has a partitive sense. Such a sense is, however, impossible where "all" or "both" are concerned. We must therefore conclude that phrases like "all of them," "both of them," have come into use by analogy.

(5) **"Am," "have,"** with Infinitive :—

I am or was to go= } In both the Inf. expresses future time
I have or had to go. } combined with a sense of duty.

Both constructions have come down to us from Old English :—

Hé is *tó cumenne* } = Lat. Ille venturus est.
He is to come } = Eng. He is about-to-come.

Thone calic the ic *tó drincenne* hæbbe } = The cup that I am
The cup that I *to drink* have } = about-to-drink.

Thus in Old Eng. "*be*" was used before an Intrans. verb, "*have*" before a Trans. In Mod. Eng. there is no such distinction.

Note 1.—The tenses of *am* and *was* are the only two that can be used in this construction. Thus we cannot say, "I *shall be* to go," "I *have been* to go," etc. But several other tenses can be used with the verb "have." Thus we can say, "I *shall have* to go," "I *have had* to go," "I *should have* to go," "he *would have* to go," "he *may have* to go," "he *might have* to go," etc.

Note 2.—The Perfect Infinitive cannot be used after *have*, but only after the verb *be*. We can say, "I *was* to have gone" (that is, it was settled for me to go, only something prevented me): but we cannot say, "I *had* to have gone," nor can we say, "I *had* to have drunk."

(6) **An if.** This is a reduplication = if if. *An* is a contraction of *and*, which in the Tudor period sometimes meant "if":—

Extreme self-lovers will set a house on fire, *and* it be but to roast their eggs.—BACON.

But *and if* that evil servant shall say.—*Matt.* xxiv. 48.

Now *an* thou dalliest, I am thy foe.—BEN JONSON.

An if you please to call it a rush candle,
Henceforth I vow it shall be so to me.—*Taming of Shrew*, iv. 5.

When the old meaning of *an* or *and* was forgotten, the *if* was placed after it to remove any doubt as to its meaning.

(7) **And** in Interrogative sentences:—

And art thou cold and lowly laid?—SCOTT.

Here "and" has no conjunctive force, but introduces a form of exclamation:—"Can it be that thou art cold and lowly laid?"

(8) **And all**:—

The soldiers had decamped, horses *and all*.
The strawberry-runners have been planted out, soil *and all*.

"And all" appears to be a more inclusive and more emphatic phrase than *et cetera* (=and the rest), and to have been formed on the same type. The first sentence means, "The soldiers had decamped, with their horses and everything else belonging to them." The second means, "The strawberry runners have been planted out, with their own soil."

The phrase "and all" goes back at least as far as the Tudor period:—

He took the two posts, bar *and all*.—*Judges* xvi. 3.
He razed towns and threw down towers *and all*.—SACKVILLE'S *Induction*.

(9) **As.** The uses and meanings of this word as a conjunction have been explained and exemplified in p. 81, under the five headings of Time, Manner, State, Extent, Reason.

One more use may now be added, though it has become obsolete. In the Tudor period, "as" could be used to denote effect or consequence, being in this sense equivalent to *that*:—

The mariners were so conquered by the storm *as* (=that) they thought it best with stricken sails to yield to be governed by it.—SYDNEY.

If a man have not the penetration of judgment *as* (=that) he can discern, etc.—BACON, *Of Simulation*.

(10) **As**, before a noun :—

(*a*) This box will serve *as* a table.
(*b*) We will not have this man *as* our chief.

The ellipses can be filled up as follows :—

(*a*) This box will serve us *as* a table (would serve us, if we had a table).
(*b*) We will not have this man *as* (in the way in which we would have) our chief.

(11) **As**, before an adjective :—

He considered the report *as* false.

That is, "He considered the report *as* (he would consider it, if it were) false."

(11*a*) **As**, before "*if*" and "*though*" :—

(*a*) He clung to it *as if* his life depended on it.
(*b*) He clung to it *as though* his life depended on it.

(*a*) "He clung to it, as (he would have clung to it), if his life depended on it." (*b*) "He clung to it as (fast as he could have clung to it, for he could not have clung to it faster) though his life depended on it."

(12) **"As best he could"** ("may" or "can") :—

He pacified his opponents *as best he could.*

The phrase italicised is elliptical: "in such a way as he could best do it." It appears to have risen out of the phrase, "as well as." "He did it *as well as* he could." The adverb *well* has been put into the Superlative degree, *best* (which in this connection is also an adverb), and the second *as* has been left out. The idiom "as best," etc., is chiefly used in reference to the doing of something very difficult or even impossible.

The same explanation holds good for "as best he can," or "as best he may." *Can* or *may* is used when the Principal verb is in the Present or Future tense.

(13) **As thee, as me** :—

The nations not so blest as *thee.*—THOMSON.
Even such weak minister as *me*
May the oppressor bruise.—SCOTT.

These Objectives after the conjunction "as" are blunders. The right construction is "not so blest as *thou* (art blest)," and "such weak minister as *I* (am weak)." The apologists of such a blunder might call it "a poetic licence." But writers of prose should keep clear of it.

(14) **As to** :—

I have heard nothing more *as to* that matter.

This phrase is of French origin = *quant à*, an elliptical phrase denoting "as far as relates to," etc. See above, § 373, *f.*

(15) **As to how, as to when, as to whether** :—

He applied to the "Jewish Journal" *as to how* he might best forward a petition to the Empress on his own behalf.—*Times Weekly*, 29th March 1907.

The same explanation holds good as in (14). Here the clause introduced by the Relative adverb is a Noun-clause, which is the object of the Preposition *to*. The phrase "as to how" = as to the manner in which. Although some grammarians have called the phrase *as to* an "offensive parasite," it is certainly useful; it violates no grammatical principle, and is backed by ample authority.

(16) **As usual** :—

He came at four o'clock, *as usual.*

"As" is here used as a conjunction or Relative adverb, and the verb "*is*" is understood after it:—"He came at four o'clock, at what time or in what manner is usual (with him)."

(17) **At best, at its best,** or **at the best** :—

At best he is only a moderate speaker.
He was *at his best* this morning.

In Superlative phrases of very frequent occurrence, such as "at best," "at worst," "at first," "at last," "at most," "at least," no pronoun or article is placed between the preposition and the adjective, unless we wish to particularise.

But in similar phrases that are of less frequent occurrence, a pronoun or the Definite article should be inserted :—

The wind is *at its loudest* or *the loudest.* The storm is *at its fiercest.* To-day the patient is *at his weakest.* The season is now *at its loveliest.* The air is now *at its hottest.*

(18) **At ten years old, at four miles distant** :—

(1) My son was *ten years old* when he died.
(2) My son died *at ten years of age.*
(3) My son died *at ten years old.*

(1) My house is *four miles distant* from the sea.
(2) My house is *at four miles' distance* from the sea.
(3) My house is *at four miles distant* from the sea.

Sentences (1) and (2) in both sets of examples are quite correct. Sentence (3) has arisen from a confusion between the constructions in (1) and (2). This mixed construction is not grammatically correct; and, though it is used by some writers and speakers, it is best to avoid it.

(19) **Away** (after Intrans. verbs) :—

Fight *away*, my men.

This adverb is a contraction for "on-way" (§ 162). It denotes continuity ("go on, continue fighting") and sometimes intensity ("fight hard"), because such action implies movement on the way, not rest or inactivity. After verbs of motion it generally means "off," as "go *away*," "send him *away*."

(20) **Bid fair to**, etc. :—

This institution *bids fair* (=makes a fair or good promise) to flourish for many years to come.

Here the adjective "fair" qualifies some noun implied in the verb "bid": "bids a fair bidding or promise."

(21) **But.**—The uses of this word as a preposition have been shown already in pp. 77, 78, and as a conjunction or as an adverb in p. 82. Its uses as a conjunction or as an adverb will now be shown rather more fully.

(*a*) As a Subordinative conjunction :—

(1) It never rains *but* it pours.—*Proverb.*
(It never rains *except that* it pours, or It never rains without pouring.)
(2) Perdition catch my soul, *but* I love thee.—SHAKESPEARE.
(Perdition catch my soul *if* I do *not* love thee.)
(3) It cannot be *but* Nature hath some Director of infinite power.—HOOKER.
(It cannot be, or it is impossible, *that* Nature hath *not* a Director, etc.)

Note.—This use of "but" as a Subordinative conjunction has arisen from the omission of the conjunction "that." If "that" were expressed, "but" would retain its original character as a preposition signifying "except," and the Noun-clause following it would be its object.

(*b*) As a Subordinative conjunction, with some Demonstrative pronoun understood after it. It then has the force of "*who* or *which* + *not*" (§ 82) :—

No one saw that sight *but* went away shocked.
(No one saw that sight *except that* he went away, or *who* did *not* go away, shocked.)

Note.—It was not always the custom to omit the Demonstrative pronoun after "but." Thus we have in Shakespeare :—

I found no one *but he* was true to me.

(We now usually, though not necessarily, say, "I found no one *but* was true to me.")

(*c*) As an Adversative conjunction of the Co-ordinative class:—

He is rich, *but* discontented.

(*d*) As an Adverb in the sense of "only":—

There is *but* (=only) a plank between us and death.
We can *but* die (nothing worse than death can befall us).

(22) **"But" misused for "than" or "when."**—Avoid the error of using *but* for *than* after "no sooner," or for *when* after "scarcely," "hardly," "not":—

Hardly was Charles dead, *when* the publication of *Eikon Basilike* (the Royal Likeness), which professed to have been written by Charles himself, produced a reaction in his favour.—RANSOME, *History of England*, p. 253. (Correct.)

No sooner do the bells leave off *than* the diligence rattles in.—BROWNING. (Correct.)

Philocles *no sooner* espied the lion *but* she ran to the lodge-ward.—SYDNEY'S *Arcadia*. (Wrong. Change *but* to *than*.)

Nor had we received him on board half an hour *but* we put out to sea.—DE FOE, *Voyage Round the World*, p. 208. (Wrong. Change *but* to *when*.)

He had *scarce* rubbed his eyes, *but* Darius fled.—H. MORE, *Exp. Dan.* ii. 35. (Wrong. Change *but* to *when*.)

(23) **But he, but they.**—The use of a Nominative as object of the preposition "but," though grammatically indefensible, has the support of custom, which cannot be set aside.

What stays (=supports) had I but *they*.—SHAKESPEARE.
You know my father hath no child but *I*.—*Ibid.*
Every one can master a grief but *he* that has it.—*Ibid.*

The boy stood on the burning deck,
Whence all but *he* had fled.—Mrs. HEMANS.

And was he not the earl? 'Twas none but *he*.—W. TAYLOR.

Note 1.—The Nominative after "but" appears to have arisen from a confusion between "but" as an Adversative conjunction of the Co-ordinative class and "but" as a preposition. "Whence all had fled, *but he* had not fled,"—that is, all had fled except him.

Note 2.—In the curious phrase "*But* me no *buts*" (Shakes.), *but* is used as a verb in the Imperative mood, and *buts* as a noun in the Plural number. *Me* is the Dative or indirect object. *Buts* is the direct object. Compare the following in Scott:—"*Woman* me no more than I *woman* you: I have not been called Mistress to be *womaned* by you."—*Peveril of the Peak.*

(24) **But that, but what:**—

(*a*) I cannot say *but what* you may be right.
(*b*) Not *but what* he did his best.
(*c*) For who would fardels bear,
To grunt and sweat under a weary life,
But that the dread of something after death, etc.
Hamlet, iii. 1.

Here "what" has come into use as a substitute for "that." In all these sentences "but" is a preposition signifying "except," to which the following Noun-clause is the object.

(*a*) This sentence could be reworded thus:—"I cannot say anything *except* or *against* the fact that-you-are-right,"—that is, anything to the contrary of your being right.

(*b*) This sentence is elliptical. The ellipse could be filled up as follows:—"I do not say anything except that he did his best, or to the contrary of his having done his best."

(*c*) Here, as before, "but" is a preposition followed by a Noun-clause as its object. In signification **but that** = if not. "If the dread of something after death did not," etc.

(25) **By thousands, by little, by himself,** etc.:—

(*a*) The ants came streaming out *by thousands.*
(*b*) The water oozes out *little by little.*
(*c*) He went out of the room *by himself.*

From denoting cause or agency, the preposition "by" came to denote manner or number; in which sense it often does the work of a Distributive adjective. In (*a*) "by thousands" means "in the manner or to the number of thousands,"—that is, "a thousand at a time," or "one thousand after another." In (*b*) "little by little" is elliptical for "by little and by little"; as in Pope:—

Loth to enrich me with too quick replies,
By little and by little (he) drops his lies.

In (*c*) the phrase "by himself," which is often used for "alone," is founded on the analogy of the above phrases:—"He went out by himself,"—that is, "he went out himself at a time," or "he went out *alone*, unaccompanied by any one else."

(26) **Came to pass, came to be regarded,** etc.—In this construction (which is very common) the Infinitive is not the Simple or Noun-Infinitive, but the Gerundial or Qualifying (§ 127), and the "to" denotes effect or result:—

How *came* her eyes so bright?—*Mids. Night's Dream*, ii. 2.

This is equivalent to saying, How came her eyes to be so bright? or, How did her eyes become so bright?

(27) **Can but, cannot but**:—

(*a*) We *can but* die.
(*b*) We *cannot but* die.

In (*a*) the word "but" is an adverb: "We can *only* die,"—that is, we cannot come to anything worse than death. See (21) *d*. In (*b*) the word "but" retains its original character as a preposition:—"We cannot do anything *except* die." Here "die" is the Noun-Infinitive (§ 127) used as object to the preposition "but."

(28) **Come**:—

(*a*) It will be two years, *come* next Christmas.
(*b*) This is the heir; *come*, let us kill him.—*Matt.* xxi. 38.
(*c*) *Come, come*, no time for lamentation now.—MILTON.

In (*a*) the construction is elliptical. "Come" is here used without an auxiliary (which must be understood) with reference to a definite future time that is expected. "It will be two years, when next Christmas will come." This is a colloquialism, not suited to written composition.

In (*b*) "come" is in the Imperative mood, and is used to excite attention or to invite persons to some joint action.

In (*c*) the repeated "come" (which is in the Imperative mood like the preceding) indicates rebuke.

(29) **Come, go**:—

(*a*) Are you *coming* to the meeting to-day?
(*b*) Are you *going* to the meeting to-day?

In sentence (*a*) the use of the verb "*come*" implies that the questioner himself intends to be present at the meeting, and he inquires whether the person addressed will be present also. The person addressed might say in reply, "Yes, I shall be there with you"; or "No, I shall not join you there."

In sentence (*b*) the use of the verb "*go*" is perfectly general; and hence the person addressed might reply: "Yes, I am going to the meeting; are you?" or "No, I am not going; are you?"

"*Come*" means motion *towards* a person or place; "*go*" means motion *from* a person or place. Thus we say, "The sun is *coming* up," or "the sun is *going* down"; "The plant is *coming* into *flower*," or "the plant is *going* to *seed*,"—that is, it has passed its prime, and is beginning to fade or pass away.

He has *come* to grief.
He has *gone* to the dogs.

These colloquial phrases mean almost the same thing. There is no saying why "come" is used in one and "go" in the other.

(30) **Come and go**.—This combination means "to appear

and disappear," and is much to be preferred on account of its brevity :—

The colour of the king doth *come and go.*—*King John*, iv. 2.

(31) **Dare, dares, dared, durst** :—

(*a*) For I know thou darest,
But this thing (Trinculo, the jester) *dare* not.—SHAKESPEARE.

(*b*) Here boldly spread thy hands; no venomed weed
Dares blister them, no slimy snail *dare* creep.
BEAUMONT AND FLETCHER.

(*c*) That man hath yet a soul, and *dare* be free.—CAMPBELL.

(*d*) Why then did not the ministers use their new law? Because they *durst* not.—MACAULAY.

Dare is one of those verbs which originally was an old past tense, but is now used for a present, and thus "he *dares*" is grammatically as bad as "he *shalls*," "he *mays*," "he *cans*." Nevertheless in the fifteenth century the practice sprang up of using *dares* for *dare* in the Third Person Sing.: the example quoted in (*b*) shows that in the Tudor period the two forms could be used promiscuously.

Durst is a Weak past tense formed by adding the suffix *-te* to the stem *dors*: thus in A.S. the form is *dors-te*. *Durst* is the proper past tense, as in example (*d*), though *dared* has also come into use.

The following uses of *dare, dares, dared*, and *durst* appear to be getting more and more established in current idiom :—

Dare is used for the Third Person Sing. when the sentence is negative, *or* when the Infin. following is unaccompanied by *to* :—

He dare not *go*.
He dare *be* free. See example (*c*).

Dares is used, whenever the sentence is affirmative, *and* whenever the Infin. following is accompanied by *to* :—

He dares *to* insult me.

Dares is also used, whenever the verb is followed by a personal object, in the sense of "challenge" :—

He *dares* me to my face.

Dared is much used with reference to direct assertions, and *durst not* with reference to hypothetical ones :—

He durst not do it = He would not dare to do it.

Durst is not used in affirmative sentences. We do not say, "He durst do it," but "He dared to do it."

(32) **Dependent on, independent of** :—

I am not at all dependent *on* your help.
I am quite independent *of* your help.

These two sentences mean precisely the same thing. Why then is the same preposition not used with both adjectives? "On" is used after "dependent," because this preposition denotes rest, support, as on some foundation. "Of" is used after "independent," because this preposition denotes "separation," and the same meaning is implied in the adjective "independent."

(33) **Do**, in the sentence, "That will do."—The explanation usually given is that this *do* is not from A.S. *do-n*, but from A.S. *dúg-an*, to avail, to be sufficient. Hence "That will do" = That will suffice. This explanation is probably the true one. In Middle English the original verb *dúg-an* took the form of *dow*, and still appears as *dow* in Burns. From *dow* we get the past tense *dowed* or *dought*, whence "doughty." In the Dutch language the verb is spelt as *deug-en*.

(34) **Doubt that, doubt but** :—

(*a*) I do not doubt *that* he is ill.
(*b*) I do not doubt *but* or *but that* he is ill.

These two sentences amount to the same thing. They might be rewritten as follows :—

(*a*) I do not doubt (=question) the fact that he is ill.
(*b*) I do not doubt anything *against* the fact that he is ill.

In (*b*) the word "but" is a preposition, and the Noun-clause "that he is ill" is its object; or if "that" is omitted after "but," the "but" is a conjunction.

Note.—It is only after the verbs "doubt" and "deny" that "but" can be substituted for "that."

(35) **Each other, one another.**—In these phrases we have a Distributive adjective (*each*, *one*) combined with a Demonstrative adjective (*other* or *another*). *Each* is Nom., *other* is Object.; cf. Lat. "alius alium."

(*a*) "**Each other**" is generally used for *two* persons :—
The two men struck *each other* (that is, *each* man struck the *other* man).

(*b*) **One another** is used for *more than two* persons :—
They all helped *one another* (that is, each man helped every other man).

The drift of a Distributive adjective can also be expressed in the following ways :—

(*a*) They went out two *by* two, or *by twos* (in separate pairs).
(*b*) They went out *two and two* (in separate pairs).
(*c*) They went out *two at a time* (in separate pairs).
(*d*) The twenty men had a gun *a piece* (had each a gun).
(*e*) They went to their *respective* homes (each to his own).

Note.—Such phrases as "to each other," "from each other," "with one another," etc. (where *each* or *one* is in the Nominative case), are permitted by English idiom :—

The two men spoke *to each other* =
The two men spoke,—each man spoke,—to the other.

In all such sentences *each* or *one* is in apposition with the preceding noun.

(36) **Either.** This word is usually followed by its correlative "or," and the two together make a pair of correlative conjunctions (§ 294). Sometimes, however, "either" is used independently of "or," and may stand at the beginning, or somewhere in the middle, or at the end, of a sentence.

(*a*) *Either* how canst thou say to thy brother, etc.?—*Luke* vi. 42.
(*b*) If John had said this, or William *either*, I could believe it.
(*c*) If you do not go, I will not go *either*.

In all of these examples "*either*" can be parsed as an *adverb*, signifying "on the other side of the question." It is not here a conjunction, for it joins nothing. The use of "either" exemplified in (*a*), though common in Tudor English, is now almost, or quite, obsolete.

(37) **Elliptical uses of "that" in a Relative sense** :—

(*a*) Equivalent to "when" or "in which time" :—
Now *that* he is dead we must find a successor.
The moment *that* he left the house they pursued him.
(*b*) Equivalent to "with which" :—
He shouted with the loudest voice *that* he could (shout).

Note.—Sometimes the antecedent to "that" is borrowed from the verb of the preceding clause :—

Have you ever met him before? Not (a meeting) *that* I can remember.

(38) **Even** (as an adverb) :—

(*a*) The hearing ear and the seeing eye, the Lord hath made *even* both of them (not merely one, but both alike).—*Prov.* xx. 12.
(*b*) *Even* so (just in the same way) did the Gauls occupy the coast.
(*c*) Thou wast a soldier *even* to Cato's wish (fully up to the level of Cato's wish).—*Coriolanus*, i. 4.

Even is thus an intensifying adverb, signifying "precisely," "quite," "fully up to the mark." In A.S. *efn*, the adjective, means "level." The adverb is from A.S. *efn-e*, which has become *even*.

(39) **Excuse, excuse not**:—

(*a*) I hope you will excuse my coming here to-day.
(*b*) I hope you will excuse my *not* coming here to-day.

These two sentences amount to the same thing, and could be rewritten as follows:—

(*a*) I hope you will excuse (=dispense with, not insist on) my coming here to-day.

(*b*) I hope you will excuse (=pardon) my *not* coming (my neglect to come) here to-day.

Observe that the verb "excuse" is used in different senses in these two sentences. Owing to the ambiguity of the verb "excuse," sentence (*a*) might mean "I hope you will excuse or *pardon* the fact of my having come here to-day." So it is best to avoid construction (*a*).

(40) **Far from, anything but, the reverse of**:—

His manners are *far from* pleasant.
His manners are *anything but* pleasant.
His manners are *the reverse of* pleasant.

These three sentences all mean the same thing. If we insert the gerund "being" before "pleasant," the phrase "being pleasant" is the object of the three prepositions *from*, *but*, and *of*.

(41) **Few, a few, the few.**—Each of these expressions has a distinct meaning of its own:—

(*a*) **Few** is a *Negative* adjective, and signifies "not many":—

He read *few* books (he did *not* read *many* books).

(*b*) **A few** is an *Affirmative* adjective, and signifies "some at least":—a certain number, however few:—

He read *a few* books (that is, he read *some* books *at least*, though the number was small). For a suggested explanation of "a few" see below (65).

(*c*) **The few** implies two statements, *one Negative* and *the other Affirmative*:—

He read *the few* (or *what few*) books he had.
That is (1) The books that he had were not many. (*Negative.*)
(2) He read all the books that he had. (*Affirmative.*)

(42) **First importance, last importance**:—

(*a*) This is a matter of the *first* importance.
(*b*) This is a matter of the *last* importance.

Though "first" and "last" are usually of opposite meanings, yet in the above phrases their meaning is the same. In (*a*) "first" denotes "foremost,"—taking precedence of everything else. In (*b*) "last" denotes "utmost," "greatest,"—which comes to the same thing as "foremost."

The opposite phrase to "of the first or of the last importance" is "of the least importance":—

This is a matter of the *least* importance (=of little or no importance, of less importance than anything else).

(43) **For to,** before an Infinitive. There is a reduplication in this phrase, since the two prepositions, *for* and *to*, both of which express a purpose, are equivalent in meaning. Compare *an if* in No. (6) and *or ere* in No. (82). The phrase *for to* is now obsolete, though it is still heard as a colloquialism in low life. It was once used by the best English writers.

They presently let in their swine *for to trample* their corn-seed into the earth.—HOLLAND'S *Pliny*, xviii. 18.
He carried away all his goods *for to go* to Isaac his father in the land of Canaan.—*Gen.* xxxi. 18.

We still use this idiom in another form by placing a noun or pronoun between the two prepositions. In this construction the inserted noun or pronoun is the object of "for" and the Infinitive is the object of "to."

It is hard *for thee to kick* against the pricks.—*Acts* ix. 5.
there was too much excitement *for the horse to remain* long without a rider.—SCOTT.

(44) **Had as lief, had rather, had better, had as soon,** etc.—These phrases, preceded by a noun or pronoun in the Nominative case and followed by a *to*-less Infinitive, are well-established idioms:—

I had as lief not be, as live to be
In awe of such a thing as I myself.—SHAKESPEARE.
I had rather be a kitten, and cry mew.—SHAKESPEARE.

But the original construction was different. What is now in the Nominative case was once in the Dative (see above, § 360), and some form of the verb *be* was used where we now use *had*:—

And *leever me is* be poure and trewe.—*Cursor Mundi.*
(=And it is more agreeable to me to be poor and true.)

But in the transition between the old and the present constructions we find the Dative case used with *had* instead of the Nominative, and the Nominative used with *be* instead of the Dative:—

A man *were better* relate himself to a statue or picture than, etc.
—BACON, *Of Friendship.*
Poor lady! *she were better* love a dream.—SHAKESPEARE.
You were best hang yourself.—BEAUMONT AND FLETCHER.
Me rather had my heart might feel your love.—SHAKESPEARE.

This is the history of the construction. But in parsing such a sentence as, "I had as lief do this as that," we must now paraphrase it into, "I should have it as agreeable to me to do this as that." Observe that "had" in "I had as lief" is in the Subjunctive mood. *Lief* is from A.S. *léof*, dear, agreeable; cf. *love.*

(45) **He to deceive me**, and similar phrases:—

> (*a*) *I* to be so foolish!
> (*b*) *He* to deceive me!

These exclamatory sentences are elliptical. (*a*) "Am I a person to be so foolish?" (*b*) "Could he be a person to deceive me?" The Infinitive is here Gerundial, and qualifies the noun or pronoun going before. The change of the above sentences from the Interrogative to the exclamatory form has necessitated a corresponding change in the punctuation.

(46) **His**, as a Possessive inflection after Proper names. The Possessive inflection *-es* was sometimes spelt as *-is*. As this syllable was sometimes written apart from the noun, especially if the noun was a foreign Proper Name, it became confounded with *his*, owing to the uncertainty of the initial "*h*." (On the uncertainty of *h* see above, § 230.)

> Argal *his* brother.—LAYAMON, A.D. 1200.
> Decius Cæsar *his* tyme.—TREVISA, A.D. 1380.
> For Jesus Christ *his* sake.—*English Prayer-book.*
> Tongues in Heliogabalus *his* kitchen—DEKKER, 1609.

Note.—It was once supposed that the *his* gave rise to the Possessive *-es* or *'s*. This theory is ridiculous, for two reasons—(1) the Possessive suffix *s* gave rise to the Possessive pronoun *his*, and not *vice versa*; (2) the same suffix is used with Feminine nouns, as "Jane's bonnet," and with Plural nouns, "men's work." We could never have said, "Jane *his* bonnet," or "men *his* work."

(47) **His**, as neuter, superseded by "*its*." "Its" has displaced the Old English neuter "his," which lasted not only throughout the Tudor period, but far into the Stuart period.

> As the star moves not but in *his* sphere.—*Hamlet*, iv. 7.
> Put up again thy sword in *his* place.—*Matt.* xxvi. 22.

Along with this use of *his* in a neuter sense we find in the fourteenth century an uninflected Possessive *hit*, which in the Tudor period appears in the unemphatic form of *it*, the initial *h* having been lost through want of accent.

> The hedge-sparrow fed the cuckoo so long,
> That it's (= it has) had *it* head bit off by *it* young.—*King Lear*, i. 4.

Such a monstrosity as a Possessive *it* could not remain in force for ever. But *its*, the form now universally used before a neuter noun, took a long time in coming. It occurs only three times in Milton's *poetry* (this does not apply to his prose), only once (*Lev.* xxv. 5) in the version of the Bible printed in 1611, and in only a few passages in Shakespeare. Dryden is the first great writer who is quite familiar with its use, besides being quite consistent himself in using it.

His as a neuter Possessive (= its) is found as late as 1670.

Goutwart (a vegetable substance) easeth the pains of the gout, and had not *his* name for nothing. (Quoted in *Oxford Dict.* under *His*, p. 301, third column.)

(48) **How do you do?**—

The first *do* is the Auxiliary, which is used for asking a question in the present or past (Indefinite) tense (§ 114).

The second *do* may be explained as an imitation, or rather translation, of the French *faire*, in the old French sentence: *Comment faites-vous?* How do you make or do?

It has been also suggested that *do* is from A.S. *dúg-an*, to will. This is possible; see above (33). But more probably the phrase "How do you do" is an adaptation from French.

(49) **I do you to wit** (from A.S. *dón tó witanne*).

This quaint and almost obsolete expression means "I cause you to know." In Old English the verb *dó-n* (= do) meant (amongst other things) "cause," and this was very freely used in Middle English, when our language had lost the power of forming fresh Causal verbs, like *raise* from *rise*. See § 99.

Moreover, brethren, we *do you to wit* of the grace of God bestowed on the churches of Macedonia (2 *Cor.* viii. 1).

(50) **I beg to**, etc.:—

I *beg* to inquire whether I may go home.

This is a common ellipse for "I beg leave to," etc. It is now more common to omit the noun "leave" than to insert it.

(51) **I take it**:—

You will win in that case, *I take it.*

This is a common phrase for "in my opinion."

(52) **I was given to understand**:—

If this sentence is converted from the Passive form to the Active, it becomes:—"Some one gave or caused me to understand." Here "me" is the Indirect object, and "to understand" (Noun-Infinitive) is the Direct. By the rule given in

§ 106, a verb which has two objects in the Active voice can retain one in the Passive. Hence in the sentence "I was given to understand," the Noun-Infinitive ("to understand") is *Retained object* to the Passive verb "was given."

(53) **I wis**: this is now used by poets, as if it were a verb in the first person, = I know.

> Our ship, *I wis*,
> Shall break in other form than this.
> —LONGFELLOW.

> *I wis* in all the Senate
> There was no heart so bold.—MACAULAY.

In reality, however, it is an adverb signifying "certainly," or "probably," A.S. *gewis*, which in Middle English was respelt as *ywis* or *iwis*. The last spelling made it look like a verb in the first person. In the following examples *ywis* or *iwisse* is merely an adverb:—

> "*Ywis*," quod he, "it is full dear, I say."
> —CHAUCER (1340-1400).

> *I-wisse*, all their sport in the park is but a shadow to that pleasure that I find in Plato.—ASCHAM (1515-1568).

> A right good knight and true of word *ywis*.
> —SPENSER (1552-1599).

(54) **If.**—This conjunction has three different uses:—

(*a*) For asking a question in the Indirect form of narration:—

> I asked him *if* (=whether) he would return soon.

(*b*) For expressing a condition or supposition:—

> *If* you return to us to-morrow (=in case you return, or in the event of your returning), we shall be glad to see you.

(*c*) For making an admission or concession. (Here the verb must be Indicative, because it concedes something as a *fact*.)

> *If I am* dull (=though I admit that I am dull), I am at least industrious. (I am dull *indeed*, *but* industrious all the same.)
> Considering how ill I was, it is no wonder *if* (=that) I made some mistakes yesterday.

Note.—The use of *if* in sense (*a*) might in some contexts be confounded with its use in sense (*b*). Should there be any such risk, it would be better to substitute *whether* for *if* in sense (*a*).

(55) **If only.**—This phrase is sometimes used to express a wish. In such cases the clause containing it is not followed by any clause expressing the consequent.

> If only gold could be found on this estate!

This is equivalent to saying, "If only gold could be found on this estate, we should be very fortunate."

(56) **If you like, if he likes :—**

You can do this, *if you like* : so can he, *if he likes.*

We now regard *you* as the subject of the verb *like* ; and this construction is so well established in usage, that we can also say, *if he likes, if we like*, etc. But originally the wording was, "If it like you," *i.e.* if it be agreeable to you. Cf. what Shakespeare says in *Hamlet*, "it likes us well." Here "like" or "likes" is an impersonal verb, followed by a pronoun in the Dative case ; § 360 (*c*). In the sentence "if it like you," the verb "like" is in the Subjunctive mood after "if."

(57) **In respect of, with respect to :—**

He is senior to me *in respect of* service.
We must have a talk *with respect to* that subject.

In such sentences as the above the phrases quoted are not identical in meaning. "In respect of" means "in point of," and qualifies the adjective "senior." "With respect to" means ncerning" or "about," and qualifies the verb "talk."

He is senior to me *in point of* service.
We must have a talk *on* that subject.

This distinction, however, is not always observed ; for we find "in respect of" used (with questionable propriety) in almost any kind of context. In the following example it signifies "on account of," or "on the grounds of" :—

The position that he has gained is entirely his due *in respect of* his long fidelity to the Liberal party.—*Daily Telegraph*, 12th December 1905, p. 9.

This use of the phrase, though it is uncommon, cannot be considered wrong ; for the phrase was so used in the Tudor period.

They dedicated an altar to Friendship *in respect of* (= on account of) the great dearness of friendship between them two.—BACON, *Of Friendship*.

Under no circumstances should the two phrases be mixed, as they are in the following :—

He was unable to say whether *in respect to* the regulations on food he would see that equality was maintained on British and on foreign vessels.—Quoted in *Daily Telegraph*, 21st March 1905, p. 7.

(58) **In that :—**

In that he died, he died unto sin once.—*New Testament*.

The words "in that" might be called a conjunctional phrase. But strictly speaking *in* is a preposition, having as its object the noun-clause "that he died." Here *that* is the Introductory conjunction, or if we say, "In the fact that," it is the conjunction of Apposition. See § 169 (*a*).

(59) **In thorough working order**:—

Here "thorough" is an adjective qualifying the compound noun "working-order" (order suitable for working). The two nouns should be joined by a hyphen. It does not qualify either *working* or *order*, but the compound noun made up of both.

(60) **It.**—This pronoun has three distinct modes of reference:—

(*a*) To a *noun* going before. In this sense it is merely a Demonstrative pronoun used in the ordinary way:—

The sun has risen; *it* (= the sun) shines brightly.

(*b*) To a *clause* going before:—

I have treated him as he deserved; and he knows *it*. (Here "it" points to the clause "I have treated him as he deserved.")

(*c*) To a *phrase* or *clause* coming after:—

{ *It* is sad *to hear such bad news*. (*Phrase.*)
{ It—viz. "to hear such bad news"—is sad.
{ *It* is probable *that rain will fall to-day*. (*Clause.*)
{ It—viz. "that rain will fall to-day"—is probable.

Sometimes the word "*it*" is used instead of some Personal pronoun to express endearment or contempt:—

What a pretty little girl *it* is (= she is)! (*Endearment.*)
What an ass *it* is (= that man is)! (*Contempt.*)

Sometimes this word is made the cognate object of an Intransitive verb, as has been shown in § 96 (*c*).

Whether the charmer sinner *it* or saint *it*,
If folly grow romantic, I must paint it.—POPE.

Here "sinner" and "saint" are used as verbs. "Sinner it" means "act the part of a sinner": "saint it" means "act the part of a saint." The *it* at the end of the second line is used in the same way as in (*a*); for it merely refers to "folly" going before.

(61) **It,** as subject of Impersonal verbs: see § 148.

(*a*) Impersonal verbs denoting *physical* events were used with "it" in Old English, as now, and were not less common:—

Hit rinth = *it* rains. *Hit* fréoseth = *it* freezes.

(*b*) But verbs denoting *mental feelings* have undergone an important change. The Dative of the person (§ 360, *c*) has become the Subject, in the Nominative case. The change was gradual, and Impersonal verbs were more common in Shakespeare's time than now:—[1]

It yearns me not.—*Hen. V.* iv. 3.
It dislikes me.—*Othel.* ii. 3, 49.
It likes us well.—*Hamlet*, i. 2, 81.
Where it thinks (seems) best unto your royal self.—*Rich. III.* iii. 1.

Sometimes the "it" was not expressed, as in "meseems," "methinks" (§ 148). An example occurs so late as A.D. 1784:—

There they are free
And howl and war, as *likes them*, uncontrolled.
—COWPER, *Task*, vi. 405.

In the Tudor period we sometimes meet with sentences in which the two constructions are mixed. Such mixture marks the transition from the Impersonal to the Personal.

The king said to him that whatsoever he were, *he should not repent him* (=it should not repent him, or he should not repent) of putting himself into his (the king's) hands.—BACON, *Hist. of Hen. VII.*

(62) **It's me, that's him**:—

These phrases are condemned by grammarians, because "me" and "him" are Subjective complements to the verb "is," and such complements must be in the same case as the Subject,—that is, in the Nominative case (see § 176, 2).

Nothing can be said in defence of "that's him."

It is better grammar to say "it is I" than "it's me." But the phrase "it's me" has been defended on two grounds: (1) because it is the counterpart and exact translation of the French "*c'est moi*," which is recognised as an established idiom by the best French writers; (2) because "me" is an adopted or borrowed objective of "I," and might be used as a complement, though not as a subject.

(63) **Lesser, less.**—"Lesser" is a Double Comparative, which is used for euphony to balance the sound of "greater":—

The *greater* light to rule the day, and the *lesser* light to rule the night.—*Old Testament.*

Note.—Observe "lesser" is always an adjective. But "less" may be either an adjective or an adverb.

[1] "An abundance of Impersonal verbs is a mark of a very early stage in a language, denoting that a speaker has not yet arrived so far in his development as to trace his own actions and feelings to his own agency."—ABBOTT, *Shakspearian Grammar*, p. 208.

(64) **Little, a little, the little.**—Each of these expressions has a distinct meaning of its own :—

(*a*) **Little** is a *negative* adjective, and means "not much."

He had *little* money (= not much money).

(*b*) **A little** is an *affirmative* adjective, and means "some at least" :—a certain quantity, however little.

He had *a little* money (=some money at least, although the amount was small). For a suggested explanation of "a little" see below (65).

(*c*) **The little** implies two statements—one *negative*, and the other *affirmative.*

He spent *the little* (or *what little*) money he had.
That is—(1) The money he had was not much. (*Negative.*)
(2) He spent all the money that he had. (*Affirmative.*)

Note.—When "little" and "a little" are used as Adverbs, the same distinction holds good :—

I *little* expected (=did not expect) such treatment.
I am *a little* (rather, slightly) tired.

(65) **Many a, a many.**—The former phrase is followed by *Singular* nouns, and the latter by *Plural* ones :—

(*a*) **Many a.**—Here "a" = "one"; "many a man" means "many times one man," or "many men." Hence "many" has here the force of a Multiplicative numeral (§ 51) :—

Many a youth and *many a* maid
Dancing 'neath the greenwood shade.—MILTON.

(*b*) **A many.**—Here "many" has the force of a *Collective noun*, and "*of*" is understood after it :—

They have not shed *a many tears,*
Dear eyes, since first I knew them well.—TENNYSON.

A many of our bodies.—SHAKESPEARE, *Hen. V.* iv. 3.
A many of us were called together.—LATIMER.
This many summers on a sea of glory.—*Hen. VIII.*

In prose it is more common to put in the word "great" between *a* and *many*. "A great many men" means "a large number *of* men," the "*of*" being understood, and *many* being a Collective noun. Similarly in such a phrase as "a few books," we might regard *a few* as a Collective noun, the "*of*" being understood after it. In the phrase "a little money" we might similarly regard "a little" as a noun denoting quantity,—"a little (of) money." Compare "the whole of the day."

Note.—In Old English "menigu" was a Collective *Noun*, signifying "a multitude or large number," and "manig" was an Indefinite Numeral *Adjective*, signifying "many." In Modern English the same word "many" stands for both; for it is equivalent to "menigu" in the phrase *a many*, and to "manig" in the phrase *many a* or simply *many*.

Definite Numeral Quantities are sometimes Collective nouns, where "*of*" must be understood after them in Mod. Eng. In Mid. Eng. the sense of *of* was expressed by the Possessive Plural. Similarly, in A.S. *twelf scēapa* means "twelve of sheep." All numerals in A.S. were followed by a Possessive Plural

> *A dozen* (of) sheep; *a million* (of) apples.
> *A hundred* (of) years; *a thousand* (of) years.
> *A hundred-thousand* (of) years.

(66) **Methinks, I think** :—

The two verbs, though spelt alike in Modern English, are from different roots. *Methinks* = it seems to me; the *me* is in the Dative case (see § 360, *c*), and the *thinks* (impersonal) is from A.S. *thync-an*, to seem. The *personal* verb exemplified in "I think" is from A.S. *thenc-an*. See § 148.

(67) **Mean, means.**—It is a distinct loss to our language we are now, through force of custom, debarred from using *mean*, when we wish to denote a Singular, and are compelled to use *means* in a Singular sense as well as in a Plural one. In Tudor English *mean* was still in common use :—

> It is the solecism of power to think to command the end, and yet not to endure the *mean*.—BACON.
> The virtuous conversation of Christians was a *mean* to work the conversion of heathen to Christ.—HOOKER.

Even now the Singular *mean* can hardly be considered extinct, as the following quotations show :—

> You may be able by this *mean* to review your own scientific acquirements.—COLERIDGE (1772-1834).
> Philosophical doubt is not an end, but a *mean*.—Sir W. HAMILTON (1788-1856).

(68) **My, mine** :—

An explanation has been given in § 68 as to the three uses of the second form of the Possessive according to present idiom. A fourth use of *mine*, *thine* remains to be told.

In poetry, if the Possessive is followed by an open vowel or by a silent *h*, the form "mine" or "thine" is commonly used; and in the Tudor period it was commonly used in prose also. In fact in the Tudor period it was the exception not to use this form of the Possessive before an open vowel.

Believe me for *mine honour*; and have respect to *mine honour* that you may believe.—*Julius Cæsar*, iii. 2.
Drink to me only with *thine* eyes.—BEN JONSON.
I kept myself from *mine iniquity*.—*Psalms*, xviii. 23.
Look through *mine eyes* with thine.—TENNYSON.

Note.—It is worth noticing that *mine*, or rather A.S. *mīn*, was the original and once the only form of the Possessive, and that *my* is merely a secondary form of *mīn*, the final *n* having been cancelled for the sake of euphony before a consonant; as "*my* (for *mine*) garden." In the south of England peasants still say *hisn, hern, ourn, yourn, theirn.*

(69) **Mistaken.**—This is the Past Part. of *mistake*, which is here used Intransitively.

He is a *mistaken* man (=a man who made or makes many mistakes).

This construction has been explained in § 134. In further illustration of this use of the Past Part. we have in Milton the curious phrase, "The *grazéd* ox," *i.e.* the ox whose habit it is to graze; and in Shakespeare, "The ravined (=ravenous) salt-sea shark."—*Macbeth*, iv. 1.

(70) **More than,** with adjectives and verbs:—

(*a*) It is *more than* probable that he will fail. (*With Adj.*)
(*b*) He *more than* hesitated to promise that. (*With Verb.*)

The construction is elliptical. The two sentences could be written at greater length as follows:—

(*a*) It is not only probable, but more than this,—it is practically certain, that, etc.
(*b*) He *did* more than *hesitate* (that is, he refused) to promise. (The Noun-infinitive "hesitate" is object to "than"; § 163.)

(71) **Mutual friend**:—

The word "mutual" implies reciprocity; as "our friendship is mutual,"—that is, "I love you, and you love me in return." But the phrase "a mutual friend" has come into vogue in a sense quite different from that of reciprocity. "I made his acquaintance through a *mutual* friend,"—that is, a *common* friend, some one who was a friend to myself as well as a friend to him. We could not speak of two persons having "mutual ancestors."

(72) **Nay, aye, yea, or rather,** as conjunctions. These have very much the same force as *not only—but also.*

(*a*) **Nay.**—This negative adverb, by appearing to deny the first statement, places the second one in a stronger light:—

He was accused, *nay* convicted (accused, and what is more, convicted) of the crime by the magistrate.

(*b*) **Aye, yea.**—These have practically the same force as *nay*, although *nay* is the negative form of *aye*. They mean "more than this," and are used to mark the introduction of a more specific or more emphatic clause :—

I therein do rejoice, *yea*, and will rejoice.—*Phil.* i. 18.

Sometimes they are used to introduce a clause with the sense of "indeed," "truly," "verily."

Aye, call it holy ground.—MRS. HEMANS, *Pilgrim Fathers.*

Yea, hath God said, Ye shall not eat of every tree of the garden? —*Genesis* iii. 1.

(*c*) **Or rather.**—This has very much the same force as "nay." It corrects the first statement in order to place the second one in a stronger light :—

He was injured, *or rather* ruined altogether, by the failure of that bank.

(73) **Never so, ever so** :—

(*a*) He refuseth to hear the voice of the charmer, charm he *never so* wisely.—*Old Testament.*

(*b*) He refuseth to hear the voice of the charmer, charm he *ever so* wisely.

These two phrases mean the same thing, although the one is negative and the other Affirmative. In (*a*) the dependent clause written out in full would be, "although he charm *so* wisely as he had *never* charmed before." In (*b*) the clause can be rewritten "however wisely he may charm." The phrase "*ever so*" is the one now used ; "*never so*" was used in the sixteenth century.

Note.—The phrase *ever so* is sometimes used colloquially as follows :—

Ever so many persons called here to-day.

Here "ever so many" means a larger number than usual, or a larger number than I care to count. Here *ever* is a mistake for "never" ; and the sentence written in full would be—

Never so many persons called here before as called here to-day.

(74) "**No,**" "**none,**" as adverbs :—

(*a*) He is *no* scholar.

(*b*) He is *none* the wiser for all his experience.

In (*a*) the word "no" = in no respect. In (*b*) "none" = in no degree. "None" is used in this adverbial sense only when it is followed by such a phrase as "the wiser,"—that is, by "the" and a Comparative. Similarly we can say "*all* the better," where "all," like "none," is used adverbially.

But we can use "no" before a Comparative, whenever the Comparative is not preceded by "the" :—

He is *no better* than he ought to be.

Here "no" is an adverb, signifying "in no degree."

(75) **No more**, preceded by some Transitive verb :—

I will *do no more* than I can help.

"More" in this sentence cannot be a noun, since it is followed by "than." We must therefore suppose that some noun such as "work" is understood after "more." "No" is an adverb qualifying "more."

But *more* can be used as a noun when it is not followed by *than*, in the same way as *much* can be :—

Let knowledge grow from *more to more*.—TENNYSON.
Oliver Twist went up and asked for *more*.—DICKENS.

(76) **None of them** :—

None but the brave *deserves* the fair.—DRYDEN.
None of them *were* present.

"None" is properly a Singular = not one, or no one. But the phrase "none of them" takes a Plural verb by attraction :— "they none." Or the Plural may be explained by analogy to the phrases "all of them," "some of them," etc. See above (4)

(77) **Not but what, not that I do not**, etc.

We have introduced the policy of Preference to Great Britain and towards all the British Empire. *Not that I do not* value American trade.—*Daily Telegraph*, 4th April 1907, p. 10.

The italicised phrase is elliptical. "*I do not say this, because I do not* value," etc. Sometimes the phrase takes the form of "*Not but what* I value," etc. = I do not say anything against the fact that, etc. Here a negative is implied in the word *but*, which is here a preposition followed by a Noun-clause, *what* being substituted for *that*.

(78) **O that** :—

This elliptical phrase is frequently used for expressing (*a*) a wish, (*b*) regret.

(*a*) O (I wish) that Ishmael might live before thee!—*Genesis* xvii. 12.

(*b*) O (it is sad) that such eyes should e'er meet other object!—SHERIDAN KNOWLES.

(79) **One more . . . and** :—

(*a*) *One more* whistle, *and* the train started.
(*b*) *One more* such loss, *and* we shall be ruined.

In each of these sentences there is an ellipsis of some verb in the Principal clause. (*a*) "*There was* one more whistle, and the train started,"—that is, *after* one more whistle, the train started.

(*b*) "*We must incur* one more such loss, and then we shall be ruined,"—that is, *if we incur* one more such loss, we shall be ruined. This sentence therefore expresses a condition and its consequence.

Any noun signifying number or space can be used in the same way as "one more":—

A mile or two farther, and we shall reach home.
A few more words, and he finished his speech.

(80) **Or.**—This conjunction has four different meanings:—

(*a*) An alternative or exclusive sense (§ 167, *b*):—

Either this man sinned *or* his parents.

Note.—If the writer wishes to emphasise the exclusive character of the alternative, he should take care not to omit, as sometimes happens, the *either* that should precede the *or*.

(*b*) An inclusive or non-alternative sense. Here the "or" is nearly equivalent to "and."

Such trades as those of leather, *or* carpentry, *or* smith's work flourish best in large cities.

(*c*) To indicate that one word is synonymous or nearly monymous with another:—

The tribes *or* castes of India are very numerous.

(*d*) As an equivalent to "otherwise."

You must work hard; or (= otherwise = if you do not work hard) you will lose your place in the class.

(81) **Or, nor,** in Negative sentences:—

He was not a clever man in books *or* in business.

The question has been raised whether "or" is correct in such sentences, or whether "nor" should be written in the place of it.

The answer is that the "or" is correct. The sentence, however, is elliptical; and the ellipse would be filled up as follows:—

He was not clever *either* in books *or* in business.

If "nor" is used instead of "or," the sentence must be rewritten in the following form, which is rather cumbersome:—

He was not clever in books, *nor* was he clever in business.

(82) **Or ere, or ever:**—

(*a*) It shall be moon or star or what I list,
Or ere I journey to your father's house.—SHAKESPEARE.

(*b*) Would I had met my dearest foe in heaven,
Or ever I had seen that day, Horatio.—SHAKESPEARE.

(a) It is generally explained that *or* is a corruption of *ere*, and that hence the phrase *or ere* is merely a reduplication.

(b) "Or ever" (=ere ever) has been compared to such compound conjunctions as *whenever*, *wherever*, *however*, etc. Some, however, think that *ever* has been confounded with *ere*, misspelt as *e'er*. In this case the phrase *or ever* would be another instance of reduplication.

(83) **Other than, other besides** :—

(a) No person *other than* a graduate need apply.
(b) No other person *besides* my friend applied.

These two phrases are often wrongly confounded.

In (a) "other than" means "different from," "except," "but":—"No one *except* a graduate, no one *but* a graduate." The word "than" is here a preposition (not a conjunction). On the prepositional use of *than*, see § 163. Observe that the word "other" has the comparative ending—"ther," like *farther*, *further*. It is, in fact, by etymology a comparative adjective, and is therefore correctly followed by "than."

In (b) "other besides" means "other in addition to" "No other person besides (or in addition to) my friend applied."

(84) **Out, out and out** :—

(a) *Out*, brief candle!
(b) He was quite *out* of it.
(c) *Out* upon it!
(d) He was beaten *out and out*.
(e) He proved to be an *out and out* deceiver.

In (a) *out* is an adverb compounded with some verb "go" understood. In (b) *out* is an adverb qualifying the preposition *of*; § 149 (a). In (c) some verb is understood, as in (a), before the adverb *out*. The phrase is exclamatory, and is used to express indignation. In (d) the adverb is repeated for the sake of intensifying it: the reduplicated adverb means "utterly." In (e) some participle is understood with the reduplicated adverb, which gives it the force of an adjective signifying "utter"; see § 151. Or the student may, if he prefers it, adopt the alternative explanation given in § 352, according to which "out and out" might be parsed as an adverb (or adverbial phrase) used as an adjective.

Note.—As regards (c) it should be noticed that the preposition *upon* is sometimes used, as it is here, in a hostile sense.

The Philistines be *upon* thee, Samson.—*Judges* xvi. 9.

Out *upon* it! (Let the word "out," *i.e.* utter rejection or utter contempt, be pronounced upon it.)

(85) **Out of temper, in a temper** :—

(*a*) He is *out of temper* (angry).
(*b*) He is *in a temper* (angry).

These phrases mean the same thing, and written in full would be, (*a*) out of his *ordinary* or *good* temper, (*b*) in a *bad* temper.

(86) **Own.**—For the sake of giving emphasis, this adjective can be placed after the Possessive forms of any of the personal pronouns :—

My own, mine own. Thy own, thine own. His own, her own, its own. Our own, your own, their own.

"Own" is never placed after *double* Possessives, like "ours," "yours," "theirs." It means literally "possessed," and was originally spelt *ägen*, the p.p. of *äg-an* (A.S.), to possess.

Sometimes we have the doubly emphatic phrases, "my own self," "your own self," etc.

Who *his own self* bare our sins upon the cross.—*New Test.*

(87) **Please,** followed by an Imperative or by an Infinitive :—

(*a*) *Please write* more legibly.
(*b*) *Please to write* more legibly.

In (*a*) "please" cannot be in the Imperative mood, since an Imperative comes immediately after it. We must regard it as elliptical, signifying "If it please you."

In (*b*) "please" signifies "have the pleasure," "be willing." There is ample authority for using "please" in this sense :—

Heavenly stranger, *please* to taste
These bounties.—MILTON, *Par. Lost.*

That he would *please* to give me my liberty.—SWIFT.

(88) **Provided, providing.** "Provided" (an elliptical form for "it being provided" = Lat. *proviso*) may be used as a conjunction either with or without *that* coming after it. It is not correct, however, to use *providing* as an equivalent, though the custom has been springing up of late: the change is not at all needed, and sometimes causes obscurity.

(*a*) *Provided that* nothing in this Act shall prejudice existing rights.
(*b*) *Provided* British rule is reasonably fair, they will not be slow to recognise its manifold advantages.—*Fortnightly Review*, May 1900, p. 861.
(*c*) There is every desire to give the preference to British firms *providing* that their charges are low. (Change *providing* to *provided*.)

In (*c*) as it stands there is some ambiguity; for *providing* might be taken for a participle qualifying "firms." The sense would then be—"to British firms which provide or make provision that," etc.

(89) **Reliable.**—There are some pedants or purists who consider this word to be wrong on the ground that it must be followed by *on*. The objection, however, is groundless; for there is ample authority for dispensing with the preposition:—

The best means and the most *reliable* pledge of a higher object.
COLERIDGE.
His own village was not much more *reliable*.—W. IRVING.

There is also abundant analogy. Thus we say "to laugh at," but not "laughable *at*"; "to avail of," but not "available *of*"; "to dispense with," but not "dispensable *with*."

(90) **Save he, save we,** etc.:—

There was no stranger in the house save *we* two.—*Old Testament.*
No man hath seen the Father, save *he* which is of God.—*New Test.*
All the conspirators, save only *he*.—SHAKESPEARE.
None shall be mistress of it save *I* alone.—SHAKESPEARE.

This Nominative (which is now gradually going out of use is a survival of the Nominative Absolute, which was used when "save" was still an Adjective used absolutely, and had not been changed into a Preposition. See above, § 370.

(91) **Self, myself, himself,** etc.—The explanation of these forms is a very simple matter, if we attend to their history and avoid conjecture. We find in A.S. such forms as *mín self-es* (of me the same, Possessive), *mé self-um* (to me the same, Dative), *mec self-ne* (me the same, Acc.).

The first thing to be noted, as in fact the above forms show, is that *self* was originally not a noun, but an adjective which signified "same," as it still does in the following line; cf. *self-same* (adj.):—

At that *self* moment enters Palamon.—DRYDEN.

"Self" is still an adjective in the phrase *himself* (him the same). But, like many other adjectives, it came in modern times to be used as a noun, and acquired a plural *selves* formed on the analogy of "shelf, shelves." We must regard it as a noun in the phrase *my-self* (lit. my identity), *our-selves* (our identities). In the Tudor period *his-self* (his identity) was as common as *himself*:—

Who *his* own *self* bare our sins.—1 *Peter* ii. 24.

In low life we still hear the phrase, "He hurt *hisself*."

The phrase *themselves* is due to a confusion of construction. Here *selves*, which should be the adjective "self" qualifying *them* (as in "himself" the "self" qualifies "him"), has received the form of a plural noun by attraction to the plural "them."

Note.—We can now see why it is wrong (as pointed out in (10), page 167) to use *myself*, *himself*, etc., as the subject of a verb. Such phrases signify that the corresponding personal pronoun has been mentioned already. "I *myself* (the identity of me, the very same person as the speaker) saw it." "He did it *himself*" (*i.e.* by himself, or for himself, or to himself). *Him* is here the Dative case, which in Old English required no preposition.

(92) **Shortly, briefly**:—

> I will write *shortly* (= in a short time).
> I will write *briefly* (= in few words).

The adverb "shortly" is used to denote shortness only of *time*, and only of *future* time. We cannot say "He went away *shortly*" (a short time ago); nor can we say, "He lived there *shortly*" (for a short time). The adverb "briefly" is used only in the sense of shortness or brevity in *language*.

(93) **So.**—This adverb is sometimes used predicatively in contexts, where we should ordinarily use "such." (On the predicative use of adverbs, see § 159, *b*.)

> My business is urgent; you will find it *so* (*i.e.* urgent).
> Is he an enemy? Indeed he is *so* (*i.e.* an enemy).

For "so" we could easily substitute the equivalent phrase "of such a character."

(94) **So and so, or so, so so, and so on**:—

> (*a*) He asked what I meant, and I told him *so and so*.
> (*b*) I shall return in a week *or so*.
> (*c*) *So so* it works: now, mistress, sit you fast.—DRYDEN.
> (*d*) He disliked dances, plays, picnics, *and so on*.

In (*a*) "so and so" is the adverbial form of the compound Indefinite adjective "such and such" (§ 54). "I told him *so and so*," might be rewritten "I gave him *such and such* an answer" or "such and such a remark." These two adverbs are used when the speaker avoids entering into particulars.

In (*b*) "or so" is also used Indefinitely. The sentence might be rewritten, "I shall return in a week or such-like time,"—that is, a week more or less.

In (*c*) "so so" means "fairly well," and is used when the

speaker does not wish to be more precise. When the phrase is preceded by "but," it means something less than "well":—

"His leg is but *so so*."—SHAKESPEARE, *As You Like It*, iii. 5.

In (*d*) the phrase "and so on" means "and such-like," or "etc." (*et cetera*). The adverb "on" means "forward,"—that is, to the end of the list:—

He disliked dances, plays, picnics, and so on =
He disliked dances, plays, picnics, and such-like amusements.

(95) **So or so as,** in the sense of condition.—In Tudor English and later we find "so" or "so as" used as equivalent to "provided that":—

Distribution is the life of dispatch, *so as* (= provided that) the distribution be not too subtle.—BACON, *Of Dispatch*.

Though all the winds of doctrine be let loose upon the earth, *so* (= provided that) truth be in the field, we do injuriously to misdoubt her strength.—MILTON, *Areopagitica*.

(96) **So as,** for "so that," in the sense of consequence.—In Tudor English we sometimes find "so as" used to express an effect or consequence in contexts where we now use "so that":—

He raised a cry *so* piteous and profound
As (= that) it did seem to shatter all his bulk.—*Hamlet*, ii. 1.

The third part of the sun was smitten, and the third part of the moon, and the third part of the stars, *so as* (= so that) the third part of them was darkened.—*Rev.* xviii. 12.

As more naturally follows *so* than *that*. But this use of *as* is now obsolete. It is, however, very likely that this old use of *so as* helped to form the still common and useful construction described in the next item (No. 97).

(97) **So as to,** etc.:—

I got up at six A.M. *so as to be* certain of being in time.

This construction is elliptical, and the ellipses should be filled up as follows:—"I got up at six A.M. *so* (= in such a way) *as* (= in which way I should get up) to be certain," etc. The Infinitive in such phrases is Gerundial, expressing a purpose.

(98) **So kind as to,** and similar phrases:—

He was *so* kind *as to* take me into his house.

"He was so (to that extent) kind as (to which extent a man would be kind) to take me (for taking me)," etc. Here too the Infinitive is Gerundial. The sentence is equivalent to "He was kind *enough* to take me."

(99) **Somehow or other, anyhow:**—

He managed *somehow or other* to pay off his debts.

Here "how" has been substituted for the corresponding noun. "He managed some how or other how = in some *way* or other (way) to pay off his debts." Compare the noun-use of *where* = "place" in the word *somewhere* :—

Thou losest here, a better *where* (= place) to find.—*K. Lear*, i. 1.

(100) **Thank you.**—This is merely an ellipse for "I thank you."

(101) **That,** as a Relative pronoun.—It has been shown in § 83, *Note*, that "*that*" is pre-eminently the *Restrictive* relative, and "*who*" or "*which*" the Continuative.

The use of "that" as an indeclinable Relative pronoun is by no means modern. It occurs in its present indeclinable form in A.S., and was the Relative chiefly used in Mid. Eng. In the Tudor period and later the Relative "that" yielded to the influence of "who" and "which," and almost disappeared. About Addison's time it again came into fashion, and has held its ground ever since as the Restrictive Relative.

Addison, however, who was evidently not acquainted with the history of our language, protested against the change. In his "Humble Petition of 'Who' and 'Which'" he makes the petitioners say :—"We are descended of ancient families, and kept up our dignity and honour many years, till the Jack Sprat *that* supplanted us."

Note.—There is another use of *that* which we often meet with in Tudor English, but seldom in more recent English :—

To do always *that* (= that which, or what) is righteous in thy sight. —*Eng. Liturgy.*

He pretends to be *that* (= what) he is not.—BACON, *Of Simulation.*

(102) **That,** as a conjunction, expressed or understood.—There is no conjunction in our language so variously used, or so frequently left out in contexts where it was originally used, as the conjunction "that." It is difficult for this reason to find for it a name sufficiently wide.

(*a*) In § 169 it has been called the conjunction of "Apposition," because the Noun-clause which it serves to introduce is in apposition with the noun going before [1] :—

I heard *the news that* you had come.

[1] This tallies with what Dr. Abbott says in *How to Parse*, p. 257 :—"Distinguish the above use of 'that' from its use when introducing a clause in Apposition to a previous noun" :—

They made *an agreement that* they would share equally.

(*b*) It often happens, however, that there is no noun going before. In this case the *that* is merely introductory, and the Noun-clause introduced by it is the complement or the subject or the object of some verb, or the object of some preposition.

My terms are *that you pay cash.*	(*Comp. of Verb.*)
That you were absent is certain.	(*Subject of Verb.*)
I heard *that you had come.*	(*Object of Verb.*)
In *that he died* he died unto sin once.	(*Object of Prep.*)

(*c*) The same conjunction placed after certain nouns has transformed the noun followed by *that* into a conjunctional phrase :—

The moment that (=in the moment in which) he saw me, he fled.

But the *that* is often omitted ; nothing is then left except the noun to represent the conjunction :—

The moment he saw me, he fled.

This, though common, is rather slovenly, and might cause obscurity. It would therefore be better to say "as soon as."

(*d*) The same conjunction is often placed after certain adverbs, and is apt to be similarly omitted :—

Directly that or *Directly* he saw me, he fled.
Now that you are well enough, you can leave your bed.
But *now* he is dead, wherefore should I fast?—2 *Samuel* xii. 23.

This use of *now* as a Subordinative conjunction, *i.e.* the use of *now* unassisted by *that*, is not to be commended.

(*e*) The same conjunction is similarly placed, and sometimes similarly omitted, after the elliptical absolute participle "provided" (§ 190, *Note* 2) :—

Provided that or *provided* you sign your name to this, I accept your terms.

Note.—*It being provided* (the full form) has been cut down to *provided*=Latin, *proviso.* See above (88).

(*f*) The same conjunction is similarly placed and similarly omitted after certain prepositions. The omission of *that* transforms the preposition into a conjunction :—

Except thou bless me, I will not let thee go.—*Gen.* xxxii. 26.
Without you keep yourselves in breath with exercise, you will never live to my age.—SIR P. SYDNEY.
Urijah the priest made it, *against* King Ahaz came from Damascus. —2 *Kings* xvi. 11.

The use of these prepositions as conjunctions is now obsolete.

(*g*) The same conjunction was originally expressed, but is now understood, after the phrases *in case*, *for fear* :—

In case (that) you fail, we shall all suffer.

For fear (that) our people call you lily maid.—TENNYSON.

Note 1.—In such a sentence as the following it is better to consider *that* a Relative pronoun :—

Did you ever see him? Not *that* (=a sight that) I remember.

Note 2.—Observe the precautions given in p. 174 (52) against using *that* as a general hack that can be freely substituted for any other conjunction.

(103) **The other day (or night).**—This phrase is Indefinite—some day (or night) a little preceding the present, that is, a few days (or nights) ago. Perhaps *the other day* meant originally "the second day," that is, two days from now, two or three days ago; for in Old English "other" meant "second." The idiom is not of recent date :—

The other night (=two or three nights ago) I fell asleep here behind the arras.—1 *Hen. IV.* iii. 3.

He said *this other day* (=two or three days before this day), you ought him a thousand pound.—1 *Hen. IV.* iii. 3.

(104) **"The whom," "the whose," "the which,"** etc.—In Middle English and in the Tudor period we find the Relative particularised by the Def. article. But modern idiom is against it, even in poetry :—

The whose power as now is falle.—GOWER.
Your mistress, from *the whom* I see
There's no disjunction.—*Winter's Tale*, iv. 4.

(105) **This much, so much, so much for :**—

(*a*) *This much* at least we can promise.
(*b*) He is now *so much* better that we need not be alarmed.
(*c*) *So much for* his courage; now as to his honesty.

In (*a*) "much" is used as a noun: "this much" is equivalent to "this amount," "this quantity."

In (*b*) "much" is an adverb qualifying the adjective "better"; and "so" is another adverb qualifying "much."

In (*c*) the first clause written out in full would be :—"*For* (=in defence of) his courage, *so much* has been or can be said." Here there is a confusion between "this much" as a noun and "so much" as an adverb. The phrase "so much" is here used as the subject of some verb understood. "This is all that need be said about his courage; now let us see what can be said about his honesty."

(106) **Though,** in the sense of "however."—"Though" is, properly speaking, a Subordinative conjunction signifying concession or contrast, and is used for introducing an Adverb-clause.

See § 169. But sometimes it stands alone, no clause of any kind being placed after it. It is then placed, not at the beginning, but in the middle or at the end of the sentence[1] :—

That is another matter, *though*.—Quoted in *Daily Telegraph*, p. 9, 6th April 1906.
A good cause would do well, *though*.—DRYDEN.
It was found, *though*, that the cause was a bad one.

This is not a modern idiom, since not only is it used by Dryden, but it occurs in Shakespeare :—

Norf. This priest has no pride in him ?
Suf. Not to speak of ;
I would not be so sick, *though*, for his place.

The speech by Suffolk written out in full would be :—"Though he has no pride to speak of, I would not be so sick for his place as he is." When *though* has no clause following it, we must regard it as a weak co-ordinative conjunction used in the sense of "however" or "but."

(107) **Though, but.**—Both of these conjunctions signify concession or contrast ; but there is an important difference in their use, for which the reader can consult § 171.

(108) **To be sure** :—

Did he promise ? *To be sure* he did.

Here the Infinitive is the Gerundial or Qualifying (§ 127, II.). The phrase *to be sure* is colloquial, and it signifies "certainly." The phrase "Well, to be sure !" is a colloquial form of exclamation signifying astonishment.

(109) **To boot.**—This phrase almost always stands at the end of its sentence. It was common in the Tudor period, but is now almost or quite obsolete in prose :—

I would not be the villain that thou think'st,
For the whole space that's in the tyrant's grasp,
And the rich East *to boot*.—*Macbeth*, iv. 3.

A man's heaviness is refreshed long before he comes to drunkenness ; for when he arrives thither, he hath but changed his heaviness and taken a crime *to boot*.—JER. TAYLOR.

"To boot" means "in addition," "over and above," "by way of an extra." "Boot" has always meant "profit" ; and is of the same root as the first syllable in *better*. The prep. *to* is here used in the sense of purpose, as in the following :—

[1] At the end of a sentence such a word as "though" appears to be very unsuitable. But I have given the sentence as I found it. It would have been better to say, "That, however, is another matter."

God will preserve them (our cattle) *to* our use from all diseases.—LATIMER'S *Sermons*.

(110) **What not.**—This phrase is placed after a string of nouns or verbs, and denotes that many more might be added, but that there is no need to mention them :—

Steam propels, lowers, elevates, pumps, drains, pulls, and what not (what else does it not do?).

Persians, Copts, Tartars, Medes, Syrians, and what not (=several other nations that I need not name) were brought under the dominion of Alexander the Great.

(111) **What was, what was not** :—

(*a*) *What was* my astonishment on seeing this!

(*b*) *What was not* my astonishment on seeing this!

These two sentences come to the same thing, in spite of the "not." The first means "How great was my astonishment," etc.; the second means "No astonishment could be greater than mine was," etc.

(112) **What with, somewhat** :—

The phrase "what with," repeated before two or more nouns, is sometimes used for enumerating a series of things :—

What with the cunning of his methods, *what with* the flattery of his tongue, and *what with* the influence of his money, he soon became the leading man in the town.

It might be supposed that "what with" is an elliptical phrase for "what *he effected* with cunning," etc. But more probably "what" is here an Indefinite Demonstrative used as an adverb in the sense of "partly." The compound word "somewhat" is still used sometimes as a noun signifying "something," and sometimes as an adverb signifying "to some extent" or "partly":—"I am *somewhat* tired of this book." In colloquial English we still say, "I tell you what," which means "I tell you something," or "I have something to tell you." The following examples show that this use of "what" is by no means of recent date :—

Love is bought for litil *what*.—GOWER (1400).

Come down and learn the little *what*
That Thomalin can sayne.—SPENSER.

With promise of his sister and *what* else.—SHAKESPEARE.

I tell you *what*, Antonio.—*Ibid.*

(113) **Whatever.**—This word has three different uses :—(*a*) as a noun; (*b*) as an adjective; (*c*) elliptically.

(a) *Whatever* Earth, all-bearing mother, yields.—MILTON. (*Noun.*)

Here "whatever," used as a noun, is the object of "yields."

(b) *Whatever fortune* stays him from his word.—SHAK. (*Adj.*)

(c) There being no room for any physical discovery *whatever* (*i.e.* whatever it might be).—WHATELY. (*Elliptical.*)

Note.—Such colloquialisms as the following are not suitable for written composition:—"*Whoever* is that? *Whyever* did you do it? *Whichever* is it?" Here (as above and as shown in § 79, c) *ever* has the sense of totality. Thus *whoever* = who among all men, who on earth? *Whyever* = why on earth, why in the world?

(114) **Whether.**—This word has in its time had three different uses, but the third is now the only one that is not obsolete or obsolescent in prose-composition:—

(a) As an interrogative pronoun signifying "which of two":—

Whether of them twain (=which of the two) did the will of his father?—*Matt.* xxi. 31.

It shall be tried, before we do depart,
Whether (which of the two) accuseth (the) other wrongfully.
HEYWOOD, *Edw. IV.* ii. 3.

Whether (which of the two) dost thou profess thyself,—a fool or a knave?—*All's Well*, iv. 5.

(b) As an interrogative adverb, offering a choice between two alternatives:—

Whether had you rather lead mine eyes, or eye your master's heels?—*Merry Wives of Windsor*, iii. 2.

(c) As a conjunctive adverb, introducing a Noun-clause, but not in an Interrogative sense:—

You have said; but *whether* wisely or no let the forest judge.—*As You Like It*, iii. 2.

Note.—The reader will have perceived from the above examples that the word *whether* signifies a choice between two things. This is well in keeping with the second syllable "-ther," which was once a comparative suffix, like al-*ter*, u-*ter* in Latin, and like fur-*ther*, far-*ther*, o-*ther*, ei-*ther*, af-*ter*, un-*der*, ne-*ther* in English.

(115) **Which,** in a selective sense. See § 84.

Between two blades, *which* bears the better temper?
1 *Hen. VI.* ii. 4.

(116) **Which,** as a Neuter Relative.—The restriction of **which** to antecedents of the neuter gender or to the names of animals is of rather recent date. In the Tudor period *which* was used where we now use *who*:—

> Then Warwick disannuls great John of Gaunt,
> *Which* did subdue the greatest part of Spain.
> 3 *Hen. VI.* iii. 1.

(117) **While, whilst,** as a conjunction.

Properly speaking, "while" is a noun signifying "time." Originally this was its only use; and this use of the word, though now less common than it was, is not extinct.

> The mighty queen may no *while* endure.—CHAUCER.
>
> (Some guest that) hath outstayed his welcome *while*,
> And tells the jest without the smile.—COLERIDGE.
>
> I will go forth and breathe the air a *while*.—LONGFELLOW.

In the line last quoted *while* must be parsed as a noun in the adverbial objective case; see § 178 (5). It must be similarly parsed in the word "mean*while*," which signifies "in the mean (intervening) time," though we are now justified in considering "meanwhile" as an adverb. It is certainly a noun, and nothing else than a noun, in the phrase "worth *while*," *i.e.* worth the time and trouble required.

While became a conjunction through having *that* placed after it. (Compare the parallel case of "moment" in (102, *c*).

> *While that* the Sun with his beams hot
> Scorchèd the fruits in vale and mountain.
> TRENCH'S *Household Poetry*, xvi. 1.

But "*that*" is now always left out after "while"; and thus "while" becomes transformed into a full-blown conjunction. As a conjunction it is used in three different senses:—

(*a*) To denote the *simultaneity* of two events:—

> You can sit down *while* (at the same time that) I stand.

(*b*) To denote *indefinite duration*:—

> *While* (so long as) the world lasts, human nature will remain what it is.

(*c*) To denote some kind of antithesis or contrast:—

> Men of understanding seek after truth; *while* (=whereas) fools despise knowledge.

Note.—An older form of the conjunction is *whiles* (Possessive, see § 367):—

> Agree with thine adversary, *whiles* thou art in the way with him.—*Matt.* v. 25.

From *whiles* we get *whilst* with added *t*, as in *amongs-t, amids-t, agains-t.*

(118) **Who,** in the phrase "*as who should say*," where *who* is used as an Indefinite demonstrative pronoun:—

The cloudy messenger turns me his back
And hums, as *who* should say, You'll rue the time
That clogs me with this answer.—*Macbeth*, iii. 6.

Aye me! This long abiding
Seemeth to me, as *who* saith
A prolonging of a dying death.—WYATT.

The expression is still seen, though it has now become rather uncommon:—

"Is the present generation of young men at Oxford affected to any appreciable degree by the traditions of the place?"
"Oh, yes," replied my host, *as who should say*, "We haven't altogether gone to the dogs."—*Quiver*, May 1894.

(119) **Withal, wherewithal** (with + all).

The word *withal* is going more and more out of use. It can be either an adverb or a preposition.

(a) *Adverb*, signifying "at the same time," "in addition":—

How modest in exception, and *withal*
How terrible in constant resolution.—*Hen. V.* ii. 4.

(b) *Preposition*; equivalent to "with," but always placed after its object, and at the end of the sentence or clause to which it belongs:—

This diamond he greets your wife *withal*.—*Macbeth*, ii. 1.

Whatsoever uncleanness it be, that a man shall be defiled *withal*.—*Lev.* v. 3.

I for my part knew the tailor that made the wings she flew *withal*.—*Merch. of Venice*, iii. 1.

"Wherewithal." In this compound word the adverb "where" does duty for a noun as object of the preposition "withal."

Wherewithal (= by what means, or in what way) shall a young man cleanse his way?—*Psalms* cxix. 9.

Sometimes "wherewithal" is used as a noun:—

(Builders of Babel) still with vain design
New Babels, had they *wherewithal*, would build.—MILTON.

Here "had they wherewithal" signifies "if they had the means."

(120) **Would-be.**—This elliptical phrase is now well established. It is used as an adjective to denote "one who wished to be something or to do something, but failed or could not." As we had no word to express all this, *would-be* was useful for filling up the gap.

A *would-be* murderer, who wishes his victim to be removed by other hands than his own, has to open negotiations with third parties.—*Daily Tel.* p. 9, 22nd Dec. 1905.

(121) **Write you, write to you** :—

I will *write you* a letter on this matter.
I will *write to you* soon.

We can use the phrase "*write you,*" when "you" is the Indirect object to the verb and is followed by a Direct object. But if there is no Direct object and the verb "write" is used Intransitively (§ 145, *a*), we must say "*write to you.*"

Questions on Chapters XXVIII. and XXIX.

Collected from London Matriculation Papers set from January 1879 to July 1905.

1. Explain the construction of *self.* What part of speech is it? Trace its history. (Jan. 1879.)

2. Correct or justify:

(*a*) That's him.
(*b*) Many a day.
(*c*) I expected to have found him better. (Jan. 1879.)

3. State clearly the rules of English accidence regarding the use of *will* and *shall* in Interrogative sentences. (Jan. 1880.)

4. Discuss with reference to the history of their usage, the words *ye* and *you, that* and *which* (as Relatives). (June 1880.)

5. Tell what you know of the origin and present use of *a* and *the.* How would you place them among the parts of speech, and why? (June 1881.)

6. What is a Relative pronoun? Point out and explain the different uses of *that, what, which, whether.* (June 1881.)

7. What is the real power of the Genitive (Possessive) case? (Jan. 1882.) Distinguish its uses according to meaning.

8. Tell the history of the forms *a* and *an,* and discuss their grammatical use. (Jan. 1883.)

9. Take six of our common English prepositions, and show in what way each has been taken to represent different relations of place, time, and causality. (Jan. 1883.)

10. Discuss the syntax of the following:—

(*a*) I meant to have written to you.
(*b*) I heard of him running away.
(*c*) It's me. (Jan. 1883.)

11. Explain how you would classify the words *aye, yea, yes, no, nay* among the parts of speech. (June 1883.)

12. How do you classify pronouns? Parse the word *what* in the sentences:—

(*a*) I will tell you *what.*
(*b*) He was some*what* weary.

(c) *What* o'clock is it?
(d) *What* man is this?
(e) *What* with the wind, and *what* with the rain, it was not easy to get on. (Jan. 1885.)

13. Explain and parse the following phrases:—*methinks; woe is me; I had as lief.* (June 1884.)

14. Define the terms *inflexion, analysis, synthetic, interjection; strong* and *weak* as applied to verbs; *abstract* and *concrete* as applied to nouns; *simple* and *complex* as applied to sentences. (June 1885.)

15. What exactly is meant by a *Pronoun*? What by a *Relative pronoun*? Mention any differences in usage between *who* and *that*. (June 1885.)

16. Write some short sentences to show the various meanings of the prepositions *at, with, of, from, against.* Explain:—

(a) He did his duty *by* him.
(b) *Under* these circumstances.
(c) Ten *to* one it is not so.
(d) Add ten *to* one.
(e) Keep up *for* my sake. (June 1885.)

17. Parse *after* and *out* in each of the following:—

(a) *After* him then, and bring him back.
(b) *After* he came, all went wrong.
(c) You go first, and I will come *after*.
(d) *After* that I will say no more.
(e) *Out*, brief candle.
(f) He was quite *out* of it.
(g) *Out* upon it!
(h) He was beaten *out and out*.
(i) He proved an *out and out* deceiver. (June 1885.)

18. Parse each of the four words, *But me no buts.* What other parts of speech may *but* be? Would you say, *They all ran away but me*, or *They all ran away but I*? (Jan. 1886.)

19. What is meant by an *idiom*? Mention two or three English idioms, and try to explain them. (Jan. 1886.)

20. Point out what is idiomatic in these phrases:—

(a) There came a letter.
(b) Let me fight it out.
(c) We spoke to each other.
(d) Many a man would flee.
(e) What an angel of a girl!
(f) What with this, and what with that, I could not get on. (June 1886.)

21. What errors have crept into these phrases?—

(a) Ever so many.
(b) To do no more than one can help.
(c) These sort of things.

Suggest some explanation of "*of*" in such phrases as "a friend *of* mine." (June 1886.)

22. Parse the italicised words and phrases:—

(a) *Down* with it!
(b) His *having been beaten* once only made him the more determined to succeed.
(c) *Seeing* is *believing*.
(d) The *hearing* ear and the *seeing* eye, the Lord hath made *even* both of them.
(e) *Whatever* sceptic could inquire for,
For every *why*, he had a *wherefore*.
(f) *Let* knowledge grow from *more* to more. (Jan. 1887.)

23. Distinguish between *farther* and *further*, *gladder* and *gladlier*, *nearest* and *next*, *latest* and *last*, *peas* and *pease*, *genii* and *geniuses*. (Jan. 1887.)

24. Give instances of common nouns becoming proper, and of proper becoming common. How does the possessive of personal pronouns differ from the genitive? (June 1887.)

25. Discuss these phrases:—

(a) He found them *fled*, horses *and all*.
(b) Fight *away*, my men.
(c) Get *you* gone.
(d) I gave him this *to boot*.
(e) He overslept *himself*.
(f) How did he come *by* such a fortune? (June 1887.)

26. Define the words, *grammar*, *etymology*, *syntax*, *gender*, *number*, *case*, *mood*, and *tense*. (Jan. 1888.)

27. Correct or justify:—

(a) Thinking of them, my pen tarries as I write.
(b) It's me.
(c) I intended to have written to him. (Jan. 1888.)

28. Give the sources of the following expressions, pointing out the objection to their use as English idioms, and showing how the meaning might in each case be properly conveyed:—

(a) That window *gives* upon the street.
(b) That affair came *upon the carpet*.
(c) That goes *without saying*.
(d) He is feeble *as to* his mind.
(e) *Solidarity* of interests.
(f) He *affected* the latest fashion.
(g) To *exploit* a new invention. (June 1888.)

29. Notice any differences in usage between the relatives, *that*, *who*, *which*. (Jan. 1890.)

30. Point out any grammatical errors that are common in ordinary colloquial speech. State exactly what you understand by "good English." (Jan. 1890.)

31. Write several sentences illustrating the correct modern usage of *shall* and *will* in Interrogative sentences, giving any explanations that appear to be necessary. (June 1890.)

32. Why are Prepositions so called? Discuss the use of *past* in "He went *past* the house"; of *of* in "The island *of* Great Britain"; of *by* in "Do your duty *by* the University." (Jan. 1891.)

33. What do you understand by a Pronoun? What by a Reflexive

pronoun? Point out the inconsistency of saying *I myself*, and yet *He himself*, and account for it. (Jan. 1892.)

34. Give the meaning and origin of the following prepositions:—*maugre*, *but*, *between*, *notwithstanding*, *during*. And mention as many as you can of the various senses in which *by*, *to*, *with* are used. (Jan. 1892.)

35. Explain and illustrate the terms *inflexion*, *assimilation*, *etymology*, *phonetics*, and *accidence*. (June 1892.)

36. Discuss the verbal forms in italics:—

(*a*) How *do* you *do*? (*b*) I *do* you *to wit*.
(*c*) Woe *worth* the day. (*d*) *Seeing* is *believing*.
(*e*) He that hath ears to *hear*, let him *hear*.
(*f*) The hawthorn bush, with seats beneath the shade,
For *talking* age and *whispering* lovers made. (June 1892.)

37. Parse the words italicised in the following:—

(*a*) *Please* write clearly. (*b*) *Thank* you.
(*c*) If you *like*. (*d*) From *bad* to worse.
(*e*) Get *you* gone. (*f*) He was accused of *having run* away. (June 1893.)

38. Discuss carefully these words and ways of speaking:—*talented*; *a friend of mine*; *reliable*; *neither he nor she are at hand*; *they all hoped to have succeeded*. (June 1893.)

39. Define and illustrate the terms:—*dialect*, *slang*, *technology*, *archaism*, *neologism*, *solecism*. (Jan. 1894.).

40. Parse *but* in the following sentences, and explain carefully its idiomatic usage in each case, with reference to its original meaning:—

(*a*) There is none here *but* hates me.
(*b*) And was not this the earl? 'Twas none *but* he.
(*c*) He would have died *but* for me.
(*d*) He is all *but* perfect.
(*e*) There's not the smallest orb which thou behold'st,
But in his motion like an angel sings.
(*f*) He is *but* a madman. (Jan. 1895.)

41. Distinguish between the comparative degree of an adjective and an adjective with comparative force. To which class belong—*former*, *inferior*, *older*, *elder*, *outer*, *utter*. (June 1895.)

42. Point out any defects in the grammar or style of the following:—

(*a*) Homer was not only the maker of a nation, but of a language.
(*b*) He is better versed in theology than any living man.
(*c*) Shakespeare frequently has passages in a strain quite false, and which are entirely unworthy of him.
(*d*) Nothing can hinder this treatise from being one of the most considerable books which has appeared for the last half-century.
(*e*) A statute inflicting the punishment of death may be and ought to be repealed, if it be in any way expedient. (June 1896.)

43. Differentiate the following as regards usage:—*further*, *farther*; *late*, *latter*; *older*, *elder*; *outer*, *utter*; *foremost*, *first*. (Jan. 1897.)

44. Classify the uses of *shall* and *will*, and their past tenses. Show how far the following examples fall within your classification:—

(*a*) He shall not go abroad with me again.

(b) You should be more accurate in your calculations.
(c) They would be astonished at his audacity.
(d) Shall you take your fishing-rod with you?
(e) They would go in spite of the rain.
(f) If you should see him, tell him what I have said.
(July 1905.)

45. Explain the construction of the words in italics:—
(i.) There sleeps Titania sometime *of the night*.
(ii.) I have lived my *life*.
(iii.) *His* equal could nowhere be found.
(iv.) He is a *well-read* youth.
(v.) The little dog laughed *to see* such sport.
(vi.) The fear *of the Lord* is the beginning of wisdom.
(July 1905.)

46. Illustrate the various uses of "that." (July 1905.)

47. Point out and correct the irregularities in the following:—
(i.) We had hoped to have been present on the occasion.
(ii.) A large and small glass was on the table.
(iii.) He was not only celebrated for his wealth, but his learning.
(iv.) The wall was of about ten feet high.
(v.) O Thou my voice inspire,
Who touched Isaiah's hallowed lips with fire.
(vi.) What is the sense of you making such a remark?
(vii.) Being interested in fishes, an aquarium is always to be found in his house. (July 1905.)

48. Illustrate the vulgar use of:—and which—seldom or ever—like—between. (July 1905.)

49. Comment on any errors of expression in the following:—
(i.) As I am the best man in the world to keep my own counsel, and my landlord the fishmonger not knowing my name, this accident was never discovered (ADDISON).
(ii.) My coffee comes into my chamber every morning without asking for it (ADDISON).
(iii.) No confederacy can exist, of which England is not only a part, but the head (BURKE).
(iv.) Tickets once nipped, and the passengers once admitted to the platform, will have to be delivered up to the Company.
(v.) All love literature of some kind or another. Some like sentimental stories; others have a fascination for novels of adventure. (July 1904.)

50. For each of the following phrases substitute a single word of equivalent meaning and write a sentence illustrating its use:—
(i.) The original pattern or model of a work.
(ii.) A remedy for all diseases.
(iii.) Not having a backbone.
(iv.) Happening at the same time.
(v.) A remedy to counteract the effects of poison.
(July 1904.)

51. Account fully for the construction of the words in italics:—
(i.) The *king's* flatterers.
(ii.) Knock *me* at this gate.

(iii.) To go on board *a ship*.
(iv.) He is a great friend of my *father's*.
(v.) They heard her *come*. (Jan. 1905.)

52. Correct any faults of expression in the following sentences, and give reasons for your corrections :—

(i.) I never remember having met his equal.
(ii.) His failure was rather due to his stupidity than from the neglect of his teacher.
(iii.) Neither in writing for the learned or for the general reader was he very successful.
(iv.) The reason why the disaster occurred was on account of an error by the signalman.
(v.) There are people at whom we all smile yet secretly dislike.
(vi.) He much preferred trudging through the mud than to take the Tube-railway. (Jan. 1905.)

53. Comment on any errors in the following sentences :—

(*a*) His chief among many responsible duties was to provide for the welfare of the staff.
(*b*) The index to the book is very imperfect. The editor has paid little attention to such matters as indices and dates.
(*c*) He resembles one of those animals that has been forced from its forest to gratify human curiosity.
(*d*) They hoped to procure the original document which had been mislaid, but which they have not been able to do.
(*e*) His sister was the best letter-writer in the family, him only excepted.
(*f*) In a short time he succeeded in mastering the three first books of Paradise Lost. (June 1905.)

54. Alter, where necessary, the order of the clauses or phrases in the following sentences so as to express the ideas more clearly, and indicate why the order is faulty :—

(*a*) Some years afterwards I had an editorial successor, who had all the wit for which I toiled in vain, without making any pretension to it.
(*b*) He erected a pavilion in the garden, around which he kept the air always cool by artificial showers.
(*c*) You will find the world, which you imagine smooth and quiet as a lake in the valley, a sea foaming with tempests and boiling with whirlpools. (June 1905.)

55. Comment on the construction of the words in italics :—

(i.) We hoped this for *both their* sakes.
(ii.) He passed the examination, *which* pleased his friends.
(iii.) On his return *home* he recovered his health.
(iv.) The game is not worth the *candle*.
(v.) *Do* what he may, he will not succeed.
(vi.) There was one point which they considered *it* important to answer. (Sept. 1905.)

56. Point out and correct any errors of expression :—

(i.) He disliked books and all those sorts of things.

(ii.) This happened in William's and Mary's reign.
(iii.) Nobody in their senses could do such a thing.
(iv.) He was of as great use and even greater than his father.
(v.) He was kind, but lacked either prudence or cleverness.
(vi.) Some one or other, I don't know whom, struck the blow.
(Sept. 1905.)

57. Express the following ideas by changing some of the parts of speech into others, and state your reasons for the alterations in each instance:—

(*a*) The result would be a hopeless confusion of thought by such a statement of the theory of evolution without any modification.
(*b*) His assertion that the combination of the two elements will be the effect of extreme pressure was a manifestation of his ignorance of recent discoveries.
(*c*) The king's favouring the extreme party, in spite of their declaration against the war, gave deep offence to his well-wishers.
(*d*) Humble origin is no bar to the attainment of greatness, while pride of birth is a frequent cause of humiliation.
(*Lond. Matric.* Sept. 1904.)

58. (*a*) Explain the Demonstrative pronouns in :—

(i.) The busy sylphs surround their darling care ;
These set the head, and those divide the hair.
(ii.) Two principles in human nature reign,
Self-love to urge, and Reason to restrain :
Nor this a good, nor that a bad we call ;
Each works its end, to move or govern all.

(*b*) Illustrate the use of *whose* as a Relative pronoun, and state to what class of nouns its use is chiefly confined.

(c) Discuss the correctness of *whom* in the following sentences :—

(i.) Tell me whom you saw.
(ii.) He could name politicians whom he knew were above such considerations.
(iii.) Whom do they say the agent represents ?
(iv.) Belial came last, than whom a spirit more lewd
Fell not from heaven. (*Lond. Matric.* Sept. 1904.)

Miscellaneous Questions.

59. What does *will* express in the following sentences ?—

(*a*) He will leave England in May.
(*b*) I will take care that your interests do not suffer.
(*c*) Will you take this woman for your wedded wife ? I will.
(*d*) When will he come ?
(*e*) *Elizabeth.* Leave me now.
Will you, companion to myself, sir ?
Bedingfield. Will I ?
With most exceeding willingness, I will.—TENNYSON.

60. Correct any errors that you may find in the following, giving reasons for your corrections:—

(a) "Yield thee, Minotti, quarter take
For thine own, thy daughter's sake."
Never, renegado, never,
Though the life of thy gift would last for ever.—BYRON.

(b) I will be happy to visit you.
(c) If I go up in a balloon, I will probably lose my life.
(d) I shall never submit to this disgrace.
(e) I am sure that I will not fail twice in this examination.

61. Explain the meanings of *shall* and *should* in the following sentences:—

(a) Shall you go?
(b) You shall go.
(c) Thou shalt not oppress the poor.
(d) Heaven and earth shall pass away, but My words shall not pass away.—*Mark* xiii. 31.
(e) This room shall be kept open for the future.
(f) My voice shall sound, as you do prompt my ear.
(g) You promised he should marry one of my daughters.
J. AUSTEN.

62. What are the different meanings of *would* in the following sentences?—

(a) You said it would rain.
(b) Would that I were dead.
(c) He would talk the whole day, when in familiar circles.
(d) I wished him to go, but he would not.

63. Correct anything that you find amiss in the following, or give reasons for making no correction:—

(a) Anger is like
A full-hot horse, who being allowed his way,
Self-mettle tires him.—SHAKESPEARE.

(b) The reader will put down Mr. W. Richmond Smith's volume, *The Siege and Fall of Port Arthur*, describing in the most interesting way the author's experiences with General Nogi's army as special correspondent for the Associated Press and Reuter's Telegram Company, with somewhat mixed feelings.—*Times Weekly*, p. 392, 17th Nov. 1905.
(c) The man named is of a particularly evil character; for he has been by turns of the Greek and Roman faith, and finally becomes a Protestant.—*Daily Telegraph*, p. 12, 8th Nov. 1905.
(d) This will not prevent his book's being useful to a large circle of readers, to whom the sources from which he draws are not accessible.—*Times Weekly*, p. 374, 3rd Nov. 1905.
(e) England as the leading maritime nation may have been expected to have led the way in organising some method of averting the perils of shipwreck.—*Dr. Wynter on Lifeboats.*

64. Comment on the uses of *do* in the following sentences:—

(a) I do one or two sums every morning.
(b) How do you do?

(*c*) I like him better than you do.
(*d*) That will do for the present.

65. Comment on the objectives after the verbs in the following sentences :—

(*a*) Earl Walter, rest him God.—SCOTT.
(*b*) He had to fight his way through the world.
(*c*) He looked daggers at me.
(*d*) If left to himself, he would whistle life away in perfect contentment.—W. IRVING.
(*e*) She will sing the savageness out of a bear.—SHAKESPEARE.

66. Correct or explain and justify the use of the words italicised below :—

(*a*) Everybody was pleased to think how much *they* had always disliked Mr. Darcy.—J. AUSTEN.
(*b*) The Gardiners stayed a week at Longbourn ; and *what* with the Philipses, the Lucases, and the officers, there was not a day without its engagement.—*Ibid.*
(*c*) A famine occurs in India *every* twenty years at least.
(*d*) I tell you *what*,—if you go on refusing every offer in this way, you will never get a husband at all.—J. AUSTEN.
(*e*) I began to associate with none but disappointed authors like myself, who praised, deplored, and despised *each other*.—GOLDSMITH.
(*f*) The terms *which* are most moderate include free carriage.—*Advertisement.*
(*g*) All unawares,
Fluttering his pennons vain, plumb down he drops
Ten thousand *fathom* deep.—MILTON.
(*h*) And I shall soon
Arm'd with thy might rid heaven of these *rebelled*.—MILTON.
(*i*) There's not a wretch that lives on common charity
But's happier than *me*.—OTWAY, *Venice Preserved*, Act i.
(*j*) Vane young in years, but in sage counsel old,
Than *whom* a better senator ne'er held
The helm of Rome.—MILTON'S *Sonnets*.
(*k*) I do not like to see us gradually becoming a nation of onlookers at games, *like* the Romans had become immediately before *that* empire fell to pieces.—Letter quoted in *Daily Telegraph*, p. 10, 26th April 1906.
(*l*) It is doubtful *if* even *your* Dublin Divinity-student, let alone the world at large, has any familiar knowledge of the Primate, who, etc.—*Times Weekly*, p. 355, 5th Oct. 1906.
(*m*) Whenas St. Francis was going one day to St. Mary of the Angels, and the very bitter cold was tormenting him, he called to Brother Leo *that* was going on before, and said thus, etc.—Quoted in *Francis of Assisi*, by W. P. Swainson, p. 28.

CHAPTER XXX.—ESSAY-WRITING ON SUBJECTS MAINLY BASED ON ENGLISH HISTORY.

383. The Method.—The method followed in this chapter is the same as that followed already in Chapter XXVII. The first section consists of essays written out in full, which the student can be asked to reproduce in words of his own, without making any change in the order or in the theme of each paragraph; the second, of subjects for essays, to which a few notes have been appended; the third, of subjects without notes. The only difference between the two chapters is that here the subjects are based on English history, together with a few that are based on general geography, whereas in Chapter XXVII. the subjects are general.

SECTION 1.—ESSAYS FOR REPRODUCTION.

384. List of Essays for Reproduction.—The following is a list of the essays written out in full, which the student can be asked to reproduce:—

I. What Britain owes to her Geographical Position.
II. What Use Britain has made of her Natural Advantages.
III. The Roman Conquest and Occupation of Britain.
IV. Early English Settlements in Britain (450-600).
V. Early English Kingdoms and their Unification in 829.
VI. Did England gain or lose by the Norman Conquest?
VII. The Part played by Accident in English History.

ESSAY I.—WHAT BRITAIN OWES TO HER GEOGRAPHICAL POSITION.

In the above heading Great Britain is called "Britain" for the sake of brevity. Ireland is not included, because what we have to say about Britain does not always apply to the sister-island, or applies to it in a less degree. The phrase "geographical position" means the position that a country held or holds in relation to other countries either neighbouring or more remote. In this essay, as in the second and third, the theme of each paragraph is printed in italics on the top.

1. *Britain not originally separated from the Continent.*

From the shallowness of the sea, by which our island is separated from the neighbouring continent, it has been inferred that Britain and Gaul were once united so as to form an unbroken expanse of land. The Strait of Dover is so shallow that if St. Paul's Cathedral (London) could be put down in the deepest part of it, the dome would be seen standing out above the water. Fortunately, however, when the land that once joined Britain and Gaul subsided, the subsidence was deep enough not only to make Britain an island, but to make the waters of the Channel navigable by the largest ships along the entire route from Kent to Cornwall. The insular character that Britain thus acquired has more than anything else determined the part that she has played and has yet to play in the history of mankind.

2. *Position of Britain in ancient and mediæval history.*

From the beginning of recorded history till the close of the Middle Age, Britain was on the outermost fringe of the then known world. Until Julius Cæsar crossed over from Gaul and set foot on the coast of Kent (55 B.C.), it remained unknown to the Romans; or, if known at all, it was known only as a vague tradition. A Roman poet of that day speaks almost with pity of the "Britanni" (Britons) as a people "entirely cut off from the rest of the world." The conquest of the greater part of Britain was the last great addition that the Romans made to their empire; and it was the first great province that they gave up when their empire was on the decline. After the Romans had gone (410 A.D.), the island fell back once more into its former state of obscurity, in which state it remained for nearly two hundred years, till Augustine and his monks arrived (597 A.D.) to Christianise its inhabitants. During the later half of the Middle Age (from 1066 to 1485) the kings of England (for Britain had long before this become mainly English) played a conspicuous part in the affairs of Europe, and especially in those of its nearest neighbour, France. But even then Britain remained, as it had begun, a remote island on the circumference or outer ring of the then known world.

3. *Position of Britain in modern history.*

The discovery of America (1492 A.D.), with the outburst of colonisation and commerce that followed, transferred the island from the circumference to the centre. If we place a school-globe in such a position that Britain appears in the centre, we can from that centre see by far the largest part of the land-surface of the globe, viz. the whole of Europe and Africa, the greater part of Asia, and the whole of the New World except the southern end of the southern half of the American continent. From the waters of the North Atlantic (if we include the Mediterranean as an arm of the Atlantic, which it is), all the great historic countries of the Old and the New Worlds can be approached without difficulty.

4. *What Britain owes to her separation from Europe.*

In more ways than one the almost unbroken prosperity of Britain (under which name we refer especially to England) is mainly to be ascribed to her separation from Europe. This more than anything else gave to her people the sense of national unity, to which most of the countries of Europe long continued to be strangers. Certainly there was no such unity during the Middle Age in France, Italy, or Germany. Notwithstanding the conquest of England by Canute the Dane (1017), and the much more violent conquest by William the Norman (1066), there was no serious break in the continuity of the national life. The home-policy of Henry I., who was born and educated in England and came to the throne only thirty-four years after William the Conqueror had landed, was an important step towards the unification of Englishman and Norman. Not only did he put forth the first "charter" of our liberties, which placed English and Normans on the same level, but by his marriage with Edith, the grand-daughter of Edmund Ironside, he restored the Saxon blood to the occupants of the English throne. Further, by his invasion of Normandy and by the victory that he won at Tenchebrai (1106) with a force which was mainly English, he wiped out the dishonour of the defeat that the English had suffered at Hastings. Henceforth Normandy became an appendage of England, and England ceased to be an appendage of Normandy. The drawing up of the Great Charter (*Magna Charta*) only eighty years after the death of Henry I., was a great national movement, in which barons, sheriffs, merchants, and burgesses all took part, showing that by this time (1215) all distinction between Englishman and Norman had disappeared. Thanks to her separation from Europe, England was able to work out her own problems, both religious and political, without foreign interference, and to solve them without foreign direction. The Channel between Dover and Calais, protected as it was from hostile fleets by the bravery of her sailors, preserved her from the aggressions of Charlemagne, of Philip II., of Louis XIV., and of Napoleon; and it placed her at a safe distance from the storm-centre of the Revolution of Paris (1789-1802), which convulsed the greater part of Western Europe.

5. *What Britain owes to her proximity to Europe.*

Our island, though removed far enough from Europe to escape from many of its wars, revolutions, and pestilences, was yet near enough to profit by intercourse with the most cultivated of its inhabitants and to receive infusions of new blood. The neighbourhood of Europe supplied a stimulant from without and prevented stagnation within. For many centuries before the Romans landed in 55 B.C., Britain had had a vigorous population of her own, the Celtic, which made a stout resistance to the Romans and survived the Roman Conquest. After the Romans had gone, immigrants of various kinds poured in at intervals,—Saxons, Frisians, Angles, Danes, Normans, Flemings, Angevins, Lombards, Huguenots. All these, partly through intermarriage with the earlier inhabitants (the Celts), partly through intermarriage with one another, and partly through the use of a common language (English) and the possession of common interests, became fused into a single nation, and fused so completely that no distinctions among the component elements could be traced. "With animals and plants," says Darwin, "a cross between different varieties, or between individuals of the same variety but of another strain, gives vigour and fertility to the offspring." The mixed stock, which in spite of the mixture is for convenience' sake called English, has produced some of the greatest explorers, discoverers, poets, and dramatists that the world has seen. From the same stock came the great inventions of modern times,—the steamship, the railway engine, and the electric telegraph,—to which we must add the last great invention, the telephone, which may be fairly claimed as English, since the inventor, A. G. Bell, was born in Edinburgh, the inhabitants of which, though they are now called Scotch, are mainly descended from Angles and are therefore of the same stock as the English.

Essay II.—What Use Britain has made of her Natural Advantages.

The purport of this heading is explained in the first paragraph, which serves as an introduction to the essay. It is sometimes expedient to begin an essay by explaining the scope of the subject set, or at least the view that the writer has taken of its scope. This clears the ground, and puts the writer in a better position with his reader or readers.

1. *The scope of the essay.*

The natural advantages of a country may be discussed under three main headings,—its seaboard, estuaries, and harbours,—its soil and climate, with their respective variations,—its mineral resources. In each of these properties Britain has been very highly favoured by the bounty of Nature. The question then arises, What use has she made of them? Or, to express the same question in different words, What influence have they had in shaping the career and character of her people? This is the question to be discussed in the present essay.

2. *Seafaring, shipbuilding, and fisheries.*

The coast-line of Britain is unusually long in proportion to the land-area, being about 1 linear mile to 20 square miles, against 1 to about 200 in the continent of Europe. At intervals not very wide apart this coast-line is indented with great natural harbours, such as Plymouth or Southampton, or is penetrated to a long distance inland by estuaries or arms of tidal sea, such as those of the Thames, the Orwell, the Humber, the Tyne, the Clyde, the Mersey, the Avon, and others. In such estuaries we have ports, which, as they are not exposed to the open sea, cannot easily be attacked by hostile fleets, though once in an hour of shame the Dutch fleet sailed up the Medway, burnt three men-of-war, and blockaded the Thames (1667). These and other great harbours scattered along the coast have given us unusual facilities for shipbuilding as well as for sea-borne trade. The shallowness of the surrounding waters has given us enormous fisheries. Off the Cornish coast, for example, twelve million pilchards have been taken in a single day. "It is an amazing sight," as an eye-witness relates, "to watch an innumerable army of these fish passing the Land's End, pursued by hordes of dogfish, hake, and cod, and followed overhead by vast flocks of sea-birds ready at any moment to pounce upon any fish that may rise to the surface." The experience of sea-life gained in the fisheries along the coast has tempted the more adventurous seamen to make distant voyages abroad. Thus a large part of our population grew into a nation of sailors, whose enterprise led them to discover new lands in different quarters of the globe, to establish great colonies which are rapidly becoming sister-nations, and to found the greatest maritime empire that the world has yet seen.

3. *Pasturage and agriculture.*

The soil and climate of Britain are favourable to fertility in plants and to the vigorous growth of animal life. Notwithstanding the occurrence, especially in parts of Scotland and Wales, of rugged hill-tracts mainly covered with bare rocks, there are broad spaces which, though not fit for the plough, are useful for pasturage; and for several centuries during the Early Middle Age England was the chief wool-producing country of the west. Besides the land fit only for pasturage there is a great deal of level country suitable for agriculture, which up to the middle of the nineteenth century was the chief industry of the nation. Though farming is now much less prosperous than it was, this is not the fault either of the soil or of the climate or of the people, but is owing to the vast increase of imported food-stuffs, which can be produced elsewhere in greater abundance and sometimes at less cost than is possible in our own overcrowded island, and are admitted into our seaports free of duty. No other country produces finer cattle, finer sheep, finer horses, or finer vegetables. In no other country is the grass so rich. The climate, though irregular and subject in almost any month of the year to fogs from the ocean, is one of moderate heat and moderate cold. Countries of the same latitude in Europe and America are afflicted with much greater extremes of temperature, because their climate is not cooled in the summer, as ours is, by the equalising influence of a vast expanse of ocean, nor warmed in the winter, as ours is, by genial breezes from the south and west that sweep across the island during the greater part of the year.

4. *Mining and manufacture.*

The tin mines of Cornwall and Devonshire were known to the Phœnicians from a remote antiquity; but the Phœnicians were wise enough to keep the secret to themselves for many centuries. These mines are not even yet exhausted; but on account of the depth to which the mining has now to be carried, the industry has become less remunerative than it was. The lead mines of Somersetshire and Northumberland began to be worked under Roman rule, *i.e.* nearly two thousand years ago. Copper, manganese, China clay, and other kinds of minerals are found in various parts; and gold is found in Wales. But the deposits of coal and iron, in which Britain abounds, have in more recent times been the mainspring of her industrial prosperity. It has been calculated that of all the "metal-wealth" of Britain eleven-twelfths are of iron, and that of all the "non-metal wealth" about three-quarters are of coal. The application of these two minerals to the manufacture of all kinds of machinery, of which her own sons were the inventors, gave her the start of other nations, and placed her in the vanguard of industrial activity. The iron and the coal of England are generally found in the neighbourhood of each other,—a fact which adds greatly to the facility of working the mines and of turning their resources to practical account. The thousands of men who earn their livelihood by such industries have been drawn together into great manufacturing centres, which in proportion to the total area of the country are more numerous and more populous in Britain than in any other part of the world.

5. *Civil government and national character.*

Favoured as England has been with such unusual advantages of seaboard, soil, climate, and mineral resources, how does she stand as compared with other countries in the matter of civil government? Few, if any, will be inclined to dispute the fact that in political wisdom, if in nothing else, she has carved out a niche peculiarly her own in the great corridor of human history. At such an early date as 1215 no other country produced such a charter as that to which King John was compelled to affix his seal. But this document, far-reaching and comprehensive though it was, was but the foundation-stone on which the stately edifice of constitutional government has since been built. The coexistence of three great industries so diverse as seafaring, farming, and manufacture produced in the minds of our countrymen a balance of character that secured for them the possession of great political rights with the minimum of political disturbance. We had, it is true, a revolutionary period of our own, when the nation was determined at all risks to get rid of the Stuarts. But the amount of violence, with which this great work was accomplished, was trifling in comparison with what has happened elsewhere in times not very remote from the present. It was the mental balance and self-restraint of our countrymen that enabled them to work out for themselves a system of government limited by law, controlled by opinion, and guided by a determination, against which tyrants conspired in vain, to defend the rights of property, reputation, and person. This, then, is the example that England has set to the world. She has solved in her own way the problem of constitutional monarchy, which, with all its faults, is the best form of government that the world has yet seen; and herein lies the world's chief interest in her history.

Essay III.

"Under the Roman dominion Britain had assumed an aspect of great prosperity, which was destroyed as soon as the legions of Rome were withdrawn."—Goldwin Smith.

Subjects are sometimes set in the form of a quotation, such as the above, which is to be expanded into an essay. More briefly the subject of the present essay might have been worded—

The Roman Conquest and Occupation of Britain.

1. *How and when Britain was conquered by the Romans.*

Britain was the last great province that the Romans added to their empire; and when their empire was falling, it was the first that they gave up. "It was entirely unknown to them," as Bede tells us in his *Ecclesiastical History*, chap. ii., "before the time of Julius Cæsar." Julius Cæsar made two invasions, the first in 55 B.C., and the second in the year following. The first was made in a spirit of adventure rather than with any serious intention of conquest. The second was made with a larger military force, and was carried further inland; but, as before, no legions were left and no province was formed. For the next hundred years Britain was left alone, the Romans being too much occupied with civil wars and other troubles of their own to undertake the conquest of a distant island, of which they had not yet learnt the value. In A.D. 43, when Claudius was emperor of Rome, invasions were renewed and the subjugation of Britain was taken up in earnest. After about forty years of conflict the conquest of the Britons was completed by Agricola (A.D. 78-85). The chief heroes on the side of the defence were Caradoc, whom the Romans called Caractacus, and Boadicea, "the warrior-queen," as she is called in Cowper's ode. The former was sent to Rome to grace the triumph of the conqueror, but was afterwards reinstated. The latter, as readers of Cowper are aware, died bravely on the battlefield, unless preference is to be given to the alternative legend, that she took poison in order to escape the dishonour of defeat.

2. *What the Romans did for the protection of Britain.*

The Romans were at that time the greatest people in the world, and the ancient Britons were among the most backward; improvement therefore was bound to follow in the wake of Roman conquest. But the first thing that the Romans had to think of was the protection of the people, who had now become their subjects, from foreign and internal foes. North Britain was at that time the home of a fierce and warlike tribe of mountaineers, called the Picts. These, aided by the Scots, who came originally from Ireland and afterwards gave Scotland its name, were a constant source of danger and unrest to their neighbours who lived further south. The Romans, not considering the northern country to be worth the labour of conquest, built and fortified strong walls from east to west, the most famous being the wall of the Emperor Hadrian (117-138 A.D.), parts of which remain to this day, extending from the mouth of the Tyne to the Solway Firth. The military force that the Romans maintained in Britain consisted of three great divisions, and to each division a separate duty was assigned—the field-army, under a commander-in-chief called the "Count of Britain" (*Comes Britanniæ*)—the frontier-army, under an officer called the "Duke of the Britains" (*Dux Britanniarum*)—and the coast-army, under an officer called the "Count of the Saxon shore" (*Comes Litoris Saxonici*), *i.e.* the shore molested by Saxons; for Saxon pirates had already appeared. Great military roads, solid as the Roman character and unswerving as the Roman ambition, were carried across the island, and no obstacles arising from rivers or mountains were allowed to stand in the way. The highways best known to us at the present day converged towards "the town anciently called *Londinium*," as the Romans spelt it; which shows that even in Celtic or pre-Roman days London was the heart or chief centre of the national life. One of these roads, now known in London as Watling Street, stretched from Dover to Chester, passing through London on its way. Nearly 800 years afterwards this very road was by the Treaty of Wedmore (A.D. 879) made the boundary line between the dominions of the Saxon king, Alfred, and those of the Danish king, Guthrum.

3. *What the Romans did for the benefit of the people.*

The roads, which the Romans had made by various routes across Britain for purposes of military protection, served the not less useful purpose of promoting trade and friendly intercourse between tribes which had hitherto been strangers, if not enemies, to one another.

Britain was thus for the first time revealed to herself. Forests were cleared, new markets were opened, mines were worked, agriculture was extended, new grains and new fruits were introduced. Large towns, such as Colchester, Doncaster, Lincoln, Chester, and many more sprang up in different parts of the country.[1] London and York, both of which had existed already for several centuries as Celtic or pre-Roman towns, grew rapidly in wealth and size,—London as the great commercial centre, which it still is,—York as the political capital of Roman Britain, the dwelling-place of the Viceroy or Governor-General (*Vicarius Britanniarum*). Under Roman tuition agriculture became so prosperous at last, that grain was sometimes exported to supply the wants of Italy or of Gaul. The human sacrifices, once so zealously practised by the Druids, were either put down by force or left to die a natural death in contemptuous neglect. The Druids themselves were expelled with much slaughter from the sanctuary that had been maintained for centuries in Mona (now called Anglesey) and was supposed to be under the special protection of the national gods. Thus Druidism was hopelessly discredited, and the name of Druid is henceforth heard no more in Britain. Romans and Britons, conquerors and conquered, became Christians together from the second century onward.

4. *Why and when the Roman legions were withdrawn.*

But the Roman dominion could not last for ever. The time had come when Rome needed all the legions that she could muster for her own defence. Ever since the birth of Christ the countries that lay around the Mediterranean Sea had rested as securely as Britain had done under her protection. For 400 years she had held at bay the barbarian world contiguous with her frontiers—the Numidians of the African desert, the Parthians to the east of the Euphrates, the Teutons or Germans to the north of the Danube, and the Franks to the east of the Rhine. But the tide of barbarians overflowed the Roman barriers at last; and Rome herself, having lost much of her pristine virtue, was the less able to repel the intruder. The western provinces were the first to fall. Gaul was conquered and colonised by the Franks, who have given to ancient Gaul the modern name of France; Spain was overrun by the West Goths; Northern Africa by the Vandals; and Italy herself by the East Goths. In the year 401 Rome began to withdraw her legions from Britain; by the year 410 the withdrawal was completed.

5. *What became of the Britons after the Romans were gone.*

Britain, having no army of her own, was unable to repel the enemies who now closed in upon her by land and by sea. Here then the Roman government in Britain, much as we may admire it for the many good things it had done, stands condemned by the verdict of history. It found the natives warlike, though untrained; it left them unwarlike and helpless. The Picts and Scots renewed their incursions from the highlands of the north, to which they could retreat in safety with the plunder that they had seized. Saxons and other tribes of hardy sea-rovers poured

[1] The names *chester*, *caster* (from Latin *castra*, a fortified encampment), and *coln* (from Lat. *colonia*, a military settlement) disclose the origin of the towns which bear these names.

into the island by way of the Channel and the North Sea. These were the English. They had come in search of new settlements, finding their own country too narrow for them; and as the Britons had no fleet to send out against them, they landed unopposed and held their ground until new settlers arrived, which enabled them to penetrate further and further inland. In this time of suffering and sorrow all that the islanders could do was to send a letter to Ætius, the only great Roman left, inscribed "the groans of the Britons." But Rome by this time was as helpless as Britain herself. In A.D. 476 the great imperial city fell a victim to the Goths, and a Gothic king set up his court in the palace of the Roman Cæsar.

Essay IV.—Early English Settlements in Britain, A.D. 450-600.

The dates that have been given as part of the heading of this essay leave no possibility of doubt as to what is meant to be included and what excluded by the words, "Early English Settlements in Britain." The essay, then, is intended to cover the period during which Britain, or at least the greater part of it, was invaded, conquered, and occupied by the English,—this being the collective name under which it is convenient to group the various tribes that left their homes in Europe in order to found new ones in Britain. By the close of this period the subjugation of the Britons is complete, the two races (the Briton and the English) have coalesced, and a missionary has come from Rome to convert the new settlers to Christianity (A.D. 597). It might be briefly called "The Period of Pagan England." Henceforth, as in some of the essays in Chapter XXVII., the student should make out for himself what the theme of each paragraph is, and write it on the top of the paragraph with a line drawn under it.

1. Long before the Romans had given up or had thought of giving up their hold on Britain, the sea-coasts facing the continent were exposed to attacks from Saxons—a brave race of warriors and pirates who crossed the Channel from the opposite seaboard of Europe. So frequent were these attacks, that the Romans found it necessary to maintain an officer called "Count of the Saxon shore" (*Comes Litoris Saxonici*), whose special duty it was to protect the south-eastern coast of Britain from the Wash to Beachy Head. "Foes are they," sang a Roman poet of the day, "fierce beyond all others, and as cunning as they are fierce: the sea is their school of war, and the storm is their friend: they are sea-wolves that live on the pillage of the world."

2. When the last of the Roman legions had been withdrawn, the invasions were renewed. But this time Saxons were not the only strangers that came. The tribes and sub-tribes were various, the three principal tribes being the Saxon, the Frisian, and the Angle; but all

these comers, to whichever tribe or sub-tribe they belonged, were men of kindred stock—Teutonic,—to whom for the sake of convenience historians have given the collective name of "English." They entered Britain by the mouths of rivers, whose courses led like open highways towards the interior of the country. Then, as their conquests were carried further and further inland, they made free use of the great military roads and the well-planned forts and camping-grounds with which the Romans had for about 350 years maintained their hold on the island. Thus the Roman dominion in Britain prepared the way for the dominion and settlement of their successors, the English. The Romans had for the most part come to conquer and to rule; the English, finding their own country too narrow for them, came to conquer and to stay. To such men Britain was a tempting field: it supplied all that they wanted,—fresh space on which they could settle, and a defenceless people on whose labours they could subsist, and from whom, if any desired it, they could obtain wives. Thus the two races,—the Celtic and the English,—easily coalesced, making a compound which should be called Anglo-Celt rather than Anglo-Saxon. As happened after the Norman conquest, the ownership of estates may have often changed hands; but the bulk of the peasantry remained Celtic as before. The completeness of the conquest is proved by the fact, that wherever an English settlement was formed, the Celtic or Cymric language perished, and some English dialect took its place; for though the conquerors borrowed the Roman letters that we now use from the Celts or Britons whom they had conquered, the number of words borrowed was very small, probably not more than 15. Henceforth a large part of Britain, amounting to more than half the island, and this the better half, may rightly be called "England."

8. The invaders did not all come at once, nor in large bands at a time. To come in large bands, as they would have done if the invasion could have been made by land, was not possible. The sea had to be crossed, and the boats by which the invaders came were neither very capacious[1] nor very numerous. The fighting men came first. When a batch of these had secured a safe landing, they sent back their boats to fetch as many of their women as were willing to join them. Each tribe or section of a tribe appears to have acted independently of every other; and Britain was large enough to offer a wide field of choice. The conquest was therefore very gradual, as slow as it was sure. About a century and a half passed before the conflicts between the old and the new inhabitants came to an end. In the course of this long contest victory was not always on the side of the invaders. In one great battle at least the Celts or Britons obtained a decisive victory, in which the Saxon leader, Cutha, was slain; we have this on the authority of the *Anglo-Saxon Chronicle* (A.D. 584), the writer of which is not likely to have been more partial to the Celts than to his own countrymen. Eventually seven kingdoms were formed,—Kent (Lat. *Kantium*),—South Saxony (Sussex),—East Saxony (Essex),—West Saxony (Wessex),—East Anglia (Norfolk and Suffolk,

[1] When Alfred the Great built his fleet about 400 years later, in order to repel the Danes and defeat them on their own element, the sea, we are expressly informed by the *Anglo-Saxon Chronicle* that, though he used the same pattern, "the Frisian," the boats that he built were of a much larger size.

and part of Lincolnshire),—Mercia (the Midland kingdom),—and Northumbria (the northern kingdom). The kingdom last named covered an area much longer than it was broad; for it embraced at first only the eastern half of this part of Britain, the western half (then called Strathclyde and Cumbria) being still unconquered and still remaining solely occupied by its original inhabitants, the Celts. On account of its length this northern kingdom was at first divided into two separate kingdoms,—Deira and Bernicia, the former extending from the Humber to the Tyne, the latter from the Tyne to the Forth.

4. It is to this period, the most obscure in English history, that we must ascribe the legend of King Arthur and the search for the Holy Grail.[1] Up to and beyond the year 600 A.D. three large tracts, inhabited by Britons or Celts, still remained unconquered by the English,—(*a*) "West Wales," as the English of that day called it; viz. the counties of Cornwall and Devon, and the greater part of Somerset; (*b*) "North Wales," which we now call simply "Wales"; and (*c*) the kingdoms of "Cumbria" and "Strathclyde" (referred to already), coextensive with the counties lying between the Mersey and the Firth of Clyde. These three tracts were never so thoroughly conquered by the Romans as the western side of the island had been; but under Roman rule or influence the inhabitants had become Christian, and Christians they remained after the Romans had gone. It is doubtful whether the legend of King Arthur is to be ascribed to (*a*) or to (*c*); both claim it, but the trend of tradition is strongly in favour of (*a*). Stripped of the mass of legend and romance that has gathered round his name, Arthur stands out to our view as a great Celtic king and warrior, who formed a league with other kings of his own race to defend the cause of the Cross against its heathen enemies,—worshippers of the god of War, the god of Thunder, and the goddess of Spring, Eostre, from which we get the name "Easter." That such a contest arose, and that it was marked by a series of conflicts of which the memory could not be wholly forgotten, is beyond all question. If the scene of it lay chiefly on the frontier of "West Wales," the triumph of King Arthur and his associates was decisive and lasted for a considerable period; for it was not till A.D. 815, or about 300 years after the kingdom of Wessex was founded, that "West Wales" was finally conquered and annexed by the victorious Saxon. Meanwhile the legend had gathered around it so many fabulous additions, that the nucleus of historical fact could not be separated from the embellishments which remained. Not only in England, but all over Western Europe, the story of King Arthur was current as a religious romance, and continued to be popular throughout the Middle Age. In recent years some portions of it have been revived by Tennyson under the title of "Idylls of the King."

5. It was stated above that the tribes and sub-tribes, under whatever names they may have come into Britain, can be reduced to three,—Saxon, Angle, and Frisian. (*a*) The Saxons were a tribe of Dutch, who came from the lower courses of the Rhine and the adjoining coast. This

[1] Camelot, one of the places where Arthur is said to have held his Round Table, has been identified with Winchester. It is alluded to in Drayton's *Polyolbion* (A.D. 1563-1631):—

> Like Camelot, what place was ever yet renown'd,
> Where, as at Caerleon oft, he kept the Table Round?

was the tribe that occupied South Britain (*i.e.* Britain to the south of the Thames) and that portion to the north of the river, which is still called Essex on the east coast and Middlesex further inland. (*b*) The Angles were a tribe of Norse (*i.e.* Scandinavians or Danes, quite distinct from Dutch), who came from the lower courses of the right bank of the Elbe and from the western seaboard of Schleswig-Holstein. This was the tribe that occupied North Britain from the Humber to the Highlands of Scotland, and that part of the western coast-land south of the Humber which is still called East Anglia. (*c*) The Frisians were an intermediate tribe, who came from the lower courses of the Ems and the Weser and from the islands which are still called Frisian. They are better known in England as Mercians, because the kingdom which they founded was surrounded by the "marches" or boundary-lines of other kingdoms. This was the tribe that occupied the wide area of Mid-Britain. The position of the Frisians, then, was intermediate in England, as it had also been in Europe before they set out from Friesland to found new homes in our island. Each of these three tribes had a distinct dialect of its own; but modern English is mainly based on the Midland or Mercian dialect.[1]

Essay V.—Early English Kingdoms and their Unification in 829.

As in the preceding essay, the theme of each paragraph should be made out by the student himself and written at the top of each paragraph, with a line drawn under it. It will be a guide to him, if he writes out and numbers the several themes, before he begins to reproduce in his own words the substance of the corresponding paragraphs. As this essay is about double the length of the others, it has been divided into two parts. One part can be taken by the student at a time.

Part I.

1. By the year 600 A.D., or about that time, the Celts or Britons amongst whom the English had settled were either completely subdued by force of arms or absorbed by intermarriage with the new settlers. The seven kingdoms, among which England was divided, having no longer any external enemies to contend with, became the enemies and rivals of one another. Apart from boundary-disputes, which must have been frequent, the main object of contention was the office of Bretwalda, "Overlord of Britain,"—an English reproduction of the Roman title *Comes Britanniæ*, "Count or Military Head of Britain." Between these two titles,—the Roman original and its English revival,—there were several links that served to keep up the tradition of an Overlord. It was from York, the capital of Roman Britain, that Constantine the Great was first declared "Emperor of Rome" (A.D. 306); since his mother, Helena, was a

[1] In Appendix I. the reader will find an explanation of the reasons why no mention has been made of the Jutes, and why prominent mention has been made of the Frisians.

British princess, the name of this emperor was long remembered and respected. After him, when the Roman empire was on the decline, more than one soldier of fortune assumed the title of Emperor of Britain, setting the authority of Rome at defiance. When the Romans were gone and the heathen English began to pour into the island, the title or something equivalent to it was assumed by King Arthur, who, as Celtic champion of the cross and leader of a band of Christian knights, is dimly seen in outline through the mists of romance and legend. To all these traditions the office of Bretwalda (so the English called it) was the natural sequel. The question was, Which among the rival kings of divided England could compel the rest to recognise him as their chief or overlord? This coveted title, which made the holder thereof the greatest king of his day, kept England divided against herself for more than 200 years, until at last in A.D. 829 the competition was brought to an end by all the kingdoms becoming united under a single sceptre,—the sceptre of Egbert. King of Wessex.

2. Of the kings amongst whom England was divided, the first to deserve special mention is Ethelbert, King of Kent. In many respects this kingdom set an example to the rest of England. It was the first of the English kingdoms that was established in the soil of Britain,—the first that discarded the heathen gods and goddesses in favour of the Christian creed,—the first that began to form a literature and establish schools of its own.[1] In 597 A.D. (about one hundred and fifty years after the first of the new settlers had landed), Ethelbert, King of Kent, consented to meet Augustine, the missionary who had come from Rome, provided that the meeting might be held in the open air; for the king was afraid that if he met him in a covered room, some spell might be cast upon him by the stranger, whose priestly garb and venerable mien had appalled him. The result of the appeal that Augustine made to his hopes or fears of a future life was that Ethelbert consented to receive Christian baptism. After this ceremony had been performed, there was no going back. His people, following the fashion of tribal discipline which then prevailed, passed at once into the allegiance of the new god. Woden, the god of War, thus yields (nominally at least) to Christ, the King of Peace. But the example of Christ appears to have been thrown away upon him. His growing ambitions henceforth went far beyond his power of carrying them into effect; and he seems to have lost much of his worldly wisdom with his change of creed. Though his kingdom was small and his people had become unwarlike, he laid claim to the office of Bretwalda, and in this self-assumed capacity he made war upon Mercia and urged his northern neighbours, the Kings of Essex and East Anglia, to receive the same creed that he had embraced himself. These kings, instead of accepting his advice, took offence at his interference. At the same time Mid-Britain or Mercia, then a small but growing and warlike kingdom, revolted against his pretensions, defeated him in battle, and placed itself under the protection of its more powerful neighbour, East Anglia, whose king thence-

[1] The story of the founding of the kingdom of Kent by Hengist and Horsa need not be repeated. Every one knows it. It is largely mixed up with fable; for Hengist is claimed by the Frisians as their ancestor no less than he is by the founders of Kent. The first settlers in Kent are said to have been Jutes. But who were the Jutes? See Appendix I., where the subject is discussed.

forward became, for a time at least, Bretwalda or overlord of Britain (A.D. 607). Never again do we hear of the kingdom of Kent possessing any political importance. One dignity, however, remained to it: Canterbury, which Ethelbert had assigned to Augustine as his place of residence, became, as it still is, the official centre of the Christian Church in this island. The Archbishop of Canterbury is still regarded as the Primate of all England.

3. The downfall of Kent made room for the expansion of Wessex, which gradually absorbed not only Kent, but all the other petty kingdoms of South Britain. The founding of this kingdom was effected on a very small scale in A.D. 495 by Cerdic, the Saxon, the great ancestor of all the sovereigns that have reigned in England since Stephen, and of most of those that had reigned before him. Little could this rough heathen adventurer, leader of a small band of pirates, surrounded by enemies on all sides, and scarcely able to effect a landing,—little could he have imagined that the petty kingdom, which by dint of hard fighting he managed to establish round the old Celtic city of Winchester,[1] was destined to become the foundress of England, of the United Kingdom, and of the British Empire. For the present, however, all that we can say in reference to Wessex is that the little kingdom founded by Cerdic obtained by degrees the mastery of the whole of South Britain excepting only the Celtic domain then called West Wales (Somerset, Devon, and Cornwall),—the realm of King Arthur, which remained under kings of its own until A.D. 815. By these successes Wessex became as large and as powerful as Mercia in Mid-Britain and Northumbria in North Britain, and was destined in the long run to prevail over both.

4. The century preceding the unification of England by Wessex is for the most part taken up with the rivalries of the two kingdoms last named,—Northumbria and Mercia. We have no space, and indeed no inclination, to give the history of these rivalries and of the battles that were fought,—battles which (as Milton says of them in his *History of England*) are not more worthy of attention than "the battles of crows and kites." The northern kingdom (Northumbria) was the first of the two to rise into fame. It was founded by Angles, a Norse or Scandinavian tribe, which accounts for the marked peculiarities of the northern or Scotch dialect of English, that have lasted to the present day; and it reached from the mouth of the Humber to as far north as the Highlands of Scotland, which accounts for the fact that the Lowland Scotch are mainly of Teutonic blood, while the Highland Scotch are mainly Celts, speaking, as many of them still do, a language that is not English. Three kings of Northumbria held the office of Bretwalda in succession. But it was in literary rather than political activity that the kingdom of Northumbria held, while it lasted, the highest place; for this was the kingdom that produced the Venerable Bede or Beda, the greatest scholar of his day,—Cædmon, the earliest and one

[1] By the Celts or ancient Britons the town was called *Caer-Gwent*, "The White City," the name White having been given to it perhaps on account of the chalk that covers the greater part of Hampshire. By the Roman historians the town is called *Venta* or *Wenta Belgarum*. *Wenta* is evidently the Roman transliteration of the Celtic *Gwent*. The town became an important Roman fort or encampment, for which reason the Saxons added to its name *chester*, the Saxon transliteration of *castra*, camp.

of the greatest of English poets,—and Alcuin, whom Charlemagne (Charles the Great) invited over to France to assist him in the education of his people. After this kingdom had fallen owing to internal divisions and to the growing power of Mercia, one honour still remained to it. Its capital, York, which during the Roman occupation of Britain had been the seat of the Roman Viceroy, continued to be the seat or see of the archbishopric of northern England, as Canterbury was of southern; and so it has remained to this day. These are interesting examples of the unbroken continuity of English history, and of the conservative character of the English people.

PART II.

5. From Northumbria we turn to the kingdom of Mercia. This kingdom was founded by Frisians, the intermediate tribe between Saxons (the southern tribe) and Angles (the northern). On account of its geographical position this midland kingdom, surrounded on all sides by the *marches* or boundary-lines of other kingdoms, acquired the name of "Mercia," just as the northern kingdom founded by Angles acquired, from its position to the north of the Humber, the name of Northumbria. The founding of the Midland kingdom by Frisians, though it is not stated in the *Anglo-Saxon Chronicle*, must be accepted as an historical necessity; for the dialect of Mercia was the ancestor of our modern English speech, and this dialect must have come to us from Friesland, because the Friese dialect to this day bears a closer resemblance to English than any other dialect spoken on the continent of Europe. This dialect is quite distinct from that of the Saxon, a kind of Dutch, and that of the Anglian, a kind of Norse; and modern English did not spring from either Saxon or Norse. Moreover, Procopius, the Roman historian of the sixth century (who is an older authority than the *Anglo-Saxon Chronicle*), informs us that in his time Britain was inhabited by three races, the Angles, the Frisians, and the Britons;[1] from which it is clear (*a*) that he included the Saxons among the Frisians, and (*b*) that Frisians took a large and active part in the colonisation of Britain. Mercia continued to be pagan after the northern and the southern kingdoms had both become Christian. King Penda in A.D. 626, a pagan, formed an unholy alliance with a Welsh Christian king for the overthrow of the newly-born Christianity of Northumbria. Edwin, the King of Northumbria, was defeated and slain, and his successors relapsed into paganism for a time. The eighth century was the period during which Mercia became the predominant power in England. Its two greatest kings were Ethelbald, who reigned for forty-one years (716-757), and Offa, who reigned for nearly forty years (757-796). An archbishop was appointed for Lichfield, the capital of Mercia; and it then seemed as if Lichfield would supersede both Canterbury and York as the spiritual capital of England. But after the death of Offa the kingdom of Mercia, as Northumbria had done, fell into a state of anarchy from which it never recovered. Lichfield ceased to be the see of an archbishop, and the chance of its becoming the royal residence of united England was lost. But one honour has survived to Mercia, though everything else has been lost; and this honour the greatest of all. Its Frisian or midland dialect, spoken in Oxford, Cambridge, and London,—

[1] Procopius, *De Bello Gothico*, ix. 20.

the dialect which Chaucer and Wycliff wrote and which Caxton printed,—became the ancestor of modern English, and is now predominant throughout the British Empire.

6. The weakness of Mercia, preceded as this had been by the fall of Northumbria, was the opportunity of Wessex, the third and last of the trio of kingdoms into which England had been so long divided. Egbert, the lineal descendant of old Cerdic, the Saxon, mounted the throne of Wessex in A.D. 800; but owing to internal disputes within the kingdom he found it expedient, before assuming the reins of government, to take refuge in the court of Charlemagne (Charles the Great), the illustrious warrior and ruler, who had brought Western Europe under his undivided sway, and had been crowned Emperor of the West by the Pope of Rome. The visit of Egbert to the court of such a man was an inspiring episode in Egbert's life, and it led to important consequences in the history of our nation; for it was during his sojourn in this court that he conceived the ambition of doing for the scattered people of his own island what Charlemagne had done on a much larger scale for the scattered nations of Western Europe. England had suffered long enough from the jealousies and ambitions of its petty kings, and it was high time for some one to arise who could weld its different parts together into a consistent homogeneous whole. Charlemagne's work died with him; for his empire fell to pieces soon after his death: but Egbert's work remained and still remains. Egbert's kingdom looks very small and insignificant by the side of the great empire of Charlemagne; but out of this little kingdom of Wessex has grown an empire that far surpasses in extent and power anything that Charlemagne could have dreamed of.

7. Before the close of the year 802 Egbert returned to his country. His first act was to subdue and annex, after many years of difficult fighting, the Britons or Celts of "West Wales," *i.e.* the area once covered by the semifabulous realm of King Arthur and his knights, and now covered by the counties of Cornwall, Devon, and the greater part of Somerset. His next act was to recover and re-annex Kent, Sussex, Surrey, and Essex, all of which had seceded from Wessex and become nominally subject to Cenwulf, the last powerful king of Mercia, who died in A.D. 821. Thus strengthened and flushed with victory, he fell upon Mercia itself; and East Anglia, disgusted with the treatment that she had received from Mercia, joined the forces of the invader. By the year 829 the whole of South Britain, and the whole of Central Britain exclusive of Wales, but inclusive of East Anglia, were united under the dominion of Egbert. The conqueror next moved against Northumbria, whose king did not dare to accept the offer of battle. Among the hills of Derbyshire the Northumbrians, as the *Chronicle* tells us, "met him and offered him obedience and peace, and with that they separated the one from the other." This treaty could only mean that the Northumbrians voluntarily accepted Egbert as their overlord. His supremacy was thus at last assured over the whole of the English portion of the island, and this to a degree much more complete than had fallen to the lot of any other king who had held the office of Bretwalda before him.

8. The unification of England by Egbert was final. Henceforth we hear nothing more about Bretwaldas; under the rule of Egbert the office died a natural death. Mercia, Northumbria, East Anglia, and Kent still for a time had kings of their own, but these were no longer independent,

and must henceforth be called "under-kings," subject to the King of Wessex as overlord. Once, and once only, after Egbert's death was the unity of England broken. But this interruption was caused, not by the revolt of any of the under-kings, but by the treaty of Wedmore, A.D. 878, when for the short period of twenty-three years England was cut in half by Watling Street, the great Roman road that ran across the island from Dover to Chester, taking London on its way. The name "Watling St." still clings to it in London; but elsewhere other names have taken its place. Whatever territory lay to the north and east of this road was conceded to the Danes,—a new race of warrior-pirates, who but for the patience and valour of Alfred the Great would have become masters of the whole of England. The incursion of the Danes, followed as it was by their occupation of one half of England under a king of their own, broke up the old traditions of the once great kingdoms of Mercia and Northumbria. Thus the temporary triumph of the Danes proved to be, as Alfred possibly foresaw, a valuable help towards the final unification of England. The opportunity for reunion was not long in coming. The Danelagh or Danish dominion to the north and east of Watling Street was re-annexed to the English crown by Edward the Elder (901-925), the son of Alfred the Great. Thus the uniting of England, that was first accomplished in A.D. 829 by Egbert, was restored more strongly than ever in A.D. 901 by the policy of Alfred and his son.

Essay VI.—Did England gain or lose by the Norman Conquest?

As this is a controversial subject, it falls naturally into the form of a dialogue. In the reproduction the student might be asked to restate the arguments on both sides in the form of an ordinary narrative. For this purpose a number has been written against each place where a new paragraph might be commenced. As the essay or dialogue is rather long, I have subdivided it into two parts, as in the case of the preceding essay.

Part I.

1. A. You told me, I remember, a few days ago, that England, as you thought, gained little or nothing, but lost much, by the Norman Conquest. Do you still hold this view?

B. I do.

A. If you are willing to discuss this question with me, can you give me some idea of the method or procedure according to which you would like the discussion to be held?

B. That is a very simple matter. Tell me, one by one, in what directions or for what purposes did England need the Norman? Choose the order of the different points yourself.

A. I agree. I will take up the several points, one after another, in the way that you suggest.

2. Firstly, then, England needed the strong arm of the Norman to unite her, to bind her people more firmly together; for at the time of Harold's accession the north of England was at enmity with the centre and the south. Tostig, aided by the King of Norway, had rebelled

against his brother, Harold, the king, and had led a hostile force into Yorkshire. Moreover, the Earl of Northumbria refused to accompany Harold to the south after William had landed; which shows that England was divided against herself.

B. You astonish me. Do you seriously believe that a passing disturbance, the like of which may be seen in almost every page of the history of those times, could not have been put right without a sanguinary conflict between the lawful King of England (for Harold had been lawfully elected king by the *Witenagemot*, or Saxon assembly) and the Norman usurper? In point of fact England had been united and pacified before William landed. You know what happened at Stamford Bridge, where Tostig, who had been justly banished for sedition and misgovernment, was defeated and slain. That was the end of the trouble. The Earl of Northumbria should, it is true, have accompanied his king to the south to meet the Norman aggressor; but as he afterwards rebelled against the Norman, when it was too late, we may safely conclude that he did not at that time realise how serious the crisis was. Let the admirers of Norman peace-makers mark the frequency of family-wars among the Normans themselves. The son of the Conqueror makes war upon his father; his sons make war upon one another; his step-brother, Bishop Odo, conspires against him in league with the Norman barons whom he himself (William) had made; Henry of Winchester abets those who are making war on his brother, Stephen; the three sons of Henry II. (a Norman on his mother's side) make war upon their father, being instigated to do so by Henry's own queen, their mother; John makes war upon his nephew, and closes his life in a civil war between himself and his barons. A happy and united family! To hold up the Normans as models of political organisation, as the indispensable unifiers of divided England, is ridiculous. England was never so harassed by disunion and internal strife as she was by the selfish ambitions of the robbers who had seized her territory. She suffered less even from the Wars of the Roses. The Norman conquest severed the Lowlands of Scotland from England, and thus put off for some centuries the union of Britain.

3. A. You have pelted me with such a shower of facts that I do not at present see how to answer you on this point. You will hardly deny, however, that the Norman conquest, even if it was not the means of uniting England to herself, was the means of connecting her more closely with the continent, of making her better known abroad, and more respected by foreigners than she had ever been before.

B. I do not deny this; but the fact tells against yourself. The possession of Normandy by the kings of England was not a blessing, but a curse. The loss of Normandy (A.D. 1453), though it seemed at the time to be a blow to the national honour, was one of the best things that ever happened to our country. What was the source out of which the Hundred Years' War arose? The possession of Normandy. What did England gain by this prolonged and sanguinary struggle? Nothing but the discredit of inflicting untold miseries on France, and of being compelled at last to give up everything for which she had fought.

4. A. Well, we will drop the subject of foreign politics. Let us turn to home politics. England needed better laws, which no country but Normandy, enlightened as it had been by the civilisation of France, was able to give her. Do you dispute this also?

B. Certainly I do. If England needed better laws, as you assert, Normandy had only worse ones to give her. The feudal system introduced by William was less patriotic and less suited to the character of the people than the Saxon Fyrd or militia-system, which flourished up to the date of the Conquest. The Fyrd was a kind of citizen-army; but William made no use of it for a very good reason—his own safety. Henry II., a much more enlightened man, revived it. The superiority of the Fyrd to the feudal system is proved by its having lasted, in some form or other, down to the present day; whereas the feudal system fell upon its own sword in the Wars of the Roses, and died out more than 400 years ago. The code issued by Alfred the Great was for its day a valuable piece of legislation, a boon to the nation. The laws of Edward the Confessor, for the restoration of which the nation clamoured after the Conquest, were based on those of Alfred. The charter of liberties granted by Henry I. (who, though a Norman by blood, was, on the whole, a friend and benefactor of the English people) was not the work of Norman jurists, but mainly the revival of the laws of Edward the Confessor. The Great Charter which the barons wrested from the tyrant, John, was avowedly based on the charter issued voluntarily by Henry I., and was therefore mainly of Saxon origin. It has been well said by Bishop Stubbs that "the Norman brought little in comparison with what he destroyed, and little that he brought was his own."[1]

PART II.

5. A. The English vocabulary, you must allow, was meagre. It needed to be enriched with a fresh stock of words. The French that came in with the Norman Conquest furnished a new source of supply.

B. The French imported by the Normans did not enrich our language. It corrupted it. We had no need of French. English words were ousted and French ones put in their place, not because the English ones were inadequate or unfit, but because for political reasons the study and use of French had come into fashion. Thus a pure Teutonic language was displaced by a medley, which, notwithstanding its alleged enrichment by Norman French, was more fitted for rhetoric and poetry than for exact thought or science, and has therefore been compelled to borrow largely from Latin and Greek ever since. Our spelling and pronunciation have become a chaos. England had a fine literature of her own,—the writings of Bede, Cædmon, Alcuin, Alfred the Great, Alfric, Layamon. Normandy had no literature of its own to give her; what little Normandy gave was not genuinely Norman, but borrowed.

6. A. I will now put one fact before you, to which you cannot, I think, take exception. The Normans introduced a finer style of architecture, especially in the building of cathedrals and castles. Norman architecture has a world-wide reputation. Do you deny this also?

B. I do not deny the superiority of what is called Norman architecture to our Old English architecture: only it was not Norman in its origin, but Gothic. As to castles, the less you say about them the better. They were an unmixed evil. To England, "Merry England," that curse had been unknown till the Norman came. It was William who encouraged his nobles to build castles, in which they could protect them-

[1] *Constitutional History of England*, i. p. 216.

selves against the Saxon earls and other nobles, whom he had robbed of their estates. The castles became centres of rapacity and oppression to all the Thanes and Saxon peasants, whose lands and homesteads lay anywhere within reach. Eventually they gave a great deal of trouble to William himself; for they were used against him by his own barons. The same castles gave a great deal of trouble to Rufus and to Henry I. The prolonged anarchy of Stephen's reign was mainly due to the unassailable castles held by his partisans or by his foes. Readers of *Ivanhoe* are aware what a curse these castles were in the reign of John. As to cathedrals, the question is of no importance. The cathedrals of that day satisfied the nation. If a better style of church-architecture was needed, it could have been got by peaceful means. For the sake of getting a better style of ecclesiastical buildings, was it necessary that the nation should be pounded to death by Norman kings and Norman barons?

7. A. Whatever you may say about cathedrals and churches to the disparagement of Normans, there is one thing that you will not deny. By the Norman Conquest England was made more thoroughly, than she had ever been before, a member of the great confederation of Latin Christendom, of which the centre was situated in Rome. Hitherto the Church had been more national than papal. The ecclesiastical authorities who now came to the front were men of far higher attainments and character than those whom they displaced.

B. Let me ask you in reply—What did this nation, what did religion gain by the change? Henceforth a sharp line is drawn between Church and State—a line of cleavage which, before the Norman came, had been unknown in England. All through the Middle Age up to the year 1535, when the connection with Rome was severed, there was a perpetual state of jealousy and contest between Church and State, between the rival claims of king and bishop. The conflict begins in the time of William himself; for you may remember that when a certain bishop claimed ecclesiastical immunity from secular law, William had him arrested and suspended from office. In point of learning the bishops imported by William were, no doubt, superior to the more homely Saxon ones; but Lanfranc, who ousted the Saxon Stigand, was an Italian, not a Norman. The new bishops did not understand English. A Norman abbot, having quarrelled with his English monks, brings archers into the church to shoot them down, and shoot them they did; all this is told in the *Chronicle*, under the date 1083 A.D. Latin becomes henceforth the language of the Church and of learning. For many a day the vernacular English is ousted from literature and from the service of religion. Was this a blessing to the nation? Was it likely that the people would venerate as spiritual pastors a class of men who were strangers to them in race and language, had seized the abbeys, and had shot the pastors of their own stock? Would they not rather look upon them as foreign ruffians? I leave you to answer the question yourself.

8. A. You give the Normans credit for nothing. Were they not better soldiers than the English? And if so, did not the infusion of Norman blood inspire the conquered people with new ambitions, and make finer and braver men of them?

B. I cannot see it. Norman blood never entered the veins of the nation as a whole. It reached only to the nobles and some of the knights. The national cause was lost at Hastings, not because the English were less brave than the Normans, but because Harold and all his brothers were slain on the field where the battle of Hastings was fought, and in the sudden emergency that arose there was no one to take the lead. The victor marched straight from the battlefield to Westminster, where he adroitly presented himself, not as a conqueror, but as lawful king, promising to respect right and to do justice. The National Assembly (*Witenagemot*), not knowing what a very serious step they were taking, had him crowned with due elective forms, and a Saxon prelate (whom William afterwards dismissed, when he had no further need of him) took part in the ceremony. This is how the national cause was lost. As to the alleged inferiority of the Saxon soldier, this is easily disproved. In the next reign, when Rufus came to the throne (1087) and made promises to the people (which he never kept), they flocked to his standard; and when Robert, his elder brother, sent over soldiers from Normandy, who landed at Pevensey, as the first William had done in 1066, it was an English army that defeated the Norman army in support of the new king. Afterwards, in 1106, when Henry I. was seated on the throne, the army which he led into Normandy, and with which he thoroughly defeated the same Robert and his Norman barons at Tenchebrai, was mainly English.

9. A. I have nothing more to urge. So far as I am concerned, the discussion is at an end. I will think over the matter again.

B. In doing so you will bear in mind, I hope, the cruelties of which William was guilty in making his clearances for the New Forest, and the still more shocking cruelties perpetrated in the ravaged north. The northern earls, who ought to have helped Harold when the Norman first landed, rebelled against the Norman when it was too late, the Norman being then seated firmly on the throne. The vengeance that he took was not confined to the earls. Towns, villages, cattle, crops, were all destroyed. More than a hundred thousand innocent people, not one of whom had wronged him, are said to have died of famine, besides those who were slain by the sword. Is this the kind of man to be extolled as the benefactor of England? Nothing succeeds like success. If Harold had been the conqueror instead of William, those who now maintain so warmly that the Norman Conquest was essential to the future greatness of England, would, with equal eloquence and warmth, be now singing the praises of Harold for having saved his country from the rapacity of the Norman adventurer.

Essay VII.

Prove the following maxim by examples taken from English history :—"Incalculable accidents, by turning the whole course of events, seem to make it impossible that history shall become a science of prediction."—Goldwin Smith.

The subject of this essay, like that of Essay III. in the present series, is given in the form of a quotation. It might easily be worded in the ordinary way, as follows :—

The Part played by Accident in English History.

1. History, as some consider, unless it can be made, like the physical sciences, a science of prediction, is of little or no practical use. We ought

to be able, they say, to predict the future from the past; given the cause or causes, we ought to be able to foresee the effect. In this view of history there is a good deal of truth; for if nothing can be learnt from the lessons of the past, we can only end as we began. No foresight, no progress. But the theory has its limits, and there are two at least that we cannot get rid of—(*a*) the force of personal character, and (*b*) accident, or what seems to be accident. Neither of these, nor the consequences that either may lead to, can be precalculated. In the present essay we have to deal with "accident" only. There is space for only a few examples; many more might be collected.

2. The battle of Hastings (A.D. 1066) decided the fate of England. No one could have foreseen its result; no one could have foreseen the consequences of the result. Yet it was not through the superiority of William to Harold that the field was won. In valour, determination, and generalship the Saxon king was quite a match for the Norman duke. The Saxon, too, had justice on his side; for he, not William, was the lawful sovereign,—lawfully elected and lawfully crowned. But luck was against him. By a cruel accident he was suddenly called away to the north to encounter his traitorous brother, Tostig, at the very time when William was about to land in the south. To have allowed two such enemies to join their forces would have been fatal; so Harold was obliged to get rid of Tostig, aided as this traitor was by the King of Norway, at all hazards. If Tostig had not appeared and Harold could have remained in the south, free from the danger of having an enemy in his rear, it is not likely that William could have even landed; for Harold had the better fleet and the better seamen of the two, and to land a large body of men in the face of a powerful force led by a brave man, who is determined to prevent it, is wellnigh impossible. Thus by the inevitable absence of Harold in the north William was able to put his troops ashore. But worse luck was still to come in the battle that followed. Who could have predicted the flight of that fateful arrow, sent by an unknown hand, which, while the result of the battle fought near Hastings was still trembling in the balance, pierced the eye of Harold, and, penetrating to the brain, put an end to his life? Supposing that Harold had been defeated (which was very doubtful), but had left the field alive, he could have rallied and fought his enemy again. Harold with England at his back, and with the Fyrd or national army eager to serve him, would have given his enemy no peace and left him no time to recover. But William had no fresh forces to draw upon, and must in the end have been compelled either to surrender to his rival or flee back to his boats. If he had reached his boats, could he have put his men on board and rowed back to Normandy in the face of Harold's fleet? This is not at all likely. Probabilities were all in favour of Harold, but an accident, which no one could have predicted, completely turned the course of events in the opposite direction.

3. In 1216 Louis, the son of the King of France, was invited over to England by the barons who were arrayed against King John, when they found that their irregular levies were no match for the disciplined mercenaries that the tyrant was able to bring into the field. What induced Louis to come was the promise of the English crown. He accepted the bargain, brought over a large force, and was received with acclamation by the citizens of London, who were ready to crown him at once in Westminster

Abbey. But by a curious accident the crown could not be found. The coronation had therefore to be postponed; but the troops of Louis were none the less led out against John, who was defeated and compelled to take flight towards the north. Where then was the crown? It was lying buried somewhere in the muddy bed of the Wash, where it must be lying still. John in his flight from London had by a clever piece of foresight carried off the crown with him. While he was crossing the estuary of the Wash he was caught in a rough tide, his boat capsized, and the crown and all his baggage were thrown into the water, where they sank to the bottom. John escaped being drowned, but only to die of fever a few days afterwards in the castle at Newark. With the death of the tyrant the services of Louis were no longer needed. John's son, a child nine years of age, who did not accompany his father, was at once crowned at Winchester by the resident bishop, who used for the purpose an extemporised circlet made of gold wire,—a kind of crown which it would have been an insult to offer to Louis. We must thank the Bishop of Winchester for the foresight and promptness, with which he performed the ceremony that saved England from falling under a foreign yoke. The heart of the nation turned at once from the foreign claimant to the native heir. Louis was bitterly disappointed of the prize that he had lost, but a golden bridge was made for his retreat.

4. In A.D. 1286 the throne of Scotland fell vacant by the death of Alexander III., and there was no male heir to succeed him. The only direct heir to the throne was his little grandchild, Margaret, an infant, daughter of Eric, King of Norway; she was hence called "the Little Maid of Norway." Trouble at once arose among the barons of Scotland, many of whom were ready to seize the crown for themselves, if they could get the chance. The leading men of Scotland, however, appealed for advice to the King of England (Edward I.), whom they regarded as their overlord. He recommended a regency for the time being; and his advice was acted on. His son, Edward (afterwards Edward II.), like the heiress of Scotland, was a child. The English king proposed a marriage between them, to which the Scotch baronage gladly assented. If this marriage had come off, the two countries would have been peaceably united, as they afterwards were under James I., and long years of discord and bloodshed would have been saved. The terms of the treaty, to which the two kingdoms had so readily agreed, showed much foresight and good feeling on both sides. But all this happy foresight was baffled by an accident that no one could have predicted. The Little Maid of Norway never reached England; she died on the voyage.

5. In 1642-1649 occurred the Civil Wars between king and people, which ended in the execution of Charles I. and the establishment of the Commonwealth under the Protectorate of Cromwell. It is believed that all these troubles could have been averted, had Prince Henry, the eldest son of James I. and heir to the English throne, not been cut off by death in his nineteenth year (1612). The grief felt by the nation at his death (officially ascribed to fever) found vent in whispers, that he had been poisoned by the hated favourite, Somerset, one of the evil spirits of James's reign. These whispers may have been true; for Lady Somerset had, as was proved, poisoned her enemy, Sir T. Overbury. Two such opposite characters as Prince Henry and Somerset could not coexist in the same court. Their contemporary, Francis Bacon, pays the highest

tribute to the memory of the young prince and to the hopes that the nation had formed of him. "Men of the best judgment," writes Bacon with surprising outspokenness concerning a court in which he was one amongst many other candidates for the royal favour, "were fully persuaded that his life was a great support and security to his father from the danger of conspiracies." The only thing that could have averted without risk of failure the conflict between king and parliament, of which the seeds were being already sown, was the accession of such a king as Prince Henry promised to be when he came to the throne,—a youth who took a lively interest in ships and shipbuilding, but stood aloof from the corruptions of the Court. He, and he only, could have taken up the cause of Raleigh, the brave seaman, the last of the Elizabethan heroes that had fought the Armada, whom he longed, and longed in vain, to set free. He was almost entirely Scotch by blood; but he was only ten years of age when his father came to the throne of England, and all his tastes were in sympathy with the English nation, which expected and hoped to come under his rule. Destiny mocked the dream. His death makes room for Charles, whose name is the knell of doom.

6. One more example will be given, and this perhaps the most striking of all. In 1768 Corsica was ceded by the Genoese to France. In 1793, when the war between England and the French Republic began, it was placed under the protection of England. While this protectorate lasted, Napoleon, a native of Corsica, but of Italian blood, was an obscure British subject, unrevealed to the world, unrevealed to himself. Had England retained Corsica instead of letting the French have it back, there would have been no career for Napoleon except that perhaps (though even this was not likely) he might have obtained a commission in the English army and fought against the French. But England gave up Corsica. France re-annexed the island, and with the island possessed herself of Napoleon, who used her as the tool of his ambition for the attempted subjugation of Europe, in which for a time he succeeded.

SECTION 2.—SUBJECTS, WITH NOTES APPENDED.

385. Arrangement and Selection of Subjects.—As the early period of English history has received a good deal of attention in Section 1 of this chapter, the subjects now selected relate to the later Mediæval and the Modern periods. By "the later Mediæval" is meant the period that followed the Norman Conquest, as distinct from that which preceded it.

The student can make whatever use of the Notes he or his teacher may think fit. Some of the Notes are subdivided into paragraphs. But the student is under no necessity to follow either their order or their contents.

1. Internal reforms introduced by Henry II.

By birth, treaty, or marriage Henry was lord not only of England with the subsequent addition of Ireland, but of Normandy, Maine, Anjou, Aquitaine, and presently of Brittany. He was a greater power in France than the King of France himself, but by the strange usage of feudalism he was there as the king's vassal. In England only was he king; on England only did he leave his mark. Among English kings he takes rank with the best and the greatest. He made his grandfather, Henry I., his model, and outstripped him.

His first act was to capture and demolish as many as he could of the baronial forts and castles and to rid the country of the mercenary bands that had been raised during the anarchy of Stephen's reign. Owing to this anarchy and bloodshed not much of the Norman aristocracy survived. Norman and Saxon were being rapidly blended by intermarriage. Little was now left of the distinction between the races.

His "Assize or Edict of Arms" (1181 A.D.) was a revival and re-organisation of the old Anglo-Saxon Fyrd or national militia, which, under his Norman predecessors, had been superseded by the feudal system. By this assize every freeman had to provide himself with a coat of mail, helmet, shield, and lance. This gave the king a force independent of feudal tenure.

His next great measure was Scutage, *i.e.* the payment of shield-money (Lat. *scutum*, a shield) in lieu of personal service,—which struck another blow at feudalism. He had no difficulty in carrying out this measure, as the English barons were unwilling to accompany him on an expedition to Toulouse.

He revived and strengthened the plan, first introduced by Henry I., of sending out justices in eyre, who should carry royal justice through the realm and maintain the king's peace. When the justices went their rounds, local delegates (twelve in number) were appointed to present the offenders and to bring forward and examine the evidence. This was the beginning of trial by jury. It first took form under Henry II., the first Plantagenet, but it has since gone the round of the civilised world.

The Assizes or edicts of Clarendon (1164) regulating criminal law and procedure are a landmark in legal history. Trial by ordeal and trial by wager of battle were still in force, but were no longer supreme; for a man who had passed these tests as innocent, but was afterwards found guilty in a legal trial, could be declared guilty and punished as a criminal.

2. Contest between King John and the Pope, 1206-1213.

The point of dispute was the old question whether the right of electing and appointing a prelate to the archbishopric of Canterbury or York belonged to the King or to the Pope. Two applicants from England presented themselves at Rome as candidates for the vacant archbishopric. The Pope, however, rejected both and appointed Stephen Langton.

John refused to recognise the appointment, and set the Pope at defiance. Hence the "Interdict," which lasted for six years. This was followed by the excommunication, and finally by the deposition of John from his throne, which was to be transferred at once to his sworn enemy, Philip, the King of France. So the spiritual sword of the Holy See was backed by the military sword of an earthly king. What sharpened the sword of Philip was personal ambition and the lust of power.

To such a combination John was forced to yield. He accepted Langton as archbishop, and by an instrument placed in the hands of Pandulph, the legate who had been sent out from Pope Innocent the Third, he surrendered his kingdom to the Pope, and received it back as a fief of the Holy See, for which he undertook to pay, and pledged his successors to pay, a thousand marks a year in token of vassalage.

Papal power has now reached its high-water mark in England. Henceforth, though its power was great for some time longer, it begins to recede. It was in the reign of Edward III. that the Pope's demand for arrears was flatly refused, and the bargain between the Pope and King John was cancelled for ever.

3. Baronial rising against Henry III., its causes and results.

This rising was an evil legacy from the previous reign. It arose out of the frequent demands made by the king upon the barons for the money that he needed to meet the extortions of the Pope, who, thanks to King John, held England as a fief of the Holy See. The Pope at this time was carrying on a contest with the Emperor, who in Europe was the chief representative of the secular power, as the Pope was of the spiritual.

England was beyond the sphere of the Emperor's dominion and influence. The Romans had abandoned the island in A.D. 409, and when Charlemagne was crowned Emperor of the West by the Pope (A.D. 800), he laid no claim to England. It was the folly of Henry III. which entangled England in the present embroglio. The shortsighted king had accepted for his younger son, Edmund, the bait of the kingdom of Sicily; and for this purpose he had pawned his kingdom to the Pope and applied to the barons for money.

Then arose Simon de Montford (a foreigner who had inherited the earldom of Lancaster) as leader of the opposition. This Simon was leader of the movement against Henry III., as Stephen Langton had been of the similar movement against King John.

The facts are well known—the Provisions of Oxford, 1258—the Civil War—the Mise of Lewes—the calling of the first parliament, 1265. Show in what respect the composition of this first parliament differed from that of any Council that had preceded it.

4. How Edward I. carried forward the home policy of Henry II.

Edward I. was called by Sir Edward Coke (the greatest lawyer of the Tudor period) the "English Justinian." (It was under the Emperor Justinian that the Roman laws were compiled into a code.) He carried on the work so well begun by Henry I. and continued by Henry II., and raised the study of law to the dignity of a profession.

The Church.—He insisted on the clergy contributing their proper share to the national burdens; hence the Statute of Mortmain. The days of Becket were over; the Papal power was now on the decline.

The Justiciary.—The circuits of the justices in eyre were made more regular. Their office at the same time was made more judicial and less fiscal. In the fiscal part of their office they were collectors of Crown revenue; by the exaction of dues and fines they had brought on themselves the distrust and dislike of the people.

Protection of Trade.—To this heading belongs the Statute of Merchants, which provided for the registration of the debts of traders and for their recovery by distraint of the debtors' goods. Protection, very liberal for the age, was extended to the foreign merchant.

Militia.—He regulated and strengthened the Fyrd, the old Saxon military system, which under the Norman kings had been superseded by the feudal system, but had been revived by Henry II.

Tallage.—This he gave up reluctantly. In this matter he was compelled to yield to force, and the statute *De tallagio non concedendo* ("concerning the non-granting of tallage") was passed. After he had given his seal to it (in those days kings did not sign statutes, as they now do), he made an attempt to get a dispensation from the Pope; but finally he surrendered the claim. On this point he was no better than his predecessors.

Police.—The high roads were made safe by watch and ward.

5. Trade between the British Isles and the Continent during the Middle Ages.

So long as the Channel and the North Sea were infested with pirates, external trade was impossible except at very great risk. The fleet of Edgar (959-975) swept the sea of pirates. The commercial greatness of London was growing. There was a great increase of trade in the time of Canute (1016-1035), the main traffic being in hides, ropes, and iron. Canute the Dane was not less energetic and successful than some of our Saxon kings in clearing the sea of pirates.

Show how far trade was protected by *Magna Charta.* Under Edward I. there was an active export-trade in wool with Flanders and in wine and timber with Gascony; and trade was springing up with Italy and Spain. Under Edward III. a fresh batch of Flemish weavers was settled in England (a previous batch had been settled by Henry I.). The same king (Edward III.) made a treaty with the Duke of Brabant and with the Flemish towns; this ensured their neutrality during his invasions of France. In the same reign there was a flourishing trade in fish and timber with Normandy. Any serf who could escape to a town and earn his living there for the space of one year and a day became free. This was a great aid to commerce.

The carrying trade by water was mostly in the hands of Hanse merchants, Italians, and traders living in Catalonia and Southern Gaul. But before the close of the Middle Age English shipping had become very active and prosperous; hence England, after the discovery of America, became more than a match for Spain on the Atlantic.

6. The mediæval parliament (1295-1485)—its origin, constitution, and powers.

Origin.—First principles asserted in Magna Charta—the Great Council to be held regularly henceforth three times a year. This was called *Magnum Concilium Regis et Regni,* "the Great Council of the King and the Realm." The Great Council was a continuation of the old Anglo-Saxon *Witenagemot,* "Assembly of Wise Men." It consisted (*a*) of the greater barons to be summoned by royal writ (germ of the House of Lords), and (*b*) of the lesser barons to be summoned through the sheriff (germ of the House of Commons). This was the first marking out of the ground on which the parliament of the future was to be built. In 1265 a new step was taken by Simon de Montford, who had two burghers summoned to represent each borough, in addition to the two knights from each county. The child (the parliament) was thus born.

Constitution.—Described to some extent already. But for the next thirty years following Simon de Montford's parliament no fresh parliament was called. It was in 1295 that the first regular parliament was called

for the general business of the kingdom. It consisted of the three estates of the realm,—the King, the Lords temporal and spiritual, and the Commons. The Commons had two knights from each county and two burghers from each borough,—the archetype of all the parliaments to come. Thirty-seven counties and a hundred and sixty-six boroughs were represented. The only serious flaw was that the selection of the boroughs remained at the option of the king; and this flaw was not removed till the Reform Act of 1832 was passed. In 1341 the parliament was divided into two separate houses, which henceforth sat, as at the present day, in separate buildings. A few years later the Lower House had its Speaker, as at the present day. By an Act of Henry VI. the qualification for a vote was fixed at the forty-shilling freehold, which remained in force till the Reform Act of 1832.

Powers.—Taxation was from the first the chief function of parliament as well as its key to power; but parliament did much more than impose taxes. In 1327 it deposed Edward II. It deposed Richard II. and settled the succession on Henry IV., under whom its powers reached the high-water mark. It retained its power of levying taxes and granting subsidies all through the Hundred Years' War; nor did it lose any powers during the Wars of the Roses. Edward IV. had begun to raise revenue by means of so-called Benevolences. But Richard III. during his short reign gave the power back to Parliament. Philippe de Commines, who visited England at this time, gives the following testimony:—"The King of England can undertake no enterprise of account without calling his Parliament, and therefore are these kings stronger and better served."

The parliament lost its powers (explain why) under the Tudors; but it fought for them and won them back under the Stuarts.

7. The Renascence or Revival of Learning—how it arose and what course it took in England.

"Renascence" is the name given to the intellectual revolution, which in Europe preceded the religious revolution called the Reformation. In England they came together, because the Renascence reached us later than elsewhere, while the Reformation reached us as rapidly as elsewhere. The Renascence mainly consisted in the revived study of the Greek and Latin classics, and in the formation of new literary tastes, which this study inspired.

What brought it on? For the chief cause we must go back to 1453, the date of the fall of Constantinople, which was captured by the Turks, and is Turkish still. All through the Middle Ages Constantinople was the centre of Greek learning, which was unknown in Western or Latin Christendom. When the great Eastern city fell, a large number of scholars left it, bringing with them not only the Greek and Roman literature of pagan or classical times, but the New Testament in Greek. Europe woke up at last from its long intellectual sleep and its long adherence to Latin Christianity.

Sir Thomas More, Colet, Ascham, Cheke, and Camden constituted the first batch in England of scholars versed in the new learning. Public schools and colleges adopted the new methods of study, and applied themselves to the new literature. Learning henceforth was not confined to the clergy, as it had been in the Middle Ages. Erasmus, the greatest scholar of his day, taught Greek at Cambridge (1497), from which he published his edition of the Greek Testament, setting aside for the first time the Latin version called the Vulgate.

In the Elizabethan age the three great representatives of the Renascence were Spenser, author of the *Faerie Queene*; Shakespeare, master of the drama; and Bacon, founder of a new method of research.

8. The state of England during the Wars of the Roses, A.D. 1455-1485.

These wars were marked with savage slaughters, ruthless executions, and shameless treachery on both sides; there was no nobleness of aim, no chivalry in its battles, no honour in the final result. But what was the state of the people or nation? The answer is given by Philippe de Commines, a philosopher and statesman, who visited England while the wars were still going on:—"There are no buildings destroyed by the war, and the mischief of it falls only on those who make the war." This is very valuable testimony.

The towns stood aloof and escaped. Once or twice, as at Towton, where the most decisive and sanguinary battle was fought (1461), a town was drawn into the struggle; but this was very rare. While feudalism was falling on its own sword, the towns were prospering and trade was increasing. Formerly the foreign trade of England was chiefly in the hands of Italians, or of the Hanse merchants, or of traders in Catalonia or Southern Gaul. But it gradually passed into English hands. English merchants were settled in Florence and in Venice. English merchant-ships were seen not only in the Mediterranean, but in the Baltic. Banking or money-lending was in the hands of the Jews until the time of Edward I., when Lombards stepped into their place. By the time of Edward IV. Lombards had either become Englishmen or had been superseded; for the name "Lombard" is heard no more. It lives only in the word "lumber-room" (Lombard-room.)

Justice remained undisturbed by the civil war. The law-courts were held, as usual, at Westminster. The judges went on circuit, as they had done in the reign of their founder, Henry II. Trial by jury took more and more its modern form by the separation of jurors from witnesses. "Among all the world's lordships," says Philippe de Commines, "England is that where the public weal is best ordered, and where least violence reigns over the people." This is what he saw while the Wars of the Roses were still going on around him.

Agriculture was less prosperous. A change was inevitable with the decline of feudalism. Smaller holdings were thrown together, the amount of tillage was diminished, more space was laid out for pasture; this tended to produce a floating labour-class, which became turbulent when it could not find work. Commons, which hitherto had been public grazing lands, were enclosed. Philippe de Commines, however, found no fault either with the state of agriculture or with the lot of the farm labourer.

9. Condition and growth of towns in the Middle Age and up to the end of the Stuarts.

In the time of William I. the chief towns were London, Westminster, Winchester, York, Lichfield, Lincoln, Chester, Canterbury, and Bristol. London the chief commercial city of the east, Bristol of the west.

Explain why London surpassed Bristol. Say anything that you know about the other towns. Towns suffer in Stephen's time, why?

They thrive under Henry II., who granted municipal charters, and under Richard I., who sold them. Show how the charters and liberties of towns were protected by Magna Charta. Show also how towns were recruited by serfs who could escape. Towns sided with the feudal lords, if the king was oppressive (as in the reigns of John and Henry III.), and with the king, if the feudal lords were oppressive. In either case they found or bought their way out of feudal thraldom. Show what fresh powers towns obtained under Edward I.

In Stuart times they were not much disturbed till Charles II. revoked their charters, and then sold them back again as a means of raising revenue without summoning Parliament.

10. Manufactures and inventions in mediæval and modern England.

In the early Middle Age England was the great wool-producing country in the west, but for some time longer was not skilled in wool-manufacture. In 1105, and afterwards in 1339, weavers were brought into England from Flanders, after which England became a manufacturer and exporter of woollen stuffs.

In 1685 the silk industry at Spitalfields was introduced by Huguenots from France; it flourished greatly for some time, but suffered eventually from competition with France, as it suffers still.

In the latter half of the eighteenth century extraordinary progress was made in all directions—coal-mining, iron-smelting, discovery of the power of steam, invention of the spinning-jenny by Hargreaves (1764), of the spinning machine by Arkwright (1768), of the mule by Crompton (1776), of the condensing steam-engine by James Watt (1736-1819); invention of smelting iron by coal instead of by charcoal; improvements in pottery by Wedgwood (1730-1795).

In 1813 came the invention of the steam-boat, which has developed into huge steamships for purposes of trade and huge battleships for purposes of war. In 1830 came the invention by Stephenson of the railway and locomotive engine. In 1837 came the invention of the electric telegraph by Wheatstone and Cooke.

These inventions, all made in England, in addition to her great wealth in iron and coal, and to her unequalled activity in shipbuilding and seafaring, gave her the start of other nations, led to an extraordinary expansion of her Colonial and Indian empires, and made her the richest country in the world.

11. The birth of the standing army in England and what preceded it.

The birth of the army was Oliver Cromwell's New Model, 1645, from which time every English sovereign had a standing army of some kind. This was preceded by (*a*) the Fyrd, or Anglo-Saxon militia, still in force, though not quite in the same form; (*b*) the feudal contingents introduced by the Duke of Normandy; (*c*) paid troops (by means of scutage) in lieu of feudal or personal service; scutage became common under the Plantagenets. It was the refusal of Parliament to grant the money needed by Charles I. for maintaining a standing army that led to the Civil War.

The New Model was an army of 80,000, with which Cromwell first overthrew the King, then the Long Parliament, then Ireland, then Scotland.

12. The struggle for the right of self-imposed taxation: (*a*) in England during the reign of Charles I.; (*b*) in America during the reign of George III.

The main facts regarding (*a*) and (*b*) can be seen in any history. What the writer has to do is to select the most important, so that not more than two paragraphs need be written concerning each. In order to connect the two subjects and thus add to the unity of the essay (§ 340), a fifth and final paragraph might be written showing that the Civil War, by which each struggle was accompanied, was due to the obstinacy of a king, for which the nation was not to be blamed. The two contests furnish a good example of an historic parallel, both events occurring within the same nation, and the one being separated from the other by an interval of only 134 years. The lesson of A.D. 1642-1649 was thrown away on George III., who had no knowledge of history and no common sense.

13. The great archives of English liberties—under what circumstances and for what purpose they each came into existence.

(1) The Charter voluntarily granted by Henry I., A.D. 1100.
(2) The Great Charter wrested from King John, A.D. 1215.
(3) The Renunciation of Tallage, A.D. 1297.
(4) The Petition of Right, A.D. 1628.
(5) The Habeas Corpus Act, A.D. 1679.
(6) The Bill of Rights, A.D. 1689.
(7) The Reform Act, A.D. 1832.

14. Attempts made before the death of Queen Elizabeth to unite the crowns of England and Scotland by peaceful means.

The first attempt was in 1290, by means of the proposed marriage of the "Little Maid of Norway" (see Essay vii. para. 4) with Edward (afterwards Edward II.), then a child, son of Edward I.

Two under-kings or guardians of the realm were appointed by Edward I. as overlord; but the first (Baliol) was deposed by the Scotch in 1296, and the second (Comyn) was slain in 1298.

Henry VII. bound England and Scotland together for a time by bestowing (in 1502) the hand of his daughter Margaret on the King of Scotland; but this union was dissolved by the strife with France which followed the accession of Henry VIII.

The next attempt was made by Henry VIII., who desired that his son and successor (Edward VI.) should be married to Mary, the heiress of the Scotch throne; but he did not live long enough to see the marriage accomplished.

The last attempt was a proposal made in 1563 by the Scotch themselves (who by this time had been drawn to England by the Reformation), that the Earl of Arran, heir presumptive of the Scottish crown, should become the husband of Queen Elizabeth; but the English queen declined the honour.

15. What the United States gained and what they lost by separation from England.

The first thing that they gained, and this stands above everything else, was self-respect; they resented the brutal indifference shown by George III. for their feelings; their Declaration of Independence was one of the noblest utterances ever made by an infant state.

The next thing gained was full freedom of action in the management of their own affairs; this, however, they might have got without separation, if Chatham had lived to carry out his plan, which was to grant absolute freedom in all matters pertaining to self-government, reserving only a federal union with the mother-country such as now exists between England and Canada, or between England and Australia.

By entirely separating themselves from England the States incurred two very serious losses: (*a*) They lost touch with the statute passed by William III., that judges shall hold their offices for life, whereas in the States they are changed with every change of President, *i.e.* every four years, which opens the door to all kinds of corruption. (*b*) They lost the chance of getting rid of slavery. Had the States remained under the English flag, the Civil War of 1861-1865 would not have occurred; for in 1833 slavery was abolished in all the British dominions. The States are now confronted with a very serious problem, viz. 10,000,000 discontented negroes, who are a constant source of anxiety and trouble.

16. Coalition Cabinets.

What we call a cabinet is a small body of men (seldom or never above twenty, and usually much below it), deputed to represent the king or queen in parliament, and united by a sense of common political convictions and common interests. They are entitled to remain in office so long as they retain a majority of votes in the House of Commons. This (as history teaches) was the origin and is still the mainstay of party government in our constitution. The phrase "Coalition Cabinet" has a bad sound, because it implies that the cabinet in question contains not one party, but two.

In 1763 the king was in the hands of a coalition cabinet, Whig in name, but to a large extent Tory in character. In this cabinet George Grenville, a moderate Whig, was the premier; and the Duke of Bedford, a moderate Tory, was the patron. It was George Grenville who in 1765 imposed the Stamp tax on the American colonies: in the same year he went out of office; but the mischief was done.

The worst example of a coalition cabinet was in 1783, when Lord North the Tory formed a coalition with Fox the Radical, who for many years past had been his bitterest opponent. This unholy alliance disgusted every one, and it soon broke up.

In 1806 was formed "The Ministry of all the Talents,"—a coalition ministry consisting of Fox, the leader of the Radicals or popular Whigs—Lord Grenville, leader of the aristocratic Whigs—and Lord Sidmouth, leader of the Tories. It was an honest combination directed against Napoleon for the defence of England. They passed one grand measure, the abolition of the slave trade (1807).

In 1895 the Conservative party, led by Lord Salisbury, entered into an alliance or coalition with Mr. J. Chamberlain and his associates (all of

whom were Liberals), for the preservation of the union between Great Britain and Ireland, a cause which (rightly or wrongly) they considered to be important enough to override all political differences. This, like the preceding, is an example of a coalition, actuated by a genuine disinterested conviction on both sides, and involving no infringement of political honour. This alliance forms what is called the Unionist party.

17. "Character does not suddenly change in an adult, but aims sometimes do." Give examples of this from English history.

Becket took an active part in the secular policy of Henry II. until he was made Archbishop of Canterbury. From that date his aims became purely ecclesiastical.

Stephen Langton was appointed Archbishop of Canterbury by the Pope, and it was John's refusal to accept him that led to the interdict. But after John had surrendered to the Pope, Langton sided with the barons against John in direct disobedience to the Pope.

Henry V., while his father was still alive, spent his time in amusements; but on coming to the throne he took his office as king very seriously.

Henry VIII. began his reign as a very strict Papist, and for his pamphlet against Luther was surnamed by the Pope, "Defender of the Faith"; but in order to get rid of his first wife he afterwards threw the Pope over.

Thomas Wentworth began his career as a parliamentarian, but after 1628 he became the right-hand man of the King, for which he paid the forfeit with his head as soon as it suited the treacherous King to sign his death-warrant.

Oliver Cromwell had no personal ambitions at first; he had decided to emigrate to America, if the Grand Remonstrance had not been passed by the Long Parliament. But he must have had personal ambitions after 1649.

Burke, the author of *Thoughts on the Present Discontents*, was in 1788 a follower and associate of Fox, and a member of the Coalition Cabinet of North and Fox. But in 1790, before the French Revolution had entered upon its most violent phase, he brought out his *Reflections on the French Revolution*, which had an astounding influence in preventing the reforms of which he had formerly been such an eloquent advocate.

Robert Peel began his political career as a Tory. In 1823 he joined the Cabinet of Wellington, who was then the leader of the Tory party. But in 1835, when he became Prime Minister, he brought his party round to a much more moderate Toryism, and rebaptized it "Conservative." Finally, in 1846, he veered completely round, and brought in his Bill for the repeal of the Corn Laws, which placed a great gulf between himself and the owners of landed estates, all of whom were Conservatives or Tories.

18. Laws for the regulation of the Press, and their repeal.

The regulations made by Henry VIII. subjected the Press to the censorship of the Star-Chamber. In the struggle which bears the name of the "Martin Marprelate Controversy," it was ruled by the Star-Chamber that no one could print without a license, 1585. Even the

Long Parliament laid a heavy hand on the Press, which called forth Milton's *Areopagitica*, a speech supposed to be addressed by him to the Parliament of England in defence of the "Liberty of Unlicensed Printing," 1644. The Licensing Act was relaxed under the Commonwealth, but revived in full force in 1662. The Licensing Act, which required annual renewal, lapsed in 1679, through an oversight on the part of the press-censor, and was never again re-enacted.

A new and indirect method of checking the power of the Press was the Stamp Act of Queen Anne, 1712, which imposed a duty on the amount of paper used by a daily or a weekly journal. The duty was raised to a much higher figure by George III., and the law in his time was so strictly enforced that there were more than 700 prosecutions for the publishing of journals on unstamped paper. The tax on knowledge was at last cancelled, and the Stamp Act repealed in 1855.

19. Great issues in English history decided at sea.

The fleet built by Alfred the Great and manned by Frisian sailors, together with the additions made to it by his son and other successors, kept the Danish pirates out of England, and forced them to turn their attention to the French coast, where they helped to found Normandy.

The long struggle between England and Spain was fought out at sea, the Armada being defeated in 1588, and the island of Jamaica captured in 1655.

The attempts made by Louis XIV. to reinstate his guest, James II., on the throne of England, were frustrated by the battle off Capo la Hogue in 1692.

The question of American Independence, though ostensibly fought out on land, was really decided at sea; for the French navy, that had been sent out in defence of the revolted States, deprived England of the free command of her sea-base; and thus Cornwallis, cut off as he was on a tongue of land at York-town, was forced to surrender.

Napoleon's design of founding an Eastern empire was frustrated in Aboukir Bay, A.D. 1798. His so-called "Continental System" was frustrated by Nelson's other victories.

Section 3.—Subjects for Essays without Notes.

386. Arrangement of Subjects.—This section consists of subjects to which no notes have been appended. Here the student is thrown entirely on himself. The subjects have been arranged under headings (*a*), (*b*), and (*c*).

The subjects under (*a*) relate to the *modern* period of English history, *i.e.* the period that begins with the reign of Henry VII., and are given for the most part in chronological order. They have been restricted to the modern period of our history, because a great deal of attention has been given in the previous section to the mediæval period preceding it.

The subjects under (*b*) have not, like those under (*a*), been prepared by myself, but have been selected from subjects set in the examinations for London Matriculation and for the London School-leaving Certificate. In making this selection I have given preference to those subjects that relate to our modern history; but it was not possible in all instances to arrange them in chronological order.

The subjects under (c) relate to Geography or to questions mainly based on Geography. They have been selected for the most part from the same source as those given under (b).

(a) Subjects on Modern England, mainly in chronological order.

1. The reasons for which the reign of Henry VII. is regarded as the close of the Middle Age and the starting-point of our Modern history.

2. "Assuredly, if by Protestantism is meant liberty of private judgment, no one was ever less a Protestant than Henry VIII." Expand and justify.

3. The progress of the Reformation during the reign of Edward VI.

4. "Great monarchies were being consolidated in Europe, and their example acted on the Tudors, as that of Louis XIV. afterwards acted on the Stuarts." Expand.

5. The contest with Spain by sea and by land from 1572 to 1588.

6. "Though Wyat's rebellion was repressed, the Queen, as the bride of Spain, was henceforth fatally estranged from her own people." Expand.

7. The progress made during the reign of Queen Elizabeth in seafaring, science, the drama and other forms of poetry, prose-fiction, the writing of history, and other forms of prose literature.

8. Religious parties, together with their political aims and actions, during the reigns of James I. and Charles I.

9. The Solemn League and Covenant—its origin, objects, and history.

10. Ship-money—its origin and subsequent exaction for use or misuse by English sovereigns.

11. Monopolies under the Tudors and the Stuarts.

12. Describe under a few main headings the proceedings of the Long Parliament in the years 1640-1649.

13. In the first civil war between Charles and the Parliament, 1642-1647, show which of the two combatants was the aggressor, relate the main events, and describe the battle which brought it to a close.

14. "The act for which Charles morally deserved to suffer, whatever might be its legal character, was the conspiracy by which he brought on the second civil war while he was carrying on friendly negotiations with the Parliament." Expand and justify.

15. Relations between England and Scotland, 1650-1660.

16. Victories over foreign enemies during the Commonwealth and the Protectorate.

17. The four irregular courts used by Charles I., but not restored by Charles II.

18. "Now were heard for the first time (1679) the two party-names famous in English history, and borne by the two great political parties almost down to the present day." Expand.

19. The year of rejoicing, 1660.

20. The year of shame, 1667.

21. The year of release, 1688.

22. The Popish Plot, and who are to be blamed for the idea of such a plot having arisen and for its having lasted so long.

23. The Rye-house Plot.

24. "Ostensibly the Revolution of 1688 was merely a change of dynasty. In fact it was a great historical landmark,—not only a British, but a European, event of the first order; it redressed the balance of power in Europe." Expand and justify.

25. Origin and growth of the Cabinet as an instrument of government.

26. The non-jurors.

27. James's reign in Ireland after his flight from England.

28. The victories of Marlborough and the resultant peace.

29. The age of Queen Anne at home and abroad.

30. "The Bill of Rights, with the annual Mutiny Act, makes the monarchy in England constitutional." Expand and explain.

31. The Act of Union, 1707, and its effects on the two countries concerned.

32. The Seven Years' War,—the causes that led to it and the terms of the peace by which it was closed.

33. "From the hour of Chatham's death England entered on a conflict with enemies whose circle gradually widened, till she stood single-handed against the world." Expand and explain.

34. The methods used by George III. for overriding the constitution.

35. "To the French monarchy the reward of its vindictive and hypocritical league with American rebellion (1782) was bankruptcy followed by Revolution." Expand and explain.

36. "Never was England so near her ruin as in 1779-1782." Give particulars and describe the upshot.

37. The Gordon riots.

38. Grattan's parliament.

39. The year of danger, 1797.

40. "Prussia, with mean and purblind selfishness, held aloof from a coalition (1805) that had been formed by Pitt's diplomacy; but she afterwards paid at Jena for her disloyalty to the cause of nations." Expand and explain.

41. Napoleon's designs in the East and how they were frustrated.

42. The Peninsular War.

43. "The effect of the 'Continental System' on Napoleon, its author, was to drive him to aggression after aggression in order to maintain the material union of Europe against Britain." Expand and explain.

44. "The growth of English liberty was due to the faults rather than to the virtues of her kings." Discuss this, justifying your arguments on either side by facts taken from English history.

45. The three great continental monarchs against whom England has had to contend—compare the nature of their power and the extent of their dominions, and show how their ambitions were thwarted.

46. Compare the relations between England and Ireland in the reigns of Elizabeth, William III., and George III. respectively.

47. The career of Wellington as soldier and as statesman.

48. Compare the Reform Bill of 1832 with that of 1867.

(*b*) *London Matriculation and School-leaving Certificate*, 1904, 1905.

1. The effect on Scotland of the union with England.
2. The Tudor and Stuart dynasties contrasted.
3. The growth of our large towns since the Revolution (1688).
4. The development of party-government in England, and its results whether beneficial or otherwise.
5. The objects of Henry VII.'s foreign policy, and how far they were successful.
6. Stages in the secularisation of Church property under Henry VIII. and Edward VI.
7. The questions in dispute between Charles I. and his parliament.
8. Account for the popularity of the Restoration, and show what principles were asserted by it.
9. The War of Spanish Succession.
10. The circumstances that led to the Irish union of 1800, and how far it was a success.
11. The progress and decline of Wolsey's influence at home and abroad.
12. The chief points of interest in the last twelve years of Elizabeth's reign.
13. The abuses alleged against the domestic administration of James I.
14. Comparison of the Parliamentary with the Royalist forces during the Civil War.
15. The part played by the Presbyterians in the reign of Charles II.
16. The fall of Walpole and the change of policy that followed it.
17. The impeachment of Warren Hastings.
18. How the lack of sea-power influenced the policy of Napoleon I.
19. The progress and effects of Catholic Emancipation.
20. Representative government in mediæval and modern England.
21. The life and career of the first Earl of Shaftesbury.
22. The policy and strength of the Whig party in 1714 as compared with those of the Tory party.
23. The attitude of the American colonists towards England in 1765-1775.
24. The distribution of political power in Ireland during the time of Grattan's parliament.
25. State, and account for, the change in the relative influence of the houses of Lords and Commons since 1832.
26. The development of industries and commerce in modern England.
27. Compare the foreign policy of Henry VIII., of Queen Mary, and of Queen Elizabeth respectively.
28. The progress of events in Ireland from the English Revolution (1688) to the Treaty of Limerick.
29. The extent to which George III. succeeded in breaking up the domination of the great Whig families, and the means that he employed for so doing.
30. The European settlement effected by the Congress of Vienna, and to the extent to which it has been modified by subsequent events.

SECTION 4.—SUBJECTS FOR ESSAYS RELATING TO GEOGRAPHY.

387. Sources of the following subjects.—The subjects given below have all been taken from examination papers recently set for London Matriculation or the London School-leaving Certificate. The subjects have been quoted simply as they stand in the examination papers. I give one essay as a specimen of the manner in which a geographical subject might be dealt with. The theme of each paragraph is printed above it, as in previous essays.

THE PHYSICAL STRUCTURE AND NATURAL DIVISIONS OF INDIA.

1. *India partly Continental and partly Peninsular.*

It is a mistake to call India a peninsula, when more than half its area is shut up in the continent of Asia. It is partly continental and partly peninsular. These are the two great sections into which the country as a whole is divided by nature, the northern or continental section being much the larger of the two.

2. *The boundaries of Continental India.*

No country has its land-boundaries more clearly marked out by nature. India is bounded on the north by the snowy crest of the Himalayas; on the west by the Sulaimán and Hála ranges; on the east by the Nága, Patkoi, and Barel ranges; on the south by irregular lines of hills, the chief of which is called the Vindhya range. The first separates India from Thibet and Central Asia, the second from Afghanistan and Baluchistan, the third from Upper Burma and the hill-tracts of Arakan, the fourth from Southern or Peninsular India. This area is sometimes called Northern India, sometimes also Hindustán.

3. *The boundaries of Peninsular India.*

This area commences from the head of the Arabian Sea or (to be rather more precise) from the Gulf of Cutch on the west, and ends at the head of the Bay of Bengal on the east. It juts out into the Indian Ocean like a wedge, the two sides meeting at Cape Comorin. Cape Comorin is the vertex of the triangle. The base is a line nearly parallel with the Tropic of Cancer. This area has been called Dekhan, or the "South."

4. *The Himalayan Region.*

The region so called consists of the long line of mountainous country lying between the snowy crest and the sunburnt base of the Himalayas. It is the mountainous portion of what was called above "Continental" India, being in length about 1500 miles, but in width comparatively narrow, more extended at the west than at the east. Here lie the independent, but protected states of Bhután, Sikkim, Nepál, and Cashmere. In the tracts lying between or below the states named are situated the plantations of tea, or of cinchona, from which quinine is extracted. Here too are the great hill-stations to which Englishmen resort for rest and change of air. At the eastern terminus (long. 95) a great river of Thibet makes a sudden bend round into India, where it takes the name of Brahmaputra. At the western terminus (long. 75) a similar bend is taken by another Thibetan river, the Indus. The one flows into the Bay of Bengal, the other into the Arabian Sea.

5. *The Great Northern Plain.*

This is the great plain that lies between the base of the Himalayas and that of the Vindhya range,—the greatest and most valuable portion of Continental India. It contains the most densely inhabited provinces and most of the great cities of India. The greater part of the plain is well watered and fertile, but a portion of it (Rajputana) is for the most part desert. This plain contains three great river-systems:—(1) The Indus, with its great affluent, the Sutlej, and four tributaries between them. (2) The Jumna and the Ganges, with their numerous tributaries north and south, running mainly parallel with the Himalaya range. The watershed between the Sutlej and the Jumna is raised so little above the general level as to be imperceptible. (3) The Brahmaputra, which unites with the Ganges as it approaches the Bay of Bengal. Before reaching the Ganges it flows through the fertile valley of Assam, noted for its tea-gardens.

6. *The Southern or Peninsular Region, the Dekhan.*

The Dekhan, the name usually given to Peninsular India, mainly consists of a three-sided mountainous region of nearly the same outline as the coast-line of the peninsula; the Vindhya mountains on the north, the Western Gháts on the west, and the Eastern on the east. The western range has a much higher level than the eastern, and hence the main rivers of the Dekhan flow into the Bay of Bengal. A few other rivers flow northward into the Ganges. Within the area of Peninsular India lie five smaller divisions: (1) the peninsula of Kathiawar, (2) the valley of the Narbada, with hills north and south, (3) the valley of the Tapti, with hills north and south, (4) the narrow strip of plain between the sea and the Western Gháts, (5) the broader strip between the sea and the Eastern Gháts.

7. *How the History of the Indian People has been affected by the Physical Structure of their Country.*

The isolation of India by means of its strong mountain-barriers to the north, the west, and the east, and by the long lines of ocean to the south, has had three effects on the history of the country. (1) It kept India free of invasion for many hundreds of years. The only invasion recorded in ancient history is that by Alexander the Great. (2) It favoured the growth of a very singular form of society,—the minute subdivision of the people into a system of castes, of which the Brahman caste stands at the head. The growth of such a system would have been stunted, if not prevented altogether, had the country been exposed, as most other countries are, to foreign conquest or invasion. (3) It gave India time and leisure to produce a religion—Buddhism, which, though it was extinguished by the Brahmans in India itself, has overspread Thibet, China, and the Indo-Chinese peninsula.

(*c*) *Subjects relating to Geography, General and Physical.*

1. A railway journey from London to Penzance.

2. The mines and manufactures of Great Britain.

3. A description of *either* China *or* the Italian peninsula with reference to physical features, products, and population.

4. The influence of rivers and mountains on commerce.

5. Describe the basin of *either* the Tay *or* the Shannon, pointing out the course of the main stream, the chief tributaries, and the nature of the country through which they flow.

6. Divide Italy into natural regions, taking into account configuration, climate, and vegetation.

7. Name the regions in which salt-lakes are found, describing and, as far as you can, explaining the peculiarities of the climate, the surface forms of the land, and the vegetation in those regions.

8. The great land-routes between Europe and India in the Middle Ages.

9. The foreign trade of Great Britain.

10. The Russian empire.

11. The three principal *types* of islands found in the Atlantic and Indian oceans, their differences in structure and origin, and in their fauna and flora.

12. Compare the configuration, climate, and products of Africa and South America between the Tropic of Capricorn and the Equator.

13. Geographical discoveries during the last fifty years.

14. The sea-ports of Southern Europe.

15. Describe the configuration (land relief) and the river-system of the English Lake district, and point out how the two are adjusted to each other.

16. Compare the physical characteristics of the west coast of Ireland with those of the west coast of Scotland.

17. The position and climate of Egypt, and the sources of its agricultural prosperity.

18. Discuss the differences between the climates of India and North-Eastern China, and point out how they affect the nature of the products of the two regions.

19. The main characteristics of the railway system of Australia, and the extent to which they have been controlled (*a*) by the position of the ports, (*b*) by the configuration or the climate or the products of the interior.

20. Describe the course of the Mississippi and its tributaries, together with the physical characteristics and vegetation of its basin.

21. The commercial towns of France and Belgium.

22. The mining industries of Europe.

23. The races, products, and physical features of North Africa.

24. The inland seas of Europe.

25. A description of the Balkan peninsula.

26. The historic towns of England.

27. The courses of the rivers which flow into the Wash, and the nature of the country which they drain.

28. Explain (*a*) the causes of the neap tides, (*b*) the reason why the time of high tide changes daily, (*c*) the special tidal conditions of the Thames estuary, which facilitate its use by shipping.

29. The physical features of Ulster and the control which they exercise (*a*) on the position of four of the chief towns, and (*b*) on the course of the canals.

30. Compare the climates of the east and west coastal regions of North America between 30° and 50° N., and explain the differences between them.

31. The distribution of lakes in Africa, with a classification of them according to the nature of their basins.

32. Describe the Rhine as a waterway and its four chief ports, and explain when the river is highest, and why then.

33. The chief economic products (two animal, two vegetable, and two mineral) of Queensland, the places where they are found, and the ports which are the terminations of the chief railways to the interior.

34. The states bordering on India, with a description of the positions of the capital of each.

35. The courses of the rivers which flow into the Humber, and the nature of the country which they drain.

36. The Nile as a waterway, four of the chief places on it, the season when the river is highest and the reason thereof.

37. The six chief economic vegetable products of India, their distribution, and the ports most convenient for the export of each.

38. The mountain ranges and rivers of Scotland and Ireland.

39. The products, manufactures, and towns of Hindustan.

40. The great lakes of Europe.

41. The physical features of the Cotteswold and Edge Hills, the courses of the main rivers, the routes of two railways that cross the hills, and the positions of two important towns on each railway.

42. The geographical distribution of active and recently extinct volcanoes; the characteristic features of a volcanic district.

43. The causes of ocean currents, and the courses of the main currents in the Pacific ocean.

44. The characteristics of the mountain systems of Asia.

45. The waterways of the St. Lawrence basin, the positions of four of the chief river- or lake-ports, the more important hindrances to navigation, and the extent to which these hindrances have been overcome.

46. The physical features, climatic conditions, and natural products of the Transvaal.

PART V.—AIDS TO THE STUDY OF ENGLISH LITERATURE.

CHAPTER XXXI.—FIGURES OF SPEECH.

388. **Figure of Speech defined.**—A Figure of Speech is a deviation from the plain and ordinary use of words with a view to increasing or specialising the effect.

Thus we can say, "There are six *pillars* on either side of this colonnade." Here the word *pillars* is used in its literal sense.

Again, we can say, "This law is one of the *pillars* of the commonwealth." Here *pillar* is used in a figurative or non-literal sense, and signifies "main support."

389. **Classification of Figures.**—The figures of speech can be arranged under six main heads, of which an outline is shown below:—[1]

Based on			
	(1)	*Resemblance:* Metaphor, Simile, etc.	I.
Intellect	(2)	*Difference:* Antithesis, Epigram, etc.	II.
	(3)	*Association:* Metonymy, Synecdoche, etc.	III.
Imagination		Personification, Apostrophe, Vision, etc.	IV.
Indirectness		Innuendo, Euphemism, Irony, etc.	V.
Sound		Alliteration, Rhyme, Assonance, etc.	VI.

The three classes first named have their origin in the three chief faculties of the human intellect, viz. (1) comparison or the perception of resemblance, (2) discrimination or the perception of difference, and (3) association or the impression of contiguity.

I. When *like* objects come under our notice, we are struck

[1] The classification relating to the first three headings has been borrowed from Bain's *Rhetoric and Composition*, vol. i. The other three classes, which Bain lumps together under the heading Miscellaneous, were differentiated by myself, and first appeared in print in my *Senior Course of English Composition*, A.D. 1904.

with the resemblance. The figures named Simile, Metaphor, and Allegory are based on similarity or resemblance. These figures therefore belong to Class I.

II. When *unlike* objects come under our notice, we are struck with the difference. The figures named Antithesis, Epigram, and the Condensed Sentence are based on contrast or difference. These figures therefore belong to Class II.

III. When two impressions *occurring together* become permanently associated (joined together) in the mind, the thought of the one calls up the thought of the other, as a storm suggests shipwreck, wealth suggests gold, etc. This is called the law of Contiguity, and is the chief foundation of memory or the retentive faculty. The figures of speech named Metonymy, Synecdoche, and the Transferred Epithet are based upon Contiguity. These therefore belong to Class III.

IV. The fourth class consists of those figures that are based on the power of Imagination,—the power by which we can imagine things to be something different from what they are. This is what happens when we speak of lifeless objects as if they were alive, and of things absent or things past or future as if they were before our eyes—present in time, or in space, or in both. To this class belong such figures as Personification, Apostrophe, Vision, and others.

The fifth and sixth classes are of a type entirely distinct from any of the four hitherto named. They are not based on any particular faculty either of the Intellect (Classes I., II., III.) or of the Imagination (Class IV.), but depend merely on dexterity in the manipulation of words.

V. In the fifth class are placed those figures which exemplify in different ways Indirectness of speech, *i.e.* the art of saying things by implication rather than by direct or simple assertion. Indirectness of speech gives rise to such figures as Innuendo, Irony, Sarcasm, and others.

VI. The sixth and last class has been reserved for those figures that depend merely on "Sound," as when we make the sound of the words suggest the sense, or when we drive a point nearer home, or fix it more firmly in the memory, by the use of Alliteration, Rhyme, or Assonance.

Note.—To a beginner figures of the last three classes will be of little or no help for composition; but they will be useful to him as aids to the study of English literature. This latter is the main purpose for which Part V. has been written.

Class I.—Figures based on Resemblance.

390. Simile: lit. "a thing like" (neuter of Latin *similis*, like).—A simile is the explicit statement of some point of resemblance conceived to exist between two things, *that differ in all other respects.*

Observe, in the simile and in all other figures based upon Resemblance, the comparison is, not between things of the same kind, but between things *of different kinds.* Thus there is no figure, if we compare a camel with a dromedary, but only when, for example, we compare it with a ship and call it "the ship of the desert."

> Errors, *like* straws, upon the surface flow ;
> He that would search for pearls must dive below.—DRYDEN.

> The tribes (on the North-west frontier of India) hung upon the flanks of our retreating columns *like* wasps.—*Review of Reviews*, Jan. 1898, p. 5.

A simile is usually introduced by some words, such as *like*, *as*, *as—so*, which draw attention to the likeness. But this is not necessary. All that is necessary to the simile is that both sides of the comparison shall be stated :—

> No man can walk abroad save on his own shadow. No dramatist can create live characters save by bequeathing the best of himself to the children of his art, scattering amongst them a largess of his own qualities.—WALTER RALEIGH, on *Shakespeare*, p. 7, ed. 1907.

> The repose of repletion may not be a very heroic attitude to a great nation like the English ; but even a lion sleeps after a full meal.—*Review of Reviews*, Jan. 1898, p. 8.

391. *Pointless Similes.*—Similitudes which add nothing to the clearness, impressiveness, or beauty of the narrative are useless, if not misleading. In the following examples we look in vain for the point of the comparison :—

> Just as a painter is limited by the fact that he has to imitate solid bodies on a flat surface, so the playwright is limited by the fact that he has to interest a crowd.—*Literature*, p. 292, 14th April 1900. (What resemblance is there between the two kinds of limitations ? or how does the one kind throw any light on the other ?)

> As Christ was crucified between two thieves, so is England degraded and destroyed by a pack of villainous Socialists between two great political parties who both look on complacently.—*Fortnightly Review*, October 1900, p. 555. (Neither of the thieves looked on complacently ; one was penitent, the other reproachful. This simile is not merely useless ; it confounds the sense.)

392. Metaphor: lit. a transfer (Gr. *meta*, across; *phor-e*, carrying).—A metaphor is a *potential* or *implied* simile. In a simile both sides of the comparison are stated; but in a metaphor one side is stated, and not the other. Thus when we say, "He *curbs* his passion," we mean that he restrains his passion, as a man would curb a restless horse. If both sides of the comparison were to be given, this is how the simile would be expressed.

> The town was *stormed* after a long siege.
> He was fond of *blowing* his own *trumpet* (praising himself).
> He *swam* bravely against the *tide* of popular applause.
> Can'st thou not minister to a mind diseased,
> *Pluck* from the memory a *rooted* sorrow?—SHAKESPEARE.

393. *Confusion of Metaphors.*—Metaphors borrowed from more than one source must not be combined in the same phrase or in the same sentence. The brevity of the metaphor as distinct from the simile renders it peculiarly liable to this misuse. The best test of the purity of a metaphor is that it will bear expansion into a simile. In the examples of confusion quoted below I have given in brackets, wherever it was possible, the word or words which would remove the confusion:—

> Traders should once and for all abandon the hope that Yunnan is a rich *mine* waiting only to be *tapped* (opened).—*Contemporary Review*, Feb. 1898.
>
> It is but cold comfort to know that a religion *grafted* upon science will *come to the birth* (germinate) only by the slow process of evolution.—*Times Weekly*, 4th March 1898.
>
> There are *phrases* of music that go home to the centre of our being, and five minutes' dwelling on them at sunrise will give a *keynote* that will sound for the day, the morning *bath* of the mind.—*National Review*, Feb. 1898. (Hopelessly confused.)

394. Allegory, Fable, Parable.—These are the same at bottom, and, like metaphors, are based upon Resemblance.

An Allegory is a tale consisting of a series of incidents analogous to another series of incidents, which it is intended to illustrate. The object of such a tale is to exemplify and enforce some moral truth; as in Bunyan's *Pilgrim's Progress*.

A Parable is a short allegory, as the Sower, the Ten Virgins, the Prodigal Son, the Grain of Mustard Seed, the Lost Sheep, etc. In the Old Testament the parable of the Ewe Lamb was intended to bring King David to a sense of his guilt by putting a parallel case before him; and it succeeded.

The following is an example of a parable or short allegory:—

They tell us of an Indian tree,
  Which, howsoe'er the sun and sky
May tempt its boughs to wander free
  And shoot and blossom wide and high,
Far better loves to bend its arms
  Downwards again to that dear earth,
From which the life that fills and warms
  Its grateful being first had birth.
'Tis thus, though wooed by flattering friends
  And fed with fame (if fame it be),
This heart, my own dear Mother, bends
  With love's true instinct back to thee.—MOORE.

The Fables of classical literature, in which birds and beasts are made to think, speak, and act like men, all teach some moral, as allegory and parable do.

Many of our proverbs and precepts, besides being true literally, admit of an allegorical application, and are now quoted chiefly for this purpose :—

A bird in the hand is worth two in the bush.
It is difficult for an empty sack to stand upright.
A stitch in time saves nine.
Make hay while the sun shines.
If two men ride a horse, one must ride behind.
Strike while the iron is hot.

Class II.—Figures based on Contrast or Difference.

395. Antithesis.—It is a first principle of the human mind, that we are affected, whether we like it or not, *by change of impression.* Among the many consequences of this law is the efficacy of contrast in verbal composition.

Antithesis is a Greek word signifying "setting against," that is, setting one word or one idea against another.

He can *bribe*, but he cannot *seduce*; he can *buy*, but he cannot *gain*; he can *lie*, but he cannot *deceive*.

A *friend* exaggerates a man's *virtues*, an *enemy* his *crimes*.

Between fame and true honour there is much difference; the former is *a blind* and *noisy applause*; the latter is an *internal and more silent homage.*

Antithesis should not be sacrificed to brevity. Compare the following, and see which of the two is the more pointed :—

(*a*) The *posthumous* fame of Buddha is far greater than what accrued to him during his life.

(*b*) The *fame which has gathered round the name of Buddha since his death* far exceeds that which accrued to him during his life.

Observe that in (*b*) not only is one clause balanced against another, but the Present Perfect tense "has gathered" is contrasted with the Past Indefinite "accrued."

396. **Epigram**: lit. an inscription (a Greek word, *epigramma*), the name given by the Greeks to a short piece of verse inscribed on a public monument.—Brevity is still one of the distinguishing marks of epigram. But the word has been made to denote any kind of pointed saying, and especially one in which the words appear to be contrasted, or at least to contain some kind of incongruity. It is therefore based upon the perception of Difference, and is closely allied to Antithesis.

"The epigram is an apparent contradiction in language, which, by causing a temporary shock, rouses our attention to some important meaning underneath" (Bain).

> The *child* is *father* of the man.—WORDSWORTH.
> By *merit* raised to that *bad* eminence.—MILTON.
> Loveliness
> Needs not the foreign aid of ornament,
> But is, when *unadorned*, *adorned* the most.—THOMSON.
> *Conspicuous* by its *absence*.—DISRAELI.
> In the midst of *life* we are in *death*.—*Proverb*.
> He lived a life of *active idleness*.
> 'Tis all thy *business*, *business* how to shun.—POPE.

397. **Pun.**—In this figure the incongruity consists in using the same word in different senses. The figure is used chiefly for purposes of humour. (Called in Greek *Paronomasia*.)

> The leopard changes his spots, as often as he goes from one *spot* to another.
> Is life worth living? That depends on the *liver*.

398. **The Condensed Sentence.**—This figure consists in bringing together, under one verb or in one enumeration, ideas so different, that we should ordinarily give a distinct clause or an entirely distinct sentence to each of them:—

> The Russian grandees came to Elizabeth's court dropping pearls and vermin.—MACAULAY.
> She dropped a tear and her pocket-handkerchief.—DICKENS.
> Smelling of musk and of insolence.—TENNYSON.

399. **Climax.**—"Climax" is a Greek word signifying "ladder,"—a term that well expresses the object for which this figure is used. In using it the writer leads the reader up to his main point by degrees, beginning from the lowest rung of the ladder, *i.e.* the lowest stage in the argument, and ascending gradually to the final one. Every new stage is contrasted with the last in degree of intensity; and hence the figure is based on Antithesis. A climax is a rising scale of antitheses.

Some books are to be tasted, others swallowed, and some few to be chewed and digested.—BACON.

The invasions of the Northmen may be divided under three heads: first, they came to plunder; then to settle; and thirdly, to conquer and rule England.—RANSOME, *Short History of England*, iv. 23.

400. Anticlimax, or Bathos.—This is the opposite of climax—descent from a higher to a lower. When this is done from inadvertence, it is a serious fault. But it may be done intentionally for the sake of humour or ridicule:—

In his most impressive perorations he was a master of bathos. After sentencing a tailor to death for stabbing a soldier, he wound up:—"Not only did ye murder him, whereby he was bereaved of life; but ye did thrust, or push, or pierce, or project, or propel the lethal weapon through the breeches, which were His Majesty's."—Quoted in *Cornhill*, April 1901.

Class III.—Figures based on Contiguity.

401. Metonymy: lit. "a transfer of name" (Gr. *meta*, across; *onoma*, name).—This figure consists in describing a thing by some *accompaniment*, instead of by its own name.

(*a*) *The symbol for the person or thing symbolised:*—

He succeeded to the *crown* =(royal office).
He is too fond of *red tape* (=official routine).
From the *cradle* to the *grave* (=from childhood to death).
Leather (=shoe-making) pays better than learning.
Grey hairs (=old age or old men) should be respected.
Show deference to the *chair* (=the chairman's ruling).

(*b*) *The instrument for the agent:*—

The *pen* has more influence than the *sword*.
Give every man thine *ear*, but few thy *voice*.
He is a good *hand* at composition.
To carry *fire* and *sword* (=a desolating war) into a country.
How shall we attract men to the *colours* (=the army)?

(*c*) *The container for the thing contained:*—

He drank the *cup* (=the contents of the cup).
He is too fond of the *bottle* (=the liquor in the bottle).
The *kettle* (=the water in the kettle) boils.
The conquerors smote the *city* (=inhabitants of the city).

(*d*) *The effect for the cause, or the cause for the effect:*—

Effect. He desperate takes the *death*
With sudden plunge.—THOMSON.
(Here the *death* is the angler's hook seized by the fish.)
Cause. O for a beaker full of the *warm south*!—KEATS.
(Here wine is described by the *warm south*, that is, the warm sun

of the south, which ripens the grape from which the wine is produced. This is a metonymy three deep.)

(e) *The maker for the thing made; the place for the thing:*—

I have never read *Homer* (= the poems of Homer).
This is a common phrase in *Tennyson*.
I am not fond of *Euclid* (= geometry).
I am fond of old *china* (= crockery made in China).
A book bound in *morocco* (= leather of Morocco).

(f) *The name of a passion for the object of the passion:*—

She is coming, my *life*, my *fate*.—TENNYSON.
For Lycidas, your *sorrow*, is not dead.—MILTON.
Soul of the age!
The *applause*, *delight*, and *wonder* of our stage!
My Shakspeare rise!—BEN JONSON.

402. Syn-ec-do-che: lit. "the understanding of one thing simultaneously with another" (a Greek word transliterated into English).—This figure is distinguished from Metonymy by the fact that the sign, which is made to represent the thing signified, may be any kind of symbol except an *accompaniment*, this last being the exclusive property of Metonymy. Perhaps, however, the best way to distinguish these two figures is as follows:—

In synecdoche one name is substituted for another, whose meaning is more or less *cognate* with its own.

In metonymy one name is substituted for another, whose meaning is wholly *foreign* to itself.

(a) *The less general put for the more general:*—

They *sank* as *lead* in the mighty waters.—Exodus xv. 10.
All *hands* employed, the royal work grows warm.—DRYDEN.
Return to her? and fifty men dismissed?
No, rather I abjure all *roofs*, and choose
To be a comrade with the *wolf* and *owl*.—SHAKESPEARE, *King Lear*.
Do men gather *grapes* of *thorns*, or *figs* of *thistles*?—*New Test.*

(b) *An individual for a class.*—A well-known individual is sometimes made to represent a class: in this way a Proper noun becomes a Common noun, see § 23, *Note* 2:—

A *Daniel* (very wise judge) come to judgment.—SHAKESPEARE.
Smooth *Jacob* still robs homely *Esau*.—BROWNING.
He's *Judas* to a tittle, that man is.—*Ibid.*
I would have such a fellow whipped for o'erdoing *Termagant*; it out-*Herods Herod*.—SHAKESPEARE.
Sternhold himself he out-*Sternholded*.—SWIFT.

(c) *The more general for the less general.*—As the usual tendency of general words is to weaken the effect rather than to strengthen it, this form of Synecdoche is rather uncommon:—

We say *vessel* for "ship"; *measure* for "dance" or for "poetry"; the smiling *year* for the smiling "season," spring or summer; the Christian *world* for the Christian Church; *liquor* for intoxicating drink; *action* for "battle"; *company* for a "commercial firm."

A very general term can be used to express contempt, pity, or endearment:—

Contempt.	A poor *creature.*	A wretched *individual.*
Pity.	Poor *thing*!	Poor *body*!
Endearment.	Dear little *thing*!	

(*d*) *The concrete for the abstract*:—

> I do the most that friendship can,
> I hate *the Viceroy*, love *the man*.—SWIFT.
> An English muse is touched with generous woe,
> And in the unhappy man forgets *the foe*.—ADDISON.

(*e*) *The abstract for the concrete*: see § 27:—

> All the *rank* and *fashion* came out to see the sight.
> The *authorities* put an end to the tumult.
> Up goes my grave *Impudence* to the maid.—*Tatler*.

The same figure appears in such phrases as, *His Majesty* for "king," *her ladyship* for "lady," *his lordship* for "lord."

(*f*) *The part for a whole*:—

> A fleet of fifty *sail* (=ships).
> *Pin* money (a lady's dress allowance).
> A man of seventy *winters*.[1]

(*g*) *The material for the thing made*:—

> A foeman worthy of his *steel* (=sword).
> The speaking *marble* (=statue of marble).
> He was bound in *irons* (=fetters made of *iron*).
> Have you any *coppers*? (=pence made of copper).

403. Transferred Epithet.—When two impressions are associated together in the mind, an epithet that properly belongs to one only can be transferred to the other:—

> He lay all night on a *sleepless* pillow.
> Melissa shook her *doubtful* curls.—TENNYSON.
> And bells made *Catholic* the trembling air.—GEORGE ELIOT.
> A lackey presented an *obsequious* cup of coffee.—CARLYLE.
> And *drowsy* tinklings lull the distant fold.—GRAY.

Such phrases as the following are common:—A *virtuous* indignation; a *happy* time; an *unlucky* remark; a *foolish* observation; a *learned* book; a *criminal* court; the *Colonial* Office; the *Foreign* Office; *easy* circumstances; a *weary* journey; *melancholy* news; an

---

[1] We are now justified perhaps in calling this an example of Synecdoche. But in A.S. the word *winter* meant "year," and this use of the word seems to have never wholly died out.

eloquent speech; *hysterical* appeals; *brutal* threats; the *smiling* morn; a *furious* wave; the *angry* ocean; a *prattling* brook; the *dimpling* waves; the *blushing* rose; a *dishonest* calling, etc.

Class IV.—Figures based on the Imagination.

404. Personification.—More common in poetry than in prose. The use of this figure arises from the inborn tendency of man to invest inanimate things with activities, designs, and passions similar to his own, and to describe them in terms expressive of such attributes. This figure is sometimes called the Personal Metaphor, because it speaks of inanimate objects as if they were alive. The figure called the Transferred Epithet (§ 403) often takes the same kind of form.

> Perhaps the vale
> *Relents* awhile to the reflected ray.—THOMSON.

The *voice* of thy brother's blood *crieth* unto me from the ground.—Gen. iv. 10.

> *Weary* wave and *dying* blast
> *Sob* and *moan* along the shore;
> And all is peace at last.

While Japan was a *hermit* nation, she was able to supply herself with everything necessary.—*Rev. of Rev.* p. 563, Dec. 1900.

Note.—An extreme form of this figure is called the **Pathetic Fallacy**, by which external objects are made to sympathise in all the emotions of the agent, feeling exactly as he does, and hearing and understanding what he says to them. At the time when Cromwell was dying, a furious storm was raging outside, "as if in sympathy," says Hallam, "with the mighty soul that was passing away from the earth."

In Tennyson's *Maud* there is a canto in which the rose, the lily, the passion-flower, etc., are (according to the poet's description) as eager as the lover himself to hear or see the maiden come out from the ballroom to meet him "at the gate, alone."

The following is an example from journalism:—

Gale and Thunderstorm in London.

The weather seems to have been infected by the fitful fever of the General Election. The issue of the writs was marked by a confusion of the elements yesterday which would have filled the breast of a Roman senator with the gravest apprehension.—*Daily Telegraph*, p. 9, 10th Jan. 1906.

405. Apostrophe: lit. "turning away."—By this figure the speaker turns aside from his audience or the writer from his reader, and addresses himself direct to the person or thing that has taken possession of his thoughts. This figure (common in poetry) is seen only in the most impassioned prose:—

Industry, liberating and sacred Industry, it is thou who consolest! Under thy steps ignorance vanishes, evil flees. By thee mankind, freed from the servitude of might, mounts without ceasing towards that luminous and serene region where is one day to be realised the ideal and perfect accord of power, justice, and kindliness.—Quoted in *Review of Reviews*, p. 415, May 1900.

Unhappy man! and must you be swept into the grave, unnoticed and unnumbered, and no friendly tear be shed for your sufferings or mingled with your dust?—ROBERT HALL (in reference to the wounded in war).

406. Vision.—By this figure the writer or speaker, in relating something past, or describing some anticipated future, employs the *present* tense instead of the *past* or *future*, and thus makes it appear as if the event were actually passing before his eyes. The same figure can be used for describing something neither past nor future, but purely imaginary.

(*a*) *Some past event.* This is called the Historic Present (§ 112, *e*):—

The sack and carnage of Delhi lasted from three o'clock in the morning until three in the afternoon. The streets echo with the shouts of brutal soldiery and with the cries and shrieks of the inhabitants. The atmosphere reeks with blood. Houses are set on fire, and hundreds perish in the flames. Husbands kill their wives, and then destroy themselves. Women throw themselves into the wells. Children are slaughtered without mercy, and infants are cut to pieces at their mothers' breasts.—WHEELER'S *India*.

(*b*) *Some anticipated future*:—

I see and behold this great city, the ornament of the earth and the capital of all nations, suddenly involved in one conflagration. I see before me the slaughtered heaps of citizens lying unburied in the midst of the ruined country. The furious countenance of Cethegus rises to my view, while with a savage joy he is triumphing in your miseries.—CICERO.

(*c*) *Something imaginary*:—

What beckoning ghost along the moonlight shade
Invites my steps, and points to yonder glade?
'Tis she. But why that bleeding bosom gored?
Why dimly gleams the visionary sword?—POPE.

407. Hy-per-bol-e (a Greek word signifying exaggeration).—This is usually a fault. But when the departure from truth does not offend one's sense of the truthful, it is a recognised Figure of Speech, as in the following examples:—

They were swifter than eagles, they were stronger than lions.—*David's Lament for Saul and Jonathan.*

All the perfumes of Arabia will not sweeten this little hand.—SHAKESPEARE (Lady Macbeth).

Such an example as the following appears, however, to be extravagant and artificial :—

> The sky shrunk upward with unusual dread,
> And trembling Tiber dived beneath his bed.—DRYDEN.

Class V.—Figures based on Indirectness of Speech.

408. Innuendo : lit. "by making a nod"; *i.e.* by hinting or implying a thing without plainly saying it.—In the use of this figure the writer abstains from expressing his point in direct terms, but says enough to enable the reader to infer it without difficulty. This mode of speech is sometimes more effective than the direct form of statement :—

I do not consult physicians; for I hope to die without them.—SIR W. TEMPLE.

To my steward I have left nothing, as he has had charge of my income and expenditure for the last 15 years.—*Extracts from a Will.*

We need not pry too deeply into the motives which actuated the minister in disregarding the interests of his country (China): Russia does not employ an auditor-general.—*Daily Telegraph*, 9th Sept. 1898.

409. Irony.—By this figure the writer or speaker says the opposite to what he means, but does not intend or expect his words to be taken literally :—

The Holy Alliance (Russia, Prussia, Austria) was minded to stretch the arm of *its Christian charity* across the Atlantic and put republicanism down in the western hemisphere as well as in its own.—GOLDWIN SMITH, *United Kingdom*, ii. 324.

Sunday was the twenty-fifth anniversary of the Sultan's accession, and was celebrated with a *geniality* peculiarly Hamidian by numerous arrests of Armenians and the distribution of half-salaries to the Turkish functionaries.—*Daily Telegraph*, p. 7, 3rd Sept. 1901.

Note.—The term "irony" is sometimes used metaphorically when it is applied to events which turn out the very opposite to what might have been expected.

It is surely the *irony* of political destiny that our occupation of Egypt should be represented as the principal obstacle to the realisation of patriotic schemes, the conception of which among the Egyptians is due to our own action.—*Daily Telegraph*, p. 11, 4th April 1907.

410. Sarcasm.—In Sarcasm a man does not, as in Irony, say the opposite to what he means. He says what he means, but says it in a way that implies ridicule, disapproval, or contempt :—

If ideas were innate, it would save much trouble to many worthy persons.—LOCKE.

When the clergyman is approved, there is a disposition to respect him, to smooth his path—always with the exception of any consent to increase his stipend.—*Spectator*, p. 618, 3rd Nov. 1900.

411. Euphemism (Gr. *eu*, well; and *phem-i*, I speak).—By this figure we speak in gentle, if not favourable, terms of some person, object, or event which is ordinarily seen in a less pleasing or in a very unpleasing light. This is effected sometimes by a single word, but usually by a periphrasis or circumlocution:—

China is a country where you often get different accounts of the same thing (=where many lies are told).—*Lord Salisbury's Speech.*

He kneeled down, and cried with a loud voice, Lord, lay not this sin to their charge. And, when he had said this, he fell asleep.—Death of Stephen, *Acts* vii. 60.

412. Lit-o-tes (a Greek word signifying plainness, simplicity).—The name is now given to that figure of speech, by which we place a negative before some word to indicate a strong affirmative in the opposite direction:—

He is no *dullard* (=decidedly clever).
A citizen of *no mean* (=a distinguished) city.—*New Test.*

Note.—By this figure such words as "infamous," "unprofessional," "unchristian," etc., have acquired a strongly affirmative sense. Thus *infamous* has a very different sense from *not famous* (=obscure), *unprofessional* from *not professional* (=private), *unchristian* from *not Christian* (=pagan, etc.).

413. Interrogation.—Usually when we ask a question, we do so for the sake of information. As a figure of speech, interrogation is used (*a*) to express a strong affirmative or negative, no answer being needed, or (*b*) to call attention to some important fact and then furnish the answer:—

(*a*) Can the Ethiopian change his skin, or the leopard his spots? —*Old Testament.*

(*b*) Seest thou a man wise in his own conceit? There is more hope of a fool than of him.—*Old Testament.*

Note.—The expository value of (*b*) is so great, that school-manuals are sometimes written in the form of question and answer.

414. Exclamation.—What an Interjection is in grammar, Exclamation is in rhetoric. It is a mode of expressing some strong emotion without describing it in set terms:—

O, what a fall was there, my countrymen!
Then you, and I, and all of us fell down,
Whilst bloody treason flourish'd over us.—SHAKESPEARE.

But she is in her grave, and oh!
The difference to me!—WORDSWORTH.

415. Identical Statement.—This figure, though it assumes the disguise of a truism, is in reality an indirect way of stating a fact that is not apparent on the surface. The disguise of self-evidence leaves no handle for attack or contradiction.

What I have written I have written.—*New Testament.*
(The inscription that I have placed on the cross was written once for all and must remain.)
We English are ourselves and not anybody else.—FREEMAN.
(Englishmen have a national character of their own and need not follow Continental models.)

416. Circumlocution: "saying a thing in a roundabout way" instead of saying it at once.—This figure may be used either for poetic ornament, as in example (1); or for giving greater prominence to a thought, as in example (2); or for Euphemism, as in example (3); or for humour, as in example (4):—

(1) The sightless couriers of the air (=the winds).—SHAKESPEARE.
(2) The very source and fount of day (=the sun)
Is flecked with wandering isles of night.—TENNYSON.
(3) She declared that neither she nor her husband was suffering from the domination of stimulant (=was tipsy).—*Daily Telegraph*, 9th March 1898.
(4) The driver of the engine played a sweet symphony with the steam whistle, then he caused it to whoop wildly, and finally made the steam hiss and puff like Vesuvius in a state of eruption; but all was in vain, the cow still held the line.—*Ibid.*

Class VI.—Figures based on Sound.

417. Sound suggestive of Sense: Onomatopœia. — We have a considerable number of words whose origin is clearly imitative. No one can fail to recognise the imitative origin of such words as *clucking* (hens), *gobbling* (turkeys), *cackling* (geese), *quacking* (ducks), *croaking* (frogs), *cawing* (rooks), *cooing* (doves), *hooting* (owls), *booming* (bitterns), *chirping* (sparrows), *twittering* (swallows), *chattering* (pies or monkeys), *neighing* or *whinnying* (horses), *purring* or *mewing* (cats), *yelping*, *howling*, *growling*, *snarling* (dogs), *grunting* or *squealing* (swine), *bellowing* (bulls), *lowing* (oxen), *bleating* (sheep). Thus, when words are so selected and arranged that "the sound," as Pope says, "seems an echo to the sense," we are following by conscious imitation one of the methods that language itself followed spontaneously and unconsciously in the early stages of its growth:—

The meeting of the Liberal party has come and gone, and left things very much as they were. In truth, all that was done at the Reform Club on Tuesday was to prepare a soothing poultice in the shape of a resolution and apply it to the party. But poultices, though greatly believed in by old women of both sexes in the nursery and in politics, are nevertheless very weakening things, and Tuesday's *s*oft, *s*qua*s*hy, *s*teaming poultice, though it may *s*oothe for the present, will only make the tis*s*ues of the Liberal party *s*ofter and flabbier than ever. —*Spectator*, p. 44, 13th July 1901.

In the frequent repetition of the letter *s* we almost hear the steaming and simmering of the poultice in the saucepan.

The following may be quoted as an example in poetry :—

Then he looked at the host that had halted he knew not why,
And he turned half round and he bade his trumpeter sound
To the charge, and he rode on ahead, as he waved his blade
To the gallant three hundred whose glory will never die—
'Follow,' and up the hill, up the hill, up the hill,
Follow'd the Heavy Brigade.—TENNYSON.

In all these lines, and especially in the last two, the ring of the metre appears to suggest the sense.

418. Alliteration.—The recurrence, either immediate or at short intervals, of the same initial letter or letters. Like the figure just described, it adds nothing to the sense, but is a mere device for impressing the memory or pleasing the ear :—

On the American side *p*latform and *p*ul*p*it s*p*outed *p*atriotic fire.—GOLDWIN SMITH, *United Kingdom*, ii. 213.

For a generation we have been limiting competition within the State and restraining its *cr*ude and *cr*uel violence.—H. W. WILSON, *Fortnightly Review*, p. 87, July 1901.

419. Rhyme.—This figure, like the preceding, should not be used in prose, except for the sake of emphasis.

It could not perhaps have been avoided, and it cannot now be *healed* or even con*cealed*.—*Lord Rosebery's Speech*, 17th July 1901.

The two men, though of course well known to each other by *name* and *fame*, had never met.—*Fortnightly Review*, p. 663, April 1901.

The following is a curious example of the mixture of rhyme and alliteration in the same sentence :—

Who can persuade where *treason* is above *reason* and *might* ruleth *right*, and it is had for *lawful* whatever is lust*ful*, and *com*mot*ioners* are better than *commissioners*, and common *w*oe is named common *w*ealth.—CHEKE.

420. Assonance.—The name given to similarities of sound

not included in Alliteration or Rhyme. Further particulars on Assonance are given in § 432.

A stitch in *time* saves *nine*.—Proverb.

John Carker, what is the league between you and this young man, in virtue of which I am *haunted* and *hunted* by the mention of your name?—DICKENS, *Dombey and Son*, chap. xiii.

421. Play upon Words.—This figure consists in using the same word in different shades of meaning within the same sentence:—

"Sportsmen," says Mr. H. S. Salt, "are men of slow perception, who find it easier to *follow* the hounds than to *follow* an argument."—*Fortnightly Review*, p. 50, July 1901.

The Guardians have decided that she shall learn *weaving*. To use Shakespeare's phrase, the idea does not *weave* itself perforce into one's mind.—*Daily Telegraph*, p. 10, 12th Sept. 1900.

He *weighs* his words as carefully as an apothecary *weighs* his drugs. —*Ibid*. 21st March 1907.

Point out the Figure or Figures of Speech exemplified in each of the following quotations:—

(*a*) *Selections from Poetry.*

1. I'll have this crown of mine cut from my shoulders,
Before I'll see the crown so foul misplaced.—SHAKESPEARE.

2. Is't not enough, unhappy thing, to know
Thou art?—BYRON.

3. Be witness to me, O thou blessèd moon!—SHAKESPEARE.

4. Old Gaunt indeed, and gaunt in being old.—*Ibid.*

5. Lamented chief! not thine the power
To save in that presumptuous hour,
When Prussia hurried to the field.—SCOTT.

6. The moon wheels her pale course.—MILTON.

7. How often have I loitered o'er thy green!—GOLDSMITH.

8. Hungry for honour, angry for his king.—TENNYSON.

9. What, shall they seek the lion in his den,
And fright him there? and make him tremble there?
O let it not be said.—SHAKESPEARE.

10. The happy night
That to the cottage and the crown
Brought tidings of salvation down.—SCOTT.

11. But all unconscious of the coming doom,
The feast, the song, the revel here abounds.—BYRON.

12. 'Tis but the tender fierceness of the dove.—*Ibid.*

13. Her heart and morning broke together in tears.—MORRIS.

14. Then wander forth the sons
Of Belial, flown with insolence and wine.—MILTON.

15. Night's candles are burnt out, and jocund day
Stands tiptoe on the misty mountain-tops.
Romeo and Juliet, iii. 7.

16. The insane root
That takes the reason prisoner.—SHAKESPEARE.

17. A needless Alexandrine ends the song,
That like a wounded snake drags its slow length along.—POPE.

18. High minds of native pride and force
Most deeply feel thy pangs, Remorse.—SCOTT.

19. But I—that am not shaped for sportive tricks,
Nor made to court an amorous looking-glass.—SHAKESPEARE.

20. But not to rank nor sex confined
Is this vain ague of the mind.—SCOTT.

21. Hearts firm as steel, as marble hard,
'Gainst faith and love and pity barred.—*Ibid.*

22. A trusty mate art thou, to fear
A single arm, and aid so near.—*Ibid.*

23. Give me my Romeo; and when he shall die,
Take him and cut him out in little stars,
And he will make the face of heaven so fine,
That all the world shall be in love with night,
And pay no worship to the garish sun.—SHAKESPEARE.

24. Such wonders speed the festal time,
While Curiosity and Fear,
Pleasure and Pain sit crouching near,
Till childhood's cheek no longer glows
And village maidens lose the rose.—SCOTT.

25. As vapours, breathed from dungeons cold,
Strike Pleasure dead.—WORDSWORTH.

26. To curb the crosier and the crown.—SCOTT.

27. For men must work and women must weep.
KINGSLEY (*Lond. Matr.* Jan. 1905).

28. Ill fares the land, to hastening ills a prey,
Where wealth accumulates and men decay.—GOLDSMITH.

29. And they blessed him in their pain, that they were not left to Spain,
To the thumbscrew and the stake, for the glory of the Lord.
TENNYSON.

30. On our quick'st decrees
Th' inaudible and noiseless foot of time
Steals, ere we can effect them.—SHAKESPEARE.

31. Cursed be good haps and cursed be they who build
Their hopes on haps.—Sir P. SIDNEY.

32. And though the terrors of the time be past,
There still remain the scatterings of the blast.

33. Sceptre and crown
Must tumble down
And in the dust be equal made
With the poor crooked scythe and spade.—JAMES SHIRLEY.

34. But look, the Morn in russet mantle clad
Walks o'er the dew of yon high eastern hill.—SHAKESPEARE.

35. Our stern alarums changed to merry meetings,
Our dreadful marches to delightful measures.—*Ibid.*

36. Hark, rising to the ignoble call,
How answers each bold Bacchanal!—BYRON.

37. Here files of pins extend their shining rows,
Puffs, powders, patches, bibles, billet-doux.—POPE.

38. While Cook is loved for savage lives he saved,
See Cortez odious for a world enslaved!
Where wast thou then, sweet Charity, where then,
Thou tutelary friend of helpless men?—COWPER.

39. She sat like Patience on a monument,
Smiling at Grief.—SHAKESPEARE.

40. The gentleness of heaven is on the Sea:
Listen, the mighty Being is awake,
And doth with his eternal motion make
A sound like thunder—everlastingly.—WORDSWORTH.

41. Wrapt in my careless cloak, as I walk to and fro,
I see how love can show what force there reigneth in his bow.
SURREY.

42. For modes of faith let graceless zealots fight:
He can't be wrong, whose life is in the right.—POPE.

(b) *Selections from Prose.*

1. That is a failing indeed! Implacable resentment is indeed a shade in the character.—J. AUSTEN.

2. An ambassador is an honest man sent abroad to lie for the good of his country.—SIR HENRY WOTTON.

3. I appeal to you, I call you to witness, O ye hills and groves of Alba.—CICERO.

4. You young Argus! you may look with all your hundred eyes and see that we play fair.—THACKERAY.

5. Miss Bolo returned in a flood of tears and a sedan chair.—DICKENS.

6. There is not a single view of human nature, which is not sufficient to extinguish the seeds of pride.—ADDISON.

7. His proceedings did not amount to much, but they were sufficient to provoke local irritation and to sand the cog-wheels of diplomacy, when other matters arose for settlement.

The foreign ministers on both sides of the Channel were determined to clear the machinery of grit, to the advantage of two very friendly nations. —*Daily Telegraph*, p. 9, 15th Dec. 1905.

8. In other words, the spectre of a military dictatorship looming on the horizon is slowly gaining in consistency and sharpness of outline.—*Ibid.* p. 9, 7th Dec. 1905.

9. Nevertheless, the winds which had slumbered in the Colonial trade were again let loose.—GOLDWIN SMITH, *United Kingdom*, ii. p. 212.

10. If he (George III.) granted Catholic emancipation, his logical mind told him the kingdom would depart from his house and go to the Catholic house of Savoy.—*Ibid.* ii. p. 298.

11. He was untruthful enough to believe his own untruths.—*Ibid.* ii. p. 320.

12. Between monarchical and elective government there was an awkward interval, in which the court, having lost its responsibility, retained its influence. In the human body there is an intestine, the survival of a previous stage of development, no longer serving any good purpose, but still serving to generate disease.—*Ibid.* ii. p. 308.

13. Pitt has been damned as a war-minister. Assuredly he was no Chatham. He had no eye for military or naval merit, no promptness in calling it to the front; he could inspire nobody, nobody could leave his presence a braver man.—GOLDWIN SMITH, *United Kingdom*, ii. p. 269.

14. He (Burke) speaks of it (the revolutionary party in England) with contempt, comparing it to half a dozen grasshoppers chirping noisily under a fern, while thousands of great cattle chew the cud silently beneath the oak; and his description was borne out by the facts.—*Ibid.* ii. p. 264.

15. The new wine of the Gospel burst the old bottle of State religion, and the evangelist in his own despite was driven forth to found outside the Church of England the free church of the poor.—*Ibid.* ii. p. 163.

16. A bishop could hold a see in which he was never seen.—*Ibid.* ii. p. 162.

17. Tory leaders found it necessary to resort to a swamping creation of twelve peers. One man in the representative house had the spirit to decline the ignominious honour.—*Ibid.* ii. 151.

18. In the nation at large, at least in its political classes, the party of the Revolution was in a minority; so the prime minister had to keep the pyramid balanced on its point.—*Ibid.* ii. 171.

19. The war was misconducted; Minorca was lost, and Newcastle basely sought to appease national indignation by the execution of Byng, the naval commander, for failing to relieve it,—shooting an admiral to encourage the rest.—*Ibid.* ii. 190.

20. Hill districts, where the flotsam of races is left eddying in a back-water, while the tide of conquest sweeps over the plains, are naturally designed to be ethnographic museums.—*Times Literary Supplement*, p. 138, 3rd May 1907.

CHAPTER XXXII.—PROSODY AND KINDRED SUBJECTS.

422. Prosody (Gr. *pros-odia*, literally "a song set to music") treats of the laws of metre and verse-building, just as grammar treats of the laws of accidence and sentence-building. Prosody might therefore be called "the grammar of verse."

Closely allied to prosody are the subjects of rhythm, rime (misspelt as *rhyme*), alliteration, and assonance, all of which enter largely into the mechanism of poetry. These therefore must be discussed along with prosody in the present chapter. They are dealt with in Section 1.

SECTION 1.—RHYTHM, RIME, ALLITERATION, ASSONANCE.

423. Rhythm (Gr. *rhuthm-os*, "even flow," or "even motion"). —For literary purposes rhythm may be defined as the "musical flow of language."[1] This is produced for the most part by a well-balanced recurrence of pauses and accents. Rhythm has nothing to do with rime (misspelt *rhyme*). It is a saying as old as Aristotle that "prose must be rhythmical, but not metrical" (*Rhetoric*, 8, § 3). Rhythm is quite as necessary to an orator as to a poet. In fact, there is scarcely any kind of written prose, which is not made more attractive by the recurrence of pauses and accents at suitable intervals. Even in an expository treatise, provided that there is no sacrifice of precision, the argument or description is made more impressive when vigour and clearness are reinforced by rhythm.

The following may be quoted as a short and simple example of a well-balanced sentence :—

> In passing judgment on the policy of a king, we must bear in mind not only the character of the matter with which he had to deal, but that of the instruments with which he had to work.—GOLDWIN SMITH, *United Kingdom*, vol. i. 86.

The two sentences which follow (both by the same author as the sentence already quoted) might be improved in point of rhythm :—

> (*a*) As the Spaniard was to the Mexican, so was the Norman with his mailed horsemen and his bowmen to the naked Celt.—*United Kingdom*, i. 102.

The noun "bowmen" requires some epithet, such as "skilful," "practised," as a balance to the epithets "mailed" and "naked": or the rhythm could be improved by a mere change of order—"with his bowmen and his mailed horsemen." The latter is the best emendation that could be made, because it sets the two epithets *mailed* and *naked* in immediate antithesis to each other.

> (*b*) Weakness he (Charles I.) inherited from his father, and it appears, together with his likeness to James, in the portrait of him by Dobson, though not in the somewhat idealised portrait by Van Dyck.—*Ibid.* i. 469.

This ill-balanced sentence requires to be recast altogether. It might be reconstructed in the following way: "Weakness he (Charles I.) inherited from his father. Not only was this trait conspicuous in his living likeness to James, but it is depicted in the portrait of him by Dobson, though in the somewhat idealised portrait by Van Dyck it is not allowed to appear."

---

[1] Rhythm has been elsewhere defined as "a principle of proportion introduced into language" (Abbott and Seeley's *Eng. Less. for Eng. People*, p. 143). This definition appears to be defective on one point: it makes no mention of *sound*, which is the chief characteristic of rhythm. Rhythm appeals to the ear, not to the eye. It is only the practised reader who can perceive "the proportion of language" without reading the composition aloud.

One short example of rhythm in poetry must suffice. In Shakespeare, whose ear for rhythm or balance was perfect, we have examples such as the following, in which the rhythm is carried on from one stanza to the next :—

1

Blow, blow, thou winter-wind,
Thou art not so unkind
As man's ingratitude, etc.

2

Freeze, freeze, thou bitter sky,
Thou dost not bite so nigh
As benefits forgot, etc.

424. Rime (A.S. *rīm*, "number," misspelt as *rhyme* from a supposed, but utterly groundless, connection with Gr. *rhuthm*-os) is a repetition of the same sound at the end of two or more lines. The effect of rime, however, is not produced unless the riming lines are near enough to each other for the resemblance of sound to strike the ear. In the following extract the tax upon the ear is greater than what most ears will easily bear :—

Slight, to be crushed with a tap
Of my finger-nail on the sand,
Small, but a work divine,
Frail, but of force to withstand
Year upon year the shock
Of cataract-seas that snap
The three-decker's oaken spine
Athwart the ledges of rock,
Here on the Breton strand.—TENNYSON, *Maud*, Part I.

Here there are four lines between *tap* and *snap*, four between *stand* and *strand*, and three between *divine* and *spine*. Such riming will not please the ear of most readers. On the use of rime as a figure of speech in prose see § 419.

425. Rimes of more than one Syllable.—A rime is usually of *one* syllable. But rimes can also be in two or more syllables, provided that the first syllable is accented and the rest are unaccented ; as, *motion, ocean* ; *behaviour, saviour.* Double rimes are called in French, and sometimes in English, female or feminine, while a single rime is called a male. Double and treble rimes are more commonly used in comic than they are in serious poetry :—

He humbly hopes by this expedient
To prove himself your most obedient,
(Which shall be always his endeavour),
And jump into their former favour.—COWPER.

Servant. "Please, Mr. Winter has called for the taxes."
Theod. Hook. "Then give Mr. Winter whatever he axes.
Mr. Winter's a man who'll stand no flummery;
His name may be Winter; his process is summery"
(summary).
W. THOMSON.

Double and treble rimes, however, are sometimes used quite seriously. The treble rime in the first extract quoted below occurs in one of the most pathetic elegies in our literature:—

One more unfortunate,
Weary of breath,
Rashly importunate,
Gone to her death.—HOOD, *The Bridge of Sighs.*

Seven goodly scions in their spring did flourish,
Which one self root brought forth, one stock did nourish.
DRAYTON, *Heroical Epistles.*

426. Perfect Rimes.—A rime is perfect under three conditions:—

1. The vowel or vowels in the riming syllable or syllables, *no matter what the spelling may be*, must produce precisely the same effect on the ear.

Thus *bear* and *fear*, though the spelling is identical, are not perfect rimes, because the vowel-sounds do not tally.

2. If any consonant or consonants come after the riming vowel or vowels, these, *no matter what the spelling may be*, must produce precisely the same effect on the ear.

Thus ap-*peased* and re-*leased* are not perfect rimes, because, though the spelling is identical, the effect produced on the ear is different in two respects: (*a*) the *s* in ap-*peased* is sounded as *z*, while that in re-*leased* is sounded as *s*; (*b*) the *d* in ap-*peased* is sounded as *d*, while that in re-*leased* is sounded as *t*.

3. The consonant that precedes the riming vowel or vowels in each line must, *no matter what the spelling may be*, produce a different effect on the ear.

But no perfection is so abso-*lute*,
That some impurity doth not pol-*lute*.—*Lucrece*, 122.

The italicised syllables are not perfect rimes, since they violate the third condition. The consonant "*l*" in "abso-*lute*" fails to produce a sound different from the sound of the "*l*" in "pol-*lute*."

427. Long Vowels riming with short ones.—Among English poets we often find that long vowels are made to rime with the corresponding short ones. Such rimes are not perfect, but they are far less faulty than rimes, such as *heat*, *great*, which, though they are spelt alike, produce nothing but discord to the ear.

> No more? A monster, then, *a dream*,
> A discord. Dragons of the prime,
> That tare each other in their slime,
> Were mellow music matched with *him*.—*In Memoriam*.

If the reader will refer to Chapter XIV. p. 122, § 222, he will be reminded that the sound of *ee*, as in *seem* or *dream*, is the long sound, not of ĕ in *them*, but of ĭ in *him*. It is not at all likely that Tennyson made a study of English phonetics, but his poetical ear, accurate by nature, and improved by practice, was well able to guide him correctly in such a matter.

428. Changes in Vowel-Sounds.—The main cause of all our trouble in the matter of rime, as also in that of our spelling, is that at different periods in the history of our language the vowel-sounds underwent great changes, which in many cases were not accompanied by changes in spelling.

Take the digraph *ea* as an example. It was in the Tudor period that this digraph first came into use. It had then the sound that it has still in such words as *great*, *break*, *steak*, etc.; but for the most part it has shifted to the sound that it now has in *breach*, *steal*, *grease*. Between the two there was a rather long interval, during which the sound was dubious.

(*a*) Examples in the Tudor, and part of the Stuart periods, when the sound of *ea* was fixed :—

(1) That ten-years-travell'd Greek, return'd from *sea*,
Ne'er joyed so much to see his Ithacā, etc.
DRAYTON (1563-1631).

(2) E'en like two little bank-dividing brooks,
That wash the pebbles with their wanton *streams*,
And having ranged and searched a thousand brooks,
Meet both at length in silver-breasted Thāmes.
QUARLES (1592-1644).

(3) Jack makes the hedge which others break,
And ever thinks what he doth *speak*.—CAMPION (1566-1620).

(*b*) Examples of the dubious sound of *ea*, from Pope to Cowper (incl.) :—

(1) Grant, gracious goddess, grant me still to *cheat*,
Oh, may thy cloud still cover the deceit.—*Dunciad*, iv.

(2) Here thou, great Anna, whom three realms obey,
Dost sometimes counsel take and sometimes *tea*.
Rape of the Lock, iii.

(3) The wing'd inhabitants of air,
The day, the night, the various *year*.—GAY, *Fable* 49.

(4) I am monarch of all I survey,
From the centre all round to the *sea*.—COWPER.

(5) But I beneath a rougher *sea*,
And whelmed in deeper gulfs than he.—COWPER.

(*c*) Since the time of Cowper (the two lines just quoted were the last two that he ever wrote), *ea* has been sounded as *ee* in all words except *yea, steak, break, great, jean, bear* (noun), *bear* (verb), *wear, tear* (verb), *pear, swear* (eleven words in all).

429. Medial Rimes.—When a rime occurs in the middle of a line, it usually produces an unpleasant jingle, as in the following couplet, the authorship of which, though it appears in Goldsmith's *Traveller*, has been ascribed to Johnson :—

How *small*, of *all* that human hearts endure,
That part which *laws* or kings can *cause* or cure.

It reminds one of Cicero's celebrated line, which called forth the ridicule of Juvenal :—

O fortu*natam natam* me consule Romam !—*Satire X*.
How fortu*nate* a *nat*al day was thine,
O Rome, in that *late* consu*late* of mine !—GIFFORD.

On the other hand medial riming may be used for the sake of melody, or to give point to an antithesis, or for any other rhetorical effect. Examples of this are very numerous in Coleridge's *Ancient Mariner* :—

If he may *know* which way to *go*, etc.
Fly, brother, *fly* more *high*, more *high*, etc.
For *slow* and *slow* that ship will *go*, etc.
We were the *first* that ever *burst*, etc.
The ship was *cheered*, the harbour *cleared*, etc.
It cracked and *growled* and roared and *howled*, etc.

In Tennyson the internal riming is more subtle :—

I *fal*-ter where I firmly trod,
And *fal*-ling with my *weight* of cares
Upon the *great* world's *al*-tar-stairs
That slope through darkness up to God.—*In Memoriam*.

430. Alliteration (Lat. *ad*, "to"; *litera*, "letter").—The use of alliteration in *prose* has been exemplified already in § 418, where it is classed among those figures of speech that are dependent on "Sound." In *poetry* not only is the figure more commonly met with, but it is used in a greater variety of forms.

(*a*) *Alternate alliterations of consonants* :—

Our *dr*eadful *m*arches to *d*elightful *m*easures.—SHAKESPEARE.

Who *b*reaks his *b*irth's invidious *b*ar,
And *g*rasps the skirts of happy chance,
And *b*reasts the *b*lows of circumstance,
And *g*rapples with his evil star.—TENNYSON.

The *b*rood of *f*olly without *f*ather *b*red.—MILTON.

(*b*) *Medial alliteration of consonants* :—

*M*yriads of *r*ivu*l*ets hu*rr*ying th*r*ough the *l*awn,
The *m*oan of doves in i*mm*e*m*oria*l* e*lm*s,
And *m*ur*m*u*r*ing of innu*m*e*r*ab*l*e bees.—TENNYSON.

In these three lines the letter *r* occurs nine times, the letter *l* five times, and the letter *m* nine times. In reading these lines aloud we seem to hear the rippling of rivulets, the moaning of doves, and the buzzing of bees.

(*c*) *Vowel alliteration* (comparatively rare) :—

Jehovah, who in one night when He passed
Through *E*gypt marching, *e*quall'd with one stroke.—MILTON.

The alliteration of the prefix *un-* seems to have cast a spell of fascination over English poets :—

Un-bodiéd, *un*-soul'd, *un*-heard, *un*-seen.—SPENSER.
Un-seen, *un*-mark'd, *un*-pitied, *un*-rewarded.—FAIRFAX.
Un-housel'd, disappointed, *un*-aneled.—SHAKESPEARE.
Un-respited, *un*-pitied, *un*-reprieved.—MILTON.
Comes *un*-prevented, *un*-implored, *un*-sought.—*Ibid.*
Un-shaken, *un*-seduced, *un*-terrified.—*Ibid.*
Un-humbled, *un*-repentant, *un*-reformed.—*Ibid.*
With pangs *un*-felt before, *un*-pitied and alone.—GRAY.
Leave me *un*-blest, *un*-pitied here to mourn.—*Ibid.*
Un-quenched by want, *un*-fann'd by strong desire.—GOLDSMITH.
Un-altered, *un*-improved the manners run.—*Ibid.*
Un-wept, *un*-honour'd, und *un*-sung.—SCOTT.
Un-knell'd, *un*-coffin'd, and *un*-known.—BYRON.
But more than all, *un*-plumb'd,
Un-seal'd, *un*-trodden is the heart of man.—M. ARNOLD.

431. Alliterative Poetry.—Alliteration is the principle on which Icelandic verse is founded to this day. We, however, have an interest in it peculiarly our own ; for it furnishes the key to Anglo-Saxon verse and to much of early English verse. In the history of our literature the last great specimen of alliterative poetry was the poem called *Piers the Ploughman* by Langland, a contemporary of Chaucer. The following lines with spelling modernised will serve as an example :—

But in a *M*ay *m*orning | on *M*alvern hills
Me be*f*ell a *f*erly | of *f*airy methought ;
I *w*as *w*eary of *w*andering | and *w*ent to rest
Under a *b*road *b*ank | *b*y a *b*urn-side ;
And as I *l*ay and *l*eaned | and *l*ooked on the waters,
I *sl*umbered in a *sl*eeping, | it sounded so merry.

In this kind of verse each line is divided in the middle by a pause that the reader has to make in reading it aloud. (This has been indicated by the short perpendicular line printed in the middle of each of the above lines.) Each part of the divided line has, or ought to have, two accented syllables. Of the four accented syllables contained in each line the first three were alliterative, *i.e.* they began with the same consonant. The fourth accented syllable could begin with a different consonant; but here too alliteration was preferred.

This kind of poetry lasted far into the fourteenth century. But it yielded at last to the riming couplet or the riming stanza. Alliterative poetry had nothing but its own inherent merits to depend upon, and these were never very great. But rime, its rival, had more than one powerful ally to back it. It was backed (1) by the solemn echoes of Latin hymns chanted in churches and high-arched cathedrals:—

Dies iræ, dies *illa*
Splendet sæclum in fav*illâ*.

(2) by the growing prestige of French poetry, the study of which was coming more and more into fashion; (3) by the rising reputation of Italian poetry, which was beginning to find its way into England; and (4) by the genius and popularity of Chaucer, our greatest poet of the Middle Age, and one of the greatest in all our literature.

But there was a period of transition, during which alliteration, though it had ceased to be used as a basis of verse-composition, was still patronised to some extent by riming poets. What is most noticeable in the poets who preceded the Elizabethan Age is the fact that they sometimes used alliteration in the first two or three lines, as if they considered the old system entitled to some recognition at starting, and then dropped it altogether to the end of the poem. The following are a few examples:—

There sat I down among the *f*aire *f*loures,
And saw the *b*irdes trippe out of her *b*oures.
The Cuckoo and the Nightingale.
Fly fro the prease and dwell with soothfastnesse,
For *h*orde *h*ath *h*ate and climbing tikelnesse.—CHAUCER.
Ye that in *l*ove find *l*uck and sweet abundance,
And *l*ive in *l*ust and *j*oyful *j*ollity.—WYATT.
*M*y *M*other's *m*aids, when they do *s*ew and *s*pin,
They *s*ing a *s*ong *m*ade of the fieldish *m*ouse.—*Ibid.*
The *g*olden *g*ift that nature did thee *g*ive,
To *f*asten *f*riends and *f*eed them at thy will
With *f*orm and *f*avour.—SURREY.

432. Assonance (Lat. *ad*, "to"; *sonantia* (verba), "sounding words").—The word assonance denotes not a rime, but an approximation to one (for an example in prose see § 420). The typical form of Assonance is that in which the vowel or vowels in the last words or the last syllables of lines represent an identical sound, while the consonants represent a different one, as in *slumber*, *thunder*; *time*, *nine*; *came*, *blade*. "The assonance," says Hallam, "is peculiar to the Spaniard"; which means that Spain is the only country in Europe, where Assonance is admitted as a substitute for rime in the classical poetry of the nation. The only example in English, so far as I know, of an ode in which Assonance is used throughout, occurs in the "Spanish Gypsy" by George Eliot. I quote the first stanza:—

> Maiden crown'd with glossy *blackness*,
> Lithe as panther forest-*roaming*,
> Long-armed Naiad, when she *dances*
> On a stream of ether *floating*—
> Bright, O bright, Fedalma.

Though we have no ballad-literature, as the Spaniards have, in which Assonance is used instead of rime throughout, we have several isolated examples, of which I now quote a few:—

> But reason, lo! hath at my folly *smiléd*;
> For youth led me, and falsehood me mis-*guided*.—WYATT.
> I wish to perish, yet I ask for *health*;
> I love another, and I hate my-*self*.—*Ibid.*
> My fever comes, with whom I spend my *time*
> In burning heat, while that she list as-*sign*.—*Ibid.*
> Crying I burn in a lonely desire,
> With my dear mistress that may not *follow*,
> Whereby mine absence turneth me to *sorrow*.—*Ibid.*
> And other time the same doth tell me he is *come*
> And playing, where I shall him find, with his fair little *son*.
> SURREY.
> Divers thy death do diversely be-*moan*:
> Some that in presence of thy livelihed
> Lurkéd, whose breasts envy with hate had *swoll'n*.—*Ibid.*
> The only debt that dead of quick may *claim*,
> Where Christ is taught, we led to Virtue's *train*.—*Ibid.*
> False and untrue, enticéd oft to *treason*,
> Ah! bitter sweet, in feeling as the *poison*.—*Ibid.*
> Whose hidden virtues are not so unknown,
> But lively dooms might gather at the *first*,
> Where Beauty so her perfect seed hath sown
> Of other graces follow needs there *must*.—*Ibid.*
> What harvest half so *sweet is*,
> As still to reap the *kisses*
> Grown wild in sowing?—CAMPION.

I have been all day looking *after*
A raven feeding upon a *quarter*.—BEN JONSON.
A crafty lawyer and pick-*pocket*,
A great philosopher and a *blockhead*.—BUTLER.
No Indian prince has to his *palace*
More followers, than a thief to the *gallows*.—*Ibid.*
When maidens such as Hester die,
Their place ye may not well supply,
Though ye among a thousand try
    With vain en-*deavour*.
A month or more hath she been dead,
Yet cannot I by force be led
To think upon the wormy bed
  And her to-*gether*.—C. LAMB.
Half a league, half a league,
  Half a league *onward*,
Into the valley of death
  Rode the Six *Hundred*.—TENNYSON.

Use of assonance in proverbs.—With all its defects as a riming instrument assonance is much used in proverbial sayings:—

(1) A stitch in *time* saves *nine*.
(2) A stitch in time saves ten.

The two lines mean the same thing; for *nine* in (1) is not intended to stand for any number in particular; it merely represents an undesignated Figure of Speech, viz. the use of numbers for things incapable of strict numerical estimate; as in "He is one in a *hundred*." Yet if we change *nine* into *ten*, as in sentence (2), the proverb appears to lose half its force.

433. Medial Assonance.—Assonance, as has been shown already, mainly consists of similar vowel-sounds enclosed within dissimilar consonants. We sometimes find this effect in the middle, not always at the end, of a line:—

Where wild Oswégo spreads her damps around,
And Niagára *stuns* with *thund*'ring sound.—GOLDSMITH.
Than living *dul*-ly *slug*-gardised at home.—SHAKESPEARE.

In the following stanza of four lines we have a curious mixture of Assonance with Alliteration:—

The *moan*-ings of the *home*-less sea,
  The sound of *s*treams that *s*wift or *s*low
  *D*raw *d*own Æ-*on*-ian hills and *s*ow
The *d*ust of continents to be.—*In Memoriam*, XXXV.

Here the assonance is in the medial syllables, *moan*-, *home*-, and -*ōn*-; and the same vowel-sound reappears in the rimes, *slow*, *sow*. The alliteration is first seen in *s*, which occurs four times in the second line and once in the third; and then in *d*, which occurs twice in the third line, and once in the fourth.

SECTION 2.—PROSODY OR THE LAWS OF METRE.

434. Accent (Lat. *ad*, "to"; *cant*-us, "song").—"When we lay stress upon a single syllable, *i.e.* pronounce it more *loudly* and more *distinctly* than any other syllable or syllables of the same word, the stress so laid is called Accent" (§ 218). In the examples given below and in all the subsequent ones of this chapter, the accentuation of a syllable is denoted, as in the Oxford Dictionary, by a full stop placed against the upper part of the vowel belonging to the accented syllable :—

Re-be·l (verb), re·b-el (noun). Sup-ply·, si·m-ply.

Every word of two syllables must have one accent, but seldom more than one. For words of more than two syllables no rule as to the number of accents can be laid down.

Vo·l-un-tee·r (two accents, three syllables).
Hu-mi·l-i-ty (one accent, four syllables).
Co·m-bi-na·-tion (two accents, four syllables).
U·n-de-si·r-a-ble (two accents, five syllables).
Va·l-e-tu·-din-a·-ri-an (three accents, seven syllables).

Note.—Emphasis must not be confounded with accent. Accent applies to only one syllable of a word; but emphasis applies to the whole word (§ 218). A syllable is accented for the sake of metre; but a word is emphasised for the sake of drawing more attention to the sense. Emphasis in itself has nothing to do with metre. Nevertheless a writer of poetry usually takes care that a monosyllable, which he wishes to emphasise on account of the sense, shall also receive an accent for the sake of the metre.

435. Metre (Gr. *metr*-on, measure) is rhythm regulated by the rules of prosody. It depends on two factors :—

(*a*) The accentuation of syllables;
(*b*) The number of *accented* syllables to a line.

436. Quantity.—"Quantity" means the amount of time required for pronouncing a syllable distinctly (§ 218). In Latin prosody syllables were subdivided by quantity into Long and Short. In English versification, however, quantity is of no importance excepting so far as it affects accentuation. It is entirely subordinated to accent, and has to take its chance of being observed or not.

And E·- | den rais'd | in the· | waste wi·l- | der-ness.—*Par. Reg.* 1. 7.

Here the short syllable "the," one of the shortest syllables in our language, has to be accented, so far as it will bear the process, in order to satisfy the demands of metre, while "waste," which is as long as any other monosyllable that could be found, is denied the honour of an accent, because the metre does not require an accent in that place.

Though Quantity can thus be overruled by accent, *i.e.* by the demands of metre, yet the rhythm (*i.e.* "the musical flow of language," as rhythm has been defined in § 423) is made much more musical when the accented syllable is also a long syllable. As a rule the positions assigned to them by poets are identical, though such an irregularity as the above, provided it does not occur too often, is useful for the sake of variety.

437. Foot, Verse, Line.—A specific combination of accented and unaccented syllables is called a **foot**. The number of syllables to a foot may be either two or three, but it cannot be less than two or more than three, and *one of these must be accented.*

A specific series or succession of feet is called a **verse** or a **line**. Every new verse or line, when it is written or printed, begins with a Capital letter. (The word "verse" is sometimes used for "poetry" as distinct from prose.)

Note.—Sometimes a monosyllable is used at the beginning of a line as if it were equivalent to a complete foot. In Cowper's Elegy on the Loss of the Royal George we have—

Weigh | the ves- | sel up.

In Tennyson's celebrated song we have—

Break, | break, | break,

where each monosyllable stands for a complete foot.

438. The four main Feet of English Prosody.—In English prosody there are four feet, about which all authorities are agreed, two consisting of two syllables, and two of three. These four are described below:—

(*a*) An **Iambus** consists of one unaccented and one accented syllable. This is the commonest of all our feet.

Ap-pea'r, be-si'des, at-ta'ck, sup-ply'.

(*b*) A **Trochee** consists of one accented and one unaccented syllable. Not quite so common as the Iambus.

Ho'-ly, u'p-per, gra'nd-eur, fai'l-ing.

(*c*) An **Anapæst** consists of two unaccented syllables followed by an accented one.

Col-on-na'de, re-ap-pea'r, on a hi'll.

(*d*) A **Dactyl** consists of one accented syllable, followed by two unaccented ones.

Me's-sen-ger, me'r-ri-ly, pro'p-er-ty, a'c-ci-dent.

Of these four feet the last two have been much less extensively used than the first two. For the much wider use of the

Iambus and the Trochee there is a reason,—facility. It is much easier to read lines written in Iambics or in Trochees than lines written in Anapæsts or in Dactyls. Our metres, as has been shown, are based on accent, and accent is favourable to alternation. "A·c-ci-dent" (see above) has been given as an example of a Dactyl, and "re-ap-pea·r" of an Anapæst; but when we lengthen these words into *accidental* and *reappearance*, we are obliged to accent them thus:—

a·c-ci-de·nt-al, re·-ap-pea·r-ance.

439. Amphibrach.—A fifth kind of foot is sometimes added, called an Amphibrach, consisting of an accented syllable between two unaccented ones, as *re-ve·nge-ful*, *a-ma·z-ing*, *be-nigh·t-ed*. The following line from Campbell may be quoted as an example:—

There ca·me to | the bea·ch a | poor e·x-ile | of E·-rin.

It would be easy, however, to subdivide the line into anapæsts by making the first foot an Iambus, an irregularity which is of rather common occurrence in anapæstic metre:—

There ca·me | to the bea·ch′ | a poor e·x′- | ile of E·-rin,

in which *Erin* is a double rime.

But the following lines contain amphibrachs, which cannot be resolved into anapæsts:—

Most frie·nd-ship | is fei·gn-ing,
Most lo·v-ing | mere fo·l-ly;
Then heigh·ho | the ho·l-ly,
This li·fe is | most jo·l-ly.—SHAKESPEARE.

440. Spondee.—A sixth kind of foot, consisting of two accented syllables, is sometimes added. In Latin prosody this foot is called a Spondee. But in English prosody no such foot is recognised, since theoretically there cannot be more than one accent to an English foot. Sometimes, however, two accented syllables are placed together for the purpose of making the sound of the line suggestive of the sense (§ 415):—

Rocks, caves, | lakes, fens, | bogs, dens, | and shades | of death.

Here the three first feet are all spondees, which were intentionally placed there by Milton to indicate by the slowness and difficulty of the line the slow and difficult progress made by Satan in his perilous journey through chaos to the earth.

Note.—The names of all the feet are derived from Greek. *Iambus* means "aiming at," "attacking," so called because this foot was first used in Satire. *Trochee* means "running," so called because it is a rapid measure. *Dactyl* means "finger," so called because this foot, like a finger, consists of one long division followed by two shorter ones. *Anapæst* means "thrown back," because this foot is a dactyl reversed. *Spondee* means "pertaining to libations," so called because, when libations were poured out, slow and solemn melodies were sung. *Amphibrach* means "short at both sides," so called because this foot consists of one long syllable enclosed by two short ones.

441. Scanning (Lat. *scand*-ere, to climb).—To scan a line is to divide it into its several feet, and say *what kind* of feet they are, and *how many* of them there are. Lines of one foot are called *unimeters*; of two, *dimeters*; of three, *trimeters*; of four, *tetrameters*; of five, *pentameters*; of six, *hexameters*. We have no names for lines that have more than six feet; so we call them seven-foot lines, eight-foot lines (as in Tennyson's *Locksley Hall*), nine-foot lines, and so on if longer lines exist.

In scanning a line the following precautions should be noted:—

(*a*) The number of feet to a line depends on the number of *accented* syllables, not on the total number of syllables (§§ 434, 435).

(*b*) An accented monosyllable at the beginning of a line sometimes does duty for an entire Iambic foot (§ 437, *Note*):—

Stay', | the kin'g | hath throw'n | his wa'r- | der dow'n.—SHAKES.
(*Iambic pentameter*, 5 feet).

(*c*) Sometimes the Trochaic and the Iambic metres are so mixed in the same poem that we hardly know which is the predominant metre:—

Come, pe'n- | sive Nu'n, | de-vou't | and pu're,
So'ber, | stea'd-fast | and de- | mu're,
All i'n | a ro'be | of dar'k- | est grai'n,
Flow'-ing | wi'th ma- | je'st-ic | trai'n;
Come, but | kee'p thy | wo'nt-ed | sta'te,
With e'- | ven ste'p | and mu's- | ing gai't.
—*Il Penseroso.*

Here lines 1, 3, and 6 are Iambic, while 2, 4, and 5 are Trochaic.

(*d*) In the Trochaic and Dactylic metres, an accented monosyllable at the end of a line counts as an entire foot, though in the former this foot is short of one unaccented syllable, and in the latter of two:—

Li'fe is | bu't an | e'm-pty | drea'm.—LONGFELLOW
(*Trochaic tetrameter*, 4 feet).

Co·m-rades | lea·ve me | he·re a | li·t-tle, | whi·le as | ye·t 'tis |
ea·r-ly | mor·n.—TENNYSON (*Trochaic octometer*, 8 feet).
Me·r-rily, | me·r-rily | sha·ll I live | now·,
U·n-der the | blo·s-som that | ha·ngs on the | bough·.—SHAKES.
(*Dactylic tetrameter*, 4 feet).

(*e*) Metres are not always perfectly carried out. In an Iambic line the first foot is sometimes a Trochee instead of an Iambus, the fourth foot more rarely so, and still more rarely the third :—

Daugh·-ter | of Go·d | and ma·n, | ac-co·m- | plish'd ere.
MILTON.
Ma·t-ter | un-for·m'd | and voi·d, | *dar·k-ness* | profound.—*Ibid.*
Oh sha·me | to ma·n | , *De·v-il* | to De·v- | il damn'd.—*Ibid.*

(*f*) In the Anapæstic metre an Iambus is often put for an Anapæst, and this in any part of the line :—

Not a dru·m | *was hear·d,* | not a fu·- | ner-al note.
Anapæstic tetrameter.

(*g*) In scanning a line, two short syllables coming together can be counted as one for the sake of the metre :—

Wi·ng'd with | red ligh·t- | ning a·nd | impe·t- | *uous* ra·ge,
The mu·l- | ti-tu·d- | *inous* sea· | incar·n- | adi·ne.

(*h*) Two open vowels belonging to different words can be slurred, so as to be fused together and pronounced as one :—

Impre·ssed | th*e* effu·l- | gence o·f | his glo·- | r*y a*bi·des·
By he·r- | ald's voi·ce | explai·ned ; | the ho·l- | l*ow a*by·ss·
Abo·m- | ina·- | b*le, u*nut·- | tera· | b*le, a*nd w·orse·
To *in*su·lt | the poo·r | or beau· | ty i·n | distre·ss·
May I· | expre·ss | th*ee u*nbla·med, | since Go·d | is ligh·t.

Note.—This process is sometimes called *Elision,* because the vowel at the end of a word is elided or cut off by the vowel at the beginning of the next word.

442. Cæsura (a Latin word denoting "a cut").—In Latin prosody this meant the "cut" or division of a foot somewhere near the middle of the line, the cut being followed by a pause of the voice in reading the line aloud. In English prosody cæsura means merely the *pause* of the voice, by which lines of eight or more syllables are usually divided, when they are read aloud; and this pause may occur either at the end or in the middle of a foot. Rhythm greatly depends on the position of the cæsura.

In the following example the figure against each line shows the number of feet (with or without a half foot) preceding each cæsura. The two little vertical lines are intended to indicate the place in which the cæsura occurs. When a comma or other stop occurs in the same place as the cæsura, the rhythm of the line is helped by the sense; but a pause or cæsura can be made independently of punctuation, if the rhythm of the line is improved thereby. Sometimes a line has no cæsura; that is, neither the rhythm nor the sense of the line requires that any pause should be made in reading or repeating the line aloud:—

> 3½ Of man's first disobedience ‖ and the fruit
> 3 Of that forbidden tree, ‖ whose mortal taste
> 0 Brought death into the world and all our woe
> 2⅓ With loss of Eden, ‖ till one greater Man
> 1⅓ Restore us ‖ and regain the blissful seat,
> 2 Sing, heavenly Muse, ‖ that on the secret top, etc.
>
> *Par. Lost* (the opening lines).

Observe that monotony is avoided and the rhythm of the lines enhanced by the variety of places assigned to the cæsura or pause.

Observe also that the rhythm of the third line does not suggest or require any such pause.

443. Blank Verse.—"Blank" means "unrimed," *i.e.* poetry in which there is no riming between the last syllables or words of the different lines.

(*a*) Blank verse is much used in Epic and Dramatic poetry, the usual metre being that of the Iambic pentameter. This is the noblest of all verse; and though it may seem to be the easiest, it is in fact the most difficult to write effectively. An example of epic blank verse has been quoted already from *Paradise Lost* in § 442, under the heading of "Cæsura."

Blank verse in the Iambic pentameter was borrowed from Italy. It was first used in our language by the Earl of Surrey (1520-1546), who translated Virgil's *Æneid*, Books ii. and iv., in the metre named. It was Christopher Marlowe who in 1587 first used it for the drama in his play *Tamberlaine*.

Milton gives the following description of blank verse as used by himself in the composition of his great epic:—"The measure is English Heroic verse without rime, as that of Homer in Greek and of Virgil in Latin; rime being no necessary adjunct or true ornament of poem or good verse, but trivial and of no true musical delight, which consists only in apt numbers, fit quantity of syllables, and *the sense variously drawn out from one verse into another*."

The last words have been printed in italics, because they

express Milton's own view concerning the changeable position of the Cæsura. It is satisfactory to find that this view confirms what has been stated in § 442.

Since Milton's time, the best blank verse in our literature may be seen in Thomson's *Seasons*, Cowper's *Task*, Keats's *Hyperion*, Wordsworth's *Excursion* and *Prelude*, Southey's *Roderick the Last of the Goths*, Rogers's *Italy*, Tennyson's *Idylls of the King*, dramas, and rustic tales, and George Eliot's *Spanish Gypsy*.

(*b*) In Longfellow's *Hiawatha* we have a solitary example of blank verse in Trochaic tetrameters. The poem opens with the following lines, the metre of which is preserved without any change through 22 different divisions or cantos :—

Should you | ask me, | whence these | stories ?
Whence these | legends | and tra- | ditions,
With the | odours | of the | forest,
With the | dew and | damp of | meadows,
With the | curling | smoke of | wigwams,
With the | rushing | of great | rivers, etc.

(*c*) As will be seen below, in §§ 448-450, stanzas consisting of three, four, or five lines have been written in blank verse by some of our poets, especially by Tennyson.

Matthew Arnold (1822-1888) has written a poem called *The Strayed Reveller* in an irregular kind of blank verse, of which I will not attempt to describe the metre. A youth, overpowered with wine and sleep in the portico of Circe's palace, addresses the goddess in the following lines, with which the poem opens :—

Faster, faster,
O Circe, goddess,
Let the wild, thronging train,
The bright procession
Of eddying forms,
Sweep through my soul.

In this kind of metre (if metre it can be called), the poem rambles on to the end, nothing but blank verse being used in the lines, and the lines being kept studiously short.

(*d*) Some attempts have been made to introduce into English the kind of hexameter in which Homer's *Iliad* and Virgil's *Æneid* were written. The best-known examples of this kind of hexameter in English are Longfellow's *Evangeline* and Kingsley's *Andromeda* ; but the earliest attempt was that made by Southey in his *Vision of Judgment*. The following are the opening lines of the poem by Longfellow :—

This is the | forest pri- | meval. The | murmuring | pines and the | hemlocks,
Bearded with | moss, and in | garments | green, indis- | tinct in the | twilight,
Stand like | Druids of | old, with | voices | sad and pro- | phetic,
Stand like | harpers | hoar, with | beards that | rest on their | bosoms.

If the attempt had been successful enough to find imitators and admirers, this would have constituted a new kind of blank verse in our literature. But this metre, grand and stately though it is in the Greek and Latin originals, never became popular in English. It does not suit the genius of our language, because in English metre is ruled by accent, while in Latin and Greek it is ruled by quantity; see §§ 435, 436. The claim that Milton makes for his own metre to be "the English heroic verse without rime, as that of Homer in Greek and of Virgil in Latin," is universally admitted.

444. **Mixture of Metres.**—Metres are sometimes so mixed, especially in Tennyson, that we cannot always decide at a glance whether the prevailing foot is Iambic, Trochaic, Anapæstic, or Dactylic.

(*a*) Here is a well-known example:—

Brea·k, | brea·k, | brea·k,
  On thy co·ld | gray sto·nes, | O Sea· !
And I wou·ld | that my to·ngue | could u·t-ter
  The thou·ghts | that a-ri·se | in me·.

O we·ll | for the fi·sh- | erman's boy·,
  That he shou·ts | with his si·s- | ter at play !
O we·ll | for the sai·l- | or la·d,
  That he sin·gs | in his boa·t | on the bay· !
And the sta·te | ly shi·ps | go o·n
  To their ha·v- | en u·nd- | er the h·ill ;
But O· | for the tou·ch | of a va·n- | ish'd ha·nd,
  And the sou·nd | of a voi·ce | that is sti·ll !

Brea·k, | brea·k, | brea·k,
  At the foo·t | of thy cra·gs, | O Sea· !
But the te·n- | der gra·ce | of a day· | that is dea·d
  Will ne·v- | er come ba·ck | to me·.

TENNYSON.

This little ode or elegy is well in keeping with the principle that Coleridge lays down in the preface to his *Christabel* :— "Count the accents, ignore the number of syllables." Out of 16 lines we find that all except two contain 3 accents, the exceptions being the eleventh and the fifteenth, each of which contains 4 accents. So on Coleridge's principle of counting only the accents and ignoring the syllables there are only two irregularities of metre.

But if we count the syllables we find a great deal of irregularity :—15 Iambuses, 27 anapæsts, 1 amphibrach (see the last foot in line 3), and 6 monosyllabic feet of the kind described in § 437, *Note*. So the anapæsts win the day : yet we can hardly call such a poem anapæstic ; it would be more correct to say that it is written in no particular metre. In spite of the absence of any uniform metre the lines are so full of melody, that they have been set to music.

(*b*) The following example is also by Tennyson :—

We fee·l we | are no·th-ing ; ‖ for a·ll | is Thou· | and in Thee· ;
We fee·l we | are so·me-thing ; ‖ that a·l- | so has co·me | from Thee· ;
We know· we | are no·th-ing ; ‖ but Thou· | wilt he·lp | us to be·.

Each of the above lines is divided into two nearly equal parts. The division is indicated by the double line that has been printed between them, by the semicolon that closes the first half, and by the differences of metre. The first half of each line consists of two amphibrachs ; in the second half of line 1 there are two Iambuses and one anapæst ; in that of line 2 there is an Iambus, an anapæst, and another Iambus ; in that of line 3 there are two Iambuses, and one anapæst, as in line 1.

(*c*) One more example of the mixture of metres :—

When Bri·t-ain fi·rst | at Hea·ven's | comma·nd
  Aro·se | from ou·t | the a·z- | ure mai·n,
This wa·s | the cha·r- | ter o·f | her la·nd,
  And gua·r- | dian a·n- | gels su·ng | the strai·n :
Ru·le, Bri- | ta·nnia ! | Brita·n- | nia ru·les | the wa·ves.
    Bri·tons | ne·ver | sha·ll be | sla·ves.

The first four lines consist entirely of Iambic feet, which rime alternately, and each of these four lines is a tetrameter, *i.e.* consists of four feet. So far the scanning is entirely uniform. With the fifth line the discrepancy begins. The fifth line begins with two trochees, and ends with three Iambuses, which together make *five* feet instead of the *four* hitherto used. The sixth and last line consists of three trochees and a riming monosyllable. It would be impossible to find any one word that would describe the irregular metre of the last two lines except the word "irregular" itself.

SECTION 3.—SPECIAL METRES, STANZAS, SONNETS.

445. The Heroic Couplet.—In this metre lines consisting of five Iambic feet rime together in pairs. This metre is called "Heroic" because it has been much used in translating Epic or

Heroic poetry; as in Dryden's translation of Virgil, and Pope's translation of Homer.[1] Pope's translation of the *Iliad* opens with the following lines:—

Achil- | les' wrath, | to Greece | the dire- | ful spring
Of woes | unnum- | ber'd heav'n- | ly god- | dess sing!
That wrath | which hurl'd | to Plu- | to's gloom- | y reign
The souls | of might- | y chiefs | untime- | ly slain;
Whose limbs | unbur- | ied on | the na- | ked shore
Devour- | ing dogs | and hun- | gry vul- | tures tore:
Since great | Achil- | les and | Atri- | des strove,
Such was | the sove- | reign doom, | and such | the will | of Jove!

Observe that (1) each foot is marked off with a short perpendicular line, (2) each foot consists of two syllables, (3) each foot is an Iambus, the first syllable being unaccented and the second accented, (4) every line (excepting the last) consists of five feet.

446. Alexandrine.—A line of *six* Iambic feet, when it occurs in a context in which the other lines have only *five* such feet or fewer than five, is called an Alexandrine. The last line in the extract just quoted from Pope's *Iliad* is an example of an Alexandrine; it is there used to give a dignified ending to the paragraph.

In the metre described in § 445 under the name of the "Heroic Couplet," the couplet is sometimes varied by a triplet (three lines instead of two riming together), as in the following example from Dryden:—

No more | excu- | ses or | delays; | I stand
In arms | prepar'd | to com- | bat hand | to hand
The base | desert- | er of | his na- | tive land.

But usually the third line of a triplet is an Alexandrine, as in the following example from the same poet:—

The rocks | and woods | around
And moun- | tains trem- | ble at | th' infer- | nal sound;
The sa- | cred lake | of Triv- | ia from | afar,
The Ve- | line foun- | tains, and | sulphur- | eous Nar,
Shake at | the bale- | ful blast, | the sig- | nal of | the war.

447. Stanza (Ital. *stanza*, Old Ital. *stantia*, so called from

---

[1] The name "Heroic," however, is much too narrow to cover the various uses to which this metre has been put. This is the metre used in almost all our Pastoral poetry,—in almost all our satires, such as Pope's *Dunciad*, Dryden's *MacFlecknoe*, Byron's *English Bards and Scotch Reviewers*,—in much of our poetry of Reflection, such as Pope's *Essay on Man*, Johnson's *Vanity of Human Wishes*, or Campbell's *Pleasures of Hope*. A great many of Dryden's dramas are in riming couplets. It would be difficult to say whether the Heroic couplet or Blank verse has been the more widely and more variously used.

the stop or pause at the end of it).—A certain number of lines, forming a division of a song or poem, and agreeing in metre and in the number of lines with all the other divisions or parts of the same poem, is called a stanza. The number of lines of which each stanza is composed, though fixed and uniform in the same poem, may vary in different poems from three to nine inclusive. As will be shown below, we have examples of each variety in our poetic literature.

The Heroic couplet cannot, for the reason that will now be stated, be regarded as a stanza, and in point of fact it never has been so regarded. In a poem that is divided into stanzas, a space is left between the last line of one stanza and the first line of the stanza following. The space so left is intended to indicate the separation of one stanza from another. No such space is left in a poem written in the metre of the Heroic couplet. The lines go on continuously, as in prose, till the end of the paragraph is reached; and the paragraphs, as in prose, may be of very different lengths.

Note 1.—A distinction, however, has been drawn between the metre of the "rhyming couplet" and that of the "narrative rhyme" (Abbott and Seeley, pp. 205, 206).

In the former, the sense and sentence come to an end with the end of every second line, each couplet being complete in itself; this is what almost always happens; the exceptions are rare. This is the true type of the "Heroic couplet," of which an example from Pope's translation of the *Iliad* has been quoted in § 445.

In the latter, *i.e.* in the so-called Narrative Rhyme, the individuality of the couplet is not preserved to the same extent as in the Rhyming Couplet. The sense of the second line may be entirely separate from that of the first. The first line of the riming pair may be the winding up of a sentence or a paragraph, and the second may be the beginning of a new one. This is the metre of Keats's *Endymion* and of Morris's *Jason*. Observe the full stop after "shook" in the example quoted below:—

And on | his head | he had | a rus- | set hood;
And in | his hand | two spears | of cor- | net-wood
Well steel'd | and bound | with bra- | zen bands | he *shook*.
Then from | the Cen- | taur's hands | at last | he took
The to- | kens of | his birth, | the ring | and horn.

MORRIS, *Jason*.

Note 2.—**Distich.** A couple of riming lines, standing quite alone, and expressing some popular maxim, is called a distich (Gr. *dis*, twice, and *stich*-os, a line or row).

(1) He who complies against his will
Is of the same opinion still.

(2) River is time in water; as it came,
Still so it flows, yet never is the same.

448. The Triplet or Three-line Stanza.—A three-line group is the shortest compass to which a stanza can be reduced. It is obvious from the nature of the case that there can be little or no variety of form in such a stanza.

(1) We have a well-known example of the three-line stanza in Tennyson's *Two Voices.* I quote the first two stanzas :—

A still | small voice | spake un- | to me,
Thou art | so full | of mis- | ery,
Were it | not bet- | ter not | to be?

Then to | the still | small voice | I said;
"Let me | not cast | in end- | less shade
What is | so wond- | erful- | ly made."

The above poem is in 133 stanzas or metrical divisions. Each stanza or division, it will be seen, is separated from every other by the space left between them and by a change of rime.

Another well-known example is furnished by Cowper in the lines addressed to Mary Unwin. The only point of difference between this and the previous example is the refrain "My Mary" at the close of each stanza. This makes the separation of one stanza from another still more complete.

The twent- | ieth year | is well- | nigh past,
Since first | our sky | was o- | vercast;
Ah would | that this | might be | the last!
My Mary!

Thy spir- | its have | a faint- | er flow,
I see | thee dai- | ly weak- | er grow;
'Twas my | distress | that brought | thee low,
My Mary!

(2) Almost all stanzas are in rime. But Tennyson has given us more than one example of stanzas in blank verse. The following is an example of a blank verse triplet; here one stanza is separated from another partly by the space that is left between them, and partly by the completion of the sense in each stanza.

O Swal- | low, Swal- | low, fly- | ing, fly- | ing South
Fly to her, | and fall | upon | her gild- | ed eaves,
And tell | her, tell | her what | I tell | to thee.

O tell | her, Swal- | low, thou | that know- | est each,
That bright | and fierce | and fick- | le is | the South,
And dark | and true | and ten- | der is | the North.

Besides the absence of rime, the difference between these and the preceding stanzas is that each line consists of *five,* instead of *four,* Iambic feet.

Note.—The **Terza Rima.** This is a kind of metre which, though common in Italian poetry, never became popular in English. It is a kind of triplet or three-line stanza, the first and third lines riming together, and the middle line being unrimed. There is a pause in the sense at the end of every such triplet; and so every triplet must be considered to constitute a stanza. The unrimed line is taken up in the stanza or triplet that comes next, so that the order of the riming lines is as follows:—

a, b, a | *b, c, b* | *c, d, c* | *d, e, d* | *e, f, e* | *f, g, f* | etc.

This is the metre of Dante's *Divine Comedy*. Byron, so far as I can find, was the first to use it in English. He used it in his own poem, *The Prophecy of Dante*, and in his rendering of Dante's *Francesca of Rimini*, from which I quote a few lines as a specimen:—

a The land | where I | was born | sits by | the seas,
b Upon | that shore | to which | the Po | descends,
a With all | his fol- | low-ers | in search | of peace.
b Love, which | the gen- | tle heart | soon ap- | prehends,
c Seiz'd him | for the | fair pers- | on which | was ta'en
b From me, | and me | e'en yet | the mode | of-fends.
c Love, who | to none | be-lov'd | to love | a-gain
d Re-mits, | seiz'd me | with wish | to please, | so strong
c That, as | thou see'st, | yet, yet | it doth | re-main.

449. The Quatrain or Four-line Stanza (Fr. *quatre*, Lat. *quatuor*, "four").

Henceforth to the end of this series of stanzas, I shall give at the head of each class one stanza, to be called the "typical stanza," *i.e.* the form of stanza that has been most frequently used by English poets and used with the greatest variety of subjects.

(1) *The Typical Stanza.*—Among quatrains or four-line stanzas the most typical is that in which the lines rime alternately. The examples given below are well known to every one. The fact that they are so well known and that the subjects are so various shows how very much this form of the quatrain has been used by English poets.

1. *a* The cur- | few tolls | the knell | of part- | ing day,
b The low- | ing herd | winds slow- | ly o'er | the lea,
a The plough- | man home- | ward plods | his wear- | y way,
b And leaves | the world | to dark- | ness and | to me.
GRAY'S *Elegy*.

2. *a* Happy | the man, | whose wish | and care,
b A few | pater- | nal a- | cres bound,
a Content | to breathe | his na- | tive air
b In his | own ground.—POPE'S *Ode on Solitude*.

3. *a* John Gil- | pin was | a cit- | izen
b Of cred- | it and | renown;
a A train- | band cap- | tain eke | was he
b Of fa- | mous Lon- | don town.—COWPER.

4. a When the | British | warrior | queen,
b Bleeding | from the | Roman | rods,
a Sought with | an in- | dignant | mien
b Counsel | of her | country's | gods.—COWPER.

5. a Not a drum | was heard, | not a fu- | neral note,
b As his corpse | to the ram- | parts we hurried;
a Not a sol- | dier discharg'd | his fare- | well shot
b O'er the grave | where our he- | ro we buried.—WOLFE.

6. a Tell me | not in | mournful | numbers
b Life is | but an | empty | dream:
a For the | soul is | dead that | slumbers,
b And things | are not | what they | seem.—LONGFELLOW.

Among these six examples there is much variety of every kind. The metre of the fourth and the sixth is Trochaic, of the last but one Anapæstic, of the rest Iambic. The lines are of various lengths. The subjects are as various as the lines and the metres. The only point on which the quotations agree is the structure of the stanza, *i.e.* the number of lines, together with the order of the rimes.

(2) There is another form of quatrain, in which the rimes do not alternate, but go in pairs: *a*, *a*, *b*, *b*. This, however, is far less common than the preceding. The space that is left between one stanza and another, and the completion of the sense in each stanza, are the only things to indicate that any stanza exists.

a Come, live | with me, | and be | my love,
a And we | will all | the pleas- | ures prove,
b That hills | and val- | leys, dale | and field,
b And all | the cragg- | y moun- | tains yield.

a There will | we sit | upon | the rocks,
a And see | the shep- | herds feed | their flocks
b By shal- | low riv- | ers, to | whose falls
b Melo- | dious birds | sing mad- | rigals.—MARLOWE.

(3) The stanza used by Tennyson in his great poem *In Memoriam* is another kind of quatrain. In this poem the lines of each stanza do not alternate, but are given in the order of *a*, *b*, *b*, *a*. This metre was not, as is often supposed, originated by Tennyson; for it was occasionally used by Sandys in his metrical paraphrase of the Psalms, A.D. 1636. I find, too, that there is at least one example of its use by Campion, whose death took place in 1622. I can find no other example belonging to that early date. The metre is an admirable one of its kind; but it has been very little used by English poets. Tennyson, in fact, is the only poet, so far

as I know, who has used it largely, and this only in a single poem.

a What prof- | it can | my blood | afford,
b When I | shall to | the grave | descend?
b Can sense- | less dust | thy praise | extend?
a Can death | thy liv- | ing truth | record?

Psalm cxxx.—SANDYS.

a Follow | thy fair | sun, un- | happy | shadow!
b Though thou | be black | as night
b And she | made all | of light,
a Yet fol- | low thy | fair sun, | unhap- | py shadow!

CAMPION.

Note.—In the stanza by Campion, it will be observed, the order of rimes is the same as that used by Tennyson and by Sandys; but the number of feet to each line is different, the first and fourth lines being pentameters, and the second and third trimeters. The first line is Trochaic, the fourth Iambic.

(4) Quatrains, like triplets, are almost always in rime. The first example, so far as I can find, of a quatrain written in blank verse is given by the same Campion in a short ode on *Silent Music.* The metre is trochaic, the first and fourth lines being dimeters, and the second and third tetrameters. I quote the first stanza:—

a Rose-cheek'd | Laura, | come!
b Sing thou | smoothly | with thy | beauty's
b Silent | music, | either | other
a Sweetly | gracing.

More recently, we find that Collins's *Ode to Evening* is a quatrain in blank verse. The metre is Iambic, the first and second lines being pentameters, and the last two trimeters.

a If aught | of oat- | en stop | or past'- | ral song
a May hope, | chaste Eve, | to soothe | thy mod- | est ear,
b Like thy | own sol- | emn springs,
b Thy springs | and dy- | ing gales.

450. The Sextain or Six-line Stanza (Lat. *sext*-us, sixth).

(1) *The Typical Stanza.*—Among sextains the typical stanza is merely a continuation of that described in § 449 as the typical stanza of quatrains. The sextain is made by the addition of a riming couplet to the end of the quatrain. The rimes therefore are in the order of *a*, *b*, *a*, *b*, *c*, *c*.

a E'en as | the sun | with pur- | ple-col- | our'd face
b Has ta'en | his last | leave of | the weep- | ing morn,
a Rose-cheek'd | Ado- | nis hied | him to | the chase;
b Hunting | he loved, | but love | he laughed | to scorn;
c Sick-thought- | ed Ve- | nus makes | amain | unto him,
c And like | a bold- | faced suit- | or 'gins | to woo him.

SHAKESPEARE, *Venus and Adonis.*

a My days | among | the Dead | are passed;
b Around | me I | behold,
a Where'er | these cas- | ual eyes | are cast,
b The might- | y minds | of old:
c My nev- | er fail- | ing friends | are they,
c With whom | I con- | verse night | and day.
SOUTHEY, *The Scholar in his Library*.

In the former example all the lines are pentameters. In the first four lines of the latter tetrameters alternate with trimeters, and in the final couplet both lines are tetrameters.

(2) Another form of the sextain (not much used by English poets) is produced by the mere addition of two more alternately riming lines to what I have called the "typical" form of the quatrain. The rimes, therefore, are in the order of *a*, *b*, *a*, *b*, *a*, *b*.

a She walks | in beau- | ty, like | the night
b Of cloud- | less climes | and star- | ry skies,
a And all | that's best | of dark | and bright
b Meet in | her as- | pect and | her eyes;
a Thus mel- | low'd to | that tend- | er light,
b Which heav'n | to gau- | dy day | denies.—BYRON.

(3) Another form of the sextain (more commonly used by English poets than the preceding) is exemplified in the following quotation:—

a Thus Na- | ture spake. | The work was done;
a How soon | my Lu- | cy's race | was run!
b She died | and left | to me
c This heath, | this calm | and qui- | et scene,
c The mem- | ory | of what | has been
b And nev- | er more | will be.—WORDSWORTH.

In the following example the difference lies, not in the order of the rimes, but in the length of the lines:—

a The joy, | the tri- | umph, the | delight, | the madness,
a The bound- | less, o- | verflow- | ing, burst- | ing gladness,
b The va- | p'rous ex- | alta- | tion not | to be | confin'd!
c Ha! ha! | the an- | ima- | tion of | delight,
c Which wraps | me like | an at- | mosphere | of light
b And bears | me as | a cloud | is borne | by its | own wind.
SHELLEY.

(4) One more form remains, the least common of all:—

a Come, Sleep, | and with | thy sweet | deceiving
b Lock me | in de- | light a- | while;
b Let some | pleasing | dreams be- | guile
c All my | fancies; | that from | thence
c I may | feel an | influ- | ence,
a All my | powers of | care be- | reaving.
BEAUMONT AND FLETCHER.

Here all the lines except the first are trochaic. The first is iambic.

451. The Octave or Eight-line Stanza (Lat. *octav*-us, eighth).

(1) *The Typical Stanza.*—This is best known by the name "Ottava Rima," the name given to it in Italian literature, from which it was borrowed by English poets. It is merely an extension of the "typical stanza" of the sextain, and is formed by the insertion of two more alternately riming lines. The rimes, therefore, follow one another in the order of *a*, *b*, *a*, *b*, *a*, *b*, *c*, *c*. An Alexandrine is never seen in the last line of this stanza.

a 'Tis sweet | to hear | the watch- | dog's hon- | est bark
b Bay deep- | mouth'd wel- | come, as | we near | our home;
a 'Tis sweet | to know | there is | an eye | will mark
b Our com- | ing, and | look bright- | er when | we come;
a 'Tis sweet | to be | awak- | en'd by | the lark,
b Or lulled | by fall- | ing wa- | ters; sweet | the hum
c Of bees, | the voice | of girls, | the song | of birds,
c The lisp | of chil- | dren and | their ear- | liest words.

BYRON.

(2) In the following example there are four sets of rimes instead of the three contained in the "typical stanza." The metre of the example quoted is anapæstic. The form of the stanza consists of two quatrains added together, each quatrain having lines that rime alternately.

a I am mon- | arch of all | I survey;
b My right | there is none | to dispute;
a From the cen- | tre all round | to the sea
b I am lord | of the fowl | and the brute.
c O Sol- | itude, where | are the charms
d That sa- | ges have seen | in thy face?
c Better dwell | in the midst | of alarms
d Than reign | in this hor- | rible place.—COWPER.

(3) In the next example, as in the preceding, there are four pairs of rimes; but the order of the last two pairs is different. The metre is iambic. The stanza winds up with an Alexandrine, which is never seen in the Ottava Rima or "typical stanza."

a Daughter | of Jove, | relent- | less power,
b Thou tam- | er of | the hu- | man breast
a Whose ir- | on scourge | and tor- | turing hour
b The bad | affright, | afflict | the best!
c Bound in | thine ad- | aman- | tine chain
c The proud | are taught | to taste | of pain,
d And pur- | ple ty- | rants vain- | ly groan
d With pangs | unfelt | before, | unpit- | ied and | alone.—GRAY.

A variety of the same form is seen in the following. The rimes are of the same number and follow the same order; but the fifth and sixth lines are dimeters, and there is no Alexandrine at the close.

a The glor- | ies of | our blood | and state
b Are shad- | ows, not | substant- | ial things;
a There is | no ar- | mour a- | gainst fate;
b Death lays | his i- | cy hand | on kings:
c Sceptre | and crown
c Must tum- | ble down,
d And in | the dust | be e- | qual made
d With the | poor crook- | ed scythe | and spade.

J. SHIRLEY.

(4) One more form of the eight-line stanza remains to be mentioned: in general structure, the number of rimes, and their order, it bears a close resemblance to form 3 of the six-line stanza described in § 450.

a Her pa- | rents held | the Qua- | ker rule,
a Which doth | the hu- | man feel- | ing cool;
a But she | was trained | in Na- | ture's school,
b Nature | had blessed her.
c A wa- | king eye, | a pry- | ing mind,
c A heart | that stirs | is hard | to bind;
c A hawk's | keen sight | ye can- | not blind,
b Ye could | not Hester.—C. LAMB.

452. The Quintette or Five-line Stanza (Lat. *quint*-us, fifth).—The octave is the last of the even-lined stanzas that will be described in this chapter. We now come to those stanzas which have an odd number of lines (five, seven, or nine). The names assigned to them are quintette, septette, and nonette respectively.[1] The quintette, the first of the new series, though not often used by English poets, has been used with a great deal of variety.

[1] Regarding the names given to the different stanzas the following explanation is offered. *Quatrain* is the word used by Dryden to describe a stanza of four lines. *Sextain* (formed on the analogy of *quatrain*) is given in Webster's *Dictionary* as the term used in Prosody for a stanza of six lines; the corresponding Italian word is "sestina." *Octave* is the name (well known already) for a stanza of eight lines, or for the first part of a sonnet described below in § 457. Then come the three words "quintette, septette, nonette" that I have used as names for the three stanzas containing an odd number of lines each. *Quintette* and *septette* are both freely used for any sets of objects (lines being, of course, included) consisting of five and seven respectively. *Nonette*, Ital. "nonetto," denotes in music a composition for nine instruments or nine voices. I have taken the liberty of applying it to a stanza of nine lines, as some descriptive name of this kind was needed.

(1) *The Typical Stanza.*—In this stanza the rimes follow the same order as in the typical stanza of four lines described in § 449; viz. *a*, *b*, *a*, *b*. All that is needed to change the four-line to a five-line stanza is to add a fifth line riming with *b*.

a You vi- | olets | that first | appear,
b By your | pure pur- | ple man- | tles known,
a Like the | proud vir- | gins of | the year,
b As if | the spring | were all | your own,—
b What are | you, when | the rose | is blown?
SIR H. WOTTON.

In the above stanza every line is of equal length,—a tetrameter. In the following form of it the first and third lines are dimeters, while the rest are all tetrameters. In both stanzas every foot is an Iambic.

a Go, love- | ly Rose!
b Tell her, | that wastes | her time | and me,
a That now | she knows,
b When I | resem- | ble her | to thee,
b How sweet | and fair | she seems | to be.—WALLER.

(2) In the following form of the five-line stanza the order of the rimes is very nearly the same, the only difference being in the fourth line, which here rimes with the first and third lines instead of riming with the second and fifth:—

a A few | brief years | have pass'd | away,
b Since Brit- | ain drove | her mil- | lion slaves
a Beneath | the trop- | ic's fie- | ry ray:
a God will'd | their free- | dom; and | to-day
b Life blooms | above | those is- | land graves.—WHITTIER.

(3) In the following form the order of the rimes is *a*, *a*, *b*, *b*, *a*. The last line only is a pentameter, the rest being tetrameters.

a Oh snatch'd | away | in beau- | ty's bloom,
a On thee | shall press | no pon- | derous tomb;
b But on | thy turf | shall ro- | ses rear
b Their leaves, | the ear- | liest of | the year,
a And the | wild cy- | press wave | in ten- | der gloom.
BYRON.

(4) In the following stanza the order of rimes is again different, though nearly the same as in (3):—

a O World! | O Life! | O Time!
a On whose | last steps | I climb,
b Trembling | at that | where I | had stood | before;
a When will | return | the glo- | ry of | your prime?
b No more, | Oh nev- | er more.—SHELLEY.

(5) Lastly, Tennyson has given us five-line stanzas in blank verse: the following is an example. Every line is an Iambic pentameter.

Tears, i- | dle tears, | I know | not what | they mean,
Tears from | the depth | of some | sublime | despair
Rise to | the heart | and gath- | er to | the eyes,
With look- | ing on | the hap- | py aut- | umn fields
And think- | ing of | the days | that are | no more.

453. The Septette or Seven-line Stanza (Lat. *sept*-imus, seventh).

(1) *The Typical Stanza.*—This stanza is generally known by the name of *Rime Royal*, because it was the metre used by James I. (of Scotland) in the composition of his poem called "The King's Quair" (the King's book). The same metre had already been used by Chaucer (whom the Scotch king made his model) in the poem called "Troylus and Creyseyde." (This was the poem which Shakespeare afterwards consulted in writing his drama *Troilus and Cressida.*) The metre used by Chaucer and by the King of Scotland was used by Shakespeare also in his poem "The Rape of Lucrece." After Shakespeare we find that it was used by Milton in the four stanzas with which he introduces his "Hymn on the Nativity." I quote the first of the stanzas by Milton :—

a This is | the mouth, | and this | the hap- | py morn,
b Wherein | the Son | of Heaven's | etern- | al King,
a Of wed- | ded maid | and vir- | gin moth- | er born,
b Our great | redemp- | tion from | above | did bring ;
b For so | the ho- | ly sa- | ges once | did sing,
c That he | our dead- | ly for- | feit should | release,
c And with | his Fa- | ther work | us a | perpet- | ual peace.

The reader will have noticed already that the first five lines are, so far as the order of the rimes is concerned, an exact reproduction of the "typical" stanza quoted in § 452, and that the stanza has been raised from a quintette to a septette by the mere addition of a riming couplet to the end of it. The last line is an Alexandrine.

(2) The above form has been much used. The only other form of septette that I have been able to find is the following. Here too the last line is an Alexandrine.

a Awake, | awake, | my Lyre !
b And tell | thy si- | lent mas- | ter's hum- | ble tale
b In sounds | that may | prevail ;
a Sounds that | gentle | thoughts in- | spire :
c Though so | exalt- | ed she,
c And I | so hum- | ble be,
c Tell her | such dif- | ferent notes | make all | thy har- | mony.

COWLEY.

454. The Nonette or Nine-line Stanza (Lat. *non*-us, ninth).

(1) *The Typical Stanza.*—This is well known as the Spenserian stanza, because it was Spenser who designed and was the first to write it. It has had many patrons since; for it is used by Thomson in his *Castle of Indolence*, by Byron in his *Childe Harold*, and by Worsley in his translation of the *Odyssey*. The ninth and last line is always an Alexandrine. The following extract is from *Childe Harold*, Canto IV.:—

a Roll on, | thou deep | and dark- | blue O- | cean, roll,
b Ten thou- | sand fleets | sweep o- | ver thee | in vain:
a Man marks | the earth | with ru- | in; his | control
b Stops with | the shore; | upon | the wa- | t'ry main
b The wrecks | are all | thy deed; | nor doth | remain
c A shad- | ow of | man's rav- | age save | his own,
b When for | a mo- | ment, like | a drop | of rain,
c He sinks | into | thy depths | with bub- | bling groan,
c Without | a grave, | unknell'd, | uncof- | fin'd, and | unknown.

BYRON.

In the following example the order of rimes is the same; but the length of every line (except the Alexandrine at the end) is one foot shorter than in the corresponding lines of the Spenserian stanza:—

a The sun | is warm, | the sky | is clear,
b The waves | are danc- | ing fast | and bright,
a Blue eyes | and snow- | y moun- | tains wear
b The pur- | ple moon's | transpa- | rent might;
b The breath | of the | moist earth | is light
c Around | its un- | expand- | ed buds;
b Like man- | y a voice | of one | delight—
c The winds', | the birds', | the o- | cean floods',
c The cit- | y's voice | itself | is soft | like Sol- | itude's.

SHELLEY.

(2) In the following stanza the order of the rimes in lines 5, 6, and 7 is entirely different, and the number of rimes is raised from three to four:—

a And thou | art dead, | as young | and fair
b As aught | of mor- | tal birth;
a And forms | so soft | and charms | so rare
b Too soon | return'd | to Earth!
c Though Earth | receiv'd | them in | her bed,
c And o'er | the spot | the crowd | may tread
b In care- | lessness | or mirth,
d There is | an eye | which could | not brook
d A mo- | ment on | that grave | to look.—BYRON.

(3) In the following stanza, quoted from the celebrated

Ode on the Battle of the Baltic, the order of the rimes is again different. The metre is mainly trochaic; but the first line is Iambic, and the fifth line is so irregular, that I have not attempted to subdivide it into feet. I quote the opening stanza:—

> *a* Of Nel- | son and | the North
> *b* Sing the | glorious | day's re- | nown,
> *a* When to | battle | fierce came | forth
> *b* All the | might of | Denmark's | crown,
> *c* And her arms along the deep proudly shone:
> *d* By each | gun the | lighted | brand
> *d* In a | bold de- | termin'd | hand,
> *d* And the | Prince of | all the | land
> *c* Led them | on.—CAMPBELL.

455. Summary of Stanzas.—The Spenserian stanza of nine feet is the last of the "typical stanzas" to be mentioned in this list. Stanzas of greater length can be found in English poetry; but there is no name for them, and they are of very rare occurrence. The following scheme shows how easily one kind of stanza can appear to grow out of another:—

Quatrain (4 lines).	Sextain (6 lines).	Octave (8 lines).	Quintette (5 lines).	Septette (7 lines).	Nonette (9 lines).
a	*a*	*a*	*a*	*a*	*a*
b	*b*	*b*	*b*	*b*	*b*
a	*a*	*a*	*a*	*a*	*a*
b	*b*	*b*	*b*	*b*	*b*
	c	*a*	*b*	*b*	*b*
	c	*b*		*c*	*c*
		c		*c*	*b*
		c			*c*
					c

Thus the sextain is formed from the quatrain by adding a riming couplet to the end of it, the octave or Ottava Rima from the sextain by wedging an additional pair of alternately riming lines into the middle of it. Similarly the septette or Rime Royal is formed from the quintette by adding a riming couplet to the end of it, and the nonette or Spenserian stanza from the septette by wedging a pair of alternately riming lines into the sixth and seventh places of the septette.

456. Refrain.—In a poem consisting of a succession of stanzas, a phrase or sentence repeated at the close of each stanza is called a Refrain. A refrain is especially common at the close of a stanza consisting of three lines. I give two examples:—

Forget | not yet | the tried | intent
Of such | a truth | as I | have meant;
My great | travail | so glad- | ly spent,
Forget not yet.—SIR T. WYATT.

The twent- | ieth year | is well- | nigh | past,
Since first | our sky | was o- | vercast;
Ah! would | that this | might be | the last,
My Mary.—COWPER.

The first extract is from a lyric of five stanzas, the second from one of thirteen stanzas. In each poem the same words are repeated at the close of each stanza from beginning to end.

The following is an example of a refrain occurring twice in each stanza, once in the middle and once in the end. The metre is Iambic. This double refrain is maintained in a lyric of five stanzas:—

Like to | Diā- | na in | her sum- | mer weed,
Girt with | a crim- | son robe | of bright- | est dye,
Goes fair | Samē- | la;
Whiter | than be | the flocks | that strag- | gling feed,
When washed | by Ar- | ethu- | sa faint | they lie,
Is fair | Samē- | la.
ROBERT GREENE (1561-1592).

In the national air *Rule Britannia*, of which one stanza is quoted in § 444 (*c*), the last two lines are repeated as a refrain at the close of every stanza.

457. The Sonnet.—Borrowed from Italy. It consists of fourteen Iambic pentameters, of which the first eight lines are called the octave, and the last six lines the sestette.

(1) The Italian octave (followed by Milton, and since Milton's time by Wordsworth, Keats, and Tennyson) has *two* rimes, in the order of *a b b a, a b b a*. The sestette has either two or three rimes, and their positions are various. The following is an example of a sonnet by Keats, in which the riming lines of the octave are in the same order as those of the Italian octave:—

Octave.
a Much have I travelled in the realms of gold,
b And many goodly states and kingdoms seen;
b Round many western islands have I been,
a Which bards in fealty to Apollo hold.
a Oft of one wide expanse had I been told
b That deep-browed Homer ruled as his demesne;
b Yet did I never breathe its pure serene
a Till I heard Chapman speak out loud and bold.

Sestette.
c Then felt I like some watcher of the skies,
d When a new planet swims into his ken;
c Or like stout Cortez when with eager eyes
d He stared at the Pacific,—and all his men
c Looked at each other with a wild surmise,—
d Silent, upon a peak in Darien.

In the above example the first portion, the octave, is in the form of two quatrains added together, each quatrain being in the form of a stanza from *In Memoriam*. See § 449 (3).

The second portion (the sestette) is divided rather sharply from the first portion (the octave), not only by the full stop after "bold," but also by a turn in the thought or argument. Such division of thought, however, is not always made by our English poets. According to Wordsworth the aim of the sonneteer should be not to separate the sense of the octave from that of the sestette, but to diffuse one main thought as evenly as possible throughout the whole poem. For the same reason he deprecates, and very rarely employs, a riming couplet at the end of the sonnet.

The sestette (on the pattern of Petrarch) contains three rimes which occur in the order of *c, d, e, c, d, e*; and the same system has been followed by Milton and his successors. Sometimes, however, our poets have only two rimes in the sestette; in which case the rimes generally occur in the order of *c, d, c, d, c, d*, as in the example quoted above from Keats.

(2) Shakespeare's sonnet avoids the Italian model altogether. It consists of fourteen lines, as the Italian sonnet does; but differs from it in every other respect. It really consists of three stanzas, in each of which there are four lines that rime alternately, and it ends with a riming couplet. The following is an example :—

a When to the sessions of sweet silent thought
b I summon up remembrance of things past,
a I sigh the lack of many a thing I sought,
b And with old woes new wail my dear time's waste.

c Then can I drown an eye, unused to flow,
d For precious friends hid in death's dateless night,
c And weep afresh love's long-since-cancell'd woe,
d And moan the expense of many a vanish'd sight.

e Then can I grieve at grievances foregone,
f And heavily from woe to woe tell o'er
e The sad account of fore-bemoanéd moan,
f Which I now pay as if not paid before.

g But if the while I think on thee, dear friend,
g All losses are restored and sorrows end.

Shakespeare was not the inventor of this form of sonnet; he had been preceded by Surrey. But his example was followed by most of the Elizabethan poets. It was Milton who set the example of reverting to the Italian model.

SECTION 4.—NAMES OF THE DIFFERENT KINDS OF POETRY.

458. Epic: from Gr. *epik*-os, that which pertains to "words" (Gr. *ep*-os, a word). Heroic legends, such as those contained in Homer's *Iliad* or *Odyssey*, were originally recited, not written. For a long time they existed only in the memories of professional reciters: they were not collected and put into writing until about 527 B.C.: hence such poems were called "verbal"; *i.e.* unwritten.

An epic poem, as defined by Arnold, "treats of one great complex action in a grand style, and with fulness of detail." It is therefore always a long poem. The "great complex action" is historical or is believed to be so.

459. Lyric: from Gr. *lurik*-os, adapted to the lyre. A lyric is always short; it expresses one incident, situation, or emotion. Its subjects (among others that might be named) are love, as in Ben Jonson's *Drink to me only with thine eyes*; battle-scenes, as in Campbell's *Hohenlinden*; appeals to patriotism, as in Cowper's *Queen Boadicea*; or scenes of banqueting, as in Dryden's *Alexander's Feast*.

A very short lyric is called a **song** or a **ditty**; a longer and more dignified kind of lyric is often called an **ode**, such as Gray's *Bard*, or Tennyson's *Ode on the Death of the Duke of Wellington*. (On the origin of the word "ode," see below, § 460, *Note* 2, and § 463, on "Monody.")

460. Dramatic: from Gr. *dramatik*-os, that which pertains to action or acting. Tragedy is written in verse, comedy in prose.

There are many dramas, too, which are neutral, *i.e.* neither Tragedy nor Comedy, as Shakespeare's *Tempest* or *Merchant of Venice*.

There are also some dramas that are based on rustic life, such as Shakespeare's *As You Like It*, Ben Jonson's *Sad Shepherd*, Beaumont and Fletcher's *Faithful Shepherdess*, and Milton's *Comus*.

Note 1.—Thus in the name "Epic" the idea of recitation is prominent; in "Lyric," the music; and in "Dramatic," the acting.

Note 2.—The word "Lyric" is now loosely used for almost any kind of short poem. Originally it meant an "ode" (a Greek word signifying "song), that expressed the emotions of the poet himself. The metre may be either regular or irregular.

461. Pastoral: from Lat. *pastor*, a shepherd. The name is given to poems that describe rural life. They usually consist of conversations between shepherds about their love-affairs, their losses, the state of their flocks, the prospect of the coming harvest, etc.

The greatest pastoral in our literature is the *Shepherd's Calendar*, by Spenser (1553-1599), divided into twelve parts or months, in which, under the guise of idyllic dialogues, the poet describes the operations of husbandmen and shepherds in the different seasons and months of the year. He gives a national aspect to his work by depicting English scenery and the English climate, by selecting English names for his rustic persons, and by infusing into their language many provincial and now obsolete expressions.

Spenser, however, was succeeded by poets (such as Pope, Gay, Shenstone, Collins) who made the classical eclogues of ancient Greece and Rome their models. These models had come into fashion from Dryden's translation of Virgil's *Bucolics* into the riming couplet. The names given to the rustic persons were not national, as Spenser's were, but Greek or Roman names, such as Phyllis, Corydon, Lycidas, Alexis, Gallus, etc. Milton, as the reader is aware, adopts the name *Lycidas* (Greek) in his celebrated monody.

All poetry of this exotic kind has gone completely out of fashion; but a new kind of pastoral or rustic poetry is coming into vogue, which is perfectly genuine and national. Examples :—Wordsworth's *Michael*, and Tennyson's *Aylmer's Field*, *Enoch Arden*, etc. Such poetry is in blank verse, and is expressed in language of the severest simplicity.

462. Elegy: from Gr. *elegeia*, a lament of some kind told in metre. In our literature the name is given to any kind of serious poem that is not long, such as Gray's *Elegy in a Country Churchyard* (one of the best poems of the kind ever written). Most of the elegies in our literature are of shorter length than this. I give as an example the first stanza of Cowper's lines on the Shrubbery :—

O hap- | py shades, | to me | unblest,
  Friendly | to peace, | but not | to me,
How ill | the bower | that of- | fers rest
  And heart | that can- | not rest | agree!

463. Monody: from Gr. *mon*-os, alone or one, and *od*-e, a song. Literally, "monody" means "a song for one voice." It now signifies a poem, in which a single mourner gives vent to his grief over the loss of some friend. The best-known monodies in our literature are Milton's *Lycidas*, in which he laments the death of his friend Edward King, who was drowned in the Irish Sea in 1637; and Shelley's *Adonais*, in which the poet laments the untimely death of his friend and fellow-poet, Keats. The former is written in the style of a pastoral.

We cannot always distinguish between an Elegy and a

Monody. Every monody might be regarded as a kind of elegy; but not every elegy as a monody. Tennyson's *In Memoriam* is a prolonged monody, unique of its kind, in which the poet gives vent to the numerous thoughts and speculations that are suggested to his mind by the untimely death of his young friend, Arthur Hallam.

464. Ballad: from Old French *balade* (Low Latin, *ball-are*, to dance); lit. a dancing song, a song to be sung by dancers. It now means a short tale told in a light and rapid metre, and in the simplest language. Examples:—*Chevy Chase*; Southey's *Ballads of the Rhine*; Cowper's *John Gilpin* (comic).

Macaulay's *Lays of Ancient Rome*, though written in the ballad-metre, belong to a higher order of narrative poetry than that of ballads.

465. Romance.—The word was originally applied to the legends of popular heroes, told in mediæval verse. It is now applied to any tale of striking adventure, with or without a legendary basis, whether told in prose or in verse. Scott's metrical romances, such as *Rokeby*, *The Lady of the Lake*, etc., are good examples of poetry of this class. In the same class we may place Coleridge's *Christabel* and *Ancient Mariner*.

466. Satire (Lat. *satira*, *satura*, an abridgment of *satura lanx*, a dish full of mixed foods, a medley).—The name is now given to the poetry of Censure, such as Dryden's *MacFlecknoe* (aimed at his rival Shadwell); Pope's *Dunciad* (the Iliad of the Dunces, an ill-natured and malicious invective against contemporary authors); Cowper's *Tirocinium, or Review of Schools*, an honest exposure of the evils existing in his day.

Note.—Such poetry has now gone quite out of fashion. We have had no poem, which can be called a Satire, since Byron's *English Bards and Scotch Reviewers*, which was aimed at contemporary poets and at the Editor of *The Edinburgh Review*, who had attacked his first attempts at poetry. Sometimes, however, we get satirical outbursts in poems, which are not of that character in other parts, as in Tennyson's *Maud*, the first canto of which is a very keen satire directed against the commercial dishonesty that was prevalent in England at the time when the poem was written.

467. Didactic (Gr. *didaktik*-os, instructional).—Such poetry is of the character which in prose we call "Technical." It consists of instruction set forth in verse and embellished as far as possible with poetic ornament and illustrative anecdotes. The best poetry of the kind in our literature is Pope's *Essay on Criticism*, *Essay on Man*, and *Moral Essays*; and Cowper's *Truth*,

Table Talk, *Expostulation*, etc. These, however, might all be ranked under the poetry of Reflection—a higher class of poetry than what is generally implied by the word "Didactic."

We have poems, however, of a far more technical or didactic character, such as Armstrong's *Art of Preserving Health*, Dyer's *Fleece*, Green's *Spleen*, Grainger's *Sugar-Cane*, Philips's *Cider*. All such poetry is of an inferior order, and has gone completely out of fashion.

468. Sonnet (from Fr. *sonnet*; Ital. lit. "a little strain").—A short poem limited to the exposition of a single thought or sentiment, which may be amatory, reflective, patriotic, or of any other kind. The metre has been described in § 457.

Exercises on Chapter XXXII.

A. *Give the name by which each of the stanzas quoted below should be designated* (see *Section* 3). *Give also the name by which each line should be called, the name being determined by the number of feet* (see § 441). *Give also the name of the foot or predominant foot exemplified in each line* (see §§ 438, 439). *Mark off each foot in each line by a short perpendicular line, as is done in the extracts quoted in Section 3 of this chapter. If the metre in any line or lines is mixed or irregular* (see examples in § 444), *point out the irregularity. If any rime appears faulty, show in what respect it is faulty* (see §§ 426-428).

1. We only know
That we are passing through a world of change;
As buds that blow
Run into fruit, so to a state most strange
We from our present forms are born to grow.
GREGORY (1907).

2. Spirits to chains of earth confined
Discourse by sense;
But ours, that are by flames refined,
With these weak ties dispense.
Let such in words their minds display,
We in a kiss our mutual thoughts convey.
THOMAS STANLEY (1625-1657).

3. Sleep is a reconciling,
A rest that peace begets:—
Doth not the sun rise smiling,
When fair at even he sets?
Rest you, then, rest, sad eyes,
Melt not in weeping,
While she lies sleeping
Softly, now softly lies
Sleeping.—*Anon.*

4. Never love, unless you can
Bear with all the faults of man.
Men sometimes will jealous be,
Though but little cause they see,
And hang the head as discontent,
And speak what straight they will repent.—CAMPION.

5. Take, O, take those lips away,
That so sweetly were forsworn;
And those eyes, the break of day,
Lights that do mislead the morn:
But my kisses bring again,
Bring again,—
Seals of love, but seal'd in vain,
Seal'd in vain.—SHAKESPEARE.

6. On Linden when the sun was low,
All bloodless lay the untrodden snow,
And dark as winter was the flow
Of Iser rolling rapidly.—CAMPBELL.

7. Days, that need borrow
No part of their good morrow
From a forespent night of sorrow:

Days, that in spite
Of darkness, by the light
Of a clear mind are day all night.—CRASHAW.

8. Over the mountains
And over the waves,
Under the fountains
And under the graves;
Under floods that are deepest,
That Neptune obey;
Over rocks that are steepest,
Love finds out the way.—*Anon.*

9. Stay, stay,
Until the hasting day
Has run
But to the even-song;
And having prayed together we
Will go with you along.—HERRICK.

10. Weigh the vessel up,
Once dreaded by our foes,
And mingle with our cup
The tears that England owes.—COWPER.

11. "I have no name;
I am but two days old."
What shall I call thee?
"I happy am;
Joy is my name."
Sweet joy befall thee!—W. BLAKE.

12. I arise from dreams of thee
In the first sweet sleep of night,

When the winds are breathing low
  And the stars are shining bright:
I arise from dreams of thee,
  And a spirit in my feet
Hath led me, who knows how?
  To thy chamber-window, Sweet.—SHELLEY.

13. Now joy, old England, raise,
  For the tidings of thy might,
By the festal cities' blaze,
  Whilst the wine-cup shines in light:
And yet amidst that joy and uproar
  Let us think of them that sleep
  Full many a fathom deep
  By thy wild and stormy steep,
    Elsinore!—CAMPBELL.

14. I remember, I remember
  The roses red and white,
The violets and the lily-cups,
  Those flowers made of light,
The lilacs where the robin built,
  And where my brother set
The laburnum on his birthday;—
  The tree is living yet.—T. HOOD.

15. One more unfortunate,
  Weary of breath,
Rashly importunate,
  Gone to her death!

Take her up tenderly,
  Lift her with care;
Fashioned so slenderly,
  Young and so fair.—T. HOOD.

16. Hail to thee, blithe Spirit!
  Bird thou never wert,
That from heaven or near it
  Pourest thy full heart
In profuse strains of unpremeditated art.—SHELLEY.

B. (1) *Subdivide each of the following extracts into lines; (2) Subdivide each line into feet by writing a short perpendicular line which shall separate one foot from another, as has been done in the text; (3) Say what is the prevailing foot or metre in the extract as a whole; (4) Give the correct punctuation throughout; and (5) Give capital letters wherever they are needed in words that are not proper names:—*

1. My own Œnōné beautiful-brow'd Œnōné my own soul behold this fruit whose gleaming rind engraven for the most fair would seem to award it thine as lovelier than whatever Oread haunt the knolls of Ida loveliest in all grace of movement and the charm of married brows.—*Lond. Matr.* Sept. 1905.

2. I am going a long way with these thou seëst if indeed I go for all my mind is clouded with a doubt to the island-valley of Avilion where falls not hail or rain or any snow nor ever wind blows loudly but it lies deep-meadow'd happy fair with orchard lawns and bowery hollows crown'd with summer sea.—*School Leav. Cert.* (London), July 1905.

3. What is complete in all this little life through which we run with flying fleet unto a future that we cannot shun and a new life that hope would have more sweet?

4. Curse on him quoth false Sextus will not the villain drown but for this stay ere close of day we should have sacked the town heaven help him quoth Lars Porsena and bring him safe to shore for such a gallant feat of arms was never seen before.—*Preceptor's Exam.* June 1892.

5. Oh love they wrong thee much that say thy sweet is bitter when thy rich fruit is such as nothing can be sweeter fair house of joy and bliss where truest pleasure is I do adore thee I know thee what thou art I serve thee with my heart and fall before thee.

6. Absence hear thou this protestation against thy strength distance and length do what thou canst for alteration for hearts of truest mettle absence doth join and time doth settle.—J. DONNE.

7. The world's a bubble and the life of man less than a span in his conception wretched from the womb so to the tomb curst from his cradle and brought up to years with cares and fears who then to frail mortality shall trust but limns on water or but writes in dust.

8. What harvest half so sweet is as still to reap the kisses grown ripe in sowing and straight to be receiver of that which thou art giver rich in bestowing there is no strict observing of times' or seasons' swerving there is ever one fresh spring abiding then what we sow with our lips let us reap love's gains dividing.—CAMPION.

9. Then all my thoughts should in thy visage shine and if that aught mischanced thou should'st not moan nor bear the burden of thy griefs alone no I would have my share in what were thine.—W. ALEXANDER.

10. And he shall he man her last work who seemed so fair such splendid purpose in his eyes who rolled the psalm to wintry skies and built him fanes of fruitless prayer who loved who suffered countless ills who battled for the true the just be blown about the desert dust or sealed within the iron hills.—TENNYSON.

11. My heart in me keeps him and me in one my heart in him his thoughts and senses guides he loves my heart for once it was his own I cherish his because in me it bides my true love hath my heart and I have his.—SIR P. SIDNEY.

12. This life which seems so fair is like a bubble blown up in the air by sporting children's breath who chase it everywhere and strive who can most motion it bequeath and though it sometimes seem of its own might like to an eye of gold to be fixed there and firm to hover in that empty height that only is because it is so light but in that pomp it doth not long appear for when 'tis most admiréd in a thought because it erst was nought it turns to nought.—W. DRUMMOND.

13. E'en such is time which takes on trust our youth our joys our all we have and pays us back with earth and dust which in the dark and silent grave when we have wandered all our ways shuts up the story of

our days but from this earth this grave this dust my God will raise me up I trust.—SIR WALTER RALEIGH.

14. The crow the slanderous cuckoo nor the boding raven nor chough hoar nor chattering pie may on our bride-house perch or sing or with them any discord bring but from it fly.—BEAUMONT AND FLETCHER.

15. What is the world tell wordling if thou know it if it be good why do all ills o'erflow it if it be bad why dost thou like it so if it be sweet how comes it bitter then if it be bitter what bewitcheth men if it be friend why kills it as a foe vain-minded men that over-love and lust it if it be foe fondling how dar'st thou trust it.—J. SYLVESTER.

16. So serious should my youth appear among the thoughtless throng so would I seem among the young and gay more grave than they that in my age as cheerful I might be as the green winter of the holly tree.—SOUTHEY.

17. One short moment would explain what all philosophy has sought in vain would clear all doubt and terminate all pain why should I drag along this life I hate without one thought to mitigate the weight whence this mysterious fearing to exist when every joy is lost and every hope dismissed.—LADY MARY MONTAGU.

CHAPTER XXXIII.—POETIC DICTION.

469. How Poetry is distinguished from Prose.—Poetry is distinguished from prose not only by the possession of metre, but by certain peculiarities of diction and of thought. The most prosaic matter may be expressed in the most prosaic language, and yet in the most perfect metre. Perfection of metre does not make either the matter or the language poetical.

> Something had happened wrong about a bill,
> Which was not drawn with sound commercial skill;
> So to amend it I was told to go
> And seek the firm of Clutterbuck and Co.—CRABBE.

The following extract—written in blank (unrimed) verse —is little, if at all, better than prose:—

> Arms through the vanity and brainless rage
> Of those, that bear them in whatever cause,
> Seem most at variance with all moral good
> And incompatible with serious talk.—COWPER.

470. Peculiarities of Poetic Diction.—The chief peculiarities of the diction of Poetry as distinct from that of Prose may be summed up under the following headings:—

I. The use of archaic or less common words;
II. The omission of words required by prose;
III. The use of uncommon constructions;
IV. Deviations from the regular order of words;

V. The substitution of adjectives or participles for clauses;
VI. The use of epithets for the sake of ornament;
VII. A freer use of graphic or picturesque language;
VIII. A freer use of the figures of speech.

We have now to take these headings in their order and quote examples under each of them.

I. The use of archaic or less common words:—

Poetry pays little or no attention to changes in current speech. At the same time, it likes to distinguish itself from prose. It therefore avoids common words, and it retains words, which were used by former poets, after they have gone out of general use. The most remarkable instance of this in our literature is the poetry of Spenser. Though in point of age he was only ten years senior to Shakespeare, his language as a rule is much more archaic. Some of it was obsolete even for his own day. His subject, *The Faërie Queene*, threw him back into the old spirit of chivalry, which led him to study its literature and imitate the style. His diction has been well described as "a studiously archaic artificial compound, partly Chaucerian, partly North Anglian, partly factitious."

Nouns.—Poetry generally uses *swine* for *pigs*; *swain* for *peasant* or *husbandman*; *billow* for *wave*; *main* for *sea* or *ocean*; *maid* or *damsel* for *girl*; *nuptials* for *marriage*; *vale* for *valley*; *steed* or *charger* for *horse*; *ire* for *anger*; *woe* for *sorrow* or *misery*; *thrall* for *distress*; *might* for *strength*; *marge* for *margin*; *spouse* for *wife*; *numbers* for *verse* or *metre*; *bower* for *summer-house*; *quest* for *search*; *guile* for *deceit*; *bliss* for *happiness*; *bane* for *poison* or *mischief*; *ken* for *perception*; *troth* for *veracity* or *faithfulness*; *chanticleer* for *cock*; *combat* for *battle*; *goblet* for *cup*; *aught* for *anything*; *naught* for *nothing*; *eve* for *evening*; *meed* for *reward*; *morn* for *morning*; *mead* for *meadow*; *realm* for *kingdom*; *scribe* for *writer*; *victor* for *conqueror*; *foe* or *foeman* for *enemy*; *yeoman* for *peasant* or *husbandman*; *tilth* for *tillage* or *agriculture*, etc.

Pronouns.—*Thou* (or *ye*), *thy*, *thine*, *thee* for *you*, *yours*, *your*, *you*; *mine*, *thine* for *my*, *yours*.

Adjectives.—Poetry often uses *lone* or *lonesome* for *lonely*; *drear* for *dreary*; *dread* for *dreadful*; *lovesome* for *lovely*; *intrepid* or *dauntless* for *courageous*; *yon* for *yonder*; *rapt* for *delighted*; *hallowed* for *holy*; *baleful* for *pernicious*; *doleful* for *sorrowful*; *artless* for *innocent*; *hapless* for *unlucky*; *lowly* for *humble*; *forlorn* for *distressed*; *sylvan* for *woody*; *sequestered* for *retired*; *joyless* for *unhappy*; *jocund* for *merry*; *aweary* for *weary*; *stilly* for *still*; *reckless* for *careless*; *bootless* for *unprofitable*; *ingrate* for *ungrateful*; *recreant* for *unfaithful*; *mute* for *silent*; *darksome* for *dark*; *quenchless* for *inextinguishable*; *fond* for *foolish*; *wrathful* for *angry*; *dire* for *dreadful*, etc.

Adverbs.—Poetry often uses *scarce* for *scarcely*; *haply* for *perhaps*;

sore for *sorely*; *oft* for *often*; *erst* or *whilom* for *formerly*; *of yore* or *of old* for *in ancient times*; *erewhile* or *erewhiles* for *lately*; *anon* for *at once*; *amain* for *violently* or *suddenly*; *hard by* for *close* or *very near*; *full* for *very*, as in "full many a gem," etc.; *right* for *very* or *precisely*, as in "right against the eastern gate" (Milton).

Verbs.—Poetry often uses *quit* for *leave*; *wax* for *grow*; *quoth* for *said*; *list* for *listen*; *sojourn* for *lodge* or *dwell*; *trow* for *believe*; *tarry* for *remain* or *stay*; *hearken* for *hear* or *attend*; *obscure* for *darken*; *fare* for *walk*; *vanquish* for *conquer*; *quaff* for *drink luxuriously*; *cleave* for *stick*; *hie* or *speed* for *hasten*; *smite* for *hit* or *strike*. *-Est* and *-eth* are still commonly used for the second and third persons respectively. The older or Strong forms of past tenses are used in preference to the modern or Weak ones; as *wrought* for *worked*: *bade* for *bid*; *begat* for *begot*; *clove* for *cleft*; *crew* for *crowed*; *drave* for *drove*; *throve* for *thrived*; *clomb* for *climbed*; *stove* for *staved*; *clad* for *clothed*. Chap. VI., sect. 13. Poetry has retained the archaic verb *wit*, *wot*, *wis*, which prose has discarded :—

And so, God *wot*, his shield is blank enough.—TENNYSON.

Wit you well, my child,
Right fain were I to learn this knight were whole.—*Ibid.*

Conjunctions.—Poetry often uses *what though* or *albeit* for *although*; *ere* or *or ere* for *before*; *nathless* for *nevertheless*; *an if* for *if*; *eke* for *also.*

Prepositions.—Poetry has retained the otherwise obsolete *withal* for *with*, and often has *adown* for *down*, *'neath* for *beneath*, *'twixt* for *betwixt*, *'gainst* for *against*.

Long words and short.—Poetry prefers the use of short words to that of long ones. In the list of words given above, most of the shorter ones are on the side of poetry and the longer ones on that of prose. Long words are appropriate, only when the grandeur of the thought has need to be sustained by grandeur of language, as when Shakespeare says—

The multitudinous seas incarnadine.[1]—*Macbeth.*

When Tennyson uses a long word, he does so with the object of making the sound suggestive of the sense :—

The murmuring of innumerable bees.—*Princess.*

Even in *Paradise Lost* big words are not very common. In the first twenty-six lines only three words have more than three syllables; and even three-syllabled words are not plentiful. Big words easily degenerate into bombast, as in the following couplet :—

Whose peaceful day Benevolence endears,
Whose night congratulating Conscience cheers.—JOHNSON.

---

[1] "Incarnadine" simply means "to redden," *i.e.* to give a thing the colour of blood. Shakespeare was the first to use this word as a verb, and the second to use it at all. The one earlier use given in the *Oxford Dictionary* is that by Sylvester, with whom "incarnadine" is not a verb, but an adjective, *Du Bartas*, I. v. 609 (1591). *Macbeth* is believed to have been written in 1605. If this date is correct, Sylvester may claim priority of use. The word was borrowed through French from Italian.

II. Omission of words required by Prose :—

In the examples given below the omitted word or words are shown in brackets. By such omissions not only is the metre preserved, but the diction is made less like that of prose.

Examples from many Different Poets.	*The parts of speech omitted.*
The brink of (the) haunted stream . . . . . Creeping like (a) snail unwillingly to school . . . Makes satire a lampoon and fiction (a) lie . . .	*Article.*
(He) who steals my purse steals trash . . . Lives there (the man) who loves his pain? . . .	*Noun or pronoun.*
For is there aught in sleep (that) can charm the wise? I have a motion (that) much imports your good. . 'Tis distance (that) lends enchantment to the view . But our Robin takes From *whom* (those who) he knows are hypocrites and liars . . . . But were I Brutus, And Brutus Antony, there were an Antony (Who) would ruffle up your spirits, etc. . . .	*Relative as subject of verb.*
Mean though I am, (I am) not wholly so, etc. . . Happy (is) the man, whose wish and care, etc. . . To whom thus Adam (spoke) . . . . . . She knew not (that she was) eating death . . . (Let us) hover through fog and filthy air . . . Their acrid temper turns, as soon as (it is) stirred, The milk of their good purpose all to curd. . . Who (is there) but must laugh, if such a man there be? I do entreat you, (let) not a man depart, Save I alone	*Finite verb.*
I'd rather be a dog and bay the moon Than (be) such a Roman	*Infinitive.*
Will either quite consume us, and reduce To nothing this essential; happier far Than (being) miserable to have eternal being . . That ten-years-travell'd Greek, (having) return'd from sea, Ne'er joyed so much to see his Ithaca . . . Soldier rest, thy warfare (being) o'er, etc. . . . My ramble (being) ended, I returned	*Participle.*
He knew himself (how) to sing . . . . . . Permit (that) I marshal thee the way. . . . . "Hand must not be raised, (Nor) foot stirred, nor voice be uttered," said the chief For I have neither wit, nor words, nor worth, (Nor) action, nor utterance, nor the power of speech To stir men's blood	*Conjunction.*

Examples from many Different Poets.	*The parts of speech omitted.*
He mourned (for) no recreant friend	
Through the dear might of Him that walked (on) the waves	
Peace is despaired (of); for who can think (of) submission?	
For (in) what are men better than sheep or goats? .	*Preposition.*
Despair and anguish fled (from) the struggling soul .	
On either side (of) the river lie Long fields of barley and of rye	
But grant me still a friend in my retreat (To) whom I may whisper, "Solitude is sweet" . .	

In poetry a verb is often used alone, where in prose it would have an auxiliary verb attached to it:—

Long *die* thy happy days before thy death!
(*May* thy happy days die, etc.)
This day *be* bread and peace my lot!
(*May* peace and bread be, etc.)
Gives not the hawthorn bush as sweet a shade?
(*Does* it not *give*, etc.)
Tell me not in mournful numbers, etc.
(*Do* not tell me, etc.)
He goes to do what I *had* done, if, etc.
(What I *should have* done, if, etc.)

III. **The use of uncommon constructions**:—

(*a*) An Adjective substituted for an adverb to qualify a verb: see above, § 181:—

First they praised him *soft* and *low*.—TENNYSON.
The green trees whispered *low* and *mild*.—LONGFELLOW.
For she guides him *smooth* or *grim*.—COLERIDGE.
He stood abashed, then answered *grave*.—SCOTT.
I'll have this crown of mine cut from my shoulders,
Before I'll see the crown so *foul* misplaced.—SHAKESPEARE.

Note.—Sometimes an Adjective is coupled with an Adverb:—

Trip it *deft* and *merrily*.—SCOTT.

(*b*) An Adverb used as an adjective to qualify a noun. This point has been discussed already in § 352.

My *almost* drunkenness of heart.—BYRON.
My bride to be, my *evermore* delight.—TENNYSON.
Scarce half made up,
And that so *lamely* and *unfashionable*
That dogs bark at me as I halt by them.—SHAKESPEARE.
All which *secure* and *sweetly* he enjoys.—*Ibid.*

(*c*) The use of the Imperative in the first person. In older English this was not so uncommon; in modern it is seldom seen except in poetry.

Thither our path lies; wind *we* up the height.—BROWNING.
"Now rest *we* here," Matilda said.—SCOTT.
Well, sit *we* down,
And let us hear Bernardo speak of this.—SHAKESPEARE.
Thence turn *we* to her latest tribune's name.—BYRON.

(*d*) The formation of Comparative adverbs by changing "ly" into "lier." This is never done in prose, and rarely even in poetry.

You have taken it *wiselier* than I meant you should.—SHAKESPEARE.
Destroyers *rightlier* called, the plagues of men.—MILTON.
Divine*lier* imaged, clearer seen.—MATTHEW ARNOLD.
Loved deep*lier*, dark*lier* understood.—TENNYSON, *In Memor.* cxxix.
That scorn'd alike concealed or open foes,
And with the rising tempest *proudlier* rose.—MANNERS.

Note.—This form of the Comparative adverb occurs, however, in the familiar word "earlier," which can be either an adverb or an adjective.

(*e*) The employment of a pronoun as well as a noun for the same verb. This superfluity is rather common in poetry.

The wedding guest *he* beat his breast.—COLERIDGE.
My banks—*they* are furnished with bees.—SHENSTONE.
They tremble—the sustaining crags.—TENNYSON.
The smith a mighty man is *he*.—LONGFELLOW.
Tired nature's sweet restorer, balmy sleep,
He, like the world, his ready visit pays,
Where fortune smiles.—YOUNG.

(*f*) A freer use of the Subjunctive mood, where in prose the Indicative mood would be equally correct or might even be used in preference:—

The summer's flower is to the summer sweet,
Though to itself it only *live* and *die*;
But if that flower with base infection *meet*,
The basest weed outbraves his dignity.—SHAKESPEARE.
I do entreat you, not a man depart,
Save I alone, till Antony *have* spoke.—*Ibid.*
Over the vast abrupt ere he *arrive*.—MILTON.
Though heaven *be* shut
And heaven's high arbitrator *sit* secure.—*Ibid.*
Oh, if thou *have*
Hid them in some flowery cave.—*Ibid.*
Ere my soul *retire*,
I'll make my own Elysium here.—MOORE.
Thy kingly intellect shall feed,
Until she *be* an athlete bold.—TENNYSON.

(*g*) The substitution of an epithet (adjective) for the noun that would have been qualified by it, if the noun had been expressed. In the following examples not only is the epithet used for the noun, but the epithet itself is qualified by another:—

Below the chestnuts, when their buds
Were glistening to the breezy *blue* (=sky).—TENNYSON.
And sudden *pale* (=pallor) usurps her cheeks.—SHAKESPEARE.
Sailing with supreme dominion
Through the azure *deep* of air.—GRAY.
And all the sea from one entire *globose*
Stretched into longitude.—MILTON.
And through the palpable *obscure* find out
Over the vast *abrupt* ere he arrive.—*Ibid.*
These passed, if any pass, the void *profound.*—*Ibid.*
Yet did I never breathe its pure *serene.*—KEATS.

Every adjective used as a noun in the above examples denotes some abstract quality or some inanimate object. In the following extract, however, the adjective so used denotes *persons.* Such examples are very rare.

Among innumerable *false* (=traitors), unmoved,
His loyalty he kept, his zeal, his love.—MILTON.

(*h*) The formation of new compound words :—[1]

Love-whispering woods and *lute-resounding* waves.—POPE.
Hast thou not heard
That haughty Spain's *pope-consecrated* fleet
Advances to our shores?—SHERIDAN.
The *always-wind-obeying* deep.—SHAKESPEARE.
Or in the *violet-embroidered* vale.—MILTON.

In Tennyson we find a large number of new coinages of this kind :—*proxy-wedded, crimson-circled, slow-arching, heavy-shotted, hammock-shroud, hundred-throated, breaker-beaten, flesh-fallen, gloomy-*

[1] Prose-writers, however, as well as poets are quite within their rights, if it suits them, as it sometimes does, to form new compounds: the only difference is that prose is less in need of the practice than poetry is. Yet we frequently come across such examples as the following:—

The book was a *publisher-prompted* enterprise, and a poorly remunerated one.—*Times Weekly*, p. 42, Feb. 9, 1906.

Over half a million *coal miners* left their work on Saturday: but many of the *bituminous coal owners* have now conceded higher wages.—*Ibid.* p. 209, April 6, 1906.

In the example last quoted the italicised words are really compounds, which have not been joined by hyphens, as they ought to have been. This shows how little truth there is in the oft-repeated assertion that "the power of making new words by the combination of other words seems to have perished through the influence of the Norman French: at any rate our language possesses it no longer" (West's *English Grammar*, p. 17, ed. 1895). The Norman Conquest has quite enough to answer for already; there is no need to lay to its charge offences that have no foundation in fact. Compounds are being formed anew every day, whenever they are wanted.

gladed, lady-laden, mock-meek, rain-rotten, tongue-torn, work-wan, hollower-bellowing, beautiful-browed, fool-fury.

(*i*) A freer use of impersonal verbs for personal ones; as *methinks* for *I think*; *melists* for *it seems to me*; *meseems* for *it seems to me*—which in prose have become obsolete :—

Methinks there is none other I can love.—TENNYSON.
Him thought he by the brook of Cherith stood.—MILTON.
When in Salamanca's cave
Him listed his magic wand to wave,
The bells would ring in Notre Dame.—SCOTT.

(*j*) The use of the Superlative degree as a substitute for the Positive degree preceded by "very" :—

Or where the gorgeous east with *richest* hand
Showers on her kings barbaric pearl and gold.—MILTON.
But hail! thou Goddess sage and holy!
Hail *divinest* Melancholy!—*Ibid.*

(*k*) The substitution of a Possessive noun for an adjective. This is much less common in prose than in poetry.

Pity and *woman's* (=womanly) compassion.—LONGFELLOW.
The *mother's* (=motherly) nature of Althea.—LOWELL.
O love, you were my crown. No other crown
Is aught but thorns on my poor *woman's* brow.—G. ELIOT.
Old wishes, ghosts of broken plans,
And phantom hopes assemble;
And that *child's* heart within the man's
Begins to move and tremble.—TENNYSON.

(*l*) The use of a simple Personal pronoun, where in prose a Reflexive would be used :—

I thought *me* (=myself) richer than the Persian king.
BEN JONSON.
How close she veils *her* (=herself) round.—KEBLE.
Then Satan first knew pain
And writhed *him* to and fro convolved.—MILTON.
Cheer *thee*, my child, the abbess said.—SCOTT.

(*m*) The use of "and" in an Interrogative sentence, to express a passionate sense of grief :—

And art thou cold and lowly laid.—SCOTT.
And wilt thou weep, when I am low?—BYRON.

(*n*) In prose the Noun-Infinitive is used after the preposition "about" (see § 127, *b*), but after no other, as "about to die." But in Spenser we find it used after "from." This, however, is very rare even in poetry.

But not to have been dipped in Lethe's stream
Could save the son of Thetis *from to die* (=from death).

(o) In Milton we have the interjection "hist," which denotes a command for silence, turned into a verb and as such invested with a causal sense :—

> And the mute Silence *hist* along,
> 'Less Philomel will deign a song.—*Il Penseroso*, 55.

(p) The free use of Possessive personal pronouns (1) as furnishing an antecedent to a Relative, or (2) as standing in apposition to a noun, or (3) as qualified by an adjective or participle :—

> (1) Say to her sons, Lo, here *his* grave,
> *Who* victor died on Gadite wave.—SCOTT.
> (2) Creation's *heir*, the world, the world is *mine*.
> GOLDSMITH.
> (3) Yet will I mourn no more *thy* fate,
> *Ingrate* in life, in death *ingrate*.—SCOTT.

Observe that in (1) *his* = "of him," and *him* is the antecedent of *who*; in (2) *mine* = "of me," and *heir* is in apposition to *me*; in (3) *thy* = "of thee," and *thee* is qualified by *ingrate*. For further examples see § 372.

(q) The use of Proper names, which are in fact Proper nouns, as if they were adjectives qualifying the noun that follows :—

> He's embarked
> With such loud reason to the *Cyprus wars*.—*Othello*, i. 1.
> Two several times by night,—at Sardis once,
> And this last night here in *Philippi fields*.—*Jul. Cæs.* v. 5.
> There is no world without *Verona walls*.—*Rom. Jul.* iii. 3.

Sometimes a common noun is similarly used in poetry :—

> Can the quick current of a *patriot* heart
> Thus stagnate in a cold and weedy converse?—SHERIDAN.
> To shake thy senate, and from heights sublime
> Of *patriot* eloquence to flash down fire.—COWPER.

In prose we should have said "patriotic" or "patriot's."

(r) The use of a noun, participle, or other word in an anticipatory sense, *i.e.* to express an expected result, before the result itself has been realised :—

> (1) So those two brothers and their *murdered* man
> Rode past fair Florence.—KEATS.

Here "*murdered* man" means "the man whom they intended to murder." This is a very bold instance of poetic license.

> (2) There many a youthful *knight*, full keen
> To gain his spurs, in arms was seen.—SCOTT.

In prose we should say, not "knight," but "candidate for knighthood."

(s) The use of Latinisms. Examples of this, however, are mainly seen in Milton.

Our supreme foe in time may much remit
His anger; and perhaps thus far removed
Not mind us not offending, satisfied
With *what is punished*.—*Paradise Lost*, ii. 210-14.

The words italicised mean "with the punishment already inflicted." No modern poet except Milton, so far as I know, has used a dative absolute similar to those shown above in § 359.

(*t*) The use of Past Participles of Intransitive verbs,—a practice not admissible in prose, as has been shown in § 133 (*b*):—

Others more mild,
Retreated in a silent valley, sing
With notes angelical to many a harp.—MILTON.
And I shall soon,
Arm'd with thy might, rid heaven of these *rebelled*.—*Ibid.*

Here *retreated* means "who had retreated" or "having retreated": *rebelled* means "who have rebelled."

IV. **Deviations from the regular order of words**:—

(*a*) By placing the adjective or participle after its noun:—

O shame to men! Devil with devil *damned*
Firm concord holds; men only disagree
Of creatures *rational*.—MILTON.

(*b*) By placing the verb before its subject:—

Rose a nurse of ninety years,
Placed his child upon her knee.—TENNYSON.

Note.—This position of the verb is common in prose also, in certain contexts. But in prose the verb is not made the first word in the sentence, as it is in the above lines. See § 153 (2), *Note*, and § 287 (*a*).

(*c*) By placing the object before its verb and the subject after it:—

A transient *calm* the happy *scenes* bestow.
No *hive* hast *thou* of hoarded sweets.

(*d*) By placing a qualifying phrase before, instead of after, the noun that it qualifies:—

Thou sun, *of this great world* both eye and soul.—MILTON.

(*e*) By placing the preposition after its noun, instead of before it:—

They dashed that rapid torrent *through*.
Where Echo walks steep hills *among*.
Like children bathing on the shores
Buried a wave *beneath*.
This diamond he greets your wife *withal*.
(He greets your wife with this diamond.)

(*f*) By placing the Infinitive before the verb on which it depends :—

> When first thy sire *to send* on earth
> Virtue, his darling child, designed.—GRAY.

(*g*) By placing the complement before its verb, instead of after it, even when the complement is not emphatic :—

> *Grieved* though thou art, forbear the rash design.
> *Fresh* blows the wind, a western wind.

(*h*) By placing an adverb before an Intransitive verb instead of after it (see § 281) :—

> *Merrily, merrily* goes the bark.
> *Full lowly* did the herdsman fall.—SCOTT.

(*i*) By placing an adverb before, instead of after, the verb with which it is compounded :—

> *Up* springs from yonder tangled thorn
> A stag more white than mountain snow.—SCOTT.
> *Out* spake the victor then.—CAMPBELL.

(*j*) By using *or—or* for *either—or*, and *nor—nor* for *neither—nor* :—

> Remote, unfriended, melancholy, slow,
> *Or* by the lazy Scheldt, or wandering Po.—GOLDSMITH.
> *Nor* grief nor pain shall break my rest.

V. The use of adjectives or participles instead of clauses :—

This is done mainly for the sake of terseness. Poetry does not patronise Relatives and Conjunctions so liberally as prose does. It likes to express as much as possible in the fewest words.[1]

(1) He can't combine each well *proportioned* part.

That is, he cannot make the different parts proportionate to one another and then combine them into a symmetrical whole.

(2) I may alarm thee, but I fear the shame
I must incur, *forgetting* Howard's name.—COWPER.

Here *forgetting* means "if I forget," *i.e.* "if I neglect to mention."

(3) Kneel now, and lay thy forehead in the dust!
Blush if thou can'st; *not petrified*, thou must.—*Ibid.*

Here *not petrified* means "unless thou art petrified."

---

[1] Sometimes, but rarely, we meet with this construction in prose also.

> He feels that the exclusion of "II Peter" from the Canon would be a serious loss, and in that conviction he has lavished toil upon it, to the great advantage of the *instructed* reader.—*Times Weekly*, p. 131, April 26, 1907.

Here "the instructed reader" means "the reader who gains much instruction thereby."

(4) Great Xerxes comes to seize the *certain* prey,
And starves *exhausted* regions in his way.—JOHNSON.

Here *certain* means "which he looked upon as certain." *Starves exhausted* means "reduces to starvation and exhaustion."

(5) But he who hurts a *harmless* neighbour's peace,
Insults *fallen* worth or beauty in distress.—POPE.

Here *harmless* stands for "though he is harmless," and *fallen* for "*when* it is fallen."

(6) Moral truth
How lovely, and the moral sense how sure,
Consulted and obeyed, to guide his steps.—COWPER.

Here *consulted and obeyed* means "when it is consulted and obeyed."

VI. **The use of epithets for the sake of ornament :—**

This peculiarity is in keeping with the chief aim of poetry, which is to please rather than to instruct. An epithet is ornamental, when it is in no respect essential to the sense.

The breezy call of *incense-breathing* morn,
The swallow twittering from its *straw-built* shed,
The cock's shrill clarion, and the echoing horn,
No more shall rouse them from their lowly bed.—GRAY.

Here the epithets "breezy," "twittering," "shrill," and "echoing," are all conducive to the sense; but *incense-breathing* and *straw-built* serve no purpose other than that of ornament or description.

Ornamental epithets are italicised in the following lines :—

(1) Oh mother Ida, *many-fountain'd* Ida,
Dear mother Ida, hearken ere I die.
(2) Then answer made the *bold* Sir Bedivere.

In the following lines the italicised epithets are essential :—

As shines the moon in *clouded* skies,
She in her *poor* attire was seen.

The *golden* harvest; the *swift* stag; the *tawny* lion; the *briny* deep; the *mighty* deep, etc., are all stock phrases common in poetry. The epithets are merely ornamental.

VII. **A freer use of picturesque language :—**

This peculiarity, too, arises from the desire to please. Language is graphic or picturesque, when it calls up some image to the mind by dwelling on the particular rather than on the general, on the concrete rather than on the abstract.

Arise, my love, my fair, and come away; for, lo! the winter is past, the rain is over and gone, the flowers appear on the earth; the time of the singing of birds is come, and the voice of the turtle is heard in our land; the fig tree putteth forth her green figs; and the vines with the tender grapes perfume the air. Arise, my love, my fair, and come away.—*The Song of Solomon.*

The mountain wooded to the peak, the lawn
And winding glades high up like ways to heaven,
The slender cocoa's drooping crown of plumes,
The lightning flash of insect and of bird,
The lustre of the long convolvuluses,
That coiled around the stately stems, and ran
E'en to the limit of the land, the glows
And glories of the broad belt of the world.—TENNYSON.

It was shown in paragraph VI. that epithets are often used in poetry purely for the sake of ornament, without any reference to the requirements of the context. In the same way and for the same purpose a simile is often prolonged far beyond the requirements of illustration :—

He scarce had finished, when such murmur filled
Th' assembly as when hollow rocks retain
The sound of blustering winds, which all night long
Had roused the sea, now with hoarse cadence lull
Sea-faring men o'erwatch'd, whose bark by chance,
Or pinnace, anchors in a craggy bay
After the tempest.—*Paradise Lost*, ii.

In this passage Milton describes the murmur of applause with which the speech of Mammon was received in Pandemonium. But the simile has carried him a good deal further than the comparison with which he started.

VIII. **A freer use of figurative language** :—

In the following example there is a succession of no fewer than four similes to show how suddenly and how rapidly pleasures pass away :—

But pleasures are like poppies spread,
You seize the flower, its bloom is shed ;
Or like the snowfall in the river,
A moment white, then melts for ever ;
Or like the Borealis race,
That flit ere you can point their place ;
Or like the rainbow's lovely form,
Evanishing amid the storm.—*Tam O' Shanter*.

Of the figure called "The Transferred Epithet" (§ 403), prose as compared with poetry makes but a sparing use, and rightly so. A bold example of this figure is given by Pope :—

Whom e'en the Saxon spared and bloody Dane,
The *wanton victims* of his sport remain.—*Windsor Forest*.

Here the epithet could easily be transferred to "sport," and the metre would have been quite as good, if the line had been—

The victims of his wanton sport remain.

But Pope with truer insight into the spirit of poetic diction uses the phrase "wanton victims" to signify "the men and women wantonly victimised (turned out of house and home) to make room for the huntsman's sport."

I mention one more figure which prose cannot frequently use without trespassing into the domain of poetry,—the figure of "Sound suggestive of Sense" (Onomatopœia), § 417.

(1) This is he that far away
Against the myriads of Assaye
Clash'd with his fiery few and won.
TENNYSON, *Ode on the Death of the Duke of Wellington.*

This alludes to the great victory of Assaye, fought against overwhelming odds, and won by a mere handful of men almost at a single dash. Those three short lines are all that the poet has given us concerning it, and all that he had need to give. A longer description would not have had half the effect.

(2) Once more upon the waters, yet once more;
And the waves bound beneath me as a steed
That knows his rider; welcome to the roar!
BYRON, *Childe Harold.*

Here the rhythmical bounding of the lines suggests the bounding of the ship on the waves.

(3) O love, they die in yon rich sky,
They faint on hill, or field, or river:
Our echoes roll from soul to soul,
And grow for ever and for ever.
Blow, bugle, blow; set the wild echoes flying;
And answer, echoes, answer, dying, dying, dying.
TENNYSON, *Princess.*

Nothing can surpass the suggestiveness of the last two lines of the above stanza.

Exercise on Chapter XXXIII.

In dealing with the following extracts the student is requested (1) *to fill up any ellipse that he may find,* (2) *to change any word that he may consider archaic or otherwise unfit for modern prose,* (3) *to put the words into the order of prose,* (4) *to comment on any peculiarity of phrase or construction,* (5) *to point out the Figure of Speech, if he finds one.*

1. Whate'er our household gods protect of dear
Are gathered round us.
2. New presbyter is but old priest writ large.
3. My song, its pinions disarranged of might,
Drooped.
4. High and majestic was his look,
At which the foulest fiends had shook.
5. All loose her negligent attire,
All loose her golden hair,
Hung Margaret o'er her slaughtered sire.—SCOTT.

6. Rather proclaim it, Westmoreland, through my host,
That he which hath no stomach to this fight,
Let him depart.—SHAKESPEARE.
7. Pray go to see them, ere it be too late.
8. From Venice—once a race of worth
His gentle sires—he drew his birth.—BYRON.
9. Seemed to the boy some comrade gay
Led him forth to the woods to play.—SCOTT.
10. On either side the river lie
Long fields of barley and of rye.—TENNYSON.
11. Come, loiterer, come! A Douglas thou
And shun to wreathe a victor's brow!—SCOTT.
12. Thence more at ease their minds and somewhat raised
By false presumptuous hopes, the rangéd powers
Disband.—MILTON.
13. O Thou my voice inspire,
That touched Isaiah's hallowed lips with fire.—POPE.
14. Pretty in amber to observe the forms
Of hairs, or straws, or dirt, or grubs, or worms.—*Ibid.*
15. My noble father—
Three times to-day I holp him to his horse.—SHAKESPEARE.
16. Coumourgi—can his glory cease,
That latest conqueror of Greece?—BYRON.
17. Dagon presumed,
Me overthrown, to enter lists with God.—MILTON.
18. You hear the learned Bellario, what he writes.
Merch. Ven. iv. 1.
19. The skilful shepherd peeled me certain wands.
20. Death grinned horribly a ghastly smile.—MILTON.
21. The louring element
Scowls o'er the darkened landskip snow and shower.—*Ibid.*
22. And him destroyed
For whom all this was made, all this will soon
Follow.—*Ibid.*
23. Let He who made thee answer that.—BYRON.
24. Fare thee well! and if for ever,
Then for ever fare thee well.
25. Move upward working out the beast,
And let the ape and tiger die.—TENNYSON.
26. Whether the charmer sinner it or saint it,
If folly grow romantic, I must paint it.—POPE.
27. Be thou me, impetuous one.—SHELLEY.
28. Still restless as a second Cain
To Scotland next my route was ta'en.—SCOTT.
29. Your "if" is your only peacemaker.—SHAKESPEARE.
30. Fair is foul, and foul is fair,
Hover through fog and filthy air.—*Ibid.*
31. Cheer thee, my child, the abbess said.
32. For those that fly may fight again,
Which he can never do that's slain.
33. But bend their weapons on the slain,
Lest the grim king should rouse again.

34. Then come kiss me, sweet-and-twenty,
Youth's a stuff will not endure.—SHAKESPEARE.

35. (I) that have given thee my heart
Never for to depart.—*Ibid.*

36. He stood abashed, then answered grave.

37. I should be content
To dwell in peace, but that my country calls.—SOUTHEY.

38. She will sing the savageness out of a bear.—SHAKESPEARE.

39. You know my father hath no child but I.—*Ibid.*

40. And roam green Erin's lovely land.

41. Senseless trees they cannot hear thee,
Ruthless beasts they will not cheer thee.—BARNEFIELD.

42. Alas, she hath no other cause of anguish
But Tereus' love, on her by strong hand wroken.—SIDNEY.

43. Melissa tinged with wan from want of sleep.—TENNYSON.

44. Him I accuse
The city-ports by this hath entered.—SHAKESPEARE.

45. My own heart's heart and ownest own, farewell.—TENNYSON.

46. Eternity so spent in worship paid
To whom we hate.—MILTON.

47. Till oft converse with heavenly habitants
Begin to cast a gleam on the outward shape.—*Ibid.*

48. And she,
Like some wild creature newly caged, commenced
A to-and-fro.—TENNYSON.

49. Thus treacherous scouts,—yet sure they lie
Who say thou cam'st a secret spy.—SCOTT.

50. There be none of beauty's daughters
With a magic like thee.—BYRON.

51. His trust was with the Eternal to be deemed
Equal in strength, and rather than be less
Cared not to be at all.—MILTON.

52. Wan was her cheek
With hollow watch, her blooming mantle torn,
Red grief and mother's hunger in her eye.—TENNYSON.

53. Of man's first disobedience and the fruit
Of that forbidden tree, whose mortal taste
Brought sin into the world and all our woe,
Sing, heavenly Muse, etc.—MILTON.

54. But not alone the bitter tear
Had filial grief supplied.—SCOTT.

55. And weaponless except his blade.—*Ibid.*

56. No one came
But he was welcome; no one went away
But that it seemed she loved him.

57. The nightingales thy coming each-where sing;
Make an eternal spring.—DRUMMOND.

58. Here may you keep your arms from rust,
May breathe your war-horse well.—SCOTT.

59. Romantic boys
Pine themselves sick for airy toys.

60. Deformed, unfinished, sent before my time
Into this breathing world, scarce half made up,
And that so lamely and unfashionable,
That dogs bark at me, as I halt by them.—SHAKESPEARE.

61. And the rebel king
Doubled that sin in Bethel and in Dan,
Likening his Maker to the grazéd ox.—MILTON.

62. Why then not hasten the decisive hour,
Still in my view and ever in my power?
LADY MARY MONTAGU.

CHAPTER XXXIV.—STYLE IN PROSE AND VERSE.

471. What is meant by Style.—"The style of a man," says Gibbon, "should be the image of his mind; but the choice and command of language is the fruit of experience." It may be asserted rather more explicitly, that style *is* the image of the writer's mind, unless he has distorted this image by a vain attempt to imitate the style of some one else. Style, then, is the personal factor in composition It cannot be taught to others; it cannot be imitated by others; and it cannot be discarded by the writer himself. It was remarked by the late James Anthony Froude that "style is not like a coat that can be put off, but like the skin, an essential part of the living organisation"; and this is well in keeping with the saying of Boileau, *Le style c'est l'homme*, "The style is the man."

Gibbon himself has furnished us with a good example of the individuality of style. His great work, *The Decline and Fall of the Roman Empire*, is characterised from beginning to end by an elevated and stately kind of diction, that is well adapted to the grandeur of his subject. There is nothing grand or elevating in his private life; yet in writing the story of his own life he cannot get rid of the stateliness of diction, which was evidently part of his nature. I give one short extract from his *Autobiography*—an extract in which he records his first experiences in Parliament:—

> I was not armed by nature with intrepid energy of mind and voice. Timidity was fortified by pride, and even the success of my pen discouraged the trial of my voice. But I assisted at the debates of a free assembly; I listened to the attack and defence of eloquence and reason; I had a near prospect of the character, views, and passions of the first men of the age.

A great many more examples of the personal character of style could be quoted. Among the many absurdities of the theory, which ascribes to Francis Bacon the authorship of the plays and poems that were written by Shakespeare, none is greater than the notion that a man can write prose with one head on his shoulders and poetry with another. This is what the theory comes to; for a man can no more change his style than he can change his head. Between the prose of Bacon and the poetry of Shakespeare there is not a sign of similarity of style, such as we see between the prose of Scott and the poetry of Scott, or between the prose of Milton and the poetry of Milton, or between the prose of Johnson and the poetry of Johnson.

472. **Classification of Styles.**—Since style is determined by the mental temperament of the individual, the varieties of style must be as numerous as the temperaments of writers. In a large number of instances the variations may be too subtle to be traced, but the differences must be there.

> If thrice ten thousand meet together,
> How scarce one face is like another!
> If scarce two faces can agree,
> Two hearts alike there seldom be.—STRODE.

If hearts or characters are so various, not less various (if Gibbon and others are to be believed) must the styles of writers be. If faces, in spite of their variety, can be classified according to certain types or standards, so must it be with styles also. The following classification of styles is offered:—

Too little of the Standard Quality.	*Styles or Standards.*	*Too much of the Standard Quality.*
1. Mannerisms 2. Euphuism 3. Pedantry	I. **Simple**	1. Doggerel. 2. Colloquialisms.
1. Rhetorical 2. Rambling	II. **Direct**	*Nil.*
Diffuse	III. **Terse**	Obscure.
Pointless	IV. **Vigorous**	Exaggerated.
Colourless	V. **Graphic**	Prolix.
1. Involved 2. Abrupt 3. Slovenly	VI. **Elegant**	1. Laboured. 2. Florid.
Bathos	VII. **Elevated**	Bombast.

From the above scheme it will be seen that (with one slight exception) every style or standard may be carried to an extreme either on the side of deficiency or on that of excess. The one exception is II. **Direct.** This word means "straight." If a statement or exposition is straight, *i.e.* goes straight to the point, it cannot be made straighter. Hence in respect of straightness there can be no extreme on the side of excess; but a writer may easily err on the side of deficiency, *i.e.* of not being straight enough.

I. The Simple Style.

473. Main Characteristics of the Simple Style.—Simplicity of diction consists in the avoidance of big words, uncommon words, roundabout phrases, long complex sentences, and complicated constructions. Whatever the nature of the subject may be, the Simple style has a charm of its own and need not by any means be confined to the treatment of simple subjects. It is peculiarly adapted to that kind of literature, in which the story, not the diction, is the main object of interest, so that the reader can unconsciously give his whole attention to what is said, without giving a thought to the manner in which it is said. Hence it has been the style mainly used in ballads, such as *Chevy Chase*,—in metrical romances such as Scott's *Lady of the Lake*,—in prose romances such as De Foe's *Robinson Crusoe* (the first of its kind),—in novels of character and manners such as Richardson's *Pamela* (the first of its kind),—in allegories such as Bunyan's *Pilgrim's Progress*,—in tales or descriptions of rustic life such as George Crabbe's *Village* or Tennyson's *Enoch Arden* (poetry) or Goldsmith's *Vicar of Wakefield* or Miss Mitford's *Popular Village Tales* (prose),—in fairy tales such as *Alice in Wonderland*,—in folk-tales or legends such as Malory's *Morte d'Arthur*,—and in elementary history such as Dickens's *History of England*. In all of these and in many more examples that might be named, Simplicity of language is the predominant key, the most suitable that could have been chosen.

It is the style used in our Authorised Version of the Bible. As this version has penetrated to every part of the world in which English is spoken, the Simple style has gained and still holds a wider currency than any other in our literature.

It is hardly necessary to quote examples, since the books named are within reach, if they are not in the possession, of every one. I give one example, however, of a dramatic soliloquy, in which Hamlet discusses within himself the reasons for and the reasons against suicide:—

For who would fardels bear,
To grunt and sweat under a weary life,
But that the dread of something after death,
The undiscover'd country, from whose bourne
No traveller returns, puzzles the will,
And makes us rather bear those ills we have
Than fly to others that we know not of?
Thus conscience does make cowards of us all, etc.

There is nothing original in the thought expressed in these lines. It is the ease and simplicity of style, combined with the undefinable genius of the author, which has made them immortal.

474. Deviations on the side of Defect.—On the side of defect, *i.e.* where the style or diction is not simple enough, there are three kinds of offences against Simplicity, viz. (1) Mannerisms, (2) Euphuism, (3) Pedantry.

(1) *Mannerisms* :—

The habitual and frequent use by a writer of some particular word, phrase, or construction is called a mannerism. Mannerism has been brought forward as an offence against Simplicity, not because it occurs only in those writings in which the Simple style predominates, but because it is in such writings that we least expect to see it.

Carlyle is full of mannerisms. I mention only one—his inveterate habit (which is opposed to prose-idiom) of using an adjective in the Superlative degree without placing before it the definite article or some noun or pronoun in the Possessive case :—

(1) Brave Sea-captain, Norse Sea-king,—Columbus, my hero, *royalest* Sea-king of all.
(2) In which, too, so many *noblest* men have both made and been what will be venerated to all time.
(3) Struggling with objects, which, though it cannot master them, are essentially of *richest* significance.

Dickens's mannerism is well known : it consists in the habit of repeating some phrase or some clause at the beginning or at the end of a succession of sentences :—

I have summoned you here to witness your own work. *I have summoned you here to witness* it, because I know it will be gall and wormwood to you. *I have summoned you here to witness* it, because I know the sight of everybody here must be a dagger in your mean, false heart.—*Martin Chuzzlewit*, ch. 52.

Only two pages further on we get the following :—

He cannot say I have not given him opportunity. *He cannot say* I have ever led him on. *He cannot say* I have not left him freely to himself in all things.

Journalism, too, has its mannerisms. I give a few examples:—

(1) We are now *within measurable distance* of a new election.

This almost unmeaning phrase happened to be used by Gladstone in one of his vaguest speeches. It has been echoing ever since.

(2) *Once* the enemy were got rid of, other things had to be attended to.

Say *when once*. "Once" by itself is an adverb, not a Subordinative Conjunction. To use it as a Subord. Conj. is against literature.

(3) British firms, *providing* prices are the same, are to be preferred to foreign ones.

The proper word "provided" (Lat. *proviso*) is rapidly disappearing before the upstart "providing," which in the above sentence almost causes an ambiguity: for on first reading it seems as if the Pres. Part. "providing" were intended to qualify the noun "firms." See p. 351.

(4) *Quite* a marked fall occurred in the death-rate yesterday.—*Daily Tel.* p. 8, April 17, 1907.

Say "a very marked fall" or "a remarkable fall" occurred, etc. This curious and indefensible use of *quite* is becoming more and more common every day: "quite a sensation"; "quite a little crowd"; "quite a readable essay." See p. 172 (40).

(2) *Euphuism*:—

This word must not be confounded with Euphemism (§ 411). Euphuism is the name given to the kinds of mannerism that occur so frequently in Lyly's book called *Euphues and his England*, published in A.D. 1580. I have space for only one short extract, in which he holds up English women as models for imitation by the women of Greece and Italy:—

> Here, ladies, is a glass that will make you blush for shame and look wan for anger. Their beauty comes by nature, yours by art; they increase their favours (good looks) with water, you maintain yours with painters' colours; the hair that they lay out grows on their own heads, your seemliness hangeth upon others; theirs is always in their own keeping, yours often in the dyer's; their beauty is not lost with a sharp blast, yours fadeth with a soft breath; not unlike unto paper-flowers, which break as soon as they are touched, resembling the birds in Egypt called ibes, who being led lose their feathers, or the serpent Serapie, which being but touched with a brake bursteth.

Paragraph after paragraph is crowded with antitheses and similes such as the above, until the reader is wearied with them. The labour with which they have been spun out is transparent, and must have wearied the author himself.

Macaulay's greatest admirers are aware that his style is marked by more than one kind of mannerism. In fact it has been called by some critics Euphuistic; but such criticism is too severe to be applied to such a clear and brilliant writer.

The best known perhaps of all his mannerisms is his habit of beginning a sentence with "every schoolboy knows." So often does this occur in his *Essays*, that an article once appeared in a monthly journal, professing to give a memoir of this wonderful schoolboy, showing what books he had read, how and where he had been trained, what were his favourite pursuits and amusements, and what uses he had made of his talents and opportunities during his boyhood. All these particulars were compiled from allusions occurring in Macaulay's *Essays*.

(3) *Pedantry*:—

Pedantry consists in using big, uncommon, or learned words for simpler ones that are not only well established in use, but are well adapted to express the writer's meaning. Such a habit is the mark of an ill-informed mind, that seeks to hide its emptiness under high-sounding phrases, like the drum in the fable that gave a booming sound, but was found on inspection to be hollow within. Nothing is gained by saying *in all human probability* for "most likely" or "most probably"; *lunar effulgence* for "moonlight"; *the tender passion* or *the amorous affection* for "love"; *pharmaceutical chemist* for "apothecary"; *caudal appendage* for "tail"; *the nasal organ* or *the prominent feature* for "nose"; *skilful agriculturist* for "good farmer" or "good husbandman"; *partake of lunch* for "take lunch" or "lunch" (verb); *inebriate* or *dipsomaniac* for "drunkard"; *minatory expressions* for "threats"; *ruminating* for "chewing the cud"; *location* for "site"; *tonsorial artist* for "barber" or "hair-cutter"; *expression* for "word"; *adumbrate* for "foreshadow"; *to donate* for "to present" or "give"; *culinary department* for "kitchen"; *maternal relative* for "mother"; *the lower extremities* for "legs" or "feet"; *potables* for "drinkables"; *arcana* for "secrets"; *pedagogue* for "teacher"; *impeccable* for "faultless"; *germane* for "relevant" or "allied"; *infructuous* for "fruitless," "barren of results"; *apologue* for "fable"; *the sacred edifice* for "the church"; *the sacred day of hebdomadal rest* for "Sunday"; *animadversion* for "blame" or "censure"; *vituperation* for "abuse"; *exacerbate* for "embitter"; *multitudinous* for "manifold"; *incarnadine* for "dye red"; *evangel* for "gospel"; *contumacy* for "obstinacy"; *exemplar* for "model"; *cleptomaniac* for "thief"; *eventuate* for "come to pass"; *circumambient air* for "surrounding air"; *disembogues its waters* for "empties its waters"; *metamorphosis* for "change"; *precipitate* for "throw down," etc.

475. Deviations on the Side of Excess, *i.e.* where Simplicity is overdone. If this quality is carried to an extreme, the diction may degenerate into either (1) Doggerel, or (2) Colloquialisms.

(1) *Doggerel.* One example will be sufficient :—

> O plump head-waiter at "The Cock,"
> To which I most resort,
> How goes the time? 'Tis five o'clock.
> Go fetch a pint of port.—TENNYSON.

The heading given to the stanzas, from which the above extract has been quoted, is *Will Waterproof's Lyrical Monologue made at The Cock*,—which shows that the doggerel was intentional on the part of the author.

(2) *Colloquialisms* :—

This is the name given to that kind of diction which, though admissible in conversation, is beneath the dignity of written composition, except in the dialogues of novels or in correspondence between friends and equals. I give a few examples :—

Personal enemies he has none. But he is a rare exception. And to assume, as he does, that the *tag-rag and bobtail* of the bureaucracy will, when occasion calls for it, display similar heroism is a mistake which, generous in an individual, is baleful in a political leader.—*National Review*, p. 319, Oct. 1906.

Philip *played the devil with* Edward's *little game* of subduing the Scots.—Dr. MACKINNON, *Hist. Scotland*. (Say, "thwarted Edward's design of subduing," etc.)

> And now night falls,
> Me, tempest-tost, and driven *from pillar to post*
> A poor worn ghost,
> This quiet pasture calls;
> And dear dead people with pale hands,
> Beckon me to their lands.
>
> E. DOWSON, *Lines on a Breton Cemetery.*

Europe instructing China is rather like *teaching one's grandmother to suck eggs*.—*Spect.* p. 412, 29th Sept. 1900.

II. THE DIRECT STYLE

476. The Direct Style and the Rhetorical.—The Direct style, though nearly allied to the Simple, is by no means identical with it: for language can be Direct without being Simple, but it can hardly be Simple without being Direct. Directness as a quality of composition consists in saying things in the most explicit and straightforward way, instead of saying them circuitously by implication, suggestion, allusion, innuendo, irony, or any of the other rhetorical devices, which in Chap. XXXI have been placed under the general heading of "Indirectness" (see §§ 408-416). The Direct method is the one most suited to narrative, description, or exposition: for such purposes the mode of statement can hardly be too explicit. The Indirect or circuitous method, though useful at times in narrative or description as a relief or for any other purpose, is more frequently seen in rhetoric or oratory, and has therefore been called Rhetorical.

477. The Direct and Rhetorical Styles in History.—By way of exemplifying the two methods in historical narrative, I give two extracts from Froude's *History of England*.

(1) The Direct Style:—

The State of English Life in the Time of Henry VIII.—In such frank style the people lived, hating three things with all their hearts,—idleness, want, and cowardice; and for the rest, carrying their hearts high, and having their hands full. The hour of rising, winter and summer, was four o'clock, with breakfast at five, after which the labourers went to work and the gentlemen to business, of which they had no little. In the country every unknown face was challenged and examined. If the account given was insufficient, he was brought before the justice; if the village shopkeeper sold bad wares, if the village cobbler made "unhonest" shoes, if servants and masters quarrelled, all was looked to by the justice; there was no fear lest time should hang heavy with him. At twelve he dined; after dinner he went hunting, or to his farm, or to what he pleased. It was a life unrefined perhaps, but coloured with a broad, rosy, English health.

(2) The Indirect or Rhetorical Style:—

The Close of the Middle Ages and the Dawn of Modern History.—A change indeed was coming upon the world, the meaning and direction of which even still is hidden from us, a change from era to era. The paths trodden by the footsteps of ages were broken up; old things were passing away, and the faith and the life of ten centuries were dissolving like a dream. Chivalry was dying; the abbey and the castle were soon together to crumble into ruins; and all the forms, desires, beliefs, convictions of the old world were passing away, never to return. A new continent had risen up beyond the western sea. The floor of heaven, inlaid with stars, had shrunk back to an infinite abyss of immeasurable space; and the firm earth itself, unfixed from its foundations, was seen to be but a small atom in the awful vastness of the universe. In the fabric of habit, which they had so laboriously built for themselves, mankind were to remain no longer.

Now what does the second of these paragraphs tell us concerning "the change that was coming upon the world"? The only *facts* that it mentions, and even these by implication rather than by direct assertion, are expressed in the following words :—"The faith of ten centuries was dissolving"; "chivalry was dying"; "the abbey and the castle were soon to crumble into ruins"; "all the forms, desires, beliefs, convictions of the old world were passing away"; "a new continent had risen up beyond the western sea"; "the floor of heaven, inlaid with stars, had sunk back to an infinite abyss of immeasurable space; and the firm earth itself, unfixed from its foundations, was seen to be but a small atom in the awful vastness of the universe." This is all that the paragraph tells us concerning the facts or events which mark the transition from mediæval to modern history. Whatever else there may be in the paragraph is merely a reassertion (disguised by verbal changes) of the theme expressed already in the first sentence.

To any one who is already acquainted with the facts, the above description of them would probably be sufficient. But to any one who does not possess this knowledge, and who desires to know in plain language what the facts were, it would be more satisfactory to have them enumerated to him in some such terms as the following :—"the decay of chivalry or the knightly spirit; the dying out of the feudal system, and the disappearance of feudal tenures; the breaking up of the baronial castles, which throughout the Middle Age were a check upon the independence of the crown; the more absolute and more centralised kind of monarchy that was about to take the place of the feudal monarchy; the rise of an industrial middle class; the growth of towns; the substitution of free labour for serfdom; the enclosing of commons; the increasing use of fire-arms on the battlefield in partial supersession of the bow; the growing slackness of discipline in religious houses; the decline of faith in the authority of the Pope; the rise of Protestantism and of national churches; the waning influence of monasteries and (in our own country at least) their impending dissolution; the revival of classical as distinct from mediæval studies, and especially the revived study of Greek; the introduction of printing; the improvements in navigation; the discovery of America; the discovery of a new route to India and to the Far East; the diversion of commerce into new channels outside the Mediterranean; the adoption of new methods for exploring the secrets of nature; the new discoveries in astronomical science;

and the broader views that men acquired from this science concerning the place that our planet holds in the vastness of the universe."

478. The Direct and Rhetorical Styles in Oratory.—A very good example of the contrast between the two styles as seen in oratory is furnished by the two orations that are delivered (in Shakespeare's drama) over the body of Julius Cæsar,—the one by Brutus, who is made to address the multitude in prose, because the issue that he puts before them needs no ornaments of language and no tricks of rhetoric, but has only to be stated as directly and precisely as possible, "Will they or will they not rise to the dignity of citizens in the free republic of Rome, which Julius Cæsar by his assumption of imperial power had destroyed?"—the other delivered by Mark Antony, who is made to speak in metre, because he has to use every trick or device of rhetoric that he can muster, in order to destroy the effect that the unvarnished, patriotic appeal of Brutus had had on the minds of the audience.[1]

In oratory it usually happens that there are two sides to be represented, and that a good deal can be said for each of them. The speaker adopts the Indirect or rhetorical method when he feels that the evidence runs short, or that plain, blunt speaking might offend his audience, and the Direct, when he considers the evidence to be conclusive, and is not afraid of giving offence.

479. The Rambling or Discursive Style.—Another kind of deviation from the Direct style occurs when the writer goes away from the point and drags into his sentences matter that has no connection, or at least a very slender connection, with

---

[1] The reason that I have given why Brutus's oration is in prose and Mark Antony's in verse is not the same as that given in *English Lessons for English People*, p. 148:—"In addressing the people he (Brutus) refuses to appeal to their feelings, and affects a studiously cold and unimpassioned style: his speech serves in this respect as a useful foil to Antony's highly impassioned harangue." It appears to me, however, that Brutus's speech, far from being "studiously cold and unimpassioned," is a highly spirited and pointed appeal to the pride and patriotism of the Roman people, and that Antony's speech is cunning, cold, and cautious at starting, and does not become impassioned until about half of it is finished, by which time he was able to assure himself that he could carry the multitude with him. The reason why Antony's speech prevailed over Brutus's was because Antony appealed to lower passions, while Brutus appealed to the sentiment of pride and patriotism, which the people did not feel with an equal degree of keenness.

his argument. Composition, in which this fault occurs, is called Rambling or Discursive. I give two examples :—

> At length the sun approaching melts the snow, sets longing men at liberty, and affords them means and time to make provision against the next return of cold. It breaks the icy fetters of the main, where vast sea-monsters pierce through floating islands with arms which can withstand the crystal rock; whilst others, who of themselves seem great as islands, are by their bulk alone armed against all but man, whose superiority over creatures of such stupendous size and force should make him mindful of his privilege of reason, and force him humbly to adore the great composer of these wondrous frames, and the author of his own superior wisdom.—SHAFTESBURY.

The sentence should have come to an end with the word "man," in the 7th line. The four lines that follow this word are all beside the mark. If the comment contained in them was needed at all, it should have been put in a sentence of its own. Standing where it does, it constitutes a violation of unity (§ 317).

The next example is from Smiles's very valuable book on "Character." He is apt, however, sometimes to ramble away from his point.

> Nor is the unjust intolerance, displayed towards men of science in the past, without its lesson for the present. It teaches us to be forbearing towards those who differ from us, provided they observe patiently, think honestly, and utter their convictions freely and truthfully. It was a remark of Plato that "the world is God's epistle to mankind"; and to read and study that epistle, so as to elicit its true meaning, can have no other effect on a well-ordered mind than to lead to a deeper impression of His power, a clearer perception of His wisdom, and a more grateful sense of his goodness.—Page 128.

The quotation from Plato throws no light on what precedes it. What follows this quotation is entirely irrelevant to both. The subject which Smiles was discussing is headed "The Martyrs of Faith," *i.e.* the hostility with which new views used to be received and the persecution that great discoverers have in times past been compelled to undergo. He weakens his argument by the irrelevant matter that he has dragged into it after the word "truthfully."

III. THE TERSE STYLE.

480. Terseness and Diffuseness exemplified.—Occasions may arise in which repetition adds force to a sentence (see § 298). As a general rule, however, brevity or terseness gives as much force to language as diffuseness takes from it. A word that does no good does harm. Attention given to superfluous words represents a loss of attention that might have been given to the matter. Here is an example :—

For seeing those things which are equal must needs have all one measure, if I cannot but wish to receive all good, even as much at every man's hand as any man can wish unto his own soul, how should I look to have any part of my desire herein satisfied, unless myself be careful to satisfy the like desire which is in other men?—HOOKER.

This is a diffuse and clumsy way of saying:—

I cannot expect to have my own desires satisfied, if I pay no heed to those of other men.

If the reader should ask for the name of any one author, who may be regarded as a model of terseness in prose, I should name Bacon, and refer him to Bacon's *Essays or Counsels Civil and Moral*. In this respect Bacon was in advance of his age: for most prose-writers of the Tudor period, such as the one quoted above, erred on the side of diffuseness.

If the reader should ask for the name of a poet, whose style is remarkable for terseness, I should name Pope. In one short couplet, for example, he accounts for the origin of society:—

His safety must his liberty restrain:
All join to guard what each desires to gain.

I give one more example from Pope, taken from the close of the First Epistle of the "Essay on Man," in which he sums up his views regarding our duty of absolute, uncomplaining submission to the wisdom of Providence:—

All Nature is but Art unknown to thee;
All chance, direction, which thou canst not see;
All discord, harmony not understood;
All partial evil, universal good:
And spite of pride, in erring reason's spite,
The truth is clear, Whatever is, is right.

481. Obscurity: Brevity overdone.—Brevity may be carried too far. The desire to get rid of superfluous words may tempt the writer into omitting words that are vital to the sense. Besides over-brevity, there are many other causes (see Chap. XXII.) from which obscurity may arise. But a writer who aims at terseness must be especially on his guard. "I labour to be brief," said Horace, "and become obscure." Perspicuity, however, must be the first consideration, and should on no account be sacrificed to brevity.

Lady Ellesmere. Without translating, gentlemen must not talk Latin, nor smoke, nor swear, in the presence of ladies.

Ellesmere. She thinks now she has been very epigrammatic. The men may swear, if they translate it? The commonest form of muddlement in sentences is occasioned by the endeavour to be brief. You apply two or three nominatives to one verb, or two or three verbs to one nominative, which do not agree together, if you look at them separately. What she did mean was,—that in the presence of ladies men must not smoke without permission, must not swear at all, and must not quote Latin without translating it.—HELPS'S *Realmah.*

482. Diffuseness not always a Fault.—Obscurity is always a fault; not so diffuseness. Sometimes the dignity of the subject is such as to demand a copious and expanded description in preference to one that is short and condensed. The following is an example,—Burke's eulogy of Howard the Philanthropist, a long and eloquent sentence, which ought not to be reduced:—

He has visited all Europe,—not to survey the sumptuousness of palaces or the stateliness of temples; not to make accurate measurements of the remains of ancient grandeur, nor to form a scale of the curiosity of modern art, nor to collect medals, or collate manuscripts: but to dive into the depths of dungeons; to plunge into the infections of hospitals; to survey the mansions of sorrow and pain; to take the gauge and dimensions of misery, depression, and contempt; to remember the forgotten, to attend to the neglected, to visit the forsaken, and to compare and collate the distresses of all men in all countries.—BURKE, *On the Career of Howard the Philanthropist.*

IV. THE VIGOROUS STYLE.

483. Vigour and how it is produced.—A style is said to be Vigorous when it stimulates the attention of the reader without exacting from him any effort above the ordinary. "Vehement" is the word used by Blair: "energetic" by Whately; "impressive" by Bain; "vivacious" by Campbell; "forcible" by Abbott and Seeley. But the word most current in popular speech is "Vigorous," and for this reason it has been here adopted. A noun sometimes used to express this quality is "verve."

The modes in which vigour or verve is produced are various. Many of them have been shown already in Chap. XX. The reader's attention is also invited to Chap. XXXI. on the Figures of Speech. These figures may serve more purposes than one; but almost all, if they do nothing else, are in different ways conducive to vigour, force, or impressiveness.

A few more of the devices by which this quality may be produced will now be given.

(*a*) *Dilemma.*—An alternative, in which both conclusions are to be deprecated alike, but one or other is inevitable. The two conclusions are called "the horns of a dilemma."

If he believed, in spite of all the evidence to the contrary, that our ministers and our soldiers who served in South Africa had been guilty of barbarous and loathsome practices, he was a fool. If he did not believe it, but was only saying so for partisan purposes, and in order to inflict discredit on this Government, he was a knave.—Quoted in *Daily Tel.* p. 6, 25th Nov. 1901.

(*b*) *Balance.*—A kind of sentence in which a word or phrase in one part is balanced against and contrasted with some word or phrase in another part. The word "balance," as an element in composition, is almost synonymous with "rhythm" (see § 423).

The great Napoleon once said that an army marches on its belly; and it certainly might be said that in these days a fleet moves on its coal.—*House of Commons*, 14th Aug. 1901.

The soldier possesses the knowledge without the power. The civilian minister has the power without the knowledge.—*Daily Tel.* p. 9, 5th March 1901.

The notice that you have been pleased to take of my labours, had it been early, had been kind; but it has been delayed, till I am indifferent and cannot enjoy it; till I am solitary, and cannot impart it; till I am known, and do not want it.—JOHNSON.

The last is the memorable answer that Dr. Johnson gave to the belated offers of help from Lord Chesterfield. It is a model of terseness, simplicity, and vigour,—not at all in Johnson's usual style. Here there is no pomposity. He wrote as he felt.

(*c*) *Condensed Statement.*—The following extract contains an admirable example of vigour or verve produced by a condensed statement, that is followed immediately afterwards by a comment of greater length. (The words in which the condensed statement is expressed have been printed in italics.)

A nation is a living organism. Never was attempt so disastrous as that of the pedantic theorists, in what has been called the murderous work of the French Revolution, to treat a state as a formal structure, which could be pulled down by political architects and raised up at will to its former height and strength upon a new design. *Nations are not built to rule or line.* They grow by the inward law of their being, and all that is great in the inspiration of a people must still rise, like the sap of "patrician trees," from their roots.—*Daily Tel.* p. 9, 29th June 1901.

(*d*) *Sarcasm.*—The occasional use of this figure (§ 410) gives point to an argument.

Every one knows that all is not well with our industries. Opinions differ as to the extent of the sickness, but none denies its existence except perhaps on the platform, where men have to say what they do not think.—*Times Weekly*, p. 122, 19th April 1907.

(e) *The use of Proverbs and familiar sayings.*

India must learn to cut her coat according to her cloth; but she has the plainest right to ask that she shall not be made to pay for the coats of other people.—*Pioneer Mail*, p. 3, 19th May 1900.

(f) *Surprise.*—The attention is aroused, if the thought is so expressed as to impart a shock of surprise.

Thus says Mr. R. B., who is looked up to by Socialists as somewhat of a great man. Well, great he is—great as an advocate of thieving by Act of Parliament.—*Fort. Rev.* p. 53, Oct. 1900.

"Gentlemen," he said, "you must not mistake me. I admit that the French Emperor is a tyrant. I admit that he is a monster. I admit that he is the sworn foe of our nation, and, if you will, of the whole human race. But, gentlemen, we must be just to our great enemy. We must not forget that he once shot a publisher."—*A Saying by Campbell the Poet* (1777-1844).

(g) The following is quoted as a very good specimen of vigorous writing. It contains a portion of the author's summing-up of the character of Napoleon III.:—

Yet we must not forget that from first to last the story of the Empire is the story of a conspirator. Through plot and counter-plot he made his way to the throne; through plot and counter-plot he moved to the Italian War, which was the commencement of his downfall; through plot and counter-plot he drifted into the final struggle which ended at Sedan. His idea of statesmanship was intrigue. Like the mole, he burrowed underground. Like the mole, his course was so tortuous and so concealed that those who were nearest to him were frequently unable to see whither he was trending.—SIR SPENCER WALPOLE, *Studies in Biography*.

The style is so natural and easy, and yet so full of point and energy, that we hardly like dissecting the author's diction to see where the vigour lies, and by what means it has been produced. Terseness, antithesis, balance, repetition, and simile are all exemplified in the above extract. Yet the author appears to be, and probably he was, quite unconscious of the arts that he was using.

484. Deviations from the Vigorous Style.—As has been shown in § 469, there are two kinds of deviations from the vigorous style: the pointless, which errs on the side of deficiency; and the exaggerated, which errs on the side of excess.

(1) *The Pointless.*—One short example must suffice:—

The solemnity of his (Clarendon's) antiquated virtue was oppressive to Charles and to the new morality of his court and harem. Having been Charles's tutor in exile, he had not doffed the tutor.—GOLDWIN SMITH, *United Kingdom*, ii. 26.

The sentences quoted furnish an admirable example of vigour, until we come to the last word, when we feel that something more is needed to give the second sentence the requisite degree of point. To balance the phrase "in exile" we can say: "He had not doffed the tutor *when Charles was on the throne*."

(2) *The Exaggerated.*—To strain after effect by using words that exaggerate the fact is vain: it carries no conviction with it (see remarks on Hyperbole in § 407). This is a common fault in the writings of Carlyle. In his description of the voyage of Columbus he has written as follows:—

> Brother, these wild water-mountains, bounding from their deep bases (ten miles deep, I am told), are not entirely there on thy behalf! Meseems they have other work than floating thee forward, etc.—*Past and Present.*

There is more than one extravagance in the above extract. (*a*) To speak of waves as being mountains-high is a trite and exploded commonplace. The highest Atlantic wave observed by Scoresby, who made a special study of the subject, was 43 feet. (*b*) The so-called water-mountains are said to bound up from bases ten miles deep. It is well known that only the surface of the ocean, and this a very shallow one, is ever stirred at all by the roughest wind. (*c*) The deepest measurements yet taken barely exceed five miles.

V. The Graphic Style.

485. Main Characteristic.—The graphic style, of which the main quality is called by Bain "picturesqueness," is an attempt to rival, by the inferior instrumentality of language, the effects of a painted picture—to make the reader see with the mind's eye the objects or events that are put before him in words. The vigorous style appeals chiefly to the understanding, the graphic to the imagination. Each in its own way excites attention and takes hold of the memory.

In words the quality most instrumental in producing a picturesque effect is their speciality. The more general the term is, the fainter is the picture; the more special, the more vivid. Compare the two sentences given below:—

(1) In proportion as the manners and amusements of a nation are cruel and barbarous, the regulations of their penal code will be severe.

(2) In proportion as men delight in battles, tourneys, bull-fights, and combats of gladiators, they will punish criminals by hanging, beheading, burning, and the rack.

The first of these two sentences is not wanting in vigour; but the second one goes a step further. The terms used being special, and not general, the sentence is not merely vigorous, but graphic. Each mode of diction is good in its way. We need the general for laying down principles, and the special for fixing them in the memory. If I were asked to name some writer whose compositions may be regarded as typical examples of the graphic style, I should name Daniel De Foe, whose *Robinson Crusoe* and *History of the Plague* are so liberally stocked with vivid detail, that readers have often been beguiled into taking them for actual history.

486. The Graphic Style exemplified.—I give one example in verse, and two in prose :—

(1) *A Winter Evening.*

Now stir the fire, and close the shutters fast,
Let fall the curtains, wheel the sofa round,
And while the bubbling and loud-hissing urn
Throws up a steaming column, and the cups
That cheer, but not inebriate, wait on each,
So let us welcome gentle evening in.—COWPER.

(2) *Changes in Social Life in England.*

It is certain that William the Conqueror ate with his fingers and never saw a coal fire, that the 2000 cooks of Richard II. could make neither a plum-pudding nor mince-pies, that Chaucer never saw a printed book, that Queen Elizabeth never heard of tea nor saw a newspaper (yet the first newspaper is given as being printed in 1588), that George I. had no umbrella, and that Queen Victoria was the first sovereign of our island-home who had not to depend on wind and weather to leave her kingdom.

Articles now considered necessities were luxuries to our forefathers, or entirely non-existent. Thus they lived without sugar till the thirteenth century; without coal till the fourteenth; without butter on their bread till the fifteenth; without tea, coffee, and soap till the seventeenth; without umbrellas, lamps, and puddings till the eighteenth; without trains, telegrams, gas, matches, and chloroform till the nineteenth.—MISS M. B. SYNGE.

(3) *The Great Frost of January* 1684.

9th January.—I went across the Thames on the ice, now become so thick as to bear not only streets of booths, in which they roasted meat and had divers shops of wares quite across as in a town, but coaches, carts, and horses passed over.

24th January.—The frost continuing more and more severe, the Thames before London was still planted with booths in formal streets, all sorts of trades and shops furnished and full of commodities, even to a printing press, where the people and ladies took a fancy to have their names printed, and the day and year set down when printed on the Thames. Coaches plied from Westminster to the Temple, and from several other stairs to and fro as in the streets, sleds, sliding with skates, a bull-baiting, horse and coach-races, puppet-plays and interludes, cooks, tippling and other lewd places, so that it seemed to be a bacchanalian triumph or carnival on the water, whilst it was a severe judgment on the land, the trees not only splitting as if lightning-struck, but men and cattle perishing in divers places, and the very seas so locked up with ice that no vessels could stir out or come in. The fowls, fish, and birds, and all our exotic plants and greens universally perishing. Many parks of deer were destroyed, and all sorts of fuel so dear that there were great contributions to preserve the poor alive. London, by reason of the excessive coldness of the air hindering the ascent of the smoke, was so filled with the fuliginous steam of the sea-coal, that hardly could one see cross the streets, and this filling the lungs with its gross particles exceedingly obstructed the breath, so as one could scarcely breathe. Here was no water to be had from the pipes and engines, nor could the brewers and divers other tradesmen work, and every moment was full of disastrous accidents.—EVELYN'S *Diary*, 1620–1706.

487. Deviations from the Graphic Style.—There are two kinds of deviations from the graphic style: the prolix, in which the enumeration of details is excessive; the colourless, in which it is not sufficient.

(*a*) *The Prolix.*—This is the best name that I can find for describing by a single word the superabundance of graphic detail. "The chief law of description," says Bain, "is to unite a comprehensive plan with an orderly enumeration of parts." Details that are suitable to the plan should be selected and mentioned with sufficient prominence; those that are unsuitable or superabundant should be left out, no notice being taken of them.

I give an example from Keats's *Endymion*, in which the author does not appear to have made any selection from the images or ideas that crowded on his imagination, or to have formed in his mind any comprehensive plan or outline. The description is so bewildering that we feel much relieved when we have come to the end of it:—

So with unusual gladness on he hies
Through caves and palaces of mottled ore,
Gold dome, and crystal wall, and turquois floor,
Black polished porticoes of awful shade,
And at the last a diamond balustrade,
Leading afar past wild magnificence,
Spiral through ruggedest loopholes, and thence
Stretching across a void, then guiding o'er
Enormous chasms, where, all foam and roar,
Streams subterranean tease their granite beds;
Then heightened just above the silvery heads
Of a thousand fountains, so that he could dash
The waters with his spear; but at the splash,

Done heedlessly, those spouting columns rose
Sudden a poplar's height, and 'gan to inclose
His diamond path with fretwork streaming round
Alike, and dazzling cool, and with a sound
Haply, like dolphin tumults, when sweet shells
Welcome the float of Thetis.

For an example (in prose) of description overdone I give the following. This extract, however, would have served equally as well as an example of obscurity (§ 481); for the meaning of certain parts of it is by no means obvious. The punctuation has been reproduced exactly as I found it in print:—

He looked about in his small despair; he crossed the hotel court, which, overarched and glazed, muffled against loud sounds and guarded against crude sights, heated, gilded, draped, almost carpeted with exotic trees in tubs, exotic ladies in chairs, the general exotic accent and presence suspended, as with wings folded or feebly fluttering, in the superior, the supreme, the inexorably enveloping Parisian medium, resembling some critical apartment of large capacity, some "dental," medical, surgical waiting-room, a scene of mixed anxiety and desire, preparatory, for gathered barbarians, to the due amputation or extraction of excrescences and redundancies of barbarism.—H. J., *Golden Bowl*, p. 165.

(*b*) *The Colourless.*—This is the opposite extreme to the Prolix. I give one example, from Roger's *Pleasures of Memory*:—

From Guinea's coast pursue the less'ning sail,
And catch the sounds that sadden every gale;
Tell, if you canst, the sum of sorrows there,
Mark the fixed gaze, the wild and frenzied glare,
The racks of thought, the freezings of despair.

This is all that he tells us about a shipload of men and women, that have been dragged from their homes by the slave-hunter and driven by the whip to the Guinea coast, from which they have been placed in chains on board the ship that is to take them across the Atlantic: some will die of their sufferings on the voyage, while those who survive will be sold like cattle to a hard task-master in a land of strangers. Contrast this colourless description of a slave-ship with the account that Goldsmith gives of an emigrant-ship (see lines 363-384 of the *Deserted Village*) that is about to cross the Atlantic, and of the scenes on shore, when the emigrants tear themselves away from the homes that they will never see again.

Observe the difference between the two following extracts. The first is a mere colourless enumeration of the names of birds.

The second is not merely an enumeration of birds, but a description of their music.

> Now too the feather'd warblers tune their notes
> Around, and charm the listening grove. The lark,
> The linnet, chaffinch, bullfinch, goldfinch, greenfinch.—SHERIDAN.

> The merry lark her matins sings aloft,
> The thrush replies, the mavis descant plays,
> The ousel shrills, the redbreast warbles soft:
> So goodly all agree, with sweet content,
> To this day's merriment.—SPENSER.

VI. THE ELEGANT STYLE.

488. Main Characteristics of Elegance.—"Elegance," says Whately, "requires that all homely and coarse words and phrases shall be avoided even at the expense of circumlocution, though these may be the most apt and forcible that language can supply. And elegance implies a smooth and easy flow of words in respect of the sound of sentences, though a more harsh and abrupt mode of expression may often be equally energetic."

Briefly, then, elegance may be defined as "beauty of thought combined with beauty of diction." This definition applies to prose no less than to poetry.

For beauty of diction, or (as Whately calls it) "the smooth and easy flow of words in respect of the sound of sentences," the reader is referred to Chap. XXI. on Euphony.

The other requirement—the avoidance of coarse words and coarse subjects—is more peculiarly the property of elegance even than euphony is. For euphony, though it is indispensable to the elegant style, is not confined to it: "a smooth and easy flow of words" may accompany any of the five qualities of composition that have been described already—Simplicity, Directness, Terseness, Vigour, and Picturesqueness. But the second requirement—the avoidance of coarse words and coarse subjects—is the peculiar property of elegance. It is this property that places elegance on a higher level than any other style that has been mentioned hitherto.

Pope's description of the Billingsgate fish-market, as it was in his own days, is Graphic, but not Elegant.[1] He has

[1] Another word for *elegant* is "graceful." This is the word used by Abbott and Seeley in their *English Lessons for English People. Elegant* is the word used by Blair, Lord Kames, Campbell, and Whately. I have adopted it, because it has a large majority in its favour.

honoured these squalid details with a Spenserian stanza (§ 454),—a stanza never before and never since, so far as I know, used for so mean a purpose.

> And on the broken pavement here and there
> Doth many a stinking sprat and herring lie;
> A brandy-and-tobacco shop is near,
> And hens and dogs and hogs are feeding by,
> And here a sailor's jacket hangs to dry.
> At every door are sunburnt matrons seen,
> Mending old nets to catch the scaly fry,
> Now singing shrill, and scolding oft between;
> Scolds answer foul-mouthed scolds;—foul neighbourhood, I ween.

By way of contrast take the following extract from *The Merchant of Venice*, v. i:—

> How sweet the moonlight sleeps upon this bank!
> Here will we sit, and let the sounds of music
> Creep in our ears; soft stillness and the night
> Become the touches of sweet harmony.
> Sit, Jessica. Look how the floor of heaven
> Is thick inlaid with patines of bright gold;
> There's not the smallest orb which thou beholdest
> But in his motion like an angel sings,
> Still quiring to the young-eyed cherubims:
> Such harmony is in immortal souls;
> But whilst this muddy vesture of decay
> Doth grossly close it in, we cannot hear it.

For beauty of thought combined with beauty of diction it would be difficult to find any passage in English or in any other literature, ancient or modern, that surpasses these exquisite lines. On the beauty of thought I need not dwell. As regards the beauty of the diction, see how this would be marred if we put *platters* for "patines," *always singing in concert with the rest* for "still quiring," *come into our hearing* for "creep in our ears," *slanting ground* for "bank," *this corruptible body* for "this vesture of decay," *the solid firmament* for "the floor of heaven," etc.

489. Poetic Prose.—"Poetry," as Whately has told us in another place (see above, § 333, p. 244), "is not distinguished from prose by superior beauty either of thought or of expression, but is *a distinct kind of composition*; and they produce, when each is excellent in its own way, distinct kinds of pleasure." This is true; and the difference in point of form and diction between the two kinds of composition has been for the most part observed by all our best writers. But we sometimes meet with a kind of elegance in prose, which consists in using the diction, and to some extent even the form, *i.e.* the metre, of poetry. Some critics object to poetical prose under any circumstances; others do not object to it, provided that it is used very sparingly, and only when the character of the narrative at that particular point is such as to justify exceptional treatment. We meet with examples of such prose in Milton's *Areopagitica*, in Wordsworth's *Guide to the Lakes* (1810), in Coleridge's prose, in Ruskin's works, and sometimes even in Dickens's.

I give one example from Dickens: it occurs at the close of chap. xxviii. in *Martin Chuzzlewit*, where Jonas administers a cowardly and unprovoked blow to his wife. The scene, painful as it is, is handled by the author with so much delicacy, that it involves no offence against Elegance.

> Not with a blow? Yes. Stern truth against the base-souled villain, with a blow.
> No angry cries; no loud reproaches. Even her weeping and her sobs were stifled by her clinging round him. She only said, repeating it in agony of heart, How could he, could he, could he! And lost utterance in tears.
> Oh woman, God-beloved in the old Jerusalem! The best among us need deal lightly with thy faults, if only for the punishment thy nature will endure, in bearing heavy evidence against us, on the Day of Judgment.

The above extract can be divided into lines and feet, in which the metre of every line, except the fifth, which is a little too long, is perfect. The metre is that of blank verse in the form of Iambic pentameter (§ 443, p. 446).

Not with | a blow?
Stern truth | against | the base- | soul'd vil- | lain, yes,
Yes, with | a blow! | No an- | gry cries, | no loud
Reproach- | es. E'en | her weep- | ing and | her sobs
Were sti- | fled by | her cling- | ing round him. She only said,
Repeat- | ing it | in ag- | ony | of heart,
How could | he? and | lost ut- | terance | in tears.
Oh wom- | an, God- | belov- | éd in | the old
Jerus- | alem! | The best | among | us need
Deal light- | ly with | thy faults, | if on- | ly for
The pun- | ishment | thy na- | ture will | endure
In bear- | ing heav- | y ev- | idence | against us
O' the Day | of Judg- | ment.

490. Deviations on the Side of Defect.—On the side of defect the three chief offences against the Elegant style are (1) the Involved or mis-shapen sentence, (2) the Abrupt or rugged, and (3) the Slovenly or slipshod.

(1) *The Involved.*—It has been pointed out already (§ 335) that within the modern period of our literature two very different styles of prose prevailed in succession, (1) the *Older*, commencing from about A.D. 1500, and lasting for nearly two centuries; (2) the *Newer*, commencing from about A.D. 1688, and continuing up to the present day.[1] A description of both is given in § 335, and there is no need to repeat. The Older, *i.e.* the Involved style, was adopted from a mistaken notion of elegance. During the Renascence or Revival of Learning, Latin and Greek authors were regarded with an almost superstitious reverence, and were supposed to be the best models for composition in English; and thus the natural English style which writers of that day might have used, and which, in fact, some writers, such as Latimer in his *Sermons* and Bacon in his *Essays*, *did* use, was sacrificed to a false conceit. Some writers, such as Clarendon, who wrote the *History of the Great Rebellion* (the first great work on the history of our country), went out of their way to imitate the style of Cæsar or Livy. The following may be quoted as a specimen:—

> It was not thought fit to pursue Lambert, who being known to be a man of courage and conduct, and his troops to be of the best, was suspected by so disorderly a retreat to have only designed to have drawn the army another way to disorder and disturb their march, which they resolved to continue with the same expedition they had hitherto used, which was incredible, until they should come to such a post as they might securely rest themselves.

Such a sentence (if the student can make out the meaning of the last two lines, which I can scarcely make out myself) could easily be translated into the equivalent Latin; and the author no doubt considered that, as he had caught the Latin style so well, he had written an elegant and scholar-like piece of English prose.

(2) *The Abrupt.*—This epithet has been applied to the style of

[1] The Restoration (1660 A.D.), according to Matthew Arnold, "marks the real moment of birth of our modern English prose. Men of lucid and direct mental habit there were, such as Chillingworth, in whom before the Restoration the desire and the commencement of a modern prose show themselves. There were men like Barrow, weighty and powerful, whose mental habit the old prose suited, who continued its forms and locutions after the Restoration. But the hour was come for the new prose, and it grew and prevailed." If any year is to be mentioned, I prefer the year 1688 to 1660, because the former will include Clarendon, one of the strongest representatives of the Older style.

Carlyle, which is supposed (wrongly, as some might think) to make up for its lack of elegance by its possessing an unusual abundance of vigour or impressiveness. (Parts of the following extract have been quoted already in p. 491 and in p. 503 for other purposes.)

> Brave Sea-captain, Norse Sea-king,—Columbus my hero, royalest Sea-king of all! it is no friendly environment this of thine, in the waste deep waters; around thee mutinous discouraged souls, behind thee disgrace and ruin, before thee the unpenetrated veil of Night. Brother, these wild water-mountains bounding from their deep bases (ten miles deep, I am told) are not entirely there on thy behalf! Meseems *they* have other work than floating thee forward:—and the huge Winds, that sweep from Ursa Major to the Tropics and Equators, dancing their giant-waltz through the kingdoms of Chaos and Immensity, they care little about filling rightly or filling wrongly the small shoulder-of-mutton sails in this cockle-skiff of thine! Thou art not among articulate-speaking friends, my brother; thou art among immeasurable dumb monsters, tumbling, howling wide as the world here. . . . Thou shalt be a Great Man. Yes, my World-Soldier, thou of the World-Marine Service,—thou wilt have to be *greater* than this tumultuous World here round thee is; thou in thy strong soul, as with wrestler's arms, shalt embrace it, harness it down, and make it bear thee on,—to new Americas or whither God will.—*Past and Present.*

In this quotation, taken at random from the writings of Carlyle, and copied with all the stops and all the capitals as I found them, there is much that is extravagant, if not rabid, in the diction. *Huge* is a curious epithet to apply to "wind." *Royalest* is a strange superlative (strange in form as well as in position, since no definite article is placed before it). *Meseems* is practically obsolete: it does not occur in Shakespeare, who, however, uses "it seems to me" three times (*M. N. D.* iv. 1; *Jul. Cæs.* ii. 2; *Tit. And.* ii. 4): to rake up such a word for use in modern prose was a flagrant piece of pedantry. Nothing is gained by using the phrase "shoulder of mutton,"—the name given by seamen to sails of a certain shape: where does the vigour,—where does the beauty, come in?

Nothing is gained by the arbitrary use of capitals that are thickly scattered over these staggering sentences,—Sea-captain, Sea-king (twice), Night, Winds, Tropics, Equators (is there more than one?), Immensity, Great Man, World-Soldier, World-Marine Service. Capitals look big to the eye; but this does not make the meaning of the words any bigger. "They are the last resource," as a critic has remarked, "of the forcible feeble." Wrongly used as they are in the extract quoted, they are merely blunders.

(3) *The Slovenly or Slipshod.*—These terms are applied literally to carelessness of dress, metaphorically to carelessness of diction. If a writer takes no trouble to correct little faults of idiom, phrase, or grammar, and makes no attempt to improve

the euphony or rhythm of what he writes, his style is stigmatised as slovenly. The subject has been dealt with already in Chapters XVIII. and XXI., and incidentally in other parts of this book. In this place, therefore, it will be enough to give a few additional examples :—

(1) "How was it possible that material of this kind could be published without having first obtained my permission?"—Quoted in *Nat. Rev.* p. 389, Nov. 1906.

It is necessary to insert *his* or *her* or *their* before *having*. The grammar is not complete without it.

(2) For months past we have advised the Peers, for practical tactical reasons, of which we are in no way ashamed, because they correspond with national interests, to accept this Bill substantially as they find it.—*Nat. Rev.* p. 585, Dec. 1906.

The jingle of *practical tactical* is inexcusable.

(3) He quotes at length that ringing poem *Clifton*, and in each verse introduces one or more of the lovely features of the scenery of the Isle of Man, which he loved with passionate devotion, and which all who love that island will delight to read.—*Daily Tel.* p. 6, 30th Jan. 1907.

The first *which* has for its antecedent "the Isle of Man"; the second one has no antecedent at all, though the writer must have had in his mind the word "poem."

(4) Sir,—May I, since privately urged to do so, ask for the hospitality of your columns in order to add my opinion to that of many others recently published concerning the construction of a Channel Tunnel, from a patriotic point of view?

This letter appeared in the *Times Weekly*, 1st Feb. 1907, over the signature of Alfred Austin. Observe the wrong order of the concluding phrase. The first line, too, is open to criticism. It could be improved by inserting *I have been* after *since*.

(5) Like its great rival, the Prussian State has been created by its Monarchs, aided by a powerful bureaucracy; and like that rival, over-centralisation has brought it to the verge of ruin.

Quoted from a writer (whose initials are given as O. A.) on the subject of "Local and Central Government." The rhythm of the last sentence is marred by his having neglected the rule of Parallel Construction (§ 329). He should have written—"it has been brought to the verge of ruin by over-centralisation."

(6) Grown out of small beginnings, the Vulkan has, by striving forward restlessly and ever conscious of its goal, taken a position which commands respect among similar works in the world. —*Daily Tel.* p. 9, 31st Jan. 1907.

The collocation of *restlessly and ever conscious* produces a very awkward sound. The writer could easily have said "by striving restlessly forward and keeping its goal steadfastly in view." Moreover, the first word "grown" has an awkward sound and is of questionable accuracy (see § 133). It could be left out altogether without any altering or weakening of the sense. If it is not left out, it should be preceded by "Having."

(7) He has no eye not only for such ethical differences as have to be divined from slender indications, but for great moral contrasts when embodied in man.—*National Rev.* p. 318, Oct. 1906.

The *no* and the *not* coming so close together in the first sentence constitute what Bain calls "a clash of negatives." It would have been quite as easy to say—"He has no eye either for such ethical, etc., or for great moral," etc. Insert "they are" after "when."

(8) He has demonstrated that under existing conditions of taxation no relief can be given either to the payers of indirect taxation or of direct taxation, and that there is absolutely no surplus.—*Daily Tel.* p. 10, May 4, 1907.

The order of the words is wrong. The order should have been "no relief can be given to the payers of either indirect or direct taxation" (see § 294 (5)).

(9) We find holy men who are credited with miraculous powers and with close communion with the deity, who live in drunkenness and immorality and who are capable of elaborate frauds on others.—*Times Weekly*, p. 326, 24th May 1907.

Change *who are credited* to *that are credited.* The second *with* is not required by the sense and might be cancelled for the sake of euphony. Cancel the *who* before *are capable.*

491. Deviations on the Side of Excess.—On the side of excess the two chief offences against the Elegant style are (1) the Laboured, (2) the Florid. In both of these the striving after elegance defeats its own object.

(1) *Laboured Diction.*—The labour of correction and revision can seldom be avoided by those writers who wish to make the best display of their natural gifts.

True ease in writing comes from art, not chance,
As those move easiest who have learnt to dance.

True: but the art lies in concealing the art. If the labour is perceived, "the *easy* flow of words," on which elegance largely depends, is gone. Such labour appears sometimes in the style of George Eliot, although in most places her diction is as easy and natural as that of her sister-novelists, Jane Austen and Charlotte Brontë. The following extract is from *Romola*:—

The delicious sun-rays fell on Romola and thrilled her gently like a caress. She lay motionless, hardly watching the scene, rather feeling simply the presence of peace and beauty. While we are still in our youth, there can always come, in our early waking, moments when mere passive existence is itself a Lethe, when the exquisiteness of subtle indefinite sensation creates a bliss which is without memory and without desire. As the soft warmth penetrated Romola's young limbs, as her eyes rested on this sequestered luxuriance, it seemed that the agitating past had glided away like the dark scene in the Bargello and that the afternoon dreams of her childhood had come back to her.

Compare the above, which is obviously laboured and in places is not easy to understand, with the elegance, ease, and lucidity of the following extract from *Shirley* by a sister-novelist:—

He laboured faithfully in the parish. The schools, both Sunday and day schools, flourished under his sway like green bay trees. Being human, of course, he had his faults. These, however, were proper, steady-going, clerical faults. The circumstance of finding himself invited to tea with a Dissenter would unhinge him for a week. The spectacle of the Quaker wearing his hat in church, the thought of an unbaptized fellow-creature being interred with Christian rites—these things could make strange havoc in Mr. Macarthey's physical and mental economy. Otherwise he was sane and rational, diligent and charitable.—CHARLOTTE BRONTË.

(2) *Florid Diction.*—Pedantry, as we have seen (§ 474, 3), searches for words and phrases that have a show of book-learning about them. In florid writing no such search is made; but fine-sounding and sometimes startling words are dragged in for the sake of the ornament that they are supposed to give. Two examples must suffice, the first from a very recent writer, the second from a writer who lived in the time of Charles I.

Hedges of aloe brandished zincen (*sic*) swords and darts; cacti sprawled and leered along the roadside; set in the vivid green of ripening grain, olive groves seemed carved from jade; or the bare rosy shoulders of sloping hill-sides turned by contrast their pale tints to tarnished silver. Vines with young gold leaves trailed the purple earth; avenues of acacia dripped perfumes; and as the sun leaned towards the west, the quivering pink light on violet mountains gave to Andalucia the vivid, almost violent, colouring one sees in sensational posters.—WILLIAMSON, *The Car of Destiny*, chap. xxiv.

The Light of Reason is a pleasant light. All Light is pleasant; 'tis the very smile of Nature, the gloss of the world, the varnish of creation, a bright paraphrase upon bodies. Whether it discover itself in the modesty of a morning blush, and open its fair and virgin eyelids in the dawning of the day; or whether it dart out more vigorous and sprightful beams, shining out in its noonday glory; whether it sport and twinkle in a star; or blaze and glare out in a comet; or frisk and dance in a jewel; or dissemble and play the hypocrite in a glowworm; or epitomise and abbreviate itself in a spark; or show its zeal and the ruddiness of its complexion in the yolk of the fire, etc. —CULVERWELL, *Light of Nature*.

VII. The Elevated Style.

492. Main Characteristics.—In § 488 the Elegant style was declared to be "beauty of thought combined with beauty of diction." Similarly the Elevated style may be defined as "loftiness of thought combined with loftiness of diction." In each of these styles the thought must be worthy of the diction, and *vice versâ*.

The Elegant style will admit a subject that is familiar, so long as it is not repulsive. The Elevated style rejects both, *i.e.* it will not admit a subject that is either familiar or repulsive, and herein lies one of the main differences between them.

If this view is correct, we must regard such passages as the following, both of which occur in *Paradise Lost*, as beneath the dignity of Elevated poetry; in the first the subject is too familiar, in the second it is repulsive:—

(1) Raised of grassy turf
Their table was, and mossy seats had round;
And on her ample square from side to side
All Autumn piled, though Spring and Autumn here
Danced hand in hand. Awhile discourse they held,
No fear lest dinner cool.—v. 391-6.

(2) All maladies
Of ghastly spasm, or racking torture, qualms
Of heart-sick agony, all feverous kinds,
Convulsions, epilepsies, fierce catarrhs,
Intestine stone and ulcer, colic pangs,
Demoniac phrensy, moping melancholy
And moon-struck madness, pining atrophy,
Marasmus, and wide-wasting pestilence,
Dropsies and asthmas, and joint-racking rheums.—xi.

Barring such passages as those just quoted, which are very rare, the best examples of the Elevated style in English poetry are to be seen in *Paradise Lost*, and with less frequency in *Paradise Regained*. Other examples will be found in several stanzas of the Third and Fourth Cantos of *Childe Harold*, especially in those addressed to the Ocean near the end of the Fourth Canto. Examples occur also in the course of Shakespeare's dramas; in Gray's Odes, *The Bard* and *The Progress of Poesy*; in some passages of Thomson's *Seasons*, especially that part of the poem which deals with "Winter"; in Tennyson's *In Memoriam*, and in George Eliot's *Spanish Gypsy*.

In prose the best examples, so far as I know, will be found

in Milton's *Areopagitica*, in Gibbon's *Decline and Fall of the Roman Empire*, and in the writings of Burke.

493. Pomposity or Bombast.—This is one of the faults into which the Elevated style is apt to fall, especially when the diction is pitched in a higher key than what the subject will bear. This style is sometimes called Johnsonese, after Dr. Johnson, who made a habit of using it. Other names in common use are "turgid," "inflated."

The following passage might have been written by Johnson. It is with no little surprise that we find it was written by Wordsworth; for there is certainly a tone of pomposity about it.

> Humble and rustic life was generally chosen, because in that condition the essential passions of the heart find a better soil in which they can attain their maturity, are less under restraint, and speak a plainer and more emphatic language; because in that condition of life our elementary feelings coexist in a state of greater simplicity, and, consequently, may be more accurately contemplated and more forcibly communicated; because the manners of rural life germinate these elementary feelings, and from the necessary character of rural occupations are more easily comprehended, and are more durable; and, lastly, because in that condition the passions of men are incorporated with the beautiful and permanent forms of Nature.—WORDSWORTH, *Preface to the Lyrical Ballads.*

Sometimes a pompous tone is assumed for the sake of humour. An example occurs in Tennyson's *Aylmer's Field*—a poem that deals with a simple subject, and, except in the passage quoted below, is written in a severely simple style:—

> Sir Aylmer Aylmer, that almighty man,
> The county god—in whose capacious hall,
> Hung with a hundred shields, the family tree
> Sprang from the midriff of a prostrate king—
> Whose playing wyvern weather-cocked the spire,
> Stood from his walls and winged his entry-gates
> And swang besides on many a windy sign—
> Whose eyes from under a pyramidal head
> Saw from his windows nothing save his own.

494. Bathos.—Among the Figures of Speech bathos has been described in § 400 as "a descent from a higher thought to a lower." Of this an example occurs in Homer, who, in describing how Athene turned aside an arrow which Pandarus had aimed at her favourite hero, Menelaus, accompanies his description with the following simile:—

> As when a mother from her infant's cheek,
> Wrapt in sweet slumbers, brushes off a fly.

Exercise on Chapter XXXIV.

To each of the following extracts the student is asked to apply one, or (if he sees reason) more than one, of the terms given in § 472 for describing the seven Standard-styles and the deviations therefrom. He should quote a few words from the extract to show in each case why he considers the term or terms to be applicable. If he finds none of the terms given in § 472 to be applicable, he can mention some term that, in his opinion, fits better. He may also name any figure of speech that he considers to be exemplified in the example before him.

1. No! rather let the fountain of your valour
Spring through each stream of enterprise,
Each petty channel of conducive daring,
Till the full torrent of your foaming wrath
O'erwhelm the flats of sunk hostility!
Lond. Matr. Jan. 1905.

2. And like the baseless fabric of this vision,
The cloud-capped towers, the gorgeous palaces,
The solemn temples, the great globe itself,
Yea, all which it inherit, shall dissolve!
Lond. Matr. Jan. 1905.

3. Mark him of shoulders curved, of stature tall,
Black hair and vivid eye and meagre cheek,
His prominent feature like an eagle's beak.
Lond. Matr. Jan. 1905.

4. Graced as thou art with all the power of words,
So known, so honoured at the House of Lords.
Lond. Matr. Jan. 1905.

5. It haunted me, the morning long,
With weary sameness in the rhymes,
The phantom of a silent song,
That went and came a thousand times.
Lond. Matr. Jan. 1905.

6. A truly interesting son of earth and son of heaven. A great shock of rough dusty-dark hair, bright, laughing, hazel eyes, massive aquiline face, most massive yet most delicate, of sallow brown complexion, almost Indian-looking; clothes cynically loose, free, and easy; smokes infinite tobacco. One of the finest looking men in the world.—CARLYLE *on Tennyson*, *Lond. Matr.* Sept. 1905.

7. Shocks and the splintering spear, the hard mail hewn,
Shield-breakings, and the clash of brands, the crash
Of battle-axes on shattered helms.—*Lond. Matr.* Sept. 1905.

8. And she bent o'er him, and he lay beneath
Hushed as a babe upon its mother's breast,
Droop'd as the willow when no winds can breathe,
Lull'd like the depth of ocean when at rest,

Fair as the crowning rose of the whole wreath,
  Soft as the callow cygnet in its nest';
In short, he was a very pretty fellow,
Although his woes had turned him rather yellow.
Lond. Matr. Sept. 1905.

9. The power of speech in the direction of public affairs becomes more and more obvious, developed, and irresistible as we advance towards the culminating period of Grecian history—the century preceding the battle of Chæroneia. That its development was greatest among the most enlightened sections of the Grecian name, and smallest among the more obtuse and stationary, is matter of notorious fact; and it is not less true, that the prevalence of this habit was one of the chief causes of the intellectual eminence of the nation generally.—*Lond. Matr.* Sept. 1905.

10. When you speak of a South African river, be it ever so large, it by no means follows that there is any water there. The channel is the river, not the stream.—*Empire Review*, April 1901, p. 292.

11. But no one challenged the vote, when the second reading was put to the House. So the Lords allowed the Bill to pass its second reading by the silence of an overwhelming majority against it.—(*Debate in House of Lords*) *Daily Express*, 5th Nov. 1906.

12. Then the progeny that springs
  From the forests of our land,
Armed with thunder, clad with wings,
  Shall a wider world command.—COWPER.

13. What we are considering is an elevation of tone above the highest utterance of man, prompting us to raise our thoughts to a region pure from the faintest admixture of those selfish elements which even men of loftiest aspiration are unable wholly to dispense with when they gird themselves to their best endeavour.—*Notes on the Sermon on the Mount.*

14. At Tanguanika Burton will to all time be honoured as its indomitable Columbus, with a Maupassantian taste for low life, its humours and laxities. Despite thorny cares, they (Burton and wife) threw themselves heartily into the vortex of society.—WRIGHT, *Life of Sir R. Burton.*

15. Macaulay was incapable, both in a good and bad sense, of Swift's trenchant misanthropy. His dislike to Walpole was founded not so much upon posthumous jealousy—though that passion is not so rare as absurd—as on the singular contrast between the character and intellect of the two men.—LESLIE STEPHEN, *Hours in a Library.*

16. DEAR GEORGE—I agree with you entirely in the pleasure you take in talking over old stories, but can't say but I meet every day with new circumstances, which will be still more pleasure to me to recollect.—*From a Letter by Horace Walpole.*

17. Sometimes, misguided by the tuneful throng,
I look for streams immortalised in song,
That lost in silence and oblivion lie
(Dumb are their fountains and their channels dry),
Yet run for ever by the Muse's skill,
And in the smooth description murmur still.
ADDISON, *Letter from Italy.*

18. The water is whipped into serpents of foam coiling about the rocky head thrust above the surface, betraying with added ferocity the rage they would seem to conceal.—G. W. BROWNE, *St. Lawrence River.*

19. They can make it the fountain and the source from which the whole of their hopes may be fulfilled.—Quoted in *Times Weekly*, 11th Jan. 1907, p. 26.

20. Your conduct has not only offended the Almighty, but it has seriously displeased me.—Quoted by *Daily Telegraph* in p. 9, 6th Jan. 1906.

21. Will all great Neptune's ocean wash this blood
Clean from my hand? No; this my hand will rather
The multitudinous seas incarnadine,
Making the green one red.—*Macbeth*, ii. 1.

22. But now we must admit the shortcomings, the fallacies, the defects, as no less essential elements in forming a sound judgment as to whether the seer and artist were so united in him as to justify the claim first put in by himself and afterwards maintained by his sect to a place beside the few great poets, who exalt men's minds and give a right direction and safe outlet to the passions through the imagination, while insensibly helping them towards balance of character and serenity of judgment by stimulating their sense of proportion, form, and the nice adjustment of means to ends.—LOWELL, *Among my Books*.

23. Labour, capital, and business-ability are the three legs of a three-legged stool; neither is the first, neither is the second, neither is the third. There is no precedence, all being equally necessary. He who would sow discord among the three is the enemy of all.—Quoted in *Review of Reviews*, p. 345, April 1901.

24. My brother Jack was nine in May,
And I was eight on New Year's day;
So in Kate Wilson's shop
Papa (he's my papa and Jack's)
Bought me last week a doll of wax
And brother Jack a top.—*Rejected Addresses*.

25. See there the olive-grove of Academe,
Plato's retirement, where the Attic bird
Trills her thick-warbled notes the summer long;
There flowery hill Hymettus with the sound
Of bees' industrious murmur oft invites
To studious musing.—*Paradise Regained*, iv.

26. The effect of Protection on London would be as commercially deplorable as industrially it would be disastrous to Battersea.—Speech as reported in *Daily Telegraph*, 6th Jan. 1906.

27. Men think according to nature, speak according to precept, but act according to custom.—BACON.

28. Sow an action, reap a habit; sow a habit, reap a character; sow a character, reap a destiny.

29. An idler is a watch that wants both hands,
As useless if it goes as if it stands.—COWPER.

30. The Right Honourable gentleman is indebted to his memory for his jests and to his imagination for his facts.—SHERIDAN.

31. The sun is set,
The stars came out by twos and threes;
The little birds are piping yet
Among the bushes and the trees.—WORDSWORTH.

32. Here thou, great Anna, whom three realms obey,
Dost sometimes counsel take and sometimes tea.—POPE.

33. And be these juggling fiends no more believed,
That palter with us in a double sense,
That keep the word of promise to our ear,
And break it to our hope.—SHAKESPEARE, *Macbeth*.

34. To ignorant pretenders to Surgery and Medicine we award our contempt and scorn; on time-serving or treacherous Counsellors, and on cruel or partial Judges, we inflict our detestation and abhorrence; while on rapacious, corrupt, perfidious, or tyrannical Statesmen and Legislators the voice of human nature cries aloud for execration and vengeance.—WILLIAM COBBETT, *Letter* 11, *on Grammar*.

35. Under every guilty secret there is hidden a brood of guilty wishes, whose unwholesome infecting life is cherished by the darkness. The contaminating effect of deeds often lies less in the commission than in the consequent adjustment of our desires—the enlistment of our self-interest on the side of falsity; as on the other hand the purifying influence of public confession springs from the fact, that by it the hope in lies is for ever swept away, and the soul recovers the noble attitude of simplicity.—*Romola*, chap. ix.

36. Those who go weekly to church and there have doled out to them a quantum of belief, which they have not the energy to work out for themselves, are simply spiritual paupers.

37. But neither breath of morn, when she ascends
With charm of earliest birds, nor rising sun
On this delightful land, nor herb, fruit, flower
Glistening with dew, nor fragrance after showers,
Nor grateful evening mild, nor silent night
With this her solemn bird, nor walk by noon
Or glittering star-light, without thee is sweet.
Par. Lost, iv. 654.

38. I will give £100 to a Liverpool charity if you can prove your statement, if you will agree to give half that sum to any Herts charity, if you cannot.—Quoted in *Daily Telegraph*, 4th Jan. 1906, p. 3.

39. Last year a paper was brought here from England called a dialogue between the Archbishop of Canterbury and Mr. Higgins, which we ordered to be burnt by the common hangman, as it well deserved, though we have no more to do with His Grace of Canterbury than you have with the Archbishop of Dublin, whom you tamely suffer to be abused openly and by name by that paltry scoundrel of an observator; and lately upon an affair in which he had no concern, I mean the business of the missionary of Drogheda, wherein our excellent prelate was engaged and did nothing but according to law and discretion.—SWIFT, *Letter from Ireland*.

40. Mean men assume greater airs and are pretentious in all that they do; the higher their elevation, the more conspicuous is the incongruity of their position. The higher the monkey climbs, the more he shows his tail.—SMILES, *Character*.

41. Hence the various classes of bodies represent parallel series, each corresponding with and modifying the order of the other; classes of which the rational arrangement follows with inherent necessity from their genetic coherence.—OSCAR SCHMIDT, *Doctrine of Descent*.

42. This wretched poetaster has written some volumes of detestable verses on religious subjects, which by mere puffing in magazines and

newspapers have had an immense sale; I really think we ought to try what effect satire will have upon this nuisance.—MACAULAY.

43. The result is looked upon by Polish nationalists as a great triumph in their sempiternal struggle against the Prussian government.—*Daily Telegraph*, 7th Jan. 1907, p. 11.

44. In youth our steps are light, our minds are ductile, and knowledge is easily laid up; but if we neglect our spring, our summers will be useless and contemptible, our harvest will be chaff, and the winter of our old age unrespected and desolate.—SIR W. SCOTT'S *Letter to his Son*.

45. He is daily progressing in learning,—not so learned as he is poor, not so poor as proud, not so proud as happy.—SOUTHEY (said of himself).

46. For only sign of life, two carrion-crows wheeled in sluggish flight near the house; and one, as I passed, lighted on the low stump of a tree, opened his beak, and emitted a hoarse croak.—O. CRAWFORD, *In Green Fields*.

47. The swan with archéd neck,
Between her white wings mantling proudly, rows
Her state with oary feet.—MILTON.

48. I wonder how it comes to pass that there has never been any law against him (the miser). Against him, do I say? I mean for him, as there is a public provision made for other madmen.—COWLEY, *Essay on Avarice*.

49. The hero of fiction, who said that he could only think when he spoke, was not so ridiculous as he was considered; for this hero is everybody.—*Fort. Review*, May 1901, p. 813.

50. And Pity, like a naked new-born babe
Striding the blast, or heaven's cherubim, horsed
Upon the sightless couriers of the air,
Shall blow the horrid deed in every eye,
That tears shall drown the wind.—*Macbeth*, i. 7.

51. One voice is heard upon the chimney-top. It is the starling's. Talkative little ventriloquist, February's changefulness affects him not at all. In storm or in sunshine, heat or cold, he has his lesson to rehearse, and very bravely will he go through all the notes he has learnt in the quiet winter days afield or on the moor, that when the nesting time has come he may arouse the darling of his heart, and teach his younglings clear articulation, the art of mimicry, and the parts of speech.—RAWNSLEY, *Months at the Lakes*.

52. The first thing she did was to make shipwreck of her happiness with a handsome man, whose conversation Addison valued more than any man's living.—Quoted in *Times Literary Supplement*, 3rd May 1907, p. 140.

53. In the granting of all these pardons and indulgences it is quite true that the Church made some kind of distinction between the temporal and spiritual (or, as it were, bodily) penances. But scarcely anybody could understand what this distinction meant.—GUEST, *Lectures on Hist. of England*.

54. As the lark rose higher, he sank deeper into thought. As the lark poured out her melody clearer and stronger, he fell into a graver and profounder silence. At length when the lark came headlong down, he sprang up from his reverie.—DICKENS.

APPENDIX I.—NOTE ON JUTES AND FRISIANS.

(*See pages* 383, 384, *and* 386.)

Jutes.—The *ancient* Jutes, who according to Beda and the *A.-S. Chronicle* took possession of Kent and the Isle of Wight, have been rashly identified with the *present* inhabitants of Jutland, the name now given to the northern province of Denmark. If this identification were correct, it would prove that the earliest colonisers of Kent were a tribe of Scandinavians or Norse, which is absurd; for the extant remains of the old Kentish dialect are Saxon, not Norse, which proves that those earliest colonisers were of the Saxon stock, a tribe of Low Dutch. Considering that the Dutch or Saxons of the Continent were nearer to Kent than any other Teutonic tribe of Europe, this is exactly what was to be expected. Freeman appears to have seen no difficulty in this glaring contradiction, the reason being, as we may presume, that he had made no study of the ancient dialects. The question of the origin of the so-called Jutes is discussed in *Social England*, vol. i. pp. 162, 163, and in the *Political History*, vol. i. chap. vi. Neither author is satisfied that they came from Denmark, but neither of them sees his way to any definite conclusion. The following letter, which I received from Professor Skeat, and which I now publish with his permission, appears to furnish a satisfactory solution:—

"I do not think there is any real difficulty. It is not likely that any Jutes came to us from Jutland. Some Jutes came over to Kent (whence we know not), and partly settled there. *Other* Jutes *afterwards* went to Jutland and remained there, and gave their name to that country. (Similarly a tribe of Scots went over to North Britain from Ireland, and gave their name to Scotland. Similarly too Normans, a Norse tribe from Scandinavia, went over to a part of France, and gave their name to Normandy.) We ought to remember the easy way in which these various Germanic tribes went about roving, without any settled home. The Danes who came over here in Alfred's time used to go from place to place at pleasure. The same men were in Hertfordshire one day, and very soon afterwards made a forced march to a place near Bridgenorth. See how the Norsemen went to Sicily and all over the Mediterranean. Look at the Lombards. The Lombards were a Saxon tribe, speaking a language which is almost Anglo-Saxon (the Wessex dialect spoken by Alfred the Great). Some of these Saxons went *north*, and got to England, and are here now. Others went *south* and took Lombardy, and are there now. If the latter had preserved their language instead of learning Italian, we might almost make it out.

As for the name '*Jute*,' I think it is a dialectic variant of *Goth*. Beda calls them *Jutæ*, Gen. *Jutarum*. The *Anglo-Saxon Chronicle* (copying from Beda) calls them *Iūtan* or *Iōtan*. The Icelandic is *Iōtar*, Nom. Plur. An old spelling of that would be *Iūtar*. But *Goth* is a Latin mis-spelling of the name by which the Goths called themselves in their own language. We have not the Gothic Nominative plural; but it must have been *Gūtus*, as the Gothic for 'Gothic people' is Gūt=*þiuda*. It looks as if *Gūt* and *Iūt* merely vary from hard *g* to *y*. Compare English *yard*, Anglo-Saxon *geard*, with Northern *garth*.

This explanation about the Jutes is not original; it has been said before. Prof. Morley said that, if any Jutes had come from *Jutland* to Kent, they would have given names to places ending in *-by*, as in Lincolnshire. But Kent knows nothing of *-by*."

"Jute" then is nothing more than a comprehensive name for the Gothic, *i.e.* Germanic or Teuton, race as a whole, and the word "Goth" is merely a Latin mis-spelling of it.

This identification is undesignedly confirmed by Procopius, a Latin writer of the sixth century A.D. He was author of a book which he called *De Bello Gothico*, *i.e.* "Concerning the Gothic War," the war between Roman on one side and Teuton or German on the other. Among his "Goths" he includes the tribes that invaded and colonised Britain, and he calls them Angles and Frisians. He never once mentions Jutes as a separate tribe; for no such separate tribe existed.

Another confirmation of the theory which identifies *Jute* with *Goth* is furnished by the fact that the account given by Beda, and by the *A.-S. Chronicle* which followed Beda, is very largely mixed up with fable. The real name of the tribe which first colonised Kent had been forgotten by the time of Beda, who lived about 200 years after the event. The only thing remembered was that the first colonisers from Europe were Jutes, *i.e.* Goths,—an equivalent name for Germans or Teutons.

Frisians.—These are alluded to in several places in the *Anglo-Saxon Chronicle.* They were evidently a great naval people in that early period, as they have been ever since. The German Ocean, or at least the southern part of it, was called after them "the Frisian Sea." Alfred the Great built his fleet after the "Frisian pattern," though on a larger scale, as we are told, and he manned it with Frisian sailors. Tacitus in his *De Moribus Germanorum*, the oldest authority that we possess for the German tribes of the Continent, includes Frisians more than once in his list. Procopius, the next great Latin authority, in his *De Bello Gothico*, iv. 20, says that Britain in his time (the sixth century) was inhabited by three races, the Angles, the Frisians, and the Britons. He never once mentions Saxons; from which we may infer two things, (1) that he included Saxons amongst Frisians, (2) that Frisians took an active part in the invasion of Britain, and are here still. Where then are we to locate them? Undoubtedly in Mercia or Mid-Britain; for the Mercian dialect was Frisian, and the Frisian dialect spoken to this day in Friesland is more like modern English than any other form of speech spoken on the Continent. The Mercian dialect was quite distinct from both Anglian and Saxon, and, as has been shown in Essay V. para. 5, pp. 386, 387, became the ancestor of modern English.

APPENDIX II.—On Certain Technical Terms not hitherto defined.

For terms defined elsewhere the reader must consult the Index.

Accidence (Lat. *accidentia*, Neut. Plur., "things which befall"): the collective name for all those changes of form that are incidental to certain Parts of Speech.

Anacoluthon (Noun), **anacoluthic** (Adj.): Greek *an*, "not," and akolūthŏn, "following." The name "anacoluthon" is given to a construction, in which the latter part of a sentence does not furnish a proper sequence or conclusion to the former part:

They hoped to procure the original document, which had been mislaid but which they have not been able to do.

Here the second *which* has not the same antecedent as the previous one.

Reckless adventure abroad and wholesale plunder at home, we have been governed by them (the outgoing Government) without a policy.—*Trade-Union Circular*, quoted in *Daily Telegraph*, p. 9, 15th Dec. 1905.

Here there is no sequel, *i.e.* no verb, to the two Nominatives "adventure" and "plunder." What the authors of the *Circular* intended to say was: "Their Government has been without a policy, but not without reckless adventure abroad and wholesale plunder at home."

Analytic (Gr. *ana*, "up," *lusis*, "loosening").—See the word **Synthetic** explained below.

Anomaly (Gr. *anomalia*, "unevenness of ground"): a solitary or very uncommon deviation from what usually occurs in Accidence, Syntax, or Idiom.

Antecedent (Lat. *ante*, "before," *cedent*-em, "going").—This word has two senses. It may signify (1) the noun or pronoun going before, to which a Relative or a Demonstrative pronoun refers; (2) the Conditional clause that precedes or goes before the Consequent, § 122 (3).

Antonomasia (Gr. *anti*, "instead of," *onom-as-ia*, "the giving of a name").—An awkward and clumsy designation of the particular kind of *Synecdoche* which is described in § 402 (*b*).

Aphæresis (Gr. *apo*, "from," *hæresis*, "taking").—The loss of an initial syllable through want of accent.

Spend from Lat. *dispendere*; *spite* for *despite*; *sport* from Lat. *disport-are*, Fr. *desport*; *gin* for *en*-gine; *sample* for *en-sample*; *cheat* for *es-cheat*; *dropsy* for *hy-dropsy* (Gr. *hydropsis*); *drawing-room* for *with-drawing-room*.

Aphesis (Gr. *apo*, "from," *hesis*, "sending away").—The loss of an initial vowel through want of accent.

Mend for *amend*; *fray* for *affray*; *peal* (as of bells) for *appeal*; *pert* (saucy) for Fr. *apert*; *prentice* for *apprentice*; *vanguard* for Fr. *avant-garde*; *bishop* from Lat. *episcop-us*; *scutcheon* for *escutcheon* (Old Fr. *escurson*); *special* for *especial*; *sterling* for *casterling*; *squire* for *esquire*.

Apocope (Gr. *apo*, "from," *kop-e*, "cutting"): the cutting off of a final vowel through want of accent. The most common example is the cutting off of final *e*,—one of the marks that distinguish Modern from Mediæval English; as *beast* for *best-e*; *riches* for *richess-e*; *alms* for *ælmess-e*.

Apo-siōpēsis (Gr. *apo*, "from" or "off," *siopesis*, "making silence").—An ungainly and unnecessary Greek word, applied to that kind of construction in which the speaker or writer suddenly breaks off from what he was going or was expected to say, and leaves his sentence unfinished.

Why urge thy chase so far astray?
And why so late returned? and why—
The rest was in her speaking eye.—SCOTT.

Appellative (Lat. *ad*, "to," *pellat*-um, "to address"): a designation applied to a thing or personage of a certain class; as *Czar* (=Emperor of Russia); *Kaiser* (=Emperor of Germany); *Pharaoh* (old name for King of Egypt); *Sultan* (=Emperor of Turkey); *Khedive* (=Viceroy of Egypt).

Archaism (Gr. *archai*-os, "ancient"): the use of a word that was once in general vogue, but has become obsolete or almost obsolete. Such words may survive in poetry, after they have disappeared in prose, as *clomb* for *climbed*.

We *clomb* the high hill and we forded the river.—BYRON.

Aspirate (Lat. *ad*, "to," *spirat*-um, "to breathe"): the name given to the letter *h*, provided that the *h* is meant to be distinctly sounded, as in *hope*. If the syllable beginning with *h* is unaccented, so that the *h* is scarcely heard or is not heard at all, as in "an *historical* novel," the *h* cannot be considered an aspirate; see § 55.

Assimilation (Lat. *ad*, "to," *similat*-um, "made like"): the process by which one consonant is made to take the form of another through the influence of contact; as in *as* (=ad)+*similation*; *ac* (=ad)+*cept*.

Asyndeton (Gr. *a*, "not," *syn-det-on*, "bound together").—A sentence is said to be **asyndetic**, when its different parts are not bound together by connective words, such as conjunctions.

I slip, I slide, I gleam, I dance.—TENNYSON.

Heal the sick, raise the dead, cleanse the lepers, cast out devils; freely ye have received, freely give.—*Matt.* x. 8.

Attraction (Lat. *ad*, "to," *traction*-em, "drawing").—This is the name given to that kind of blunder, in which some violation of Concord or Construction is produced by the greater nearness of some word or words, with which the Concord or Construction has nothing to do.

(1) A great deal of bad blood and bad language *have* been shed during the dispute.—*John Bull*, p. 170, 23rd Feb. 1907.

The subject is "a great deal," and therefore the verb should be *has*, not *have*. But the greater proximity of "bad blood and bad language" (two singular nouns connected by *and*) has wrongly produced a plural verb.

(2) Few, if any, town or village in the south of England *has* a name ending in *-by*.—HARRISON, *Eng. Language*.

The sentence should have been:—"Few, if any, towns or villages, etc., *have*, etc." But the Singularity of "town or village" has led the author to write *has* for *have*. Attraction has been well called by Dr. Abbott "the error of proximity." See also my "Errors in Eng. Compos.," § 5.

Balance (Lat. *bi*, "twice," *lanc*-em, "dish," or "scale of a balance").—See § 423, on Rhythm; and § 483 (*b*), on Balance.

Dialect (Gr. *dialekt*-os, "discourse"): a local or provincial form of speech characterised by some peculiarities of accent, pronunciation, or grammatical usage, which distinguish it from the standard speech of the nation, such as the Yorkshire dialect or the Dorsetshire dialect. Until some national standard has become established, the different local varieties of kindred speech are of coequal rank. But when a standard speech has been formed (such as was formed in England out of the Frisian, Mercian, Midland, or London dialect), and no other dialect is used for literary purposes, the local varieties of dialect, if any such survive, fall into a lower rank, and are regarded as the speech of the unlearned

Ellipsis (Gr. *en*, "in," *leipsis*, "leaving"): an omission (allowed by idiom or custom) of a word or words, which must be mentally supplied in order to make the phrase or sentence grammatically complete. The adjectival form is *elliptic* or *elliptical*.

I must (go) to Coventry.—SHAKESPEARE.

It is more than probable, etc. (*i.e.* it is not only probable, but something more).

En-al-lag-e (Gr. *en*, "in," *allagē*, "change" or "substitution").—This awkward-looking word was not needed. "Substitution" was quite sufficient. The Greek word has been used to denote (1) a change from one part of speech to another; (2) a change in the natural order of words.

(1) He has come from *beyond-the-sea* (a phrase substituted for a noun).

(2) Female infanticide and the *living* cremation of widows were abhorrent, etc.—*Times Weekly*, p. 786, 15th Dec. 1905.

In (2) the word "living" belongs by the sense to "widows," not to "cremation," but appears to have been given to "cremation" as a balance to the phrase "female infanticide." This is merely an example of the Transferred epithet (§ 403).

Episode (Gr. *epi*, "besides," *eisod*-os, "a coming into"): a side-incident, not belonging to the main current of the story, but arising from or suggested by it. In prose such an irrelevancy is generally called "a digression"; in poetry "an episode." Such incidents, provided they are short and rare, are admissible in a long story, because they give variety.

Epithet (Gr. *epi*, "in addition to," *thet*-os, "placed").—This word is merely the Greek equivalent to Lat. "adjective" (*ad*, "to," *jact*-us, "thrown" or "placed"). A distinction, however, has been drawn. An epithet is said to be more distinctive than an adjective, especially when it is made to qualify an individual, as "Charles the *Simple*." An adjective qualifying a noun makes a kind of compound noun, as "a noble man" or "nobleman."

Etymology (Gr. *etum*-os, "true," *log*-os, "word"): that branch of the study of language which traces out the true beginning or origin of words. Sometimes, however, the word "Etymology" is used as an equivalent to "Accidence."

Genitive (Lat. *genitiv-us*, "producing"): occasionally used in books on Eng. Grammar to denote the case that is usually called the "Possessive."

Grammar (Gr. *gramma*, a letter; Old Fr. *gramaire*): an exposition, partly practical and partly theoretical, of the various forms and methods employed in any given language for the expression of thought. This definition, since it makes no reference to time, is wide enough to include the forms and methods formerly used (Historical Grammar) as well as those in present use (Modern Grammar).

Hendiadys (a bad coinage from Gr. *hen*, "one," *dia*, "through," and *dis*, "twice"): the name sometimes given to the construction described and exemplified in § 186, (*a*) and (*b*). One more example is here given:—

Which understood
Not instant, but of future time, with *joy*
And tidings fraught, to Hell he now returned.
Par. Lost, x. 345-6.

Here *joy and tidings* = joyful tidings or tidings of joy.

Heterogeneous, homogeneous (Gr. *heteros*, "another"; *homos*, "the same"; *gene*-os, "kind").—The former word is sometimes applied to a sentence which violates, and the latter to a sentence which observes, the Rule of Unity described in § 317.

Homonym (Gr. *homos*, "the same"; *onom-a*, "a name").—This name is applied to words that are both spelt and sounded alike, but differ in sense and in origin; as (1) *bear*, verb (A.-S. *ber*-an; Sanskrit, *bhar*; Lat. *fer*-re; Gr. *pher*-ein); (2) *bear*, noun (A.-S. *ber*-a; Sanskrit, *bhall*-a).

Homophone (Gr. *homos*, "the same," *phon*-e, "voice or sound").—Words sounded, *but not spelt*, alike; as *some, sum*; *grate, great*; *all, awl.*

Hypallage (Gr. *hypo*, "under," *allag-e*, "change").—An unnecessary word; the equivalent to sense (2) of *enallage* (see above). Thus Virgil has *dare classibus austros*, "to give the south-winds to the fleet," by which he really meant "to give the fleet to the winds."

Impropriety (Lat. *in*, "not," *propri*-us, "proper"): the using of a word in a sense that does not properly belong to it, or in a context for which it is not suited; as "to *perpetrate* a good action." The verb italicised, although by its etymology it merely signifies "to perform or do anything," is now always used in a bad sense.

Inflexion (Lat. *in*, used in an intensive sense, *flexion*-em, "a bending").—"By inflexion," says Sweet, "we understand an addition to a whole class of words expressing some grammatical function or a meaning so general as not to constitute a new word. Thus the inflexion *s* is added to *tree* to express plurality, the meaning of which is so general that we feel 'trees' to be essentially the same word as the uninflected singular 'tree.'"

"Inflexion," then, must not be confounded with "Suffix." The adding of a suffix makes a new word, whereas the use of an inflexion does not. Thus *duch-ess* is not an inflexion of *duke.*

Neologism (Gr. *neos*, "new," *log*-os, "word," with Gr. suffix *ism*, see p. 137): the introduction of new words, or the use of an old word in a new sense. Examples:—*altruism*, the habit of living for others in contrast with selfishness; *solidarity*, entire union of aims, duties, and interests.

Oxymoron (Gr. *ox-us*, "sharp," *mōr-on*, "a foolish thing"): an extreme form of epigram (§ 396).

A damn-ed saint, an honorable villain.—*Rom. and Jul.* iii. 2.

Paragoge (Gr. *para*, "aside"; *agōgē*, "leading"): a needless addition to the end of a word; as, without, without-*en.*

Paraleipsis (Gr. *para*, "at one side"; *leips-is*, "a leaving"). In rhetoric the word denotes the trick of *professing* to pass over certain points, but not doing so in fact.

> Of the honesty of such a speech we will say nothing. Our readers can form their own opinion on this head, etc.—*Nat. Rev.* p. 827, Jan. 1906.

As a figure of rhetoric paraleipsis belongs to Class V., "Indirectness," p. 424, § 408-416.

Parenthesis (Gr. *para*, "at one side," *en-thes-is*, "insertion").—This word is used to designate a phrase or sentence inserted by way of comment or explanation into a larger sentence that is completely formed without it. It thus bears some resemblance to an interjection (§ 17) or to an Absolute construction (§ 348).

Parody (Gr. *para*, "at one side," *ōd-e*, "a song or ode"): an imitative poem, in which the metre and some of the words of the original are retained in dealing with an entirely different subject. The object of a parody is humour. The best collection of parodies in our literature is that contained in the volume called *Rejected Addresses*.

Paronym (Gr. *para*, "beside" or "aside," *onom*-a, a name).—This word is used in two different senses:—(1) allied in origin, as *manhood, mankind, manly*; (2) as equivalent to "homophone," *i.e.* of the same sound, but of different spelling; as *write, rite, right, wright*.

Parse (Lat. quæ *pars* orationis, "what part of speech").—To parse a word is (1) to show to what part of speech it belongs; (2) to account for its inflexions, if it has any; (3) to show what *part* it plays, *i.e.* what work it does, in the construction of the sentence. An interjection can be parsed only in the first respect; other kinds of words can be parsed in all three.

Periphrasis (Gr. *peri*, "around," *phrasis*, "saying"): the Greek equivalent to circumlocution (Lat. *circum*, "around," *locution*-em, "saying"). On Circumlocution see § 416.

Philology (Gr. *phil-os*, "a friend," *log*-os, "word" or "speech"): literally, the study of words; but usually in a more specific sense—the comparative study of kindred languages, such as the Teutonic group, to which the English language belongs.

Phonetics (Gr. *phonetik*-a, things pertaining to the sounds of the voice): that branch of grammar that deals with speech-sounds (Chap. XIV.).

Pleonasm (Gr. *pleonasm*-os, "more than enough"): the Greek equivalent of Lat. "redundancy" (Lat. *re* or *red*, "again," *undant*-ia, "flowing over"): example, "a *sole* monopoly."

Pluperfect (Lat. *plus*, "more," *perfect*-us, "complete"): another name for "Past Perfect," see § 113 (2). The name "Past Perfect," however, is to be preferred, because it draws attention to the distinction between *Present*-Perfect, *Past*-Perfect, and *Future*-Perfect.

Poetic licence: a licence or liberty allowed to poets, but not to writers of prose. This has been fully exemplified already in Chap. XXXIII., especially under headings II., III., and IV. Poets, however, are not allowed to make blunders, as in Byron's "There let him *lay*" for "There let him *lie*." I know of no bolder example of poetic licence than that by Tennyson in the following extract:—

> But our Robin takes
> From *whom* he knows are hypocrites and liars.

Here for *whom* we must write *those who*; otherwise the verb *are* has no subject.

Polysyndeton (Gr. *polus*, "much" or "many," *syndeton*, "joined together").—This is the opposite to *asyndeton*, defined above. A sentence is said to be polysyndetic, when its different parts are joined together by a liberal use of connective words (conjunctions):—

> (Satan) pursues his way,
> *And* swims, *or* sinks, *or* wades, *or* creeps, *or* flies.—*Par. Lost*, ii. 950.

Potential (Lat. *potent*-em, "able").—The name of a supposed mood, which was once included, but is not now recognised, as an element in the conjugation of a verb. It is expressed by *can* and *could*. This, however, is not an Auxiliary, but a Notional, verb, and therefore it cannot make a Mood; see § 102, *Note* 3.

Preterite (Lat. *præterit*-us, "past"): a name sometimes given to the Past Indefinite tense (§ 111).

Prolepsis (Gr. *pro*, "beforehand," *lepsis*, "taking").—The adjective form is *proleptic*, "anticipatory." For examples see p. 480 (*r*).

Prose. See **Verse**, below.

Prosōpo-pœia (Gr. *prosōpon*, "face," *pœia*, "making").—This figure consists in making the event appear to be passing before the reader's face, things inanimate being addressed as if they were alive, things absent as if they were in sight, and the historic or graphic present being used for the Past Indefinite; § 112 (*c*). After all, however, "prosopopœia" is nothing but an awkward and ungainly equivalent to "vision" described in § 406.

Purity (Lat. *puritat*-em, "purity").—As applied to our language, this word is intended to exclude (1) the use of obsolete words; (2) the use of foreign words or phrases, when suitable English ones exist, such as saying Lat. *de die in diem*, "from day to day," or Fr. *à propos* for "with reference to"; (3) the use of slang words; as "jolly" for "very."

Rhetoric (Gr. *rhetor*, "a public speaker"): the theory and practice of eloquence either spoken or written; the art of using language in such a way as to persuade others to do something or to believe something.

Root (A.-S. *wyrt*, a "wort" or "root").—The last element to which a word can be reduced, when search is made for its origin. Thus if we search for the origin of *bairn*, we find the A.-S. *bearn*. But we must not stop there; for we find that A.-S. *bearn* is itself a derivative from A.-S. *ber*-an, to bear or produce. We cannot discover in Anglo-Saxon any word more elementary than *ber*-an; so *ber*- is the Root. To the same root can be traced such words as *barm* (lap), *barrow* (wheel-barrow), *berth*, *birth*, *bier*, *burden*. (Anglo-Saxon belongs to the Teutonic group of languages; but the Teutonic group itself is one of a much wider group, which is called "Aryan" and includes Greek, Latin, Sanskrit, and several other languages. Thus *ber*-an shows the root in A.-S., *fer*-re in Latin, *pher*-ein in Greek, *bhri* in Sanskrit.)

Slang (Icelandic *sleng*).—This word is used in two senses; (*a*) vulgar language, (*b*) a mode of speaking peculiar to some particular place or calling; as stockbroker's slang (*e.g. bull*, *bear*, *slump*). "Slang" in this sense is equivalent to "cant" in one of the meanings of this word. Slang words sometimes rise into general acceptance and become part of the national speech, as *donkey*, *dunce*, *jingo*, *to boycott*, *whig*, *tory*.

Solecism (Gr. *Soloikos*, "a dweller at Soloi"): a town notorious in ancient days for speaking bad Greek. This word in our language signifies (*a*) a violation of accidence or syntax, (*b*) a violation of idiom.

(*a*) *Whom* do men say that I am? (*Whom* for *who*.)
(*b*) He died *with* fever. (*With* for *of*.)

Stem (A.-S. *stæfn*, *stefn*, or *stemn*, "the trunk of a tree").—Stem is that part of a word which remains unchanged, or (if changed at all by assimilation, see above) very slightly changed, whatever prefixes, suffixes, or inflexions are added to it. "Stem" must not be confounded with "root" (see above). Thus in the words for-*bear*-ance, un-*bear*-able, over-*bear*-ing, the stem is *bear*. The root, however, as shown above is A.-S. *ber*-an, "to bear."

Surprise (derived through Old Fr. *sorprise* from Lat. *super*, "above," and *prehens*-ionem, "seizing").—The way in which surprise can be used as an element in composition has been described and exemplified in

§ 483 (*f*). By some writers it is included among the Figures of Rhetoric; the Latin name for the figure was *Prœter expectatum*, "beyond what was expected."

Syllepsis (Gr. *sun*, "with," *lepsis*, "a taking"): an unnecessary Greek name for the figure called "The Condensed Sentence"; § 398.

Syn-cop-e (Gr. *sun*, "with," *kop-e*, "a cutting"): the cutting out of a medial syllable, which disappears through want of accent (see above, "Apocope")—

> *Punch* for *punish*; *clerk* for *cleric*; *French* for *Frenc-isk* (Frankish); *butler* for *bot-il-er* (a bottle-man); *chimney* for *chim-en-ce*; *laundress* for *lav-end-er-ess*; *crown* for *corone* (Lat. *corona*); *parlous* (as in Shakespeare) for *perilous*; *partner* for *parc-e-nere*; *wardrobe* for *gar-de-robe*; *damsel* for *dam-o-sel*; *mar-shal* for *mar-es-chal*; *proxy* for *pro-cur-a-cy*; *palsy* for Middle Eng. *pal-e-sy* (Fr. *para-lys-ie*, Gr. *para-lys-is*); *sexton* for *sacr-ist-an*.

Syntax (Gr. *syn*, with, *taxis*, arrangement): that part of Grammar that deals with the order of words in a sentence and with their relations to one another in the construction of a sentence.

Synthetic (Gr. *sun*, "with," *thet*-os, "placed").—A language is said to be in the *synthetic* stage when the different parts of a word are formed by adding inflexions to the stem:—in the *Analytic* stage, when it has discarded most of its inflexions and makes a very frequent use of separate words (such as prepositions and Auxiliary verbs) to take their place. Old English was mainly Synthetic, Mod. Eng. is Analytic.

Tautology (Gr. *to auto*, "the same," *log*-os, "a word"): the employment of a superfluous word or words in the same grammatical relation with some other word, as "safe *and secure*."

Technology (Gr. *techn-e*, "art" or "science," *log*-os, "word"): an explanation of technical terms, as when a word has some specific meaning in connection with some art or science, different from that in general use. Thus *elbow* has one sense in bridge-building, and another in navigation, besides that which it bears in ordinary use.

Verse, prose.—"Prose" is from Lat. *pro*, "forward," and *versa*, "turned." *Proversa* (oratio) has been shortened first to *prorsa*, and then finally to *prose*. The word signifies composition that goes "straight forward," the opposite to verse (Lat. *versus*), that turns back and makes a new beginning with every new line.

Vocative (Lat. *voc-at-iv-us*, "that which calls"): the Latin name for what in our grammar we call the "Nominative of Address," § 176 (4). In Latin this case had a form of its own distinct from that of the Nominative, and hence a separate name was needed for it.

Zeugma (Gr. *zeugma*, "juncture"): the name sometimes given to a faulty construction, against which the student is cautioned in p. 171 (36):—

> And deemed (that) restraint in convent strange
> Would hide her wrongs and her revenge.—SCOTT.

"Wrongs" goes very well with "hide" as its object; but "revenge" requires a new verb—"Would hide her wrongs and *ward off* her revenge."

INDEX OF SUBJECTS AND SELECTED WORDS.

THE reader is requested to give attention to the following points :—

(1) No reference is made in this index to the contents of Chapter XXIX., since the contents of this chapter are in alphabetical order already, and are therefore an index to themselves.

(2) For the same reason no reference is made to the contents of Chapter XI.

(3) For the same reason no reference is made to the contents of Appendix II., at the end of this volume.

(4) Regarding the remaining chapters, the references are to pages, not to paragraphs.

THE END